'Wollstonecraft was  were
realised through Joh Hay
interweaves in her c erous
and engaging guide, s she
exposes their frailtie nted
and devoted to Johnson; Priestley, slight and fragile, propelled by a restless
energy, walking ahead of his tall, powerful wife; Cowper, petulant and occasionally high-handed towards Johnson the 'tradesman', whom he nevertheless
acknowledges the most discerning reader and editor of his verses . . . *Dinner
with Joseph Johnson* is an admirable achievement of biography and humanis-
tic imagination' Kathryn Sutherland, *Times Literary Supplement*

'In *Dinner with Joseph Johnson*, drawing upon a body of scholarly research
into Johnson's significance that began fifty years ago . . . Hay has produced
an enlightening biography. Her detailed portrait of Johnson illuminates the
considerable risks faced by a London publisher bold enough to defy the
repressive laws issued by the nervous British government at a time when
revolution seemed worryingly likely to spread from France to England'
Miranda Seymour, *New York Review of Books*

'Today, Johnson is virtually unknown, his name obscured and his renown
eclipsed by that of the bright lights that once shone so vividly through the
shadows of his dining room. In her enthralling and intricately researched new
book, Daisy Hay, a professor of English literature at the University of Exeter,
illuminates the life of this influential publisher and bookseller. But *Dinner With
Joseph Johnson* is more than a richly detailed character profile: It also comprises
a sharply realized group portrait of those whom Johnson wined, dined and gave
voice to – "the men and women who," Ms Hay argues, "remade the literary
landscape of the late eighteenth century"' *Wall Street Journal*

'Hay's meticulously researched biography, rich in period and personal detail,
sheds light on both Johnson and the vibrant cultural world he inhabited'
Guardian

'A portrait of literary ferment . . . Daisy Hay's compendious and impressive
survey illuminates the contribution to these significant ideological shifts of
the ill-assorted men and women whose kinship was marked by their shared
participation in Joseph Johnson's hospitality . . . Instead what emerges from
Hay's elegant account is his curiosity and his moderation . . . Thrillingly,
however, *Dinner with Joseph Johnson* reminds us of the excitement of a period
in which inherited orthodoxies were forensically scrutinised and found lack-
ing. And it offers us pause for thought' *Daily Telegraph*

'Chronicling Johnson's fascinating dining companions and the changes that rocked Britain during the period, this is a feast for those interested in the eighteenth century' *BBC History Magazine*

'This delightful book by the English literature professor Daisy Hay gives the reader the feeling of being at a rather elevated party . . . Johnson's guests talked, wrote and painted about democracy, human rights, atheism, feminism, anatomy, chemistry and electricity. While dreaming of a better future, they befriended each other, loved each other and criticised each other . . . shaped an era . . . Johnson was a brilliant talent spotter and supported the best minds of his day' *The Times*

'Hay makes the most of a vivid period in English and especially London history. Her carefully poised study puts Johnson, today an obscure figure, back at the centre of his circle' *London Review of Books*

'*Dinner with Joseph Johnson* sheds much-needed light on a key figure in both the ideological and material context of the eighteenth century . . . Hay's meticulous research brings this "paper age" to life . . . Evokes the noise and excitement of an age characterised by the unceasing hum of literary debate . . . A fitting reflection of the period that Hay describes: a time when the written word could make someone's name – or cost them their liberty' *Financial Times*

'A beautifully packaged, skilfully written and detailed book that finally gives this gentle revolutionary the recognition he deserves' *Country Life*

'It makes little sense to approach a character of such extensive and various connections as the bookseller and publisher Joseph Johnson other than via the clubbable sort of method at which Daisy Hay has already proven herself adept . . . In *Dinner with Joseph Johnson*, she has again broadened her scope . . . Hay pursues lines of enquiry with patience and sensitivity to detail' *Literary Review*

'Marvellous . . . The list of Joseph Johnson's guests reads like a who's who of revolutionary politics and culture: abolitionist MPs, Jacobin agents, pioneering scientists and radical preachers . . . Panoramic and kaleidoscopic' *History Today*

'We usually think of the Romantic revolution in terms of its writers, from Blake, Wordsworth and Coleridge in poetry to Mary Wollstonecraft and William Godwin in politics. But writers need publishers and booksellers. In this regard, Joseph Johnson was the man who made the revolution possible. Daisy Hay has had the inspired idea of reading Romanticism through the prism of the "three o'clock dinners" where he brought the literary world together. The result is truly a biography of the spirit of the age' Sir Jonathan Bate, author of *Radical Wordsworth*

DAISY HAY

Daisy Hay is an award-winning biographer whose previous work includes *Young Romantics: The Shelleys, Byron and Other Tangled Lives* and *Mr and Mrs Disraeli: A Strange Romance*. She began her writing career as a doctoral student and then a Bye-Fellow at Murray Edwards College, Cambridge before moving to Oxford where she held the Alistair Horne Fellowship at St Antony's College and a Visiting Scholarship at the Oxford Centre for Life Writing at Wolfson College. She has also held a Fellowship at the Radcliffe Institute for Advanced Study, Harvard. In 2016 she was awarded a Philip Leverhulme Prize by the Leverhulme Trust and in 2018 she was elected a Fellow of the Royal Society of Literature. She is currently Associate Professor in English Literature and Life Writing at the University of Exeter and lives in Devon with her family.

DAISY HAY

Dinner with Joseph Johnson

Books and Friendship in
a Revolutionary Age

VINTAGE

1 3 5 7 9 10 8 6 4 2

Vintage is part of the Penguin Random House group of companies
whose addresses can be found at global.penguinrandomhouse.com

Penguin
Random House
UK

First published in Vintage in 2023
First published in hardback by Chatto & Windus in 2022

penguin.co.uk/vintage

Printed and bound in Great Britain by Clays Ltd, Elcograf S.p.A.

The authorised representative in the EEA is Penguin Random House Ireland,
Morrison Chambers, 32 Nassau Street, Dublin D02 YH68

A CIP catalogue record for this book is available from the British Library

ISBN 9781784701079

Penguin Random House is committed to a sustainable
future for our business, our readers and our planet. This book
is made from Forest Stewardship Council® certified paper.

In memory of my father, Michael

and for my children, Freddy and Eloise

Contents

INTRODUCTION
Dinner with Joseph Johnson

Over the course of the eighteenth century a landscape of bookshops formed in the City of London, under the shadow of St Paul's Cathedral. In Paternoster Row and St Paul's Churchyard the booksellers congregated, dealing with customers from street-facing frontages, commissioning new titles and negotiating with printers and paper-makers in back offices and workshops, eating and sleeping in warrens of rooms above their businesses.

Upstairs in one of the houses in St Paul's Churchyard there was a room with no right angles and no straight walls. Over the decades the appearance of this room altered and re-formed. For many years the most striking sight to catch the eye of visitors was a painting of a nightmare, featuring an incubus leering over a sleeping woman. The flesh-and-blood figure at the centre of the room formed an incongruous contrast to his backdrop. He was the bookseller Joseph Johnson, the proprietor of 72 St Paul's Churchyard. Johnson was a small, bewigged man, with dark eyes. One woman who had reason to be grateful to him testified to the 'tenderness' of his 'look'.[1] Another acquaintance recalled that Johnson greeted visitors with 'a good humoured face', an outstretched hand and an open invitation on his lips. 'How d'ye do Sir, I dine at three.'[2]

Once a week, between the early 1770s and the end of 1809, Joseph Johnson issued an invitation to dinner. Throughout the year he filled his dark, sloping dining room with the men and women who remade the literary landscape of the late eighteenth century. His guests did not come to dinner because of the quality of the food. Each week the fare consisted of roasted veal, boiled fish, boiled vegetables and rice pudding. There was wine to drink, although sometimes when Johnson's shop staff joined the company they insisted on bringing their own beer – a 'brutal' practice, thought one more refined guest.[3] Over the decades, Johnson entertained hundreds to

I

dine under the eye of the incubus. And the lines of their lives – and ideas – overlapped as they crossed his path.

Let us imagine, for a moment, that the men and women who dined with Joseph Johnson are gathered around the table once again, according to their centrality to Johnson's story rather than the realities of time and place. Gradually, a picture of the community he created becomes visible beneath the painting of the nightmare. Seated at Johnson's right hand, monopolising the attention of the host, is the artist responsible for the image of incubus and sleeper, Henry Fuseli. Fuseli himself acknowledges that once he starts drinking he finds it hard to control his tongue. 'A few glasses of wine cause his spirits to run away with him, and He always repents of his extravagance in conversation', reports one witness to his table manners.[4] Fuseli's chief sparring partner at dinner is a mathematician called John Bonnycastle. During working hours Bonnycastle teaches maths to trainee soldiers at the Woolwich Military Academy; during his leisure he writes books designed to reveal the beauties of mathematics to general readers. He is not an elegant eater. According to the testimony of one young guest he has an unfortunate tendency to 'goggle' over his plate, 'like a horse'.[5] When he laughs his teeth are exposed at the sides, and in Fuseli's presence he laughs and shouts in equal measure.

Sitting apart from the squabbles of Fuseli and Bonnycastle, in this imagined gathering, is Joseph Priestley. Priestley is at once a philosopher, chemist, theologian, teacher and more: there is barely an aspect of human existence to which he has not given some thought. At his own table Priestley has to be dissuaded from reading while he eats, but at Johnson's house there is too much pleasure to be had in the company of others for Priestley to be distracted by books. Chief among his friends at the table are Benjamin Franklin, a fellow chemist increasingly concerned by the deterioration in relations between Britain and his native America; and the Unitarian minister Theophilus Lindsey, whose chapel at Essex Street, further down the Strand, is another gathering place for many of Johnson's friends. Also clustered around Priestley are Richard Lovell Edgeworth and his brilliant novelist daughter, Maria; Erasmus Darwin, a doctor and poet whose girth is barely contained by his waistcoat; and from the younger generation, the quiet figure of another doctor, John Aikin, and John's sister, the writer Anna Barbauld. Barbauld is usually accompanied on her visits to St Paul's Churchyard by her husband, Rochemont, a Suffolk schoolmaster eclipsed by his brilliant wife. In letters to friends Barbauld writes of the intensity of her pleasure in the conversation to be found at Johnson's, although sometimes, like Fuseli, she writes the morning after dinner with wine-sodden wisdom of the perils of a late night on a tender head.

There are more men than there are women at dinner with Joseph Johnson, but Barbauld and Maria Edgeworth are by no means the only representatives in the dining room of their sex. Sometimes the company is joined by the white-capped figure of Sarah Trimmer, a children's writer and devout Anglican who has little in common with Johnson's more radical guests. Also present, when the boundaries of time and place are collapsed, is the poet Charlotte Smith, who finds refuge on Johnson's list in the final years of her life. His nieces Elizabeth and Hester form part of the family unit at St Paul's Churchyard, alongside their younger brother Rowland, a pupil at the Barbaulds' school who will become first Johnson's apprentice and later one of his heirs. But of all the women who gather for dinner it is the voice of Mary Wollstonecraft that can be heard most clearly across the table. It is the early opinion of another dinner guest, the philosopher William Godwin, that Wollstonecraft has a good deal too much to say for herself, but even Godwin's attention is snagged by the clarity with which Wollstonecraft makes her views known. At this end of the table Godwin would prefer to hear from Thomas Paine, whose political writings have caused a stir in both America and Britain. He is to be disappointed since Paine, as Godwin will later acknowledge, 'is no great talker.'[6] Another guest is also disappointed in Paine, although for different reasons. An aspiring poet called James Hurdis, who seriously over-estimates the extent of his own literary talent, finds Paine's appearance as objectionable as his views. In a letter to a friend Hurdis complains that Paine's face is red and 'somewhat resembling in the inequality of its surface the coat of a Seville orange.' Paine's hair is as bad: thin, 'carelessly frizzed', and untidily held back with a slip of ribbon.[7]

Jostling for space at the table alongside the men and women who come to dinner most regularly are other figures eager to make their voices heard. Amongst a group of young men trying to carve space in the conversation is the poet William Wordsworth, down on his luck after being forced by political crisis to leave France. Alongside Wordsworth in this outer group is his friend Samuel Taylor Coleridge. Some of the older guests have nursed the hope that Coleridge might channel his genius with words as a minister in the Unitarian Church, but their wishes will not be fulfilled. Also anxious for a place at the table is another chemist, Humphry Davy, who, the gossips report, sometimes runs to dinner straight from his workshop without stopping to change his shirt, and William Hazlitt, a follower of Godwin who has turned his back on the religion of Johnson and Priestley. Hazlitt wants to paint Johnson, but he cannot persuade the bookseller to sit still long enough to have his likeness taken.

Johnson is more interested in listening to others than he is in his own image. As the candles flicker, illuminating both the animated faces round the table and the strange image on the wall, he remains still. When the wine glasses have been drained and the guests at this phantasm of a dinner disappear down the stairs and into the night he is left alone in the crooked dining room. There are servants to clear the dirty crockery, their presence barely registered in the historical record. There is work to be set in train for the morning, and manuscripts to be read. The business of making and selling books is unrelenting, and within a few hours of the candles guttering in the dining room the shutters protecting the shop front will be thrown back, and into 72 St Paul's Churchyard will come once again the procession of authors, tradesmen and friends for whom dinner with Joseph Johnson offers the prospect of sustenance, conversation and safety.

✢

Joseph Johnson became a bookseller and a maker of books in an age when books appeared to have the potential to change the world. Between 1760 and 1809, the years of Johnson's adulthood, Britain experienced a period of political, social, scientific, cultural and religious change during which nothing was certain and everything seemed possible. On paper Johnson's dinner guests charted the evolution of Britain's relationship first with America and then with Europe: several were intimately involved in the struggles that reformed the world order. They pioneered revolutions in medical treatment and scientific enquiry and they proclaimed the rights of women and children. All those whose presence was documented in the dining room were white. Most, but not all, were opponents of the global trade in enslaved people. Johnson's guests lived in a clubbable century, during which multiple groups of people came together and adopted or were given names that signalled their allegiances. 'Grub Street' was one such name: so was 'Scriblerians', 'Bluestockings', 'The Club of Honest Whigs' and, towards the end of the century, 'Anti-Jacobins'.

The men and women who gathered around Johnson had no communal name and they never moved as a single group. Some, like Wollstonecraft,

Fuseli, Bonnycastle and Lindsey, frequented his shop and his dining room without waiting to be invited, treating his home as an extension of their own. Others, like Priestley and Barbauld, viewed St Paul's Churchyard as their Pole Star: the beacon towards whose light they were drawn whenever they came to London. A few – Paine, Trimmer, Darwin – are harder to place, because they left fewer textual traces of their physical presence in Johnson's house. One man, Johnson's engraver William Blake, came to dinner only rarely. At St Paul's Churchyard Blake was a tradesman, like Johnson. Few at the dining table saw him as either an author or artist: he was referred to by one of the guests simply as 'Blake, the Engraver'.[8] Also absent from dinner was the poet William Cowper. Cowper was one of Johnson's bestselling authors and among his most significant correspondents, but he never visited London and never met the bookseller in person. Despite this he made his presence felt in the dining room just as surely as did those who came to Johnson's shop and home.

Many of those who came to dinner understood that the weekly gatherings at St Paul's Churchyard were emblematic of a broader interwoven community, and that to dine with Johnson was to acknowledge one's allegiance both to the bookseller and the network he enabled. As the years went on some among Johnson's guests came to resent the way in which they were identified outside the walls via their presence in his house. All those who dined were connected by a web that spun outwards from Johnson's house through the medium of paper, as conversations begun within the privacy of the dining room stretched out – often in public view – across the country and over the decades. Johnson turned his home into a writers' house in the most capacious sense of the phrase: a place where writers of contrasting politics and personalities could come together. Some of his guests took shelter under his roof for weeks on end; others called only occasionally. A few, through either choice or necessity, sent proxies in place of themselves. The dining room provided space for thinking and talking but it also symbolised and served as a sanctuary at times of crisis. Johnson's guests had to contend with events that threatened their physical security as well as their intellectual liberty. In the tumultuous years either side of the French Revolution they faced riots, fire, exile and prison, alongside the more quotidian but no less serious threats of homelessness, mental collapse, poverty and the exigencies of childbirth. Johnson's house provided a refuge throughout, and his labours allowed his visitors to make their voices heard even when external forces conspired to silence them.

If 72 St Paul's Churchyard offered both the reality and the possibility of shelter, Johnson himself embodied a way of being in the world that many of those who sought out his company described as a kind of gift. In the historical record Johnson's voice is quieter than those of many of his guests. As a result his own story is less audible than those of his authors, through which he forms the connecting line. But although his voice is sometimes difficult to hear he remains visible through the decisions he made. He worked hard in order to make money and he died a rich man. But his professional and personal lives were characterised by generosity, and by the belief that acts of kindness contained within them a political and ethical significance that could not be gainsaid by reactionary State power. He threw open his dining room to all comers because he enjoyed the company of others and because it served his business interests, but also because the ethics of so doing underpinned every decision he took.

At St Paul's Churchyard Johnson made little distinction between public and private, or work and home. He lived according to a set of principles about the responsibilities of an individual to his friends, and those principles offered their own kind of sanctuary to the men and women who sought out his company. In Johnson's house family was not a concept bounded by claims of blood, and a friend could be someone who never crossed the threshold just as surely as someone who visited daily. His relationships with the men and women to whom he was closest were sometimes unconventional, but in all cases they demonstrated the strength of his belief in the political power of friendship. Friendship and its unknowability stand at the centre of Johnson's story, and at the centre of the communal story of the men and women who made their way to St Paul's Churchyard.

In the image of the nightmare hanging on Johnson's wall creatures lurk in the gloaming, exuding a force both potent and frightening. In the crooked dining room Johnson risks being lost in the shadows, while his guests appear in colour and light. In the one image of him that survives he looks away from the viewer, eluding discovery. Yet although Johnson has sometimes been obscured by the personalities gathered around his table he stands at the heart of the group, uniting them, giving them space and focus. In so doing he gives us a literature religious, revolutionary and Romantic. He championed the supremacy of the untrammelled creative imagination, for which Fuseli's painting stood as a symbol, but he did so alongside a commitment towards the imaginative and intellectual potential inherent in the collegiate conversations enabled at his table. In the strength of his allegiance to both shadowy nightmare and candlelit reality he was a maker of books who was also a maker of dreams. Chiselled throughout the strata of his story and the story of the dinners he held are the stories of the people, the books and the dreams he made.

PART ONE

FIRE (1760–1770)

William Hogarth, *Gin Lane*, 1751

To begin with the dining room is uninhabited and the nightmare is unpainted. There are no dinner parties, apart from those that take place in dreams. In the fantasy it is winter, in the middle years of the 1760s, and in lodgings on Paternoster Row a small group gathers around the bookseller. They are an artist, a former slave-trader, an enquirer, a politician, and a poet. The poet is a young woman who refuses to be silenced by her age or gender. Each person present has a distinctive story and they all play a part in the story of Johnson's beginning. Over dinner they talk of education, electricity, the nature of God, the cowardice of the Prime Minister and the continuance of a global trade in kidnapped Africans. The streets outside the shop can be dangerous at night, but for the men and woman gathered around the table there is security in strong walls and the company of others. The security offered by buildings is illusory. Fire in the hearth of the lodgings offers brightness and warmth, but in the bookshop below fire spreads through the paper stacked high, bringing with it destruction.

I

Authentic Narrative

Joseph Johnson was born in 1738, the last child of Rebecca and John Johnson. His father was a man of means who in 1733 bought a small estate in Everton, then a village near Liverpool. The Johnsons were Baptists and the house they bought, Lowhill, had previously been owned by Dr Fabius, a leading member of the Society of Baptists. In 1707 Fabius gave a piece of land adjoining his garden to the Baptists so they could open a chapel and burying ground. During Johnson's childhood the chapel was moved elsewhere but the burying ground remained. The house in which he was born was a solid stone building with outhouses. Its land comprised two meadows, an orchard and kitchen garden. No records survive regarding the composition of the household but a family with enough money to buy a well-built house and three acres of land would have had a small staff of indoor and outdoor servants and the Johnson children grew up with space to roam. There were three of them: John, born in 1731, Sarah, born in 1733, and Joseph.

His parents' faith was at the heart of Johnson's upbringing. To be born a Baptist in 1738 meant being marginalised and distrusted by the twin pillars of Established Church and State. This was a position borne out of religious allegiance that no amount of money could overturn. Baptists were a subset of a much larger group known as Dissenters: Christians who worshipped outside the structures of the Church of England and who rejected its oaths and allegiances. In 1649, as Charles I laid his head on the execution block, he uttered his last word: 'remember'. After the Restoration the word echoed through the country as his son, Charles II, set about ensuring that the Protestant regicides who had brought about his father's downfall were debarred from the benefits of the State unless they explicitly testified to their loyalty. In 1662 Charles II passed the Act of Uniformity, which required all clergy, schoolmasters, private tutors and fellows of Oxford and Cambridge colleges to sign a declaration promising to reject any resistance to the Crown and to adopt a revised State-sanctioned and anti-Puritan liturgy. On August 24th 1662, a day that subsequently became known as 'Black Bartholomew's Day' or 'The Great Ejection', all clergymen, schoolmasters and fellows who had refused to sign were evicted from their positions. Over two thousand men were summarily made homeless and the campaign of persecution that followed drove several to early graves. Ten years later Charles introduced a Royal Declaration of Indulgence which softened the laws against Dissenters but his government forced him to withdraw this: the following year Parliament passed the first of a series of Test Acts, penal laws imposing religious tests for public offices.

After the Revolution of 1688, with the Protestant Mary and William of Orange on the throne, ministers passed an 'Act of Toleration' which eased some of the worst penalties on Dissenters. As its name suggested the act stipulated that Dissenters were to be tolerated rather than enabled and although the active persecution stopped, the conditions under which Dissenters could worship remained stringently controlled. They were allowed to gather only in buildings granted a licence by a bishop or magistrate; they were compelled to pay church rates for the maintenance of Anglican churches they did not use. Their ministers were required to subscribe to many of the thirty-nine articles (which stipulated loyalty to the Church and King), and they had to swear an oath of allegiance. These conditions were enshrined in law by two intertwined pieces of legislation, the Test and Corporation Acts. In 1717 a Dissenting campaign for the repeal of the Test and Corporation Acts failed; similar campaigns took place with no success throughout the 1730s, during the period of Johnson's infancy.

Johnson was thus born into a community which stood apart, in which the bonds of internal loyalty were both strengthened and tested by external opposition. As a child he witnessed schisms in his own church and he grew up with the knowledge that many civic offices and professions were closed to him. He learnt early that 'toleration' was a contingent concept, one that could be withdrawn if particular groups of Dissenters pushed too hard at the limits circumscribing their existence. Yet he also knew that he had a religious lineage stretching back to Black Bartholomew's Day in which consistency, bravery and conviction were virtues to be worked at and celebrated, and that the qualities that made a man able to account for his actions and the state of his soul were more important than public approbation or social success.[1]

Johnson's older sister Sarah died aged twenty-two, leaving a widower, Rowland Hunter. The most likely cause of death for a young married woman was childbirth but if Sarah did give birth to a child the baby did not survive her. His brother John married a woman also called Sarah Hunter. In the tight-knit community of Liverpool Baptists it is probable that John's wife was related to his sister's husband. Rowland Hunter remained closely connected with both Johnson brothers, as did the children borne by his second wife. In early adolescence both John and Joseph went into trade. Although the family were comfortable there was not enough money for either son to live off the fat of their father's modest lands. John became a brewer and made his own fortune. He settled with Sarah in Liverpool, which remained his home all his life.

Joseph was sent south. On February 12th 1753 the account book of the Worshipful Company of Musicians, one of the Livery Companies of the City of London, recorded his binding as an apprentice to the bookseller George Keith.[2] Keith had served his own apprenticeship with the Musicians Company a generation earlier and for much of the eighteenth century the guild represented a variety of City trades. Johnson was fourteen when he was bound to Keith for a seven-year term. The conditions governing the behaviour of apprentices in the City were stringent. Johnson signed an indenture that required him to serve his master faithfully, 'his Secrets keep, his lawful Commands every where gladly do.' Fornication and matrimony were both forbidden during the course of the apprenticeship, as were cards, dice, gaming, the selling of goods without permission, and the haunting of taverns and playhouses. In return Keith undertook to feed and house Johnson and 'in the same Art and Mystery which he useth, by the best Means he can, [to] Teach and Instruct'.[3]

George Keith was a Baptist bookseller and religious affiliation made him the natural apprentice master for the Johnsons' youngest child. Johnson spent the second half of his adolescence at Keith's house in Gracechurch Street, near the site of one of the earliest Quaker Meeting Houses in Britain. Keith's wife Mary was the daughter of the Baptist theologian John Gill and Gill's works were a staple of the bookselling business that sustained the household. In the Dissenting tradition represented by Gill and Keith it was an act of devotion to make the Word of God accessible to all. Both men rejected the idea that a hierarchical clergy should control access to biblical knowledge, and they treated the printing press as an alternative to the pulpit. From the earliest days of his training Johnson saw that power resided with those who were able to make themselves heard. At Keith's house he also witnessed a version of bookselling in which the making of a book was an article of faith as well as commerce.

♱

The city into which Johnson arrived in 1753 to be instructed into the mysteries of bookselling while avoiding fornication, taverns, playhouses, matrimony, cards, dice, gaming and unlicensed selling was a world apart from the orchards and meadows of Everton. The old gates of the City still stood. 'Within the walls' the writ of the Livery Companies was law, although the narrow alleys and dark wynds of the old street system could be violent places. Outside the City walls the canonical image of London during this period was Hogarth's *Gin Lane*, a work completed in 1751, two years before Johnson's binding. The City was policed by an ad hoc network of local constables who were nominally under the charge of the City Marshal; in 1749 the formation of a group of six Bow Street Runners marked the advent of the first organised police force on London's streets. It was not until the early 1760s, however, that the Court of Aldermen began swearing in members of the Society for the Reformation of Manners as constables in order to police the spread of vice, and the City Marshal only had his role fully defined and staffed after 1770.

The tight overlapping networks of regulation in the City meant apprentices like Johnson knew their behaviour to be monitored and scrutinised. It did little to touch either petty crime or the vices the Society for the Reformation of Manners had in mind: sodomy, prostitution, blasphemy, Sabbath breaking, and the production of obscene prints. All were among the sights of daily life in the streets where Johnson worked out his adolescence, learning the mechanics of the bookselling trade and watching as Baptist tract after Baptist tract rolled off the presses, many of them promising damnation to souls who strayed.

In moving from Liverpool to London in 1753 Johnson was part of a demographic phenomenon. In the second half of the eighteenth century London grew at an unprecedented rate, as hundreds of thousands of young men and women from all over the country migrated to the capital. The city spread westwards and northwards as grand families moved to new houses in Mayfair and by 1760 London had outpaced Paris to become the largest metropolis in Europe. As its population grew so did the volume of printed material issued by its booksellers. Matters which had once been the preserve of a tiny elite were transmuted into text and, in the process, into subjects for mass consumption and conversation. Cheap labour made immediacy possible in an age of hand-set type. A writer might produce a pamphlet in response to a particular event in two or three days; a printer could set it and a bookseller stock it in two or three more.

'Bookseller' is a catch-all term for the trade in which Johnson was trained by Keith. The historian James Raven has positioned the bookseller as the 'foremost entrepreneur' in an overlapping network of 'distinctive crafts and employments' that met in the production of a book. Printers and engravers were crucial to the book trade and they worked for themselves, contracting work from booksellers on a case-by-case basis. The makers of ink and paper played their part in the trade; so did bookbinders and carriers and advertising agents. The trade to which Johnson was apprenticed bears a good deal of resemblance to modern publishing, because Keith was a 'wholesale bookseller', who commissioned and took on the financial risk of book production, and who issued works under his own imprint. 'Retail booksellers', in contrast, simply sold books – although to confuse matters, wholesale booksellers enacted complicated exchanges with each other to sell works they had not printed alongside those issued under their own names.

The wholesale booksellers of the City also frequently joined together to take shares in profitable reprints of older works. Many of the City's most successful booksellers made as much money from the canny trading of shares as they did from the issuing of original works and through multiple consortia they exercised stringent control over their copyrights.[4] During the seven years of his apprenticeship Johnson learnt how to navigate the labyrinthine complexities of a business that required of its practitioners knowledge of multiple trades, investment instruments and copyright law. He learnt that readers would not stand for good words on bad paper and that sometimes engravers forgot to flip their images and, if unchecked, the resulting print run could spell reputational disaster. He discovered the importance of bartering stock with other booksellers, so that customers would not grow tired of the offerings of one house. He was taught to view his fellow booksellers as collaborators, friends and competitors, and he was instructed in the niceties of the informal systems by which the booksellers regulated themselves. Copyright (the legal instrument by which authors and the publishers they licensed retained ownership of their work) was theoretically protected under the Copyright Act of 1710 by registration at the Stationers' Company, the City guild responsible for the regulations governing publishing. In reality, however, it was the handwritten registers kept by the booksellers themselves that mattered most to a man making his way in a competitive market.

✛

On May 28th 1761 Johnson was, in the phrasing of the City's Livery Companies, 'made free'. The ledgers of the Musicians Company record the moment: 'Jos Johnson free by Redm.'[5] 'Redm' stood in the shorthand of the Company's clerk for 'redemption': Johnson, or his parents, bought his freedom for eighteen shillings and fourpence. The transaction marked the end of his apprenticeship and the moment, aged twenty-two, when he became his own master.

In his first years in the bookselling business Johnson moved frequently, renting temporary premises as he sought out authors to publish. His first shop was on Fenchurch Street in the heart of the City, but within a short period he had established his business in vacant premises on Fish Street Hill, near the Monument. Many years later a friend recalled that this move was driven by Johnson's desire to attract the business of the medical students who trooped down the street on their way to the Southwark hospitals where they learnt their trade. The medical students who passed the door and window of the new shop were overwhelmingly young men of Johnson's generation who shared with him a determination to find in books the knowledge that would allow them to flourish. Baptist tracts represented the bookselling business in which Johnson had been trained but from the outset he cast his net wider than had his apprentice-master, seeking out new writers and readers from across the City and beyond.

His first bestseller came in 1764, three years after the end of his apprenticeship. Its title was An Authentic Narrative and it was the work of a Church of England minister called John Newton. Johnson and Newton found each other as a result of the tight-knit Baptist community in Liverpool in which Johnson's relations still figured largely, but the working relationship that subsequently developed took both men into new territory. An Authentic Narrative was ostensibly a conversion narrative of the kind made popular by the Evangelical revival but its popularity lay less in its moral teachings than in Newton's enthusiastic embrace of his own crimes. As a young man, he recalled, 'I loved sin, and was unwilling to forsake it'.[6] Newton was a slave-trader and for many years he earned a large income commanding slave ships. His spiritual conversion gathered pace alongside professional success but for many years he paid little attention to the irony of a ship's captain sending up prayers of thanks to a beneficent God while enslaved people lay bound in chains below decks on his orders.

There was only one point in *An Authentic Narrative* at which Newton acknowledged the ethical difficulties his story presented. 'During the time I was engaged in the slave trade, I never had the least scruple as to its lawfulness', he explained. 'It is indeed accounted a very genteel employment, and is usually very profitable ... However, I considered myself as a sort of *Gaoler* or *Turnkey*; and I was sometimes shocked with an employment that was perpetually conversant with chains, bolts, and shackles.'[7]

When Newton returned to the subject of the slave trade in the 1780s he gave a graphic account of the conditions under which the slaves on his ships were kept, in a tract which became a central text in William Wilberforce's campaign for abolition. Yet although he dwelt at length on the chains and punishments and the rape of slave women, his principal argument was less against the cruelty itself than on its debasing spiritual effect on those who practised it.

The success of *An Authentic Narrative* created new opportunities for Johnson. No longer was he the ingenue protégé of an obscure Baptist bookseller; instead he was a tradesman in his own right, with a profitable title in his catalogue and a proven eye for work that captured the mood of the moment. Newton's autobiography combined conversion narrative, romance, politics and tales of seafaring adventure. Its hybrid form proved popular with a reading public who were being shown by the new novels flooding the market that their reading could hold them in thrall to a good story even as it improved their morals.

In late 1764, buoyed by his first experience of commercial success, Johnson moved his home and business to Number 8 Paternoster Row, where he entered into partnership with a fellow bookseller called Benjamin Davenport. Little is known of Davenport, whose commitment to bookselling appears to have been driven more by religious belief than by any intrinsic interest in the trade. He served his apprenticeship as a hat-band maker and by the 1770s was working as a tobacconist.[8] Religious works formed the backbone of the lists they issued together, but by 1767 Johnson had broken with Davenport and entered into business with a bookseller called John Payne, with whom he traded from the same building. Payne was made free of his apprenticeship a year after Johnson and he closed his own shop at Number 54 Paternoster Row in order to join forces with him.

By the 1760s Paternoster Row and St Paul's Churchyard represented the centre of bookselling London. They were the streets on which the most prestigious booksellers had their premises, to which the ever-expanding metropolitan reading public went in search of new titles. Johnson's decision to move his business to Paternoster Row testifies to his determination to rival longer-established names. Number 8 was a long thin building at the eastern end of the Row, with warehouse space directly behind it, off Queen's Head Passage. Johnson and Payne settled in quarters above the shop. Each man had his own set of rooms and a maid was employed to clean and lay fires. Neither lodging allowed for large gatherings of friends or colleagues but a few doors down on the opposite side of the street was the Chapter Coffee House, which served as a communal office and living space for many of the Row's tradesmen. The City booksellers stored their handwritten copyright ledgers behind the counter, and the Coffee House was also home to regular meetings of like-minded scientific experimentalists and philosophical societies. The booksellers relied on quick and reliable information from elsewhere in Britain and Europe in order to trade competitively, and at the Chapter Coffee House they gathered to read the morning newspapers before the ink on the paper was dry. Johnson was twenty-five when he moved to the heart of the bookselling City. Here he was able, for the first time, to live according to inclination rather than the dictates of convention or financial contingency.

2

Domestic Occurrences

In the spring of 1764, as the proof sheets of *An Authentic Narrative* were being set by the printer, a young Swiss artist arrived in London. His name was Johann Heinrich Füssli. Today he is better known by the anglicised version of his name adopted after his arrival in England: Henry Fuseli. He was a small, fierce-looking man, just over five foot tall, with deep-set blue eyes. In self-portraits he consistently drew a large beak-like nose as his dominant feature and he wore his hair unpowdered in defiance of fashionable convention. His English remained heavily accented all his life but he swore proficiently and fluently.

'How do you get on with Fuseli?' an acquaintance once asked William Blake. 'I can't stand his foul-mouthed swearing. Does he swear at you?'

'He does,' Blake replied.

'And what do you do?'

'What do I do? – Why – I swear again! And he says astonished, "Vy, *Blake, you are svaring!*" But he leaves off himself.'[1]

✢

Henry Fuseli was born in Zurich in 1741, to Johann Caspar Füssli, a painter and art historian, and his wife, Anna Elizabeth Waser. All the Füssli children could draw and paint but Johann Caspar, knowing how precarious was his own existence as a portrait painter, refused to let Henry train as an artist, and instead required him to undergo ordination as a minister. During his theological training Fuseli formed an enduring friendship with Johann Casper Lavater, who would find fame throughout Europe for his pioneering work on physiognomy. In the autumn of 1762, in conjunction with a third friend, Felix Hess, Lavater and Fuseli wrote a pamphlet exposing political corruption in Zurich which brought down such opprobrium on their heads that they were forced to leave Switzerland. Fuseli travelled to Berlin, where he worked as an illustrator and an assistant to the art theorist Johann Georg Sulzer, who employed him as a contributor to his *General Theory of the Fine Arts*. In his spare time he wrote poetry and a passionate prose work entitled the *Complaints* in which he mourned his enforced separation from Lavater. His work attracted the attention of Sir Andrew Mitchell, the British chargé d'affaires in Berlin, who took him under his wing and, in 1764, brought him to London.

Despite the patronage of Sir Andrew, Fuseli's first weeks in London were hard. Many years later he told his friend and biographer John Knowles of a moment soon after his arrival that underscored his vulnerability and stayed with him all his life. 'Meeting with a vulgar fellow', Knowles wrote, 'Fuseli inquired his way to the post-office, in a broad German pronunciation: this produced only a horse-laugh from the man. The forlorn situation in which he was placed burst on his mind; – he stamped with his foot while tears trickled down his cheeks.'[2] It was a characteristic response: the quick and physically expressed anger, the readily accessible emotional reaction, the sense of self as a figure in a tableau, alone in his defiance of brute ignorance. In letters Lavater chastised him for making his life harder by putting 'on airs' around Englishmen but Fuseli refused to tame his distinctive characteristics.[3] Other new acquaintances were more sympathetic to the isolation entailed by foreign difference and domestic parochialism. One of Sir Andrew's friends wrote with news that Fuseli was managing to live on three shillings a day and that this was the minimum sum needed for survival. Any less and 'he must have been lodged in some garret where nobody could have found their way, and must have been thrown into alehouses and eating houses, with company every way unsuitable.'[4]

With the support of Sir Andrew and his friends Fuseli managed to avoid staying in garrets. Initially he took lodgings at the other end of the Strand from Johnson's shop and home at Number 8 Paternoster Row. Sir Andrew then introduced Fuseli to Johnson, Coutts the banker, and Andrew Millar, a well-known bookseller. Fuseli and Johnson subsequently developed a relationship that would sustain both men until Johnson's death.

＋

In the newspapers and journals Johnson published and sold, the columns printed under the heading of 'Domestic Occurrences' often related quotidian details of births, marriages and deaths. Here readers could learn of good, purposeful lives, lived out of the glare of the public eye. This insistence on the public value of private stories is repeated across many of the works Johnson commissioned and sold from the 1760s onwards. Of his own private story, however, he left few traces. In her 1974 biography of Mary Wollstonecraft, Claire Tomalin suggested that Johnson and Fuseli might have been lovers.[5] She acknowledged that such a suggestion took her into the realms of speculation and, unsurprisingly, there is no evidence in the historical record that the relationship between the two men was homosexual. What the record does show, however, is that Fuseli was one of the most important people in Johnson's life. Their relationship was subject to interruption, as Fuseli travelled throughout Europe and public and private loyalties pulled them in different directions. Yet in spite of this it was also characterised by a constancy and a sense of mutual primacy that set it apart from other friendships. Their partnership resisted labels. No one who knew either man ever intimated, even in the most elliptical way, that they were lovers, and close reading of the available sources suggests that they were not. But in the mid-1760s, possibly after Fuseli returned from a European visit in 1766, he took lodgings at Johnson's premises at 8 Paternoster Row. In so doing he became the first documented person with whom Johnson chose to share his life and make a home.

Cocooned in the physical and emotional security of 8 Paternoster Row, Fuseli developed new confidence in both his brush and his pen. He worked as a reader for Johnson and Payne and as a translator, rendering French, German and Italian works into English. He insisted that he was the only person in London proficient enough to write in German and English and he was scathing about the translations produced by some of Johnson's competitors.[6] He began work on his first oil painting on canvas, *Joseph Interpreting the Dreams of the Pharaoh's Baker and Butler*, which he gave to Johnson in exchange for his keep. The gift marks the first documented instance of Johnson offering a vulnerable ally physical security in exchange for creative labour. Fuseli told Lavater that 'the friends that I have made in England, and the idea that I have found the means to establish my talents here, are, God have mercy, very promising.' He described himself as 'blissfully happy with my friend, Johnson, who I pay for my accommodation by means of drawings, and sometimes with writing.'[7]

Johnson's support allowed Fuseli to test his strength on paper as well as on canvas. In 1767 he published his friend's *Remarks on the Writings and Conduct of J. J. Rousseau*, in which Fuseli supported Rousseau's assertion that art should be considered separately from morality. His pamphlet was in part a response to attacks levelled at Rousseau by David Hume and its tone was set by the frontispiece Fuseli designed, which showed Voltaire booted and spurred with a whip in his hand, riding on a supine Everyman, while the figures of Justice and Liberty hang from a gibbet above his head and Rousseau stands to one side, looking straight at the viewer and pointing at Voltaire as if to reveal his villainy. Fuseli's aim in the pamphlet was to protect and celebrate the philosophical truth of Rousseau's work. 'Truth', he wrote, 'has been – and is – the destroyer of peace – and the parent of revolution.'[8]

Despite the satirical precision of its frontispiece the testimony presented in *Remarks* had less to do with Rousseau than with Fuseli's own opinions on everything from cohabitation to the literary overabundance of metropolitan culture. From the heart of Paternoster Row he recorded an outsider's view of the world of books and bookmaking. 'I wish you would allow me a few remarks on the limits of this epidemic rage of scribbling, and the remedies against that deluge of nonsense which inundates every rank of life', he implored. The answer was to restrict the licence to publish to those who had true learning and genius, rather than allowing the freedom of the press to everyone with a passing interest in a particular subject. Literary culture might be improved, he suggested, 'did not so many bottomless officious people write their lives away, with compendiums, short and accurate views, tables, definitions, lectures, and the rest of their rudimental trash, to level, to reduce science to the conception of the *great club*.'[9] Fuseli presented clubbable, bookselling London as the object of a tongue-in-cheek evisceration even as he privately acknowledged himself to be a beneficiary of the literary hubbub he bemoaned.

Women figured in Fuseli's *Remarks* as lesser mortals, unable to follow the twists and turns of an argument. They were also emphatically not the audience for his own writing. 'You', he told his reader, who he represented as a fellow writer, 'must keep them alive by tattle, scotch the solid reason which they can neither clench nor digest of one piece.'[10] Elsewhere he arraigned the stock figures of the capital for censure, mocking Voltaire and the vice-ridden citizenry for whom he spoke. 'Rakes, bucks, bloods, beaux, connoisseurs, belles, flirts, quality, and mob of pleasure ... how often must your champions be arraigned for high treason against your sublime constitutions and privileges?'[11] Finally he turned his attention to the English people, in an account that drew on his own experiences as a young stranger in London: 'the English have no compliments for their friends; – hence the pretended neglect of salutations ... they are extremely shy to address, or to enter into conversation with a foreigner, even he speaks the language ... their shyness increases in proportion, if he does not; – hence many awkwardnesses of conduct, and the cold looks of his landladies.'[12]

The picture Fuseli presented in *Remarks* of his life in London highlighted some of the ways in which his move to Johnson's quarters liberated him. Gone were the unfriendly landladies, suspicious of strange accents and unfamiliar ways; gone too was any sense of exclusion from the world of the London booksellers. At Paternoster Row Fuseli discovered the freedom to paint and write unafraid of critical reaction, and although he later claimed to be ashamed of his early work the proclamation of his own views demonstrates both a defensiveness and a confidence in his position and ability to speak which friendship with Johnson gave him. 'The effects of united power',[13] he wrote in the pamphlet, were to allow men to combine in groups in such a way as to produce both leisure and luxury.

In the summer of 1767 Johnson took Fuseli to Liverpool to meet his family and Merseyside friends. The excursion emphasised that Fuseli's residence with Johnson was not merely a matter of convenience but an affirmation of mutual importance. Johnson's family in Liverpool now comprised a steadily growing number of nieces and nephews, some of whom were related to him by blood; others of whom were joined to him courtesy of a more elastic conception of family. Sarah Johnson's widower Rowland Hunter had six children with his second wife Elizabeth and those children, along with the offspring of Johnson's older brother John, became part of his life. Geography did little to lessen his ties to this network of Liverpool kin, and his nephews and step-nephews later wrote of the central role Fuseli played in their London uncle's life.

They made a strange pair, the bewigged bookseller and the artist of grand passions, with features 'as strongly marked as if they had been cut in marble.'[14] Paper leaves little trace of their shared domestic rhythms, or many clues about how they shared their lives. It is however possible to witness them sharing a joke. In his *Remarks on the Conduct of Rousseau* Fuseli incorporated some tart observations on the behaviour of booksellers and other tradesmen. 'Cursed marplots they are', who ought long ago to 'have been kicked out of all good company'. Enter any shop, he warned, to 'produce your scheme, drug, book [and] I'll be shot, if not all their *honest* owners with more or less contempt, just as you advance east or westward – will ... whisper ye, *"Truth! It beggars any man that keeps it; and if you mean to thrive well, endeavour to trust to yourself, and live without it."'*[15] Yet to live without truth was one thing that Johnson was unable to do. And at the end of 1764 a man entered his life for whom the search for truth was not only a guiding principle but a life's work.

3

The Enquirer

In the autumn of 1764 – the year of *An Authentic Narrative* and Fuseli's
arrival in London – Johnson and Davenport joined with the firm of Becket
and De Hondt to publish a volume entitled *Essay on a Course of Liberal
Education*. Its author was Joseph Priestley. The essayist William Hazlitt
described Priestley's body as 'the envelope of his mind' and nothing more.
'In his face there was a strange mixture of acuteness and obtuseness; the
nose was sharp and turned up, yet rounded at the end, a keen glance, a
quivering lip, yet the aspect placid and indifferent, without any of that
expression which arises either from the close workings of the passions or
an intercourse with the world.' At breakfast he sat with a book in one hand
and a notebook by the other; if you asked him a question he would answer
as if you were not there. He stammered and rushed his words together. But
he did not consider people beneath his notice. He was a generous man and
he believed it his sacred duty to make every subject in which he took an
interest intelligible to his reader. 'He wrote on history, grammar, law, politics,
divinity, metaphysics, and natural philosophy', wrote Hazlitt. 'Those who
pursued his works fancied themselves entirely, and were in great measure,
masters of all these subjects.'[1]

Priestley exemplified the spirit of enquiry which came in its turn to
exemplify the eighteenth century. He campaigned for a reformed politics,
for the right to worship freely and to acquire and disseminate knowledge.
In 1796 his friend William Enfield published the first of a series of columns
entitled 'The Enquirer' in the *Monthly Magazine*, which took as their starting
point the idea that to push at the boundaries of knowledge was the responsibility of every man. 'The power of enquiry, with which every human mind
is endued, is itself a licence from the Author of Nature for its exercise:
each individual comes into the world possessed of this birth-right, and can

neither resign it without folly, nor be deprived of it without injustice.'[2] Priestley personified this idea. There was hardly a field of active enquiry which did not at some point attract his ambitious attention. To enquire was for him not simply a question of satisfying curiosity, scoring a point or proving oneself. It was a calling.

Priestley was born in 1733 into a Dissenting family. As a young man he rejected the Calvinism of his upbringing and adopted Arianism, a Nontrinitarian doctrine which posited Jesus, the Son of God, as a divine being distinct from and subordinate to the Father. In 1761 he was appointed to a teaching position at Warrington Academy, close to Liverpool. The Academy had been founded six years earlier with the avowed purpose of educating the sons of Dissenting families who were barred by their religion from taking places at either Oxford or Cambridge. Dissenting Academies first emerged after Black Bartholomew's Day and the subsequent passing of the Test Acts: by 1750 over sixty such institutions existed. Many – including the academies at Manchester, Newington Green and Daventry, where Priestley himself studied – became centres of learning to rival England's two universities. At Warrington Priestley was initially appointed to teach languages and belles-lettres but within a few months he was exerting his influence over broad areas of the curriculum. Warrington offered Priestley a haven of congenial company. He developed a friendship with the theology tutor, John Aikin, and watched with pleasure as Aikin's brilliant daughter Anna blossomed intellectually alongside the male scholars of the Academy. It was during frequent visits to nearby Liverpool that he developed a friendship with William Enfield, who in 1765 was minister to the Nonconformist congregation at Benn's Garden Chapel where Johnson also worshipped during his summer visits to the city.

Presented with the opportunity to design a scheme of education from first principles, Priestley and his colleagues turned their backs on the stale models offered by Oxford and Cambridge, where the only languages taught were Greek and Latin, and where students were fitted only for scholarly pleasure. Priestley and Aikin knew that lives of leisure would not be possible for most of their pupils, who were predominantly drawn from the prosperous merchant families of the north-west. These families had ambitions for their boys, whom they expected to overcome religious discrimination in order to take an active part in civic and mercantile life.

The early success of the Warrington Academy brought tangible rewards for Priestley, who was able for the first time in his life to settle into a house of his own (provided for him by the trustees) and into the pattern of reading, writing and preaching that would become central to his existence. In May 1762 he was ordained as a minister at the Warrington Provincial Meeting and a month later he married nineteen-year-old Mary Wilkinson, the sister of one of his students. Their first child – a daughter, Sarah – was born a year later. The Priestleys' marriage was enduring but Priestley did not draw his wife into the circles into which his scholarly pursuits took him. Many years later William Hazlitt recalled the sight of them together. 'His frame was light, fragile, neither strong nor elegant; and in going to any place, he walked on before his wife (who was a tall, powerful woman) with a primitive simplicity, or as if a certain restlessness and hurry impelled him on with a projectile force before others.'[3] At home with a baby and a husband who read books at breakfast, Mary Priestley found a companion in Anna Aikin, who was also nineteen. One of Anna's earliest poems was written to Mary Priestley and speaks both of her gratitude for Mary's presence in her life and her dawning realisation that the paths open to the boys amongst whom she had been educated were closed to her. 'Thy friend thus strives to cheat the lonely hour' she wrote in the ambivalent final stanza of 'To Mrs Priestley, with some Drawings of Birds and Insects':

> Yet, if Amanda praise the flowing line,
> And bend delighted o'er the gay design,
> I envy not, nor emulate the fame
> Or of the painter's, or the poet's name:
> Could I to both with equal claim pretend,
> Yet far, far dearer were the name of FRIEND.[4]

✦

In the volume that Johnson and his fellow booksellers published in 1764, *Essay on a Course of Liberal Education*, Priestley drew on his experiences in the classrooms of Warrington to propose a revised scheme of national education. This was not an education to be administered by the State: indeed, Priestley devoted a substantial proportion of his work to insisting on the importance of education being delivered free from State interference. But it was nevertheless a call for a reformed system for educating the sons of the nation in a manner that would enable them to achieve great things for their country and themselves. He proposed that a full liberal education would not be restricted to the study of Latin and Greek but would encompass history, law, mathematics (including algebra and geometry), French and extensive study of English grammar and writing. It was a nonsense, he wrote, that scholars who would be ashamed to express themselves in bad Latin should feel no shame about sloppy use of their mother tongue, 'which they considered as belonging only to the vulgar.'[5]

The starting point in Priestley's proposed curriculum was history. In the sample lecture scheme included with his *Essay* he related a version of history that would allow the subject to play its part 'in forming the able statesman, and the intelligent and useful citizen.'[6] He insisted on the importance of students being permitted and encouraged to interrupt their teachers with questions and criticisms and was alert to the fact that the model of education he proposed had the potential to shake the foundations of the established order. 'Some may perhaps object to these studies, as giving too much encouragement to that turn for politics, which they may think is already immoderate in the lower and middle ranks of men among us.' He had little sympathy with such an objection. 'Only tyrants, and the friends of arbitrary power ever took umbrage at a turn for political knowledge, and political discourses among even the lowest of the people.' No 'friend to liberty', he concluded, could possibly object to the dissemination of useful and productive knowledge through the country, and only those who knew their power to be based on corruption and ignorance had anything to fear from the onward course of progress.[7]

In the *Essay* Priestley presented himself as the embodiment of calm reason. In a rhetorical sleight of hand he depicted his proposals as so uncontentious as to be obvious, yet he was also unapologetic about the challenge his view of a reformed society posed to the established order. In a pattern that would repeat throughout his work, the subject at hand enabled a larger discussion of the barriers he saw presented by the status quo to the progress of enlightenment. Implicit in the *Essay* was a suggestion that Oxford and Cambridge no longer served a useful purpose in the education of active men and that it was therefore from amongst the Dissenters, with their alternative models of education, that the next generation of leaders would be drawn. He offered a revised version of patriotism, in which attention to the beauties and complexities of the English language was paramount. His ideal statesman was an active, metropolitan figure, fluent in French, familiar with the history of his own country and that of other European nations, able to navigate the law and international systems of commercial and cultural exchange. He expected his pupils to make their way across the globe in search of new knowledge and new ideas. 'We are probably strangers to some of the most useful productions of the earth on which we live', he lamented. 'But a general attention once excited to the subject, by teaching it to youth in all places of liberal education, would be the best provision for extending it.'[8]

These were arguments with which Johnson wholeheartedly agreed. A friendship grew between the two men following the publication of the *Essay*, sustained by letters, during Priestley's winter visits to London and Johnson's annual summer pilgrimage to Liverpool. They had much in common. Both were curious about new ideas and polymathic in their interests. Both believed that the spread of knowledge through the writing and publication of books would effect a social, cultural and political revolution that was urgently needed. Both were shaped by the experience of being born into faiths which debarred them from active participation in affairs of State and by the experience shared by all the Dissenters of being at once outsiders in their own country, tolerated but not welcomed. Both were independent-minded to a degree that set them apart from others. In adulthood each man looked with a critical eye at the religious sect into which he had been born and, over the course of the 1760s, both turned their backs on the faith of their families.

By the end of the decade Johnson had moved away from Baptist beliefs and had adopted Unitarianism as the bedrock of his religious faith. His spiritual journey mirrored Priestley's. Both men read the scriptures with great attention, and are likely to have moved towards Unitarianism as a result of the influence of William Enfield in Liverpool. For Johnson conversion to Unitarianism entailed a rejection of the doctrine of predestination preached by John Gill and the pastors of his youth, in favour of a version of religious Nonconformism in which an individual had the potential and the responsibility to shape his or her destiny in this world and in the world beyond. Unitarianism attracted significant numbers of new adherents during the second half of the eighteenth century and Johnson and Priestley both played their part in its spread. William Hazlitt, who was born into a Unitarian family, termed the latter 'the Voltaire of the Unitarians'[9] and Priestley came for many to embody the liberal curiosity that was the chief characteristic of the Unitarian position.

Unitarianism was itself a broad Church – so broad that one of Johnson's contemporaries laughingly termed it 'a feather-bed to catch a falling

Christian.'[10] Its central tenet was the rejection of the Trinity and the belief in the unity of one God. Christ stood as an exemplar whose teachings demolished ideas of Original Sin and eternal damnation as well as predestination. Unitarians also believed in the God-given supremacy of reason and rational thought: scientific discoveries were not a challenge to God's power, but rather an expression of his glory. Unitarianism allowed the men and women of the Enlightenment to pursue enquiry in a manner that celebrated rather than undermined their religious faith. In its emphasis on freedom and equality it enabled its believers to question political structures propped up by religion. The uniformity of belief insisted upon by the Church of England had no place in Unitarian churches. It was a progressive creed for an enquiring age and it gave men like Johnson and Priestley a framework within which rational thought and faith could be reconciled.

As Johnson read his way towards Unitarianism he discovered other Dissenting writers in need of an audience. One such was William Hazlitt the elder, a Unitarian minister who gave his name to his famous essayist son. In 1766 Johnson published Hazlitt's *Sermon on Human Mortality* and shortly thereafter introduced him to the notice of Priestley, who was turning his attention with renewed vigour to theological questions.[11] At the end of the decade Priestley decided to found a journal dedicated to the pursuit of theological enquiry. The *Theological Repository* was published and part-financed by Johnson, in a sign of the extent to which the bookseller made the Unitarian cause his own.

Priestley's letters for 1766 paint a vivid picture of his life in Warrington and London and illustrate the extent to which the arrival of his work on Johnson's lists expanded the bookseller's circle and horizons. In February Priestley wrote to a friend that 'I have lately been at London, & formed a most agreeable acquaintance with Dr. Franklin, Mr Canton, Dr. Watson, and other philosophers & electricians. I have been enjoined by them, to write a treatise on electricity, in which I shall give a full history of all the new discoveries in the order of time, in which they were made.'[12] In March he was back in Warrington and on the hunt for books to help with this project. To the Dissenting minister Richard Price he sent a list of books with the following plea: 'If you, or your friends, can procure me those, or tell Mr Johnson the bookseller, where to get them, you would do me an important service.' 'I take it for granted,' he continued, 'you have seen the letter I wrote, about a fortnight ago, to Dr. Franklin. I desired he would shew it to you, and Mr Canton. Writing upon a philosophical subject to any of you, I would have considered as writing to you all.'[13]

Of the names that pulse through Priestley's letters that of Benjamin Franklin most immediately catches the eye. Franklin lived in London for much of the period between 1757 and 1775 in airy lodgings on Craven Street, just off the Strand. He was famous throughout Europe for his investigations into the sources and storage of electricity. In 1752, in his famous kite experiment, he had demonstrated that lightning and electricity were one and the same. In his *History and Present State of Electricity*, published with Johnson in 1767, Priestley divided the course of electrical discoveries into periods before and after Franklin, so pivotal was his friend's work. Franklin became Priestley's chief interlocutor on scientific matters and when the latter was in London they met daily. 'It is probable', Priestley wrote after Franklin's death, 'that no person now living was better acquainted with Dr. Franklin and his sentiments on all subjects of importance, than myself.' To strangers, Priestley recalled, Franklin could be 'cold and reserved; but where he was intimate, no man indulged more in pleasantry and good-humour.'[14]

When Priestley was in Warrington it was Franklin who wandered into Johnson's Paternoster Row shop on his way to and from St Paul's Coffee House, where he congregated fortnightly with a group he affectionately termed his Club of Honest Whigs. 'I shall make all the experiments you direct', Priestley wrote to him in March. 'I am impatient to receive the books you are so kind as to procure for me ... Please also to desire Mr. Johnson to send me a copy of Theophrastus for I have not the book, tho' I remember reading it formerly.'[15] Johnson's earliest surviving letter shows him in the role of intermediary during the composition of *The History of Electricity*, facilitating communication between Priestley and Franklin. 'J. Johnson's compliments to Dr. Francklin [*sic*] and sends these MSS for his inspection by order of Dr. Priestley who will esteem himself much oblig'd to the Dr. for looking over them as soon as possible.'[16]

Franklin had returned to London in 1764 following a two-year visit to Philadelphia. His mission in Britain was to petition the King about the governance of Philadelphia, but this campaign faded into insignificance as the government introduced the Stamp Act in Parliament as part of a concerted effort to extract more from the American Colonists and to re-exert control over the Empire. The Stamp Act put taxes on paper, playing cards and legal documents produced in America as well as those exported from elsewhere. Franklin campaigned against the legislation in Parliament and in the press. His efforts positioned him as the pre-eminent defender of American interests in London and his time became absorbed by politics. Like many Americans of his generation he considered himself a proud English patriot and was appalled by the sight of his country turning aggressor against its own people. 'The unity of the British Empire in all its parts was a favourite idea of his', recalled Priestley. 'He used to compare it to a beautiful China vase, which, if once broken, could never be put together again.'[17] But when in spite of his efforts the King and his government persisted in treating the Colonists with contempt, both as a resource to be exploited and a pest to be controlled, Franklin's sense of national allegiance shifted. In London he warned against pushing the American people further than they would tolerate. He advocated for the postponement of war, hoping he would never see the day when the mother country took up arms against its own people, but as the decade went on he began to view the postponement of war as to America's advantage, giving the Colonists more time to prepare for a conflict which was beginning to look inevitable.

A few months after he sent the manuscript of Priestley's *History of Electricity* to Franklin, Johnson put the completed volume on sale. The full work ran to over 750 pages and encompassed both an extensive history of electrical experimentation and an account of Priestley's own investigations. In its opening pages he presented the development of the human mind as a sublime spectacle but he also insisted that it was impossible for individual thinkers to reach sublime heights on their own. To underline this argument he included in his summary of his own work descriptions of experiments that were failed or unfinished. He acknowledged that in so doing he ran the risk of exposing himself to ridicule. But, he argued, the greater good outweighed any potential cost. 'If electricians in general had done this, they would have saved one another a great deal of useless labour, and would have more time for making experiments really new.'[18] It was a statement of collaborative intent; of a world-view which placed the dissemination of knowledge and the pursuit of truth above individual reputation. That Johnson shared this view is apparent from the fact that he permitted Priestley to include the following promise in his Preface: 'I INTITLE the work the *history and present state of electricity*; and whether or nor there be any new editions of the whole work or not, care will be taken to preserve the propriety of the title, by occasionally printing ADDITIONS, in the same size, as new discoveries are made; which will always be sold at a reasonable price to the purchasers of the book; or given *gratis*, if the bulk be incon-siderable.'[19] Profit too was secondary to knowledge in Priestley's scheme, and in pursuit of this ideal he and Johnson evolved new forms of publishing, in which the inherent obsolescence of books during an age of rapid discovery could be overcome through collaborative ingenuity and collective deter-mination.

✢

> What principles are those, which ought to restrain an injured and insulted people from asserting their natural rights, and from changing, or even punishing, their governors, that is their servants, who had abused their trust; or from altering the whole form of their govern-ment, if it appeared to be of a structure so liable to abuse?[20]

This was the challenge to power issued by Priestley in 1768, in his *Essay on the First Principles of Government*. Johnson published the *Essay* at a moment when the aristocrats who ran Britain felt themselves assailed from every side. Opposition to the Stamp Act was growing both in America and at home; on the streets of London silk-weavers and coal-heavers rioted in protest at poor working conditions, bad pay and food scarcity. The exiled MP John Wilkes returned to England and was overwhelmingly elected by the voters of Middlesex. The subsequent decision of the government to expel him from Parliament and to subvert the will of the electorate raised major constitutional questions about the abuse of power and produced waves of further rioting and disorder. In October William Pitt resigned on grounds of ill-health, leaving his administration in the hands of the inexperienced Duke of Grafton, who found himself unable to contain the forces of unrest levelled against him. Grafton responded by clamping down on Dissent in all its forms. Wilkes was imprisoned, rioters were shot, and the army was sent into the silk-weavers' stronghold at Spitalfields to prevent the destruc-tion of the looms of wage-cutting masters. There was nothing rational or enlightened in the sights confronting Priestley, Johnson and Franklin as they congregated in the coffee houses of the City, where the effects of starvation, violence and lawlessness were everywhere visible. Priestley had been provoked to write on government by the continued existence of the Test and Corporation Acts and by the penalties Dissenters suffered as a result but his *Essay* caught the mood of the nation and identified a political malaise which affected disenfranchised people of all religions. 'Whatever be the form of any government, whoever be the supreme magistrates, or whatever be their number; that is, to whomsoever the power of the society is delegated, their authority is, in its own nature, reversible. No man can be supposed to resign his natural liberty, but on *conditions*.'[21]

The corruptions of power, Priestley argued, were neither inevitable nor unchangeable. In the Mediterranean, the people of Corsica had already proved this to be true. In 1755 the nationalist Corsican leader Pasquale Paoli had established the Corsican Republic in defiance of the Republic of Genoa, which owned the island. For over a decade Paoli successfully resisted Genoese attempts to regain control of the territory and he implemented wide-ranging constitutional changes, introducing the most extensive voting franchise in the world and significant educational reform. The Corsican Constitution was held up as a model of good government by liberal thinkers all over Europe: Rousseau praised it, as did his old adversary, Voltaire.

In 1768 Genoa ceded control of Corsica to France and French troops landed on the island to establish control. France was Britain's old enemy, and Grafton's ministry came under intense pressure to send military support to the Corsicans in their battle against French tyranny. Loudest among the voices calling for action was that of James Boswell, whose *Account of Corsica* did more than any other text to awaken public sympathy in Britain for the Corsican people. Grafton, though, was distracted by events in America, and he also knew that Britain's position within Europe was weak. Only a pan-European alliance had the capacity to counter French imperial power and Grafton's half-hearted attempt to build such an alliance with Spain and Sardinia ended in failure. Opposition Members of Parliament called in vain for the British Navy to be mobilised in Corsica's defence and in 1769 Paoli's forces were defeated at the Battle of Ponte Novu.

In Warrington the plight of the Corsicans attracted the attention of an outraged Anna Aikin. Aikin was twenty-six in 1769. Her younger brother John was away studying medicine but she remained at home with her parents, writing poetry which delineated the circumscribed sphere ordained for her sex. 'Come Muse, and sing the dreaded washing day', implored one poem in which domestic labour is made a fit subject for verse:

> For should the skies pour down, adieu to all
> Remains of quiet; then expect to hear
> Of sad disasters – dirt and gravel stains
> Hard to efface, and loaded lines at once

> Snapped short, and linen-horse by dog thrown down,
> And all the petty miseries of life.[22]

The quotidian subject of 'Washing Day' demonstrates Anna Aikin's writerly audacity, as she invokes her muse like Milton. The 'petty miseries of life', she insists, are as fit a subject for poetry as heroic deeds; the home and exist-ence to which she is restricted is well able to provide inspiration.

In 1767 Priestley moved his family from Warrington to Leeds, where he took up a position as minister to the Dissenting congregation at Mill Hill Chapel. Anna Aikin felt their departure keenly. With Mary she had learnt the strength of female friendship; from Priestley she saw that it was possible to speak truth to power. As the failure of the British State to come to the aid of the Corsicans became apparent she drew on the confidence gained from her friendship with Mary and the example of Priestley to make her own intervention in the debate. The poem she wrote in response to Boswell was called, simply, 'Corsica' and in it she harnessed the power of poetry to represent the island's abandonment as a tragedy for the cause of liberty. Parts of the poem were written before the outcome of Paoli's uprising was known; the final published sections post-dated the establishment of French control. Liberty itself she represented as 'a mountain goddess', engrained in the island's rugged mountain landscape.

The final stanza of 'Corsica', however, undercut this celebration of liberty. Like Priestley in the *History of Electricity*, Aikin argued that to fail gloriously is still to advance the cause of progress:

> Nor with the purple colouring of success
> Is virtue best adorn'd: th' attempt is praise.
> There yet remains a freedom, nobler far
> Than kings or senates can destroy or give;

The poem is poised here, ready for a conventional poetic retreat towards religious consolation, and the promise, used to compel passivity from restive believers the world over, of a better life hereafter. But Aikin ends her work on a quite different note:

> Beyond the proud oppressor's cruel grasp
> Seated secure; uninjur'd; undestroyed;
> Worthy of Gods: The freedom of the mind.[23]

Religious consolations are not enough in Aikin's scheme: what matters is the will and ability to think and speak freely. It is a right she claims for herself in spite of her gender and religious marginalisation. 'Corsica' offers no apology for its presence; it has no demurring female poetic figure acknowledging her lack of fitness to speak. Instead it plays a part in a national conversation and insists upon the right of its author to speak her mind.

Although 'Corsica' remained unpublished it did not remain unseen. It circulated in manuscript among the Dissenting circles of the north and news of it reached Priestley in Leeds. He was supportive of the idea that girls as well as boys merited an education, but he was clear about his reasons. 'Certainly, the minds of women are capable of the same improvement, and the same furniture, as those of men; and it is of importance that, when they have leisure, they should have the same resource in reading, and the same power of instructing the world by writing, that men have; and that, if they be mothers, they be capable of assisting in the instruction of their children.'[24] But in Aikin's case her blazing talent prompted from Priestley an acknowledgement of the weight a woman's voice might carry in a campaign for public sympathy. He asked her to send a manuscript copy of 'Corsica' to 'Mr Johnson in London.'[25] Aikin did as Priestley requested. Through him she was introduced to Johnson, and, as a result of his connection with Priestley, Johnson became the publisher of choice for the Dissenters of Warrington. In Anna Aikin he discovered a voice he made it his business to nurture.

Priestley was fearless in his pursuit of knowledge, his sacred duty. But he acknowledged that to demolish the structures of power in every sphere risked both his liberty and Johnson's. Writing at the end of 1769 he mused on the possibility that he and other enquirers after truth – Aikin, Franklin and Johnson among them – might find themselves muzzled. 'I should not be at all surprised if some restrictions were laid on the liberty of the press; and am not sorry that I have spoken my mind so freely before that time.'[26] The future of free speech was uncertain; the government had put soldiers on the streets and was not inclined to tolerate Dissent. But to enquire was to be free, and Priestley had no intention of ceasing to ask questions, or Johnson of ceasing to publish the results of his enquiries.

4

London

At the beginning of 1761 Johnson was an indentured apprentice to an obscure Baptist bookseller. By the end of 1769 he was a well-known figure in the London book trade, with a shop in Paternoster Row and a diverse and growing list. The speed with which he made his mark allows us to glimpse him at work. He appears as a confident, decisive figure, sure of his own mind. He is prepared to depart from tested names and genres; his acquisitions are driven by intellectual curiosity and religious faith. He takes nothing for granted: not what he should believe, nor what he should publish, nor how and with whom he should live. The relationships he forged in 1764 with Priestley, Newton and Fuseli formed the first threads in a web of writerly connections that had him at its centre and which would grow larger and more complex with every passing year.

The tradesmen of Paternoster Row had reason in 1769 to be thankful for secure homes and strong shopfront shutters. It was a year in which desperate workers rioted over food and pay and the Duke of Grafton's government turned its back on the principled patriots of Corsica in order to focus their energies westwards, as they treated the British citizens of the American colonies with dangerous contempt. Johnson, however, was by now securely established as a pillar of a productive neighbourhood of tradesmen and merchants, who were his customers as well as his competitors.

In the *General Evening Post* for the second week of January 1770 he advertised 'Johnson's complete pocket-book'; an account book expressly designed for the men of business amongst whom he lived. The pocket-book promised order and method for the industrious man; its pages were designed to record prosperity and growth. It contained, the advertisement boasted:

> a plain and concise method of keeping accounts of all monies received, paid, lent, or expended every day in the year, comprised in 52 pages properly ruled; also 52 pages ruled for entering all appointments, memorandums, and observations. Together with the following useful particulars: A correct list of the merchants and principal tradesmen in London, with their places of abode, and the numbers of their houses, compiled by a personal application to each house. A correct list of the bankers. The holidays kept at the Bank and public offices. A table of interest, at 5 per cent, for 1 day to 12 months, and for 1 pound to 1 thousand pounds.[1]

The pocket-book provides an apt illustration of Johnson's life and character: organised, methodical, punctilious and attuned to the rhythms and demands of the City trades. It was also a speculative enterprise, which involved gambling on a sufficient financial return to repay the effort of manually assembling and checking the details of all the merchants and tradesmen of London. It was the publication of a bookseller secure in his trade, able and prepared to take risks.

✝

In the same edition of the *General Evening Post* in which Johnson advertised his pocket-book a news report appeared, in a column entitled 'LONDON':

> Yesterday morning a little after six o'clock, a terrible fire broke out in the back shop of Mess. Johnson and Payne, booksellers, in Paternoster-row, which spread with the greatest rapidity, and soon consumed that house; Mr Upton's broker, which was formerly the Castle tavern; Mr Cock's printer, in Paternoster-row; Mrs Bateman's; and greatly damaged several others; it burnt indeed so extremely furious, that it seemed to threaten the whole neighbourhood.

Fire was a common occurrence in the old streets of the City, where wooden buildings and tightly packed warehouses offered few defences against its spread. But even by the standards of a community accustomed to living alongside its threat the fire that razed Johnson's shop and home at the beginning of 1770 was unprecedented in living memory. The blaze started in the early hours when most of the residents of Paternoster Row were still sleeping: 'Mr. Johnson had but just time to alarm his partner and the rest of the family', reported the *Middlesex Journal*, 'and they escaped, having only some of their books of accounts, the whole stock in trade and furniture being destroyed.'[2] The newspapers reported that Johnson and two other escapees were all slightly burnt. As the *London Evening Post* went to press, the day after the fire, Johnson's maidservant was still missing.

The scale of the blaze tested the City's firefighting capacity to the limit. The water-carrying engines were clogged with ice and snow and it took too long for them to be deployed. Volunteer firemen broke walls and used hand pumps to try and stop the spread of the flames but some hours after the fire was first contained it broke out again, spreading new fear through groups of traumatised residents. This fresh outbreak, reported the *General Evening Post*, added 'much to the distress of those individuals, who were nighest to it, and who but just collected together their scattered effects, were by this new alarm obliged a second time to remove them.' The clergy of St Paul's cancelled all their services for the day and threw open the doors of the Cathedral to those made homeless, Johnson and Fuseli among them. Slowly the occupants of Paternoster Row began counting their losses. In the days following the blaze pleas for lost possessions began to appear in the pages of the local papers. 'LOST, at the Fire in Pater-noster-row, a small Red Morocco Pocket-book with a silver lock, containing a promissory note for 100*l.* payable to the order of Samuel Acton, not indorsed, dated in November last, with sundry other papers of no use but to the owner.' Lost, 'two large silver table-spoons; a child's three tea-spoons, one pair of stone shoe-buckles, and one pair of silver, ditto'.[3]

Fuseli was not mentioned in any of the press reports of the fire, apart from the *Middlesex Journal*'s elliptical reference to 'the rest of the family'. His books, paintings, manuscripts, clothes and domestic goods all perished. Some among his Swiss friends and relations were sceptical about the reported scale of the disaster. His brother accused him of a 'lack of frugality' and received in return a reminder that Fuseli had lost 'all my clothes – apart from the gown and trousers that I had on, and all of my books, paintings, and sketches of apostles and evangelists that I had finished for Ely Cathedral which were to be copied onto glass by a painter.' The loss of the work for the Cathedral also involved the loss of the fee – 'another forty pounds.'[4]

Lavater too received his share of Fuseli's ire. 'You want proof of the fire [?] Write to London to Mr. Peyer von Schaffhausen, who lives near to the fire in Paternoster Row, or to Mr. Moser in Craven Street, Drury Lane, and ask them if it wasn't Johnson's house and what I had in there that had burned down!'[5] Fuseli found himself at a standstill, deprived of everything for which he had worked since his arrival in London. To start again in a hostile city seemed impossible. 'If it were just keeping going that mattered', he told Lavater, it might be possible to return to Switzerland or even rebuild a life from scratch in London 'and to make myself known in the disciplines of Latin, Greek, English, German, Italian, French, poetry, drawing and antiques'. He acknowledged that such a plan offered little hope of a sustainable future. 'I wouldn't be able to make ends meet and simultaneously put money aside.'[6]

In the face of ruin Fuseli determined to abandon piecemeal literary commissions and dedicate himself to art. In 1768 Sir Joshua Reynolds had advised him to travel to Italy if he was serious about his craft, in order to study the works of the Old Masters and so compensate for his lack of formal training. Coutts the banker offered to fund his travels in exchange for three history paintings that Fuseli hastily worked up from scratch. By spring the commission was fulfilled and Fuseli had gone. In November he still sounded frozen by shock at the ease with which the flames had swept the stuff of life away. He told Lavater he was unable to wrestle words or images onto the page. 'God knows just how many good things I have received from you since my stay here and how little I can do in return. I have lost the desire and perhaps the capacity to condense great thoughts and exquisite lines into three inches so that they may also glitter like a ... dagger in one's eyes.' He had tried, he promised, but his efforts were 'so substandard or so damaged by the flame ... that I beg you to forgive me.'[7]

The historical record leaves no trace of Johnson's reaction to Fuseli's departure. The press reports of the fire testify to a professional catastrophe that was absolute. Several of the City newspapers noted with sympathy that the fire had occurred during a period when Johnson and Payne were uninsured, since they had let an old policy lapse as they awaited a revaluation of their holdings. Johnson lost his home, his possessions, his income and all his stock. The fire ended his partnership with Payne and broke up the household in which Fuseli had professed himself 'blissfully happy'.[8] Fuseli responded by leaving the country to begin afresh on his own terms, as an artist rather than a literary hack for hire. Payne retired from bookselling and moved out of the City to Westminster where he attempted to make a living as a writer. Johnson left neither the profession nor the place ordained for him. It is tempting to speculate that he was bolstered by faith as he confronted the ruins of his house, or perhaps by the memory of the power of the pulpit his apprentice-master George Keith had offered the Dissenting preacher John Gill. The religion of his parents had taught him the value of strength in adversity and the stories of his Dissenting forefathers offered multiple examples of religious men triumphing over violently imposed homelessness. The surviving sources, however, offer certainty on only one point. In 1761 Johnson had been a young man alone. By 1770 he had drawn around himself a circle of friends.

PART TWO

RIOT (1770–1780)

Anonymous, *View of the entrance to St Paul's Churchyard and Paternoster Row, from Cheapside,* 1797

There is a dining room now, up a flight of stairs behind the shop. The walls are still bare since the artist is away, learning his craft. But the bookseller is not alone. As he rebuilds his life he opens his doors to friends and acquaintances who will come to call his house theirs. Anna Aikin and Joseph Priestley are already present at the table and their voices grow stronger as they are joined by new acquaintances. Prominent among the company during this first decade in the dining room is the Unitarian minister Theophilus Lindsey, whose arrival alters the geography of Johnson's spiritual existence. Many of the men who pass through the dining room, in contrast to Lindsey, are less concerned with spirituality than with the operations of the body, and they practise their faith by channelling their energies towards medical advancements that promise to alleviate suffering. Meanwhile, although Anna Aikin is still a rare female presence, in the shop below friends and customers alike are compelled to confront the logical vacuum underpinning the intellectual disenfranchisement of women. Upstairs in the candlelight, as servants clear the cod, veal and rice pudding, conversation ranges over the relationship between body and mind, the avoidable follies of an American War, the composition of the universe, the beauty of mathematics and the dangers of religious intolerance. At the end of the 1770s, however, religious intolerance is no longer merely a moral affront to natural justice. Instead it is a present danger to house, life and limb. As the shutters go up to protect those sheltering around the table, the streets outside are filled with the shouts of a rioting crowd, and the gutters run with gin, urine and blood.

5

Joineriana

When Anna Aikin's brother John recalled this period of Johnson's life it was the memory of friends that held fast. For once, in Aikin's telling, it was Johnson himself who took up the story. "'His friends,'" as he expressed it to a particular acquaintance, "came about him, and set him up again.'"[1] In manuscript notes the antiquary John Underhill repeated the suggestion that it was Johnson's friends who 'contributed to enable him to begin business again'.[2] No sources detail where Johnson slept in the nights following the fire, but by June he was trading again from temporary premises further along Paternoster Row. He was thirty-one when he lost his stock and home, and his whereabouts between mid-January and June are unknown. He appears to have raised money for his immediate needs from friends and by selling shares and copyrights[3] and it is likely that in the first few months of 1770 he was occupied in raising cash, as well as in searching for new premises and in reprinting work lost to the fire. By July he had a house.

The building on which Johnson took a lease, Number 72 St Paul's Churchyard, no longer survives. It was destroyed on December 29th 1940 in one of the deadliest raids of the Blitz, along with over five million books stored in shops and warehouses across the City, and the street-scape of Johnson's London. St Paul's Churchyard is a shadow street now, visible in outline thanks to the immovable bulwark of the Cathedral itself, which offers protection on one side to the ancient line of the thoroughfare. Paternoster Row is gone, marked only by a pedestrian passageway through to the privatised environment of Paternoster Square. The bookshops, taverns and printers in which knowledge was created and shared in the eighteenth century have been replaced by noodle bars and banks; the anarchic energy of the old street is contained by signs warning visitors that their behaviour is being monitored by security personnel. The sterile vistas of Paternoster Square are a world away from the tightly packed streets in which Johnson rebuilt his life in 1770. His was the period and the place of what one of his authors termed 'Joineriana', when men and women lived on top of their businesses and each other; when friends, colleagues, customers and competitors were drawn from the same pool of people, and where home and work nestled together under one roof.

Number 72 St Paul's Churchyard occupied a corner position on the other side of the road from the west door of the Cathedral. The great dome of St Paul's towered above the surrounding buildings, a physical manifestation of the Anglican Church from which Johnson dissented. Number 72 was one of the biggest buildings on either the Row or the Churchyard but it was nevertheless dwarfed by the scale of St Paul's. Johnson's new house was two doors along from London House Yard, where he took warehouse space, and it backed onto narrow Mitre Court and the rear of the houses on the south side of Paternoster Row. Its footprint was asymmetric, narrow at the front and wide at the back. Writing in 1839, an elderly gentleman who visited Johnson in his youth recalled how old-fashioned the building appeared. St Paul's Churchyard had none of the Georgian homogeneity of newer London streets and anyone walking eastwards to the old City would have felt themselves walking back in time.

Descriptions survive of two of the spaces at 72 St Paul's Churchyard. One is the shop itself: narrow and dark, with books displayed in the window; and with office space at the back, probably giving way to the warehouses and alleys of Mitre Court. The shop was a bookshop in the contemporary sense, open during trading hours to casual customers, with stock for sale on the shelves and in the window, but it was also the destination for those who visited Johnson on business. Suppliers or authors might start their conversations with him or one of his assistants in the shop before being ushered upstairs, if their business demanded, to continue the discussion. The other was the dining room – the room decorated with Fuseli's sketches. Here Johnson conducted negotiations by day and, as the decade drew onwards, brought his friends and authors together for dinner by night. 'I was often surprised at the quiet comfort, and ease with which he entertained the characters who assembled at his literary parties', commented one of his guests. Those parties were held 'in a plain moderate sized room, where, at other times, important transactions took place, and immense sums were paid to authors, artists, stationers, printers, and others concerned with him in trade.'[4] William Blake's biographer Alexander Gilchrist offers a further description of Johnson's dining room: 'a little quaintly shaped upstairs room, with walls not at right angles.'[5]

This odd-shaped dining room was the heart of the house. It was the space where the public and private lives of the building and its occupants met, where Johnson was simultaneously at home and at work. Priestley took up residence for weeks at a time, making the dining room his office and receiving room during long winter visits to London. Friends congregated for food and conversation; paper-sellers and printers haggled over prices at the table. Most of the time Johnson's staff pass silently through the paper traces of the house and its inhabitants, although one guest recalled that one of the shopmen, a Mr Redman, had originally trained as a schoolmaster and 'retained the cross habits and manners of the pedagogue'.[6] At least one live-in maid must have been present at all times to lay fires and cook for the crowds of visitors. The work of the servants was supervised by two Liverpool nieces who came to keep house for their London uncle. A 'Miss Johnson' (the daughter of Johnson's older brother John) and a 'Miss Hunter' (daughter of Rowland Hunter, Johnson's erstwhile brother-in-law) both appear as the recipients of thanks and good wishes in the letters written after Priestley had left London to return home.

Writing to his landlord in 1797, Johnson himself provides us with a rare glimpse of his house. 'I have been your tenant twenty seven years & have prevented the decay of your house as far as necessary repairs could do it', he opens. 'But there is no preventing the dilapidations of time. A new roof was wanted & it has had one this year. A new wall is now necessary to its being inhabited with safety, & other repairs must be made.'[7] Johnson had good reason to fear for the fabric of his house, since the fragility of the old wooden structures of the City did little to alleviate the danger of fire. There was nothing particularly comfortable or luxurious about life at 72 St Paul's Churchyard. The rooms were small and cramped, smoke and smells mingled together throughout the building, the packed closes and alleys running behind it offered little in the way of light or fresh air. Johnson's decision to re-roof the building at his own expense in 1797 suggests that there was nothing very weatherproof about the building he inhabited either. Set against all this, though, was the fact that the house represented both solidity and promise.

✢

Three vignettes reveal, in contrasting ways, the life Johnson made for himself at St Paul's Churchyard in the first half of the 1770s. In June 1774 we see him calling on the Marquis of Rockingham at his house in Grosvenor Square in the company of Edmund Burke, Whig MP and author of A *Philosophical Enquiry into the Origin of our Ideas of the Sublime and the Beautiful*. In February 1774 the House of Lords (then the final court of appeal in England) had heard the case of Donaldson v. Becket, and had ruled that booksellers' statutory copyrights lasted for fourteen years only, after which perpetual copyright reverted back to the author. London booksellers banded together to petition the House of Commons to pass legislation overturning the decision, and a bill in support of their claim was passed at the end of May.

Rockingham asked Burke to visit with Johnson in the run-up to the House of Lords vote on the Commons bill. Burke was sympathetic to the booksellers' cause and lobbied Rockingham to vote in their favour. 'I wish you would meet me in Grosvenor Square', Rockingham wrote as the vote neared. 'If you can I should be glad Mr Johnson was with you.'[8] Johnson was still a relative newcomer in the world of London bookselling when he called on Rockingham. In comparison many of his friends and competitors in the Churchyard and Paternoster Row headed famous, long-established firms. On Paternoster Row Thomas Longman had inherited his business from his uncle; and Andrew Millar, to whom Fuseli had been introduced on his arrival in London, had been trading on the Strand since the 1740s. Nevertheless it was Johnson who went with Burke to convince Rockingham of the merits of the booksellers' cause. Although the House of Lords again rejected their demands the episode established Johnson at the heart of the City committees formed to defend literary property. Burke and Johnson would subsequently find themselves on opposite sides of debates about the most fundamental questions dominating British life but at Rockingham's house they argued in support of each other.

‡

In 1772 Johnson published his friend Samuel Paterson's *Joineriana*. Paterson was a bibliophile, a bibliographer and an occasional bookseller. He ran an auction house in Essex Street, just off the Strand, but his tendency to read rather than sell his stock meant that he was often in financial difficulty. *Joineriana* is a strange work; a miscellany of observations and anecdotes. 'To write, is mechanical; but to be an Author, is no easy matter', Paterson argues. 'Those who think much, for the most part, write little – those who write much, generally, think little.'[9] The hacks who fill newspapers are 'paragraph-mongers'; bookmakers 'are the common pests of useful letters.' The bookseller, meanwhile, 'is generally a bad judge of everything – but his stupidity shines most conspicuously, in that particular brand of knowledge by which he is to get his bread.'[10] Johnson himself is quoted, in the guise of Paterson's cynical and knowing advisor. 'He talks of uncommon gratuities, which have often followed both common and uncommon Dedications – such as sinecure places and sine-cure livings', reports Paterson, in an essay on 'Dedication'. 'Surely, he must mean to impose upon my simplicity! – I should think so, if I did not know him to be a thorough honest man – for, according to my conception, there can be no such places – no such benefices.'[11] Johnson and Paterson stand together here, poking fun at the corruptions of their world, in which empty positions and tied houses can be bought for no more than a little obsequious flattery.

The figure about whom Paterson is most complimentary is that of the 'Freethinker'. 'It becomes every sensible man to be a Freethinker', he writes. 'Nay more, that it is his duty, as a rational being.'[12] Free thinking, however, is not an untrammelled right, nor something that can be disconnected from the public good. 'Men, however enlightened, are not to throw out at random – to pull down, from meer rage and wantonness of pulling down – to try experiments upon the weak and wavering ... as though they were angling for gudgeons.'[13] Instead the Freethinker has a responsibility to mould his thinking to the requirements of society, and to temper his philosophical speculations accordingly. 'He considers himself, in a great measure, born for the service of society – and if he may promulgate any good, without the hazard of bringing on a great inconveniency, he is ready, at all times, to exert his faculties.'[14] Under the guise of a self-mocking joke, and through a reworking of the miscellaneous, familiar form popularised in the period-icals of the middle of the century, Paterson argued for a tempering of his age's spirit of enquiry, for moderation and balance.

This question, about how to be a Freethinker without being a radical, about how to restore the structures of a corrupt world without tearing down its pillars, was one that increasingly preoccupied Johnson and his growing circle of authors in the 1770s. Priestley had one answer, about the extent to which Freethinkers should be prepared to go in pursuit of truth; Paterson had another. At 72 St Paul's Churchyard, men on opposite sides of the question met in the spirit of Paterson's *Joineriana*, in which miscellaneous ideas and individuals could come together to represent the spirit of their age.

✝

> There is a vice, said to be among us of late years (tho' 'tis certain our ancestors knew very little of it) – a vice, which I forbear to name – Yet the apostle PAUL has stigmatized it sufficiently – He calls it the sin of men abusing themselves with men – against which detestable and unmanly lust, a more terrific punishment, as I conceive, even than death, might be awarded – more especially to such timid, such chicken-hearted wretches – Castration.[15]

Thus writes Paterson, in an essay in *Joineriana* on 'Law and Lawyers'. The passage serves as a reminder of one possible reason why so little evidence survives regarding Johnson's private life. For much of the 1770s Fuseli remained abroad, studying in Rome in order to remake himself as the single-minded artist he had determined to become. In London, meanwhile, a new friend introduced Johnson to a different side of metropolitan life. In 1768 a young Scotsman called John Murray sank most of his wife's dowry into a bookselling business on the Strand. As a newcomer to the market he was ideally positioned to make the most of the House of Lords decision against perpetual copyright in 1774 and by the middle of the decade he had made a great deal of money and had established himself as a prominent figure in City bookselling. He formed an enduring friendship and business partnership with Johnson. Murray was well connected to medical and scientific circles in Edinburgh, as was Johnson, through Priestley, to those in London, and they pooled their connections and resources to build a joint list which represented the most exciting scientific innovations north and south of the boarder. They bought books for each other and revelled in the power their connection gave them. 'Joey Johnson and I produce wonderful Publications in the Winter', Murray wrote to a mutual friend, William Enfield. 'Tell us what we are to expect from Warrington.'[16]

In the same letter to Enfield, an ordained Unitarian minister, Murray passed on more news of their friend. 'Mr Jos Johnson is in good health', he reported. 'I hear nothing of his I-ch nor the bountifull Lady who bestowed it upon him.'[17] The cheerful familiarity of Murray's missive is striking. Venereal disease was a fact of life for any man who bought the services of the prostitutes of the City and Murray presented Johnson's complaint as an ordinary matter; the subject of an affectionate joke between men. The Johnson who frequents the brothels (or the Molly houses) of the streets running north and east from his house stands alongside the upright Freethinker who publishes Priestley. He appears next to the pillar of the bookselling community who negotiates with Rockingham and Burke; and by the side of the publisher of Paterson's suggestion that castration might enable the cleansing of vice from the soul of the nation. He is there too alongside the figure of the master of the house standing in the doorway of 72 St Paul's Churchyard, waiting to welcome those in need of shelter.

6

Freethinker

In September 1773 a Church of England vicar called Theophilus Lindsey packed up the manuscript pages of an 'Apology' to his parishioners, and handed them to the carrier for safe passage from his vicarage in Yorkshire to Johnson's shop in London. A few weeks later Lindsey and his wife Hannah sold their possessions and relinquished their vicarage, voluntarily making themselves homeless. In London that winter they took lodgings in Holborn, where piles of books served in place of table and chairs. In Johnson's dining room they found respite from the smell of horse excrement that drifted through their cramped ground-floor quarters, as they began to plan for a home they could call their own.

Theophilus and Hannah Lindsey appeared at St Paul's Churchyard in February 1774 as modern-day Black Bartholomew's Day martyrs. Lindsey resigned his position as vicar in the parish of Catterick because he could not reconcile possession of a Church of England living with his conscience. He was born into an Anglican family in 1723 and educated at Cambridge but in the 1760s decided he could no longer subscribe to the Thirty-Nine Articles. Just as Priestley and Johnson were reading their way towards Unitarianism, so Lindsey experienced a religious awakening in which the doctrine of the Trinity (adherence to which was one of the requirements of the Articles) was no longer tenable.

When Priestley looked back in old age on his friendship with Lindsey, he remembered that Lindsey had been struggling with his conscience from the point of their first meeting in the 1760s. Initially, however, Priestley encouraged him to remain an Anglican vicar and attempt reform of the Church from within. In the summer of 1771 Lindsey travelled to London, where he began collecting signatures for a document that would become known as the Feathers Tavern Petition. This Petition asked Parliament to repeal the requirement for clerical subscription and was signed by over two hundred sympathetic clergy. The petition was defeated in Parliament in February 1772 and the petitioners re-gathered, determined to present their argument once again and to escalate their campaign to do away with subscription for students entering Oxford and Cambridge. They believed the best hope for lasting reform lay with the younger generation and that it was thus particularly important that young men should not be corrupted at the outset of their university studies.

Lindsey insisted there was glory in the defeat of the petition. 'Truth and reason were all for us, and overpowered only by Power.'[1] In reality, the emphatic nature of the defeat revealed the gulf between Lindsey and his Church, and between the country at large and those who dared to think differently. In December 1771 Priestley's nomination as scientist and astronomer to Captain James Cook's second expedition was overturned because of his religious beliefs. 'Twenty years ago', Lindsey wrote, 'one so singularly qualified for the employment, might have been chosen, and his dissent in religious points, no objection; but I think our *Public* has been retrograde in those respects ever since, and we shall become less liberal eer we are more so'.[2] Reforming the Church from within had proved impossible. With the example set by the evicted ministers of Black Bartholomew's Day in 1662 in his mind, Lindsey posted a resignation letter and Hannah Lindsey started packing.

During his final weeks in Yorkshire Lindsey drafted a detailed explanation of the circumstances leading to his resignation. By the time he arrived in London Johnson had published the manuscript. Much of *The Apology of Theophilus Lindsey, M.A., on resigning the vicarage of Catterick, Yorkshire* was taken up with a biblically grounded repudiation of the doctrine of the Trinity and its publication thrust Lindsey into the limelight as one of the most controversial figures of the decade. Many commentators viewed him as a traitor to the Church and to Christ. The anonymous author of a pamphlet sold by Johnson's old apprentice-master remarked that if Lindsey was in the mood for apologising he should do so to the people of Catterick for abandoning them in order to indulge his own scruples. The writer also angrily rejected the suggestion that there was any comparison between Lindsey's situation and the privations suffered by the Bartholomew's Day martyrs. All the ejected ministers believed in the Trinity, he protested, and all suffered quietly and without show. The first assertion depended on a little historical licence; the second sought to deprive Lindsey's actions of rhetorical power by presenting his resignation as motived solely by a vain-glorious desire to appear as a martyr.[3]

While Lindsey initially tried to exercise freedom of conscience from within the Church of England, Priestley wanted the Dissenters to be free from the constraints under which they lived and worshipped. He believed his cause to be unarguable, but in both 1772 and 1773 parliamentary campaigns for Dissenting freedoms failed. After extensive discussions during the winter evenings at St Paul's Churchyard Johnson insisted that Priestley's *Theological Repository* should be halted. Johnson bore much of the cost of the *Repository* and he continued to pay for it even in the aftermath of the Paternoster Row fire, but in early 1771 he withdrew his support as it became clear that the *Repository* stood no chance of ever recouping its costs. Deprived of this platform for his work Priestley turned his attention back to a project begun in the 1760s, his four-volume *Institutes of Natural and Revealed Religion*, which Johnson published between 1772 and 1774. In the *Institutes* Priestley argued that the only possible pure religious beliefs were those that tallied with the evidence of the natural world: everything else was the result of human superstition and corruption. The *Institutes* was a powerful articulation of the Unitarian position and the work established Priestley as one of the most important exponents of a refashioned faith. At stake in the work of Priestley and Lindsey were fundamental questions about what kind of country Britain wanted and needed to be. 'Religious and civil liberty are exquisitely connected', insisted one of Lindsey's anonymous defenders. 'No man can be obsequious to religious thraldom, and at the same time genuine in his feeling of political independence.'[4]

✝

In September 1772 an argument broke out between Priestley and Johnson when Priestley was offered the post of companion to the Earl of Shelburne. The offer was tempting. The post came with a house on Shelburne's Wiltshire estate and a salary. The duties were light. Shelburne wanted someone to catalogue his books and keep his library up to date, with whom he could freely discuss politics. He was a prominent opposition politician, sympathetic to the complaints of both the American Colonists and the Dissenters, and he offered the position to Priestley at the suggestion of the Dissenting minister Richard Price.

Johnson was fiercely opposed to the idea of his friend compromising his independence for an aristocratic paymaster. The letter in which he remonstrated with Priestley has been lost, but from Priestley's account it is clear that Johnson objected to Shelburne's character and argued that employment in his household would prevent Priestley from being master of his own conduct. Yet Johnson was also blunt about the chances of any of Priestley's publications making either of them any money. 'As to the History of Experimental Philosophy, it does not appear, from Mr Johnson's last account of the sale of my History of Vision, &c, that it will be worth my while to prosecute it any farther.'[5] Prosperous friends might insist on the importance of remaining independent but none of them, Priestley complained, had any idea of the reality of his situation. He had a wife and growing family to support, and running his experimental workshop was an expensive business. Shelburne offered to take on those costs and thus enable Priestley to continue with work he knew to be important. In November 1772, as he prepared to journey from Leeds to London (sharing a coach with Lindsey and another Feathers Tavern petitioner in order to reduce the cost), he wrote to Price that he was minded to accept Shelburne's offer. 'Those who are acquainted with Lord Shelburne encourage me to accept of his proposal; but most of those who know the world in general, but not Lord Shelburne in particular, dissuade me from it.'[6] To be blind to the virtues of those whose lives were different from one's own was not, Priestley suggested, a vice from which his own friends were free. In June 1773 the Priestleys moved to a house in Calne, on Shelburne's estate. In his library Priestley resumed work on essays on the Dissenters' campaign, and in the workshop Shelburne built for him he began a series of experiments on air.

✢

As news of his impending resignation spread in the autumn of 1773, Lindsey was offered the ministry of a Dissenting chapel in Leeds. He refused. His intention was to try to gather together a group of Unitarians drawn from the Church of England, rather than to lead the worship of those who had already dissented. He planned to open a new church, where he would conduct services using a rewritten version of the Anglican liturgy. It was an enterprise which presented more of a threat to the unity of the Established Church than did the existence of disparate groups of grudgingly tolerated Dissenters. In the inaugural sermon he drafted for his church he chose as his text a verse from Ephesians: 'Endeavouring to keep the unity of the Spirit in the bond of peace.' No text, protested one of his detractors, could be less appropriate. 'And how does he himself endeavour it? why, by endeavouring to draw the good People from their national Church, the proper Place of Worship, to hear his vain Babbling in an unconsecrated Auction-room.'[7]

The 'unconsecrated Auction-room' was in Essex House on Essex Street, just off the Strand. Lindsey was offered a lease on the room thanks to the efforts of one old friend – Priestley – and two new friends in London – Franklin and Johnson. Franklin sent encouraging news of distinguished people who stood ready to support the foundation of a new chapel through their presence in the congregation, and Johnson went to work to bring the project to fruition. Essex House was in the possession of Johnson's friend Samuel Paterson, who was sympathetic to the Unitarian cause and had celebrated the figure of the Freethinker in *Joineriana*. Paterson's auction business was doing badly and Johnson knew him to be urgently in need of money. Sympathetic Unitarians in London and beyond donated funds to support Lindsey and raised £200 to rent the room for two years. Much of the money came from strangers and, Lindsey reported, 'most of them dissenters.' But he continued, 'I am now a dissenter myself.' He was, he concluded, 'happy in it. Nay, I would say to you, I glory in it.'[8]

As Lindsey moved steadily further away from the Established Church, he experienced some of the insidious ways in which the State constrained the activities of Dissenters. Two MPs summoned him for meetings in which they warned him that any remaining public sympathy would turn to hostility if he pressed ahead with his plans. Johnson went forth to do battle with the authorities for a licence for the chapel but at every stage legal obstacles were thrown in his way. At the beginning of April building work in Essex Street was finished and the liturgy worked on by Priestley, Johnson and Lindsey at St Paul's Churchyard was printed and ready, but the licence all Dissenters needed to worship legally had not been granted. Johnson ran all over Westminster and the City, pushed from pillar to post by magistrates who found a multitude of reasons to withhold permission for the chapel to open. Eventually Johnson and Lindsey managed to talk their way into the chambers of the Chief Justice Lord Mansfield, who was outraged that petty functionaries were subverting the legal framework of religious toleration because of their own prejudices. 'He came like a lion', Lindsey told a supporter. 'But we have not succeeded without striking with the great hammer.'[9]

On Sunday April 17th 1774, Lindsey preached his first sermon at Essex Street. Johnson was in the congregation, along with Priestley and Franklin. For all four men, as well as for Lindsey and Hannah, it was a defining moment in the battle for Dissenting rights. For the first time the Unitarians had a church of their own. John Lee, a lawyer who had advised Johnson during his battle to get the chapel licenced, reported that there were ten coaches at the door, and that somewhere between two and three hundred well-to-do strangers had appeared to hear Lindsey preach. The Dukes of Norfolk and Richmond were among the crowd; so were three clergyman, a handful of barristers and a government spy. 'Everything passed very well', Lindsey wrote the day afterwards. 'Some disturbance was apprehended, and foreboded to me by great names, – but not the least movement of the kind.' Many of those present commented on the difference between the experience of being in Essex Street and being in an Anglican church. 'I should have blushed', Lindsey wrote robustly, 'to have appeared in a white garment.'[10] After a few weeks the government spy melted away, rather to the amusement of those in the congregation who had been unconvinced by his professed religiosity. Within a week of the first service Johnson had rushed Lindsey's inaugural sermon into print and the ability to read the words preached at Essex Street inspired some of Lindsey's more outspoken opponents to take up their own pens once more. The author of one pamphlet termed his sermon 'poison'; another implied that a little persecution might be just what Lindsey and his fellow Dissenters required. Too much toleration, he argued, put true Christians at risk. 'If these *Unitarians* should ever gain an Establishment (which I trust they never will) I very much doubt whether we should meet with the like Indulgence.'[11]

✢

When Lindsey stood in his frock coat at his auction-room pulpit on Sunday April 17th, in front of a congregation comprised of friends and strangers, the devout and the curious, he largely kept clear of political matters. Only in one respect was the subject unavoidable. 'In later times', he acknowledged, 'great benefits have been derived to true religion, from those who have refused to submit to the impositions of civil and ecclesiastical authority in matters of faith; and who, on that principle, have had the virtue and courage to depart from the established forms in their several countries, to worship God in the way they believed most acceptable to him.'[12] The country that most completely embodied freedom of belief was America. Its first citizens crossed an ocean in pursuit of a space where they could worship freely, and its inhabitants held fast to their right to practise their faith away from the mechanisms of State control.

For the men and women sitting in Essex House, the import of Lindsey's generalisation was unavoidable. Six weeks after he preached his sermon the British government passed a set of laws known as the 'Intolerable Acts': a package of legislation designed to punish the citizens of Massachusetts for the Boston Tea Party. The Intolerable Acts closed the port of Boston, brought Massachusetts's State affairs and the administration of justice directly under the control of the British government, and required the colony to house British soldiers. A furious Benjamin Franklin responded by publishing his satirical 'Act to Enforce Obedience' in the New England newspapers, but he also offered to repay the duty on the tea damaged in Boston harbour himself in order to avert the outbreak of war.

Franklin continued to talk and write of the importance of Britain reconciling herself with her colony, even as he found himself viewed with mounting distrust by the authorities who dealt with him not as a loyal subject of the King but as a representative of a hostile enemy nation. In the spring and summer of 1774 Essex Street became a haven for Franklin in a city where he had once felt completely at home. He had friends in the congregation, and from Lindsey's pulpit he heard the Colonists praised for their bravery. 'He dreaded the war', Priestley recalled. But, 'that the issue would be favourable to America, he never doubted. The English, he used to say, may take all our great towns, but that will not give them possession of the country.'[13]

Priestley himself was in little doubt about the cause of government hostility towards the Colonists. In 1774 Johnson published his *Address to the Protestant Dissenters*, written in advance of the general election of 1774. In the first part of the *Address* Priestley urged his fellow Dissenters to vote against those MPs who had failed to support repeal of the Test and Corporation Acts; in the second part he attacked the government for its treatment of America. 'Religious liberty', he insisted in his opening, 'cannot be maintained except on the basis of *civil liberty*.' The government opposed religious liberty because the example of America made them fear for their own power should they allow it to spread. 'Can you suppose that those who are so violently hostile to the *offspring* of the English dissenters, should be friendly to the remains of the *parent stock?*' Priestley's imagery allied the

Dissenters of the mother country with the freedom fighters of the colony and he was uncompromising in his own allegiances:

> Do you imagine, my fellow-citizens, that we can sit still, and be the idle spectators of the chains which are forging for our brethren in America, with safety to ourselves? Let us suppose America to be completely enslaved, in consequence of which the English court can command all the money, and all the force of that country; will they like to be so arbitrary abroad, and have their power confined at home?[14]

In the second part of the *Address* Priestley distilled many of his conversations with Franklin. His identification of such close connections between the Dissenters and the Colonists reflected the extent to which the two men believed the political fortunes of their causes to be linked. At stake for both was the question of how to be free in a country whose government feared freedom. One solution was to create places in which it might be possible to practise freedom, and to model it for a citizenry who could then claim it for themselves. The Essex Street chapel was one such place: a hard-won refuge against prejudice where friends and fellow believers could gather to worship as they pleased. Johnson's shop in St Paul's Churchyard was another.

Essex Street offered a geographical, intellectual and spiritual contrast to St Paul's Cathedral at the other end of the Strand. The Cathedral was visible for miles around; the hierarchies of the Anglican Church were represented in stone within its walls. The centrality of the Church of England to the political and religious life of the capital and the nation was mirrored by the way the Cathedral's scale dominated the surrounding streets. St Paul's represented centuries of tradition and stability, as well as the demand that its congregation should acquiesce in the structures of belief represented in its services and architecture. Essex Street, by contrast, was a hastily fitted-out room; barely tolerated by those with the power to rule on its legality. Lindsey presented himself not as the father of his congregation, marked out as different in clerical robes, but as a fellow enquirer, who read in the Scriptures that to believe was to ask questions of power. Only a handful of the thousands who passed along the Strand each day were aware of Essex Street's existence, while the presence of St Paul's on the streetscape of the thoroughfare was inescapable. The conflict between Cathedral and chapel was asymmetric from the outset, and Johnson saw the truth of this every week as he walked from east to west to worship. But the print pulpit he offered Lindsey went some way to redressing this balance, as sermons taking place in an overlooked London auction house reverberated on paper across the country. Essex Street became a second fixed point on Johnson's compass; the spiritual counterpoint to his domestic and commercial moorings at home. He worshipped in the chapel for the rest of his life and the journey down the Strand on a Sunday morning was a central beat in the rhythm of his existence. Lindsey and Hannah became staunch supporters of both Johnson and his business, and the three remained friends all their lives.

✢

At the end of the 1770s Johnson brought out the first collected edition of Franklin's works in England. The collection was edited by Franklin's friend Benjamin Vaughan, who during production lost faith in the undertaking, swamped by a morass of errors and the extent of Franklin's work. 'These circumstances', he confessed, 'had so much affected my mind, that upon a review of the printed pages, I had determined to destroy the whole impression'. Johnson, however, 'told me that he could with the utmost care cancel the exceptionable pages, and laughed at me for low spirits.'[15] The edition appeared and Franklin's words reached a British readership. But Franklin himself had gone. On March 20th 1775 he set sail for America. Shortly after he left a warrant was issued in London for his arrest. He spent his last day in England with Priestley and together they read American newspaper reports of local towns issuing statements in support of the beleaguered citizens of Boston. 'Dr Franklin has left us', wrote Priestley a day later. 'I do not know that he has any thing particular in view. He told me in general that he thought he did no good here, and might do some in America.'[16]

7

Essays Medical and Experimental

In the dining room at St Paul's Churchyard the conversation had a tendency to turn bloody. Between 1770 and 1780 Johnson and his guests turned their attention to dentistry, uterine haemorrhage, inoculation, experimental drugs, asthma, geometry, combustion, gases, rheumatism, material science, electricity, astronomy and surgery. A few of Johnson's scientific visitors during his early years in the Churchyard were well-off men pursuing scholarly preoccupations. More were practising doctors who saw daily in their working lives the desperate consequences of ignorance and incuriousness. As a young man trading on Fish Street Hill, Johnson had sold books to the trainee doctors who passed his shop. During his first decade at St Paul's Churchyard he drew around him men of science who, like him, understood the pursuit of knowledge that alleviated suffering as an act of political kindness. The scientific books he published as he rebuilt his business reflected that understanding, offering guidance on specific subjects as well as a model of how to be a person of faith in a changing world.

In 1767, when Johnson was just six years free of his apprenticeship and still in partnership with Benjamin Davenport, he published Thomas Percival's *Essays Medical and Experimental*. Percival was one of the first pupils at the Warrington Academy and an early and devoted follower of Unitarianism. From Warrington he travelled north to Edinburgh for his medical training, following a path taken by many aspiring doctors in the eighteenth century. Dissenting students had to go to Scotland for all forms of university education because of their exclusion from Oxford and Cambridge, and Edinburgh was home to the only medical school in Britain where students were taught along the proto-clinical lines pioneered at the medical school in Leiden. Leiden and Edinburgh-trained doctors learnt their trade through anatomy classes, intensive lecturing and years of hospital ward-rounds; a model of medical education that remains largely unchanged today. During the second half of the eighteenth century Scottish-trained doctors effected a revolution in British medicine, and Johnson was one of several London publishers to provide a platform for their thinking. Percival and his contemporaries were taught to view themselves simultaneously as practitioners and scientists, engaged both in healing the sick and in battling pain and disease through research and experimentation. 'There are two methods of acquiring experience in the art of medicine; one by reading, the other by practice', Percival wrote in the volume he published with Johnson. 'Both are necessary to form the skilful and expert physician; but without the concurring assistance of our judgement and understanding, neither of them will be found of any other avail, than to perplex us with uncertainty and to lead us into error.'[1]

The doctors who gathered around Johnson took Percival's exhortation to combine theory and judgement to heart. Johnson's own interest in the qualities and conduct necessary in a physician is evident in many of the works he published. The author of an anonymous pamphlet on the subject dating from 1772 insisted that aspiring doctors must cultivate knowledge of different languages, mathematics and natural philosophy, so immense was the task confronting those who sought to understand the mysteries of the human body. 'In theology we may always refer to the Bible; in law to the settled constitution of our country; but there is no constitution so unsettled as the animal system.'[2] Four years later John Millar published his *Discourse on the Duty of Physicians* with Johnson, in which he argued that the moment was ripe for medical breakthroughs. Particularly significant was that medical science was no longer exclusively the preserve of a leisured elite. 'The chains of ignorance are broken!' he exulted. 'The charms of mystery dispelled! Monopoly and Exclusion, the last feeble efforts of despotism, abolished; and unbounded scope for emulation and industry universally established!'[3]

Millar was over-optimistic when he proclaimed the chains of ignorance to be broken. Inevitably, many of the remedies propounded by the doctors Johnson published were both incorrect and dangerous. Even when the science was wrong, however, there was much that was valuable in the medical volumes issued under his name. The doctors on Johnson's list wrote of their patients and the human body with compassionate curiosity, and they embodied an approach to scientific research which valued observation over dogma. Johnson himself was less interested in swelling the number of works on purportedly cutting-edge medical discoveries than in issuing prescriptions for improving the treatment of the sick that were straightforward to duplicate.

In this spirit he published the work of John Aikin, brother of Anna and another Edinburgh-trained doctor, on the importance of ventilation and space in crowded hospital wards. Aikin was sympathetic to the charitable instincts that drove well-meaning philanthropists to establish hospitals, but he was deeply frustrated by the obvious dangers posed by badly designed warehouses for the sick. In an account based on his own experience as a young doctor he described the despair felt by the physician '[as he] walks through the long wards of a crowded Hospital, and surveys the languid countenances of the patients, when he feels the peculiarly noisome effluvia so unfriendly to every vigorous principle of life, and compares their transient effect upon him, with that to be expected by those who are constantly breathing them and imbibing them at every pore, he will be apt to look upon the Hospital as a dismal prison, where the sick are shut up from the rest of mankind to perish by mutual contagion.'[4]

Aikin's prescription for change was revolutionary in its simplicity. He recommended that hospital wards should be built with high sash windows, opened top and bottom to allow the circulation of air and proper ventilation, that patients should be housed in cubicles rather than open wards to prevent the spread of infection, and that those well enough to be moved should be helped to get up each day to sit in communal spaces while their beds were aired.

Another Johnson doctor who believed passionately in the importance of fresh air was John Aikin's Warrington contemporary Edward Rigby. In the early 1770s Rigby was working in Norwich, where he was frequently called on to try and save the lives of women in labour. His patients lived predominantly in the city's poorest quarters and in 1776 he drew on his experiences at hundreds of births to publish his *Essay on the Uterine Haemorrhage*. Johnson was Rigby's sole English publisher, but the *Essay* was of such importance that it went through multiple editions and was translated into French and German. Rigby described placenta praevia; he gave detailed instructions about how to examine for causes of bleeding, and how to turn breech babies in utero in order to increase the chances of mother and child surviving.

The women Rigby attended were among the most marginalised and vulnerable members of society and they were often in desperate straits by the time he arrived, labouring with no medical attention in dirty and airless rooms. His volume exemplified the practical compassion that characterised many of the doctors Johnson befriended, and Johnson himself. In case after case Rigby described how his first action on arriving at a birth was to open the windows to let in fresh air; his second was to demand clean, cool water with which to sponge feverish faces and hands. Throughout his *Essay* Rigby argued against doctrinaire treatment of labouring women. What was needed, he argued, was a set of empirically observed principles that would allow physicians to consider the evidence of their eyes and to make a qualified judgement about when and how to intervene. Like others published by Johnson, he concluded by asserting his belief in the importance of writing. 'If I shall be', he concluded, 'but in a single instance, the means of saving the life of a fellow-creature, the little trouble I have had in throwing my thoughts together upon the subject, will not be lost labour, nor these pages, few as they are, be written in vain.'[5] John Aikin shared Rigby's belief that pregnancy offered no grounds upon which to infantilise women or deprive them of their individuality or agency. 'The chief source of error in the treatment of puerperal women', he wrote, 'has been considering the state of parturition too much a disease, rather than a regular operation of nature. From hence has proceeded that numerous train of arbitrary rules and customs relating to diet, confinement, and nursing, which are applied indiscriminately to all persons without regard to their particular state or constitution.'[6]

Some of the doctors who dined with Johnson were more concerned with the fundamentals of physiology than with improving methods of treatment. In 1768 he published the first of multiple editions of George Fordyce's *Elements of the Practice of Physic.* Fordyce sought to battle diseases of the human body by going back to first principles in an extended investigation of the nature of disease and its causes which drew on the work of a new generation of experimental chemists for inspiration. 'Disease', he wrote, 'is such an alteration of the chemical properties of the fluids or solids, or of their organization, or of the action of the moving power, as produces an inability or difficulty of performing the functions of the whole, or any part of the system; or pain; or a preternatural evacuation.'[7] Fordyce lived on Essex Street, near Samuel Paterson's auction room, and he combined medical work with lecturing on chemistry to groups of students who came to his house every morning. He and Johnson formed an enduring friendship and as the years went on Fordyce became a familiar presence in the dining room at St Paul's Churchyard.

It was probably Fordyce who encouraged John Hunter to send his manuscript on *The Natural History of Human Teeth* to Johnson in 1771. Hunter was a major figure in medical London and in the late 1750s Fordyce had been among the crowds of aspiring doctors who thronged to his lectures on surgery. Hunter learnt his trade first as an assistant to his brother William (another Scottish-trained physician) and then as an army surgeon during the Seven Years War. On the battlefield he saw the brutal limitations of his art. Men who suffered surgical intervention on their wounds were just as likely to die as those who went untreated and sometimes their suffering was worse. He witnessed the mysterious ways in which the body repaired itself and was forced to confront the paucity of surgical knowledge. When Hunter returned to London he devoted himself to furthering his own understanding and that of generations of students, driven forward by his belief that without a true appreciation for the intricacies of the human frame surgeons would never be able to do their patients more good than harm. He collected a menagerie of living and dead animals for the purposes of comparative anatomy and, in order to earn money, joined the dental practice of James Spence, one of the few practitioners to treat dentistry as a branch of medicine rather than a mechanical trade.

In early 1771 Hunter approached Johnson about the publication of his *History of Human Teeth*. He was anxious to publish in return for a significant sum since he was on the point of getting married and wanted to open his own surgical establishment, where he could see patients and take paying pupils. Johnson realised that Hunter's manuscript was groundbreaking, but that words alone would serve neither reader nor writer well in a volume dedicated to the systems of the mouth and jaw. He employed an artist to draw to Hunter's specification and then sent sketches out to a trusted circle of freelance engravers. The resulting images were both beautiful and macabre. Johnson wrote of them with pride. In an advertisement he boasted that Hunter's treatise was illustrated 'with Sixteen elegant and accurate Copper-plates, from the Drawings of *Riemsdyk*, taken under the Author's Inspection, and engraved by the best Masters'.[8] Sixteen elegant and accurate copper-plates represented a substantial investment, but the risk paid off and when all Johnson's expenses were paid Hunter made £1,000 from the sale of his work. Calculating contemporary comparisons for such a sum is an inexact science, but the purchasing power of £1,000 in 1771 was roughly equivalent to £85,000 today: more than enough to enable Hunter to establish a stylish home with his bride.

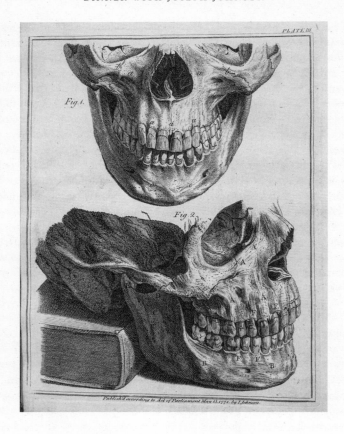

In 1774 the circle of professional and personal connections spiralling in and out of Johnson's shop brought one more doctor into his orbit. He was William Hewson, a young anatomist who conducted his work in the basement of the house where Benjamin Franklin had lodged at Number 7 Craven Street. Hewson was married to Polly Stevenson, the daughter of Franklin's landlady Margaret. In October 1772 Mrs Stevenson gave her house to Polly and Hewson and moved across the road, taking Franklin with her. Hewson's specialism was the lymphatic system and he made few concessions to the sensibilities of his readers in his description of the operations of the blood. 'Having laid bare the jugular vein of a living rabbit', he wrote in his *Experimental Inquiries*, 'I tied it up in three places; then opening it between two of the ligatures, I let out the blood, and filled this part of the vein with air.'[9]

Part One of *Experimental Inquiries* was first published by Thomas Cadell in the Strand in 1772. In 1774 Johnson republished Part One in a single volume with a newly written Part Two. At the end of Johnson's new edition there was an extensive advertisement for a course of lectures to be given by Hewson, presumably for the attention of those who wanted to see the jugular veins of living rabbits for themselves. But a few weeks after the volume's appearance, Hewson's knife slipped while he was dissecting a corpse. He died of septicaemia on May 1st. His pregnant wife was left in sole charge of two young children. 'Physician, heal thyself,' says Jesus in Luke 4:23, quoting a Greek proverb. Johnson's doctors wrote treatises, cut corpses, experimented on rabbits, delivered babies, amputated limbs and threw open windows in their pursuit of a humane medicine, but they were not immune to the dangers that continued in spite of their work to assail the body from every side.

✦

Other writers gathered around Johnson turned their attention to the stars. A Bristol maker of instruments for measuring the tides and the distance to the Moon sent him a series of instructions and worked problems to publish: readers were also told where they could buy the instruments themselves, should they wish to turn explorer. The mathematics tutor at Warrington, George Walker, published his monumental *Doctrine of the Sphere* with Johnson, a labour of love which made neither man any money. Walker had been tinkering with his manuscript for over a dozen years and when the time came to publish he had to sit down with a pair of scissors and painstakingly snip out twenty thousand illustrative figures so they could be set by the printer. 'The purchaser will not wonder at the addition to the price of the work', wrote Walker in an exhausted-sounding Preface, 'which this most tedious and fatiguing business has occasioned.'[10] The story of his labours became the stuff of legend among his acquaintances: many years later John Aikin's daughter Lucy recalled it in an account of her father and his friends. Johnson paid Walker £40 for *Doctrine of the Sphere* but when Walker discovered that Johnson had lost money on the publication he insisted on paying the advance back. The field of pure geometry was not, Lucy Aikin recalled, one in which there were liberal financial rewards.

For the experimental chemists who either came to dinner at St Paul's Churchyard or sent Johnson their work from abroad, reward was less about money than about winning a pan-European race to be the first to describe a new system of knowledge. Johnson's friendship with Priestley meant that he was aware of the potential of the work of the chemist Antoine Lavoisier earlier than were the other London booksellers. In 1776 he published the first English translation of Lavoisier's *Essays Physical and Chemical*. Lavoisier and Priestley were both in search of the same thing: an understanding of the composition of the gases in the air and the processes by which combustion happened. The two men met in Paris in 1774 and sparred with each other in pamphlets and treatises that flew back and forth across the English Channel. Both isolated oxygen, as did the Swedish chemist Carl Wilhelm Scheele, whose work Johnson also published in translation. Priestley, though, termed oxygen 'dephlogisticated air', in accordance with his championing of the so-called 'phlogiston theory' which posited the presence of an element (called phlogiston) within all combustible bodies. It was Lavoisier who developed a competing 'oxygen theory' of combustion and who gave the gas its name.

Alongside Priestley in Johnson's dining room, and Lavoisier in Johnson's scientific catalogues, there were other authors with much to say about the materials of the universe. In his spare hours John Aikin wrote on the uses and preparation of lead, and Johnson commissioned him to translate the second edition of Antoine Beaumé's 1762 *Manual of Chemistry*. Aikin's Preface to the *Manual* reads like a credo for the egalitarian version of science Johnson championed. Cutting-edge discoveries were important, but so was clarity and the dissemination of knowledge to as many people as possible. The *Manual*, Aikin explained, 'contains a large store of knowledge in a very small compass; and will, I imagine, prove eminently useful, either to the student who wishes to review his former acquisitions or to the artist, whose want of leisure obliges him to contend himself with some concise abstract of the science.'[11] Both Johnson and Aikin knew that some of their readers would be students like the young graduates of Warrington, starting their own journey through the foothills of enquiry; others would be interested working men eager to master new ways of conceptualising the composition of the Earth and sky. All could enlighten themselves by reading a book; no longer would the fate of scientific progress remain in the hands of a tiny minority. Johnson and his scientific visitors promised their readers nothing more and nothing less than knowledge democratised by ink on paper, sewn and unbound.

✠

Priestley himself was convinced that the progress of knowledge was as inexorable as 'a *wave* of the sea, or *sound*, or *light* from the sun'.[12] Between 1770 and 1780 he published, among many other works on different subjects, *Directions for impregnating water with fixed air* (1775), *Disquisitions relating to matter and spirit* (1777), *Experiments and observations on different kinds of air* (1774), *Experiments and observations relating to various branches of natural philosophy* (1779), *A familiar introduction to the study of electricity* (1777) and *A free discussion of the doctrines of materialism* (1778). From his workshop on Shelburne's estate in Calne he took on some of the most fundamental questions facing humankind in a series of investigations in which religion and science were inextricably linked. He brought a quasi-scientific methodology to bear on one of the most contested areas of eighteenth-century philosophy, the relationship between the body and the soul. Priestley followed the principles laid down by David Hartley to reject the widely held belief that the soul or spirit existed independently of the host body, 'docking' with it, in the words of the historian Roy Porter, in the womb, and leaving at death prior to final reunification at the Last Judgement.[13]

Priestley knew that in overturning this orthodoxy he would lay himself open to attack, but he believed that the reward – a new generation of 'rational christians' – was worth the risk. 'I feel a great *present ease* in the idea of publishing my thoughts with the most unreserved freedom on this important subject', he insisted. 'Though many well meaning christians may, for some time, rank me with unbelievers, some unbelievers, of a philosophical turn of mind, may, on this very account, be prevailed upon to attend to the subject.'[14] His arguments drew on the work of the anatomists, who were showing in their lecture theatres that the human body was more complex than could possibly be imagined. The true system of revelation, he wrote, was 'infinitely more consonant' to the extraordinary beauty of such complexity. God's greatness, in this reading, appeared in lace-like labyrinths of blood vessels and sinews in infinitely richer form than the teachings of the Established Church suggested.

Throughout his scientific writing of the 1770s, Priestley returned again and again to themes that formed the touchstone of his thought. He emphasised the value of collaboration, the importance of prioritising shared knowledge over individual reputation, the potential of failure and the impossibility of reaching a settled understanding in fields that kept changing. Acknowledging these ideas was for Priestley an act of worship. In *Experiments and observations on different kinds of air* he wrote that his labours would never be complete. 'My first publication I acknowledged to be very imperfect, and the present, I am as ready to acknowledge, is still more so.' But, he continued, 'this will ever be the case in the progress of natural science, so long as the works of God are, like himself, infinite and inexhaustible.'[15] He conceded that this belief presented certain difficulties for his publisher. In the Preface to *Experiments on air* he declared his intention of rewriting the volume as his knowledge increased:

> I give notice of it that no person who intends to purchase it may have reason (being thus apprised of my intention) to complain of buying the same thing twice. If any person chuse it, he may save his five or six shillings for the present, and wait five or six years longer (if I should live so long) for the opportunity of buying the same thing, probably much enlarged.[16]

Freed by his employment with Shelburne from the need to make money from his writing, Priestley was able to expand his thinking to encompass a utopian version of the book as a mutable form, immune from the pressures of profit and loss. He developed a system of shorthand so that he could write as quickly as he thought and it was all Johnson could do to keep up. Just as the body needed oxygen, so the book-writer depended on the book-maker for air. 'I am very desirous to get my two metaphysical works out', wrote Priestley to Lindsey in November 1777. 'If you can hasten Mr Johnson, you would oblige me much.'[17]

8

Paint and Washes

To you, my fair readers! this article is particularly addressed – and, heaven send it may have a happy influence upon some of you![1]

In Samuel Paterson's *Joineriana*, only one article was addressed directly to women. Its title was 'Paint and Washes' and it was on the subject of make-up. 'What a collection of filth and trumpery have we here! – PAINT and PASTES! GREASE and WASHES! – choicely disposed and carefully preserved in boxes and gallipots – in pans and platters! What a labour to live, if all these are necessary!'[2] Paterson's professed dislike of female adornment raised a question about how to be a woman in a world controlled by men. 'Think what time you waste in deforming, where you propose decoration and amendment!' he railed. 'Think to what nobler purposes, that time might be allotted!'[3]

Within the select world of literary London, Paterson's characterisation of female pursuits was anachronistic even by the time Johnson published *Joineriana*. Over the course of the eighteenth century a series of brilliant women published novels, essays, classical translations and histories, earning themselves fame – and, sometimes, notoriety – in the process. Johnson was one of several London booksellers who recognised early the spending power of well-off women readers and the consequent value of the work of women writers, but his commitment to those he published was not driven simply by commercial considerations. The women writers who sought him out were, for the most part, not elite, and they did not have the literary connections that enabled writers such as Elizabeth Montagu and her sister Sarah Scott to make themselves heard. Most were Dissenters, but unlike their fathers and brothers they were aware of the inequalities that characterised the avowedly egalitarian Dissenting community. On Johnson's list they drew attention to the structures that constrained them, to the occasional consternation of the Dissenting and non-Dissenting men amongst whom they lived.

Two Dissenting women made their name under Johnson's imprint in the 1770s. The first was a young Unitarian called Mary Scott, born in 1751 or 1752 in Milborne Port, Somerset. Her father was a local linen merchant and her mother an invalid. Little is known about Scott's early life but her brother became a Unitarian minister and Scott evidently knew enough people in the nascent Unitarian movement to meet her future husband through its networks and to win an early introduction to Johnson. After her brother left the family home for his education Scott was left behind to care for her mother and she poured her untapped intellect into reading and writing. In 1774 Johnson published her first long poem, *The Female Advocate*, which took as its themes the achievements of women and the stultifying effects of inadequate female education. *The Female Advocate* was a rebuke to unequally held power. Scott's parents forbade her marriage on the grounds that she was required at home to nurse her mother and she was unable to defy them. Her friend Anna Seward, herself the model of a dutiful daughter, described Scott as locked in 'painful combat with long-established affection',[4] and every aspect of Scott's upbringing made her struggle with parental will irrevocably uneven. Through poetry she found a way to fight back.

In *The Female Advocate* Scott marshalled her forces through overlapping layers of text. First, she laid out the deficiencies in female education in an impassioned prose preface. Second, lines of verse hymned the achievements of over sixty brilliant Protestant women from the Renaissance onwards. Third, biographical footnotes demonstrated the role played by education or its absence in those achievements, so that every poetic flight of fancy was grounded in argument and polemic. Scott drew her inspiration from John Duncombe's 1754 poem *The Feminead* and she acknowledged the role played in the cultivation of female intellects by a small number of enlightened men. Most men, though, she described as terrified of the consequences of educating women properly and she had no time for complacent critics who argued that the state of female education was already much improved. 'If they have allowed us to study the imitative arts, have they not prohibited us from cultivating an acquaintance with the sciences? Do they not regard the woman who suffers her faculties to rust in the state of lifeless indolence, with a more favourable eye, than her who engages in a dispassionate search after truth?'[5] The refusal to allow women a scientific education was particularly obnoxious, she continued, given the prevalence of a falsely gallant insistence that women were subject to more 'exquisite sensations' than men. If this was true, then surely women were in fact better positioned than men to benefit from close study of the new worlds being discovered by the chemists and natural philosophers.

Scott conceded that men were not solely to blame for the systematic subjugation of women's talents. All women of intellect had a responsibility to improve on their God-given gifts through hard reading. 'As to those Ladies whose situation in life will not admit of their engaging very deep in literary researches, it surely is commendable in them, to employ, part at least of, their leisure-hours, in improving their minds.'[6] The women whose praises she sang in poetry had done just that. The Irish poet Constantia Grierson was born in rural poverty to parents who were quick to recognise her extraordinary intellect and who made the best arrangements they could for her education. 'Wit and Learning mark'd her for their own', wrote Scott, 'though her fortune low, her birth obscure':

> With wond'rous ease, her comprehensive mind
> The various stores of knowledge all combined.

Similarly Phillis Wheatley, who was enslaved and taken to America as a child, was praised for producing poetry that demonstrated deep and complex thought rather than a simplistic response to the world around her:

> Nor be thy praise confin'd to rural themes
> Or idly-musing Fancy's pleasing dreams.

Scott made the target of her poem clear from the outset:

> Whilst LORDLY MAN asserts his right divine,
> Alone to bow, at wisdom's sacred shrine;
> With tyrant sway, would keep the female mind
> In error's cheerless dark abyss confined.

In an age when tyrants domestic and international were coming under scrutiny on both sides of the Atlantic, Scott argued that the fabric of civil society was predicated on a system of subjugation in which one half of the population was consistently denied the knowledge that was its birthright.

The intellectual disenfranchisement of women cut across boundaries of class and race, so that Grierson and Wheatley stood alongside Henry VIII's last queen, Catherine Parr. All three were united in Scott's telling by the fact that they had access to an education not usually granted to women. Grierson's parents defied the expectations of their class to send their daughter to the local vicar to learn Latin and Hebrew; Wheatley was sold into domestic slavery and became the property of an owner who encouraged her reading. Catherine Parr combined an exceptional humanist education with 'great sense' and 'singular prudence' which allowed Scott to transform her metaphorically into an instrument of heaven:

> The rage of superstition to control
> And chase the mists of error from the soul.

Scott's gallery of brilliant women were also united by their religious beliefs, and her own prejudices, like those of many Dissenting writers, were abundantly clear. A dedication to the cause of Protestantism's battle against the dark arts of Popish superstition was a defining characteristic of her portraits. Elizabeth I, for example, merited particular praise as a Protestant reformer who vanquished the 'bigot rage' that had made the land run red with the blood of martyred saints.

Despite the sharpness of her critique, Scott was not without hope about the prospects for her own century. She named the Bluestocking historian Catharine Macaulay as one who 'patriots yet unborn shall long revere' because of Macaulay's account of the importance of freedom to progress. Elsewhere she refused to believe that developments in scientific knowledge would remain permanently closed off to women. With knowledge, she argued, would come unimagined progress, until science and freedom became mutually sustaining. As Scott encountered among her fellow authors on Johnson's list a commitment to open up scientific developments to anyone with the ability to buy a book, she saw the promise of a more equal future. Some men, she concluded, might think 'the fair realms of knowledge [theirs] alone', but the efforts of others meant that their days were numbered. *The Female Advocate* ended with a vision of women toiling alongside men in workshops and laboratories, claiming for their own discoveries about the composition of the universe and the relationship between body and soul. Some, 'with arduous flight / Explore the realms of intellectual light'; others 'With unremitting study seek to find, / How mind on matter, matter acts on mind.' In every line of verse and in every note, *The Female Advocate* demolished the suggestion that the architecture of women's minds and souls mitigated against rational thought and discovery. It countered too the suggestion that the comparative frailty of female bodies compromised the ability of women to think and argue. All that mattered for progress was the presence of enquiring minds, working together:

> Alike in nature, arts and manners read
> In ev'ry path of knowledge, see they tread!

Johnson published *The Female Advocate* alongside a brief catalogue advertising Paterson's *Joineriana* as well as recent works by his Warrington authors. The specificity of the advertisements suggests he thought *The Female Advocate* might appeal to some of the open-minded, enquiring Unitarians who regularly brought his books, as well as to all those who appreciated unususal voices and literary curiosities. He included in the catalogue an edition of historical letters edited by John Duncombe, whose poem had provided Scott with inspiration, as well as an anonymous work entitled *Peregrinations of the Mind through the most general and interesting Subjects which are usually agitated in Life*. Scott's presence on his list made clear his own belief that the peregrinations of women's minds made for a subject worthy of attention in its own right. He recognised the validity of the criticisms levelled against his sex in the poem and in this he formed a contrast with the author of a critique of *The Female Advocate* in the *Monthly Review*. 'This Lady', wrote the reviewer, 'has done herself the honour to defend the literary privileges of her sex, and to assert the distinction which those privileges bring along with them, against those vile usurpers *the Men*.' He went on to bemoan the state of female education, although his view, in contrast to Scott, was that in allowing young women access to Shakespeare and Milton the defenders of women's rights had done all women a grave disservice. In contrast to Johnson and to Scott herself, the only reader the *Monthly*'s reviewer was able to encompass imaginatively was a horrified man:

> It is dreadful for a man of real knowledge and politeness to encounter one of these literary vixens.... You are offended with an empty mind, bloated with vanity; while politeness obliges you to suppress your disgust, and perhaps to feign some degree of admiration. The effects

of real knowledge are gentleness and modesty, particularly in a sex where anything approaching to assurance is intolerable.[7]

✢

The final figure in *The Female Advocate*'s pantheon of women writers was Anna Aikin. Scott believed that only Aikin was capable of rescuing her fellow women from the trap of meaningless pleasure; only she could lead her readers through the maze of 'the paths of science' in order to scan the 'open book of Nature'. Scott's confidence in Aikin reflects the speed with which the older woman's reputation was transformed. At the beginning of 1772 Aikin was without a single publication to her name. By the end of 1773, and the point at which Scott was escaping her daughterly duties to write her furious celebration of women's intellects, Aikin had become famous.

The rapidity of Aikin's rise to fame was the result of a combination of talent, serendipity and social circumstance. Although her name was unknown to most of the reading public, within certain circles her poetry circulated widely in manuscript. 'Corsica' was an early example of this; other poems followed in its wake. Several members of the overlapping Dissenting communities of Warrington, Wakefield and Manchester knew that Miss Aikin was a poet of unusual quality and Johnson's connection to those communities meant that he learnt of her work early. Aikin's brother John, meanwhile, had returned to Warrington after completing his medical training in Edinburgh. In 1772 he persuaded Johnson to publish his anonymous *Essays on Song-Writing*, to which Anna Aikin contributed six songs. The volume was positively received and with John's encouragement she gathered her poetry together in a sole-authored volume for Johnson.

Poems by Anna Letitia Aikin took its epigraph from Virgil and opened with 'Corsica'. Aikin followed her celebration of political and intellectual liberty with verses that located her at the heart of a network of Dissenting kinship. The title page was signed 'Warrington, December 1st 1772', in a deliberate artistic decision to locate herself as a poet of a particular place and community. The volume included poetry written to Mary Priestley and other celebrations of local friendships. Yet Aikin's praise of the intellectual and religious community of her youth was not straightforward. She included a parodic lament entitled 'The Groans of the Tankard' in which she gave voice to a venerable silver tankard standing on her father's sideboard bemoaning its banishment to a Puritan household in which it is permitted to hold only water. Another verse, 'The Mouse's Petition' was dedicated to Priestley and professed to be a plea from a mouse caught by Priestley for the purposes of chemical experimentation. The mouse reminds him that the values he holds dear apply to all living creatures, no matter how insignificant:

> If e'er thy breast with freedom glow'd,
> And spurn'd a tyrant's chain,
> Let not thy strong oppressive force
> A free-born mouse detain.

Some reviewers of *Poems* alighted with glee on this verse, seeing in it a valuable opportunity to attack Priestley. Aikin was moved to add a defensive note in later editions. 'The Author is concerned to find, that what was intended as the petition of mercy against justice, has been construed as the plea of humanity against cruelty. She is certain that cruelty could never be apprehended from the Gentleman to whom this is addressed.'[8] Despite her protestations, Aikin's poems directed a degree of mockery towards both her father and her intellectual mentor. In both cases Aikin staked her claim to contribute to the debates about religion and science that coloured every aspect of her domestic existence. The route she took into those debates was lateral: it involved imaginatively inhabiting the position of creatures and objects with no voice but with something to say. Humour allowed her to remind the opinionated and clever men amongst whom she was brought up that their unthinking acceptance of their own power did not tally with their theology or their professed commitment to equality.

Johnson inserted an advertisement for John Aikin's *Essays on Song-Writing* at the end of *Poems*, yoking the Aikins together as a pair of writers for discerning readers: 'Just Published, Price 3s 6d. sewed, elegantly printed, ESSAYS on SONG-WRITING, with a Collection of ENGLISH SONGS as are most eminent for poetical Merit. To which are added some Original Pieces.' Both Anna and John Aikin shared Johnson's view that together they had the potential to be a potent literary brand. 'I think we must some day sew all our fragments together and make a *Joineriana* of them', wrote Aikin to her brother. Her enjoyment of the rag-bag metaphor was

clear in her laconic characterisation of her back catalogue. 'Let me see: –
I have, half a ballad; the first scene of a play; a plot of another, all but
the catastrophe; half a dozen loose similes, and an eccentric flight or two
among the fairies.'[9]

✠

The reviews of *Poems* were double-edged. The reviewer for the *Critical
Review* thought that Aikin possessed poetic talents worth cultivating but
he disliked 'The Groans of the Tankard' and thought that some verses
revealed Muses who seemed 'on this occasion, to be drawn particularly
against their inclination into the Puritanic walk.'[10] In a leisurely two-part
commentary published in the *Monthly Review* in January and February 1773,
William Woodfall regretted the way in which Aikin's work was used as a
weapon by polemicists who refused to acknowledge the disparity of intellect
between the sexes:

> A woman is as perfect in her kind as a man; she appears inferior only
> when she quits her station, and aims at excellence out of her province.
> This is true, not only in common life, but in all the branches of the
> arts, and of philosophy. We see by the speculative turn of the man,
> for what sciences he is designed. We see by the conversation of a
> woman, in what kind of knowledge she would excel.

Any exceptions to this rule, he concluded, could only be the result of
'something like a mistake of sex.'[11]

Woodfall was in no doubt about the cause of Aikin's mistaken ambition
to tread on ground reserved for men. 'If she, as well as others of our female
writers, had, in pursuing the road to fame, trod too much in the footsteps
of the men, it has been owing, not to a want of genius, but to a want of
proper education.'[12] He evoked a parody of Warrington, in which young
men and women were educated alongside each other with complete disre-
gard for their natural stations in life. But Aikin did not sit in lecture
theatres alongside her father's male pupils and her education was signifi-
cantly more ad hoc and provisional than Woodfall suggested. Hers was not
the education of a young man, but nor was it an education Woodfall would
have considered 'proper'. In Warrington Aikin read first and watercoloured
later; 'feminine beauties', in Woodfall's phrase, were less significant to her
than were finding ways to join a conversation from which she was excluded.

The reviewers might be ambivalent about the implications of *Poems* for the power balance between the sexes, but their concerns were not shared by the readers who found their way to Aikin's poetry. The volume went through three editions within a year; two more editions followed over the next two years. The technological constraints of the hand-operated printing press meant that no single edition was very large: a few hundred copies was typical for a new work without a guaranteed audience. Nevertheless the rapidity with which Aikin's work was reprinted suggests a developing market for her work. The growth of her readership was aided by the widespread reprinting in newspapers of individual poems from her volume. As her biographer William McCarthy has noted, her physical image also developed its own value, after she was chosen by Josiah Wedgwood as a portrait subject. 'Anna Letitia', McCarthy writes, 'could have encountered her profile on other people's rings, buttons, lockets, bracelets, workboxes, and smelling bottles or inlaid in their writing tables, chairs, and cabinets. Her own family used one in a brooch.'[13]

Johnson too cashed in on the value of Aikin's image, using it to differentiate a memorandum book he published for genteel women from similar volumes advertised by rival publishers. Her portrait appeared in the volume as part of a much-reproduced grouping of the 'nine muses' of literary female worthies. Taken together, the painting, memorandum book and Aikin's continued popularity appeared to demonstrate yet again that male attempts to preserve the republic of letters from female invasion were doomed to failure. Through Aikin Johnson found his way to a female readership with money to spend on volumes of poetry and embellished appointment books, and he recognised that one of the things women readers wanted to be shown in exchange for their money was a version of their own lives. Other entrepreneurial booksellers had also identified women with disposable income as a profitable audience, but in Aikin Johnson acquired a writer who was drawn from, and spoke directly to, that readership.

Buoyed by the success of *Poems*, Aikin and her brother began work on a collaborative follow-up volume. Their version of the *Joineriana* appeared late in 1773 and was entitled *Miscellaneous Pieces in Prose*. Four of the essays in the volume were by John, the rest by Aikin. None were signed, so it was left to the reader to work out, if they so desired, whose work they were reading. In one of her contributions, 'On Romances', Aikin took up the question of access to different forms of knowledge in an essay which argued for genres with the potential to reach as many readers as possible. It was imaginative works, she argued, that had the greatest ability to change people's minds and lives. Again, her essay contained an implicit rebuke to the scholarly men who moulded her mind – George Walker, with his 500-page treatise on the sphere; Priestley, engaged in obscure theological arguments about the soul; and her father, whose writerly energies were restricted to a handful of journal essays on philosophical subjects:

> The Geometrician and Divine, the Antiquary and Critic, however distinguished by uncontested excellence, can only hope to please those whom a conformity of disposition has engaged in similar pursuits; and must be content to be regarded by the rest of the world with the smile of frigid indifference... . To the writer of fiction alone every ear is open, and every tongue lavish of applause; curiosity sparkles in every eye, and every bosom is throbbing with concern.[14]

Elsewhere in the volume she argued against a version of Protestantism that refused to admit the virtues of other religious systems. Even in collaborative publications that announced her as part of the Warrington tribe, Aikin demonstrated that she was determined to be mistress of her own mind.

✝

In the summer of 1772, several months before the first publication of *Poems*, Aikin sent Johnson an extraordinary drawing. He published it anonymously as a standalone work, entitled *A New Map of the Land of Matrimony*.[15] Aikin's map drew on a literary subculture of metaphorical cartography that allowed for the expression of both licensed and illicit emotions. It showed the Land of Matrimony surrounded by an Ocean of Love. Aikin's Ocean hid 'Rocks of Jealousy' and 'Calms and violent Tornadoes.' Sailors aiming for the Cape of Good Hope had to pass through the Straits of Uncertainty. Enchanted Islands were named for St Magdalena and were surrounded by a Gulf of Reproach and a Bay of Repentance: privateers and Syrens patrolled the seas on either side. In the north the capital of a landmass named Friesland was Singletown: Friesland's promontories included Cape Lookout and Cape Demur ('generally covered with vapours'). The Land of Matrimony itself had a Slave Coast and a Gold Coast as well as a Land of Nod. On Cape Horn were Coterie Place and the Fortress of Virtue Dismantled: both overlooked an island named Divorce.

On May 26th 1774, Aikin set sail across the Straits of Uncertainty and married a Warrington graduate six years her junior. She was thirty-one and her wedding took place in the face of her father's objections. Her bridegroom was Rochemont Barbauld, a student of the Academy's divinity course and a recent convert to Dissent. Anna Letitia Aikin became Anna Letitia Barbauld, the name by which she is best known today, and Johnson had to alter the frontispiece of the fourth edition of *Poems*. Rochemont was a mercurial young man prone to unpredictable flights of exuberance and melancholy. In later life many of his friends recognised that he was subject to some form of 'malady'. It was probably unease about Rochemont's apparent instability that made John Aikin so resistant to the idea of his daughter's marriage, since Aikin was in danger of moving beyond the age when a woman was thought eligible and Rochemont's family was impeccably respectable.

Shortly after her wedding Anna Barbauld presented a copy of her Map of Matrimony to Rochemont, with a poem in which she represented him as a sailor navigating choppy waters:

> Thus canst thou, Rochemont, view this pictured chart
> Thus does thy faithful bosom beat with joy,
> To think the tempest past, the wanderings o'er?[16]

Doubt echoes through the poem as the sailor resists the domination of love and the speaker worries about his constancy. 'But soon', fears the speaker:

> the restless seaman longs to change
> His bounded view and tempt the deeps again:
> So shall not thou, for no returning prow
> E'er cut the ocean which thy bark has past;
> Too strong relentless Fate has fixed her bars,
> And I my destined captive hold too fast.

Bars, captives, the gift of a map with a slave coast: these are not images which suggest a bride filled with optimism about her future. Yet her marriage won Barbauld a form of freedom. With Rochemont by her side, she left her parents' house in Warrington to make a life and a home of her own.

After their wedding the Barbaulds went to London, where they remained for some weeks. They saw the sights and met many people who were eager to be introduced to the author of *Poems*. Horace Walpole issued an invitation to his house at Strawberry Hill; Elizabeth Montagu asked them to dine. So too did Johnson, whom Barbauld met for the first time. When her niece Lucy Aikin came to write a biography of her famous aunt, she depicted this and subsequent visits to London as transformative:

> At the splendid mansion of her early and constant admirer Mrs Montague, Mrs Barbauld beheld in perfection the imposing union of literature and fashion; – under the humbler roof of her friend and publisher, the late worthy Joseph Johnson of St Paul's Church-yard, she tasted, perhaps with higher relish, 'the feast of reason and the flow of soul,' in a chosen knot of lettered equals.

This chosen knot in the mid-1770s included Priestley, Barbauld's friend of old, as well as Johnson's friends Fordyce and Lindsey, the latter of whom reported in early 1775 that 'Mr and Mrs Barbauld have been in Town. They seem to go on well in their new situation.'[17]

Barbauld's arrival in London marks one of the earliest documented occasions on which Johnson gathered passing writers, friends and readers for dinner. It is likely that he instituted the habit of hosting weekly dinners in his oddly shaped dining room shortly after his move to St Paul's Churchyard, but before 1774 documentary evidence for the gatherings is scarce. 'Dinner' in the 1770s fell in the middle of the afternoon at 3 or 4 p.m., before the winter light had faded. Visitors who were left unsatisfied by veal, cod and vegetables might choose to eat a 'supper' elsewhere later in the evening, but frequently the dinners at St Paul's Churchyard stretched into the night. 'Our evenings, particularly at Johnson's, were so truly social and lively, that we protracted them sometimes till ...' Barbauld reported to her brother John. 'But I am not telling tales.'[18]

The 'new situation' to which Lindsey referred saw the Barbaulds move in July 1774 to the village of Palgrave in Suffolk, where Rochement had accepted the position of minister to a Dissenting congregation. There they opened a school for boys, which offered an education for younger pupils modelled along the lines Rochemont had experienced and Barbauld had witnessed at Warrington. Several of Barbauld's new-found London friends and admirers were dismayed at the prospect of her turning schoolmistress in a Suffolk village but the school was a success and Barbauld threw herself into its management. Through Johnson she procured books and stationery and she also sent him clothes orders to pass on to other tradesmen. She kept writing, publishing a work of devotional pieces in 1775, and during vacation visits to London she met the friends and fellow writers who sustained her literary imagination. Simultaneously, she turned her attention to the education of the very young.

The story of Barbauld's decision to turn children's writer starts with a letter she sent in 1776 to her brother John:

> Our request then, in short, is this: that you will permit us to adopt one of your children; which of them, we leave it to you; – that you will make it ours in every sense in which it is possible to make it, – that you will transfer to us all the care and all the authority of a parent; that we should provide for it, educate it, and have the entire direction of it as far into life as the parental power itself extends.[19]

When John received this letter he was the father of three small boys: Arthur, born in 1773; George, born in 1774; and Charles, born in August 1775. His wife was expecting a fourth baby. Barbauld and Rochemont had been married for three years but no children had come and Barbauld evidently felt their absence keenly. It was, nevertheless, an audacious request, and it is instructive that she took many paragraphs to argue her case, suggesting that she feared an immediate rebuff. 'Perhaps you will entirely deny it; and then we must acquiesce: for I am sensible it is not a small thing we ask; nor can it be easy for a parent to part with a child.' But, she continued, from a number, '*one* may more easily be spared'.

Barbauld's letter was answered by her sister-in-law Martha, and although that letter has not survived it is evident from Barbauld's reply that her sister-in-law was made very anxious by the proposal:

> I wonder not that your softness takes alarm at the idea of parting with any of your sweet blossoms. All I can say is, that the greater the sacrifice, the more we shall think ourselves obliged to you, and the stronger ties we shall think ourselves under the supply, as far as possible, to the child of our adoption the tenderness and care of the parents we take it from.[20]

Somehow Martha Aikin was persuaded to overcome her anxieties and in June 1777 Barbauld went to bring home two-year-old Charles to Palgrave.

He cried on arrival, Barbauld reported to his parents, but, after a long sleep, had cheered up and 'has been very busy today, hunting the puss and the chickens.'[21] Charles learnt to call Barbauld 'Mother' and Rochemont 'Father', although he continued to address John Aikin by the title of 'Father' too. Posterity does not record what he called the mother from whom he was taken, and her reaction to his loss is not represented in the historical record.

The ruthlessness underlying Barbauld's adoption of Charles is inescapable. She always wrote of him with great tenderness and he was happy in her care, but her motives in claiming him were not simply maternal or emotional. He was to be the subject of her great experiment in education. In 1778 Johnson published the first results of this experiment, in an anonymously issued volume entitled *Lessons for Children from Two to Three Years Old*. In the prefatory Advertisement to the volume Barbauld explained that 'it was made for a particular child, but the public is welcome to the use of it.'[22] Every sentence was addressed to Charles, so that infant readers saw in the text an image of themselves and the parent who taught them. 'Pray give me a raisin', demands 'Charles' at one point:

> Here is one.
> I want another.
> Here is another. One, two.
> I want a great many; I
> > Want ten.
> Here are ten. One, two,
> three, four, five, six, seven
> eight, nine, ten.[23]

Elsewhere Charles asks for pudding with his dinner; and cries that he is hungry. He is told to lay the table; in return he demands that 'mamma' put down her work to play with him. He chases butterflies in the fields and pleads to be carried. He behaves, in short, in completely recognisable ways, evoked in simple words and sentences designed to keep the attention of a very young reader. This version of childhood was quietly revolutionary. Barbauld showed Charles being a child, and she described a mode of child-rearing in which he was given safe and stable boundaries and then allowed to run free. He was not left unchecked or neglected in the name of progress but nor was he expected to behave like a miniature adult. Barbauld-the-mother, in both text and reality, taught Charles about the world around him according to the principles of John Locke, by encouraging him to follow the logic of his senses. Charles is never shown sitting solemnly at a desk. Instead he is encouraged to use his mind, eyes, ears and nose to make connections and work things out for himself.

Charles learnt his first lessons as he decoded this version of himself, letter by letter, at Barbauld's knee. Having proved to herself that her method for teaching him to read was successful, she wrote a series of follow-up volumes for three- and four-year-olds. Johnson responded to her ideas by producing volumes designed for the hands of their intended readers, with print that looked and felt distinctive. Other London publishers had already pioneered the publication of books aimed at small readers: Thomas Boreman's two-inch-high *Gigantick Histories* dated from the early 1740s, as did one of the earliest books written specifically for children, John Newbery's *Pretty Pocket-Book*. Barbauld drove Johnson to push the innovations in children's book publishing further. Writing to her brother John in response to an early proof she complained that 'Charles's little book is very well, but my idea is not executed in it. I must therefore beg you will print one as soon as you can, on fine paper, on one side only, and more space and a clearer line for the chapters.'[24]

Johnson responded to her demands by issuing *Lessons* on good paper, with a maximum of nine lines of type to a page. In the Advertisement to the first volume Barbauld asserted the distinctiveness of the form she and Johnson had evolved. Other volumes for children were marred by 'the want of good paper, clear and large type, and large spaces.' She represented herself as both mother and teacher, uniquely well-positioned to pronounce on the needs of small children. 'They only, who have actually taught young children, can be sensible how necessary these assistances are. The eye of a child and of a learner cannot catch, as ours can, a small, obscure, ill-formed word, amidst a number of others equally unknown to him.'[25] Bad paper and bleeding ink had no place in *Lessons for Children*; neither did words that sought to instruct children without celebrating their experience and perspective.

Both Barbauld and Johnson believed in the importance of education in improving an imperfect world; both asserted the right of all people, regardless of background, to have access to a world of books. Both knew that the form as well as the content of a book could break new ground. And both saw too the potential benefits to themselves of being among the first to produce a new kind of book for a new kind of audience. *Lessons for Children* ran to multiple volumes and from 1778 onwards Johnson reprinted the titles in the series every year in order to keep up with demand. A plethora of imitations followed from other publishers and authors keen to capture the market Johnson and Barbauld had shaped, but even as the field she had established became crowded Barbauld continued to reign supreme. Of the child celebrated in *Lessons* she wrote to John: 'I am afraid to tell you much about him, lest you should fall in love with him again, and send somebody to kidnap him; though I think Charles would have a great many defenders in the house if you did.'[26]

COME hither Charles, come to mamma. Make haste.

✢

In 1826 Barbauld's niece Lucy Aikin gathered together some of her aunt's unpublished works in a volume she called *A Legacy for Young Ladies*. She included an essay entitled 'Fashion: A Vision' in which Barbauld pointed out that hard-won political liberties were of no use to young women 'if there exists a tyrant of our own creation, who, without law or reason, or even external force, exercises over us the most despotic authority; whose jurisdiction is extended over every part of private and domestic life; controls our pleasures, fashions our garb, cramps our motions, fills our lives with vain cares and restless anxiety.'[27] The essay unfolds as a nightmare vision of the court of the Queen of Fashion, where girls are trussed up in tortuous whalebone corsets and frightened into conformity through the threat of social exclusion; and where rules are frequently and arbitrarily changed through a system of nods and whispers. 'As the Spartan mothers brought their children to be scourged at the altar of Diana, so do the mothers here bring their children, – and chiefly those whose tender sex one would suppose excused them from such exertions, – and early inure them to this cruel discipline.'[28] The result is a landscape of deformed bodies as ludicrous as they are frightening:

> Of some, the ears were distended till they hung upon the shoulders; and of others, the shoulders were raised till they met the ears: there was not one free from some deformity, or monstrous swelling, in one part or other; either it was before, or behind, or about the hips, or the arms were puffed up to an unusual thickness ... some had no necks; others had necks that reached almost to their waists; the bodies of some were bloated up to such a size, that they could scarcely enter a pair of folding doors; and others had suddenly sprouted up to such a disproportionate height, that they could not sit upright in their loftiest carriages.[29]

Clothes that constrict and deform become a metaphor in the essay for a world in which women are oppressed and constrained by a toxic combination of autocratic dominance and internalised inferiority. Like Paterson in 'Paint and Washes', Barbauld viewed the absurdities of female adornment as damaging to her sex, although she offered a much more sophisticated explanation as to why women submit to such tortures than Paterson countenanced. Paterson dismissed women as vain and shallow; Barbauld recognised the insidious ways in which male domination and an expectation of female submission warps the intellects of young women until they connive in the systems that keep them powerless. To change that, she argued, you have to start by seeing yourself clearly, and you have to identify the systems that hold you in check.

Whalebone corsets represented one way of restricting women; the laws of the land offered another. In 1777 Johnson published an anonymous treatise on *The Laws Respecting Women*, in which the writer set out, in painstaking detail, the ways in which a range of interconnected laws relating to marriage, property and inheritance reduced women to legal nonentities. The treatise's author did not enter into lengthy protests or complaints about the injustice of this: instead she let the facts make her argument for her. Like Barbauld in 'Fashion: A Vision' she showed her readers the world as it was and then left them to exercise their agency and form their own conclusions. A severely beaten woman cannot sue her abuser, she notes, but her husband can enter an action against the assailant for trespass on his property. A woman cannot hold property; a fiction that collapses because exceptions are made for the wife of the king. The only time a woman takes on legal characteristics of her own is if she offends. She can be tried as a scold, a libeller and a bigamist but after marriage she has virtually no recourse to legal protection in her own right.

Only in the Preface did the writer offer an opinion about the state of affairs she described. No society, she argued, could reach a state of advanced progress while riven by inequality:

> A nation of men characterised for bravery, generosity, and a love superior to mean suspicions, must consider the happiness of women as inseparably blended with their own. When public virtue prevails, each individual will have the justest idea wherein his own private happiness really consists.[30]

This argument runs through the works Johnson published in the 1770s by and about women, in volumes united by a demand that readers consider the evidence of their eyes. Mary Scott let the size of her pantheon of brilliant women make her argument for her; Barbauld showed that she had a mind of her own and the will to use it. Both insisted that education offered the best hope for reform, and both showed that the fate of the nation depended on its ability to address long-standing injustices. Both stressed that the democratisation of knowledge posited as a sacred duty by their Unitarian fathers was nothing more than a hollow gesture if women were forbidden to explore and test the discoveries of men. A narrow focus on whether the women who took up their pens had overstepped the boundaries of acceptable female behaviour was, they argued, of no use at all. In the end, as the anonymous author of *The Laws Respecting Women* revealed in a deliberate sleight of hand, what mattered was the idea and the book:

> The author of a book is not like a conjurer, or a rope dancer, who must exhibit themselves personally to make their skill apparent. A book is like current coin, if it has weight and intrinsic value, it is not the less current because the image and inscription cannot be ascertained; and it in vain looks splendid if these essentials are wanting.[31]

9

The American War Lamented

In the first weeks of 1775, Johnson and his friends looked on in dismay as Britain prepared for war. 'One sees the red coats preparing themselves in Hyde-Park and St James's every day', wrote Lindsey. 'Their rulers are persuaded that the Americans, the Bostonians in particular, will throw down their arms at the sight of our troops. My acquaintance, who are better informed, say quite the reverse.'[1] Merchants in London banded together to petition the government to avoid war and the disastrous consequences for British trade that would inevitably follow its outbreak; further petitions arrived from groups of manufacturers in Bristol, Wakefield, Halifax, Bradford and other industrial towns. Cutting off relations with their biggest trading partner was, the petitioners insisted, a self-inflicted wound that threatened the economic growth on which Britain's international power was founded. Their protests went unheeded as Lord North's administration concentrated its attention on massing troops and warships along the eastern seaboard of New England. 'Providence seems to hasten our ruin and the independence of America', Lindsey wrote to a friend in Wakefield. 'If so ... we may all of us have reason to rejoice, that there will be a place in the globe where Englishmen may be free.'[2]

The majority of those who gathered around Johnson's dining table in 1775 believed that war with America was both completely unnecessary and a national disaster. Priestley had watched his friend Franklin driven out of London by the impending conflict and he saw America as a beacon of religious permissiveness; Lindsey viewed the government's race towards confrontation with despair. On April 18th 1775 the silversmith Paul Revere rode out of Boston to warn the farmers and smallholders scattered throughout the New England countryside that the British were marching on a rebel arms store outside Concord. Shots were fired and the British infantry were chased back to Boston by a rapidly assembled but extremely effective Patriot militia. In June the British attempted to seize control of a Patriot fort on Bunker Hill overlooking Boston; one thousand British soldiers were killed in the effort. In America the Second Continental Congress created an army and put George Washington in command; in Britain George III declared the colonies to be in open rebellion. Lindsey reported these events in regular letters to friends in the north of England, basing his information on officially sanctioned reports that tended to reach London earlier than the rest of the country and on accounts sent in private letters from American friends and religious sympathisers. His correspondents were clear from the outset that a British victory was doubtful. 'Nothing but ruin can follow from the attempt to subdue the americans and keep an armed force in their country', Lindsey wrote in December.[3] Yet this was a course upon which North and his ministers appeared determined.

In March 1776 Lindsey reported that a motion for conciliation had been defeated in the House of Lords, despite the Duke of Richmond reminding the Bishops sitting in the House of the immorality of their being 'instruments of blood' and warning them that 'in the probable ruin, their rich, overgrown preferments would be the first things that would be seized.'[4] For Lindsey and Priestley the sight of Church of England bishops voting for the continuance of war epitomised all that was rotten in Britain. The bishops represented a Church corrupted by politics and a hierarchical religious system more concerned with secular riches than spiritual matters.

The war dragged onwards and in 1777 Lindsey wrote that it seemed likely France and Spain would join forces with America to defeat Britain. Eighteen months later, with no end in sight, he reported that 'poverty and misery may come with great strides upon us; for our manufacturers now are drooping every where'. Only government contractors flourished: 'they continue to vilify the Americans and cry out for the war'.[5] When news of peace finally reached Britain, following the signing of the Treaty of Versailles on September 3rd 1783, Lindsey could hardly bring himself to celebrate. Even the weather seemed determined to underscore the whole affair as a national disgrace. 'We have had a great hubbub in the streets and noise at the proclaiming of Peace', he told his friend John Lee. 'But they have had a dismal day for it, which is likely to help to increase the discontents of the Mob.'[6]

✢

Johnson's authors responded to the war in pamphlets and treatises, but also in poems, sermons and familiar letters that shone a light on the human consequences of the conflict. Andrew Hunter's *Advice from a Father to a Son, just entered into the army* gave voice to a parent faced with losing a child in battle. 'War is the offspring of the irregular passions of men; it proceeds usually from the immoderate love of power from resentment, or from mistaken views of interest.' Still, Hunter continued, it was the duty of his soldier-son to follow the orders he was given with dignity and honour. 'I recommend you to the care of God, and pray that you may be happily instrumental in restoring good order and lasting tranquillity in our American dominions.'[7]

An early poem by Mary Robinson entitled *Elegiac Verses to a Young Lady, on the death of her brother who was slain at the late engagement at Boston* appeared under Johnson's imprint in 1776. When she wrote for Johnson, Robinson was incarcerated in the Fleet prison with her debtor husband. Poetry offered one way to make money, although her first volume, published by a rival bookseller in 1775, had been a commercial failure. When her husband was released in the summer of 1776 Robinson sought work on the stage, again in an attempt to boost her family's income. She would later become famous as 'Perdita', the actress who caught the attention of the Prince Regent, but in 1776 her existence was precarious and she was on the alert for subjects for popular poetry. In *Elegiac Verses* she seized the opportunity offered by a sentimental, conventional poetic form to level stringent criticism against British military conduct. She contrasted the unjustness of Britain's 'self-convicting cause / That lately crimson'd Boston's carnag'd plain' with the honour demonstrated by individual soldiers. She did not doubt the rights of a country to defend itself against tyranny. 'Should haughty nations fire BRITANNIA's rage, / And spurn her claim to Freedom's general laws' it would be entirely proper for a government to mount a defence. But in the case of America, the opposite was true:

> But can she see what discord has prevail'd,
>> What horrors mark'd that inauspicious day
> When parent states their offspring's peace assail'd,
>> To force allegiance to despotic sway?[8]

In her final stanza Robinson retreated to conventional piety, although her assertion of the much-repeated and contested statement from Pope's *Essay on Man* that 'whatever is, is right', was undermined by the graphic presentation of bloodshed in the rest of the poem.

The theme of religious consolation in the face of conflict was one to which other writers published by Johnson turned in their efforts to rationalise irrational violence. In Taunton the Dissenting minister Joshua Toulmin preached a sermon on *The American War Lamented* which Johnson subsequently published. Toulmin avoided political arguments but nevertheless made it clear that he considered peace and reconciliation to be the only outcomes for which a conscientious Christian could possibly wish. Obliquely he drew attention to the economic self-sabotage inherent in the government's actions. 'With united hearts, with united voices, pray, that the God of peace, who ruleth among nations, may banish from our borders civil discord ... that commerce may continue to pour in her blessings upon our coasts, to cloath the countenances of the industrious with chearfulness and smiles.'[9]

For some writers on the American War, the conflict raised fundamental questions about liberty. Johnson was one of several publishers of Richard Price's *Observations on the Nature of Civil Liberty*, five editions of which appeared in February and March 1776. 'Our colonies in NORTH AMERICA appear to be now determined to risque and suffer everything, under the persuasion, that GREAT BRITAIN is attempting to rob them of that Liberty to which every member of society, and all civil communities, have a natural and unalienable right', Price explained. It was therefore important to investigate the essential components of liberty itself. He divided liberty into four categories: physical, moral, religious and civil. The innate characteristics of civil liberty pointed to an unavoidable conclusion: 'a country, that is subject to the legislature of another country, in which it has no voice, and over which it has no control, cannot be said to be governed by its own will. Such a country, therefore, is in a state of slavery.'[10]

Like others in Johnson's circle, Price was appalled at the rank folly inherent in Britain knowingly exploding its most valuable trading relationship. 'Some have made the proportion of our trade depending on *North America* to be near ONE HALF. A moderate computation makes it a THIRD. Let it, however, be supposed to be only a FOURTH. I will venture to say, this is a proportion of our foreign trade, the loss of which, when it comes to be felt, will be found insupportable.'[11] Elsewhere Price compared the situation of the American Patriots to that endured by the Corsicans in 1769: Britain, in this comparison, was firmly on the wrong side of history.

He believed that the war was producing a moment of national reckoning in which British subjects on both sides of the Atlantic would have to decide what price they were prepared to pay for freedom. Yet unless the corruptions inherent in Britain's governmental structures were rooted out, he concluded, 'I think it totally indifferent to the kingdom who are *in*, or who are *out* of power.'[12]

Not all those who wrote for Johnson on the subject of America saw the colony as a beacon of liberty. One pamphleteer noted sternly that it was the height of hypocrisy for Americans to protest about liberty while simultaneously enslaving their fellow creatures:

> These American contenders for freedom, so far from being animated by a general love of liberty any further than concerns themselves, never think of emancipating their poor slaves, but look on them as little better than beasts of the field, or domestic animals, though men as well as they, possessed of the same feelings, and only differing from them in colour.[13]

Men who fought to topple those in power over them while paying no attention to the plight of others, were guaranteed, the anonymous pamphleteer continued, to respond to power by themselves turning into tyrants and despots. In the reports emerging from America in newspapers and private letters of battles, skirmishes, retreats and bloody encounters of every kind, it was increasingly clear that neither side was emerging with much credit.

꜠

As Britain and America tore themselves asunder over questions of freedom, the slave trade received renewed attention. In Liverpool, a young friend of Johnson's called William Roscoe looked out across the Mersey from his home at Mount Pleasant and saw only symbols of national disgrace. As he watched the ships set sail he followed them in his mind's eye down to the west coast of Africa, where men and women were torn from everything they knew and loved:

> Shame to Mankind! But shame to BRITONS most,
> Who all the sweets of Liberty can boast;
> Yet, deaf to every human claim, deny
> That bliss to others, which themselves enjoy.[14]

Roscoe was a member of William Enfield's Unitarian chapel in Liverpool and it was through Enfield that he met Johnson. He was fifteen years younger than Johnson and was more prosperous than were most of Johnson's authors, but despite the disparity in age and social status the two men became close, drawn together by religious sympathy and a shared love of Liverpool. Roscoe's attachment to the city was so great that he rarely travelled out of it, but on the occasions that he did venture to London he made for the sanctuary of St Paul's Churchyard.

During Johnson's summer visits to Liverpool Roscoe was a welcoming presence. He was passionately devoted to the arts and determined that Liverpool could become a great cultural centre. In 1773 he was instrumental in founding a Society for the Encouragement of the Arts, Paintings and Design, through which he organised the first public exhibition of paintings to take place in England outside London. Enfield drew him into the circle of rational enquirers at Warrington and encouraged him to write. His 1777 poem, *Mount Pleasant*, was the first overtly abolitionist work Johnson published. In verse Roscoe celebrated the bustle of industrial Liverpool while simultaneously drawing attention to the torment funding the city's expansion. No city could be great – no country proud – while its success depended on the sufferings of others. 'Whence these horrors?' he asked:

> Is it, our varied interests disagree,
> And BRITAIN sinks if AFRIC's sons be free?
> No – Hence a few superfluous stores we claim,
> That tempt our avarice, but increase our shame;
> The sickly palate touch with more delight,
> Or swell the senseless riot of the night.[15]

Roscoe wrote his poem ten years before the formation of the Society for the Abolition of the Slave Trade. In 1777, when the attention of the country at large was turned towards the conflict in America, the plight of the enslaved African people caught between two warring nations attracted little interest. In a brief notice of *Mount Pleasant* in the *Critical Review* one reviewer praised the poem's elegancies but made no acknowledgement of its subject. 'He who can be satisfied with an elegant picture of Liverpool, its public buildings, &c. in agreeable poetry, has not occasion to travel any farther than to our author's Mount Pleasant'.[16] The *Monthly Review*'s summary similarly focused solely on Roscoe's depiction of Liverpool. In both cases the wider scope of the poem was ignored, its politics diminished to invisibility. As war dragged on, sapping the economic and intellectual energies of the country, Johnson's friends and authors saw their arguments against the confrontation ignored and their cries against global injustices go unheard. In this climate Johnson's decision to keep publishing work that went against the grain of the national mood was a political act with which he kept faith.

'No man', wrote Anna Barbauld, 'expects to preserve oranges through an English winter; or when he has planted an acorn, to see it become a large oak in a few months.'[17] Against an unsettled national backdrop, the men and women who gathered for dinner at 72 St Paul's Churchyard pressed on with the work they believed would result in reformation. In Suffolk Barbauld and her husband took more pupils every year, educating them on the rational, egalitarian principles of Warrington. In Norfolk John Aikin tended to the sick; in London George Fordyce did likewise. In Calne Priestley continued his efforts to understand the structures of the mind and the air. At Essex Street Lindsey enlarged his congregation until, in 1778, he had enough money from subscriptions to buy the building, build a proper chapel above the old auction room and, in one corner, furnish living quarters of his own. Lindsey raised the money but it was Hannah who raised the roof. 'She has been this whole week seven or eight hours each day on the spot, to see everything done and despatched as it ought to be.' Hannah worked, Lindsey continued, with 'the zeal and the intelligence of any of our most enlightened reformers.'[18] At the end of June Lindsey was able to write to a friend from a new address: 'Essex-house, Essex-Street, Strand'. 'The house', he reported, 'is not yet all of it habitable – but after being cooped up 4 years and a half in lodgings, crouded with other guests, it is a great refreshment to have one or two rooms to ourselves at this hot season.'[19]

From 72 St Paul's Churchyard Johnson set his printers to work day after day. He summoned William Enfield from Liverpool to be on hand while his *Biographical Sermons* were corrected and printed; he sent Priestley's books to small groups of sympathetic readers scattered all over the country. He bought remaindered copies of obscure religious tracts at the sales of other booksellers, determined that rigorous philosophical enquiry should see the light of day. He issued a steady stream of sermons, addresses, works on Dissent and Dissenting liberties and theological enquiries. But he also published books that did nothing more or less than contribute to the enjoyment of life. He was part of a consortium of publishers who issued an enlarged edition ('with all the modern improvements') of Hannah Glasse's *Art of Cookery* in 1778, which included chapters on 'Cheesecakes, Creams, Jellies, Whip-Syllabubs' and 'fifty receipts for different articles of perfumery'.[20] In another consortium he published a new edition of John Abercrombie's *Every Man his own Gardener* which boasted of encompassing 'not only an account of what work is necessary to be done in the Hot-House, Green-house, Shrubbery, Kitchen, Flower, and Fruit-Gardens, for every Month of the Year; but also ample Directions for performing the said Work, according to the newest and most approved Methods now in Practice among the best Gardeners.'[21] He published poetry by anonymous young ladies, picaresque novels, and plays of all descriptions. The only books he would not publish were those for which he foresaw no audience, and as his confidence grew so did his bluntness towards those authors who overestimated the size of their potential readership.

In 1778 the French Navy joined forces with American ships to harry British vessels back to port and Johnson brought out a capacious two-part account of *New Discoveries Concerning the World and its Inhabitants*. It contained, his advertisement promised, an account

> of all the islands in the South-Sea, that have been lately discovered or explored; the Situation, Climate, and Soil of each; their natural Productions, including many Species of Animals and Vegetables hith-erto unknown; the Persons, Dresses, extraordinary Manners and Customs, Manufactures, Buildings, Government, and Religion of the various Inhabitants; their domestic Utensils, and Weapons of War; their Ingenuity, mental Endowments, Skill in Navigation, and other Arts and Sciences.[22]

New Discoveries appeared seven years after Cook's first voyage in 1771; Hawkesworth's history of the second voyage had been published only a year previously. Johnson's compendium account of the voyages was an up-to-the-minute summary, designed to disseminate new knowledge as it emerged. He kept his gaze and that of his readers resolutely outwards, focused on the world beyond corrupt domestic politics and a shameful war. He issued books on English grammar, history and biography alongside pocket dictionaries and shorthand guides for students. The readers of Johnson's books could know the history of their own country, be well-grounded in the essentials of their language and have models of eminent people on which to base their own conduct. They could learn about countries beyond Britain and the responsibilities attendant on being a citizen of the world. They could take pleasure in reading poetry, drama, novels and advice manuals, even as they drew religious guidance and consolation from works of theological enquiry. They could understand the beauty of a complex universe and they would know how to treat the poor, the vulnerable and the sick. From Johnson's list, in short, a rising generation could receive an education that would enable them to avoid the mistakes of their forefathers as they remade the world in the image of the books they read.

10

Thoughts on the Devotional Taste

On the morning of Friday June 2nd 1780 a crowd of between forty and fifty thousand people gathered at St George's Fields, a little south of Westminster Bridge. Many of them had blue cockades in their hats, a sign of their membership of a body called the Protestant Association. Shortly before midday the crowd formed itself into four divisions, each with its own flags and banners, and began a march via separate routes to the Houses of Parliament.

The gathering at St George's Fields was orchestrated by Lord George Gordon. Gordon was an MP, former soldier, and ardent anti-Catholic. Under his leadership the Protestant Association's primary goal became to compel Parliament to repeal the Catholic Relief Act, a piece of legislation passed in 1777 primarily to enable Catholics to enrol in the army and to boost the overstretched troops fighting in America. The professed intention of the June 2nd marchers was to present a petition for repeal of the Act to Parliament, but as the crowd reached the Palace of Westminster Gordon lost control of his followers. As members of the Commons and Lords drove through the gates of the Palace their carriages were attacked, their wigs torn off and blue feathers were rammed in their hats. One peer was pelted with mud; another was briefly held captive by the crowd. The Archbishop of York was dragged from his carriage and compelled to say, 'No Popery!' repeatedly as he attempted to escape.

Gordon presented the petition and made a speech advocating calm. His attempts to quell his supporters were ineffectual. Eventually the crowd was persuaded to disperse and although there were outbreaks of violence and rioting in the streets around Westminster for the rest of the evening it seemed as if the unrest was dissipating. An uneasy calm prevailed throughout Saturday

June 3rd but on Sunday afternoon the crowds reassembled and rioters began systematically attacking houses and chapels in the predominantly Catholic neighbourhood of Moorfields. On Monday the violence spread, as the houses of Catholic-sympathising parliamentarians were set on fire. The shopkeepers of the City hastily boarded up their windows and scrawled, 'No Popery!' on their buildings in the hope this would defend them from attack.

By Tuesday morning civil order in London had broken down. Rioters destroyed the house of Lord Justice Hyde in Leicester Fields, as well as that of Sir John Fielding, the Bow Street magistrate. They moved on to Newgate prison, where they burnt down the doors and released the prisoners. From there the crowd roared onwards and that night the house of the reforming Lord Chief Justice Lord Mansfield (who had insisted that his clerks issue a licence for the Essex Street Chapel) was consumed by fire. Mansfield's library contained thousands of priceless manuscripts, all destroyed in retaliation for his support of the Catholic Relief Act. By the end of the following day, which became known as 'Black Wednesday', the London skyline was alight. In Holborn the crowd set fire to the house of Mr Langdale, a distiller, and the streets ran with un-purified gin. Drunk on adrenaline, power, violence and spirits, the rioters moved from prison to prison, setting inmates free as they went, before finally alighting on the Bank of England as their ultimate target. Only there were they repulsed by the militia. Gradually, over the following days, the government regained control of the streets. Hundreds of people were killed and seriously injured in the violence. Twenty-five more deaths came in July, when those identified as ringleaders in the destruction were hanged.

One of the first published accounts of the riots was by Thomas Holcroft, who based his *Plain and Succinct Narrative* on newspaper reports, anecdote and the events he had seen unfold:

> Let those who were not spectators judge what the inhabitants felt when they beheld at the same instant the flames ascending and rolling in vast and voluminous clouds from the King's Bench and Fleet Prisons, from New Bridewell, from the Toll-gates on Blackfriars Bridge, from houses in every quarter of the town.[1]

Although he had been a witness to the destruction, Holcroft found it almost impossible to describe his experiences. Faced with the failure of language to evoke violence, he deployed journalistic details to convey the scale of desolation:

> Men, women, and children were running up and down with beds, glasses, bundles, or whatever they wished most to preserve. In streets where there were no fires, numbers were removing their goods and effects at midnight. The tremendous roar of the initiate and innumerable fiends who were the authors of these horrible scenes, was heard at one instant, and the next the dreadful report of soldiers muskets, as if firing in platoons, and at various places, in short, every thing which could impress the mind with the idea of universal anarchy, and approaching desolation, seemed to be accumulating. Sleep and rest were things not thought of; the streets were swarming with people, and uproar, confusion, and terror reigned in every part.[2]

+

At Essex Street Theophilus Lindsey refused to bar his windows. On Black Wednesday he received news that rioters had been heard discussing an attack on the chapel. Essex Street was to be targeted, friends reported, because 'our heresy in denying the deity and worship of Christ was said to be what made us next to, if not worse than the Papist.' Instead of revealing to the rioters that he feared them Lindsey orchestrated the removal of papers and valuables. On the night of June 7th he and Hannah took refuge with friends, leaving, he told one correspondent, 'a person or two in the house' (whose safety, by implication, was of less concern). The violence abated and Essex House remained unharmed but the fear the riots had instilled in Lindsey's congregation took longer to quell. 'I received several applications from the members of our society and anonymous letters from others, to blot their names out of their prayer-books in the chapel, lest they shd be made use of to their prejudice', he told a friend. 'As this had been the way in which the associators had come to the knowledge of many of the unfortunate R. Catholics.'[3]

Today historians tend to read the Gordon Riots as the result less of anti-Catholicism than as a proto-revolutionary uprising against power, an expression of anger by a hungry and disenfranchised population.[4] It is certainly the case that the cause for which Gordon's petitioners marched on June 2nd was seized upon by a much broader array of individuals and groups, some of whom were caught up in the enthusiasm of the crowd and some of whom were intent on the spread of violence. Yet the attack on religious diversity that sparked the riots remained a central feature of the 'Days of June' for those who had to fight for their right to religious independence. Many Dissenters shared the anti-Catholic sentiments of their Church of England counterparts and attacked Catholicism's idols and hierarchies with ferocity. But others recognised it was a logical fallacy to demand toleration for themselves while denying it to others.

Priestley led the way in this. He was personally deeply suspicious of Catholics but insisted that a reformed State would allow them to worship freely – and, indeed, that religious freedom might actually work to prevent the secret spread of idolatrous beliefs. Lindsey detested Catholicism, which he viewed as antithetical to individual religious freedom, but he also believed that the Gordon Riots were the product of State-sponsored religious prejudice that was poisoning the nation. In the meantime, when a city the size of London could be engulfed in a conflagration of flames and fear, only the closest and most loyal friends were to be trusted. 'I cannot but look upon our country and the name of Englishman disgraced by this spirit of cruel bigotry which is now shewing itself', he wrote. 'I add no more at present, only that we do not mention their intentions against us but to particular friends, for obvious reasons.'[5]

The Gordon Riots made real the anxieties of those who felt themselves to be marginalised in and unprotected from their country. In the aftermath of the violence Johnson published a sermon by an 'R. Harrison' entitled *The Catholic Protestant*, which argued that intolerance towards other religious practices was a fundamentally anti-Christian position. Yet Harrison also argued for the existence of what he termed 'sinless anger': anger that was fully justified by circumstance. 'Sinless anger' would become a touchstone of Dissenting politics: the phrase encompassing both the right of self-defence and the responsibility of marginalised patriots to argue and write their way towards national reformation. The Gordon Riots brought the fears of those excluded in the name of religious toleration into focus and demonstrated that it was no longer possible for Unitarians and other Nonconformists to hold themselves aloof from the institutions of the State. Harrison was clear about this:

So long as we hold a just estimate and concern for our own safety or peace, it is neither wise nor possible to bear in silence all the abuse and cruelty causeless rage or malice would heap upon us. The injuries of bad men might take encouragement and grow with the absolute tameness of our submission; nay, that very sympathy and good-will which humanity dictates, and religion prescribes, in behalf of helpless, innocent, and virtuous sufferers, call aloud for our assistance, and demand proper expressions of severity to restrain the lawless, savage oppressors of our brethren.[6]

On the frontispiece Johnson made the connection between the sermon and the riots explicit: it had been preached, read the description, 'during the Peril and Sufferings of Great-Britain by domestic Riots, and her foreign Wars against the united Powers of France, Spain, and her revolted Colonies in North-America.'

France formally entered the war on America's side in 1778; Spain followed in 1779 and Holland in 1780, leaving Britain with no allies. Faced with fire at home and superior fire-power abroad, Britain seemed to her citizens to be in crisis. In 1780 Johnson published a pamphlet in defence of the Catholic Relief Act, written the previous December, before the Riots. 'I can say', promised the anonymous writer, 'that if I were possessed of all the kingdoms of the world I would not touch a hair of any man's head on account of his opinions in religion ... As a private man, however, I believe Popery to be a corrupt religion; and therefore to be opposed. – But how is this to be done? – Not by force; but by reasoning: not by penalties; but by persuasion.'[7] It was a sentiment shared by many of those who sought literal and metaphorical shelter with Johnson. But during the hot 'Days of June' 1780, when the sky itself appeared on fire, persuasion and thoughtful pamphlets proved ineffective defences against the strength of the crowd.

Within Johnson's immediate circle persuasion also revealed its limits. In 1775 Anna Barbauld wrote a provocative essay entitled 'Thoughts on the Devotional Taste'. She published it in an innocuously titled volume, *Devotional Pieces*, which, apparently even more innocuously, she dedicated to her father. In the essay itself, however, she dissected the follies and contradictions of the religious tradition of Warrington and her own family. She opened with a challenge to Priestley, her old intellectual mentor. 'In the first place, there is nothing more prejudicial to the feelings of a devout heart, than a habit of disputing on religious subjects. Free inquiry is undoubt-edly necessary to establish a rational belief; but a disputatious spirit, and fondness for controversy, gives the mind a sceptical turn, with an aptness to call in question the most established truths.'[8] Too much philosophy rendered God unimaginable, she continued. A little superstition, on the other hand, was no bad thing. She characterised Dissenting sects as fit places of worship only for those with the capacity to think for themselves. For everyone else the music, traditions and structures of the Established Church offered more to encourage moderate religious feeling. She insisted that religion was a matter of feeling as well as thought and she poked fun at the Dissenting men who had brought her up. 'The dissenting teacher is nothing', she wrote, 'if he have not the spirit of a martyr; and is the scorn of the world, if he be not above the world.'[9]

Barbauld's essay generated a furious response from Priestley. In a long letter he chastised her for daring to criticise Dissent. He made it clear that his opinions were shared by others in their circle. 'Many serious persons,' he told her, 'are more especially offended, and I think justly, at your comparing devotion to the passion of love, thinking it to be a profanation of the subject.'[10] He attacked her repeatedly for betraying their cause. 'To balance my opinion, you have secured the applause of the high clergy, (as I know in several instances,) of the decent part of the polite world in general, and of those Dissenters in particular who wish to have their defection from us made easier to them than it would otherwise have been.'[11] Although he insisted that she was free to write as she wished, he simultaneously cajoled her to alter her public position. 'If, upon reflection you should think there may be something of weight in any of these remarks, I could wish that, for the sake of many serious persons who esteem and love you, and who are exceedingly hurt by your later publication, you would, in a second edition, qualify some of the expressions, as far as regard to your real persuasion will admit.'[12]

Barbauld would not be persuaded. Her essay advocated a retreat from extreme positions and showed that it was possible to value the good in the opinions and practices of those who thought differently. The only change she made in later editions was to insert a final concluding paragraph in which this point was made explicit. 'We may see much good in an establishment, the doctrines of which we cannot give our assent to, without violating our integrity; we may respect the tendencies of a sect, the tenets of which we utterly disapprove. We may think practices useful which we cannot adopt without hypocrisy. We may think all religions beneficial, and believe of one alone that it is true.'[13] Barbauld recognised the failings of toleration among her own people. She compounded the crime of pointing this out by exercising independence of thought, one of the most important attributes Priestley sought to instil in his pupils. His response revealed the limits to his own tolerance, expressed in barely concealed outrage that a daughter of Warrington should dissent from his teachings so openly. As the 1770s drew to a close, divergent devotional tastes fractured friendships as well as skulls and windows. Barbauld was prescient when she wrote in 1775 that religion was a matter of the heart as well as the head and that those who ignored this essential truth – men like Priestley and her father – did so at their own peril:

> It is the character of the present age to allow little to sentiment, and all the warm and generous emotions are treated as romantic by the supercilious brow of a cold-hearted philosophy. The man of science, with an air of superiority, leaves them to some florid declaimer who professes to work upon the passions of the lower class, where they are so debased by noise and nonsense, that it is no wonder if they move disgust in those of elegant and better-informed minds.[14]

✢

In amongst the darkness of an embattled city, the turn of the decade also witnessed at St Paul's Churchyard the ascension of bright stars. In 1779 a young engraver called William Blake completed his apprenticeship. As a child Blake saw visions of angels in trees and prophets in fields and his shopkeeper parents sought a trade for him that would harness the intensity of his visual imagination. The apprentice-master they chose was the printmaker James Basire, who introduced the adolescent Blake into intellectual London life, putting him to work engraving illustrations for publications emerging from the Royal Society and the Society of Antiquaries. Blake learnt his trade quickly and by the time he had completed his apprenticeship was a highly competent engraver. One of his first steps as a free man was to enrol as a student at the Royal Academy, which gave him access to both the fine art and sculpture collections. Johnson was among the earliest booksellers to employ Blake and in 1780 he put him to work to copy a painting by Thomas Stothard for a new edition of William Enfield's *The Speaker*. Blake stood apart from the writers who congregated at Johnson's shop. He was a contractor, not an author; a skilled tradesman who provided a service in the production of the work of others. Other booksellers made use of his services too but it was Johnson who became Blake's chief employer.[15]

1780 also saw the first joint enterprise between Johnson and a mathematician called John Bonnycastle. In the first work he published with Johnson, a *Scholar's Guide to Arithmetic*, Bonnycastle described himself as a private teacher of mathematics. Within two years of his first work appearing he had been appointed mathematics master at the Royal Military Academy in Woolwich. Bonnycastle was neither a Dissenter nor disenfranchised: he was, instead, a respectable Establishment figure, connected to the military and widely respected by the generations of officers he taught. He and Johnson became firm friends. In his published works Bonnycastle attempted to unravel mathematics and the mysteries of the universe for his readers, writing books that were modest in conception but grand in scope. His was a deeply democratic project and in Johnson he found an ideal publisher, who insisted on bringing out books in inexpensive editions in order to make them available to as many people as possible. Without access to a rudimentary understanding of science, Bonnycastle insisted, it was impossible for thoughtful readers to form a judgement about the great discoveries of their age. All his energies were devoted to enlightening those 'whose situations in life, or confined education, may have prevented them from applying to a subject, which has commonly been thought of so abstruse and difficult a nature, as to be utterly unattainable without a previous knowledge of many other branches of science.'[16] He enlivened subsequent texts with quotations from poetry, in order to relieve 'minds unaccustomed to the regular deduction of facts by mathematical reasoning, and to enliven those parts, where a simple detail of particular must, from its necessary length, become languid.' Poetic descriptions, he continued, 'generally leave a stronger impression on the mind, and are far more captivating than simple unadorned language.'[17]

From 1780 onwards Bonnycastle appeared frequently at the dinners Johnson held at St Paul's Churchyard. Many years later a fellow guest described the strange sight he presented at the table: 'a tall, gaunt, long-headed man, with large features and spectacles, and a deep internal voice with a twang of rusticity in it'.[18] Others who met Bonnycastle at Johnson's described him as a man rich in anecdotes with a passion for poetry and drama and a genius for friendship. His books sold in large numbers and went through multiple editions because he had the ability to catch his passions on the page and to inspire his readers with his joy at beauty in all its forms, whether mathematic, astronomic or poetical. Johnson put Blake to work on engravings to sit alongside Bonnycastle's prose and the mathematician thus brought to the artist's vision a register of measurement and scales that would reappear in the latter's later work. Johnson simultaneously engaged Blake to engrave illustrations for new medical texts, and the sinews of the body in motion would likewise reappear in the images the younger man now began to create in the snatches of time between commissions.

✝

One evening early on in their acquaintance, a voice was heard on the stairs as Johnson and Bonnycastle were sitting down to dinner. The noise prompted Johnson to offer Bonnycastle a warning. 'I will now introduce you to a most ingenious foreigner, whom I think you will like; but, if you wish to enjoy his conversation, you will not attempt to stop the torrent of his words by contradicting him.'[19] The voice on the stair was that of Henry Fuseli, who in 1779 returned to London after an absence of almost a decade. During his years in Rome Fuseli achieved his ambition and established a reputation as one of the leading artists of his generation. On his way back to London he made a brief return to Switzerland, where he was accorded celebrity treatment and acknowledged as a returning hero. But his determined progress onwards made it clear that London was now his home. He took lodgings on Broad Street in Soho, just a few doors away from the house Blake still shared with his parents, and began a series of large-scale pictures for exhibition at the Royal Academy.

At St Paul's Churchyard Fuseli set up his materials and went to work on preparatory sketches of a young woman fast asleep with a leering creature perched atop her chest. Johnson meanwhile took Fuseli back to Liverpool as soon as the summer lull permitted and introduced him to William Roscoe, now established as a patron of artists and the arts. Once again Johnson and Fuseli knitted their lives together, sharing friends and work in ways that were long-lasting. Between Bonnycastle and Fuseli a warm friendship also developed, although Bonnycastle was never able to heed Johnson's advice to hold his tongue while Fuseli talked. 'They came and went away together, for years, like a couple of old schoolboys', recalled one acquaintance. 'They also, like boys, rallied one another, and sometimes made a singular display of it.'[20]

Amongst the hubbub of voices at St Paul's Churchyard, Johnson himself was quiet. Guests at his table in 1780 would have heard any number of argumentative people jousting with each other over their rice pudding: Barbauld, holding her own against Priestley and Lindsey; Bonnycastle and Fuseli, bickering comfortably; George Fordyce, John Aikin and their fellow doctors deep in discussion about new discoveries. Not all these men and women lived in London and while some dropped in to dinner frequently others only did so during their occasional visits to the city. The one constant was Johnson himself, keeping his own counsel. Many years later one friend described him at these gatherings. 'All were delighted when he took his share in the conversation, and only regretted that the gentleness and modesty of his nature led him to do it so rarely.' When he did make himself heard, however, it was to some effect. 'He was always found an advocate on the side of human nature and human virtues, recommending that line of conduct which springs from disinterestedness and a liberal feeling, and maintaining the practicability of such conduct.'[21] In 1780 to be an advocate on the side of human nature was to be an optimist, since it involved believing that people were better than smouldering buildings, religious divisions and an unjust war suggested. Thus as the 'Days of June' came to an end and the rioters melted away, Johnson opened his doors, summoned his authors, workshop-hands, engravers and printers and set them to work once again.

PART THREE

REVOLT (1780–1789)

William Blake, Frontispiece to Mary Wollstonecraft's
Original Stories, 1791

It is the 1780s now, and the list of people who are part of the conversation at St Paul's Churchyard is growing. New voices in the dining room include Erasmus Darwin, an enormous presence in every sense of the word; Sarah Trimmer, a children's writer with the reformation of the nation's morals in her sights; and Mary Wollstonecraft, who gets off the stagecoach and comes to stay with Johnson before becoming, along with Fuseli, a central figure in his life. During the day letters and manuscripts from a new author, William Cowper, cover the table, but Cowper's presence fades when the room is cleared of work and those who inhabit the house in person arrive to dine. Sometimes over dinner single voices ring out, as the stories and ideas of individuals take on particular significance in both Johnson's life and in the world of letters he is in the business of creating. At other moments verses comprising singular histories give way to a chorus – or cacophony – in which the men and women of the dining room interrupt each other to speak of the work of writing, making and reforming the world upon which they are engaged. As the decade draws to a close it is possible not only to imagine a better future but to see in both Britain and France the intimations of a new beginning. Across the Channel a Parisian crowd hammers on the doors of a hated prison, and, as excitement builds in St Paul's Churchyard, the noise of the dining room spills outside its walls and into the world beyond.

The Task

At the end of May 1780, two days before violence erupted in London and Johnson shuttered his shop windows, an evangelical minister called Martin Madan published a treatise entitled *Thelyphthora*. Madan's central argument was simple: men should be held responsible for the virgins they had sex with and any man who seduced a woman should be obliged to marry her publicly, even if she was already married. He attacked the insistence on monogamy in the civil marriage code and proposed that polygamy offered the best hope for cleansing society of evil.

In the noisy world of eighteenth-century letters airing such an *outré* proposal was akin to throwing a well-aimed grenade. A petition against *Thelyphthora* gained six thousand signatures; over twenty separate attacks on Madan were published in pamphlets and magazines. He was forced to resign from his position as chaplain at Lock Hospital in central London, an establishment that ministered to reformed prostitutes, and many acquaintances turned their backs on him. Among them were the author of Johnson's first bestseller, John Newton, who tried to persuade Madan to withdraw from publishing his ideas, and a cousin of Madan's named William Cowper.

✣

William Cowper was drawn towards the circles surrounding 72 St Paul's Churchyard by Newton, who in 1764, the year of *An Authentic Narrative*, took holy orders and accepted the curacy of the parish of Olney in Buckinghamshire. By the time Newton moved to Olney he was one of the best-known figures of the Evangelical Revival, and in 1767 a new household settled in the town in order to worship under the light of his ministry. It comprised Mary Unwin, a widow of two months standing, her grown-up daughter Susannah, and Cowper.

Cowper would become one of Johnson's most successful authors but he did not find fame until middle age. As a young man he pursued an aimless course in London, paying only the most desultory attention to the legal work his family insisted he train for, preferring instead to frequent the theatres and scribble classically inspired verses. His father's death in 1756 left him with a modest income and his path to a comfortable existence appeared assured after his uncle Ashley Cowper, an official in Parliament, offered him a valuable clerkship. Another candidate for the same position objected and Cowper was told he would need to testify to his credentials at the bar of the House of Lords. To withdraw was impossible but Cowper believed himself to be incapable of success. A few days before his examination he attempted suicide, first by buying laudanum he was unable to swallow, then by stabbing himself, and finally by hanging himself. He was found by his landlord and brought round, but his sanity was in tatters and he sank into despair, believing himself destined only for damnation. Relatives placed him under the care of a Dr Cotton in St Albans, who ran a genteel asylum for the insane.

Cowper remained in Dr Cotton's care for over a year, during which he attempted suicide again and experienced day after day the blackness of despair. Many years later he wrote a detailed account of this period of his life in a conversion narrative that, like Newton's, does not shy from the horrors that come before redemption. In Cowper's case, however, these horrors were internal. 'Life', he recalled, 'appeared now more eligible than death only because it was a barrier between me and everlasting burnings.'[1] The blackness lifted slowly during the months he spent in St Albans and one day he picked up a Bible and experienced revelation. 'In a moment', he recalled, 'I believed and received the Gospel'.[2] From this point on Cowper's recovery developed in tandem with his own Evangelical awakening. He swore never to visit London again, viewing the city as the place where he had been driven to the sins of despair and self-destruction. His friends and brother, recognising that his recovery was fragile and his mental state perilous, arranged to supply him with an income of £100 a year so that he would be protected from the demands of public life. Armed with this resource Cowper moved to Huntingdon in Cambridgeshire, where he met the Unwins. They recognised in him a lost soul searching, like them, for salvation, and offered him room and board at a heavily reduced rate.

Cowper sometimes referred to Mary Unwin as his mother, but at forty-four to his thirty-six she was quite evidently not his parent. Nor, though, as was apparent to all who met them, was she his mistress. The entry for Cowper in the *Oxford Dictionary of National Biography* describes her as his 'keeper' but this is to underestimate the complexity of a relationship that defied social convention and description. It is certainly the case, however, that from 1767 onwards Mary Unwin was, and felt herself to be responsible for, keeping Cowper alive. Throughout their life together his despair would return. During these periods, which lasted for months on end, she would sit with him all night, hardly sleeping herself, acting as protector from the mental terrors that tormented him.

Cowper lived every day with the certainty that he was damned for eternity, shut out from God's love because of his suicide attempt. During daylight hours he was sometimes able to block thoughts of what awaited him by walking with Mrs Unwin, tending the cucumbers and melons he grew under glass, caring for his menagerie of hares and writing long letters to a small circle of friends. At night the horror came, in visions of hell that were brilliant and terrifying. His cousin Martin Madan's treatise on polygamy appeared to offer an open invitation for thoughtless men and women to condemn themselves to damnation. Cowper was deeply distressed that his cousin should have allowed himself to become carried away by his passions at the expense of reason: a reaction founded in part on his own awareness of the dangers of an unchecked imagination. 'Judgement falls asleep upon the bench', he wrote after a particularly bad night. 'While Imagination, like a smug, pert, counsellor, stands chattering at the bar, and with a deal of fine-spun, enchanting sophistry, carries all before him.'[3]

To write despite the certainty of eternal torment was not easy. 'Such nights as I frequently spend, are but a miserable prelude to the succeeding day, and indispose me, above all things, to the business of writing.'[4] Yet in the closing months of 1780, anger at Madan's folly prompted Cowper to sit down with fresh paper at a rickety table that creaked and tilted as his pen travelled across the page. By December he had produced a two-hundred-line poem in response to Madan. He called it *Antithelyphthora*. It was a vociferous verse satire, similar in form to the poems he had dashed off as a young lawyer before mental illness overtook him. Madan appears in the poem as Sir Airy del Castro, who is engaged in an illicit relationship with Dame Hypothesis. Cowper wrote in a grand tradition of eighteenth-century anonymous satirical attacks, harnessing both humour and brutality in his assault on his subject. When his pen faltered, as it did in November, Mrs Unwin told him to keep going and suggested he might like to include an attack on the Church of England authorities for allowing moral corruption to infect their flock. 'She thought there was a fair Opportunity to give the Bishops a Slap', Cowper told Newton. 'As it would not have been civil to have denied a Lady so reasonable a Request, I have just made the Powder fly out of their Wigs a little.'[5]

In December he sent the completed poem to Newton who gave it to Johnson. Cowper was anxious about the thought of his work moving through the press without him but was nevertheless grateful to Newton for what he termed his 'obstetrical assistance.'[6] Johnson and Newton agreed that Cowper's name should be kept out of the business and both entered into the subterfuge with enthusiasm. 'Either Johnson does not know the author, or is not at liberty to tell', Newton wrote disingenuously to a friend. 'When asked the question he shrugs, and bows, and looks very profound. I shall not be the first to extort the secret from him.'[7]

Madan was unmoved by the attacks that rained down on him and in January he published a second edition of *Thelyphthora*. Cowper concluded that his stubborn cousin was simply burning unread the broadsides aimed at him, and few critics paid much attention to Cowper's own response. But the experience of writing *Antithelyphthora* revealed to him that poetry had the potential to keep nightmares at bay. In January he began a direct conversation with Johnson. His opening gambit was hardly that of a debutante poet anxiously seeking a bookseller's approval: if they were to work together, he announced, Johnson would need to ensure his printers left off tampering with the verse. Under no circumstances would he allow his work to be tidied to suit modern ears. 'Give me a manly, rough line, with a deal of meaning in it', he insisted. 'There is a roughness on a plumb, which nobody that understands fruit would rub off, though the plumb would be much more polished without it.'[8]

✢

Cowper and Johnson never met but the relationship that developed between them on paper changed both their lives. Johnson recognised immediately that Cowper had a voice like no other and within a few weeks of their first exchange of letters he had offered to publish any poetry Cowper wrote, sight unseen. In a development of his professional practice he appointed himself as Cowper's editor, and Cowper came to value his suggestions in spite of his early protestations. The partnership made Johnson rich. Long after both men were dead an acquaintance calculated that Johnson had made over £10,000 from the sale of work by Cowper: ten times the handsome profit earned by the surgeon John Hunter for his *Natural History of the Human Teeth*. The profits from Cowper's work allowed Johnson to invest more funds into the intricate copyright share schemes that contributed substantially to the wealth accrued by the most successful London booksellers, and the dividends that resulted in turn enabled Johnson to publish work that he considered important but that had little chance of offering any financial return. But Cowper's gifts to Johnson were not merely financial. Johnson's passionate interest in creative people bound him to Cowper, as together they discussed editorial amendments, forms of publication and the tastes of their audience. Johnson's voice, so often muted elsewhere, rings through his correspondence with Cowper in letters that showed distance was no barrier to working together.

By early spring 1781 Cowper was writing steadily and letters were flying back and forth between him, Johnson and Newton about plans for a volume of poems. In March Cowper agreed that Johnson could use his name on the title page, provided he announce him to the world via his old professional association: 'William Cowper Esqr. of the Inner Temple'. He did so with some reluctance, at Johnson's insistence, and on condition that the authorship of *Antithelyphthora* should never be revealed. Explaining his change of heart he acknowledged that writing had become one of his principal ways of staving off the blackness and that he could not bear to deny himself the chance of finding readers. 'If a Board of Enquiry were to be establish'd, at which Poets were to undergo an Examination respecting the Motives that induced them to publish', he told Newton, his answer would be straightforward: 'there is nothing but this, no Occupation within the Compass of my small Sphere, Poetry excepted, that can do much towards diverting that train of Melancholy thoughts, which when I am not thus employ'd, are for ever pouring themselves in upon me.' To write for the void was no solution either. 'If I did not publish what I write, I could not interest myself sufficiently in my own Success to make an Amusement of it.'[9]

In his letters to Newton and to Mrs Unwin's son William, Cowper presented the writing of poetry as a respite from pain, to be abandoned when the sun shone again and the garden and greenhouse beckoned. Soon, he promised Newton in April, he would lay down the character of author and become again a gardener, with little need to trouble Newton with instructions to the printer. Yet poetry was far more than a therapeutic diversion. He approached the creation of a volume of poetry with the same intensity he brought to carpentry and the cultivation of exotic fruit. He was interested in the mechanics of bookmaking and was simultaneously elated and frustrated by delays which both allowed him to add more lines to the volume and at times made its eventual publication seem a distant prospect. Some days, when he was unable to write poetry, he filled letters to Newton with speculations about the progress of his book. In April he mused about the eventual length of the volume; by May he was able to tell Unwin he thought it would stretch to 2,500 lines. He felt himself to be a shaky investment – 'But Johnson has heroically set all peradventures at defiance, and takes the whole charge upon himself – so Out I come.'[10]

Publishing a book at a distance from bookseller and printer in 1781 was a stressful and time-consuming business. To avoid the costs of postage becoming exorbitant as proof sheets travelled between St Paul's Churchyard and Olney, Johnson and Cowper had to cajole sympathetic friends to procure them franks from corruptible members of Parliament, who were able to use the postal system for free by marking their own signatures with an official stamp. Larger parcels had to be sent by an erratic network of private carriers and Cowper lived in dread of letters and corrected proofs being mislaid. Sometimes he worried that his distance from Johnson's shop made it easy for the bookseller to ignore him and he was quick to attribute delays in printing to neglect. Even paper had to be ordered in from elsewhere, since nowhere within walking distance of the village had stock of an adequate quality for writing and rewriting. Newton acted as Cowper's proxy at St Paul's Churchyard, sometimes popping in to prod Johnson into action; at other times visiting to investigate progress. In May Johnson decided to hold publication back until the beginning of the new London season, to Cowper's frustration. 'Man, especially Man that writes verse, is born to disappointments, as surely as Printers and Booksellers are born to be the most dilatory and tedious of all Creatures.'[11] Yet delay also made it possible for Cowper to correct the proof sheets himself rather than rely on Newton to do it for him. Over the summer he steadily asserted more control over the production of his work and his relationship with Johnson. His letters for this period show him tiring of Newton's bombastic encouragement, and wary of the proprietorial interest of others in the progress of the volume.

As Cowper's confidence in his work grew so did his tolerance of criticism. His reliance on Newton's approval lessened as his faith in Johnson's judgement increased. When Newton told him that Johnson was muttering about the need for improvements, Cowper listened. 'I had rather submitt to Chastisement now, than be obliged to undergo it hereafter. If Johnson therefore will mark with a marginal Q, those Lines that He or His, object to, as not Sufficiently finished, I will willingly retouch them, or give a reason for my refusal. I shall moreover think myself obliged by any hints of that sort.'[12] He grew to enjoy the competitive camaraderie of working alongside someone as committed as him to bringing out a book in the best state possible. 'Johnson is printing away and I am writing away as if it was a race between us.'[13] The pace of Johnson's printers ebbed and flowed and Cowper lived with the fear that his mental state would collapse before work was completed. In September 1781 he intimated this to Johnson, establishing an understanding about the fragility of his mind. 'I never write except when I can do it with facility', he explained, 'and am rather apprehensive that the Muse is about to forsake me for the present; ever since I could use a pen I have been subject to such Vicissitudes.'[14] Still the volume continued to grow, until in October Cowper sent the final poem to Johnson. With the volume completed, he reported to Newton, he could return to the important business of preparing his greenhouse for the winter.

The printers kept working, laboriously setting each line of type in great metal frames, letter by letter. In February 1782 Cowper was finally able to tell Newton that he had his proofs. Correcting them was a tedious business but for the experience of professional authorship he had only gratitude. To bring a volume into the world was 'bewitching'. Moreover, 'the quieting and composing effect of it was such, and so totally absorbed have I sometimes been in my rhiming occupation, that neither the past nor the future ... had any longer a share in my contemplation.'[15] To Johnson he sent a final list of errata and an acknowledgement of the work they had done together. 'I now reckon the book finished, and therefore once for all and very unfeignedly return you my thanks for the many usefull hints you have given me. And if I were to prefix an Advertisement to the Reader, would most willingly acknowledge my self indebted to my Bookseller, as my very judicious, and only Corrector.'[16]

In April 1781, when the shape of the volume was still unknown, Cowper had asked Newton to write a Preface for the poems. Newton seized on the invitation as an opportunity to yoke Cowper's poetry to the Evangelical cause. Newton's Preface related in oblique terms the story of Cowper's despair and withdrawal from the world, caused, in Newton's telling, by having 'lived without God'. God enabled Cowper's recovery in rural peace and watched over him as he was again afflicted by 'a long indisposition.' The published poems, meanwhile, everywhere demonstrated Cowper's 'perceptions of the truth, beauty, and influence of the religion of the Bible.'[17] Elsewhere in the Preface Newton presented himself as the volume's presiding genius, deciding which poems should be included and which omitted. God and Newton watch over Cowper in equal measure in Newton's telling and the Preface reads as a powerful testament to Newton's self-belief as well as his faith.

Johnson printed Newton's Preface and had it bound with half a dozen trial copies of Poems. But having seen the effect of it in print he decided that it should be omitted. Religious readers might plough through the Preface in order to get to the poetry, he told Cowper, but those who did not share Newton's views would put the volume aside in disgust before they discovered Cowper's voice. 'It appears to me wrong to insert a preface which has a direct tendency to prevent readers of very different senti-ments from the writer of it from turning over a single page, & which will infallibly prejudice the critics against the work before they have read a single line.' He offered no insult to Newton, he insisted: indeed, 'few men stand so high in my esteem ... or have so great a share of my love.'[18] Although Johnson left the final decision to Cowper he also offered to tell Newton that his work would not be required and Cowper agreed. 'I have found Johnson a very judicious man on other occasions', he explained to William Unwin, 'and am therefore willing that he should determine for me upon this.'[19]

With Newton himself Cowper prevaricated, explaining that he was putting his own wishes aside in order to accede to Johnson's superior know-ledge of public taste. Distance allowed him to take refuge from the squalls of literary men and he instructed Johnson to make the final decision himself once he had seen Newton. But in March he sent Newton a decisive letter, shrugging off Newton's unhappiness and the Preface's unsuitability as symp-toms of debased times. 'I can only repeat what I said some time since', he wrote with finality. 'The world is grown more foolish and careless than it was when I had the honour of knowing it.' For Johnson himself he had nothing but praise. 'I have reason to be very satisfied with my publisher. He marked such lines as did not please him, and as often as I could, I paid all possible respect to his animadversions.... I do not know where I could have found a Bookseller who could have pointed out to me my defects with more discernment.'[20] Newton knew himself to be dethroned as Cowper's chief mentor and he struggled to disguise his anger. Their friendship survived but it was never again as close and the balance of power between them had shifted irrevocably.

Cowper's first published volume combined moral satires with shorter, observational pieces that sought to capture the essence of the everyday in poetry. The satires were formal and, for the most part, serious, although in 'The Progress of Error', the first poem Cowper wrote for the volume, both Madan and dilatory printers came in for ridicule. Newton was right when he wrote that the poems attempted to express the experience of living a life of religious devotion and wrong in his insistence that devotion was their only theme. Cowper explored ideas such as truth, charity, conversation and retirement in the volume but he also drew attention to the great events of public life (notably in lines on the burning of Lord Mansfield's Library during the Gordon Riots and in 'The Modern Patriot') and to the texture of his own existence. The volume included poems addressed to William Unwin and to Newton as well as verses in which Cowper articulated the hope that he might one day be free of mental suffering:

> Come, peace of mind, delightful guest!
> Return and make thy downy nest
> Once more in this sad heart.

Lines like these marked Cowper out from other aspirant poets crowding the stage. Others might write satires in heroic couplets; many scribbled verses on affairs of State. In 1782 few offered their readers a window into their own emotional existence as starkly as this:

> But fixt unalterable care
> Foregoes not what she feels within,
> Shows the same sadness every where,
> And slights the season and the scene.

Cowper wrote of himself but although his own torments were particular to him, the washed-out colours of the world seen by those experiencing periods of grief and melancholy were not. Elsewhere he described the restorative power of sympathy and love and he even included a poem on the tantalising sight of a pineapple growing behind glass, inspired by watching a bee frantically trying to breach the greenhouse at Olney and by the experience of seeing the beauties of the world while shut out from joy:

> Our dear delights are often such,
> Expos'd to view but not to touch.[21]

If Johnson expected the critics to join him in acclaiming his new author when *Poems* was finally published in March 1782, he was disappointed. The *Monthly Review* thought that Cowper's voice was indeed unusual: 'his style of composition, as well as his modes of thinking, are entirely his own.'[22] But the *Critical Review* was unimpressed. Cowper's verses, it decreed, 'are, in general, weak and languid, and have neither novelty, spirit or animation to recommend them.'[23] Cowper himself was pleased by the praise of friends and by the sense that the volume offered him a way back into the world he could no longer enter physically. 'I shall be glad if my Book might afford you any amusement', he wrote to a friend who was preparing for a journey. 'It is long since you and I were in a Chaise together; perhaps I am more agreeable in print than in person.'[24] Meanwhile William Unwin took on Newton's old role as Cowper's proxy at St Paul's Churchyard and praised the book to all and sundry with the zeal, in Cowper's phrase, of a trumpeter.

✢

In the summer of 1781 Cowper met a visitor to Olney. She was Ann Austen, called Lady Austen by all who knew her. A close friendship formed between her, Mrs Unwin and Cowper. In the winter of 1782–3 Lady Austen returned to Olney and established herself in the other side of the vicarage where Cowper and Mrs Unwin had made their home. She became almost as attuned as Mrs Unwin to the fluctuations in Cowper's mental state and in the summer of 1783 attempted to shake him out of creeping melancholy by challenging him to write a poem on the subject of the sofa in his parlour. Cowper accepted and began once more to write. The writing table was now wobbling beyond repair so together with Mrs Unwin he hauled an old card table out of the lumber room and put it in the cramped parlour. The card table had divots that sent glasses flying and a splintered edge on which Mrs Unwin periodically tore her skirts, but its feet were steady and its surface stable.

The poem that Cowper produced in response to Lady Austen's challenge was over five thousand lines long and its vision ranged far beyond the sofa.

Throughout six books entitled 'The Sofa', 'The Time-Piece', 'The Garden', 'The Winter Evening', 'The Winter Morning Walk' and 'The Winter Walk at Noon', Cowper evoked his world in all its dimensions. As well as the sofa he wrote of the Olney lanes through which he and Mrs Unwin walked, of the changing seasons, of rural work and domestic comforts, of contemporary politics, slavery, Milton and Isaac Newton. He described himself as a 'stricken deer that left the herd / Long since'[25] and when the first generation of Romantic poets discovered his work in the 1790s it was the virtuositic combination of the personal and the political that spurred their own experiments in verse.

Book I started with the sofa and ended with a meditation on the terrible glory of London, the city of Cowper's descent to damnation. He described it as the home of Reynolds and Bacon, where art reaches unsurpassed heights. It is the place where scientific discoveries are made and where commerce triumphs, but it is also a cruel and capricious mistress:

> more prompt
> T' avenge than to prevent the breach of law.
> That she is rigid in denouncing death
> On petty robbers, and indulges life
> And liberty, and oft-times honour too
> To peculators of the public gold.
> That thieves at home must hang: but he that puts
> Into his overgorged and bloated purse
> The wealth of Indian provinces, escapes.[26]

One of Cowper's most quoted aphorisms comes just after this passage: 'God made the country, and man made the town.' But he was neither nostalgic nor naive about the hardships of rural life. He showed his reader the hay wain with its wheels clogged with mud, a noiseless 'moving hill of snow' drawn by an exhausted team led by a man who shuts his eyes against the weather and holds on to his hat with his hand. He wrote of the housewife trembling as she lights her tiny stock of brushwood, knowing how briefly it will keep her children warm. He evoked the numbing boredom of poverty; the way it strips life of joy. 'Where penury is felt the thought is chain'd, / And sweet colloquial pleasures are but few.'[27] Yet elsewhere he described the delights of small things with such acuity it is hard to remember how fleetingly he experienced joy himself. The arrival of the newspapers at the beginning of 'The Winter Evening' is the signal for settling into the warmth – 'Now stir the fire, and close the shutters fast, / Let fall the curtains, wheel the sofa round' – and for roaming imaginatively through the widest vistas of the newspaper, advertisements and all:

> Cataracts of declamation thunder here,
> There forests of no-meaning spread the page
> In which all comprehension wanders lost;
> While fields of pleasantry amuse us there,
> With merry descants on a nation's woes.
> The rest appears a wilderness of strange
> But gay confusion, roses for the cheeks
> And lilies for the brows of faded age,
> Teeth for the toothless, ringlets for the bald,
> Heav'n, earth, and ocean plunder'd of their sweets,
> Nectareous essences, Olympian dews,
> Sermons and city feasts and fav'rite airs,
> Aetherial journies, submarine exploits,
> And Katterfelto with his hair on end
> At his own wonders, wond'ring for his bread.[28]

There are contemporary references aplenty in the poem – here, to a Prussian conjuror, elsewhere to Pitt, Shelburne and Grafton, the men who, for better or worse, were making Britain anew. Yet the world Cowper painted is timeless as well as specific, and the mode of being he described has no historical limits. 'My ear is pain'd, / My soul is sick with ev'ry day's report / Of wrong and outrage with which earth is fill'd', he writes at the beginning of Book II.[29] He asked what it means to be alive and arrived at this answer: 'I think, articulate, I laugh and weep'.[30] He dwelt on the triumph of the gardener when trees train as they are meant to do, and on his own hope that when his end came he would rest in his garden:

> So glide my life away! and so at last
> My share of duties decently fulfilled,
> May some disease, not tardy to perform
> Its destin'd office, yet with gentle stroke
> Dismiss me weary to a safe retreat,
> Beneath the turf that I have often trod.[31]

✝

It took Cowper almost a year to write this poem, which he called *The Task* in reference to Lady Austen's challenge. The winter of 1783–4 was one of the coldest on record and Cowper wrote huddled by the fire during mornings in which his garden and greenhouse were impassable. By late summer 1784 he was beginning to tell his friends he had another poem ready for Johnson. In September he finished transcribing the entire poem for the printer and sent the manuscript to William Unwin, with the request that he should deliver it to St Paul's Churchyard. If Johnson 'should stroak his chin and look up to the ceiling and cry Humph!', Unwin was to offer the volume instead to another publisher.[32] He did not mention the poem to Newton, who found himself shut out of negotiations between author and bookseller. Only at the end of October did Cowper casually mention that 'I am again at Johnson's.'[33] To Unwin he speculated on Newton's reaction with a certain ruthlessness. 'He will be surprized and perhaps not pleased, but I think he cannot complain, for he keeps his own Authorly secrets without participating them with me.'[34] When Newton did write, it was in a letter in each line of which Cowper heard 'the soft murmurs of something like mortification', but he was unrepentant.[35] Johnson accepted the volume with alacrity and Cowper responded by sending a collection of shorter poems to swell it to the required length.

With the manuscript of the poem safely in Johnson's keeping and Unwin established as Cowper's authorial 'Go-between',[36] the uneven rhythm of long-distance publication was once again heard in both Olney and St Paul's Churchyard. First came the business of illegally acquiring franks from friendly Parliamentarians; then anxieties about the reliability of the post, followed by long months of frustration on Cowper's part at the slow pace of Johnson and his printers. 'The Press proceeds like a broad-wheeled wagon, slow and sure', he complained in February. 'After the correction of the two first sheets, a complete month intervened before I received two more.'[37] Cowper pleaded with Unwin to put his head through the door of Johnson's shop to remind him of Cowper's existence and in April wrote angrily to Johnson himself. To Unwin he criticised his bookseller in terms that reveal an unspoken but ever-present awareness of the class barrier between a gentleman author and the tradesman bookseller. 'The man Johnson', he wrote, 'is like unto some vicious horses that I have known. They would not budge 'till they were spurred and when they were spurred they would kick. So did He. His temper was somewhat disconcerted, but his pace was quicken'd and I was contented.'[38] Johnson was unabashed and wrote to Cowper to suggest he might like to improve the final poem in the volume before it was printed.

The Task appeared in print at the beginning of July 1785. Even at the end there were delays, and a few days before publication Cowper told Newton he had given up asking questions. 'I know not what Johnson is about, neither do I now enquire.... . He might, I suppose, have published by this time without hurrying himself into a fever, or breaking his neck through the violence of his dispatch.'[39] But the reaction of both friends and strangers to the volume made the wait worthwhile. The *Critical Review* was complimentary, in contrast to its dismissive account of *Poems*, and the reviewer for the *Monthly* wrote that *The Task* represented a watershed in the development of English verse. 'Amidst the multitude of dull, or flimsy, or insipid things that issue from the press under the name of poems, we are now and then relieved by a production of real genius; though it is very seldom that we are furnished with an entertainment that mingles delight and improvement in so perfect a degree as the present ingenious and truly original publication.'[40]

⁂

When Cowper embarked on the task set him by Lady Austen, to hymn the sofa in his parlour at Olney, he did so in order to keep despair at bay. At the close of 1785, with *The Task* published, he turned his attention to a project that he hoped would prove equally rewarding. Rather than embark on the composition of more original poetry he decided to publish a new translation of Homer's *Iliad* and *Odyssey*. The work was absorbing and the business of producing proposals and raising subscriptions kept him connected to the literary world from which he was physically separated. Johnson was reluctant to agree to Cowper's plan to raise money for his translation by subscription rather than by selling him the copyright outright, but in a sign of Cowper's increasing confidence he refused to be dissuaded from a plan he believed would allow him to retain greater control over his work. He aimed to produce a version of Homer to rival that of Alexander Pope, heralded as the standard English translation since its first appearance in 1715. Cowper overturned a decades-old critical orthodoxy when he drew attention to the defects in Pope's work and declared he could do better. It was one thing to tell a trusted coterie of correspondents that he considered

Pope's reworking 'bloated and tumid' but quite another to offer a translation to the public in which radically stripped back verse produced its own rebuke to a literary giant.[41] Cowper aimed to give readers who had no Greek the experience of reading Homer in its original form; he promised to transmit nothing less than 'the Spirit and manner of the Poet'.[42] Newton, William Unwin and an aristocratic cousin, Lady Hesketh, were sent forth as Cowper's emissaries to raise subscriptions among their friends while Cowper himself went to work, translating between forty and fifty lines a day. He was full of entrepreneurial optimism, seeing in the project the possibility of clearing a profit of over £1,000 as well as maintaining a hard-won mental equilibrium and intervening decisively in a rejuvenated, inventive literary culture. 'Once an Author and always an Author', he told one correspondent. 'Hitherto I have given away my Copies, but having indulged myself in that frolic twice, I now mean to try whether it may not prove equally agreeable to get something by the bargain.'[43]

Johnson agreed to let Cowper control the means of publication for his Homer but he did not take Cowper's estimation of the quality of his work on trust. Faced with an author who was at once confident and fragile and who was proposing to up-end classical enquiry, Johnson turned to Fuseli for advice. Fuseli was a fluent reader of Greek, Latin, French, Hebrew, Italian and English as well as his native German and Johnson knew he was unafraid of overturning conventions. Fuseli cast his eye and his pen over Cowper's sample manuscript and Johnson sent the heavily annotated results back to Olney, with the stipulation that he would publish if Cowper agreed to have the rest of his work similarly scrutinised. Cowper's agreement set the scene for one of the most eccentric and productive relationships to be forged at St Paul's Churchyard. Cowper and Fuseli never met but on paper they were fired by each other's intellect. 'I am delighted with taste, judgement, and learning, that discover themselves in the strictures of your friend, and will submit my translation to them with all my heart', Cowper told Johnson at the end of January. 'In every article I have amended my copy according to his recommendation.'[44] For Johnson's own uncompromisingly high standards, and the gentleness with which he delivered the news that the translation required more work, Cowper was grateful. 'I account myself highly obliged to you for the friendly anxiety, that you express on this occasion'.[45] Occasionally he rejected Fuseli's suggestions and two weeks into their correspondence he wrote angrily that he was overwhelmed by the extent of the changes demanded. But the difficulties were smoothed over.

Fuseli agreed to compare Cowper's work strictly with Homer's original, rather than with Pope, with the result, Cowper told Lady Hesketh, that 'we shall now jog on merrily together.'[46]

As his working relationship with Johnson and Fuseli strengthened, Cowper occasionally acknowledged how much he had lost in his decision to turn his back for ever on London. 'You are very happy in being so intimately acquainted with Mr Fuseli', he wrote to Johnson in March. 'I am only sorry that my distance from town permits me not (at least at present) the pleasure of an introduction to one to whom I am to be so much indebted.'[47] 'Town' crept closer during 1786, as the growing list of subscribers compiled by Cowper's satellites revealed the extent of his following in the social circles he avoided. By Fuseli himself Cowper was continually surprised and unsettled. 'I have put my work into the hands of the most extraordinary Critic', he told William Unwin. 'He is Swiss; a Painter in the Historical way; has an accurate knowledge of English, and for his knowledge of Homer has, I verily believe, no fellow.'[48]

Faced with the overwhelming detail of Fuseli's response Cowper withdrew his manuscript from other friends and regular readers, trusting to Fuseli's judgement alone. In July he wrote again to Johnson, expressing the hope that he and Fuseli might one day visit him in Olney. Although Cowper wrote of his indebtedness to Fuseli, he was unsure of the artist's motives. He repeatedly told his friends that Fuseli received no money for his services, although it is possible that Johnson paid Fuseli without revealing the payment to Cowper. Fuseli's first biographer, however, who knew both him and Johnson well, insisted that Fuseli worked on Cowper's manuscript without any expectation of payment. For his part Cowper began to adapt his translation to Fuseli's tastes, pre-empting his criticisms with increasing accuracy. 'I now perfectly understand what it is that he requires in a translation of Homer', he wrote in September. 'Being convinced of the justness of his demands, will attempt at least to conform to them.'[49] To thank Fuseli for his efforts he sent him a hare by the London coach, and then worried that the gift might make the artist less rigorous in his criticism.

The tranquillity that translating Homer brought Cowper was shattered at the end of 1786 by the sudden death of Mary Unwin's son William, shortly after Cowper and Mrs Unwin had moved their household from Olney to the nearby village of Weston Underwood. In January 1787 Cowper told Johnson that an 'indisposition of the feverish kind' was slowing his work; a few days later he fell silent.[50] Between January and July he remained

trapped in a black depression, bringing to an abrupt halt the exchange of
letters and ideas with Fuseli and others that had characterised the previous
year. In great anxiety Johnson wrote to Mrs Unwin asking for reassuring
news but she could give none. It was not until October that Cowper himself
was able to pick up his pen to write to Johnson, in a letter that reveals
how deeply he felt the loss of time and momentum he had suffered. 'All
interruptions of poetical labors are prejudicial ... because the mind by disuse
becomes prosaic.'[51] To Fuseli, his 'kind coadjutor', he could offer nothing
more than good wishes, but to others he wrote that he was grateful to
Johnson for summoning him back to work.

By the end of the year Cowper was writing again, half-dreading the day
when the translation was finished and his mind would once more be free
to contemplate the abyss. Johnson's dilatoriness now became almost a
blessing, extending the haven of gainful occupation onwards by days and
weeks. Back and forth he sent his manuscript, holding on to the work with
an iron grip. 'He who has Homer to Translate may well be contented to
do little else', he told Lady Hesketh in January 1788. It was a relief to be
able to work again, and to see in work the possibility of his own restoration.
'It is now become so habitual to me, to spend half my time with Homer,
that it is impossible for me not to apprehend a tremendous Vacuum, when
this work shall be accomplished', he confessed to one correspondent, who
had been into Johnson's shop and seen a box of Cowper's manuscript
waiting. 'But thanks to the excellent and long-winded old Greecian, what
with the difficulties with which he presents me, and the necessity that I
find of sifting and searching and improving for ever my most successful
attempts to represent him so as not grossly to wrong him, that dreaded
consummation seems yet at a distance.'[52]

✦

Cowper believed that the presence of a sympathetic publisher in his life
was of paramount importance. 'I could no more amuse myself with writing
verse, if I did not print it when written, than with the study of Tacticks
for which I can never have any real occasion.'[53] To write was to publish,
and to publish was – temporarily – to escape the nightmare. As he looked
back on the period he had spent absorbed in work, Cowper saw the task
of the poet ever more clearly as a defence against visions of damnation.
'Dejection of Spirits, which I suppose may have prevented many a man
from becoming an Author, made me one. I find constant employment

necessary, and therefore take care to be constantly employ'd. Manual occupations do not engage the mind sufficiently, as I know by experience, having tried many.'[54]

Cowper's work continues to bear witness to the way the act of writing lights the darkness. In public poetry and private prose he articulated the experience of living with despair. His description of his mental fragility was greeted with remarkable understanding by strangers who admired his verse and by the unorthodox family who gathered around him in person in Olney and on paper in London. Even more remarkable is that out of despair Cowper produced one of the greatest – and most neglected – poems in the English language. Cowper brought new artistry and vision to Johnson's list and Johnson's circle, expanding the creative reach of his network as well as Johnson's capacity for commercial success. It is striking that of the hundreds of authors with whom Johnson worked it was Cowper whose work he edited most carefully; Cowper who inspired in him the desire to produce a book that lived up to the genius it promised. Their working relationship was not easy, but it shaped them both.

12

Trade Winds

At the beginning of 1781 Joseph Priestley packed up his laboratory and moved his family to Birmingham. Lord Shelburne's parliamentary career was in the ascension and Priestley had little in common with the Whig faction Shelburne led. Shelburne offered Priestley a pension of £150 a year and friends and supporters banded together to raise more money to support him. His brother-in-law John Wilkinson had made a fortune in iron and offered to buy the Priestleys an elegant house at Fair Hill, just south of the city. In December Priestley was appointed minister at the New Meeting, one of the largest and most influential Dissenting congregations in England. He marked his appointment in characteristic fashion, sending Johnson his acceptance sermon for printing. 'As far as I can judge', he wrote in March, 'I have a prospect of being very useful and happy here.'[1]

Priestley later recalled his decision to move to Birmingham as the happiest event of his life. The city was at the forefront of the industrial transformation sweeping through Britain and was home to a group of brilliant industrialists, inventors and entrepreneurs who were, in the words of their biographer Jenny Uglow, 'without a doubt, men who changed the world.'[2] They included Matthew Boulton and James Watt, who worked together to harness the power of steam for a new age. Priestley formed close friendships with the chemist James Keir and the doctor William Withering, having been drawn into their circle by Josiah Wedgwood, whose pottery outside the city was transforming British manufacturing. At the monthly meetings of the Lunar Society – so called, Priestley explained, 'because the time of our meeting was near the full moon'[3] – Priestley also met Erasmus Darwin, a doctor of enormous intellect and girth whose spirit of enquiry matched his own.

Birmingham offered ample scope for a man of Priestley's restless energy. At the New Meeting he instituted an ambitious Sunday School programme, in which children and young adults were taught reading and writing as well as scripture. He re-started the *Theological Repository* and entered into theological debate with the city's Dissenting clergymen. He peppered Johnson with pamphlets and sermons for publication, with requests for copies of books – his own, and those by others – and with invitations to visit Fair Hill. Each winter he continued his habit of de-camping to St Paul's Churchyard for weeks on end, shuttling between Johnson's quarters and the Lindseys' parlour at Essex Street with contented regularity.

At St Paul's Churchyard Priestley paid fatherly compliments to Sarah Johnson and Elizabeth Hunter, Johnson's niece and step-niece, both of whom were now in their mid-twenties. Elizabeth's younger sister Hester was another frequent visitor but after her marriage to Henry Newnum in 1783 she came to dinner as a guest rather than a member of the household. Also under Johnson's care was Elizabeth's youngest brother Rowland, born in 1773. Johnson made no distinction between the nieces and nephews to whom he was related by blood and those to whom he considered himself connected by kin. From 1780 onwards, as the Hunters turned their attention to the question of a trade for their son, he assumed quasi-paternal responsibility for Rowland. In 1781 when Rowland was eight Johnson sent him to Anna Barbauld's school in Palgrave. Rowland's entry on the school roll makes it clear that he arrived in Suffolk at Johnson's behest and expense. 'From Liverpool', it reads. 'Sent by Mr Johnson Bookseller St Paul's Churchyard.'[4] Barbauld's letters to Johnson for the period are punctuated with affectionate messages from Rowland to his uncle and sister and with details of arrangements for the child's vacations. Once or twice the Barbaulds took Rowland north when they visited Warrington in the summer, enabling his safe travel to his parents in Liverpool. For much of the time, though, it was Elizabeth and Johnson who were sufficiently near to stand *in loco parentis* to Rowland, for whom St Paul's Churchyard became a second home.

Johnson's proxy family also encompassed the Lindseys. Lindsey acted as Johnson's emissary to the religious men of Warrington and Birmingham who clamoured for new books. Knowing his friend's tendency to delay, he lingered at St Paul's Churchyard when Priestley's works were in press. Unlike those who sniped at Johnson's work rate from afar Lindsey saw at first hand the daily frustrations of bookselling life: inadequate paper, dilatory stationers and demanding authors. Despite his loyalty to Priestley he recognised that to be Priestley's publisher was no sinecure. When Johnson agreed to publish

Priestley's *History of Early Opinion* at his own risk, freeing him of the need to hawk his work around for subscribers, Lindsey was alert to the generosity of this agreement. 'I should be sorry however, if Mr Johnson shd lose by it, as he is an honest man, and far from any meanness about money, though he is not supposed to abound in it.'[5] The Lindseys did not abound in money either but they were generous with their time and acted for Johnson as readers and advisers. Hannah Lindsey was particularly ruthless in her strictures on one *Introduction to the Reading of the Holy Bible* and comprehensively redrafted it. She did so to the ire of its author, Lady Mayne, who appeared in Johnson's shop several months later in high dudgeon. Johnson gave her short shrift: Mrs Lindsey, he replied, had no idea who the author was, 'or whether in the land of the living.'[6] Lindsey's account of this scene reveals his proprietorial interest in the works Johnson produced. 'We published here a new Edition of The Introduction to the reading of the Bible', he told a friend. 'I shall rejoice if it has been farther improved.'[7]

Meanwhile letters, books and manuscripts moved between Priestley and Johnson: the gift of a copy of John Bonnycastle's *Introduction to Algebra* acknowledged; family news exchanged; advice given and – sometimes – accepted. 'As a bookseller, I believe you judge very well', wrote Priestley in February 1783, when Johnson told him that his newest proposal had no chance of making any money. 'But there are other considerations, of which you cannot be so good a judge, as I am.'[8] When professional differences arose both men worked hard to ensure they left no mark. 'We shall be very happy to see you at Birmingham, & hope you will not disappoint us, this year, as you did the last', wrote Priestley in 1787. 'Our connection is, now, of long standing, & is, I hope, founded on friendship, as well as mutual interest.'[9]

✦

Amongst the 'Lunar Men' of Birmingham Erasmus Darwin loomed large. His physical presence was enormous, his intellect capacious and his enthusiasm boundless. 'He was somewhat above the middle size', wrote his neighbour Anna Seward:

> The traces of a severe small-pox; features, and countenance, which, when they were not animated by social pleasure, were rather saturnine than sprightly; a stoop in the shoulders, and the then professional appendage, a large full-bottomed wig, gave, at that early

period of life, an appearance of nearly twice the years he bore. Florid health, and the earnest of good humour, a sunny smile, on entering a room, and on first accosting his friends, rendered in his youth, that exterior agreeable, to which beauty and symmetry had not been propitious.[10]

In 1781, a few months after Priestley's arrival in Birmingham, Darwin moved his own household to Derby at the insistence of his new wife, Elizabeth Pole. Darwin was fifty when he moved; and father to three legitimate sons and two illegitimate daughters. He met Elizabeth when she brought her children to him for medical attention in 1775 and for five lovesick years he mourned her unavailability, until the death of her husband in 1780 freed her. Although he spent his days practising medicine, travelling miles through the Midlands to visit patients, his interests ranged far beyond medicine and the body. He created a botanic garden at his house in Lichfield and was an ardent supporter of the experiments with steam carried out by other members of the Lunar Society, as well as an inventor with a passion for exciting contraptions. As a young man he had written poetry and in the throes of his passion for Elizabeth he turned once more to verse as a way to ease his emotional torment.

Shortly after his remarriage Darwin visited London, where he made the acquaintance of Henry Fuseli. When they met Fuseli was at work on *The Nightmare*, the painting for which he is now chiefly remembered. Fuseli made several versions of *The Nightmare*: the canvas on which he was working when he first met Darwin was designed for exhibition at the Royal Academy. The painting's representation of a Gothic and highly sexualised monstrousness caused a sensation when it was first exhibited and Fuseli delighted in the frisson of shock and excitement it elicited from its viewers. Darwin saw in both canvas and painter the image of an imagination as adventurous and unafraid as his own and went to work in verse to capture the genius he saw:

> Such as of late amid the murky sky
> Was mark'd by FUSSELI's poetic eye;
> Whose daring tints, with SHAKESPEAR's happiest grace,
> Gave to the airy phantom form and place. –
> Back o'er her pillow sinks her blushing head,
> Her snow-white limbs hang helpless from the bed;

> While with quick signs, and suffocative breath,
> Her interrupted heart-pulse swims in death.

Darwin followed his own imagination into the darkest recesses of the nightmares endured by Fuseli's sleeping woman, charting her mental journey through captured towns echoing with shrieks; past the body of a fallen lover to a 'headlong precipice' where she finds she can neither flee nor scream:

> In vain she wills to walk, swim, run, fly, leap;
> The WILL presides not in the bower of SLEEP.
> – On her fair bosom sits the Demon-Ape
> Erect, and balances his bloated shape;
> Rolls in their marble orbs his Gorgon-eyes,
> And drinks with leathern ears her tender cries.[11]

Fuseli was delighted by Darwin's characterisation of his work and later insisted that it should form an epigram for his picture. Darwin and Fuseli moved in different worlds but each recognised the other as a fearless interpreter of the mysteries of the universe and they found that the contrasting mediums in which they worked complemented each other in unexpected ways.

By the time Fuseli and Darwin met, Darwin had been at work for several years on an epic poem inspired by his garden at Lichfield. *The Botanic Garden* fell into two parts: *The Economy of Vegetation* and *Loves of the Plants*. *Loves of the Plants*, on which Darwin was working when he was introduced to Fuseli, was a poetic response to the work of the Swedish botanist Carl Linnaeus, who developed a system of botanical taxonomy based on the sex organs of plants. Other English botanists who had adopted Linnaeus's system had stripped it of its sexual elements. Darwin embraced the metaphor. *Loves of the Plants* is set in a garden and features the Spirit of Botany describing the plants populating the borders via their Linnean classifications. Surrounding this structure are a cascade of epic metaphors, through which Darwin addresses the central issues of his age: slavery, industrialisation, rationalism, art.

Interspersed between the four cantos are three 'Interludes' with a Bookseller, in which the poet discusses poetry itself. The Bookseller is particularly concerned with the relationship between the poem and the extensive prose notes that accompany it: 'Your verses, Mr Botanist, consist of *pure description*, I hope there is *sense* in the notes.'[12] The notes themselves more than meet this requirement: they surround the poem with a system of knowledge so comprehensive as to be overwhelming. Darwin himself viewed poetry as the servant of science; the imagination as the flag bearer of progress. The general design of his poem, he explained in an advertisement, was 'to inlist Imagination under the banner of Science; and to lead her votaries from the looser analogies, dress out the imagery of poetry, to the stricter ones which form the ratiocination of philosophy.'[13] In his hands poetry was to do nothing less than articulate the structure and evolution of the natural world for readers who would more willingly pick up a volume of verse than they would a scientific treatise.

Although Darwin had a grand vision for *The Botanic Garden* its composition was never his primary activity. He wrote much of the poem in his chaise as he bounced along bad country lanes from patient to patient. When Fuseli pressed him to publish, his first thought was that he could only do so anonymously, lest appearing in public as a poet damage his medical practice. Johnson wrote to Darwin expressing his willingness to proceed on the strength of a sample of the manuscript and Fuseli's recommendation. 'I have the favour of your note in a letter from Mr Fuseli', Darwin replied. 'From the ingenuous manner of your proposal to me, and the character from Mr Fuseli and others, have no doubt of relying on your honour, and of putting intire confidence in you.'[14] Darwin refused to part with the copyright, explaining that both parts of the poem were still evolving, and he also made clear that he was motivated to publish by the prospect of having his work illustrated by Fuseli himself. Johnson commissioned original plates for the poem from Fuseli and engravings from Blake and went to work on the text himself. 'Pray send me any general or particular criticisms which may have occurred to you,' Darwin asked. 'And particularly if you think it is too long, and would wish any part to be omitted, as I am unacquainted with what is like to make a book sell.'[15]

✣

Darwin's appearance in Johnson's life widened the reach of the currents blowing in and out of 72 St Paul's Churchyard. As the London bookseller of both Darwin and Priestley, Johnson became the principal means through which the industrialists of Birmingham and the West Midlands, like the theologians of Warrington and the north-west before them, sought to disseminate their work. His reach extended east to Suffolk as well, where

Anna and Rochemont Barbauld were growing their school. Rochemont's letters for the period are full of requests for new books and stationery; Barbauld responded to parcels from Johnson by suggesting ways in which the books themselves might be made better. 'We think some excellent, more pretty, & a good many mediocre', she wrote by way of thanks.[16] Children's books that were sloppy or condescending to their readers also received short shrift: 'the stile is not elegant, plain & simple it should be no doubt but it ought to have all the elegance of perfect clearness & correctness.'[17]

At other times Barbauld treated St Paul's Churchyard less as a bookshop than as a sorting office and personal administrative centre. She positioned Johnson himself as the conduit between groups of friends and relations in the west and north. Priestley had been in town, she thought. 'Pray tell me if he looks well.' Johnson was instructed to negotiate with her dress-maker: 'Be so good as to desire Mr Kinder to enclose ... two turbans such as I had before.' Her brother had not received parcels she had sent via Johnson: 'Do me the favour therefore to let me know by a line whether they got to you & whether they have been put into the post.' Elsewhere there was family news: 'Hunter is a good boy and very well. I suppose he stays here during the vacation.' And always, there were shopping lists: 'Please to send by the very next waggon, 2000 quills, 3 doz copy books. The Anatomist. Florizel & Perdita. Faces. A Shakespeare's Henry 4th if to be had.'[18]

To fulfil all the functions demanded by Barbauld and others while also running a growing business and serving as the connecting charge between overlapping groups of writers and friends made demands on Johnson that at times he found impossible to fill. Authors gossiped to each other about his slowness and at the beginning of 1784 his old friend John Murray (who in the 1770s had passed on a cheerful account of Johnson's 'itch' to William Enfield) complained that Johnson's inability to meet his many commitments served him badly. Johnson had failed to honour a promised exchange of work and had withdrawn into himself rather than take others into his confidence. His unfriendliness was distressing, Murray wrote. 'Conscious of the Integrity of my Intentions respecting you at all times, & the real friend-ship I have borne you, independent of all business, my Mind sits easy with regard to my behaviour.'[19] There is little sign that Johnson responded to complaints of slowness by changing his working habits but when fourteen-year-old Rowland Hunter completed his education at Palgrave in 1785 it was to St Paul's Churchyard that he went, to take up his place as his step-uncle's right-hand man.

In a note to *The Botanic Garden* Darwin expounded on the competing theories of Priestley and Lavoisier on the composition of air, and attempted to describe the qualities and behaviour of the globe's dominant air currents. He wrote of the physical properties of 'trade-winds' that enabled British ships to forge routes across the oceans in pursuit of goods and new territories, demonstrating the interdependence between humanity and nature. But he also envisaged a future in which knowledge might develop sufficiently for man to harness the wind for his own ends. 'We may still suspect that there exists in the arctic and antarctic circles, a BEAR or DRAGON, yet unknown to philosophers, which, at times, suddenly drinks up, and as suddenly, at other times, vomits out ... part of the atmosphere'. Maybe, he concluded, 'some future age will learn how to govern and domesticate a monster which might be rendered of such important service to mankind.'[20]

To govern and domesticate the wind was a grand ambition, but as technology shrank the distances between Britain's cities and the trading outposts of the globe, anything seemed possible. Through the new roads along which the mail coach sped a doctor in the Midlands forged a connection with a bookseller in London and in the process both found new ways to make themselves heard. But others in Johnson's circle had a different view about the things in life that really mattered. Lindsey was not interested in taming the winds but rather in sustaining a way of living that made him happy. 'Seldom a day but we see Dr Priestley here, or meet with him some part of it at a third friends', he wrote in April 1784. 'I desire no higher happiness hereafter than to be always with such friends, lovers, and seekers of truth and virtue.'[21]

13

Thoughts on the Education of Daughters

One afternoon in the autumn of 1787 a literary hanger-on called William Beloe joined the company at Johnson's table. Beloe had come to London from Norwich in 1780. He was determined to make his name in the literary world and immediately after arriving in the capital he went to St Paul's Churchyard to seek Johnson out. If he expected Johnson to welcome a stranger hawking manuscripts he was disappointed. Many years later he recalled the crushing way in which Johnson rejected work: a 'Sardonic grin' would be followed by a 'sneering laugh' and a refusal to offer any explanation. Beloe rejected the liberal underpinning of Johnson's politics and accused him of imbibing the 'sourest manners' of the 'old Presbyterian school'. Yet in spite of himself he was drawn to Johnson and badly wanted a place at his table. He saw Johnson make generous bargains with needy authors and recognised that the 'dry Bookseller' kept an open table because he knew that some of those who came to dinner could hardly afford to feed themselves. As an old man Beloe recalled the friends he had met at Johnson's and looked back on the dining room at St Paul's Churchyard as the symbol of a more tolerant age. It was a place, he wrote, 'where, previously to the calamity of the French Revolution, individuals of all parties and persuasions, political and religious, used to meet in easy and agreeable familiarity.'[1]

When he came to dinner in 1787 Beloe was riding high. After multiple rejections he had finally persuaded Johnson to accept one of his works for publication, a volume of *Poems and Translations*. Over dinner he joined in the conversations of Priestley, Barbauld, John Aikin, Richard Price and others, and he revelled in the sensation of being part of their world. At St Paul's Churchyard he also met two women who, like him, were recent additions to Johnson's circle. One was a devout Anglican, a writer for children and mother of twelve called Sarah Trimmer. The other was Mary Wollstonecraft. Wollstonecraft's presence in Johnson's house is well-documented but Beloe is one of the only witnesses to place Trimmer in the dining room alongside her. After the French Revolution Trimmer and Wollstonecraft found themselves on opposite sides of a polarised national debate and they came to represent everything against which the other stood. But when they met through Johnson they did so as two women who were attempting to make their way in a male-dominated literary world, with a shared determination to shape a better future for their daughters. Both were following in the footsteps of Anna Barbauld, who showed by example just how much an intelligent woman could achieve with a friendly publisher at her side.

＋

When Sarah Trimmer met Johnson she had just turned forty and long years of childbearing were finally behind her. Ten of the twelve children she bore between 1763 and 1780 were still alive, although her baby Annabella was very fragile. Her eldest daughters were young women facing uncertain futures and her youngest children were in need of an education. Anna Barbauld's reading primers were family staples, used by Trimmer and her older daughters as they taught the nursery children to read. Trimmer was grateful for Barbauld's books, which she considered a distinct improvement on anything else available, but she was also convinced that she could do better. She wrote in the early hours of the morning, getting up at four or five o'clock to work by candlelight while her family slept. Her first biographers viewed her early waking as a symbol of her virtue, but it speaks too of a need for time to think undisturbed. Trimmer did not reject the roles of wife and mother stipulated by her Anglican upbringing: indeed, she embraced her position at the heart of a large family. But despite the orthodoxy of her beliefs she could not give up the parts of her existence which were separate from the position society ordained for her. Her descendants insisted that she published only at the insistence of friends and in order to do good, but her private papers tell a different story. In 1784 she wrote to Johnson about an advertisement for her multi-volume work, *Sacred History*, which she wanted Johnson to puff in a new edition of William Enfield's *Speaker*. 'I begin to be very impatient to have my Work go on', she explained. And, with some exactness, 'I hope no new cause of delay has arisen, and that you will be so good as to hasten it.'[2]

Johnson was not the only London publisher to discover Trimmer, but in the early days of her career as an author he was among the most encouraging. William Beloe credited him with being the first to encourage Trimmer 'to systematize and publish her various excellent performances for the benefit of mankind' and over dinner at St Paul's Churchyard Beloe bore witness to the way Trimmer responded to such encouragement.[3] Trimmer was implacably opposed to Unitarianism but in spite of their religious differences she trusted Johnson, sending friends his way when they visited London; joining with him to produce new kinds of books for children. Barbauld had worked out that children learning to read needed large, clear type and stories that would not bore them. Trimmer took these innovations a stage further. She published picture books for very young children, in which stories from the Bible were related through images, and she drew on classical and folk traditions to introduce children to big ideas through tales of birds and animals. Illustrations and animals stories are now so commonplace in children's publishing that it is hard to imagine a time when either were radical or new, but the line of inheritance of the bears, mice and Gruffalos of today's children's books stretches all the way back to the family of robins who star in Trimmer's *Fabulous Histories*, first published by Johnson in conjunction with three other firms in 1786.

Like Barbauld, Trimmer spoke directly to her readers. Unlike Barbauld, she never missed an opportunity to underline a moral lesson, or to join the dots between the activities of her animal protagonists and orthodox Anglican teaching. Trimmer's fictional children misbehave at their peril: they are thrown from the horses they mistreat and are constantly reminded of the importance of studying the Bible. Cosmopolitan adventuring serves only to underline the superiority of the English. 'You are an Englishman', she tells her fictional reader. 'So you must love England the best.' Yet she is also alert to the wonder in new scenes. 'When you go to London', she reports, 'you will be quite astonished at the multitudes, for they crowd along the streets in the city like bees in a hive.'[4]

In prefaces and advertisements Trimmer insisted on the originality of her work, disclaiming any desire to compete directly with Barbauld. In a letter to her friend Hannah More she described herself around this time as 'a mere bookseller's fag',[5] but all the evidence suggests she thrived as she carved out a place for herself independent of her family. As her own children grew up she turned her attention to the fate of those who she could not reach through books alone. In 1787, the year that Beloe convinced

Johnson to take him on, Trimmer opened a day school for girls who would be compelled by financial necessity to earn their own living. Middle-class orphans she trained as teachers; working-class girls were equipped with a trade that might allow them to carve out a modicum of independence. Simultaneously she published a work, *The Oeconomy of Charity*, in which she set out the principles on which her school was run, so that other women might follow her example.

Trimmer had little interest in the causes of poverty and no desire to crusade against inequality. Neither did she want to educate girls out of their roles as wives and mothers: the roles in which she described herself as having found most happiness. Nevertheless, she also found fulfilment in the professional spaces she carved and she equipped her own daughters to do likewise. The girls she educated in charity schools had fewer opportunities, but she made sure they were warm, clothed and fed and she gave them the skills that might protect them from poverty.

Her vision of the power and purpose of education was diametrically opposed to the views of many others who gathered around Johnson's table. When impoverished charity school children were marched to St Paul's to give thanks for the beneficence of others in their regimented thousands, for example, she saw those children not as victims of an unjust society, but as subjects ripe for moulding into good, obedient citizens. They were future 'Fathers and Mothers, who will either train up their children in the way they should go, or lead them into the practice of wickedness – As Sons and Daughters, who will either prove a blessing or a curse to their parents – Brothers and Sisters, who will promote each other's happiness, or divide families by domestic broils – Masters and Mistresses of Schools, who will instil useful knowledge into the minds of the children, or leave them in ignorance of their duty.' Most importantly, they were 'Subjects, who will be supporters of the State, by the proper exertion of their humble talents, and obedient submission to its laws, or the ready and willing tools of *faction*, *sedition*, and *rebellion* for its overthrow.'[6]

✥

Eighteen years separated Sarah Trimmer and Mary Wollstonecraft, and when they met the disparity in their circumstances was marked. Trimmer had experienced success and financial security; Wollstonecraft knew too well what it was to live precariously on the margins of society. As Wollstonecraft struggled to make an independent existence for herself she turned to Trimmer for advice, following up an acquaintance made at Johnson's table with a visit to her house in Middlesex. Trimmer, Wollstonecraft told her sister, was 'a truly respectable woman.'[7] Five years later, when Wollstonecraft published her *Vindication of the Rights of Woman*, Trimmer found herself unable to return the compliment. Her own husband had just died and she confessed herself baffled by the younger woman's views. 'I can say nothing more', she wrote to a friend, 'than that I found so much happiness in having a husband to assist me in forming a proper judgement, and in taking upon him the chief labour of providing for a family, that I never wished for a further degree of liberty or consequence than I enjoyed. Miss Woolstonecraft is a woman of extraordinary abilities, I confess; I cannot help thinking they might be employed to more advantage to society.'[8]

Mary Wollstonecraft had good reason to mistrust the social structures in which Trimmer placed her faith. The relationship she formed with Johnson existed outside those structures and it altered the pattern of her existence. Johnson's support of Wollstonecraft changed his life as well as hers, and he behaved towards her in ways that were replicated nowhere else in his story. Although money and work were the forces that connected them they displayed towards each other an affection and loyalty that enriched them both.

In her girlhood Wollstonecraft lived with the threat of male violence. At times she resorted to sleeping on the landing outside her mother's bedroom door in the hope she might be able to protect her from her father's attacks. She watched her mother fade in the face of violence, withdrawing from all her children apart from her favourite son. In adolescence Wollstonecraft tried to take the care of her younger siblings upon herself, setting up a quasi-maternal relationship within the family on which the younger children would both rely and come to resist. As a young woman she rescued her sister Bess from another abusive marriage and watched her dearest friend, Fanny Blood, succumb after her wedding to a deadly combination of tuberculosis and pregnancy.

In the aftermath of the collapse of her sister Bess's marriage Wollstonecraft attempted to form a family unit that was not based around matrimony. In Newington Green, just north of London, she set up a school with Bess and their sister Everina. From the outset the school's finances were shaky but it did allow Wollstonecraft to form friendships with men who were sympathetic to her ideas and connected to Johnson. One such friendship was with the Welsh divine Richard Price, author of *Observations on the Nature of Civil Liberty*, published by Johnson during the American War. In the chapel at Newington Green Price led one of the liveliest Nonconformist congregations in England. Wollstonecraft had been brought up in an Anglican family but she found herself drawn to Price's rational, reform-minded version of Christianity. Price objected to tyranny in all its forms, including in the classroom. He thought that children should be taught to think for themselves, rather than have their heads filled with meaningless jargon. Wollstonecraft discovered in him a friend who showed in every aspect of his being that religion, politics and education were all capable of improvement, and she was deeply influenced by his example. In her school she put the ideas honed in Price's company into practice. 'Whenever a child asks a question, it should always have a reasonable answer given it', she wrote later.[9] She encouraged her pupils to read books that caught their fancy, rather than restricting them to a narrow diet of approved moral tales: all she asked in return was that they brought their curiosity and critical faculties to their reading.

At Newington Green Wollstonecraft also made friends with the Anglican priest of the neighbouring village of Shacklewell. John Hewlett was an ambitious, well-connected twenty-two-year-old, who was in the process of negotiating publication of his first volume of sermons with Johnson and two other publishers when he and Wollstonecraft met. He took her to meet an ageing Dr Johnson and volunteered to help find a publisher for her own work. Like Price and Priestley, Hewlett expressed great confidence in human knowledge; like them he argued that curiosity and intellectual enquiry enabled rather than undermined religious devotion. He believed too that knowledge was derived from experience and that emotional experience in particular should be honoured. 'The calamities and disappointments which happen to ourselves', he told his parishioners, 'are the counsellors that will make us wise and good; unless in despite of reason and of nature, we let life glide away unnoticed, without improvement in knowledge or in virtue.'[10]

Wollstonecraft's intellectual horizons expanded as she joined in the conversations swirling around her. Very little sense of these conversations survives in her letters for the period, which are mostly concerned with the practical difficulties of running a school and holding her household together. Instead her voice emerges in the work she began to produce in rare moments of quiet, in which she distilled her thinking in a series of essays on the education of girls. She acknowledged that she was not the first person to turn her attention to this subject: yet, 'it occurred to me, that much still remained to be said.' And, with a certain confidence: 'I shall not swell these sheets by writing apologies for my attempt.'[11] She understood that to be a wife and mother was the fate of most of her pupils and in her first treatise on the position of women she was careful to emphasise that the life of the mind could not be pursued by a woman at the expense of domestic accomplishments. Her chief concern, though, was for the fate of young women who had neither parents nor husband to support them. 'A teacher at a school is only a kind of upper servant, who has more work than the menial ones', she observed with some bitterness. Poverty she described as the enemy of friendship; the task of education was to equip women isolated by circumstance to depend on their own intellectual and emotional reserves so that they might embrace unhappiness rather than have their minds narrowed by misfortune. It was a bleak prospectus, which stared straight at the painful consequences of John Hewlett's account of the development of knowledge. But it also allowed Wollstonecraft to try for the first time to make sense of the condition of being female in a world which expected women to be helpless ornaments but which also provided no material support for the women who acceded to this demand. *Thoughts on the Education of Daughters* returns consistently to one theme, namely that the woman who wants to survive with her sense of self intact will need to turn inwards for emotional, moral, intellectual and practical support. Yet Wollstonecraft herself was unable to banish her desire for more. 'How earnestly does a mind full of sensibility look for disinterested friendship, and long to meet with good unalloyed.'[12]

A lack of both money and pupils forced the closure of Wollstonecraft's school and by the middle of 1786 debts associated with the business threatened to overwhelm her. She instructed her sisters to find jobs elsewhere and, through her network of Newington Green supporters, secured a job offer herself, as governess to the children of Lord and Lady Kingsborough. While she compounded with creditors, organised her sisters and turned her attention to her own pressing need to earn money, she also managed to turn her observations on female education into a book. Hewlett took the manuscript of *Thoughts on the Education of Daughters* to Johnson who promptly offered ten guineas for the copyright. Wollstonecraft made the journey from Newington Green to St Paul's Churchyard to meet the man who would exchange money for ideas and who was prepared to usher her work into the world.

In Johnson's presence she laid out her difficulties with a frankness that set her apart from the other writers crowding his table. He encouraged her not to despair, reminding her of Barbauld's success at forging her own path in her Suffolk school. But he also listened with sympathy as she described her fear of the future. 'As I mentioned to you, previous to my departure, that I entered on my new way of life with extreme regret – I am vain enough to imagine you wish to hear how I like my situation', she wrote after their meeting. 'A state of dependence must ever be irksome to me, and I have *many* vexations to encounter, which some people would term trifling – I have most of the [n]*ative* comforts of life – yet weighed with liberty they are of little value.'[13] It was an astonishing letter to send to a man she had met only once and with whom she had a strictly professional relationship, and Wollstonecraft kept hold of the letter for over a month before sending it. Yet although she vacillated, ultimately the memory of the kindness of the man she affectionately called 'little Johnson' (in reference to his short stature) prevailed. In response he sent her books, including Hewlett's *Sermons*, Cowper's *Poems* and an early copy of her own work, which she posted on to friends with pride.

Wollstonecraft spent almost a year working for the Kingsboroughs, first at Mitchelstown Castle in County Cork, then at their town house in Dublin, and finally for a few unhappy months during their summer residence at Bristol Hotwells. In the 1770s Wollstonecraft's employers had demolished the old castle at Mitchelstown and replaced it with a fashionable Palladian building which Wollstonecraft nevertheless compared unfavourably to the Paris Bastille. Her pupils were the three older Kingsborough daughters, Margaret, Caroline and Mary, who had successfully dispatched a series of governesses prior to Wollstonecraft's arrival. The household existed in varying states of emotional disarray: Lady Kingsborough was more interested in her dogs than her children and she had little in common with either her clever governess or her sensitive eldest daughter. In Margaret Kingsborough Wollstonecraft earned herself a devoted admirer but the affection of a child was not enough to compensate for the isolation that was a governess's lot. Governesses and ladies' companions were caught between the worlds of drawing room and servants' hall and knew themselves to be welcome in neither. Wollstonecraft had predicted her own future when she contemplated this state in *Thoughts on the Education of Daughters*. Such a woman was 'above the servants, yet considered by them as a spy, and ever reminded of her inferiority when in conversation with the superiors'. In the meantime, she continued, quoting both Cowper and Hewlett, 'life glides away, and the spirits with it.'[14]

In the spring of 1787 Wollstonecraft wrote again to Johnson. It was another frank letter, detailing the bodily suffering occasioned by mental torment. It mattered to her that Johnson should understand her unhappiness was rooted in circumstance; that it was not merely the product of weakness or ill-temper. 'I am desirous to convince you that I have *some* cause for sorrow'. How, she demanded, 'can I be reconciled to life, when it is always a painful warfare, and when I am deprived of all the pleasures I relish?' What she needed was 'rational conversation, and domestic affections' and her future offered neither.[15] Other writers depended on Johnson for money, logistics and food but few entered into an extended conversation with him about how they might live a better and more fulfilled life. Wollstonecraft's plight exemplified many of the ideas articulated by the women Johnson published – first by Scott and Barbauld in their rejection of intellectual inequality; then by Trimmer and Wollstonecraft herself. Johnson responded to her by insisting that she had the capacity to become mistress of her destiny and he offered to stand by her as she forged her own path.

At the end of August 1787 Wollstonecraft left the Kingsboroughs and travelled by coach to London. From the coaching inn where she was set down she went on foot to 72 St Paul's Churchyard, where Johnson offered her a room for as long as she needed shelter. In the note he wrote about this period many years later, he explained simply that 'Mary came from Ireland in 1787 (Augt) & resided with me having determined to try to live by literary exertions & be independent.'[16] Wollstonecraft was not the first of Johnson's authors to make a temporary home at St Paul's Churchyard – indeed Priestley did so every winter – but her sex made the arrangement notable. It is possible that one or both of Johnson's unmarried nieces still lived with him during this period. Elizabeth Hunter is the more likely candidate, since her fourteen-year-old brother Rowland had recently left school and was learning his trade at Johnson's side. No documentary evidence survives to indicate how long Elizabeth lived with her uncle so it is a matter of conjecture to suggest that she was present when Wollstonecraft sought refuge with her publisher. Elizabeth's presence would have made the arrangement less socially anomalous, but it was nevertheless unusual enough for Wollstonecraft to keep the details of her accommodation secret from her sisters. For almost two weeks she experienced the unfamiliar sensation of living free of responsibility: none of her siblings or creditors knew where she was and as Johnson's guest she was liberated from domestic drudgery. When the shop was closed and the dinner guests had departed she and Johnson talked about her future. She showed him the manuscript of the novella she had written at Bristol Hotwells, in which she took aim at the marriages of both her parents and the Kingsboroughs, and he undertook to publish it as *Mary: A Fiction*. But he also made a more radical proposal. He offered to find Wollstonecraft a house and a servant and to pay for both. She would earn her keep by writing original works and by acting as his staff reviewer and translator.

When she eventually revealed this plan to her sister Everina, some weeks after she was settled in a home of her own, Wollstonecraft wrote as one who could scarcely believe her change in fortune: 'Mr Johnson, whose uncommon kindness, I believe, has saved me from despair, and vexations I shrink back from – and *feared* to encounter; assures me that if I exert my talents in writing I may support myself in a comfortable way. I am then going to be the first of a new genus.'[17]

This 'new genus' was the professional woman writer. In many respects she was not the first, as the examples of Barbauld, Trimmer and several others testified. Her distinctiveness lay in the fact she decided to turn professional writer despite having no other sources of income on which to rely. The other women on Johnson's list were not obliged to earn enough through writing to feed themselves and pay for shelter: financial security liberated their pens. Johnson knew this and he offered Wollstonecraft comparable security free of the restrictions of domestic life. For other writers Johnson provided a sanctuary and a platform, but for Wollstonecraft he created the conditions that allowed her to write. His private papers offer few clues about his motivation for so doing, but in the account he later drew up of this period in Wollstonecraft's life he stressed three aspects of her story that go some way to explaining his desire to help her. The first was Wollstonecraft's intense productivity in the period after her return to London, and the variety of the material she produced. Johnson valued her talent, both as an independent voice and as a shrewd reader and translator of others. The second was the number of people who relied on her and the extent of her efforts to support her younger brothers and sisters. Johnson knew what it was to be the rock to which others clung and he later inter-vened decisively in the tangles surrounding the Wollstonecraft estate and the struggles of the younger members of the family. As a young man he had been alone in an unfriendly city and when fire demolished everything he had worked for in 1770 his friends helped him stand upright again. In 1787 he did the same for Wollstonecraft and only in one respect did he pay any attention to her gender. When he found her a house he also found her a servant, in the form, she later reported, of one of his relations, 'sent to me, out of the country.'[18] He understood that to live in a house was also to have work at a house, and he freed her from the female burden of lighting fires, washing linen and sourcing food.

The final quality in Wollstonecraft which Johnson stressed in his account was the frankness with which she allowed him to see how mercurial were her moods. 'She was incapable of disguise', he wrote. 'Whatever was the state of her mind it appeared when she entered, & the turn of conversation might easily be guessed; when harassed, which was very often the case, she was relieved by unbosoming herself.'[19] In the chill of September evenings, as the hum of activity at Number 72 fell quiet, Johnson saw both Wollstonecraft's strength and her vulnerability. He developed an affection for her which was all the stronger for being platonic. There was never any suggestion between Wollstonecraft and Johnson of a romantic attachment and the unspoken acceptance of this fact rings through Wollstonecraft's letters. He became her doughtiest defender, and for his presence in her life she was passionately and unsentimentally grateful. 'I wish to introduce you to Mr Johnson', she told Everina in November. 'You would respect him; and his sensible conversation would soon wear away the impression, that a formality – or rather stiffness of manners, first makes to his disadvan-tage – I am sure you would love him did you know with what *tenderness* and humanity he has behaved to me.'[20]

The house Johnson found for her was just south of the river in Southwark, at Number 49 George Street. The relative from the country was summoned. Nothing is known of her identity, but she is likely to have been known by or connected to Johnson's sprawling Liverpool family. To get to St Paul's Churchyard from George Street Wollstonecraft had to walk through the streets and alleys of Southwark to Blackfriars, where she joined the traffic crossing the bridge, picking her way over piles of horse dung, flattening herself away from mud splashes as carriages flashed by. The bridge was new but the wynds and alleys of Southwark and the City were not, and it took a certain independence of mind for Wollstonecraft to step out into the gloaming and make her way home alone as Johnson's guests parted company after dinner. It also took hardiness to undertake the daily journey on foot and in all weathers while encumbered by skirts that soaked up every puddle. Wollstonecraft walked while knowing most of her fellow diners had drier feet and warmer knees than she did and the knowledge did nothing to quell her sense of the injustices faced by her sex. 'You have no petticoats to dangle in the snow', she told a male friend some years later. 'Poor Women how they are beset with plagues – within – and without.'[21]

In the second week of September, while Johnson set about the business of finding her lodgings, Wollstonecraft left St Paul's Churchyard and travelled to Henley, where Everina was working in a school. She said nothing to Everina of her altered circumstances but hugged her secret close, writing to Johnson of the unaccustomed tranquillity she was experiencing. She walked alone along the river and listened with renewed attention to the sounds of autumn: leaves rustling, a robin singing, water rushing through the race of the local mill. 'Have you heard yet of an habitation for me?' she asked. 'I often think of my new plan of life.' To the benefactor who had placed such confidence in her she made a kind of promise. 'Let me tell you, I never yet resolved to do, any thing of consequence, that I did not adhere resolutely to it, till I had accomplished my purpose.' Yet simultaneously she emphasised that she would work for her own material and intellectual fulfilment, and not because she felt herself beholden. Her anxiety about the asymmetry in their relationship is apparent in the prickles of hostility of the letter she sent from Henley, written at a point when the emotional nuances of the life Johnson promised remained unknown. 'Every obligation we receive from our fellow-creatures is a new shackle, takes from our native freedom, and debases the mind, makes us mere earthworms.' Yet, she warned Johnson, she would not be debased in mind or in spirit. 'I am not fond of grovelling.'[22]

Together and apart, Wollstonecraft and Johnson negotiated a relationship for which they knew no precedent. Away from him, worries about indebtedness and a new kind of serfdom reasserted themselves; back in his company briefly, in late September, those worries subsided. Wollstonecraft travelled back through London to Leicestershire, where her sister Bess was working, and Johnson saw her onto the coach. From Market Harborough she sent him a gossipy letter about the dull fellow passengers in whose company he had left her, in which she poked fun at one tradesman's boorish attempts at gallantry. 'I was not surprised by any glimpse of the sublime, or beautiful, though one of them imagined I should be a very useful partner in a good *firm*.'[23] From Bess as well as Everina she kept her plans secret, sheltering briefly in their ignorance from reassuming the burden of their unhappiness. Back in London in October she turned her attention to finding more congenial posts for both her sisters, but it was not until November that she revealed to them the change in her own life. She promised both Bess and Everina a home in sickness and a refuge for their holidays but she did not invite either to form part of her household. 'I wish to be a mother to you both', she insisted. But it was a need rather than a wish that drove her actions. To offer support was easy, to give up what she had gained was not. 'I must be independent.' And, finally, and in defiance of Everina's misery: 'freedom, *even* uncertain freedom — is dear.'[24]

Wollstonecraft's letters for this period reveal that it took her some time to accustom herself to her new situation. In multiple letters she dwelt on Johnson's kindness and confidence, rebuilding in words the sanctuary he offered. 'He insisted on my coming to his house', she told Everina, with an emphasis on Johnson's actions that suggests Everina was worried by the risks her headstrong older sister was taking. 'You can *scarcely* conceive how warmly, and delicately he has interested himself in my fate. He has now settled me in a little house, in a street near Black-Friars-Bridge, and he *assures* me I may earn a comfortable maintenance if I exert myself. I have given him *Mary* — and before your vacation, I shall finish another book for young people, which I think has some merit.'

Every sound and smell of her new house spoke of peace and security — the barrel-organ piping melancholy tunes under her window, the tread of her servant on the stair. To Everina, living among strangers still, Wollstonecraft knew herself to be writing of an impossible idyll, but she was unable to conceal her good fortune. 'All this', she conceded, 'will appear to you like a dream; whenever I am tired of solitude, I go to Mr. Johnson's, and there I meet the kind of company *I* find most pleasure in.' In guilty recognition of her good fortune she tried to emphasise how spartan was her existence in barely furnished rooms, but her lack of furniture also made it possible for her to keep Bess and Everina at arm's length. She promised them a share of Johnson's bounty but she also turned down his generosity on their behalf. 'Mr J. knows that next to obtaining the means of life, I wish to mitigate [Bess's], and your fate.' But, firmly: 'J. offered you both a bed at his house; but that would not be pleasant.' For whom the presence of her sisters at St Paul's Churchyard would be unpleasant Wollstonecraft did not say. Johnson was her friend, her bulwark against the world, and she would not share him with her family. Her brother Charles wrote her an angry letter: she agreed to meet him only at Johnson's, and only if he behaved. Piously she thanked 'Providence' for her deliverance, but her 'Providence' was a short, bewigged man with dark eyes and a countenance that invited confidences.[25]

Wollstonecraft spent a little over three years at George Street. In the mornings she worked and in the afternoons she went to Johnson's, where she became friends with Bonnycastle, George Fordyce and a young accountant called George Anderson, and where she was introduced to Fuseli. New friends were welcome after the isolation of life with the Kingsboroughs, and she wrote with pleasure of hearing John Hewlett preach a sermon inspired by her gratitude, on the 'recognition of our friends in a future state.' Yet in spite of the pleasure she took in the company of new friends and old it was Johnson who remained the central compass point of her newfound stability. 'My good friend, Mr Johnson, every day displays more goodness of heart', she wrote in March 1788. 'I often visit his hospitable mansion – where I meet some sensible men, at any rate my worthy friend – who bears with my infirmities.'[26]

On the days that Wollstonecraft did not make the journey over the river she and Johnson exchanged letters. Usually these were brief notes about the progress of work, but sometimes the written word allowed her to express the things she could not say to Johnson's face. Early in 1789 she wrote asking him to procure her a German grammar so that she could extend her usefulness by becoming a translator. She was as determined as ever to earn her independence, she told him, but that did not render her any less grateful for the life he had given her. 'Without your humane and *delicate* assistance, how many obstacles should I not have had to encounter.' In giving her security, she continued, Johnson had restored her capacity to see the good in life. Without him, 'too often should I have been out of patience with my fellow-creatures, whom I wish to love!' And so, 'Allow me to love you, my dear sir, and call friend a being I respect.'[27]

Johnson's generosity towards Wollstonecraft was extensive, but it was offered in the expectation of a return. The intensity with which she worked reveals that she understood this. She translated lengthy works from French and German: Jacques Necker's *On the Importance of Religious Opinions* and Christian Gotthilf Salzmann's *Elements of Morality for the Use of Children*, as well as a more substantially reworked version from a French edition of Maria van de Werken de Cambon's juvenile *Young Grandison*. She finished *Mary: A Fiction* and embarked on a new work of fiction entitled *The Cave of Fancy* which she subsequently abandoned. Her confidence was boosted by the success of *Thoughts on the Education of Daughters*, which was excerpted in the fashionable *Lady's Magazine* in the months following its publication. She produced an anthology for use in teaching girls entitled *The Female Reader*, modelled on Enfield's *The Speaker*. Her selection was orthodox: Cowper, Barbauld and Trimmer all featured prominently, as did the theme of duty towards a benevolent God. Her works for this period stress the importance of rationalism and social responsibility, and for the most part her views and tastes sat comfortably within the traditions of Johnson's list.

In *Original Stories*, a collection of moral tales for children published in 1788, Wollstonecraft's fictional daughters read Trimmer's *Fabulous Histories* in the cause of moral improvement. Yet in this work there are also glimpses of her burgeoning resistance to the mental straitjacket of convention and unthinking piety. Reason is crucial 'to make religion an active, invigorating director of the affections, and not a mere attention to forms', she insists.[28] She envisaged her stories as a prompt to reason; that they should act as the basis of a conversation between teacher and pupil about how best to be in the world. The fables in *Original Stories* are related to fourteen-year-old Mary and twelve-year-old Caroline by a family friend, Mrs Mason, who is horrified by the prejudices into which they have been led by negligent parents. Mrs Mason makes Mary and Caroline confront the evidence of their eyes as she teaches them through storytelling and example to control their passions, to think of the needs of others and to act according to their intellects rather than their inclinations. She shows them the reality of poverty and offers them a vision of the kind of women they might be if they take responsibility for their own behaviour.

Johnson commissioned Blake to provide illustrations for the *Original Stories* and in Blake's plates Mrs Mason appears as a Christ-like figure, her arms outstretched as she shows her juvenile disciples how to live. Together, image and text suggested that salvation for a new generation of girls lay not in the Bible but in the example of independent, assertive women who combined religious devotion with attention to social injustice and who rejected the corruptions attendant in vanity and female artifice. Wollstonecraft felt herself to be swimming against the tide in *Original Stories* and she had little faith in matters improving without her involvement. 'To wish that parents would, themselves, mould the ductile passions, is a chimerical wish', she wrote in the Preface. 'The present generation have their own passions to combat with and fastidious pleasures to pursue, neglecting those pointed out by nature: we must therefore pour premature knowledge into the succeeding one; and, teaching virtue, explain the nature of vice.'[29] Johnson attempted to persuade Wollstonecraft to cut this passage, perhaps because he worried that offending the people with the purchasing power to buy books for their children was too great a commercial risk, but she would not be persuaded and the Preface remained unaltered. 'I hate the usual smooth way of exhibiting proud humility', she explained. 'Believe me, the few judicious parents who may peruse my book, will not feel themselves hurt – and the weak are too vain to mind what is said in a book intended for children.'[30]

As Wollstonecraft honed her voice through the practice of professional authorship she remained determined to protect the sanctuary she had won. To her sisters she offered everything short of a revival of the community they had built briefly at Newington Green. For her first Christmas in George Street she invited Bess and Everina to stay and let down her guard long enough to introduce both to Johnson. Bess carried the memory of his 'look of tenderness' back with her to Market Harborough but Everina refused to return to her drudgery in Henley.[31] Wollstonecraft enlisted Johnson's help and he turned to Fuseli, who wrote to friends in Paris enquiring for a situation for a young but 'not rich' woman.[32] When Everina left, Wollstonecraft walked with Johnson to the inn from where the French mail was departing in order to dispatch words of encouragement to her younger sister. Johnson added the occasional greeting himself, although unlike Wollstonecraft he refrained from peppering Everina with instructions. 'Your sister told me I might add a postscript', he scribbled at the bottom of a letter in March. 'See what room she has left me, not to make love surely! only to express my good wishes for your happiness.'[33] Occasionally he also stepped in to help with the difficult business of keeping her troublesome younger siblings in any gainful occupation, settling her brother Charles's debts so he could be sent from London to Wales and later arranging for another brother, James, to study maths with John Bonnycastle in Woolwich in the hope that more education might enable him to settle to a profession.

The sense that she no longer carried her burdens alone prompted Wollstonecraft to characterise Johnson as a one-man replacement for the family who had failed her. 'You forgot you were to make out my account', she reminded him towards the end of 1788. 'I am, of course, over head and ears in debt; but I have not that kind of pride, which make some dislike to be obliged to those they respect'. Wollstonecraft was not able to ignore the financial asymmetry between her and Johnson, but she was grateful to him for support that was never merely financial. He cared for her as did nobody else and he carried with her the burden of care for her own family. 'When I involuntarily lament that I have not a father or brother, I thankfully recollect that I have received unexpected kindness from you and a few others.' Johnson restored her faith in humanity. 'So reason allows, what nature impels me to', she concluded. 'For I cannot live without loving my fellow-creatures – nor can I love them, without discovering some virtue.'[34]

✝

Of the four paintings of Wollstonecraft that survive, three date from the period between 1787 and 1792 when she was living and working in London. One of these was by John Opie, who sometimes joined the company at Johnson's. Opie's painting shows an austere intellectual dressed in dark stripes, with a curled and powdered wig and a full white fichu standing in for the neckties of her male contemporaries. It is an image that projects strength and male equivalence: the philosopher, stripped of all ornament. Wollstonecraft is caught looking up from a book with dark brown eyes, as if the painter has suddenly attracted her attention. Opie captures in oil and canvas a woman who surveys the world and thinks a great deal about what she sees, but who nevertheless keeps her own countenance. A less well-known image, attributed to the Irish artist John Keenan, shows a younger woman. Her gaze is still acute but curls creep out from under a soft grey cap and there is colour in her cheeks. Her dress is restrained and her fichu is black but her figure is visible and she has rolled a single sleeve back in a gesture that gives Keenan's image a sense of the breath and pulse of his sitter. In this painting, like Opie's, Wollstonecraft glances up from a book. Both portraits represent Wollstonecraft as the professional woman writer; both capture the intensity of her attention and her engagement with the world. Keenan's painting shows something else too: the woman of quicksilver moods described by Johnson, who is sometimes barely able to spare the time to change out of wet skirts or settle her sleeves and hair before picking up her book again. Looking at this image it is hard to avoid the sensation that you are an unwelcome visitor in the parlour at George Street. Faced with this piercing gaze, the only course of action is surely to apologise for the interruption and slip away.

14

The Paper Age

By the late 1780s passing visitors to Johnson's dining room could rely on meeting Wollstonecraft, Fuseli and Bonnycastle at dinner; Lindsey, Priestley and Barbauld joined the company as often as geography and circumstance allowed. Blake kept his distance from the sociable gatherings at the table but was nevertheless a familiar presence in the room, especially during working hours when the dining table served as Johnson's desk. Authors, printers and paper-sellers whose business was important enough to merit an invitation to talk to Johnson in the privacy of his home witnessed the table strewn with documents: with manuscripts, accounts, proposals, proofs and, above all, with letters.

As the 1780s drew to a close the men and women who inhabited the dining room in person and on paper attempted to roll back an incoming wave of political crisis. In poetry, paintings, treatises, sermons and pamphlets they tried to stem the tide of Dissenting repression, and to preserve a space where they could think freely. As they did so their conversations travelled out of the house into the city and country beyond its walls. Paper allowed the abolitionists among Johnson's guests to protest the trade in enslaved Africans with renewed vigour. It permitted the exchange of ideas and plans between men who were determined to gather together in formal societies in order to effect political reform, and it allowed those who were debarred from public life to protest their exclusion. In 1788 it also allowed Johnson to bring the voices of his guests together in a journal that united in chorus many of the men and women who gathered at St Paul's Churchyard. The journal enabled him to capture those ephemeral conversations, and transformed him into the bookselling equivalent of Priestley in his workshop, isolating gases in glass vials and releasing new discoveries into the air.

✛

To resist an intolerant politics, however, required actions as well as words. At the beginning of 1787 a committee of Dissenters met to plot a new campaign for the repeal of the Test and Corporation Acts, the statutes that prevented them from holding public office. The leaders of the campaign believed that the young Prime Minister, William Pitt, was sympathetic to their cause, and that the moment was ripe for the passage through Parliament of an enlightened piece of legislation. The Dissenters' committee met at the King's Head Tavern in the Poultry, the name given to the eastern extension of Cheapside just a few minutes' walk from St Paul's Churchyard, where the poulterers and scalders killed and prepared their stock. Between January and March 1787 Johnson attended six meetings of the committee, advising on publication of their manifesto and the circulation of proof sheets. Although he never formally joined the campaigners he offered them practical assistance, publishing over fifty defences of the Dissenting position during the months in which the committee was most active. George III was vehemently opposed to Repeal and Pitt's cautious early support wavered in the face of opposition from the Monarch, the Church and the aristocrats of his own party. Johnson's house was crowded with friends who travelled from the English regions to follow the progress of a debate about whether or not they were to be considered full citizens with equal rights in their own country. 'The hive is now full', wrote Barbauld to her brother John in January. The Barbaulds had recently moved to the capital, following their decision in 1785 to resign from their school at Palgrave, and Barbauld was struck by the noise of her new home. 'Almost everybody that intends to come to town is come, and the streets rattle with carriages at all hours.'[1]

On April 5th Priestley and Lindsey sat together in the gallery of the House of Commons from twelve noon until one in the morning, listening as the Bill for Repeal was rejected by a margin of seventy-eight votes. It was providential that Priestley was there, Lindsey thought, since it fired him with ideas for a letter to Pitt himself. Priestley excoriated Pitt for his feeble populism in personal terms. 'There was the appearance', he told the Prime Minister in a letter Johnson published, 'of your being farther embarrassed and misled by your situation; and that your attention to the real merits of the question was distracted by a wish to recommend yourself to a majority of the people, without offending the minority.' Such a vain ambition, Priestley continued, was a symptom of Pitt's callow immaturity, and 'an object, Sir, which much older statesmen than yourself have seldom been able to accomplish.'

He was equally scathing about the result of the failure of Repeal. The Church Establishment might have succeeded temporarily in keeping Dissenters out of their universities, but they did so at their own expense. 'Our institutions', he taunted Pitt, 'are more liberal, and therefore better calculated to answer the purpose of a truly liberal education. Thus while your Universities resemble pools of *stagnant water* secured by dams and mounds, and offensive to the neighbourhood, ours are like *rivers*, which, taking their natural course, fertilize a whole country.'[2] Priestley's imagery was deliberately provocative in its presentation of the irresistible force of the Dissenters' efforts to reform the nation. It was only a matter of time, he implied, before the corrupt coupling of Church and State would be undone. In Birmingham, Church supporters responded to Priestley's call for change by banning the purchase of his books by the local subscription library, in an attempt to shut down Dissent that inevitably propelled him to take up his pen in protest once again.

As Priestley became the bogeyman of the Church in popular culture, a Christ-denying alchemist conjured to frighten children, Lindsey marched out in defence of his friend, addressing an extended *Vindiciae Priestleiane* to the students of Oxford and Cambridge, the two universities Priestley had castigated. Priestley, Lindsey insisted, had 'no interest in view, but that of truth, nor any desires but to have that in the best way promoted and established.'[3] Lindsey's vindication of Priestley took the form of an extensive theological enquiry rather than a straightforward defence, but his friend's notoriety gave him an opportunity to seize attention for his work.

Meanwhile Johnson joined the newly formed London Revolution Society, appearing on its list of committee members on the opening pages of the Society's minutes.[4] Its ostensible purpose was to celebrate the Glorious Revolution of 1688 and to assist in the dissemination of what the founding committee members maintained were the ideals underpinning the accession to the throne of William and Mary: freedom of the press, the right of trial by jury and individual intellectual and religious liberty, as well as the idea that political power was only legitimate if it derived from the people. Celebration of the events of 1688 gave respectable cover to the reforming zeal of the Society's members, many of whom were tradesmen, merchants and ministers drawn from London's Dissenting communities.

The attempts of the first members of the Revolution Society to begin a conversation about national political reform coincided with the most serious constitutional crisis to face Britain in decades. In November 1788, just after the Society held its first commemorative dinner on the anniversary of the Glorious Revolution, George III was struck with a malady which rendered him physically and mentally incapacitated. His illness left him unable to open Parliament and a bitter political struggle erupted between Pitt and Charles Fox's Whigs about the relationship between political power and the Monarch. The Foxite Whigs pushed hard for the Prince of Wales to be made Regent, motivated by the knowledge that he was their friend and supporter. Pitt held on to power by declaring that without the King's consent Parliament could not function, and that the statutory instruments necessary for the declaration of a Regency did not exist. The affair brought into the open a set of interlinked questions about the power of the Monarch and Parliament and although George III recovered before a Regency was declared the fragility of the British constitution had been laid bare. If Parliament could act without having been opened by the King, as happened at the end of 1788, the basis of the informal constitutional settlement of 1688 was more permeable than defenders of the status quo had ever predicted or reformers had dared hope.

᛭

The possibility of reform of the nation's constitution, politics and character spurred Johnson's authors into an attack on the great stain of their age. In *Loves of the Plants* Darwin thundered in capital letters against the parliamentarians who allowed the slave trade to continue through inertia: 'HE, WHO ALLOWS OPPRESSION, SHARES THE CRIME.'[5] But he thought that in some cases images and objects spoke louder than words. 'I have just heard that there are muzzles or gags made at Birmingham for the slaves in our islands', he wrote to Josiah Wedgwood. 'If this be true, and such an instrument could be exhibited by a speaker in the house of commons, it might have great effect. Could not one of their long whips, or wire-tails be also procured, and exhibited? But an instrument of torture of our own manufact[ure] would have a great effect.'[6] In February 1788 Barbauld wrote hopefully to her brother about an apparent groundswell of resistance to the slave trade in both the press and the country's pulpits: surely, she argued, the demand for abolition would not be resisted 'if the pleadings of eloquence of the cry of duty can be heard.'[7] One of those who castigated slavery from the pulpit was Priestley, who published a sermon *On the Subject of the Slave*

Trade in the same month. Priestley's attack was double-pronged. He simultaneously went to work on the emotions of his readers, asking them to imagine how they would feel if they were kidnapped and forced across the world, and on their consciences. 'No less guilty are we ourselves, who, in order to have our sugars, and other West-India commodities, a little cheaper ... connive at, and encourage, these iniquitous proceedings.'[8]

Priestley and Darwin knew that slavery was embedded in every part of the British economy and they were convinced that nothing less than a revolution in national morality was needed if the trade were to be abolished. Priestley drew on the language of the increasingly popular sentimental novel in order to compel his readers to look the enslaved in the eye. 'The cruel separation of the nearest relations and friends, husbands and wives, parents and children, both when they are put on board the ships, and at the place of sale, would be heard with horror by all but those who are habituated to this traffic.'[9] No Christian, he continued, of any denomination, could countenance such barbarity; nor could any patriot who believed in the Englishman's natural love of liberty. Lindsey walked up the Strand to St Paul's Churchyard to discover that the first print run of Priestley's sermon had already sold out, which he hoped was a sign it was being read widely and seriously.

In another part of London a deputation of abolition campaigners called on John Newton, now one of the most ardent exponents of the evils of slavery, to ask him to use his influence with Cowper on their behalf. They wanted Cowper to contribute to the growing canon of abolitionist poetry by composing a ballad on the slave trade that could be printed in large numbers and sung on street corners. Cowper responded with a trio of poems, the composition of which caused him much anxiety. He went to work nevertheless, overcoming his personal abhorrence of confronting a subject which offered 'only images of horror' for the sake of the cause.[10] 'If you hear Ballads sung in the Streets on the subject of the hardships suffer'd by the poor Negroes in the islands, they are probably mine', he wrote in March. Like Darwin he was sceptical about whether words alone could do away with slavery, but he understood the argument that the public had to be made to understand their own culpability in the trade. 'Since the public attention has been riveted to the horrible theme, and we can no longer plead either that we did not know it, or did not think of it, woe be to us if we refuse the poor captives the redress to which they have so clear a right, and prove ourselves in the sight of God and man indifferent to all considerations but those of gain.'[11] His most enduring ballad on the subject of slavery was 'The Negro's Complaint'. Like Priestley he forced his readers to occupy the emotional torment of the enslaved:

> Still in thought as free as ever,
>   What are England's rights, I ask,
> Me from my delights to sever,
>   Me to torture, me to task?

Physical difference offered no justification for denying the humanity of others:

> Skins may differ, but affection
>   Dwells in white and black the same.

Finally he turned the label of slave back on those who wilfully ignored suffering for their own gain. A country which could connive in the enslavement of men, women and children was a country enslaved to profit at the expense of its soul:

> Slaves of gold, whose sordid dealings
>   Tarnish all your boasted powers,
> Prove that you have human feelings,
>   Ere you proudly question ours![12]

Cowper had lived long enough with the prospect of his own damnation to fear when others mortgaged their own eternities for luxury goods and cheap sugar. Lady Hesketh reported that the nation's aristocrats showed little sign of being moved by public agitation for abolition: their indifference, Cowper responded, was a national shame. 'Hereafter ... we cannot be wrong'd by the most opprobrious appellations. Call us, who will, deliberately cruel and Tyrants upon principle, we are all guilty and must acknowledge it.'[13]

In the campaign for abolition, however, one voice was pre-eminent. Olaudah Equiano's *Interesting Narrative* told the story of his capture aged eight by slave-traders, and of the events that led to him experiencing the Middle Passage in the hull of a slave ship:

> At last, when the ship we were in had got in all her cargo, they made ready with many fearful noises, and we were all put under deck, so

that we could not see how they managed the vessel. But this disappointment was the least of my sorrow. The stench of the hold while we were on the coast was so intolerably loathsome, that it was dangerous to remain there for any time, and some of us had been permitted to stay on deck for the fresh air; but now that the whole ship's cargo were confined together, it became absolutely pestilential. The closeness of the place, and the heat of the climate, added to the number in the ship, which was so crowded that each had scarcely room to turn himself, almost suffocated us. This produced copious perspirations, so that the air soon became unfit for respiration, from a variety of loathsome smells, and brought on a sickness among the slaves, of which many died, thus falling victims to the improvident avarice, as I may call it, of their purchasers. This wretched situation was again aggravated by the galling of the chains, now become insupportable; and the filth of the necessary tubs, into which the children often fell, and were almost suffocated. The shrieks of the women, and the groans of the dying, rendered the whole a scene of horror almost inconceivable.[14]

Never before had English readers been confronted with the reality of the Middle Passage seen through the eyes of an individual who had survived its horrors. Johnson's name appeared at the head of a list of booksellers from whom readers could buy *The Interesting Narrative of the Life of Olaudah Equiano, or Gustavus Vassa, The African, Written by Himself*. The book, priced 7 shillings, was published in a two-volume, small duodecimo edition – a format often used for memoirs and novels. Equiano organised the printing himself, raising money by subscription. His subscribers included a number of well-known abolitionists, but also members of the Royal Family and House of Commons, as well as dozens of peers and bishops. Within a few months the first edition had sold out. Nine further editions appeared in five years, all of them funded by Equiano's tireless campaign for subscribers from all over Britain.

The Interesting Narrative was published with a frontispiece depicting Equiano in the clothes of an English gentleman, with book in hand. Everything about the volume combined to proclaim him as the voice for a new dawn, an era in which those who were oppressed would be heard as clearly as those who dreamt up spurious philosophies to sustain oppression. Equiano himself, however, wrote with painful clarity about the extent to which his freedom depended on the willingness of international governments to uphold the law. In Britain he was protected by the Mansfield declaration of 1772, which decreed that an enslaved person could not forcibly be removed from Britain, and he concluded his *Narrative* by expressing the hope that the freedom flickering in his adopted country would spread all over the world. 'May Heaven make the British senators the dispersers of light, liberty, and science, to the uttermost parts of the earth', he prayed. 'Then will be glory to God in the highest, on earth peace, and good-will to men.'[15]

᛭

In the spring of 1788 Johnson made a decisive intervention in the world of letters. With the assistance of a young Scot called Thomas Christie he founded a journal, the *Analytical Review*. In his early twenties Christie had embarked on medical training, first in London and then in Edinburgh, and during his visits to the capital he became a familiar presence at St Paul's Churchyard. He met Bonnycastle at Johnson's table, and witnessed the mathematician's shy romance with a young woman called Bridget Johnstone, who joined the company for tea and who Bonnycastle subsequently married. Back in Edinburgh Christie worked briefly as an *accoucheur*, or man-midwife, and had to encounter the prejudice of men who had never witnessed a baby being born but nevertheless felt themselves qualified to comment on the necessity, or not, of expert medical support during childbirth. In 1787 he embarked on a tour through England, during which he met Darwin, Priestley and Barbauld. As he travelled the prospect of ensconcing himself at the heart of Johnson's circle grew more attractive, and his wide reading of foreign literary journals convinced him that there was a space to be filled in the English market.

Johnson provided the money and logistical support and Christie nominally held the role of editor of the journal they founded together, but from the outset Johnson himself took command of much of the enterprise. It was he who appointed Wollstonecraft as a staff reviewer, and who convinced Cowper, Fuseli and John Aikin also to turn reviewers on his behalf. In a sign of his determination that the journal should not simply become yet another vehicle for disgruntled Dissenters he appointed the Catholic theologian Alexander Geddes as the *Analytical*'s chief theological reviewer. Geddes was an irascible figure, a slight man made furiously angry by anyone who dared to oppose his views. When Blake began to produce his visionary reworkings of the scriptures in a series of prophetic books it was Geddes's *Prospectus of a New Translation of the Holy Bible* that formed his most important intertext.[16] Others in Johnson's circle were less impressed with his arrival in their midst. Fuseli and Geddes were unable to meet without their conversation descending into open warfare. On one occasion Fuseli made Geddes so angry that the latter burst out of Johnson's dining room and stormed round the Cathedral in a vain attempt to calm down. On another Fuseli provoked his antagonist into calling him a 'Son of a bitch' and into a second march around St Paul's.[17] The clash of voices in the *Analytical* was a deliberate attempt on Johnson's part to replicate the stimulating, sometimes disputatious conversations between his guests in print so that the charged atmosphere of St Paul's Churchyard could be heard outside his walls.

From the outset Johnson and Christie had to work out how to make their journal prominent in a cacophonous literary marketplace. Periodicals already crowded for attention and several – the *Critical*, the *Monthly*, the *Gentleman's Magazine* – were powerful and well-established. In the Prospectus for the *Analytical* Christie denounced their competitors with unabashed ferocity. The journals no longer contained serious literary news, he insisted: they were partial and corrupt, more interested in puffing off their own work and opinions than in allowing their readers a snapshot of the new knowledge in all fields. Reviewers had wilfully perverted the meanings of authors in order to create controversy; shady financial transactions allowed booksellers and writers to buy favourable coverage in important journals. Reviews were superficial, concerned with 'trifling and temporary works' rather than those that deserved serious attention. They were also absurdly parochial, ignoring works published overseas at all costs. Christie made it clear that he and Johnson expected more from their reviewers:

> In the judgements given on books, writers will endeavour to conduct themselves with that degree of modesty which is most suitable to their character. Where absurdity and immortality are to be imposed on the public, they will certainly think themselves authorized to raise the rod of criticism, but will not deem themselves entitled to interfere in a dictatorial manner, when authors of approved learning and genius have produced a work containing an elaborate chain of facts and arguments, nor pretend by the hasty reading of an hour to confute the labour of years.

It mattered to Christie and Johnson that their reviewers were writers before they were critics: that they understood what it meant to labour on and publish a volume, and that they were not merely hacks for hire. It also mattered to them that they were, and were seen to be, independent of any single party or faction. Geddes's involvement was crucial to this, leavening the Dissenting bias of many of the journal's other contributors. They also wanted the journal to be a place where knowledge could be shared, and to which readers as well as regular critics might bring their expertise. Early on in the journal's existence they asked readers 'to favour us with communications relative to the state of literature and arts, new discoveries, new publications.' Only through receipt of such information, they proclaimed, could they make the journal representative of new knowledge in all parts of the country.

Of utmost importance was the *Analytical*'s vision of a Europe without boundaries, in which books and knowledge could pass between countries in an endlessly productive exchange. In the reach of their international ambitions, Johnson and Christie broke new ground. Each issue of the *Analytical* had a section on 'Literary Intelligence', in which news was summarised from learned societies all over Europe and in which major European journals were excerpted and aggregated. The first issue carried bulletins from the Académie Royale des Inscriptions et Belles Lettres in Paris and the Royal Society of Arts and Sciences at Metz as well as summaries of works published in Leipzig, Madrid, Naples, Stockholm, Pisa and Florence, and bulletins relating to new discoveries by the French chemists. 'So *complete* a view of foreign literature has never yet been attempted in any Journal', boasted Christie. Surely his journal had 'a just claim to the title of The HISTORY of the LITERATURE of EUROPE.'[18] With all these ambitions firmly in mind Johnson and Christie settled on a title for their enterprise which was nothing if not comprehensive: 'The Analytical Review, or History of Literature, Domestic and Foreign. On an Enlarged Plan. Containing scientific abstracts of important and interesting works, published in English; a general account of such as are of less consequence, with short characters; notices, or reviews of valuable foreign books; criticisms on new pieces of music and works of art; and the literary intelligence of Europe, etc.'

The *Analytical*'s thematic scope was as broad as its geographical reach. Theological works featured in every issue, alongside reviews of medical texts, scientific proceedings, narratives of travel and exploration, classical translations, mathematical texts, educational works, novels, poetry, musical scores, dramas and reports on visual art. Works published by Johnson received a liberal hearing, but so did those produced by rival booksellers. Faults were not overlooked, but they were fairly considered. Johnson sent many of the new novels requiring review to Wollstonecraft: so many that in July she protested. 'If you wish me to look over any more trash this month – you must send it directly.' But, she continued, 'I shall soon want some paper – you may as well send it at the same time – for I am trying to brace my nerves that I may be industrious.'[19] Of many of the novels she was unsparing, although she did her best to accede to the *Analytical*'s dictum that its reviewers would not write vitriol for its own sake. 'Few of the numerous productions termed novels, claim any attention', she bemoaned in an early review of Charlotte Smith's *Emmeline*. 'While we distinguish this one, we cannot help lamenting that it has the same tendency as the generality, whose preposterous sentiments our young females imbibe with such avidity.'[20] Reviewing fiction aimed squarely at bored young ladies left Wollstonecraft ever more convinced that the female state had become debased by a culturally required decorative uselessness, and on this subject above all she refused to temper the severity of her judgement. She watched with interest as the established periodicals issued indignant statements of their independence in response to the *Analytical*'s insurgent announcement of its intellectual purity. 'The Appendix to the Monthly afforded me more amusement', she told Johnson. 'Though every article almost wants energy and a *cant* of virtue and liberality is strewed over it; always tame, and eager to pay court to established fame.'[21]

In the early days the amount of work required by the scale of the *Analytical*'s ambitions threatened to overwhelm Johnson and Christie. The first volume contained a hastily inserted apology for inaccuracies of style. They pleaded forgiveness on the basis of 'how much time is required, to pursue such a number of letters, printed papers and foreign Journals, as we are obliged to do, in order to extract the essence of them for our readers.'[22] Elsewhere in the periodical they made it clear that their preference was for plain and clear language, which sought to elucidate meaning rather than draw attention to itself. The reviewer of Andrew Kippis's *Life of Captain Cook* argued that since 'entertainment appears to us the principal object of biographical publications', unadorned language was infinitely preferable than 'the verbose, tumid, and highly figurative style so fashionable at present.'[23]

Elsewhere the journal reflected the old preoccupations of Johnson's list, covering works on subjects ranging from the scandal of the deaths of too many women in childbirth, through to chemical discoveries, Dissenting disputes, educational innovation and the boundaries of the known universe. An early reviewer disavowed controversy, terming it 'foreign' to the purpose of the *Analytical Review*[24] but the journal did not shy away from the debates convulsing the nation. It covered the profusion of rapidly produced pamphlets in which authors of every political allegiance shouted their views on the Regency Crisis, as well as the multitude of works which told the story of the failed attempt to repeal the Test and Corporation Acts. Not all those who contributed reviews shared the same outlook on the world: while the reviewer of Kippis's *Life* of Cook approved of biography, the critic of his *Biographia Britannica* took a dim view of the genre. He conceded that a 'Complete Biography' would be welcome, but lamented the reality that such a work entailed 'a task so irksome and laborious, that persons of real abilities, without very extraordinary encouragements, can seldom be prevailed upon to undertake it.' The result, he concluded, was most unfortunate. Biography 'has therefore too frequently fallen into the hands of dull and tasteless compilers, who accumulate facts and dates without any ingenuity of remark, depth of investigation, or beauty or sentiment to enliven the tedious and insipid chronicle.'[25]

✦

The *Analytical Review* offered a vision for both its readers and its writers of how to be in the world: enquiring, curious, open-minded, inviting. It ignored national boundaries and the creeping swell of Establishment parochialism and offered optimism as an antidote to sectarianism. In paper, and the task of filling it, it saw the potential for restoration. 'This is a PAPER AGE', announced the reviewer of an updated version of Samuel Paterson's *Joineriana*. Paper had become the engine of Britain's emergent capitalist economy, as banknotes, share certificates, contracts and promissory notes circulated out from London into the provinces and across the globe. The *Analytical*'s reviewer estimated that 'nine parts out of ten' of Britain's trade relied on the medium of paper. It was also the medium through which an equally fundamental shift in the attitudes and beliefs of a country might be achieved. 'The GOLDEN, the SILVER, and the IRON AGES are long since past, the two former *never to return!* – We are now, happily, arrived at the PAPER AGE.'[26]

If the penultimate decade of the eighteenth century was the 'paper age', then at St Paul's Churchyard that age had one of its engine rooms and its temple. The tasks confronting the men and women who Johnson gathered together were daunting: to stem the flow of prejudice against those who thought and worshipped in ways feared by the State, to stamp out the abhorrent global trade in people, to create the conditions for a more enlightened age. The threat of Dissenting repression gathered strength just at the point that Johnson announced the collegiate force of his circle in the pages of the *Analytical*. Nevertheless, for a moment in 1788, as a corrupted Establishment wavered under the intellectual pressure produced by the King's affliction, it seemed possible that Darwin was unnecessarily pessimistic when he argued that whips rather than words were needed to change the political weather. Perhaps, the collective voices of the dining room suggested, a revolution in the character of the nation might for once be effected with the shedding of ink instead of blood.

15

Aphorisms on Man

In 1788, the year of the founding of the *Analytical Review* and the political crisis occasioned by George III's illness, Johnson published Fuseli's translation of Johann Caspar Lavater's *Aphorisms on Man*. When Fuseli set to work on the volume, both he and Johnson hoped that it would be a precursor for a major English edition of Lavater's *Essays on Physiognomy*. The central theme of Lavater's *Essays*, namely that specific character traits could be inferred from physical characteristics, had widespread appeal. Lavater did more than anyone to popularise the pseudo-science of physiognomy, producing in *Essays* a hybrid miscellany of observation, empirical explanation and proto-self-help instructions about how to divine character from appearance. His system was founded on a broad belief in the particular genius of the individual: it celebrated the idea that part of being alive was to have a unique inner identity that could be mapped through the close study of the outer surface. Johnson's English edition of *Aphorisms on Man* was a celebration of friendship. It opened with a letter from Lavater to Fuseli in which he avowed his devotion to his friend and translator before positing friendship itself as central to the condition of being human. 'Want of friends', ran one of his aphorisms, 'argues either want of humility or courage, or both'.[1] Blake engraved the frontispiece for *Aphorisms* from a painting by Fuseli and he read and reread his own copy, annotating it throughout with a fine-nibbed pen. On the frontispiece he drew a heart around Lavater's name and added his own directly beneath it, in recognition of how profoundly Lavater had shaped his own thinking about ways of being in the world.

Emboldened by the success of *Aphorisms on Man* and buoyed by Fuseli's enthusiasm, Johnson began to plot a large-scale edition of Lavater's *Essays*. At George Street Wollstonecraft set to work on a new translation; Fuseli and Blake were contracted to design and engrave additional illustrations.

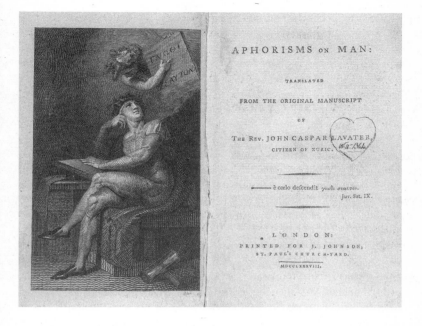

Blake began by engraving a large profile portrait of Lavater, which Johnson published in order to drum up interest in the edition. From Zurich Lavater peppered Johnson and Fuseli with instructions and suggestions. He wanted his work to appear in a large-scale, deluxe volume, quite unlike the affordable books Johnson usually produced, and he strove to exercise an iron grip on every detail of the new illustrations. Fuseli did his best to mediate between his friends, soothing Lavater with explanations about the reality of the English book market; coaxing Johnson into accepting new material from a writer who was apparently completely unable to let his text stay fixed long enough for it to be typeset.

Johnson and Fuseli knew themselves to be working against the clock as they grappled with Lavater's demands. Word reached them that the writer Thomas Holcroft was working on an affordable translation that would be completed before Wollstonecraft's, and that Johnson's old friend and rival John Murray had commissioned a translation from Henry Hunter and was planning to produce a lavishly illustrated edition of his own. Johnson threatened to publish a notice announcing that it was he who had Lavater's approval and cooperation, rather than Murray, but then thought better of doing so. In October 1787 Murray proposed that they should join together in coalition. 'I called at your shop to day to inform you of particulars, but you had just gone up stairs with a Gentleman on business', he wrote. 'No matter whose scheme here is the best; a public competition will infallibly hurt both.' And, in recognition of Johnson's inflexibility on the matter: 'Obstinacy therefore should be avoided on both sides, & all of us keep steadily in our Eye, what will tend most to the general interest.'[2] Johnson agreed, possibly with some relief at freeing himself from epistolary tangles with Lavater's ego. He cancelled Wollstonecraft's translation and joined Murray's coalition as a silent backer, bringing both financial assistance and Fuseli's ability to cajole Lavater to the project. Fuseli himself kept a close eye on Hunter's translation and Blake's engravings were handed over to Murray, who published four of them in the first of several richly illustrated volumes.

The episode of Lavater's *Essays* revealed anew the intricate network of personal and professional connections emanating outwards from St Paul's Churchyard. In the undertaking Johnson and Fuseli stood side by side, strengthened by their connection with each other. Friendship and sympathy linked Johnson with Wollstonecraft, layering their professional understanding: the same was true of his dealings with Murray, who appealed to his old friend's character as well as his business sense. Blake still worked as Johnson's staff engraver, but Johnson's growing appreciation of the depths of Blake's talent was demonstrated by his decision to publish his engravings of Lavater's profile as an independent work. Both Wollstonecraft and Blake found Johnson a demanding taskmaster but the work that they did for him gave them space and time to develop distinctive voices in both image and text. 'Who in the same given time can produce more than many others, has *vigour*', declared Lavater in the *Aphorisms*. 'Who can produce more and better, has *talents*; who can produce what none else can, has *genius*.'[3] In 1788 vigour, talent and genius were all on display amongst the men and women who formed Johnson's inner circle of trusted friends, employees and collaborators, but it was the energy with which they made books together that created the conditions in which genius could take flight.

✛

For Wollstonecraft the beginning of 1789 promised a new beginning that was personal as well as political. As a consequence of conversations at St

Paul's Churchyard that initially arose out of a shared commitment to work on Lavater, she found herself increasingly drawn towards Fuseli. In 1788 Fuseli had married Sophia Rawlins, an artist's model twenty years his junior. Sophia appears in many of Fuseli's drawings but she very rarely joined her husband at Johnson's table, and Wollstonecraft was more interested in Fuseli's 'original genius and uncommon diligence' than she was in his wife.[4] 'Painting, and subjects closely connected with painting, were their almost constant topics of conversation', wrote Wollstonecraft's first biographer, William Godwin. Godwin derived his account of her friendship with Fuseli from Johnson and Fuseli later destroyed many of the letters he received from Wollstonecraft so the surviving sources give only a partial account of the events that followed. In these sources Wollstonecraft's own voice is occluded.

Meetings at Johnson's table led to a suggestion that Wollstonecraft might visit Fuseli at home to see his paintings. Her visits were returned, breaking her self-imposed isolation in George Street. She began to relax the austerity of her appearance, swapping sober black for more fashionable clothes, and introducing domestic comforts into her spartan parlour. Fuseli's biographer presented these shifts as an attempt by Wollstonecraft to capture the artist's attention but Wollstonecraft was aware of the dangers of moulding herself to suit the tastes and inclinations of a man. Fuseli's company does appear, though, to have fired her imagination and to have convinced her that life might not need to be as rigorous and disciplined as her previous experience suggested.

During this period she wrote as one for whom a new vista had opened up, in which it seemed possible to live unconstrained by narrow social expectation. The prospect was overwhelming. 'My hand trembles', she told Fanny Blood's brother George. 'I will write again as soon as I can calm my mind'.[5] To Fuseli she wrote that he provoked in her a 'strength of feeling unalloyed by passion' but since Fuseli saved only complimentary snippets from her letters the context for this declaration has been lost. Johnson knew more of Fuseli than anyone else and he watched Wollstonecraft's developing relationship with the artist with concern. For once she spurned his advice. 'You made me very low-spirited last night, by your manner of talking', she protested, in an undated letter. 'You are my only friend – the only person I am *intimate* with'. Yet even as she rejected his caution, believing that she could forge a way of living that had no precedent, Wollstonecraft acknowledged that Johnson's care for her was without precedent too. 'I never had a father, or a brother – you have been both to me, ever since I knew you – yet I have sometimes been very petulant. I have been thinking of those instances of ill-humour and quickness, and they appeared like crimes.'[6] When Johnson came to collect his memories of this period for Wollstonecraft's first biographer he was elliptical about the nature of her emotional storms and explicit about their cause. 'F.', he recorded, 'was frequently with us'.[7]

⚓

In amongst personal dramas, the work of writing and making continued. In the first months of 1789 Darwin and Johnson were occupied with organising plates for *The Botanic Garden*; Cowper was grumbling about the volume of work necessitated by his commitment to the *Analytical Review*. At least by taking up the role of reviewer, he conceded, he had an opportunity to defend his tribe. 'I would that every fastidious judge of authors, were, himself, obliged to write,' he told his friend Samuel Rose. 'There goes more to the complication of a volume than many Critics imagine.'[8] In between the business of producing books and the *Analytical* Johnson administrated a competition for aspirant scientists, who were instructed to send their essays on the material origins of the world to his shop marked for his attention. Meanwhile Wollstonecraft was not the only woman to be attracted by Fuseli's light. In June he captured the attention of Frederica Lock, the wife of one of his pupils, who sent a breathless account of their conversation to the novelist Frances Burney. Over a leisurely breakfast Fuseli mocked Bonnycastle as a man of spectacularly little imagination, told stories 'with all the fire of poetic genius' and promised to read Burney's novels, *Evelina* and *Cecilia*. He also reported Johnson's admiration for Burney, expressed in the form of a promise by him to publish anything Burney wrote for any price she decreed, as well as Johnson's disappointment that Fuseli himself refused to read new works of fiction.[9] While Fuseli entertained Frederica Lock over breakfast and Wollstonecraft over dinner, the Lindseys left London for the summer. They made their way to Priestley's house at Fair Hill where they spent several weeks cocooned from the noise of the capital. 'The time you and Mrs Lindsey passed at Birmingham appears now as a pleasant dream', Priestley wrote, on July 22nd. It was a dream 'which I hope … will often be repeated, before we wake in a state where, I trust, we shall separate no more.'[10]

The Lindseys were still in Birmingham on July 14th 1789 when a Parisian crowd stormed the Bastille and set its inmates free. The Bastille had long

178

represented the worst abuses of the French State against its people and its destruction marked the moment when festering public anger in France tipped into revolution. The immediate trigger for the attack was the decision of Louis XVI to sack his reformist finance minister, Jacques Necker, although the tensions that led to the events of July 14th had been building for decades. France was in the throes of economic crisis and the country's political systems had been forced beyond breaking point by the actions of an intransigent monarch and an impoverished public. In May the convention of the Estates-General collapsed and the Third Estate – representatives of the people drawn from outside the ranks of the Church and the nobility – formed themselves into a redefined National Assembly, in which the representation of the people rather than the pillars of the State was paramount. Louis XVI tried and failed to shut down the National Assembly, which reconstituted itself on July 9th as the National Constituent Assembly and the supreme governing body of France. In October a crowd marched from Paris to Versailles before storming the royal palace and bringing Louis, his wife Marie Antoinette and their children back to the capital by force.

In the period immediately following the storming of the Bastille, France stood as a beacon of hope for all those who had worked and prayed for reform. Events in Paris showed that the people could make themselves heard; that a corrupt king could be deprived of his power in favour of representative government. The Revolution brought with it the promise of change and generated a spirit of renewed optimism among all those who believed in the possibility of a better future. Once again the truth of Lavater's formulation in *Aphorisms on Man* appeared to be vindicated, as the actions of men of vigour, talent and genius effected a revolution in both politics and ideas. Thomas Christie was so enthralled by the version of liberty emerging from France that he abandoned his post at the *Analytical* to travel there and witness the unfolding of revolution for himself. Lindsey saw nothing but good in the reports filtering through from Paris. 'Abroad great and most important changes are coming in'. Surely, he wrote, events in France 'will have the best effect in the moral state not of one country only but of the who[le] world.'[11] Priestley too was convinced that the conflagration of a detested prison heralded a brilliant future. His son and his brother-in-law had been in Paris in July and had beheld the birth of the Revolution at first hand. From their accounts, he wrote, only one conclusion was possible. 'There is indeed a great prospect for mankind before us.'[12]

PART FOUR
RUINS (1789–1791)

What will become of me!

William Blake, engraving for Wollstonecraft's translation of
Christian Salzmann's *Elements of Morality*, 1791

Over dinner all the talk is of revolution, of new ways of living and working and making. As the citizens of France demolish the structures of the Ancien Régime, their supporters in Britain see in their example the prospect of a more equal future. For Priestley, Lindsey, Barbauld and John Aikin it seems as if the moment has finally come for the lifting of the yoke under which the Dissenters have laboured. Darwin spies in the winds of change a chance to celebrate the technological prowess of his friends, in whose Midlands workshops a modern, prosperous country is being forged. Wollstonecraft seizes on the opportunity offered by a national conversation about rights and the source of political power to make her first substantive intervention in a debate about equality that will come to define her career. Her example will be followed by Thomas Paine who, after the events of 1789, comes to dinner for the first time. For Fuseli and Blake the great questions of the moment are about how to make art outside the confines of existing technology, untrammelled by the constraints of a market in buying and selling. For all of Johnson's guests, and for Cowper in Weston, the tension between artistic integrity and the business of earning a living colours their relationship with their host, despite the geniality of candlelit evenings around the table. Johnson himself is always aware of the responsibility of keeping his guests and dependents warm and fed, but he is also inspired by the faces gathered around him to take risks, and to test new combinations of voice and vision in print and on copper-plate. Within the confines of the dining room, amongst the safety offered by the company of sympathetic men and women, it seems in these uncertain days as if old conventions need not hold back any endeavour, whether artistic, political, religious or technological. But in another British city, outside another dining room, a crowd gathers, of angry men armed with clubs and flaming torches. They are baying for the blood of a man who is amongst Johnson's most valued dinner guests, and one of his oldest friends.

16

On Liberty

> Bliss was it in that dawn to be alive
> But to be young was very heaven! O times,
> In which the meagre, stale, forbidding ways
> Of custom, law, and state took at once
> The attraction of a Country in Romance;
> When Reason seemed the most to assert her rights
> When most intent on making of herself
> A prime Enchanter to assist the work
> Which then was going forwards in her name.[1]

This is how William Wordsworth, writing more than a decade later, recalled the excitement of 1789. For him the French Revolution was the great experience of his youth. He was nineteen when the Bastille fell and in his epic poem of self-discovery, *The Prelude*, he charted an awakening that unfolded alongside events in France. 'Bliss was it in that dawn to be alive / But to be young was very heaven!' No lines of poetry more brilliantly epitomise the sensation of witnessing the world remade.

For most of Johnson's dinner guests, however, the French Revolution was not an experience of youth. Johnson was fifty-one in 1789. Priestley was fifty-seven; Lindsey a decade older and Barbauld a decade younger. Fuseli was forty-eight. Wollstonecraft and Blake were younger – thirty and thirty-two respectively – but they too had lived long enough to experience the 'forbidding ways / Of custom, law, and state' as reality rather than arcane abstraction.

In 1792, three years after the start of the French Revolution, Johnson invited a new guest to dinner. George Dyer had spent the first part of his adulthood in Cambridge, where he moved in the Dissenting circle surrounding a recent convert to Unitarianism, William Frend. In Cambridge Dyer wrote his own *Inquiry* into clerical subscription, which Johnson republished when he moved to London. Dyer spoke with a stammer and his conversation was punctuated by a verbal tic: he would add the redundant phrase, 'Well, sir; but however' to the end of his pronouncements.[2] He was shabbily dressed, more interested in books than in his own appearance, and in later life he became so absent-minded that on one occasion he walked into a pond on the way home.

Dyer was committed to the cause of political reform with every fibre of his being, and at Johnson's he rejoiced in the company of sympathetic fellow travellers. Inspired by their conversation he wrote an ode 'On Liberty' in which he immortalised Johnson's circle in a poetic pantheon of Dissent. Priestley and Lindsey stand together in Dyer's poem as 'gen'rous friends … Alike in manners, and in worth allied'. Wollstonecraft's words 'break the charm, / Where beauty lies in durance vile opprest'. Liberty sings through Barbauld's poetry and in the work of a rabble-rouser called Tom Paine who has the potential

> to rouse the languid hearts
> Of Albion's sons, and through their feeble veins
> Dart the electric fire, which quick imparts
> Passions, which make them wonder, while they feel.[3]

The analogy Dyer made between liberty and electricity was not coincidental. In the months following the fall of the Bastille it seemed to many of those gathered at St Paul's Churchyard as if the Revolution was above all the product of Enlightenment: an expression of the end of ignorance and the triumph of knowledge. Those who understood the power of electrical charges could surely no longer be content to live under the yoke of arbitrary power. To follow the cause of Liberty was to follow the path of restoration. 'Hail! radiant form divine, blest Liberty!' wrote Dyer. 'Wher'er thou deign'st to rove, oh! Let me rove with thee.'[4] Dyer presented the followers of Liberty as both patriotic and Christian, and Liberty itself as a force that might inspire patriotism and religious devotion in those who had not yet seen the light. He was particularly interested in the way in which the light shone by Liberty attracted the attention of marginalised groups. 'I have observed', he wrote in a footnote, 'that the most sensible females, when they turn their attention to political subjects, are more uniformly on the side of liberty than the other sex'. He thought the reason for this was obvious: 'Most governments are partial, and more injurious to women than to men.'[5] For some political commentators the sight of the women of Paris marching to Versailles to bring back the royal family under guard was all the more terrifying because of the gender of the marchers, but for others it offered further confirmation of the end of a corrupted order.

⚓

'I do not doubt your attention, as well as that of everyone else, has been engaged lately by the affairs in France', wrote Barbauld to her friend Miss Dixon in August. An acquaintance had returned from Paris with graphic reports of the capture of the Bastille, 'that not impregnable castle of Giant Despair'. Even the revealed architecture of the building defied reason.

> He told us, that after all the prisoners in the common apartments had been liberated, they heard for a long time the groans of a man in one of the dungeons, to which they could not get access, and were at length obliged to take him out by making a breach in the wall, through which they drew him out after he had been forty-eight hours without food; and they could not at last find the aperture by which he was put into the dungeon.[6]

Cells without doors; prisoners reduced to animalistic groans: surely, Barbauld implied, the fall of a regime that perpetrated such horrors was to be celebrated.

Others among her acquaintance were even more enthusiastic. 'Now is the time to speak out without any fear, both on civil and religious subjects, while the advocates for tyranny are overawed', insisted Priestley.[7] He wanted to believe that events in France foreshadowed a European-wide reformation of politics and he watched developments in Paris and in neighbouring nations closely. From the confusion of rumours that emerged from France in the late summer of 1789 came the suggestion that Louis XVI was preparing to retake power through military force. 'The courtiers here will triumph', worried Priestley. But, surely, 'as the people in general are in favour of liberty ... the king cannot, I should imagine, find many to carry on a war'.[8] Disbelief that the Revolutionaries would ultimately prevail mingled with personal anxiety for Priestley, whose son William was in the thick of the disturbance at Paris. By November William had made his way to the safety of Frankfurt and Priestley was able to watch events in Paris unfold without fear.

Priestley was not the only one among Johnson's friends who struggled to balance personal and political considerations as they contemplated the subject of France. Lindsey's fellow Unitarian William Frend was also abroad when the Revolution started and Lindsey too had to wait until November for news that Frend was safely out of harm's way. 'Heaven be praised', he wrote, 'that we have gotten you safe again to our isle.' Frend had sent news of events in Paris as well as of his own safety and his observations filled Lindsey with hope. 'The revolution in France is a wonderful work of providence in our days, and we trust it will prosper and go on, and be the speedy means of putting an end to tyranny every where.'[9] Lindsey also took pleasure in the fact that the French people appeared to have effected revolution without widespread violence, to the disappointment, he thought, of many parliamentarians in London. 'The quiet and stability of the proceedings at Paris', he reported in January, 'is said to be very offensive here.'[10] In October the *Analytical Review* addressed the tension between personal gain and public good in a review of a French study of commerce. 'There are some who are of opinion', wrote Johnson's anonymous reviewer, 'that if the French become a free and commercial people, it will be much against the interest of this country; but for our part, we deem this a narrow and ill-grounded idea'. A prosperous France promised great things for English tradesmen, he countered, but in any case, some things mattered more than money:

As men, we ought to be interested in the happiness of man; as freemen, we ought to rejoice in the extension of freedom; as citizens of the world, we should wish well to all its inhabitants; and as Christians, we are bound to consider all men as our brethren. Instead of viewing their rising liberty with mean and jealous suspicion, we ought to hail the auspicious day, when the sun of freedom arose to illuminate their land.

It was only to be pitied, opined the reviewer, with blithe disdain for the balance of opinion in government, that Britain had not come to the aid of the French people as they claimed the liberty that was their birthright. In spite of that there was plenty about which to be optimistic:

We seem to be advancing to a great æra in the history of human affairs. The papal power, that scourge of nations, is declining ... The improvements in science, if our limits allowed us to enter upon them, would open a large field for speculation. More liberal ideas, both in politics and religion, are every where gaining ground. The regulation, and perhaps in time, the abolition of the slave trade, with the endeavours of societies for discovering Africa, may lead to the civilisation of some parts of that immense continent, and open new markets for our manufactures. The Americans approach fast to a settled government; and will, probably, then become a great commercial people.

Improvement for improvement's sake was one thing in the case of France, the reviewer conceded: to defeat slavery would entail deploying arguments for economic self-interest as well as appealing to a nation's morality. Yet events in France showed that anything was possible, especially if economic and moral imperatives were harnessed for the same end. Together, the review concluded, their force was unstoppable. 'The genius of commerce is gone forth among the nations of the earth; everywhere carrying peace and plenty and freedom in her train.'[11]

＋

On August 26th 1789 the National Constituent Assembly of France adopted the final article of a document entitled *The Declaration of the Rights of Man and the Citizen*. The *Declaration* gave formal expression to some of the interlinked ideas underpinning the Revolution and formed the basis for a new constitution for France. The rights described in the *Declaration* were presented as 'natural, imprescriptible, and unalienable'. 'Men were born and always continue free, and equal in respect of their rights', ran the first article. No one could be arbitrarily arrested and held; all were to be presumed innocent unless proven guilty. 'No man ought to be molested on account of his opinions', read article X, 'not even on account of his *religious* opinions, provided his avowal of them does not disturb the public order established by the law.' The freedom to speak, write and publish freely was enshrined in the *Declaration*, as was the principle of equal, means-tested taxation. Article XVI was fundamental: 'Every community in which a separation of powers and a security of rights is not provided for, wants a constitution.'[12]

With the benefit of hindsight it is easy to read the *Declaration* and Lindsey's pleasure in the stability of Paris as naive. The bloodshed of the Terror dominated later accounts of the French Revolution and the guillotine remains one of its central images. Many of those who greeted news of the Revolution with joy in 1789 were subsequently appalled by the violent excesses of its later stages. But for watchers in London who did not themselves experience the febrile atmosphere in Paris it seemed for at least a year after July 1789 as if the ideals of the *Declaration* had finally won out over tyranny. Louis XVI and his family experienced the time they spent in the Tuileries Palace as a period of imprisonment but it was also the period when Louis reigned as constitutional monarch. Many although not all of the principles expressed in the French *Declaration* echoed those encoded in the Constitution of the United States, signed in Philadelphia in September 1787. Both documents shared similarities with the English Bill of Rights of 1689, which enshrined the ideals celebrated by Johnson and his fellow committee members at the Revolution Society.

On November 4th 1789 Richard Price, the Welsh preacher who had befriended both Priestley and Wollstonecraft, gave a sermon to the Revolution Society in which he made the connection between the three texts explicit. Price entitled his sermon A *Discourse on the Love of our Country*. He opened by examining the nature of patriotism. By country he meant, 'not the soil or the spot of earth on which we happen to have been born' but community, 'or that body of companions and friends and kindred who are associated with us under the same constitution of government'.[13] To love that community was not to think it superior to all others. 'We should love it ardently, but not exclusively', Price argued. 'We ought to seek its good, by all the means that our different circumstances and abilities will allow; but at the same time we ought to consider ourselves as citizens of the world.'[14] Price rejected the idea that to be a citizen of the world was to be a citizen of nowhere. He encouraged his listeners to be patriotic but not blind to the faults of their own polity: to improve the nation was the duty of every patriotic man. 'Our first concern, as lovers of our country, must be to *enlighten* it.'[15]

Throughout Price returned to the touchstones of his own moral code: truth, virtue and liberty. These, he argued, were the chief blessings of human nature, but the structures of contemporary civil society militated against the triumph of these ideas. 'Men in power ... are always endeavouring to extend their power', he observed. 'They hate the doctrine, that it is a TRUST derived from the people, and not a *right* vested in themselves.'[16] Unequal political representation of the kind that persisted in England exacerbated the natural despotism of the powerful. But, Price insisted, events in France offered grounds for optimism. Price was sixty-seven in 1789, the same age as Lindsey. He spoke of his gratitude that he had lived long enough to see his dearest hopes come to fruition. 'I have lived to see THIRTY MILLIONS of people, indignant and resolute, spurning at slavery, and demanding liberty with an irresistible voice; their king led in triumph, and an arbitrary monarch surrendering himself to his subjects.'[17] For those who sought to hold back the tide of change he had a warning. 'You cannot now hold the world in darkness. Struggle no longer against increasing light and liberality. Restore to mankind their rights; and consent to the correction of abuses, before they and you are destroyed together.'[18]

Price's sermon epitomised the promise of the French Revolution. He used his pulpit to argue that liberty was God-given and inevitable and he offered hope to the many Dissenters who heard or read his words. In Birmingham Priestley had to wait for some weeks for a copy of Price's sermon, although he heard report of it from Lindsey, who had been in the congregation. At the end of November Priestley was still waiting for a copy but when it finally arrived in the second week of December it moved him to tears. 'His friends need be under no apprehension' he assured Lindsey, who was worried that a frail man had exposed himself to risk. 'The court will be galled, but they will never hurt him. I hope it will be reprinted in a cheap form, to distribute through the country.'[19]

✦

Three months after Price gave his sermon the connection between the Dissenters and the ideals of the Revolution finally erupted into public consciousness in a manner which suggested that the optimism felt by Johnson and his writers in 1789 had been misplaced. At the beginning of 1790 the Dissenting Deputies of London regathered to try once more to force the repeal of the Test and Corporation Acts. This time they enlisted the support of the leader of the Whig opposition in Parliament, Charles Fox. The political philosopher William Godwin recorded a series of dinners with overlapping groups of men he referred to variously as the 'Revolutionists' and the 'Anti-tests' in diary entries that show Lindsey and others meeting and mobilising once more against legislation they believed had no place on the statute books of a modern country. For a brief period it looked as if they might finally succeed. They knew that George III was against them, but, wrote Lindsey, in a pointed reference to the King's illness the year before, surely sensible parliamentarians would recognise his animus for what it was, a 'temporary insanity'.[20]

The Dissenters' cause was dealt a fatal blow on March 2nd 1790 when Edmund Burke stood up in the House of Commons to oppose Repeal. Burke was not a natural enemy of the Dissenters: he had been sympathetic to the grievances of the Americans prior to the American War of Independence and had argued consistently for Anglo-American cooperation as an alternative to war. When the Revolution broke out in France Burke initially reserved his position, but he was horrified by the sight of Parisian peasant women forcing the Royal Family back to the capital and by the end of 1789 his opposition to the Revolution was entrenched. On March 2nd he took the opportunity offered by the debate on repeal of the Test and Corporation Acts to make an explicit connection between English Dissenters and French Revolutionaries. In a long speech he bemoaned the destruction of the French State Church and suggested that indulging the Dissenters would produce the same result in England. He quoted liberally from an anti-Dissenting pamphlet formed of Priestley's writings, taken out of context so that they appeared dangerously inflammatory. Priestley had compared the spread of enlightenment ideals to gunpowder, powerful and irresistible once lit, and Burke seized on the analogy to imply that Priestley intended violence to the Church Establishment. He quoted liberally from Richard Price's sermon, chastising him for bringing politics into the pulpit. Every excerpt was carefully chosen to bolster one argument: that the Dissenters were the avowed enemies of the Church of England and that the Church itself was in danger. In alleging that the Dissenters wanted revolution at a time when both the public and the political classes feared the spread of revolutionary ideals Burke rendered Repeal politically untenable. He also laid the groundwork for the fracturing of a century of 'toleration' of Nonconformist views.

In theory the Dissenters remained free to worship as they chose provided they did not seek civil office or threaten the sanctity of the Established Church. In reality leading Dissenters found themselves represented in cartoons and in the pages of the popular press as the enemy within. Priestley was caricatured as 'Gunpowder Joe', a dangerous chemist intent on destruction of the national peace. Lindsey was represented as a lackey of the Devil. Price found himself depicted among hellish demons celebrating his treason. 'My daughter wishes much to have the print in which we are represented as going to hell', Priestley told Lindsey in May. 'I shall be obliged to you to buy it, and put it to my account. She has the former, in which we are in the same pulpit.'[21]

+

The 1790 Repeal motion was defeated in the House of Commons by 189 votes, less than a year after it had failed by a margin of only 20 votes. The knowledge that public opinion had hardened against them prompted a shift in the rhetoric of Johnson's inner circle. Priestley confronted the accusations against him head on, in a series of *Familiar Letters to the Inhabitants of Birmingham*. A group of Establishment Birmingham clerics had been preaching and publishing attacks on him that mirrored Burke's and he addressed himself directly to the parishioners. 'You have been told in a variety of publications, that I have threatened to blow up the church, if not the state also, with *gunpowder*', he acknowledged. 'Now, my good friends and neighbours, I am not actually a mad-man … my gunpowder is nothing but *arguments*, which can have no force but what you yourselves shall be pleased to give them, from your own conviction of the reasonableness of what I lay before you.'[22] In the face of defeat he promised to preach, speak and write for as long as the press remained free. In the meantime, he noted, there was little incentive for the Dissenters whose ingenuity had brought riches to Manchester and Birmingham to remain in cities that spurned them. When all the Dissenters had been vanquished from England and had established great trading cities in France and America, he promised, those who opposed them would have plenty of opportunity to rejoice in the fact that 'all the taxes, and all the tithes, then perhaps doubled, will be paid cheerfully by the *genuine sons of the church*.'[23]

Priestley labelled Pitt's Tories as supporters of arbitrary power; Fox's Whigs he characterised as friends of liberty. Burke might point to France as an example of what happened when religious freedom was unchecked but the true story of the Revolution offered a parable about the dangers of corruption from within. Church livings in the Ancien Régime and in the England of 1790 were stuffed with the incompetent younger sons of landed families and 'in the late glorious revolution in France this great abuse has not been overlooked. All the bishops, and officiating clergy in general, have been made *elective* by those whom their services respect, and neither the pope nor the king has so much as a negative on the choice of the people.'[24] If Burke and his ilk wanted to avoid revolution in Britain, Priestley warned, they needed urgently to reform corrupted systems that seemed designed to produce rather than prevent revolt.

The day after the defeat of Repeal, Anna Barbauld and her brother John Aikin sat down to write their own responses to the failure of their cause. Johnson sped both works into print, acknowledging the link between them with reciprocal advertisements. Aikin's pamphlet was angry and to the point: no one who had watched the conduct of the British government during the American war could be surprised at their authoritarian cowardice now. As much to blame as the government in Aikin's telling were middle-class Dissenters who had foolishly imagined themselves to be free. 'That nation which you have fondly thought, and which many of you have painted, as the most liberal and enlightened among mankind, has proved itself signally deficient in these qualities', he scoffed. 'So far from having caught new spirit from the noble sentiments now pervading Europe, it seems to go backwards in its policy, and to be determined by weak fears and narrow views to the rejection of every thing which is elsewhere called improvement.'[25] Aikin explicitly tied the Dissenting colours to the French Revolution, following Priestley in contrasting its glories to feeble Establishment England.

Aikin deliberately addressed the Dissenters rather than the population at large in a reflection of the way in which a national conversation was splitting along tribal lines, but his sister rejected such an approach. Barbauld addressed her pamphlet directly to the *Opposers of the Repeal of the Corporation and Test Acts*. Her rhetorical weapons were sarcasm and humour. 'Is the Test Act, your boasted bulwark, of equal necessity with the dykes in Holland; and do we wait, like an impetuous sea, to rush in and over-whelm the land?'[26] She mocked Church and State for allowing fear to spread through their ranks like an electric shock, adopting the imagery of scientific discovery to taunt them. Of the Church she was scathing. 'We desire not to share in her good things. We know it is the children's bread, which must not be given to dogs.' She accused the Church of acting like a jealous stepmother who 'with the two frequent arts of that relation' did her best 'to prejudice the State, the common father of us all, against a part of his offspring'.[27] One of the objections raised by Burke and others was that the Dissenters had not begged for Repeal with appropriate meekness. 'No, Gentlemen', Barbauld countered. 'We wish to have it understood, that we *do* claim it as a right ... We claim it as men, we claim it as citizens, we claim it as good subjects.'[28]

Barbauld expressed incredulity at the folly of those MPs who had voted against Repeal. Had the restrictions on Dissenters been lifted they would have disappeared as a homogenous and visible group, the apparent threat they represented to national unity neutered. Instead 'You have refused us; and by so doing, you keep us under the eye of the public, in the interesting point of view of men who suffer under a deprivation of rights.'[29] Repeal had offered a chance to lock the Dissenters' tongues with a golden padlock: now, with nothing to lose, nor was there anything to stop legions of previously meek men and women from rising up in protest. All the signs of the times were in the Dissenters' favour, she warned, drawing her metaphors from the work of Darwin. 'We appeal to the certain, sure operation of increasing light and knowledge, which it is no more in your power to stop, than to repel the tide with your naked hand, or to wither with your breath the genial influence of vegetation.'[30]

It was France and America, not England, who now showed the world as it might be. America offered an example of 'a mighty empire breaking from bondage'. France was nothing less than a country liberated from a nightmare:

> Her dungeons indeed exist no longer, the iron doors are forced, the massy walls are thrown down; and the liberated spectres, trembling between joy and horror, may now blazon the infernal secrets of their prison house. Her cloistered Monks no longer exist, nor does the soft heart of sensibility beat behind the grate of a convent, but the best affections of the human mind permitted to flow in their natural channel, diffuse their friendly influence over the brightening prospect of domestic happiness. Nobles, the creatures of Kings, exist there no longer; but Man, the creature of God, exists there. Millions of men exist there who, only now, truly begin to exist, and hail with shouts of grateful acclamation the better birth-day of their country. Go on, generous nation, set the world as an example of virtues as you have of talents. Be our model, as we have been yours.[31]

Barbauld's vision of pre-Revolutionary France owed a great deal to Gothic fiction. France becomes a place of darkness, dominated by the black mass of the Bastille, peopled by sinister monks and oppressed nuns. The language of fiction allowed Barbauld to cast the fate of entire groups of people in metaphor. Nobles exist no longer: their fate is simply to be disappeared in favour of 'man'. Their disappearance is the natural consequence of the diffusion of knowledge: the mechanisms by which they are dethroned are left unspecified. In March 1790 Paris appeared calm enough for the fiction of a bloodless revolution to be maintained, but Barbauld's prose contains an acknowledgement that not all men will benefit from the liberty spreading through the globe. Her conclusion, that Revolutionary France should now be the model for Britain, could hardly have been more explicit. In her final reckoning Barbauld made it clear that liberty would only prevail when a nation's citizens came together to form a community of equals. She announced that God was on her side as she established herself as the spokesperson for men and women of all faiths who wanted more for their country and themselves.

An Address to the Opposers of the Repeal of the Corporation and Test Acts was the most overtly political work of Barbauld's career. She published anonymously but her authorship was hinted at suggestively in the periodical press. In the Address Barbauld insisted on the importance of unity and looked forwardly piously to a time when religious divisions would no longer provoke discord in the country. But her rhetoric told a different story, illustrating that the actions of the Establishment had rendered national unity a forlorn hope. The Address demonstrated that there were two tribes in Britain: those who believed in Liberty and worked to aid its progress and those who feared its light. Barbauld took her argument to her enemies in order to demolish them, but at every stage she made it clear that she did so in response to a series of parliamentary manoeuvres that had translated religious difference into a national chasm. The effect of this chasm on the men and women who gathered around Johnson's dining table was profound. By the end of 1790, Barbauld, Wollstonecraft and Sarah Trimmer – women who had met at St Paul's Churchyard and who had once been united by shared professional interests – found themselves ranged on different sides of a political abyss. 'I am grieved to see by the Reviews, that Unitarian books multiply continually', wrote Trimmer in her diary in October. 'I am afraid that poison spreads itself: Oh that I could furnish an antidote to it.'[32] In Johnson's youth the making of books had been positioned by the example of his apprentice-master George Keith as an act of worship. At the beginning of the 1790s, as the Dissenters found themselves framed in the writing of others as enemies of the nation, the making of books became less a statement of faith than a proclamation of resistance.

17

Original Stories

As the old certainties of pre-Revolutionary Europe fell away, Johnson's authors embraced the creative promise offered by the experience of living through an historical moment without precedent. In concert with Darwin, Wollstonecraft and Johnson, Blake collaborated on volumes which celebrated distinctive kinds of artistic purpose. Blake was unusual among Johnson's authors in that he did not assess the value of his work in part at least through the money it earned him. For Cowper, Darwin and Fuseli, by contrast, money mattered a great deal in a world in which tired assumptions about hierarchies and value appeared to count for little. For all of these men, and for Wollstonecraft, new ideas about art, the professionalisation of creative endeavour, the nation's relationship with the past and its strengths in the present emerged as sources of possibility in a collaborative remaking of the artistic landscape.

For Johnson himself the years immediately following the outbreak of the French Revolution brought both professional success and the first intimations of physical frailty. In the August of 1790 Wollstonecraft returned to London after a short absence to find her friend looking thin and ill. When dinner was over she lingered as the other guests departed, in order to press Johnson for an explanation. 'He seriously told me', she reported to her sister Eliza, 'that some alarming symptoms in his head and arm, made him apprehend the approach of a paralytic stroke – a few years ago he had a very alarming fit – and he added, with composure, that he was settling his affairs that they might not be left in confusion.' Back home and unable to sleep for anxiety, Wollstonecraft sat up marshalling the arguments she would deploy to persuade Johnson to consult Dr Fordyce about his symptoms. She tortured herself with the memory of all the times she had poured out her sorrows to him, or when she had met his quiet care with anger. 'If I had lost a friend, who has been a father and brother to me ever since I knew him … I should be deprived of a tender friend who bore with my faults – who was ever anxious to serve me – and solitary would my life be.'[1] Wollstonecraft was not the only visitor to St Paul's Churchyard to write of Johnson's health with concern while he remained sanguine in the face of physical limitations. The composure on which Wollstonecraft remarked characterised not just Johnson's attitude to his occasionally troublesome body but also to authors and employees who brought creative disruption to the heart of his house and business.

+

Blake was chief among those with little regard for the established conventions of bookmaking and bookselling. A few months before the fall of the Bastille he effected a creative revolution on the ground floor of his house on Poland Street in Soho. He took an engraver's copper-plate and painted directly onto it, using an acid-resistant 'stop' varnish. The varnish allowed him to combine image and text on a single plate, painted in reverse. He etched away the uncovered areas of the plate and painstakingly daubed the raised surfaces protected by the varnish with a hand-mixed ink. He covered the inked plate with paper and passed it through a heavy roller press that took up an entire room of his narrow house. The press was heavy and noisy, with a great star-shaped handle that took considerable physical effort to move. Once Blake had printed the image he set it to one side to dry so that it could be ironed and stitched to others in the sequence.[2]

The first works Blake produced using this method were two short statements of his faith – *All Religions are One* and *There is No Natural Religion* – in which text and image mingled throughout. Blake later said that his decision to turn printer and take command of every stage of the bookmaking process was the result of his dead brother Robert appearing before him in a dream. In 1789 he published a book of poetry using his new method. It was called *Songs of Innocence* and was ostensibly written for children. Children appeared in virtually every poem, both in the illustrations and as speakers, subjects and auditors. In 'Introduction' Blake announced his own presence in the volume:

> And I made a rural pen
> And I stain'd the water clear,

> And I wrote my happy songs,
> Every child may joy to hear.

But Blake wrote with a machine, not a pen, and he did so in the heart of London and not by a rural stream. A child may well hear *Songs of Innocence* with joy but from those who know something of the world the volume demands more. In 'Holy Thursday' Blake memorialised the annual service of thanksgiving that gave Sarah Trimmer so much pleasure, in which charity children in their thousands were paraded for the benefit of their benefactors. 'O what a multitude they seemd these flowers of London town', Blake wrote. The children he represented as irrepressible; to their watchers he had a warning:

> Now like a mighty wind they raise to heaven the voice of song
> Or like harmonious thunderings the seats of heaven among
> Beneath them sit the aged men wise guardians of the poor
> Then cherish pity, lest you drive an angel from your door.

⁜

Blake called the works produced by his invention 'illuminated books'. He developed his printing method at a time when authors and artists had to relinquish control over their work as manuscripts were converted to type and rolled through letterpresses in a mechanised process that required the labour of several operatives. Copper-plate images had to be printed and slotted in between pages of text, making it impossible for image and words to appear on the same page. This division between two integral parts of his artistic vision was an anathema to Blake. At Poland Street he created a system in which every aspect of bookmaking (with the exception of the production of the paper itself) was within his command, freed from the commercial and logistical constraints experienced by printers and booksellers. In the illuminated books Blake brought his skill to bear on the creation of a new kind of work, in which the artist and poet could reject the transmission from manuscript to type. 'The labours of the Artist, the Poet, the Musician, have been proverbially attended by poverty and obscurity', he wrote in 1793. 'This was never the fault of the public, but was owing to a neglect of means to propagate such works as have wholly absorbed the Man of Genius. Even Milton and Shakespeare could not publish their own works.'[3]

The one thing Blake could not do alone was reach new audiences. He turned to Johnson, who had long been his most reliable and flexible employer. Johnson had given him free rein as he produced the images for Wollstonecraft's *Original Stories* and he shared Fuseli's estimation of Blake's skill. 'Blake is d—d good to steal from', Fuseli told his friends.[4] Several of those who watched them at work later recalled that Fuseli allowed Blake an exceptional degree of freedom when he passed his images to him for engraving, and that Fuseli produced his designs on the understanding that Blake would develop them further. In 1796 Joseph Farington, whose diaries offer a wealth of information about the art world of late-eighteenth-century London, recorded an evening with Fuseli during which Blake was the main subject of conversation. 'Fuseli called on me last night and sat till 12 o'Clock', Farington wrote. 'He mentioned Blake, the Engraver, whose genius and invention have been much spoken of. Fuseli has known him a great many years, and thinks He has a great deal of invention, but that "Fancy is the end, and not a means in his designs." He does not employ it to give novelty and decoration to regular conceptions; but the whole of his aim is to produce singular shapes and odd combinations.'[5]

The relationship between 'Blake, the Engraver' and Johnson was professional but cooperative. Johnson might have been Blake's employer but both were tradesmen committed to and identified by their craft. Johnson offered Blake the chance to display samples of the illuminated works in his shop so that they might be seen by passersby who knew nothing of their maker. 'You will see several more of Blake's books at Johnsons in St Ps Ch Yd,' reported an antiquary and bibliophile called Richard Twiss to a fellow enthusiast.[6] Every edition of Blake's work required a significant investment of time, physical effort and ink-and-paper resources. By showing samples at St Paul's Churchyard Blake was able to secure buyers before he printed new editions and Twiss's letter reveals that this system had some success, as news of his designs circulated among a select group of bookish connoisseurs.

Blake was an artist before he was a poet but the experience of producing the illuminated pages of *Songs of Innocence* convinced him that word as well as image offered a way to speak of his visions. In 1791 he produced a text without illustrations and handed it to Johnson, who agreed to set it in proof. Blake described it as a poem in seven books, a prophetic work. Called *The French Revolution*, it told the story of the Revolution through a series of extended metaphors. The Bastille stands at the centre of the poem, representing all that is wrong in pre-Revolutionary France. The country itself is peopled with a combination of real, fictional and mythic characters, some of whom appear elsewhere in Blake's work. Blake wrote of the American Revolution as an event which precipitated convulsion in France and he was uncompromising about the challenge both revolutions represented to tyranny.

> France shakes!
> And the heavens of France
> Perplex'd vibrate round each careful countenance! Darkness of old
> times around them
> Utters loud despair, shadowing Paris; her grey towers groan, and the
> Bastille trembles.[7]

The first book of *The French Revolution* covers the summer of 1789. By 1791, when Johnson set Blake's stanzas in type, the violence of the Revolution was apparent to all those who had initially greeted it with triumph. In the advertisement to the poem Blake promised readers that 'the remaining Books of this Poem are finished, and will be published in their Order', but the proof of the first book was never reprinted and no more books appeared. Johnson may have baulked at publishing a prophetic celebration of Revolution as news of bloodshed on the streets of Paris filtered back across the Channel. It is also possible that Blake, who was as mercurial as he was brilliant, may have diverted his enormous creative attention elsewhere.

In 1793 Blake and Johnson came together once more as publisher and author, joining as co-publishers on the title page of Blake's *For Children: The Gates of Paradise*. On this occasion it was Blake's press that produced the illuminated frontispiece and Blake who etched Johnson's name onto the title page. He may have done so to formalise Johnson's role as his chief bookseller, replicating an arrangement common with Johnson's regional authors, including Priestley, who sometimes printed close to home and who acted with Johnson to place his name on the title page so they could check proofs before sending them to London for sale. In all their dealings in the period immediately following the French Revolution Johnson and Blake experimented with a hybrid model of publication which married Blake's idiosyncratic mode of creation and production with Johnson's ability to reach a wide readership. Johnson was sometimes willing to let his authors control the means by which they disseminated their work, but only when he had confidence in the worth of the material they were producing. Blake's printing methods meant his illuminated books never reached more than a handful of readers and it was many decades before his work became more widely known. But in the early 1790s, as Blake himself was still in the throes of designing, writing, etching and heaving his star-shaped printer's wheel forward, Johnson ensured that the results of this process were on display, waiting for a reader who would recognise the engraver's genius.

The illuminated books did nothing to relieve Blake from the pressure to earn a living. Johnson understood this as intuitively as he understood Blake's need to publish his own work on his own terms. In 1791 he commissioned Blake to provide forty-four plates for an enlarged edition of Wollstonecraft's translation of Christian Salzmann's *Elements of Morality*. This was written for children and, like Wollstonecraft's own *Original Stories*, it followed Sarah Trimmer's example as it showed children the dangers of indolence and greed. Wollstonecraft drew attention to the similarity between Salzmann's work and her own in a prefatory advertisement. 'All the pictures are drawn from real life', she announced. 'That I heartily approve of this method, my having written a book on the same plan, is the strongest proof.'[8]

Wollstonecraft's translation and Salzmann's original followed an apparently well-trodden path, along which children who mistreat animals learn the error of their ways and those with money are instructed in the importance of paternalistic care for those without. Salzmann's ideas interested Wollstonecraft, but it was the necessity of paying for the roof that Johnson had put over her head that made her take up the project in the first place. Blake's illustrations, however, transformed the second edition of *Elements of Morality* into an artefact altogether more striking. The images he produced showed children as children. They offered child readers a rare thing: a sight of themselves, not as stylised dolls but as individuals who run, breathe and feel. 'What will become of me!' cries a child lost in a wood. The wood is tunnelled and dark; the child's fear is evident. When she was herself very elderly, in 1883, Barbauld's niece Anna Le Breton recalled the excitement of being given a book with pictures that captured so profoundly the experience of childhood:

Unlike the children of the present day who expect a constant supply of little novels, splendidly bound, and illustrated by the best artists, our little books were clothed in the plainest paper covers, with hardly ever an illustration, with, indeed, one exception, a translation by Mary Wollstonecraft of a German work, the text quaint and foreign, and full of wonderful pictures, which I long afterwards found out were by Blake.

Blake, she continued, was only just beginning to be recognised as a great artist, but it was his genius which 'accounted for the hold these designs kept upon my memory.'[9] The reviewer for the *Analytical* shared Le Breton's view that the quality of Blake's images was unusual, especially in a volume aimed at children. 'The prints are far superior, both with respect to design and engraving, to any we have ever seen in books designed for children.' The impact of Blake's work was all the more significant, the reviewer continued, given the different ways children experienced text and image. 'That prints, judiciously introduced, are particularly calculated to enforce a moral tale, must be obvious to every one who has any experience in education.'[10]

⁂

In the summer of 1791 Johnson handed Blake the most significant commission of their partnership when he appointed him engraver for Erasmus Darwin's new poem. *The Economy of Vegetation* formed the first part of *The Botanic Garden* and a companion piece for *Loves of the Plants*. With the whole work now complete Darwin finally agreed to sell Johnson the copyright for *The Botanic Garden*. Buoyed by the success of *Loves of the Plants*, he drove a hard bargain. 'I write for pay, not for fame', he announced to a friend.[11] It was a sentiment he repeated in January 1790 when he told James Watt that Johnson had offered £600 and that he was holding out for more. Johnson increased his offer to £800 and in February Darwin agreed to the deal. He was proud of the figure, writing to trusted friends and collaborators of the details of the agreement he had struck.

The Economy of Vegetation included lines in praise of Josiah Wedgwood's copy of the Portland Vase, as well as a long explanatory note in which Darwin attempted to describe and analyse the vase's intricate system of decorative symbols for his readers. By the early 1780s, when Sir William Hamilton acquired the Portland Vase, it had long been one of the most revered artefacts of ancient Rome. Antiquarians and art historians were particularly intrigued by the manufacturing techniques that gave the vase an almost miraculous translucency. Hamilton agreed to lend the vase to

Wedgwood for a year so that he could copy it at his manufactory at Etruria, where other classical pots collected by Hamilton had earlier provided the inspiration for Wedgwood's iconic black basalt stoneware. Wedgwood hoped that the process of replicating the vase would allow him to learn more about ancient ceramics and pioneer new artistic methods as a result. He also knew that copies of the vase, accurately rendered, would sell for high sums and offer a substantial return on the necessary investment of time and effort.

The only existing images of the original vase were protected by copyright and Johnson proposed to Darwin and Wedgwood that Blake should be entrusted with responsibility for four new plates showing Wedgwood's vase from a variety of angles. 'Blake is certainly capable of making an exact copy ... if the vase were lent him for that purpose', he wrote reassuringly. 'I see no other way of its being done, for the drawing he had was very imperfect.'[12] Although Johnson proposed the plates as an illustration for Darwin's poem both he and Darwin knew that the images would reflect as much on Wedgwood's talent and industry as on his friend's. Darwin might hymn Wedgwood's rendering of 'Portland's mystic urn' but words alone could not show the detail or the skill that Wedgwood had developed as he perfected his copy during years of expensive experimentation. Darwin included the note on the Portland Vase at Wedgwood's request and then, worrying that he had not told Johnson of this commitment, asked Wedgwood to help explain matters to the bookseller. 'I think I am rather in a dilemma about this, for I forgot to mention to Johnson that you was to have this account when I sold him property of the work', he wrote a month after he had accepted Johnson's offer. 'I think he can have no objections, since our printing that part would assist the sale of the book in my opinion.' Still, he fussed, it would be helpful if Wedgwood could add his voice in support. 'If you happen to see him in London, you will please to mention it to him.'[13]

Wedgwood agreed to the proposal that his vase should be engraved anew and Blake set to work, working either from images of the original vase or, possibly, directly from one of Wedgwood's copies. He added fig leaves to the figures of nude men, probably at the insistence of Johnson who had paid a high figure for the copyright and could not afford to jeopardise potential sales. When the poem was published the anonymous reviewer for the *Analytical Review*, who is likely to have been one of Johnson's circle and thus familiar with the intricate tangle of artistic and commercial

The Portland Vase

motivations underpinning the volume, singled out the lines on Wedgwood's genius for praise. 'Scripture and fable, the wonders of creation and the works of art, the discoveries of the philosopher and the inventions of the mechanic, are alike made to contribute to the splendour of his poem', he concluded. 'The allusions are learned, the illustrations ingenious, and the descriptions lively.'[14]

Wedgwood was not the only member of Darwin's circle to have his work featured in *The Economy of Vegetation*. Darwin's ostensible subject in the poem was the natural world but in a series of diversions and byways he celebrated the technological achievements of his fellow Lunar Men. Wedgwood's copy of the Portland Vase stands in the poem for the brilliance of British industry and as example of the unlimited potential of the symbiosis of invention, entrepreneurship, technology and art. James Watt's steam engine appeared alongside Wedgwood's vase; lines on the latter's abolitionist medallion demonstrated that the consequences of experimentation could be political as well as artistic. In 1790 Darwin sent the manuscript of the poem to his old friend Richard Lovell Edgeworth who in his turn showed it to his daughter Maria. 'My daughter says, that the manner, in which you mention your friends in your poem, shews as much generosity, as your descriptions show genius', Richard Edgeworth responded. Darwin promptly returned the compliment. 'Why don't you publish something wonderful, you who have so much invention?' he demanded. 'A century of new machines, with plates ... I should send you any, which have occurred to me – I think such a book would be new in its way, and would procure fame.'[15]

Darwin viewed poetry as the servant of science; the glories that inspired his own pen were both natural and man-made. In *The Botanic Garden* he wrote of the wonders of the natural world but also of the achievements of the friends who in workshops and factories were harnessing fire and water for their own ends. The generic hybridity of *The Botanic Garden*, in which poetry, prose notes and plates jostled for attention, was Darwin's own contribution to a conversation about how the world might be seen and made anew. It was his offering in a market where commerce drove innovation. He presented himself in letters to his friends not as a gentleman author, loftily above mercenary concerns, but as a tradesman in words, a manufacturer of verse. Johnson's willingness to pay handsomely for that verse appeared to Darwin as a vote of confidence as, between one tradesman and another, money acted as a proxy for quality. The subtle class distinctions apparent in the phrase 'Blake the Engraver' melted away as *The Botanic Garden* came to fruition, and as bookseller, engraver, potter and poet combined forces in a triumphant demonstration of their trades and their skills.

✠

In the spring of 1791, barely a month after Johnson and Darwin had agreed terms, news of their contract reached Cowper in Weston. The speed with which Cowper learnt of the £800 offered to Darwin testifies to the strength of the correspondence networks via which he kept abreast of the London literary world, as well as to the enthusiasm with which Darwin himself spread the news. Cowper learnt of Darwin's success just as he was putting the finishing touches to his translation of Homer. Fuseli had more reason than most to be relieved that the project was at last coming to an end. 'I heartily wish with You, that Cowper had trusted to his own Legs instead of a pair of Stilts to lift him to Fame', he had complained to William Roscoe eighteen months earlier. 'This I wish as much for my own Sake as for his; for I am deadly Sick of revising his foul Linen.'[16]

A year later, in September 1790, Fuseli finally washed his hands of the project, ending his unconventional professional relationship with Cowper and leaving the poet to complete the final sections of his translation alone. Johnson broke the news by letter, and Cowper responded with a formal expression of thanks for all Fuseli had done. 'It grieves me, that after all, I am obliged to go into public without the whole advantage of Mr. Fuseli's strictures.'[17] But he recognised that he had claimed enough of the artist's time. It was a wrench to part with a manuscript that had offered respite from the darkness for five years but Cowper looked forward to the prospect of receiving a substantial sum for his labours. On Christmas Day he complained that the printer was proving predictably and frustratingly slow, but in spite of the difficulties of long-distance proof correction he was optimistic about the prospect of sending his work out into the world once more. The revelation that it had been Johnson himself who had annotated the proofs of *The Task* inspired him with renewed confidence in his bookseller. 'I beg that you will not suffer your reverence either for Homer, or his Translator to check your continual examinations,' he wrote. 'I never knew with certainty, till now, that the marginal strictures I found in the Task-proofs were yours. The justness of them, and the benefit I derived from them, are fresh in my memory.'[18]

Cowper's confidence in Johnson was tested as the spring of 1791 gave way to summer. In April he was still complaining about the printer's tardiness and once again resorted to asking London friends to go to St Paul's Churchyard to check progress and exert pressure on Johnson in person. The subscription list grew steadily: Blake added his name. In June Cowper complained that Johnson was planning to go to press in July, just at the point that town emptied for the summer, at the end of the London season. The friends who wandered in and out of Johnson's shop to check on his industriousness sent contradictory news. Perhaps to pre-empt more visits Johnson called on Lady Hesketh at her London house. 'I am glad that Johnson waited on you, and glad that he acquitted himself so well in your presence', wrote Cowper in response to her report. He was pleased too, he continued, 'that he likes my prose, and [I am] fill'd with wonder that he likes my letters, because to Him I have hardly sent any but letters of Jobation.' Johnson, he concluded, was a rare being. 'I verily believe that, though a Bookseller, he has in him the soul of a Gentleman. Such strange combinations sometimes happen, and such a one may have happen'd in his instance. We shall see.'[19]

Cowper was always more conscious than Darwin and Priestley of the social distinctions between authors and tradesmen. Distance, as well as his own anomalous social position, prompted varying degrees of insecurity in his dealings with his bookseller. Sometimes he treated Johnson as his editor and critic, as an equal; at other moments, especially in letters to aristocratic friends, he wrote as if he were dealing with a pestiferous servant. At the beginning of July he received formal notice of the price Johnson was prepared to pay for his Homer, and all his finely graded social and professional anxieties burst out in a barrage of letters to both Johnson and the men and women who represented him in the world. The subscription had raised £1,144; Cowper calculated that the unsubscribed copies would bring Johnson £500 more. Johnson estimated the expense of the edition at £600 and offered Cowper £1,000 outright for the copyright, leaving Johnson a profit of £44. Cowper was outraged by the suggestion that the profits of the subscription should be his only if he sold the copyright, thus forfeiting his ownership of his work. 'This to me has much the appearance of giving me nothing for my copy', he protested to Samuel Rose. 'Or rather it has the appearance of [Johnson] being paid 44*l.* for accepting it.'[20]

Cowper's letters for July 1791 reveal the complex role money played in a relationship that was simultaneously professional and personal, and which was refracted through an intricate set of class preoccupations and distinctions. Some of Cowper's friends saw in Johnson's first offer the true character of a mean-spirited tradesman and were quick to undermine the poet's confidence in the bookseller still further. One of Lady Hesketh's acquaintances even suggested that Cowper should sign all 700 copies of the first edition to prevent Johnson from accruing a profit on clandestinely produced additional volumes. Cowper refused to do so. 'It would be calling Johnson a Knave, and telling the Public that I think him one. Now, though I do not perhaps think so highly of his liberality as some people do, and I was once, myself, disposed to think, yet I have no reason, at present, to charge him with dishonesty.' All Cowper's anxious equivocations were on display in his response to Lady Hesketh. 'I must e'en take my chance as other poets do, and if I am wrong'd, must comfort myself with what somebody has said – That Authors are the natural prey of Booksellers.'[21] Cowper's usually fluent pen stumbled when he attempted to respond to Johnson himself and in his letters he was unable to prevent professional jealousy of Darwin from breaking through. Surely, he wrote, he must have misunderstood Johnson's offer? If not, 'I should have no other reward of my labours than the Thousand pounds which you propose to give for the copyright.' This, he continued, was 'a recompense short of what I have been taught to look for, judging by the sums which have been given not long since for works of much less length and difficulty, and if, I am well inform'd, even by yourself.'[22]

Johnson was taken aback by the anger with which Cowper and his satellites greeted his proposals. At the end of the second week of July he reached an agreement with the poet's old friend, Joseph Hill, who had come to St Paul's Churchyard in order to resolve the impasse. The sums at issue remained the same but Johnson proposed that Cowper should retain the copyright to his work. To Lady Hesketh Cowper professed himself still disappointed in Johnson's conduct. 'I am not much better pleased with that Dealer in authors than yourself.'[23] Writing a day later to Hill, he expressed relief that an agreement had been reached, although he was still brooding on the treatment Johnson accorded to favoured friends. 'At least if it be true, as I have good reason to believe it is, that he gave Dr. Darwin eight hundred pounds for his *Loves of the Plants*, it then seemed strange that he should propose to get my Homer for nothing.'[24] Cowper's circumstances were sufficiently straitened for money to matter because of what it could buy as well as what it represented, but his emphasis on the disparity between Johnson's treatment of Darwin and that experienced by him revealed his fear of the effect of being out of the world. From his self-imposed isolation in Buckinghamshire it was all too easy to believe that he was of less importance to Johnson than were the authors who gathered around the dining table. The sense that he did not know the generous man praised by others worried him greatly. Even as he accepted Johnson's second offer the belief that he had been taken for a fool continued to rankle. 'He stands so fair in the opinion of some who have known him longer than I, not only as an honest book-seller but as a liberal one, that I did well hope for such an offer from him as would save both me and my friends all trouble.'[25]

The tussle over the terms for Cowper's Homer exemplified a tension at the heart of many of the relationships emanating from St Paul's Churchyard. Johnson's authors came together in his dining room as friends but also as providers of and traders in the written word. His house was a place where like-minded men and women gathered to eat and talk freely but it was also where deals were struck and from where literary reputations could be made and undone. For Cowper, who neither dined nor did business in the dining room, negotiating a relationship which was simultaneously personal and professional was fraught with difficulty. So too was the business of estimating his own quality in a world to which he had only textual access. 'The last was an anxious week with me', he confessed to Hill, 'not only for the pecuniary interest that I had at stake, but because I was desirous also to obtain such terms as might not disgrace me in the ears of the curious who shall hereafter enquire what I gain'd by my labours.' More important than the question of how he was valued in the marketplace was a perceived threat to the relationship which sustained his literary voice. 'It was irksome to me likewise to feel myself on the edge of a quarrel with a man who has not corresponded with me merely as a Trader in my commodity, but familiarly and almost as a friend.'

＋

I am sick with vexation – and wish I could knock my foolish head against the wall, that bodily pain might make me feel less anguish from self-reproach.[26]

In a series of undated letters, thought by the most recent editor of her correspondence to date from 1790, Wollstonecraft presented herself as a creature in the eye of an emotional storm. Her earliest biographer attributed the turmoil to an unrequited passion for Fuseli. This was a narrative supported by Fuseli and his first biographer John Knowles, and by Knowles's selective editing and destruction of Wollstonecraft's letters. Many subsequent biographers have taken their lead from Knowles, and a hopelessly one-sided love affair with Fuseli, in which Wollstonecraft tried and failed to insert herself as a third member of the Fuselis' marriage, remains at the heart of many interpretations of this period of Wollstonecraft's life. The fragments of letters that Fuseli kept give credence to his version of events. In those fragments Wollstonecraft told Fuseli that she loved him in spite of herself and that she had 'always thought, with some degree of horror, of falling a sacrifice to a passion which may have a mixture of dross in it.' In Fuseli she had met a man 'possessed of those noble qualities, that grandeur of the soul, that quickness of comprehension, and lively sympathy'[27] which were essential to a happy union between husband and wife. Knowles insisted that Fuseli was scrupulous in his insistence that he could offer Wollstonecraft only friendship and that she must moderate her demands accordingly.

In her 2005 biography of Wollstonecraft Lyndall Gordon cast doubt on the story of Fuseli as the innocent object of Wollstonecraft's untrammelled desire. 'Whatever it was that she had in mind', Gordon writes, 'it was a plan easy for a man of Fuseli's vanity to misrepresent'.[28] The literary scholar E. J. Clery has taken Gordon's argument further, suggesting that the remaining textual evidence speaks only of a crisis in which Fuseli was involved. His version of events, Clery writes, was 'believed without question ... by virtually every commentator since. Changes in our own work culture may at last encourage scepticism regarding this claim.'[29] The possibility Clery raises, that Wollstonecraft was harassed by Fuseli, deserves to be considered alongside the male-constructed account of Wollstonecraft throwing herself at a married man.

The physical and mental impact of Wollstonecraft's torment is visible throughout her letters. She told Johnson her stomach was violently affected by mental distress and that the pain left her barely able to bend over her desk, let alone venture out to visit him. She had borrowed more money from Johnson than usual and was too distracted to work to repay him; complications in her family's finances threatened to drive her to despair. Johnson stepped in to help her disentangle the mess and found himself lumbered with management of a row of houses in Primrose Street owned by Wollstonecraft's estranged father. When Johnson attempted to remonstrate with her about her mental state she turned on him angrily. 'I thought you *very* unkind, nay, very unfeeling, last night', she protested. 'I will say what I allow myself to think'. For his part, Johnson should do more to understand how she suffered:

> I am not the only character deserving of respect, that has had to struggle with various sorrows – while inferior minds have enjoyed local fame and present comfort. – Dr. Johnson's cares almost drove him mad – but, I suppose, you would quietly have told him, he was a fool for not being calm, and that wise men striving against the stream, can yet be in a good humour.

She was done, she continued, with listening to advice based only on heartless rationalism. God, at least, 'never disregarded an almost broken heart.' Johnson, on the other hand, was implicated in a suggestion that wounded her deeply, namely that she should marry an unattached older gentleman of his acquaintance. A friend of that gentleman had just visited. 'Pray did you know his motive for calling?' Of all people, Johnson should have known better. 'Pray tell him that I am offended – and do not wish to see him again! – When I meet him at your house, I shall leave the room, since I cannot pull him by the nose.' She was, she concluded, 'sick at heart', and she charged Johnson with meeting her pain with remorseless practicality.[30] She also told him that nothing in her circumstances gave him the right to make insensitive suggestions about her future. 'I am POOR – yet can live without your benevolent exertions.'[31] It is not clear how much Johnson knew of the particularities of Wollstonecraft's relationship with Fuseli, but from his subsequent actions it is apparent that he considered the artist to be an important figure in Wollstonecraft's life and he defended him against those who claimed otherwise. Nothing in the surviving sources suggests he suspected Fuseli of acting in a predatory way towards Wollstonecraft but little in his sex or position would have led him towards such a suspicion. Nevertheless, his attempt to secure a marriage proposal from an unknown suitor may have been prompted by a desire to separate Wollstonecraft from an entanglement he believed to be damaging. Her response demonstrated there were limits to the mingling of professional and private concerns that was increasingly a feature of life at St Paul's Churchyard. Wollstonecraft's unwelcome suitor was dismissed and Johnson did not attempt to settle his friend's future so directly again.

⚓

Johnson's own relationship with Fuseli remained at the heart of his domestic existence. When William Roscoe came to London he found artist and bookseller inseparable. Roscoe wrote happily to his wife Jane of an evening spent at St Paul's Churchyard in the company of Wollstonecraft, Johnson and Fuseli: Jane responded by reminding him that Fuseli was too egotistical to be reliable. 'To be on terms of Friendship with Fuseli there is a degree of Servility necessary.' She knew her strictures might be unwelcome to her husband. 'Don't be angry my dear R – but I never can think his merit as an artist adequate to the defects of his character in other points.'[32] For his part Roscoe was unable to resist the lure of Fuseli's conversation, despite his wife's disapproval. After one particularly tempestuous evening Fuseli had to apologise for an unspecified 'high misdemeanour', which caused Jane to retort angrily that Fuseli and Johnson had both behaved shamefully.[33] Jane rarely joined her husband in London and the descriptions she received in recompense for his absences were brief. 'On Friday our entertainment was at Johnsons' with Fuseli Bonnycastle &c', ran another of Roscoe's letters home. 'As this visit exceeds all description I must reserve it for a conversation.'[34]

In August 1790, as the capital emptied and the weather became sultry, Johnson and Fuseli left London for a seaside holiday in Ramsgate. There is no indication in the letters of either man that they were accompanied by Fuseli's wife Sophia, either on this trip or on any of the excursions they made to Ramsgate thereafter. In the 1760s and the 1780s they had journeyed to Liverpool in each other's company, visiting Johnson's family, the Roscoes and old friends from Warrington. In Ramsgate there were no comparable ties or obligations and they chose as their destination a prosperous and newly developed resort, sustained by and designed for coastal pleasure-seeking. Amidst the quiet of a town where they knew no one they wrote a joint letter to Roscoe. Much of their conversation that August was focused on the subject of Fuseli's future and they knew that Roscoe's patronage was crucial to Fuseli's reputation and survival.

Fuseli was rarely out of work but he was not his own master. At the Shakespeare Gallery in Pall Mall Johnson's rival John Boydell had developed a hybrid model for making money out of art. He paid established and emerging artists to paint scenes from Shakespeare for a fee. The paintings were exhibited at the gallery but they were also engraved in-house and the engravings offered for sale at a nascent gallery gift-shop. Visitors had the option of buying either a portfolio of prints or a luxurious illustrated edition of the plays. The profits went to Boydell himself. His innovation was to turn the book-buying middle classes into patrons of the artists and engravers whose time he bought. Fuseli produced nine paintings for the Shakespeare Gallery as well as multiple images for smaller-scale rival projects. In 1790 he was elected Royal Academician, a position which brought with it honour but no income. 'I have and am contributing to make the Public drop their gold in purses not my own', he explained to Roscoe. Were he a painter of fashionable portraits or a pet of the King it might be possible to make a living by his brush, but for the history painter to do so was impossible. But, 'I am determined to lay, hatch and crack an egg <u>for myself</u>.' More than anything he wanted to be freed to work without commission for three years, so that he might expand his artistic vision and ambition unfettered by the need to make money. Should he be able to do so he was confident in his ability to produce over twenty paintings, the sale of which would handsomely repay an investment. 'My Idea is to get a set of men (twenty perhaps, less if possible, but not more:) to Subscribe towards it. Suppose twenty pounds each annually, To be repaid either by small pictures, or drawings, or the profits of the Exhibition'.

Fuseli asked Roscoe to grant him artistic freedom. To value art in Fuseli's argument was to give the artist space to create new visions, to free him from the necessity of shuttling preparatory sketches up and down the country before granting him permission to paint. Fuseli asked for a degree of licence Johnson allowed to none of his authors, capitalising on a relationship with Roscoe that was based simultaneously on friendship and on the exchange of money for goods. Writing on the same piece of paper, and, for once, as a friend and not as a man of business, Johnson pleaded Fuseli's cause. The Shakespearean pictures produced for John Boydell offered all the proof needed of Fuseli's ever-developing talent, he reminded Roscoe. And, he insisted, he was convinced they were as nothing compared to the work Fuseli could produce if he were liberated from the need to paint to order. 'His plan has my hearty concurrence, & I have gone so far as to say that I would be one of six or even of three to support him in it; but he prefers a larger number.' With the scheme still in its infancy Johnson implored Roscoe to keep its details to himself, even as he sought to assure him that Fuseli's request stemmed from a desire for artistic autonomy rather than from financial necessity. 'It may be & I am confident it is unnecessary to tell you, but as such things are common in your experience I shall say that this is not ye. effort of a man whose circumstances are involved to save himself from sinking – our friend tho' not rich is perfectly free from incumbrances.' They would return to town together in a few days, Johnson concluded, where such matters could be discussed further.[35]

Fuseli's attempt to find twenty rich men prepared to back him without question was not successful, but Johnson did not forget his friend's dilemma. Perhaps, he reasoned, the commercial innovations pioneered by Boydell and others might be reworked to give Fuseli his freedom. Blake had taken control of his own production processes but made no money; Darwin had turned poetry into an art in itself as well as a tool of Wedgwood's trade and made himself a great deal of money in the process. What Fuseli needed was a scheme comparable to the Shakespeare Gallery, but in which he would command his own work and not simply be an artist for hire. Personal and professional threads intertwined once more as Johnson and Fuseli escaped to the seaside to plot new forms of collaborative artistic and commercial activity. Back at St Paul's Churchyard that autumn, a year after the fall of the Bastille, they were once again joined in their experiments by the writers and artists of the dining room who had new stories to tell about the potential of art and the trade in ideas in a revolutionary world, and to whom a complete reform of the nation appeared to be drawing ever closer.

18

Views of the Ruins

In November 1790 Johnson's fellow bookseller James Dodsley published a new work by Edmund Burke. It was entitled *Reflections on the Revolution in France and on the Proceedings in Certain Societies in London Relative to that Event*. From the outset it was a huge commercial success: eighteen thousand copies were sold over the course of seven rapidly printed editions in 1790 alone. Burke set the upheavals in France against a celebration of the stability of England. That stability he described as the natural consequence of a hereditary system of inheritance and governance. The owners of the great estates on which Britain's strength was founded passed their rights and responsibilities down to their sons whole and intact through the legal system of primogeniture. Similarly kings, the fathers of the nation, passed the crown down through the generations in a series of peaceful and organic transitions of power. In France, by contrast, Louis XVI and Marie Antoinette, the father and mother of the nation, had (along with their children) been assailed in the privacy of their bedchambers by the mob:

> A band of cruel ruffians and assassins ... rushed into the chamber of the queen, and pierced with an hundred strokes of bayonets and poniards the bed from which this persecuted woman had just time to fly almost naked.[1]

In these lines Burke transformed the English narrative of the French Revolution, turning a conversation about political systems and abstract rights into a Gothic horror story with a sexualised and suffering victim at its centre. He represented the Revolution as a human tragedy, in which a loving family were torn apart at the hands of a mob deprived of its senses by the incendiary rhetoric of irresponsible philosophers. The implications of the comparison Burke drew throughout his *Reflections* between French unrest and English stability were obvious. If the philosophers of England had their way – if they were allowed to corrupt an unthinking populace through utopian dreams of political liberty – then no loyal Englishman would be safe on his throne, on his land, in his house or in his bed.

Reflections on the Revolution in France became universally known after its first publication by the shortened version of its title, but for Johnson and his authors the second part of the title – *And on the Proceedings in Certain Societies in London Relative to that Event* – was of equal significance. Burke opened with an extended attack on the Revolution Society and another reform group, the Society for Constitutional Information. Both societies had sent supportive addresses to the French National Assembly and in his opening paragraphs Burke accused them of subverting the ideals of both the Revolution of 1688 and the British constitution. Johnson had been a member of the Revolution Society since its foundation in 1788 and, along with Priestley and Christie, he was also a member of the Society for Constitutional Information (known as the SCI) by 1792. The date at which Johnson joined the SCI is not known, but he acted as their publisher in 1791 or 1792 and his name appears on a subscription list from 1793, as well as on an undated list of members who contributed financial assistance to those fighting for the 'cause of freedom' in France.[2] Burke charged the SCI with sending inflammatory books and pamphlets to France, subverting their ostensibly charitable purpose. Although he thought such behaviour irresponsible he was dismissive of its impact. Nothing the SCI had achieved, he insisted, could be considered 'except by some of themselves, as of any serious consequence.'[3]

Burke regarded the threat presented by the Revolution Society as much more serious. He described it as a 'club of dissenters' who had knowingly infected their pulpits with politics. He acknowledged that there was nothing objectionable in the founding principles of the club but suggested that it had been infiltrated by those who saw it as an instrument through which national security might be undermined. Burke professed himself deeply suspicious of philosophy stripped of context, insisting that to valorise abstractions without considering the practical consequences was a dangerous game. In an analogy explicitly designed to link the investigations of Priestley and the French chemists with the chaos he saw unfolding in France he compared unregulated liberty to 'wild *gas*' broken loose. 'We ought', he cautioned, 'to suspend our judgement until the first effervescence is a little subsided, till the liquor is cleared, and until we see something deeper than the agitation of a troubled and frothy surface.'[4]

That such practical caution was 'below the transcendental dignity of the Revolution Society' was evident, Burke continued, from Dr Price's sermon on the anniversary of the English Revolution. Burke tore into Price's *Discourse on the Love of our Country* and into Price himself. He termed the sermon a 'porridge of various political opinions and reflections' that had infected other members of the Revolution Society with a dangerously incendiary spirit. It was 'the public declaration of a man much connected with literary caballers, and intriguing philosophers; with political theologians, and theological politicians, both at home and abroad.'[5] It represented an invasion of the pulpit by politics and illustrated the perversions of Dissenting belief. In this respect in particular it was an aberration. 'No sound ought to be heard in the church but the healing voice of Christian charity.'[6] He charged Price with denying kingship and set up a series of professedly logical progressions which suggested that Price had come dangerously close to treason. It was in response to Price that Burke wrote his famous defence of entailed inheritance as the principle on which Britain's stability rested:

> You will observe, that from Magna Charta to the Declaration of Right, it has been the uniform policy of our constitution to claim and assert our liberties, as an entailed inheritance derived to us from our fore-fathers, and to be transmitted to our posterity; as an estate specially belonging to the people of this kingdom without any reference what-ever to any other more general or prior right. By this means our constitution preserves an unity in so great a diversity of its parts. We have an inheritable crown; an inheritable peerage; and an house of commons and a people inheriting privileges, franchises, and liberties, from a long line of ancestors.[7]

Price and the Revolution Society had tried to overturn this principle and had compounded their crime by doing so in the religious setting of a chapel. To make matters worse, after Price's sermon was over the entire society had moved directly from chapel to tavern. The preacher in the pub was, Burke concluded, a sight to shock 'the moral taste of every well-born mind.'[8]

The immediate popularity of Burke's attack on Price, the Revolution Society and the morals of Dissenters was a blow to those who dined with Johnson. Rumours spread faster than did printed copies. In Birmingham Priestley combed the volume looking for a moment when Burke was alleged to have charged the Dissenters with triggering the Gordon Riots. Even without such outright libels the reality of Burke's argument was bad enough. The Revolution Society was rattled. At the anniversary meeting on November 4th Price himself took the chair and was warmly welcomed but a row broke out when one of the more radical members, John Horne Tooke, proposed that all peers and holders of titles should be immediately excluded. The motion was withdrawn following consternation from Lindsey and others about the damage such a decision would do to the reputation of the society and incensed members had to content themselves instead with abusing Burke to each other in private.

One of the earliest public responses to Burke came in a long review of *Reflections on the Revolution in France* in the *Analytical Review*. Johnson's anonymous reviewer was precise in his unravelling of Burke's 'monstrous and extraordinary doctrine'. Burke demonstrated an 'extravagant idolatry of ancestry and rank' and had come close to inciting the King of France to trigger a bloody civil war in his own territory. 'The truth is', the reviewer concluded, 'that brilliant as are Mr Burke's abilities, they are untampered with ... judgements. The dupe of his imagination or his passions, he despises arrangement or logical precision. He loses himself in a wilderness of words and figures.'[9] Burke, in short, had fallen into exactly the same sin with which he had charged the philosophers of the Revolution Society. He had been carried away by his own rhetoric and seduced into a position under-pinned by neither sense nor reason.

Wollstonecraft was the first member of Johnson's circle to produce a pamphlet-length riposte to Burke. She was angered by the attack on her old friend Richard Price, and by the failure of reason she saw in Burke's work. The lethargy with which she had struggled evaporated as she raced her response into print. On November 29th, less than a month after the first publication of *Reflections*, Johnson published an anonymous edition of her *Vindication of the Rights of Men*. Three weeks later he republished it, this time with her name on the title page. It was more overtly political than anything Wollstonecraft had previously published and from the first page it demonstrated that she had no intention of being bound by tame rhetorical convention. She addressed herself to Burke directly:

Sir,

It is not necessary, with courtly insincerity, to apologise to you for thus intruding on your precious time, nor to profess that I think it an honour to discuss an important subject with a man whose literary abilities have raised him to notice in the state. I have not yet learnt to twist my periods, nor, in the equivocal idiom of politeness, to disguise my sentiments, and imply what I should be afraid to utter.[10]

Burke had insulted a man of age and distinction and deserved no courtesy, either false or sincere. Had he 'as much reverence for the grey hairs of virtue as for the accidental distinctions of rank' he would not treat Price 'with such indecent familiarity and supercilious contempt.'[11] Given Burke himself appeared pathetically unable to keep his wits when he considered the plight of a barely clad Marie Antoinette, he had little right to slander Price for indulging in utopian political reveries. Wollstonecraft rebutted Burke's attack on Price point by point, but she followed his example in making the political personal. 'Observe, Sir, that I called your piety affectation', she taunted him. 'I speak with warmth, because, of all the hypocrites, my soul most indignantly spurns a religious one; – and I very cautiously bring forward such a heavy charge, to strip you of your cloak of sanctity.'[12] Wollstonecraft deliberately wrote herself into her response to Burke, aligning herself as Price's defender and friend. Friendship itself thus became explicitly political. Where Burke saw gangs of seditious literary caballers she saw friends ranged alongside each other, strong in their mutual support. She turned her emotions into a defensive weapon with which she cut through Burke's pornographically charged visions of the terrified French Queen. Even the haste with which she wrote became part of her armoury, as the enthusiastic *Analytical* reviewer noted. 'Notwithstanding it may be "the effusions of the moment"', *The Rights of Men* 'abounds with just sentiments, and lively and animated remarks, expressed in elegant and nervous language, and which may be read, with pleasure and improvement, when the controversy, which gave rise to them, is forgotten.'[13]

A *Vindication of the Rights of Men* was the first publication to appear in response to Burke and it marked the start of one of the most famous pamphlet wars in British political history. Responses to Burke flowed through printers' presses all over the City, some supportive, many deeply critical. The *Analytical* kept up a running commentary, reviewing as many of the pamphlets as space permitted. The assault on Price and the Dissenters was not a subject on which Johnson attempted to achieve balance on his list and no defence of Burke appeared under his imprint. Lindsey sent a series of agitated requests to Priestley that he would put his pen to work in support of Price and Priestley agreed, although tangling with Burke's prose left him sick at heart. 'I cannot read Mr Burke any more', he told Lindsey in December.'[14] Two days after Christmas Priestley wrote again to Lindsey to say that 800 copies of his *Letters to the Right Hon. Edmund Burke* were on their way to Johnson by carrier, and that Johnson had agreed to pay £50 for the copyright. By January the 800 original copies and the whole of a second edition of Priestley's *Letters* had sold out and Johnson was rapidly printing a third.

Like Wollstonecraft, Priestley alighted on Burke's defence of Marie Antoinette as particularly worthy of ridicule and like her, he attacked Burke for his slurs against Richard Price. Unlike Wollstonecraft, he was unable to resist the opportunity to resume the great argument of his career and his *Letters* rapidly branched out from a direct response to encompass a ringing defence of the Dissenters more generally. In *Reflections on the Revolution in France* Burke displayed all his prejudices as well as the avarice underlying his defence of the Established Church. Greed, Priestley countered, had led Burke into folly. 'Your opinion of the *sacredness*, and *majesty*, of an established church, is most conspicuous in what you say of its *revenues*. On this subject you appear to have adopted maxims which, I believe, were never before avowed by any Protestant, viz. that the state has no power or authority over any thing that has once been the property of the church.'[15] The controversy arising from Burke's inflammatory rhetoric had only increased the numbers of Dissenters worshipping in Birmingham; Burke's error was to fail to realise that sometimes events spoke louder than bombastic words. The Revolutions in France and America 'teach the doctrine of *liberty*, *civil* and *religious*, with infinitely greater clearness and force, than a thousand treatises on the subject.'[16]

Price was cheered by Priestley's defence and in an exchange of letters in January the two men consoled themselves with the thought that although they were targets for slander, world events continued to move in the right direction. To be attacked, Priestley wrote, was one of the 'necessary consequences of any man's distinguishing himself ... and there is no field in which a man is exposed to more serious hatred than that of politics.' And elsewhere they had good reason to be optimistic. 'I rejoice with you that the French Revolution goes on, to all appearance, so well', Priestley wrote. 'I hope the example will be followed in other countries.'[17] On April 19th 1791, however, as Johnson and his fellow booksellers continued to publish pamphlets in response to Burke, Richard Price died, aged sixty-eight.

Priestley preached at his funeral: William Godwin was in the congregation, as was Anna Barbauld. Priestley, Barbauld wrote, 'well delineated the character he so well knew ... He told us, [Price] had been thirty years his acquaintance, and twenty years his intimate friend.'[18] The immediate cause of Price's death was a bladder infection triggered by a cold, but his friends had seen for themselves how completely Burke had disrupted his peace and they held Burke to blame for his demise.

Two months before Price died Thomas Paine came to Johnson's shop with his response to Burke. His title, *The Rights of Man*, echoed Wollstonecraft's. In 1774, following a series of professional dead ends, Paine had sailed for America, carrying a letter of introduction from Benjamin Franklin. During the American War of Independence Paine established himself as one of the leading champions of the American cause and his pamphlet, *Common Sense*, became the most widely distributed work of the conflict. Paine's prose was clear and accessible: he spoke not to men of State but to the ordinary citizens caught up in the wars of armies and ideas. In Paine's account America represented freedom and England despotism. The clarity with which he articulated this distinction carried great power. But Paine understood that rhetoric alone could not effect change and he also pioneered a system of federal finance for the American army, founding a subscription fund which later developed into the Bank of North America. After the war arguments about the bank soured Paine's relationship with his adoptive country and in 1787 he left America to sail for France. In Paris he moved in literary and scientific circles, with whom he kept up a regular correspondence after his return to England in 1788. In London in 1790 he began work on a draft account of the French Revolution which evolved after the publication of Burke's *Reflections* into the first part of *The Rights of Man*.

Like Wollstonecraft, Paine wrote his response to Burke at speed and although he was not a gregarious or clubbable man word quickly spread through literary circles that he was preparing to do battle. By November 10th, a week after the publication of *Reflections*, Lindsey was able to report that Paine was at work, although 'as he is the most inveterate declared unbeliever I ever conversed with, he will give no proper answer to any but political matters.'[19] Paine finished his manuscript on his fifty-fourth birthday, January 29th 1791. The next day he presented it to Johnson who agreed to publish it and dispatched it to the printer to be set in type.

Paine was nothing if not direct in his attack on Burke and the corrupt systems Burke defended. An inbred aristocracy 'has a tendency to degenerate the human species' as well as to produce tyranny. The British hereditary crown had descended through tortuous inheritance patterns to 'one of the petty tribes of Germany', so that the hereditary principle had resulted in aristocrats who hated foreigners accepting one as their monarch. Representation in Britain was broken beyond repair: hamlets with no remaining inhabitants returned multiple MPs; the growing city of Manchester had none. In the face of such absurdity France offered hope. 'From what we now see, nothing of reform in the political world ought to be held improbable. It is an age of revolutions in which everything may be looked for.'[20] Paine was less interested than Wollstonecraft in defending Price but he took pleasure in assailing Burke, who he presented as a terrified tyrant. 'Through the whole of Mr Burke's book I do not observe that the Bastille is mentioned more than once, and that with a kind of implication as if he was sorry it is pulled down, and wished it was built up again.'[21] In the aftermath of the fall of the Bastille Paine had been charged by Lafayette with conveying the key of the prison to George Washington in recognition of the symbiotic connection between the French and American Revolutions. Burke's failure to acknowledge the symbolic power of the Bastille was emblematic, in Paine's argument, of moral bankruptcy.

During the three-week period in which Paine's *Rights of Man* was in press Johnson appears to have been subjected to political pressure of a kind he had never before experienced. On February 23rd, two days after the projected publication date (chosen so that Paine's work would be out before the opening of Parliament and Washington's birthday on February 22nd) Lindsey wrote to a friend that he had seen a finished copy of Paine's work and that it had many excellent passages. But, 'the book is so intirely republican, tho' full of most excellent matter, and contains such reflections on the Brunswick princes, that Mr Johnson, for whom it is printed, is advised not to sell it.'[22] Paine's biographer John Keane suggests that those who 'advised' Johnson were government agents who made repeated visits to St Paul's Churchyard while the book was in press.[23] Lindsey's cautious phrasing supports this suggestion, as does Johnson's response. On the day of publication he dramatically withdrew as Paine's publisher and Paine had to load the unbound printed sheets into a cart and drive them away. He scrambled to agree an alternative deal and, on the day Johnson withdrew, reached an agreement with J. S. Jordan on Fleet Street, to whom he took his cartful of paper. 'What is the case with respect to Mr. Paine's pamphlet?' asked Priestley two weeks later. 'Was Mr Johnson threatened, or did he take the alarm of himself?'[24]

In 1791 booksellers were as liable as authors for the contents of the work they printed. A few copies had already been bound when Johnson withdrew: Paine kept them and distributed them among friends. Lindsey knew enough about the detail of the volume to suggest that he either read an early proof copy at St Paul's Churchyard, or that he was in regular conversation with Johnson about the dangers Paine's argument represented to his bookseller. Jordan published *The Rights of Man* on March 12th, three weeks later than Paine had intended. A few days before Jordan published his edition Paine departed London for Paris, leaving final arrangements for the volume in the hands of friends. The success of Paine's pamphlet was as immediate as that of Burke's *Reflections*. On March 24th Lindsey reported that 700 copies of the third edition of *The Rights of Man* had already been sold.[25] To a correspondent who had written in praise of Paine, Lindsey was clear-sighted about the passages that had made it impossible for Johnson to publish. 'I am as much an idolator of Mr Paine's book as you are, and trust our nation will profit by it', he wrote in response. But, 'it wd have been more read if some things towards the latter end had been omitted. It still continues to sell rapidly.'[26]

The suggestion that Johnson was threatened with arrest while his printers set the pages of *The Rights of Man* is supported by the appearance of an uncharacteristically cautious review of Paine's work in the *Analytical*. The vehemence with which Burke had been attacked by Johnson's reviewers in December was replaced with a careful insistence that Burke and Paine's work enabled individuals to reach their own conclusions about the state of the nation. 'Fortunately for the present age, politics and government are no longer mysteries enveloped in the dark shades of divine right and feudal prejudice; in the present dispute men will be taught by their interests to determine on which side the force of argument preponderates.' Paine's plain speaking was just as powerful as Burke's eloquence. 'In a word, without subscribing implicitly to every principle which our author advances, we cannot in justice withhold this testimony to the work before us, that it is one of the most curious, original, and interesting publications, which the singular vicissitudes of modern politics have produced.'[27]

Johnson never knowingly took a step which compromised his ability to hold his household and business together and he never allowed one powerful author to drown out the voices of others. It is quite possible that he acted in response to institutional pressure. The prominence of the *Analytical Review* and his profile in the Dissenting community meant that by 1790 he was a person of interest to the government agents fanning out across London to prevent a recurrence in England of events in France. It is also possible that the advice not to publish came from friends concerned for his welfare (a suggestion made by Paine's friend and early biographer, Clio Rickman)[28] or that it sprang from his own natural caution and his reading of Paine's pages. The clarity of Paine's unadorned prose made him a threat in the eyes of the government; as a writer with the power to incite an unlearned citizenry to anger. However, Jordan was not arrested for publishing the first part of *The Rights of Man* and it brought him significant commercial gain, with 50,000 copies in circulation by May.

Nevertheless, the episode trained the attention of the authorities on Jordan, Johnson and Paine, and it also brought a new level of State scrutiny to the activities of writers and booksellers. Books that were written and priced for a wealthy middle-class audience represented less of a threat than those designed for mass circulation. One respondent to Burke was warned by John Scott, who became the Attorney General in 1793, to publish his work in octavo form, 'so as to confine it probably to that class of readers who may consider it coolly: so soon as it is published cheaply for dissemination among the populace; it will be my duty to prosecute.'[29] Johnson did not shy away from risk and he later offered to publish an abridged edition of *The Rights of Man* for mass circulation on behalf of the Manchester branch of the SCI, but he made every decision on its own merits and after careful consideration of the commercial, political and intellectual consequences. 'I am glad that Mr Paine's book is to be published as it was printed, though not by Johnson', Priestley wrote on March 14th. 'It will be read the more on account of the stoppage.'[30] Not everyone in Johnson's circle shared Priestley's enthusiasm. 'I have not seen Payne's book', announced Cowper in May. A copy had been offered to him (probably by Johnson) but '[I] refused to see it when it was offer'd me. No man shall convince me that I am improperly govern'd while I feel the contrary.'[31]

☩

'I hope care will be taken to prevent the repetition of the riots in 1780', wrote Priestley in March.[32] A new bill for Catholic relief was making its way through Parliament and although Priestley hoped it would succeed he feared the consequences of public anxieties about national security mingling with religious prejudice. In April, while he was in London for Price's funeral, Priestley preached a sermon to mark the anniversary of the foundation of New College in Hackney, a Dissenting academy opened with the support of Lindsey and other prominent Nonconformists five years earlier. Johnson printed the sermon and a volley of attacks rained down on Priestley in response. There was nothing new in Priestley being assailed, Lindsey reported, but this time his opponents were demanding that he be publicly called to account for his words. Meanwhile rumours were circulating that larger groups of Dissenters were plotting trouble. 'It is not easy to describe the panic fears that are entertained by many at the West end of the Town of Dissenters, Unitarians, favourers of the french revolution, as if the like was to be brought about in the same way, and that particularly the meeting to celebrate the anniversary of the French Revolution, the 14th of august, is the time assigned for the commencement of it, and a confederation at home.' Lindsey's pen slipped as he noted the date of the anniversary of the fall of the Bastille but there was no mistake in his analysis of the geographical division between the affluent, Establishment West End of London and the Dissenting merchants of the City. He was certain too that rumours of Dissenting plots had been started by members of the former tribe determined to stir up trouble. 'Those who invent these things I suppose have their views to serve their own purposes, but they often contribute to raise the ferment they wd pretend to allay.'[33]

In June the French Royal Family escaped their guards and made for the eastern frontier, where they hoped to join a group of loyalist troops and seek the protection of Marie Antoinette's brother, the Austrian Emperor. They were arrested at the town of Varennes and reimprisoned under closer guard at the Tuileries Palace. Louis XVI's fragile position as a constitutional monarch was dealt a fatal blow by his flight. No king acting of his own free will would have needed to mount an elaborate escape attempt: his actions gave his enemies all the evidence they needed that he was intent on the destruction of the reformed political order. For Priestley the episode both threatened the reforms on which he had pinned so much hope and revealed afresh the fractured nature of political debate in Britain:

Our anxiety during the King of France's escape, and our joy on his capture, cannot be described. The high-party here are mortified in the extreme. They would have had France involved in a most ruinous civil war, for the imaginary rights of one man. A majority, I fear, of Englishmen are in these sentiments, so that we are far indeed behind the French. In spite of all we can write or do, an attachment to the high maxims of government gains ground here, and the love of liberty is on the decline.

Priestley had been writing and preaching for years about the damage done by religious divisions and political tribalism and it was sobering to realise that the majority of his fellow countrymen remained slavish followers of unthinking loyalism. The influence of the Court and the government was so strong in Britain that 'nothing but public difficulties will open our eyes.'[34]

On July 14th 1791 Lindsey joined a Revolution dinner at the Crown and Anchor tavern, in the company of William Godwin, Rochemont Barbauld and other prominent supporters of the French cause. In Birmingham a celebratory dinner was organised for the same evening at Dadley's Hotel but Priestley stayed at home at Fair Hill. Rumours had reached him that local thugs were looking for trouble and he knew himself to be a prominent figure. Approximately eighty people did attend the Birmingham dinner. When they gathered in the middle of the afternoon they were heckled by a small crowd, but the diners made their way into the hotel through the shouts and the crowd dispersed. The dinner passed off peacefully and the guests had scattered before they returned, sometime after 7 p.m., to find that there was no one left to heckle. As the evening wore on the crowd became a mob, and when darkness fell, fuelled by drink and adrenaline, they armed themselves with flaming torches and made their way to the New Meeting, the Dissenting chapel of which Priestley was minister.

Priestley's biographer Robert Schofield has demonstrated that the actions of the crowd in the hours that followed were not accidental. Two days before the dinner news reached the local magistrates that a loyalist group was plotting trouble and two of the magistrates, Benjamin Spencer and Joseph Carles, were among the hecklers outside Dadley's. A third, John Brooke, lived next door to the hotel and rather than see the crowd linger outside his own house he appears to have suggested that they would be protected by the law provided they did not attack private property. Rumours circulated that a list of targets had been drawn up. Tempers rose and the Riot Act was not read. While men set fire to two Dissenting chapels (the New Meeting, and then the Old Meeting), an army recruiting party offered to help quell the disorder. Their offer was turned down. 'We have our plans', the magistrates are reported to have said. 'We have our own plans.'[35]

At Fair Hill Priestley had finished dinner and was playing backgammon with Mary when a group of young men hammered on the door. They had run all the way from town and were so out of breath they could hardly speak. Between them they gasped out the news that the New Meeting was alight and Fair Hill was the next target. Priestley scoffed at the idea that his fellow citizens would harm either him or his house but he nevertheless took the precaution of moving some of his most important papers upstairs in case there should be trouble at the door. Just as he was about to retire upstairs himself to wait out events his friend John Ryland arrived with a chaise and the news that a crowd were on their way and threatening murder. The Priestleys bundled themselves into the chaise with nothing but the clothes they stood in, leaving their grown-up sons to defend the house. They drove to the house of their friend and fellow Dissenter William Russell, who lived a mile away. From Russell's window they saw the meeting houses on fire. As they struggled to comprehend what they were seeing news arrived that the crowd had arrived at Fair Hill and were threatening to destroy Russell's house too.

The Priestleys were forced to get back into the chaise and drive on another mile to the house of Thomas Hawkes at Moseley Green. Hawkes's house was on higher ground and from his windows Priestley could see Fair Hill in the distance. He later recalled hearing shouts of exultation as the crowd arrived at his house and its defences gave way. Priestley's sons had extinguished all the hearth fires before they made their own escape so the crowd had to make do with weapons and fists as they set about destroying the Priestleys' home. They tried without success to make fire using the large electrical machine that stood in the library and in their rage they destroyed all Priestley's scientific apparatus and well as his manuscripts and valuable library. They ransacked the cellars and drank themselves into a further frenzy before finally succeeding in setting fire to the ruins. One rioter was killed by a falling cornice stone as they made their way to their next target.

For the whole of the next day, July 15th, rioters roamed the city, destroying the houses of Dissenters at will. At four o'clock on the morning of the 16th news arrived that the defences William Russell had put in place at his house were about to fail. As the crowd gathered strength for their final assault Russell's daughter Martha was among a group of women who fled the house on foot, carrying terrified children wrapped in blankets. They hid in hedgerows as drunken rioters rolled past and as she cowered in the darkness Martha heard men on horseback calling for her father's head. 'I know there's a d—d Presbyterian somewhere hereabouts, we'll have him before morning', she heard one man shout.[36]

Priestley kept moving, desperately attempting to outrun his pursuers. As the crowd drew near Moseley Green he got back into the borrowed chaise alongside Mary and travelled five miles out of town to his daughter Sarah's house at Heath-Forge. There they were greeted by the news that Fair Hill had been completely destroyed. Three more messages arrived by express warning Priestley that the rioters were making their way to Heath-Forge and that nothing less than his life would satisfy them. This time he made his escape on horseback, leaving Mary behind with her son-in-law and heavily pregnant daughter. Everywhere he went, over the course of three exhausting days and nights during which he hardly slept, he heard news that his attackers remained active and dangerous. Exhausted, he made his way to Worcester where he caught the London coach. At six in the morning of Monday July 18th he arrived in London and sought sanctuary at Lindsey's house in Essex Street. The anonymity of the capital offered some protection, but Priestley still worried that his presence put his hosts in danger. So he shuttled back and forth between Essex Street and St Paul's Churchyard, watching over his shoulder as he did so.

In the Midlands the stunned victims of the riots began to count their losses. As the violence abated Martha Russell made her way back to her childhood home to find a smouldering ruin. Everywhere she went she saw the houses of other Dissenting families smoking and blackened. William Hutton, who awoke on the morning of the riots as one of the most upstanding and prominent men in Birmingham, recounted the disorientation of finding himself, on the evening of July 17th, 'leaning on a mile-stone upon Sutton Coldfield, without food, without a home, without money, and, what is the last resort of the wretched, without hope.'[37] In London Lindsey sent letters to friends with the news that Priestley was safe and in good spirits, but information from Birmingham was patchy and Priestley was wracked with anxiety about the fate of his wife and the impact of the violence on his pregnant daughter.

For four days the crowd ran riot through Birmingham and its surrounding towns and villages. Four Dissenting chapels were damaged or destroyed, along with twenty-seven private houses. Although many of those who joined in the violence were drunk and out of control a core of approximately thirty men moved soberly and systematically across the city, apparently acting according to a premeditated plan. By the time troops arrived to quell the violence on July 17th the ringleaders had melted into the background and most of the rioters had disbanded. The Birmingham magistrates refused to arrest those responsible and ordered the release of a handful of men captured by troops or special constables. William Russell made his way to London to demand redress from the State and Priestley began to make an inventory of all he had lost. His house was gone, along with his household goods, his books, manuscripts and all his scientific equipment. Pitt's government and government-supporting newspapers treated the riots as the natural result of the loyalism of patriotic men pushed beyond endurance by Revolution-inciting, Christ-denying troublemakers. William Russell's attempt to secure compensation and justice was met with official intransigence and the authorities in Birmingham made it clear to Priestley that he was neither welcome nor safe in their city.

In Johnson's circle the news of the riots was greeted with a mixture of anger, devastation and shock. Lindsey knew better than most what it was to be exiled from house and home because of religious belief, although his exile had been voluntary rather than violent. Still, 'we, who have been wanderers without a home, have some feeling of what he and Mrs Priestley must experience, thus stripd of every thing.'[38] Johnson's horror at the plight of his friend was palpable. 'I believe that if Dr P. had been found by the high-church mob he would have been murdered', he told Darwin.[39] Darwin in turn raged to Wedgwood that the riots were 'a disgrace to mankind. Active ignorance delights in depressing the sciences they don't understand.'[40] Cowper knew Priestley only by repute but he too was appalled by the reports that reached Weston. 'All the leisure that I have had of late for thinking, has been given over to the Riots at Birmingham', he wrote to Newton. 'What a horrid zeal for the church, and what a horrid Loyalty to Government have manifested themselves there!'[41] Lindsey had a different view about who held ultimate responsibility for the riots. It was Burke, he insisted, who had 'kindle[d] the present flame', and who was not content

Self Portrait, Henry Fuseli, c. 1779.

Fuseli's representation of himself confirms the intensity of person and expression upon which many of his contemporaries remarked.

The Nightmare, Henry Fuseli, 1781.

A version of this painting, which was first exhibited at the Royal Academy's Summer Exhibition in 1782, hung in Johnson's dining room.

Left: Theophilus Lindsey by an unknown artist. This image of Lindsey was included in Thomas Belsham's *Memoirs of the Late Reverend Theophilus Lindsey*, published by Johnson's successor Rowland Hunter in 1812.

Right: Joseph Priestley by Henry Fuseli, c. 1783. This portrait hung in the dining room at St Paul's Churchyard, alongside a version of *The Nightmare*.

Joseph Priestley by John Opie, 1791.

Priestley sat for Opie at St Paul's Churchyard in 1791, in the weeks following the Birmingham Riots.

Left: Anna Barbauld, née Aikin, by John Chapman, 1798.

Chapman based his engraving of Barbauld on images that circulated widely after she first became famous.

Below: *A New Map of the Land of Matrimony, Drawn from the Latest Surveys*, Anna Barbauld, née Aikin, 1772.

On Aikin's map an Ocean of Love divides the Land of Matrimony from Friesland (capital city: Singletown). The Ocean of Love is a perilous place, with Enchanted Islands surrounded by a Bay of Repentance and a Gulf of Reproach. The Land of Matrimony requires careful navigation by explorers around the Lake of Indifference, Henpeck Bay and the Land of Nod.

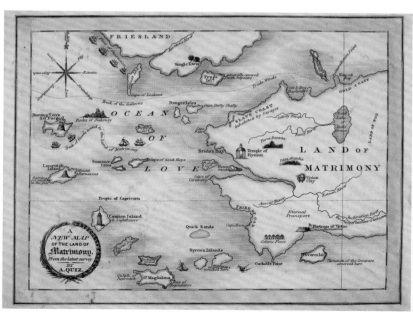

Mary Wollstonecraft by John Opie, c. 1790–1791.

In his first portrait of Wollstonecraft, which dates from the time when she was working on A *Vindication of the Rights of Woman*, Opie represents her as the philosopher interrupted.

Mary Wollstonecraft by John Opie, 1797.

Wollstonecraft sat for this portrait during her second pregnancy; after her death it hung in the study of her husband William Godwin.

Sarah Trimmer by Henry Howard, c. 1800.

Howard shows Trimmer as Grandmother of the Nation, pen in hand.

William Cowper by George Romney, 1792.

Cowper sat for Romney during his visit to William Haley at Eartham in Sussex. Cowper told Johnson that the drawing, which Romney coloured with crayons, 'is agreed by all here to be my exact counterpart.'

Erasmus Darwin by Joseph Wright of Derby, 1770.

Olaudah Equiano by Daniel Orme after W. Denton, 1789, represented on the Frontispiece to Equiano's *Interesting Narrative*.

Thomas Paine by William Sharp, after a painting by George Romney, 1793.

Iolo Morganwg by Ap Caledfryn, 1896, after an earlier drawing by an unknown artist, *c.* 1800.

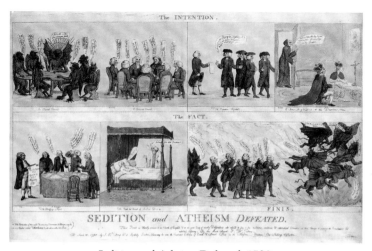

Sedition and Atheism Defeated, 1790.

The second picture from the left on the top row of this cartoon shows Priestley, Price and Lindsey in 'A Nocturnal Council' plotting sedition. In the frame on the bottom right the trio are chased by demons towards the flames of perdition. Priestley wrote to Lindsey to ask him to track down a copy of the print: 'My daughter wishes much to have the print in which we are represented as going to hell.'

The shell of Priestley's house after the riots of 1791, from
Views of the Ruins of Birmingham.

Satan and Death Separated by Sin, Henry Fuseli, 1799–1800.

This painting of Satan and Death evolved from the work on *Paradise Lost* on which Fuseli, Johnson and Cowper collaborated in 1791.

The Edgeworth Family by Adam Buck, 1787.

Maria is on the left in a beribboned hat smiling at her father Richard, who is pointing to plans lying between them on the table. Richard's third wife Elizabeth sits behind her husband with a baby on her lap; some of his many children gather round them.

with seeing Birmingham alone on fire. 'Our college at Hackney he stiles the Arsenal of sedition, as I am told by a friend, who remarked that he shd not wonder if it were some time or other set on fire.'[42] For his part Priestley told his fellow sufferer William Russell that he could only be glad Richard Price was dead and thus safe from the violence Burke's words had unleashed.[43]

At the end of July Priestley dined with Charles Fox's friend and ally, Richard Brinsley Sheridan. Fox himself stayed away from the dinner at the last minute, perhaps fearing the consequences of an overt association with Priestley. Instead he sent a message via his friend. 'They conceive that the encouragement given by the court to the high-church party was intended to crush Mr Fox, and those who took our part, and to intimidate both them and us.' Priestley sent this report to William Russell, who was spearheading a campaign for government recognition of the outrage. But Priestley himself was wary of Russell's approach and Fox's sympathy. Any acknowledgement that the violence had been politically motivated risked supporting the slanders of *The Times* and other Establishment newspapers, in which the riots were presented as a consequence of political factionalism between two warring parties.

Priestley countered this narrative with an insistence that the Dissenters of Birmingham were the victims of religious persecution which was in every way contrary to the spirit of Britain's unwritten constitution. 'I therefore differ from most of our friends here, and wish, with you, to shew no distrust of government ... our tribunal is our country and the world; and before this our court, as well as ourselves, must appear.'[44] Within six weeks of arriving in London Priestley had sped his own account of the riots to Johnson and on August 4th 1791 he watched the printers set the early pages of his narrative in type as he scribbled letters on scraps of paper gleaned from the workshop floor. With uncharacteristic caution he asked Lindsey to look at the draft of his account before it was finally set. Meanwhile William Russell had made his way back to Birmingham and was training his servants to use firearms in his shell of a house. When Russell left his grounds he carried pistols in his pockets and he wrote that more riots seemed inevitable. It was quite impossible for Priestley to return to the city, and even in London he feared for his safety.

Johnson published Priestley's *Appeal to the Public on the Subject of the Riots in Birmingham* at the end of the summer. The volume consisted of a narrative account of the circumstances that had bred religious tension in

Birmingham in the years before the riots and of the days of the riots themselves, and a reflection on the consequences of the violence. Both were
bound together with a series of appendices in which Priestley reprinted his
own letters to the papers in the days immediately following the violence,
copies of anti-Dissenting handbills that had circulated in Birmingham before
July 14th, supportive addresses from groups of Dissenters elsewhere in the
country as well as letters from Priestley's homeless congregation at the New
Meeting. In his narrative he documented his own losses – letters from
friends, his indexed library, priceless books and instruments – but he had
more to say about the losses the country had incurred as a result of a
governmental decision to allow the disorder to continue. 'It is something
extraordinary that persons used to a state of law and government should
not be struck with the impropriety of making a mob both the judges, and
executioners of law, and that in a state of intoxication, when they are not
capable of hearing any reason.' Had he been guilty of the charges ranged
against him – 'that I drank *No church, no king* and *The King's head in a
charger*, at a place where I was not present' (and where no such toasts had
been made), the most a court would have sentenced him to would have
been a fine or imprisonment. Yet the State had permitted the mob to carry
out its own punishment without allowing him any chance to prove his
innocence.

The dangers of such vigilante justice were enormous. 'If there is to be
a revolution in this country, similar to that which has taken place in France
... attempts to deter men by illegal violence from doing what the law does
not forbid, will, I am confident, bring it on in half the time. Men, who do
not like to be insulted, will at length be prepared to resist violence by
violence; and from such accidental inconsiderate sparks as these, a civil
war may be lighted up, and consequences may follow which the wisest
among us cannot foresee.'[45] Priestley framed his account of the riots as an
attack on a religious minority by an intolerant Church Establishment that
made ignorant drunkards its tools. The consequences for the character and
security of both Church and nation of so doing were severe. For the
Dissenters the riots represented the final failure of a fiction of toleration
under which they had suffered for a century. Priestley presented his own
case as proof-positive that to be a Dissenter was to be persecuted. Just as
the Dissenting ministers of Black Bartholomew's Day of 1662 had been
forced from their homes by a vengeful Establishment, so had Priestley and
the Dissenters of Birmingham, like Lindsey before them, been rendered

homeless as a result of their religious beliefs. The events of July 1791 were not a fair fight between political opponents, Priestley insisted. They were a State-sanctioned attack on a religious minority and a stain on the soul of the nation.

For three decades Priestley had thought, read, investigated, talked and written his way to enlightenment. In Birmingham he had gathered friends and congregants around him and had set no limits on the scope of his enquiries. In London in 1791 he was a refugee, driven from his home and the life he had made because of his commitment to religious and intellectual liberty. His fate suggested that for those who wanted a better future Britain was a barren land. For the supporters of freedom who struggled through the wilderness in the aftermath of the riots, the friendship of fellow believers and the prospect of a safe harbour became more important than ever. At St Paul's Churchyard, and at Essex Street, Priestley found both. In the *Appeal*, it was this that he celebrated. 'I have had such resources in my friends, and in those whom I did not before know to be my friends, as few persons in my situation could have had'. He had hoped never again to have to start afresh, but stripped of every possession he wrote that he was free to do God's will. 'Now I am light enough, and can move with more ease than ever, ready, at moment's warning, to go wherever it shall please divine providence to call me.'[46] Priestley wrote sincerely of the benefits to his faith of experiencing suffering and of the solace he found in the freedom to act according to God's bidding. But he was a scientist, a man of evidence, and his life's work was dedicated to assembling observations through which he could tell a story. The assembled evidence of the *Appeal* and the blackened shells of the ruins of Birmingham told a story not of consolation but of loss. Meanwhile in Birmingham upstanding members of the Church of England vowed to have nothing more to do with the Dissenters. The local newspapers printed article after article proclaiming that Priestley and his ilk had brought disaster upon themselves.

Priestley responded to the riots in the only way he knew. He argued his case calmly and repeatedly on paper, trusting to the day when his countrymen would finally be able to hear him. Johnson, who made his living through the production of text, understood that sometimes images spoke louder than words. In 1791 he commissioned an anonymous pamphlet, entitled *Views of the Ruins of the Principal Houses Destroyed During the Riots at Birmingham*. The pamphlet comprised a series of aquatint engravings of the ruins of Birmingham, each standing alongside brief explanatory text, simultaneously printed in English and French. The prints showed more powerfully than could any verbal description the true nature of what had happened. In a city celebrated for innovation and industrial prowess a frightened populace had been transformed into a weapon by a cowardly Establishment. The ruins of Birmingham stood for the ruins of a dream of a country in which men and women of different religious and political opinions might live peacefully alongside each other. 'Take care of yourself', wrote Priestley to Russell as the latter surveyed the ruin of his house. 'More difficult times … I fear, await us all in this country.'[47]

PART FIVE

REFUGE (1791–1795)

Thomas Lawrence, Sketch of Godwin and Holcroft at the
Treason Trials, 1794

The dining room is thronged with men and women of different generations who have come to shelter from dangerous streets. At one end of the table sits Priestley, shocked but not silenced, with Lindsey at his side. Old friends gather around them – Barbauld, Aikin, Darwin – drawing strength from shared anger and a collective determination not to be cowed by the taunts of a loyalist crowd. Others at the table also know what it is to be chased down alleyways by young men drunk on patriotism and fear: this is an experience shared by Thomas Paine and a new figure at the table, a Welsh mythmaker called Edward Williams. Clustered near Paine are Godwin and Wollstonecraft, who find during their first meeting at dinner that they cannot agree on anything. Seated amidst these individuals are less familiar faces: Mary Hays, striving to establish her voice within and without the Dissenting community; Joel Barlow and his wife Ruth, American visitors who befriend Wollstonecraft; William Wordsworth, lonely and in need of friends. Blake, as ever, appears in the dining room only briefly; Cowper remains present only through the medium of paper. At home among his visitors Johnson is still a quiet presence, but the government has decided it has heard quite enough from those who dine with him. When the bookseller speaks in the first years of the 1790s he is not in his home but in a courtroom, where he is required to account for his decision to give voice to the more radical among his guests. But although it is possible for Pitt's law officers to stem the tide of words flowing from Johnson's presses, they cannot stifle the conversations that take place over dinner. The effects of governmental action are still felt in the dining room however as, within the refuge it offers, that conversation turns towards the interlinked subjects of creative, political and physical survival.

19

Evenings at Home

'The state of things at B——m is really frightful', wrote Lindsey a month after the riots. 'Dr P. cannot come there with safety.'[1] Rumours circulated of a plan to attack Priestley in his pulpit if he returned to the city to preach. A lively literary subculture of anti-Dissenting pamphlets and handbills flourished in the Birmingham presses. During days previously occupied with writing and laboratory work Priestley sat for his portrait to John Opie, who had previously painted Wollstonecraft. The sittings took place at St Paul's Churchyard, under the shadows of an earlier portrait of Priestley by Fuseli, commissioned and painted specifically for the dining room.[2] Opie represented Priestley as contemplative philosopher, a stoic unmoved by the violence of men. In Fuseli's image Priestley is pale and his eyes are sunken. His hands are at rest and his attention has wandered from the papers by his side. Like the sleeper in *The Nightmare* his attention is elsewhere, but the background behind him is plain and dark and his visions have their foundation in work rather than dreams.[3]

In September, when Priestley travelled to the West Midlands in order to be nearby when his daughter Sarah gave birth, he was forced to avoid the main coaching route into Birmingham. Lindsey reported that it seemed sadly inevitable that 'the enemy' would succeed in driving him away from the city for good.[4] On November 6th 1791 Priestley was elected to fill Richard Price's place as minister at the Gravel Pit Meeting in Hackney by a majority of fifty-one to nineteen. Lindsey crowed that it was a decisive victory but Priestley took on his new ministry knowing a sizeable proportion of his congregation were opposed to him. He rented a house in Clapton, but the exigencies of house-hunting did little to make him feel secure or welcome. No landlord would let to him directly and in the end he was only able to secure lodgings after a supporter took a house for him in their own name. Even with such precautions the landlord took some persuading to allow the lease to be transferred so Priestley could lawfully inhabit the property.

On the first anniversary of the riots in 1792 rumours swirled that Priestley's rented house would be torched and those living nearby rushed to hide their valuables, while the mother of a local maidservant made a spirited attempt to summon her daughter home. 'On several other occasions', Priestley later wrote, 'the neighbourhood has been greatly alarmed on account of my being so near them.' And, he continued, with characteristic honesty, they had good reason to be fearful. 'I could name a person, and to appearance a reputable tradesman, who, in the company of his friends, in the hearing of one of my late congregation at Birmingham, but without knowing him to be such, declared that, in case of any disturbance, they would immediately come to Hackney, evidently for the purpose of mischief.'[5]

Priestley's house survived the first anniversary of the riots, although in Birmingham loyalists commemorated their triumph by a late-night storming of the house of William Hutton, who had remained in the city and rebuilt his property after the 1791 attack. In 1792 Hutton's house was left standing but his family were forced to the windows to profess their loyalty to Church and King before an angry crowd. Another victim of 1791, George Humphries, had his windows broken but was able to bribe his attackers before more damage was done.[6] For Priestley, who lived with the threat of violence but was beyond the reach of his most determined adversaries, the loss of the company of the friends amongst whom he had lived in Birmingham was as acute as his loss of security. At Clapton he made valiant attempts to reconstruct his library and laboratory but there was no compensating for the loss of over three thousand volumes and a lifetime's worth of manuscripts and carefully accumulated scientific instruments. Still, he took a house with space for both since 'without room for these things ... I am useless.'[7]

The Lunar Men of Birmingham donated what they could, and friends combed through the rubble at Fair Hill to salvage as much paper as possible. In the process they discovered that a locked box of correspondence from Priestley's oldest and closest friends had been opened and searched. Priestley had kept the letters as a memorial to friendships old and new, in order to have the pleasure of sometimes rereading them, and he viewed them as entirely confidential: his will stipulated that the contents of the box should be burnt without inspection. Now these documents were freely available to the authorities. In the face of this invasion of privacy Priestley resorted to a rare moment of sarcasm. 'Some of my private papers are said to have been sent to the secretary of state. But secretaries of state, I presume, are *gentlemen*, and consider themselves as bound by the same rules of justice and honour that are acknowledged to bind other men, and therefore, if this be the case, these papers will certainly be returned to me.'[8] It was brutally apparent that the only safe conversations were those that took place away from the public realm, besides hearths and over dinner tables. It was in those spaces, rather than in the poor replacement for Fair Hill which he rented in Clapton, that Priestley found relief.

⚓

When Anna Barbauld and John Aikin came to describe their ideal house they filled it with friends and paper:

The mansion-house of the pleasant village of Beachgrove was inhabited by the family of FAIRBORNE, consisting of the master and mistress, and a numerous progeny of children of both sexes. Of these, part were educated at home under their parents' care, and part were sent out to school. The house was seldom unprovided with visitors, the intimate friends or relations of the owners, who were entertained with cheerfulness and hospitality, free from ceremony and parade. They formed, during their stay, part of the family; and were ready to concur with Mr. and Mrs. Fairborne in any little domestic plan for varying their amusements, and particularly for promoting the instruction and entertainment of the younger part of the household. As some of them were accustomed to writing, they would frequently produce a fable, a story, or dialogue, adapted to the age and understanding of the young people. It was always considered as a high favour when they would so employ themselves; and after the pieces were once read over, they were carefully deposited by Mrs. Fairborne in a box, of which she kept the key. None of these were allowed to be taken out again till all the children were assembled in the holidays. It was then made one of the evening amusements of the family to rummage the budget as their phrase was. One of the least children was sent to the box, who putting in its little hand, drew out the paper that came next, and brought it into the parlour. This was then read distinctly by one of the older ones; and after it had undergone sufficient consideration, another little messenger was dispatched for a fresh supply; and so on, till as much time had been spent in this manner as the parents thought proper. Other children were admitted to these readings; and as the Budget of Beachgrove Hall became somewhat celebrated in the neighbourhood, its proprietors were at length urged to lay it open to the public.[9]

This passage is from the Introduction to *Evenings at Home*, published by Johnson in 1792. The full work ran to six volumes of stories, dialogues and essays. Aikin and Barbauld collaborated on much of the project but although Johnson capitalised on Barbauld's celebrity by emphasising her contributions it was her brother who provided most of the materials unearthed as a result of the budget rummaging. In *Evenings at Home* Aikin and Barbauld invited their readers into their own houses, giving the illusion of familiar immediacy through a fictional conceit. In their description of Beachgrove Hall they celebrated a fluid and capacious conception of family. All those who joined in the fun and contributed to the world of story-making were automatically included in the Fairborne clan.

'Home' carried great significance for Barbauld and Aikin, both of whom had been brought up at Warrington in a schoolhouse which was at once private and professional, where friends, colleagues and students ran in and out of the door. 'Home' did not entail shutting out the world or battening down the hatches; but rather in sharing its pleasures and its security with friends and fellow travellers. The children who invaded the domestic sanctuary of Beachgrove Hall to listen to stories have their counterparts in Aikin and Barbauld's readers, who are presented not just with a collection of tales but with an invitation to join the family.

In the summer of 1791 'home' was revealed as a concept that the Dissenters could not take for granted. The Lindseys had long known the reality of this truth. Now, in Priestley's plight, a new generation of religious and political dissidents saw the fragility of their own existences writ large. *Evenings at Home* was in part an elegy for the Warrington of the 1760s, and for a period before good men were driven from their houses by doctrine and flames. But it was also a proclamation of the Dissenters' continued ability to make their private spaces matter in the world: to celebrate their houses, schools and chapels as places where friendship, virtue and learning could be found.

At St Paul's Churchyard Johnson offered his writers and friends the freedom of his house and a proxy hearth. In the 1790s his dining room became a haven for men and women who were prevented by religion, politics and circumstance from claiming a sanctuary of their own. In the aftermath of the Birmingham riots the stories of Johnson's guests became ever more intertwined as they gathered around his table. In the streets beyond his walls an increasingly sophisticated apparatus of State surveillance trained its attention on the activities of all those suspected of unpatriotic disloyalty. Events in Birmingham had shown that the protections of the law were limited for those who questioned the new nationalist orthodoxy. In response Johnson made his home a refuge for all who needed to think, talk and be, and who were prepared to share the results of their thinking with the world via the medium of paper.

Simultaneously he drew around himself a family delineated by the bonds of sympathy as well as blood. Johnson's family, as constituted by the kin with whom he lived at St Paul's Churchyard in the 1790s, were all a generation younger than him. Rowland Hunter was seventeen in 1790. References to him appeared with increasing frequency in Johnson's business correspondence as he took on more of the burden of running the bookselling business and keeping an open house. Rowland's sister Hester dined with her husband Henry on many occasions and at one point sat for her portrait to Fuseli – although the results of the sitting are now lost. Johnson's brother John made periodic excursions from Liverpool.

Alongside these family members old friends gathered each week to dine and talk. Fuseli was a constant, noisy presence. John Bonnycastle often came in the company of his protégé George Anderson, a young official at the Board of Control. Lindsey shuttled up and down the Strand between St Paul's Churchyard and Essex Street, hailing chance-met friends in Johnson's shop, pestering the bookseller with orders and requests from a growing network of Unitarians scattered throughout the country. On his seventieth birthday, July 1st 1793, Lindsey retired from his ministry at Essex Street, but the chapel's board ordained that he and Hannah should be allowed to stay in the house they had built alongside it. In spite of this dispensation Hannah prepared for Lindsey's retirement with a whirlwind of repairs to the public side of the building which, she told an old friend, she was determined 'to get executed in the best manner possible, to put them in a good state into the possession of the Trustees.'[10] Hannah's energy did not dim as she aged. When Johnson fell ill in 1794, probably with an attack of asthma, she swept into his house, sorted through the post and gave a series of orders to the shopman.

Wollstonecraft was central to this constellation of kin and friends and Johnson carried the burdens imposed by her family alongside her. In 1792 she made arrangements to send her unsatisfactory brother Charles to America with the help of a new acquaintance met at Johnson's, Joel Barlow. An American adventurer, and follower of Price and Paine, Barlow had arrived in London in 1791 with his wife Ruth. He had been in Paris at the Fall of the Bastille and was a self-declared enemy of feudal and monarchical systems. He wrote Charles a letter of introduction and Johnson helped Wollstonecraft to sell part of her father's Primrose Street property to fund the purchase of a modest piece of land in Ohio for Charles to farm. It took him time to leave, and in June 1792 Wollstonecraft complained that he was lingering in London, wearing out the clothes she had bought for his voyage. In September he was still in town but Wollstonecraft was more hopeful. 'He has regained Mr J's good opinion by the propriety of his behaviour', she told her sister Everina. She attributed the change to the example set by the people Charles met in Johnson's dining room. 'The habit of order, which he is acquiring, by attending to business will, to use Mr Paine's phrase, "do him no harm in America"; besides, the company he mixes with at this social table opens his mind.'[11]

Charles might be settled, but Wollstonecraft's unloving and unsupportive father continued to claim financial support and the administration of his London property was a constant difficulty. In 1795 Johnson wrote to Charles to inform him that he had been obliged to make their father a gift of money, with the pointed implication that Charles himself might like to remember his filial responsibilities and make up the shortfall. Meanwhile Eliza and Everina continued to dog their more successful – and, in their eyes, fortunate – sister with requests for emotional support. In March 1792 Eliza wrote miserably to Everina of her need for a holiday from the drudgery of governessing at Upton Castle in Pembrokeshire, with the suggestion that it lay within Wollstonecraft and Johnson's power to offer her respite. 'Oh that M. and Johnson would spend a month at Tenby and we add our mite for never did poor wretch sigh more for society than I now do a total exile is dreadful.'[12] Wollstonecraft, though, had little interest in holidaying on the Welsh coast with her sisters. In the autumn of 1791 she moved from the house in George Street that Johnson had taken for her to larger and smarter lodgings in Store Street, near Bedford Square. John Knowles insisted that she did so in order to woo Fuseli, charging her with introducing 'furniture somewhat elegant into commodious apartments, which she took for that purpose.'[13] But in her move, as in her relationships with her sisters and brothers, Wollstonecraft was her own woman. In 1791, as the fragility of home echoed through Johnson's circle, she made a characteristically decisive move to establish a new sanctuary in a space and place of her choosing.

+

In the months following Priestley's arrival in London new faces joined the company in Johnson's dining room. William Godwin was a staff journalist on George Robinson's *New Annual Register* and a committed supporter of political reform. He and Johnson had moved in overlapping circles for years but in 1791 Johnson appeared for the first time in his diary. Godwin was an elliptical diarist and the majority of his entries are brief records of people met, calls made and received, reading and sparsely noted conversational subjects. Despite their brevity these entries are a treasure trove of information about the composition of radical and reformist circles in London. 'Tea at Johnson's, talk of Voltaire and Cicero', read the entry for December 20th 1793.[14] And, two weeks later: 'Dine at Johnson's, w. Blair, Mackintosh & Courtney'. Or, two weeks after that: 'tea at Johnson's, w. Courtenays & Blairs, talk of Brissot, Mirabeau & jurisprudence.' Many of the men and women Godwin reported meeting at Johnson's appear nowhere else in the historical record. It is thanks to Godwin that we can place Johnson's niece Hester in her uncle's house; and thanks to him too that we know the dining room at St Paul's Churchyard held a shadowy throng of writers, artists, theatrical prompters, politicians and scholars who remain unidentified, sitting alongside the relations and friends whose identities are known.

In 1791, when Godwin began to call on Johnson, he was in the throes of the composition and correction of his greatest work, *An Enquiry into Political Justice*. On November 13th Godwin made his way to dinner at St Paul's Churchyard, after a day spent mired in manuscript corrections. Johnson had invited him in order that he might talk to Paine, whose work he greatly admired. A week earlier Godwin had been left frustrated when his attempt to introduce himself and start a conversation with Paine at the Revolution Society dinner had ended in failure. A sympathetic Johnson extended an unusually precise dinner invitation to Godwin and Paine in order to allow the former the meeting he craved. In the early dusk of the afternoon of the 13th Godwin made his way from his lodgings in Moorgate to St Paul's Churchyard on foot, looking forward to stimulating exchanges with one of the most prominent political thinkers of the moment. But, as he later recounted in his biography of Wollstonecraft, the evening did not live up to his expectations. When he arrived he found Wollstonecraft in residence. He had not read her most recent work and he was sniffy about her *Vindication of the Rights of Men*, which he thought marred by grammatical and compositional offences. 'I had therefore little curiosity to see Mrs. Wollstonecraft, and a very great curiosity to see Thomas Paine.' But Paine kept silent and Wollstonecraft had plenty to say. Godwin thought her ludicrously gloomy:

> We ventilated in this way the characters of Voltaire and others, who have obtained from some individuals an ardent admiration, while the greater number have treated them with extreme moral severity. Mary was at last provoked to tell me, that praise, lavished in the way that I lavished it, could do no credit either to the commended or the commender. We discussed some questions on the subject of religion, in which her opinions approached much nearer to the received ones, than mine. As the conversation proceeded, I became dissatisfied with the tone of my own share in it. We touched upon all topics, without treating forcibly and connectedly upon any.[15]

A frustrated Godwin left the table early, retreating to the house of his friend Thomas Holcroft to complain. The best he could bring himself to say of Wollstonecraft was that she was evidently a woman of active and independent thought. For her part she thought Godwin a bore and could find nothing about him worthy of praise. 'Dine at Johnson's', Godwin recorded in his diary. 'Talk of monarchy, Tooke, Johnson, Voltaire, pursuits & religion.'

+

Other men and women who joined the company at St Paul's Churchyard in the early 1790s left less meticulous records of their presence. Joel Barlow and his wife Ruth dined sufficiently often during the months they spent in London to become friends with both Johnson and Wollstonecraft and to entrust the former with precious manuscripts when they left for Paris. In 1791 Darwin's friend Richard Lovell Edgeworth set up a temporary home at Clifton outside Bristol in order to seek medical treatment for one of his children. In November he was joined by his eldest daughter Maria, whom he had left at the family estate of Edgeworthstown in Ireland as his proxy head of household, and six of her younger siblings whom she brought across from Ireland to join their father. For two years the family remained in England. During visits to London Richard Lovell Edgeworth struck up a friendship with Johnson and, in the process, introduced his older children into the world of St Paul's Churchyard. Maria later wrote of Johnson as the most regular and reliable recipient of her father's voluminous correspondence but letters between the two men have not survived. At the beginning of 1794, once the family had returned home, she showed her father the draft of a work entitled *Letters for Literary Ladies*. The result, she told her cousin Sophy, was a manuscript 'disfigured by all manner of crooked marks of Papa's critical indignation, besides various abusive marginal notes, which I would not have you see for half-a-crown-sterling.'[16]

Edgeworth's delight in the severity of her father's comments reveals the conversational atmosphere of family life at Edgeworthstown and the intensity with which father and daughter worked together. Edgeworth did not always respond to her father's 'crooked marks' but he was her first and most engaged reader and she took his suggestions seriously. *Letters for Literary Ladies* was Edgeworth's work alone but her father was her collaborator as well as her first reader and in later educational projects they worked alongside each other as equals. In 1795 he arranged for the publication of her work with Johnson and Johnson responded by asking for more volumes. The Edgeworths went on to produce a collection of untitled stories written to help parents educate their children. 'I purpose calling them Vol I &c in the hope that you will furnish the rising generation with many more', Johnson wrote. 'I cannot think of an engaging title for I am a bad hand at it but perhaps something may occur to you.'[17]

Letters for Literary Ladies was a tripartite defence of female education and it revealed the influence of Barbauld. *Evenings at Home* 'we admire extremely' Edgeworth told her aunt in May 1794.[18] Like Barbauld and Aikin she understood the value of friendship and home, but she was more specific than them about for whom the security of home held most promise. Such security was, she insisted, crucial for women who hoped to live independent and fulfilling lives. The second part of her volume was entitled 'Letters of Julia and Caroline' and featured the wise Caroline advising giddy Julia about how to live a better life. 'Before you have formed for yourself companions in your own family, you will want a society suited to your taste', Caroline acknowledges. 'But ... the possibility of your forming such a society must depend on your having a home to receive, a character and consequence in life to invite and attach friends.'[19]

It may well have been through George Dyer that Johnson was introduced to another new guest. For Edward Williams, dinner in the warm dining room at St Paul's Churchyard provided not just intellectual or political comfort but the ability to keep body as well as soul together. Williams was a Welsh poet with a genius for reinvention. During a stint in Cardiff gaol in the 1780s, where he was sent after various business enterprises left him in debt, he wrote a treatise on the form of Welsh bardic poetry as well as copious poems in English. He also embarked on an ambitious programme of forgery, writing verse in the style of the great medieval Welsh poet Dafydd ap Gwilym which went undetected by literary scholars for more than a century. In 1791 he moved to London, leaving his wife Peggy and four children to survive by gleaning in Welsh fields. In London he rechristened himself Iolo Morganwg (Edward of Glamorgan) and invented an ancient druidic association called the Gorsedd of Bards of the Isle of Britain, whose first meeting he hosted at Primrose Hill in 1792.

Reinventing himself as the rightful son of the Welsh bards did not bring Iolo a steady income. In a laudanum-induced haze he wove his way through the London streets, battling to raise enough money to feed himself and publish his English-language poems by subscription. During the summer of 1792 he whiled away the days sleeping under hedges; at night he was tormented with visions of suicide and his children lying dead. His lodgings were just two doors away from the house where the boy-poet and fellow forger Thomas Chatterton had died from an overdose of laudanum. In Chatterton's fate Iolo saw his own end. He told Peggy he had no friends in London but in fact he was supported and championed by a network of wealthy Welshmen and he found companions among the political reformers who congregated at Johnson's shop.

Throughout 1793 Iolo lingered in the capital, watching political events at home and in France with absorbed interest. In April he learnt of the death of his three-year-old daughter and made for home. On discovering that she had been buried in his absence he had her body exhumed and reburied before he departed once more for London. By the autumn he was printing his poems and he wrote querulously to Peggy of the expense of bribing the pressmen and clothing himself. Moreover, he explained, the costs of friendship prevented him from sending more money home. 'I have so many literary friends that call on me to take an evening [c]up of tea and spend an hour or two in the morning or evening that more goes at one time on such occasions than would serve me for two or three days.'[20] But he had better news about the prospects of his poems. 'I was yesterd[ay] at Mr Johnson, St Paul's Church yard, and he told [me] that Dr Geddes, Dr Aikin and others of the first literary abilities spoke well of it and expressed a wish that I shou[ld] soon publish it.'[21] Johnson's generosity did not extend to offering to buy the copyright of Iolo's volume but for a man so concerned with reputation and self-presentation the support of literary men was still a balm. Iolo's *Poems, Lyric and Pastoral* appeared at the beginning of 1794 and he enjoyed a brief period of literary celebrity. When he finally left London, dragged home by the desperate straits to which his family had been reduced, he wrote to Johnson with a book order and 'compliments to literary friends that frequent your shop'. George Dyer, John Aikin and Anna and Rochemont Barbauld were among those he singled out, alongside Johnson himself and 'all others, all in your family.'[22] For the first part of the 1790s Iolo brought a whiff of bardic mysticism to gatherings at St Paul's Churchyard and he was evidently a figure of some fascination for Aikin and others bought up in the world of eighteenth-century rational Dissent. The exotic other was a role Iolo delighted in performing, particularly to men and women with whom he found himself in political sympathy.

✝

As the crowd who circulated in and out of Johnson's home grew larger the noise at the table grew louder. Fuseli figures in almost every account of a Johnson dinner from the 1790s. In October 1791 he wrote to Roscoe with a mixture of pride and anxiety, having heard from Wollstonecraft that Roscoe had been 'startled by the *ferocity* of my Conversation during your last Visit in Town.' Surely though, 'Affection, built on the base which, I flatter myself, ours is founded on, cannot be brushed away by the roughness or petulance of a few unguarded words.'[23] Roscoe himself wrote of Fuseli to his wife Jane with a mixture of exasperation and admiration. 'He is a wonderful man', Roscoe insisted. 'Certainly the most agreeable companion that can be when pleased, and even when not so his very anger and resentment may be tolerated for the sake of the wit and liveliness it produces.'[24] Others in Johnson's circle did not share this view. The simmering animosity between Fuseli and Alexander Geddes burst out into the open after the publication of Cowper's translation of Homer, as a row started at the dinner table continued in print. Geddes venerated Pope and was appalled by

Cowper's translation and the credit the poet accorded to Fuseli. Indeed, wrote his biographer John Mason Good, 'what appears principally to have irritated him, was Mr. Cowper's declaration towards the close of his preface of acknowledgements to "the learned and ingenious Mr Fuseli," whom he styles in the same place "the best critic of Homer I ever met with."' The result at St Paul's Churchyard, Good continued, was the throwing of 'much learned dust'. Even those at dinner who enjoyed debate grew weary of this argument. It was, Good acknowledged, 'not at all times to the amusement of the rest of the respective parties.'[25]

Fuseli squabbled with Bonnycastle almost as often as with Geddes, but between the mathematician and the artist arguments were ameliorated by long friendship. At one dinner the two men demanded that Johnson should adjudicate as to whose memory was best. Johnson responded by challenging them both to learn by heart a long passage from *Paradise Lost* at the table and against the clock. On this occasion Fuseli was declared the victor when he memorised the passage after only three readings. (Bonnycastle might legitimately have argued that Johnson had not played fair in picking the task, since at that moment there were few men in London more absorbed in Milton's poetry than Fuseli.) Sometimes conversation spilt over from the dining room into walks and carriage rides home. One evening Fuseli's confidence momentarily faltered as he and Bonnycastle travelled back to Fuseli's lodgings by coach. 'Pray Bonnycastle', he asked, 'what do you consider the reason that I am not popular as a painter, in a country which has produced Shakespeare and Milton?' Bonnycastle answered that he thought the public found Fuseli's visions alienating; that they preferred familiar subjects. Fuseli's response was uncompromising. 'Is that their taste?... Then, if I am not their painter, they are not my critics.'[26] William West, who also dined at St Paul's Churchyard and who described the food and dining room in detail, recalled that Fuseli had a rival as chief wit of the table in the form of the lawyer and radical writer John Horne Tooke, one of the leaders of the campaign for parliamentary reform. Johnson himself West remembered in marked contrast to his guests. 'He was from habit and necessity extremely temperate; and his quiet, shrewd, yet agreeable manners were sure to please; and the wit of Horne Tooke, and more particularly that of Fuseli, frequently created the greatest delight and good humour at his table.'[27] The result of all this delight and good humour, one guest recalled, was that it sometimes felt as if eighteen rather than eight people were sitting down to dinner.

Occasionally the laughter and the argument stopped completely. On April 26th 1796, Bonnycastle's friend and protégé George Anderson left the table early complaining of rheumatic pain. Four days later he was dead. Anderson was a remarkable man: the son of an agricultural labourer who taught himself mathematics by scrawling on the walls of Buckinghamshire barns. He came to Bonnycastle's attention when he entered and won a mathematical competition set by the *London Magazine* and he went to Oxford with the support of Bonnycastle and his local vicar. At his death aged thirty-six he left behind a wife and two adopted children. Johnson thought that the strain of work at the Board of Control had killed Anderson. The result, he told a fellow bookseller, was 'a dreadful chasm made in our little Society'.[28] At St Paul's Churchyard celebrity was no indicator of influence. It did not matter that Anderson's work and name died with him. He left a 'chasm' all the same.

✢

In November 1793 Priestley sent a letter to the collected members of the Birmingham Lunar Society. To his friends and fellow enquirers he confessed that 'there are few things that I more regret, in consequence of my removal from Birmingham, than the loss of your society.'[29] By the time he wrote this letter Priestley was losing faith in the feasibility of rebuilding his life in London. His three sons had already emigrated to America; he was known in the country as the old and trusted friend of an American hero, Benjamin Franklin. In February 1794 Lindsey wrote sorrowfully that the Priestleys' departure seemed inevitable. Priestley made the decision to emigrate later that month, although he wavered when his son-in-law refused to uproot his family and follow them. Priestley and Mary thus made their plans to leave England knowing it was very unlikely they would ever see their daughter Sarah again. The knowledge brought an additional sting to an exile which hardly felt voluntary. They spent March in a whirl of packing and farewells. There were sermons to be preached, farewell addresses to be written, friends to be seen. Their worldly goods were packed into nineteen enormous bales; Lindsey hardly left his friend's side. On April 9th Priestley wrote to Lindsey from Deal, where he was waiting to board a ship. 'This I hope will be the last time I shall write to you from Old England. Our Captain has just informed us, that if he falls in with the fleet of merchantmen at Portsmouth, he will join them for the sake of the convoy.'[30] Two days later he handed another letter to a sailor making landfall at Falmouth; then his correspondence fell silent as his ship pushed out into the Atlantic.

'How much we feel Dr Priestley's separation, in this house, where we commonly were happy in seeing him once or twice a week or oftener', wrote Lindsey a week later.[31] The next letter he received from Priestley himself was dated June and was posted from New York. 'I feel', Priestley reflected, 'as if I were in another world'.[32] He was anxiously waiting for a box of books from Johnson which he hoped to reprint and distribute among a liberal and enquiring populace. Of the voyage he had little to say, although Mary Priestley was more forthcoming about the strange experience of moving from one life to another and of spending weeks at sea. 'We passed mountains of ice', she told a friend, 'larger than the captain had ever seen before; and kept watch two nights, fearing we might come too near some of them ... We saw billows mountain-high, which by night appeared all on fire, and sometimes by night we were illumed around by the ship cutting her way through them.'[33] A gale made Mary angry rather than scared – she thought the sailors could have managed with more dexterity – and she advised any friends contemplating a similar voyage to lay in ample supplies of dried goods, reading material and patience. One family who did make a similar voyage was less lucky. Priestley's fellow Birmingham refugee William Russell set off from Falmouth with his wife, son and daughters the following August but four days into the voyage their ship was captured by a French frigate and they were taken prisoner. They were kept aboard for five months before being landed on the French coast in December. For six months they were marooned in Paris. The news of their capture was devastating to Priestley, who had pinned his hopes for the future on the presence of one set of familiar faces. He sent a volley of letters to influential Americans and French politicians pleading for the Russells' release but it was not until August 1795, a year after they had set out, that the family reached New York.

Deprived of the comfort of old friends, the Priestleys redoubled their efforts to make a new home. They moved from New York to Philadelphia and then to Northumberland in rural Pennsylvania, where they planned to build a farm. Johnson was dubious about the wisdom of this plan. Surely, he protested, the Priestleys would be better off in Philadelphia than in the wilds of the countryside. 'I am continually dwelling upon your wants & what you must suffer in such a wilderness, without even what we in this country call common society after having been accustomed all your life to the best.'[34] Johnson did not know, however, that the Birmingham riots had left Mary Priestley unable to contemplate beginning life again in another city. She had experienced the cruelty of crowds at first hand, and in London had lived with the knowledge that her family was at risk. After her arrival in America she refused to establish her home in Philadelphia and Priestley accepted her decision. He remained hopeful that in Northumberland he could create an ideal Unitarian community, to which fellow believers would be drawn by his presence. Meanwhile Johnson warned him not to place too much reliance on the vagaries of international mail. He would do his best to meet his old friend's demands for books and journals but Priestley should assume that three out of every four letters and parcels would be lost along the way.

✚

For Johnson – and, increasingly, for Rowland Hunter too – life at St Paul's Churchyard involved a great deal of work, as well as dinner. The faces trooping in and out of the dining room might alter in response to exile, death and more mundane changes in the daily rhythms in the lives of the guests, but the labour of running a business and keeping the larder and decanters filled went on regardless. Johnson's letters for the 1790s were concerned with transactions with other booksellers, the defence of his copyrights, the negotiation and administration of purchases and editorial suggestions, all of which came before discussion of friends met and lost, or the great political convulsions of the age.

Whether he was discussing the division of volumes with Maria Edgeworth, or plotting new editions with Cowper and Fuseli, or acting as the publisher and bookseller for Lindsey's Unitarian Society, Johnson appeared most frequently in his own words at work among his papers. Paper enabled everything that happened in his house, and occasionally his authors stopped to marvel at the miracle of their medium. Paper, Barbauld wrote in an essay in *Evenings at Home*, is 'a delicate and beautiful substance ... made from the meanest and most disgusting materials, from old rags, which have passed from one person to another, and at length have perhaps dropped in tatters from the child of the beggar.' The effort and ingenuity necessary to reanimate these scraps should, she insisted, never be forgotten. For the invention of paper 'has been of almost equal consequence to literature, as that of printing itself; and shows how the arts and sciences, like children of the same family, mutually assist and bring forward each other.'[35] Barbauld's imagery is striking. Paper and printing are, along with the arts and sciences, like siblings: part of a mutually supportive family made strong by numbers and contrasts. To work and live alongside others, in this account, is akin to binding individual sheets of paper into a book. Each sheet is fragile and easily torn, but bound together paper, like people, holds firm.

20

Things as They Are

The question now afloat in the world respecting THINGS AS THEY
ARE, is the most interesting that can be presented to the human mind.[1]

Thus announced William Godwin in the Preface to his 1794 novel, *Things
as they Are; or, The Adventures of Caleb Williams*. Godwin wrote that *Caleb
Williams* was designed to reveal 'the modes of domestic and unrecorded
despotism, by which man becomes the destroyer of man' to a readership
who devoured novels but did not have the time, education or inclination
to wade through works of philosophy. Godwin's publisher, Benjamin Crosby,
agreed to print the novel but refused to print the Preface. By 1794 any
attempt to reveal domestic despotism to a mass readership was dangerous
and Godwin knew men who had been imprisoned for so doing. Yet he
remained convinced that to speak truth required speaking of things as they
are, without fear or favour. The novel form offered an opportunity to protest
with a degree of protection from prosecution: who could possibly argue that
a mere story was seditious? To this challenge Pitt's government offered an
answer. Sedition, they proclaimed, encompassed every conceivable form of
expression, including the act of imagining itself.

✠

At the end of 1791 Tom Paine made a decisive move to increase the size
of his readership. In November he confided to a friend that he wanted
100,000 copies of the *Rights of Man* and the sequel he was writing to spread
throughout the country, with the cost to be held at sixpence.[2] He elected
to call the sequel *Rights of Man, Part the Second*. Once again he took his
manuscript to Johnson, who, in spite of his refusal to publish the first part
of *Rights of Man*, Paine considered as a trusted adviser. Johnson read the

draft and then handed it to Bonnycastle, whose politics were moderate. Bonnycastle's advice, according to Fuseli's recollection, was uncompromising. 'If you wish to be hanged, or immured in a prison all your life, publish this book.'[3] Jordan, who had published *Rights of Man*, Part I, also refused to allow his name to be put on the title page. Both Jordan and Johnson said they would sell copies of Paine's new work if he found a printer bold or foolish enough to print it, and with the help of Thomas Christie, the editor of the *Analytical Review*, Paine was able to persuade a printer called Thomas Chapman to set the manuscript in type. Chapman began work but Paine lingered over the final corrections and as he did so Chapman made a series of increasingly extravagant offers for the copyright – a hundred guineas, then five hundred, then a thousand. Chapman had nothing like the wealth needed to make such offers and it is likely that he was acting on the instructions of government agents who hoped to acquire the copyright of Paine's work and then supress it. Paine refused to part with his copyright, insisting that he would not allow his work to become a commodity to be bought and sold. According to the account he subsequently gave before a judge and jury, Chapman then thought better of publishing a work with such a 'dangerous tendency.' On January 16th 1792 Paine called on Chapman after dinner at Johnson's. He was drunk, Chapman reported, and a row erupted. Paine announced that all business between them was at an end and stormed out: a pious and upstanding Chapman told the judge he was grateful.[4]

Again Paine found himself with piles of printed sheets but no publisher. He returned to Jordan, who agreed to publish provided Paine provide him with a letter assuming full responsibility for the work. Johnson acted as Paine's bookseller and financial backer. On February 16th the first edition of the second part of *Rights of Man* was released. Within days Jordan was reprinting, probably with the aid of money advanced to Paine by Johnson. Although sales figures are difficult to estimate, it is clear that Paine's ambition for 100,000 copies to circulate through the country was rapidly realised. Cheap reprints followed Jordan's edition, enabling men and women far removed from the centres of power to absorb the stark clarity of Paine's analysis. Further revolution, he argued, was inevitable. Revolutions 'are become subjects of universal conversation, and may be considered as the *order of the day*.'[5]

The government response to the second part of the *Rights of Man* was three-fold. On May 21st 1792 they issued a proclamation against 'wicked and seditious writings' aimed directly at Paine. The proclamation gave magistrates the authority to pursue the writers and printers of so-called seditious writings, as well as all those who enabled their dissemination. One of the first victims of the proclamation was Jordan, who was charged with publishing seditious libel. Jordan immediately pleaded guilty and struck a deal with the office of the Treasury Solicitor (the equivalent of a contemporary Director of Public Prosecutions) to hand over all the paper relating to his dealings with Paine. Among the material he relinquished was a first edition of the second part of the *Rights of Man* annotated with a note that it had been bought at Johnson's shop.

Jordan had proved relatively easy to intimidate, but Pitt's law officers knew that to put Paine himself on trial involved considerable risk. Court reports and trial transcriptions circulated freely in the 1790s and to try a speaker as clarion as Paine was to give him a platform. Instead, in a second line of governmental attack, Paine was harried in person and in the press. Government agents followed him down badly lit streets. In a spot chosen for maximum publicity, outside the London Tavern in Bishopsgate, he was arrested and imprisoned for failing to pay a long-forgotten debt. These personal tribulations were gleefully reported in Establishment-supporting newspapers. One loyalist mock-heroic *Epistle to Thomas Paine* was excerpted by the *Critical Review*. The lines chosen for quotation included the assertion that it was Johnson who rescued Paine from the debtors' sponging-house:

> The time may come, when J—n's aid may fail,
> Nor clubs combin'd preserve thee from a jail.[6]

On the same day that the government issued the proclamation against seditious writings they also issued a summons for Paine to appear in court to answer a charge of seditious libel. The summons was for two weeks hence. The advance warning was deliberate: its aim was to force him into exile rather than into the dock. Again, Johnson came to the rescue. Friends found Paine a temporary lodging in a village outside the capital and Johnson hired a hackney-coach. He packed himself and Paine aboard, along with Paine's possessions. Fuseli, who heard the tale from Johnson, later related it to John Knowles. 'On their arrival at the new abode, Paine discovered that half a bottle of brandy was left behind'. A panic-stricken Paine pleaded with Johnson to drive back to fetch the bottle but Johnson was unmoved.

"'No, Mr Paine," said he, "it would not be right to spend eight shillings in coach-hire, to regain one shilling's worth of brandy.'"[7]

Paine returned to London when he heard the news of Jordan's guilty plea and the charge against him was temporarily deferred. By September rumours were circulating that the government had grown tired of his presence in Britain and was plotting his arrest. Blake's biographer Alexander Gilchrist told a story about a Johnson dinner that month during which Blake warned Paine that he was in danger. 'Paine was giving at Johnson's an idea of the inflammatory eloquence he had poured forth at a public meeting of the previous night', Gilchrist wrote. 'Blake, who was present, silently inferred from the tenor of his report that those in power, now eager to lay hold of noxious persons, would certainly not let slip such an opportunity. On Paine's rising to leave, Blake laid his hand on the orator's shoulder, saying, "You must not go home, or you are a dead man!"'[8]

The anecdote is apocryphal, but from more reliable sources it is evident that news reached Paine that his days of compromised freedom in London were over. On the evening of September 13th he left for Dover, in the company of three friends who insisted that the coach take a number of diversions to throw off suspicion. On the quay at Dover he was jostled and heckled by angry loyalists, who continued to shout and hiss as the ship carrying him to France edged out into the English Channel. In December he was tried in absentia in London and the jury delivered a verdict of guilty without retiring to consider the evidence. At the trial letters from Paine to Johnson were read out in open court and the extent of Johnson's support for a loyalist hate figure was evident for all to see. In Paine's absence his words continued to spread, as both parts of the *Rights of Man* were reprinted by reformers and campaigning societies. Surely, believed Lindsey, the volumes 'must promote no small change in the minds of men, and in time on all the governments on the earth, where such plain striking truths will probably be dispersed and adopted.'[9]

✦

In a climate of increased suspicion and paranoia, during which the friend-ship between Johnson and Paine was scorned in the conservative press, it was more important than ever for the Dissenters to hold together. When one prominent biblical scholar broke ranks to attack his brethren, the shock of Lindsey, Priestley and Barbauld was palpable. Gilbert Wakefield had served on the staff at the Warrington Academy and was an old friend of the Aikin family. He had also taught for a year at New College in Hackney, although he remained outside the circles who gathered in Hackney first around Price, and then Priestley. In 1791 he published an *Enquiry into the Expediency and Propriety of Public or Social Worship* in which he demolished the practice of communal religion and singled out the Unitarians for attack. Devotion should not be ostentatious or public, he insisted. God should not be worshipped 'as we pay our respect to earthly potentates, in crowds and pomp and tumult.' The Unitarians were particularly guilty in this respect because they claimed superiority over the Established Church. 'It much behoves those, who are so free in their censures of others, to consider, whether their own conduct be not in reality liable to *more* exception, in proportion to their louder pretences to liberality, and knowledge, and love of truth.'[10]

The Dissenters had grown accustomed to being attacked from without, but Wakefield threatened their internal unity at a point when they were particularly vulnerable. Events in Birmingham gave licence to public distrust of a group who proclaimed themselves separate and who refused to fall into line in the face of overwhelming public opinion. Wakefield did not merely attack doctrine: he undermined the religious rationale for communal solidarity. Barbauld and Priestley both raced into print with Johnson in response.

One of the most assertive responses to Wakefield, however, came from a woman barely known to Johnson's inner circle of Unitarian sympathisers. Mary Hays lived in Southwark with her mother and sisters and she worshipped intermittently at Essex Street. She knew neither Wakefield nor the men he had in his sights, but she knew how much benefit she had derived from the company of fellow congregants. 'I have myself experienced so much satisfaction, intellectual entertainment, and improvement, from an attendance on the public ordinances of religion, that I cannot without concern, see an institution which I am persuaded has been productive of consequences the most salutary, treated with acrimony and derision', she wrote, signing herself 'Eusebia'. She warned of the dangers, in an age of partisan controversy, of theologians turning against each other and treating religion as little more than a carcass to be disembowelled by argument. 'Christianity, by becoming a science, too frequently appears sour, haughty, and contentious; and in general the disputes which have disturbed the peace of mankind, have not been about justice, mercy, and love; but concerning curious, and perplexing points of speculation.'[11] Hays's *Cursory*

Remarks on an Enquiry into the Expediency and Propriety of Public or Social Worship was published by the Dissenting bookseller Thomas Knott in 1793. It drew her into precisely the kind of social and familial gatherings that Barbauld celebrated and against which Wakefield railed. She met Johnson and Lindsey and became friends with Wollstonecraft, George Dyer and Godwin. But even though the damage caused to the Dissenters' reputation by Wakefield was papered over, the divisions within the circle who frequented Johnson's shop were less easily obscured. When a group of young men studying at New College sensationally announced that they no longer believed in God, Lindsey was quick to apportion blame. It was Godwin, he insisted, who had done the damage, through his determination to spread atheistic ideas among the impressionable young. Even Johnson seemed distracted by contemporary events, and for once Lindsey found himself short of theological reading material. 'I do not know a book of any account that has lately come out', he told his old friend Russell Scott. 'Theological objects Mr Johnson says it would be fruitless at this time to strive to call mens attention to them. Nor has he any new work of that kind in hand, or has heard of any.'[12]

✢

'The approaching summer', wrote William Wordsworth in May 1792, 'will undoubtedly decide the fate of france.'[13] Wordsworth was living in the French city of Blois when he wrote this and was well-positioned to make such a judgement. He arrived in Paris in November 1791 and after a brief stay in the French capital moved on to Orléans. There he met a young woman called Annette Vallon, with whom he fell in love. By May Annette was pregnant and Wordsworth had followed her back to her home in Blois. The couple had no money and at the end of 1792 he returned to London, just at the point that Annette gave birth to their daughter, Caroline. In London Wordsworth was bereft. He had no hope of funding a speedy reunion with Annette and no clear plans for his future.

He took two poems to Johnson, who agreed to publish them as *An Evening Walk* and *Descriptive Sketches*. Johnson brought out the poems in octavo volumes and they were read with interest by the few readers who discovered them but otherwise they received little attention. Wordsworth also wrote a fiery polemic entitled *A Letter to the Bishop of Llandaff* which either Johnson refused to issue or Wordsworth thought better of publishing. The Bishop of Llandaff, Richard Watson, had attacked republicanism and the French Revolutionaries in a public denunciation of a movement he had previously supported. He hymned the British constitution as a model and Wordsworth was disgusted by his apostasy. He charged Watson with knowingly keeping the British people in a state of ignorance. 'Attempting to lull the people of England into a belief that any enquiries directed towards the nature of liberty and equality can in no other way lead to their happiness than by convincing them that they have already arrived at perfection in the science of government, what is your object but to exclude them for ever from the most fruitful field of human knowledge?'[14]

By the summer of 1793 Wordsworth had left London again, forsaking the sanctuary of St Paul's Churchyard just at the point that events in France and England rendered a reunion with Annette and Caroline impossible. Wordsworth was right when he wrote in May 1792 that France was reaching a decisive moment in the Revolutionary struggle. In August there was an insurrection in Paris. The Tuileries Palace was attacked and the Legislative Assembly was dissolved and replaced by the National Convention. In September over a thousand people were murdered in Paris's prisons, on the orders of the Revolutionary government. Over a hundred of those killed were priests. On September 22nd the National Convention proclaimed the birth of the First French Republic and the abolition of royalty. In December Louis XVI was put on trial, with Robespierre, the leader of the Jacobins in the Convention, leading the public outcry against him. On January 21st the King was executed in front of a Parisian crowd. Pitt's government broke off diplomatic relations with France and on February 1st the National Convention declared war against Britain and the Dutch Republic. France was already at war against Prussia and the Austrian Netherlands and the Revolutionary leaders were confident of their ability to export their brand of political reform across Europe through territorial conquest. With Britain and France at war, travel between the two countries became dangerous and those who remained in Paris sent back reports of systematic bloodshed and the first days of the Terror.

The government of William Pitt reacted to events in France with a series of legislative and political manoeuvres that became collectively and colloquially known as 'Pitt's Terror'. Britain had no revolution in the 1790s. No guillotine was erected on the streets of London and the King remained on his throne. But in 1793 the prospect of a violent revolution in Britain seemed all too real to the authorities. The declaration of war by Revolutionary France on Britain and the other monarchical European powers focused the minds of many parliamentarians and by 1794 parliamentary opposition to Pitt had virtually collapsed. The majority of the Whigs joined Pitt in coalition. Charles Fox, who had championed reform, was left with only a handful of MPs to defend the liberal cause. The proclamation against seditious writings in 1792 offered a foretaste of how Pitt's ministers would respond to domestic unrest, and it was followed by a series of laws that sought to clamp down on dissent wherever it occurred. In January 1793 the government passed the Alien Act, which limited immigration and banned French Revolutionaries from Britain (loyalist refugees were permitted to enter freely). Foreigners who were allowed to travel had to register with a Justice of the Peace and their presence in the country was made contingent on good behaviour. Fuseli was among the legions of international citizens who were threatened by the Act. Foreigners who offended the government could be held without bail or summarily deported. Their ability to speak freely was thus drastically curtailed.

At St Paul's Churchyard Johnson's writers felt the chill. In October 1792 Darwin had written of his pleasure at 'the success of the French against a confederacy of kings'[15] but the execution of Louis XVI meant that by the following February such statements were risky. The leaders of the campaign for political reform responded to the early intimations of a government clampdown by organising on a grand scale. In January 1792, five months before the proclamation against Seditious Writings, a shoemaker called Thomas Hardy founded the London Corresponding Society. Hardy's masterstroke was to design the LCS as a conduit through which political reform societies up and down the country could unite. The LCS had its own agenda, to campaign for political reform and universal manhood suffrage, but Hardy and his fellow founders realised they would only achieve their goals if they enabled a mass movement of political reformers that reached across the class divide. By developing a well-supported correspondence network, the LCS forged links with reform societies in the major industrial cities of the west and north as well as with the more genteel Society for Constitutional Information, of which Johnson was a member. In the spring of 1793 the leaders of the LCS coordinated a major petitioning campaign and for a few months, despite intense government suspicion, they managed to operate unimpeded.

The founders of the LCS were aware from the outset of the dangers posed by spies and they established a structure that was designed to make spying impossible. The LCS was divided into a series of divisions which were themselves subdivided into groups of ten members who lived and worked near each other. The groups of ten – known as 'tithings' – met each week to discuss political publications, petitions and possible actions, in a grassroots structure that gave the LCS depth and strength. The energy the foundation of the LCS injected into the English reform movement was matched by that demonstrated by groups of Scottish reformers north of the border. In the spring of 1792, as petitions for reform flooded into Parliament and Paine remained at liberty, it seemed as if legislative attempts to stem the flood of political pamphlets and campaigns had failed.

Pitt's government began to move against the leaders of the reform move‐ ment in both England and Scotland. In August 1793 Lindsey's friend and fellow Unitarian minister Thomas Fyshe Palmer was arrested in Edinburgh. Palmer had amended the grammar and toned down some of the fierier expressions of a pamphlet by a fellow reformer that called for universal male suffrage and protested against punitive war taxation. Palmer was arrested and charged as the author of the document and, after he refused to plead, citing a lack of evidence and his own ignorance of Scots law, the charge was changed to one of treason. He was found guilty and sentenced to seven years' transportation.

In December Palmer was sent to London in the company of two other convicted Scottish reformers, and placed aboard a prison ship – or hulk – at Woolwich, where he was held in chains. Friends and reformers younger and fitter than Lindsey made the journey there to visit Palmer and his fellow convict Thomas Muir. At the end of 1793 the Scottish reformers were joined in the hulks by other reform leaders, after the first national convention of reform societies (held in Edinburgh that autumn) ended in arrests. Lindsey was unable to believe that the government would be so vindictive as to carry out the sentence of transportation, and even after Palmer was transferred to a ship in harbour at Portsmouth he refused to contemplate the possibility that his friend would be taken across the world. In Portsmouth Palmer contracted dysentery and Lindsey made frantic efforts to send him money and medical advice. When it became clear that there was no hope of remitting Palmer's sentence his friends turned their atten‐ tion to raising money to bribe the captain so that the martyrs for reform would at least be permitted access to fresh provisions. Lindsey sent a Bible for the voyage. Hannah, hearing that Palmer's eyesight was failing, sent her own spectacles. After the ship carrying Palmer sailed out of Portsmouth he and Lindsey remained in touch over the years by infrequent letter, but although Palmer attempted to sail home after his sentence had expired he died on the journey.

Palmer's fate brought Pitt's Terror into the heart of Johnson's circle and showed how dangerous it had become to be in any way associated with the making of books that demanded reform. In May 1794 there was a further series of arrests. This time it was the turn of the leaders of the LCS and the group of which Johnson was a member, the SCI. Among those arrested were Thomas Hardy, John Horne Tooke (a regular visitor to Johnson's dining room) and the journalist John Thelwall. Shortly after Thomas Hardy was committed to the Tower of London a loyalist crowd attacked his house. His pregnant wife was injured as she fled and a few weeks later she died giving birth to a stillborn baby.

The government followed the May arrests by suspending Habeas Corpus, a manoeuvre that allowed the indefinite detention of political prisoners. In the days following the suspension government agents fanned out across London in search of paper as well as people. The homes and workshops of printers and reformers were ransacked in the search for evidence. Iolo Morganwg was one of those compelled to submit to State investigation. He told his wife Peggy that his possessions had been searched by the Privy Council. 'They are satisfied, they say, that I have seditious papers somewhere.'[16] In June Iolo found himself caught up in a drunken loyalist crowd:

> I was amongst this king-ridden mob in real danger of my life. They were egged on by parsons in abundance. I was afraid that the butchers who were parading the streets with their marrow bones and cleavers would have split my skull with one of them. They very frequently called out to the slavish mob: 'Down on your marrow bones, blast ye! and say God Save the King!' And down on their marrow bones to be sure they fell, especially the parsonic tribe, and prayed out what the butchers' boys dictated.[17]

Iolo's account reveals the extent to which the actions of government agents licensed the aggression of loyalist vigilantes, who roamed the streets with impunity, hunting for dissidents. The actions of such vigilantes in their turn licensed what the literary historian Kenneth Johnston has described as a series of 'overflow effects'. These encompassed 'university professorships denied, college fellowships taken away, expected inheritances lost, promised church livings not forthcoming, evictions from properties or tenancies, engagements broken off, reputations and businesses ruined by slander and innuendo, publications dropped, dramas gutted or rejected, contracts broken.'[18] It all amounted to a culture of surveillance and control, in which one's neighbours had the potential to be just as much of a threat as government agents. Only in places that were truly private and to which access was controlled, like Johnson's dining room, was it possible to speak freely. A sense of the relief offered by the prospect of meeting friends in safe domestic spaces comes in a letter in which Iolo accepted an invitation to dinner at the house of a fellow Welshman. 'Be it known', he wrote in the cod-legalese of government proclamations, that 'citizens and sansculottes George Dyer and Iolo Morganwg, being instigated thereunto by the devil', would visit to eat, drink and 'talk of politics, republicanism, Jacobinisms, Carmagnolism, sansculottisms, and a number of other wicked and trayterous isms against the peace of the lords, kingism and parsonism, their crowns and dignities'.[19]

In the autumn of 1794 the imprisoned campaigners for reform were put on trial. In order to charge the men with treason the government had to exercise considerable legal ingenuity. When law officers drew up the indictment against Hardy and his co-defendants, they made literal two clauses in the 1351 Act against High Treason, passed when Edward III was King. The 1351 Act made it a crime 'to compass and imagine' the death of the King, and to 'levy war' against him. The legal men who drafted the 1351 act used 'compass and imagine' to mean intend, and 'to intend the death of the King' had been the commonly accepted reading of this clause for centuries. Pitt's lawyers redefined it, so that an act of imagining alone became a crime. To commit treason one needed merely to have imagined the King's death, not to have acted to advance it. Writing and speaking thus became treasonable. The law officers also argued that since the government was appointed in the name of the King any action which threatened the security and stability of government legally constituted an attempt to 'levy war' on the King himself. Political protest thus became treasonable by its very nature. The imagination was rendered an object of political repression by this legal manoeuvring. This legal assault would, over time, provoke the poets of the 1790s into a powerful defence of the sanctity of untrammelled individual imagination. In the short term, however, it offered those charged with prosecuting Hardy and the other leaders of the LCS a powerful weapon.

Hardy's trial began first, on October 28th. It lasted nine days: an extraordinary length in a period when most trials were over within a few hours. Hardy was defended by Thomas Erskine, a former legal advisor to the Prince of Wales who had lost his job when he agreed in 1792 to defend Paine. Erskine conducted a magnificent defence. He was aided in his demolition of the government arguments by William Godwin, who in October published an article in the *Morning Chronicle* on the legal foundation of the charges, entitled 'Cursory Strictures'. Godwin accused Chief Justice Eyre, who had laid out the charge, of perpetrating 'one of the most flagrant violations of the principles of executive justice, that was ever heard or imagined.' Particularly obnoxious, Godwin wrote, was the attempt to attribute guilt necessitating the death sentence to a group of individuals on the basis of events taking place in a neighbouring country. Eyre's argument, in Godwin's analysis, rested on two fundamental flaws and threatened to undermine not just the case before the court but the British legal system in its entirety:

> He does not proceed, as a judge ought to proceed, by explaining the law, and leaving the Grand Jury to fix its application upon individuals; but leads them to the selection of the individuals themselves, and centres in his own person the provinces of judge and accuser. It may be doubted whether, in the whole records of the legal proceedings of England, another instance is to be found, of such wild conjecture, such premature presumption, imaginations so licentious, and dreams so full of sanguinary and tremendous prophecy.[20]

Godwin's rhetoric demonstrates the extent to which the imagination was politicised by the legal innovations of the Treason Trials. It also gives an indication of the brilliance with which advocates for the defendants both inside and outside the courtroom turned the government's strategy against it, accusing them of indulging in an overblown imaginative frenzy that itself came dangerously close, according to the new reading of the law, to treason. Godwin's pamphlet proved tremendously popular and he sat in court as Erskine expanded his arguments in hour upon hour of oratorical flight. Thomas Lawrence sketched Godwin sitting alongside his friend Thomas Holcroft as they listened to Erskine's defence. Both men are pictured watching intently as their friends and fellow campaigners are tried for their lives.

✦

Johnson was summoned by the prosecution to give evidence at the Treason Trials. He was examined on the witness stand by the government's prosecuting counsel, William Garrow. One of the crimes of which Hardy and John Horne Tooke were accused was to have disseminated the work of Paine and Joel Barlow, whose *Advice to the Privileged Orders* Johnson had printed. In the trials of Hardy and Horne Tooke, Johnson was called on to account for his role in the publication of works alleged by the prosecution to be seditious and potentially treasonous. Jordan, who had pleaded guilty to publishing Paine in 1792, made strenuous efforts during his own time on the stand to implicate Johnson in seditious activities. Johnson left no record of the experience of being examined in court, but his instinctive caution can be heard in his answers to Garrow's questioning. In the exchange below, recorded during the trial of Thomas Hardy, Garrow speaks first:

– You publish a great many books, and you do not always recollect the contents – did it happen to you to publish the Rights of Man?
– No.
– Did you sell any?
– Yes.
– How many copies – I do not ask you to within a thousand, – but about how many do you think you sold
– I cannot tell.
– Did you sell many or few
– I cannot tell what you mean by many
– Did you sell some dozens?
– Certainly I did – when that pamphlet was published it was supposed not to be a libel, afterwards it was proved to be one. I beg to ask the Court whether I am obliged to answer that question?[21]

Johnson knew his actions were within the law at the time he acted, but only by a slim margin. He also knew that the law itself was vulnerable to retrospective State reinterpretation. When he was called back to court during the trial of Horne Tooke, Johnson was required to explain his role in the publication of Joel Barlow's work. His evidence followed that of Jordan, who did his best to demonstrate that Johnson had acted as an informal collaborator in the publication of the second part of the *Rights of Man*. In his summing up, Chief Justice Eyre drew attention to the role played by both booksellers in the dissemination of material of which Hardy and Horne Tooke stood accused. A guilty verdict had the potential to threaten the livelihoods – and, conceivably, the lives – of the booksellers as well as those of the defendants in the dock.

The combined efforts of Erskine and Godwin were successful. In an outcome that surprised many and horrified the government, the jury at Hardy's trial found him not guilty of treason and sedition. An ecstatic crowd carried Hardy through the streets, although they remained at a respectful distance as he stood alone before the graves of his wife and child. Horne Tooke's acquittal followed a week later. In response to both judgements the government was forced to release other members of the LCS and SCI. John Thelwall remained in prison because the case against him was said to be particularly strong, but ultimately he too was acquitted. Pitt declared them all to be 'morally guilty'. The Solicitor General insisted that a not-guilty verdict was not the same as a declaration of innocence.[22] Such assertions did nothing to quell the widespread sense of liberal jubilation at the acquittals. It was a good moment in a difficult year, when reason and justice won out over repression. Nevertheless, for the men who had been imprisoned the effects of the trial were devastating. Hardy's wife and stillborn child had died as a result of his arrest; his business was ruined. Friends helped him re-establish himself in a smaller shop but he remained vulnerable to loyalist crowds carrying flaming torches. Thelwall's footsteps were dogged by government spies after his release and eventually he left London, hoping to find peace in the isolation of rural Wales. John Horne Tooke remained defiant throughout his imprisonment and trial but by the time he was released he was exhausted and his finances were strained. He had been an articulate and witty combatant at Johnson's table but in the years following 1794 his voice was muted and the SCI missed the strength of his leadership. After the Treason Trials its members gradually stopped meeting.

✦

In September 1795 Johnson wrote to Priestley to explain why he could not invest in land Priestley wanted to buy in Northumberland. Priestley had visions of establishing a Dissenting College in rural Pennsylvania and he offered Johnson the opportunity to exchange his stock for a share in the project. Johnson commended the principle but told Priestley bluntly he had misjudged his moment. 'You ask me to become a sharer not considering that I want the means', he wrote. 'Connections with the poor all my life & political connections of late have prevented me from making a fortune.'[23]

It was an uncharacteristically strained response, which revealed something of the effort it took for Johnson to keep an open house in a climate of surveillance and retrenchment. Johnson's ability to conduct his business freely was damaged by his visibility during the Treason Trials. As the political landscape darkened, the number of people who relied on him for their physical and intellectual security increased. For a man who believed in the power of peace and reason, public affairs offered little consolation. 'The last news we have here is that the French have crossed the Rhine & are carrying everything before them in Germany', he told Priestley. 'Our ministry is employed in preparing for a descent on the coast of France & sending an immense force to the West Indies, and by and by will be engaged in procuring an immense loan.' It seemed scarcely credible to him that a once civilised continent, which he had celebrated in the *Analytical Review* as a place where ideas and knowledge flowed freely between nations, should have fallen so far. 'These are the occupations of European Courts! and extermination on one side or the other the plan of ours.' Peace seemed a distant prospect; hardly a petition in its favour had been circulated. To sustain the bonds of friendship in spite of distance and political exile was ever more important and ever more difficult. 'You will oblige me in writing often, and I shall endeavour to be a better correspondent.'[24]

2 1

Things by their Right Names

The fire has been lit in *Evenings at Home*, and it is time for a story. Charles Barbauld, last seen by readers as a toddler in *Lessons for Children*, has transformed into an enquiring child with a keen eye for parental failings. 'Papa', he complains, 'you grow very lazy. Last winter you used to tell us stories, and now you never tell us one; and we are all got round the fire quite ready to hear you.' Father agrees to tell a story; Charles demands that the subject should be 'bloody murder'. Father's tale starts with a band of men, dressed all alike, marching through a deep forest in steel-capped boots. Charles interjects that they must have been 'ill-looking fellows'. No, says Father, 'they were tall personable men'. Charles presumes it must be midnight in the story. No, says Father, it is a balmy summer's morning. The band of men move forward to a village which they set on fire. Then they murder twenty thousand men. 'Papa!' exclaims Charles. 'You do not intend I should believe this. I thought all along you were making up a tale, as you often do; but you shall not catch me this time.' He scoffs at the notion such violence is possible:

C: What! they lay still, I suppose, and let those fellows cut their throats!
F: No, truly – they resisted as long as they could.
C: How should these men kill twenty thousand people, pray?
F: Why not? The murderers were thirty thousand.
C: O, now I have found you out! You mean a BATTLE.
F: Indeed I do. I do not know of any murders half so bloody.[1]

Barbauld titled the dialogue between Charles and Father 'Things by their Right Names'. In a rhetorical sleight-of-hand she recast war as mass murder, shorn of spurious justification. A child's innocence reveals the corruptions of the adult world, as Charles becomes the vehicle through which readers are enabled to see things as they are. Within a year of the first publication of *Evenings at Home* Britain had entered a war with no end in sight. An entire generation would grow up without experiencing peace. In the first years of the war Johnson and his authors sought to withstand repression at home and militarism abroad by writing of what they saw; by giving things their right names. To capture the world in ink and print became more than a vocation between 1792 and 1795. It became a means of economic and intellectual survival, but only for those who were brave enough to withstand the risk.

☩

In spite of the Proclamation against Seditious Writings, Paine's *Rights of Man* inspired a host of imitations and responses. Johnson did not publish the other great political work of the early 1790s, Godwin's *Political Justice*, although he did his best to foster a conversation between Godwin and Paine. Godwin was less interested than Paine in the passing events of the day. His concern was with the structures of philosophical thought necessary for political perfectibility. Godwin believed in the innate goodness of man: freed of State control, he theorised, man would achieve an ideal of self-government. He argued for the abolition of property rights and political institutions and he prophesied a future in which all State structures would be dissolved, allowing men and women to live together in a condition of progressive political perfection. Godwin gave voice to the optimism experienced by political radicals across Europe in the immediate aftermath of the French Revolution. *Political Justice* acted as a rallying cry for those who wanted to achieve justice by tearing down the old ideas and rebuilding a utopian – and essentially anarchic – society in its place. Godwin himself was convinced that change would come without revolution; that it was inevitable given the intrinsic benevolence of man. His work did not reach the masses as did Paine's, largely because it was longer and more expensive.

The effects of *Political Justice* were felt chiefly amongst the circles in which Godwin himself moved. At St Paul's Churchyard and the other spaces where men and women met to dissect the great events of the moment, Godwin was feted as a speaker of truth. His analysis gave hope to those who watched as their friends were arrested and transported – or at least it did to those who were able to look past his rejection of religion alongside civic structures. Lindsey could not subdue his conviction that Godwin's true intention was to convert vulnerable young men to atheism. He had also seen too much of the workings of the world to be seduced by visions of philosophical anarchism. It was left instead to the younger generation who moved in and out of Johnson's dining room alongside Lindsey to take up Godwin's ideas. Thirty-four-year-old Mary Hays was among those swept away by the grandeur of Godwin's vision. In vain she hunted for a copy of *Political Justice* and, thwarted by both the circulating library and the parsimony of friends, she wrote to the author to ask him to loan her a copy and to enter into a discussion with her about political principles. 'May then a disciple of truth, & a contemner of the artificial forms which have served but to corrupt & enslave society, request of Mr Godwin himself to be allowed an opportunity of investigating further the important & interesting subjects of moral truth & political justice?'[2] Godwin made anything seem possible; he took nothing about the status quo for granted. *Political Justice* suggested that the present was alive with possibility in spite of the best efforts of Pitt and his acolytes.

The political tracts Johnson published in the first half of the 1790s cleaved more closely to established genres, if not to established ideas. In 1792 he brought out Joel Barlow's *Conspiracy of Kings*. The poem presented a dystopian vision in heroic couplets, of kings waged against common men, defended only by Burke, Pitt and the 'impious arts' of pomp and ceremony.[3] In the same year Johnson published the first part of Barlow's *Advice to the Privileged Orders*, in which Barlow warned aristocrats across the globe of the inevitability of a new republican world order. Barlow left for Paris soon after the publication of the first part of his work, leaving the remaining portions of the manuscript in Johnson's hands. In Barlow's absence Johnson decided that Part Two was too incendiary for publication and he sent the manuscript on to Barlow in Paris. At the same time he withdrew Part One from sale. His caution was proved right when he was called to account for his role in the publication of *Advice to the Privileged Orders* during the Treason Trials. Barlow attributed the failure of his work to reach its audience to 'violent attacks on the Liberty of the Press' which suggests that Johnson's original publication of Part One may have attracted the attention of agents working on behalf of the State before the Treason Trials opened.[4]

While Barlow turned to poetry and the polemical combination of exhortation and revisionary economic analysis popularised by Paine, Barbauld took literary forms sanctioned by the State and turned them against the government. Shortly after the outbreak of war with France, George III proclaimed April 19th 1793 as a public fast-day. Publicly ordained fast-days had been part of the armoury through which the British State managed crises since the mid-sixteenth-century. During periods of war they were a ritual through which the country was brought together to pray for divine intercession in the cause of the nation. Fast-days were designed to inculcate loyalty and obedience and to remind ordinary men and women that they had a part to play in the success of the government. On such days the entire population was supposed to abstain from food, repent of its sins and attend State-prescribed religious services.

Wartime fast-days represented everything to which the Dissenters objected in State religion. Barbauld responded with a satirical fast-day discourse which countered the loyalist sermons issuing from the presses. She entitled her pamphlet *Sins of Government, Sins of the Nation* and she explicitly tied it to the ceremonies of April 19th 1793. She signed herself simply 'A Volunteer' but neither she nor Johnson made any effort to conceal her identity. Barbauld returned to the conceit of 'Things by their Right Names' in *Sins of Government*, which was both a trenchant anti-war critique and a dissection of the intellectual paucity implied by the decision to use religion to subdue the populace. Again her concern was with using words accurately:

> We should do well to translate this word war into language more intelligible to us. When we pay our army and our navy estimates, let us set down – so much for killing, so much for maiming, so much for making widows and orphans, so much for bringing famine among a district, so much for corrupting citizens and subjects into spies and traitors, so much for ruining industrious tradesmen and making bankrupts ... so much for letting loose the daemons of fury rapine and lust within the fold of cultivated society, and giving to the brutal ferocity of the most ferocious, its full scope and range of invention.[5]

Barbauld did not restrict her criticisms to the conduct of the government alone. She worked from what she called a 'plain principle': 'that the will of the minority should ever yield to that of the majority.' The two groups who were most in danger of forgetting this principle were the government and the reformers. Of those in power little more was to be expected, since the responsibilities of governance resulted in a delusion of executive power derived from the will of the governed. For the reformers she had sharp words. Barlow and his ilk had condemned Burke for writing of the populace as a 'swinish multitude' but they too showed disdain for the will of the people in their privileging of an 'aristocracy of talents.' It was the condition of reformers, Barbauld acknowledged, to breed visions of a better world, but the public were not necessarily at fault for refusing to be swept up by ideas of political futurity. 'Their plans', she wrote of the reformers, 'are often crude and premature, their ideas too refined for real life, and influenced by their own particular cast of thinking.' 'Freedom is a good thing', she insisted. 'But if a nation is not disposed to accept of it, it is not to be presented to them on the point of a bayonet.'[6]

✢

For the most part the men who dreamt of brighter political futures in the 1790s had little to say about the condition of women. Johnson had been supportive of work and writing done by women since the 1770s, when he had first published Mary Scott's *The Female Advocate*. In Mary Wollstonecraft, however, the cause of women's rights found an advocate like no other. The first intimations that Wollstonecraft was working on a sequel to her *Vindication of the Rights of Men* came in the autumn of 1791, when she broke off sitting for her portrait to tell William Roscoe (who had commissioned the painting) that the book she was writing would result in a more authentic likeness than the image. It was inevitable, she explained, that she herself would appear in the new work, 'head and heart'.[7] Godwin, who learnt the details of this period of Wollstonecraft's life from Johnson, later wrote that it took her only six weeks to produce A *Vindication of the Rights of Woman*. By January 2nd 1792, all bar the final sheet was off the press. As she laid down her pen on January 3rd Wollstonecraft told Roscoe that when she came to write a second volume she would complete the whole work before submitting it for publication, since it was harassing to write with the printer's errand boy waiting at the door. The haste with which she wrote and printed was revealed in the high number of errata in the first edition and Wollstonecraft went immediately to work on a corrected second edition, published by Johnson later that year.

Wollstonecraft dedicated the *Vindication* to Talleyrand, in the hope that those charged with drawing up a constitution for Revolutionary France would recognise the need to educate women to be full citizens and participants in the life of the State. In aristocratic Britain men had been imprisoned by 'gaudy hereditary trappings' and women by 'the arbitrary power of beauty'. Both sexes, she insisted, needed to throw off the yoke of old expectations and privileges in order to flourish anew. She attacked the manner in which women were subjugated by their own affections and senses and by the way they connived in a patriarchal valorisation of weakness. 'Fondness' she described as 'a poor substitute for friendship': 'Weakness may excite tenderness, and gratify the arrogant pride of man; but the lordly caresses of a protector will not gratify a noble mind that pants for and deserves to be respected.'[8] Wollstonecraft's ideal woman cultivated strength in body and mind and stood on her own intellectually and emotionally. Hard graft as the chief reviewer of fiction for the *Analytical* had convinced her that novels had little to offer a young woman in pursuit of self-improvement. It was difficult to become a rational creature, she explained, on a diet of sensation alone. She was suspicious of love but she celebrated friendship as the sovereign emotion for women who wished to be sustained but not enslaved by their passions:

> Friendship is a serious affection; the most sublime of all affections, because it is founded on principle, and cemented by time. The reverse may be said of love. In the great degree, love and friendship cannot subsist in the same bosom; even when inspired by different objects they weaken or destroy each other, and for the same object can only be felt in succession. The vain fears and fond jealousies, the winds which fan the flame of love, when judiciously or artfully tempered, are both incompatible with the tender confidence and sincere respect of friendship.[9]

The well-educated woman, she continued, would recognise that in marriage passion would give way to friendship and she would thus meet her husband on her own terms, rather than vainly wrestling against time and age to maintain herself as a desirable doll.

Everywhere she looked Wollstonecraft saw women rendered foolish by ignorance and upbringing. What was needed was thus a 'REVOLUTION in female manners.'[10] Should women be educated to think for themselves and to act according to the dictates of intellect rather than their senses, they would become free. 'Let woman share the rights, and she will emulate the virtues of man', she concluded. 'She must grow more perfect when emancipated, or justify the authority that chains such a weak being to her duty.'[11] Wollstonecraft located the genesis of an education that failed women and allowed them to fail themselves in the social and political structures of the old order, and she framed her manifesto for a revolution in women's lives within the context of a broader reform of outdated systems.

Johnson published A *Vindication of the Rights of Woman* in the early spring of 1792. 'Lesser wits', pronounced the *Analytical*, 'will probably affect to make themselves merry at the title and apparent object of this publication; but we have no doubt if even her contemporaries should fail to do her justice, posterity will compensate the defect.' Johnson's reviewer insisted that the nation would be 'better, wiser and happier' if Wollstonecraft's diagnosis of its ills were heeded.[12] Other reviewers were less sympathetic. The *Critical Review* spoke for many when it pronounced her conclusions an 'absurdity.'[13]

Within the inner circle of St Paul's Churchyard Wollstonecraft's achievement was a cause for celebration. Her friends wrote to each other of the need to ensure the *Vindication* was widely circulated. 'Mr J. tells me that you make the Liverpool women read my book', she wrote to Roscoe in February.[14] A curious Godwin wondered if there was perhaps more to Wollstonecraft than he had realised at their first antagonistic meeting and he paid a visit to the Barlows in order to learn more of her. Wollstonecraft and Ruth Barlow were friends and Ruth was well-placed to enlighten Godwin about Wollstonecraft's history. 'Call on Barlow', Godwin recorded in his diary. 'Read the Duellist: Richard II, 2 acts. Story of Mrs Wolstencraft. Frost, 4 days.'[15] A week later Godwin called on the Barlows again and met Wollstonecraft in person. There was talk 'of libels, & the power of mind.'[16] Wollstonecraft herself was entertained by the impact of her celebrity on one gentleman who it appeared had not read her prescription for equality within marriage very closely. 'Be it known unto you that my book &c &c has afforded me an opportunity of settling *very* advantageous in the matrimonial line', she told Everina. The suitor was unknown to her, a 'new acquaintance'. The offer was not an appealing one but she enjoyed the sensation of boasting of it. 'A handsome house and a proper man did not tempt me; yet I may as well appear before you, with the feather stuck in my cap.'[17]

For Mary Hays the *Vindication* represented an epiphany. She wrote to Wollstonecraft to express her admiration and received a formal acknowledgement in reply. A meeting followed at St Paul's Churchyard, the place to which Wollstonecraft usually directed visitors she was not prepared to admit into the sanctuary of her lodgings. Hays's ambition for her own writing was growing and she wanted Wollstonecraft's advice and access to Johnson's patronage. Wollstonecraft agreed to show the manuscript on which Hays was working to Johnson but she admonished her for the subservience with which she framed her plea. 'I yesterday mentioned to Mr Johnson your request and he assented desiring that the title page might be sent to him', she wrote in November. 'I, therefore, can say nothing more, for trifles of this kind I have always left to him to settle; and you must be aware, Madam, that the *honour* of publishing, the phrase on which you have laid a stress, is the cant of both trade and sex'. Hays had a responsibility, she explained, to model the kind of professional relationship they both desired, and to think herself worthy of equal treatment. 'If really equality should ever take place in society the man who is employed and gives a just equivalent for the money he receives will not behave with the servile obsequiousness of a servant.'[18]

The work that Hays wanted Johnson to see was entitled *Letters and Essays*. It was thoroughly influenced by the *Vindication* and it defended Wollstonecraft against every criticism. Although she shared Wollstonecraft's conviction that the debased condition of women was a symptom of broader social ills, Hays was more cautious about the costs of reform. 'Posterity', she was sure, 'will ... reap the benefit of the present struggles in France, but they are ruinous and dreadful to those actually engaged in them.'[19] Hays did not restrict herself to the subject of women's rights in her book. Other letters continued the debate sparked by Gilbert Wakefield's strictures against public worship and considered the foundations of civil liberty. Hays adopted the miscellaneous form popularised by Barbauld as she ranged across forms of address and contrasting genres. She was less censorious than Wollstonecraft about the dangers of novel-reading for impressionable young women and she was explicit about the intellectual debt she owed to the Dissenting men amongst whom she lived. In recognition of that debt she sent a copy of *Letters and Essays* to Lindsey, who wrote approvingly in reply. 'I like both your metaphysics and divinity', he told her, 'but most of all, what appears in every page, the enlightened mind, turned to virtue and to God, and ardent to inspire others with the same sentiments and engage in the same pursuits.'[20]

Wollstonecraft was less complimentary. She reviewed Hays's work in draft and sent a rebuke about the tone of the preface. Hays had pleaded for the reader's forbearance, citing the disadvantages of her education. It was a conventional gesture for a woman writer attempting to reconcile the demand for female modesty with her right to be heard. It infuriated Wollstonecraft. 'This kind of vain humility has ever disgusted me', she responded. 'I should say to an author, who humbly sued for forbearance, "if you have not a tolerably good opinion of your own production, why intrude it on the public? we have plenty of bad books already, that have just gasped for breath and died."' She told Hays to care less about pleasing men like Priestley, who spoke warmly of women's achievements in private but refused to support them in public. She thought that Hays, by aligning herself so openly with the intellectual lineage of Dissent, was contributing to an inequality she professed to abhor. 'Rest, on yourself', she insisted. 'If your essays have merit they will stand alone, if not the *shouldering up* of Dr this or that will not long keep them from falling to the ground.' She concluded her rebuke with a reminder of the central argument of the *Vindication*. 'When weakness claims indulgence it seems to justify the despotism of strength.'[21]

Later, at St Paul's Churchyard, Wollstonecraft added a postscript to her letter saying that Johnson willingly relinquished the position of Hays's publisher. Hays had simultaneously been negotiating with Thomas Knott, who had published her reply to Wakefield, and he insisted that his name should appear first in the list of booksellers connected with *Letters and Essays*. Johnson was the senior of the two booksellers by virtue of being longer established in the trade, and although he professed himself content to appear second Wollstonecraft asserted herself in his defence. 'I have just now spoken to Mr. J', she told Hays, 'who desires me to tell you that he very willingly waves the privilege of seniority, though as it is an impropriety, I should think his name might well be omitted.'[22] Johnson was her publisher and it did not suit her that he should abase himself to please a woman who appeared to have only partially learnt the lessons of the *Vindication*. With Hays kept safely at a distance from Johnson's list Wollstonecraft was able to write more generously in acknowledgment of the proofs of *Letters and Essays*, which she corrected for Hays with a pencil while the printer's boy once again stood waiting by the door.

In 1796 Hays brought out an autobiographical novel with Godwin's publisher George Robinson, entitled *Memoirs of Emma Courtney*, in which she laid bare her emotional existence for the world to see. The novel told of the torture of disappointed love and quoted verbatim from the philosophical correspondence on which she had embarked with William Godwin. Some in Johnson's circle disapproved intensely of the frankness with which

Hays anatomised her own passions. Lindsey heard that *Memoirs of Emma Courtney* was a love-letter to the ideas of Godwin and could not bring himself to read it. Hannah read it on his behalf and pronounced it an 'unedifying ... love-story'.[23] Wollstonecraft was right when she told Hays not to rely too much on the approval of elderly Dissenting men for her sense of self-worth. Lindsey and Hannah were a generation older than Hays and Wollstonecraft and they saw little appreciation in the work of either woman of the richness or complexity of their own long partnership. Wollstonecraft and Hays both asked a question central to their existence, about how to be an independent woman in a world designed for men. They located their answer in a manifesto for reform of social structures which blighted the lives of both men and women. Lindsey had spent much of his life campaigning for religious justice but the idea that women constituted a group also deserving of restitution – that the right to feel freely might be equivalent to the right to worship freely – was foreign to him. Johnson's friends and authors might share a sense that the world needed to change but their priorities and prescriptions were as various as the forms in which they wrote and the experiences that shaped them.

✢

Wollstonecraft, Godwin, Paine, Barlow and Hays attracted a great deal of attention as they dissected the conditions under which men and women thought and worked. Less noticed was the work of the scientific men on Johnson's list, who continued their enquiries about the workings of the body and the universe throughout the years of political repression. Between 1792 and 1795 Johnson published tracts on the anatomy of the bones, muscles and joints, on 'animal electricity', the nervous system, 'urinary gravel', pregnancy and labour, the management of fever and a host of other medico-scientific topics. These publications were practical, designed to increase knowledge and decrease suffering. They reflected an awareness amongst the medical men who joined Johnson's list that it was no good being free if poverty and a lack of access to medical care shortened one's life or necessitated a life lived in pain. These books were not fashionable but they were invaluable for hard-pressed doctors and the people they served. Johnson was the sole English publisher of John Elliot's *Medical Pocket-Book*, which appeared for the first time in 1781 and which he reissued twice more during the tumultuous first half of the 1790s. Elliot designed his volume as a convenient primer for those who tended to the sick. It contained 'a short but plain account of the symptoms, causes, and methods of cure, of the diseases incident to the human body: Including such as require Surgical Treatment: Together with the Virtues and Doses of Medical Compositions and Simples.' This cornucopia of information was 'extracted from the best authors, and digested into alphabetical order.'[24] Johnson continued to issue editions of old and new works by his old friend John Bonnycastle, all of which adhered to Bonnycastle's early vision of mathematical texts that would be of use to those denied an advanced education. Johnson also published work by a young chemist called Thomas Beddoes, the son-in-law of his friend Richard Lovell Edgeworth. Beddoes was a devout believer in the relationship between reformist politics and a reformist medicine and by 1793 he had acquired a reputation as something of a troublemaker. In Bristol he performed a series of experiments to test the efficacy of gas as a medical treatment, the early results of which Johnson published in 1795 as *Considerations on the Medicinal Use, and on the Production of Factitious Airs*.

The most significant scientific work Johnson issued during Pitt's Terror was Erasmus Darwin's *Zoonomia*, Volume I of which he published in 1794. Darwin was hard at work on *Zoonomia* by 1792. He wrote that the commercial success of *The Botanic Garden* brought its own pressures, and that he felt his years. The volume, he told his friend Richard Dixon, 'will be chiefly on physic.' But 'I fear it will not sell as well as the last. The worst thing I find now is this d—n'd old age, which creeps slily upon one, like moss upon a tree, and wrinkles one all over like a baked pear.'[25] Darwin's aim in *Zoonomia* was to produce a grand theory of disease. He believed that all organic life, or animal life, shared certain fundamental characteristics, and that if these were properly understood medical practitioners would have a much more robust basis for innovation and practice. Darwin's scheme united mind and body and it encompassed a description of reproduction (which Darwin called 'generation') as a proto-evolutionary process. Darwin theorised that reproduction entailed continuous development and refinement from one generation to the next: it was a suggestion that anticipated the work of his grandson Charles by half a century. In a decade in which theorists of every kind were suspected of radicalism and treated with suspicion, Darwin mounted a staunch defence of the pursuit of knowledge. 'There are some modern practitioners, who declaim against medical theory in general,' he wrote. Those practitioners had failed to consider 'that to think is to theorize; and that no one can direct a method of cure to a person labouring under disease without thinking; that is, without theorizing.' Darwin knew by which kind of doctor he himself would wish to be treated. 'Happy therefore is the patient, whose physician possesses the best theory.'[26]

In the Preface to *Zoonomia* Darwin paid lip-service to the role played in the development of life by the 'great CREATOR of all things'[27] but in his scheme generation was a natural process that operated without the involvement of any divine force. The first reviewers overlooked this. The *Analytical's* reviewer conceded that the complexity of Darwin's vision was almost beyond him. 'The very comprehension of new doctrines, founded upon a large induction, especially when the facts are of a nature by no means obvious, is attended with an effort too great to be agreeable to ordinary readers'. In short, the reviewer continued, to understand Darwin's theories required a great deal of work: 'we must make no inconsiderable exertions both of recollection and comparison.'[28] Darwin told his son he was unimpressed by the results of such exertions – 'my book is reviewed (I think not well tho') in the analytical review'[29] – but the complexity of his work protected him in the short term from a political Establishment suspicious of heterodoxy regardless of the field of enquiry in which it occurred. After 1789 the work of the French chemists with whom Priestley had sparred became indelibly associated in the popular imagination with the intellectual upheaval that produced blood on the streets of Paris. In Britain Pitt's government and its proxies were increasingly on the alert for sedition disguised as enquiry. In the 1770s Johnson's list had ranged freely across the broad vistas of eighteenth-century scientific pursuit, in a proud statement of the importance of knowledge and progress. By the 1790s the same thematic range implied an opposition to loyalist orthodoxy and was fraught with danger.

⁂

On April 18th 1791 the MP for Hull, William Wilberforce, introduced an Abolition Bill on the floor of the House of Commons. The bill was rejected by 163 votes to 88 two days later. Wilberforce had been working with Pitt to build parliamentary support for abolition since 1790, when a select committee was established to consider the subject. Events in France gave MPs opposed to abolition ample excuse to reject any change to the institution on which Britain's imperial might relied. A slave rebellion in French-owned San Domingo (modern-day Haiti) offered anti-abolitionists further ammunition in their battle against Wilberforce. Petitions in favour of abolition flooded into Parliament. In 1792 a bill did pass through Parliament that stipulated slavery would be abolished but anti-abolitionists succeeded in attaching an amendment noting that abolition should be 'gradual' which rendered it legally toothless. From Yarmouth John Aikin declared to his sister that he could no longer square the consumption of sugar with his conscience and that he had become an 'antisaccharist.'[30] During her residence in Clifton Maria Edgeworth reported to her cousin Sophy that 25,000 people in England were boycotting West Indian sugar but that she was unconvinced it would do any good and was continuing to eat apple pies made with sugar rather than honey. Her father, however, had eaten 'excellent custards sweetened with honey' at the house of a friend. 'Will it not be rather hard upon the poor bees in the end?'[31]

Edgeworth's ambivalence about the extent of the personal sacrifices required by the abolition campaign was mirrored by the decisions Johnson made about the extent of his own involvement in the debate. He published several abolitionist works, some of which, such as Alexander Geddes's furiously satirical 1792 work *An Apology for Slavery*, mocked the self-serving sophistry of the anti-abolitionists.[32] But in the same year he also published a polemic entitled *Case of the Sugar Colonies* in which a West Indian planter called John Collins defended his right to buy and keep slaves and presented himself and his fellow planters as victims of an abolitionist conspiracy. Collins accused the abolitionists of being a lobby group for the East Indian sugar producers, who stood to benefit from a boycott of the West Indian, slave-produced product. Abstract theories of human liberty might suggest that slavery was an evil; Collins responded that the violence in France proved that such theories were dangerous in practice. It was unjust that West Indian planters were less secure in their possessions than other British citizens and that the poor in Britain would suffer most if abolition resulted in a rise in the cost of sugar. Collins was utterly convinced of the righteousness of his argument, although he undermined his own rhetoric by suggesting in conclusion that the West Indian planters were being treated little better than slaves. Elsewhere he insinuated that the abolitionists were a threat not just to slave-owners but to the security of the nation. Abolition, he wrote, originated not 'in the policy of the state; but in another principle, with which policy is frequently at variance, namely a principle of humanity; which though it has always existed in a certain degree in the human mind, has never assumed so formidable a shape as until lately, when it was called forth by the zeal of certain speculative writers; and on their recommendation, associations were formed for the avowed purpose of annihilating the commerce in slaves.'[33] Collins labelled the associations of abolitionists a 'confederacy': an idea which, like 'speculation' and 'association', had already been used by the government to represent disparate groups of reformers as a united national threat.

The *Analytical*'s review of Collins's diatribe was studiously neutral: readers were invited to reach their own conclusion about the merits of his argument. Johnson's motives for giving Collins a platform are difficult to divine. He was always committed to airing both sides of a debate – except in the case of a subject, such as Dissenting rights, when his list suggests he believed the question to be beyond dispute. Johnson's business correspondence illustrates that he would not publish work he did not think would sell, unless his commitment to the argument or the author was sufficiently strong to compel him to waive financial considerations. With the exception of the Dissenting debate, there is no suggestion that he refrained from publishing work about which he had moral scruples or with which he disagreed. He may have been motivated by a desire to sustain and enable conversation about the most important topics of the day, or it may have been the result of a more ruthless business decision. The idea that Johnson was personally ambivalent about the slave trade is at odds with many of the decisions he took and the company he kept, but in the absence of any evidence of his view his list has to stand as some indication of the arguments he thought worthy of note. It is also equally possible that in publishing Collins he gave him a platform upon which to condemn himself. Collins dismissed the ideas of Paine while simultaneously presenting the West Indian planters as the most oppressed of all men, shorn of their natural rights by liberal ideology. His rhetoric made a nonsense of his argument, and on Johnson's list his voice was overwhelmed by those of writers who took up their pens to condemn everything for which he stood.

The complexity of Johnson's position in relation to the slave trade appears most strikingly in the story of his relationship with Gabriel Stedman. Stedman was a mercenary soldier who in 1771 joined a volunteer force assembled to quell a slave rebellion in the Latin American colony of Surinam. Stedman spent five years in Surinam, where he married Joanna, a mixed-race slave, and had a child, called Johnny. In 1777 Stedman left Joanna in Surinam and sailed for the Netherlands. Johnny was sent to school in England and Stedman remarried (a year before Joanna died) and had five more children. In 1783 he sold his commission and settled down to family life in England. Ten years later he entered into an agreement with Johnson for the publication of his *Narrative of a Five Years Expedition against the Revolted Negroes of Surinam*. The *Narrative* related the mistreatment of slaves in unsparing detail, alongside the daily degradations of their lives and the bravery of those who had rebelled against cruelty.

Johnson agreed to publish on the basis of Stedman's manuscript and in December 1793 advanced him £212. Then, without consulting Stedman, he engaged a hack writer called William Thomson to edit the text. Thomson was an occasional guest at St Paul's Churchyard, although not a distinguished one. On one occasion he fell asleep while Wollstonecraft was talking and snored loudly throughout tea. Before Johnson employed Thomson he had acted as a writer-for-hire for a committee of anti-abolitionists and had filled his days scribbling tracts in defence of the slave trade. The writer of Thomson's obituary, who knew him personally, went to great lengths to explain this: 'a committee formed for the express purpose of supporting this infamous traffic, actually met in the city, and holding forth *golden temptations* to needy men of letters, unfortunately prevailed on multitudes to advocate their cause.'[34] The obituarist claimed that Thomson was later ashamed of the part he played in defending slavery, but when he edited Stedman's work he was at pains to tone down the abolitionist sentiments of the manuscript. He deleted passages on the conduct of the British Navy and some of Stedman's more explicitly political commentary. Stedman's editors have argued that Thompson acted on his own initiative as he altered the text: 'we suspect that Johnson ... paid little attention to what he assumed to be largely technical editing on Thomson's part, and that he gave Thomson's text to the printer without first having compared it carefully to Stedman's original.'[35] It is certainly likely that Johnson, having decided it was necessary to employ a 'literary dry-nurse'[36] to polish Stedman's text, subsequently displayed little interest in the minutiae of manuscript changes. While Thomson went to work on the text Johnson concentrated his efforts on commissioning engravers to transform Stedman's own images for the press. Some of the work was contracted to Francesco Bartolozzi, one of London's most celebrated engravers; sixteen of the plates Johnson placed in the hands of Blake.

Blake's images showed the brutality of which Stedman wrote in stark detail. Regardless of Thomson's alterations, no one who picked up the completed edition of Stedman's narrative could be in any doubt as to the immorality of the slave trade. But when Stedman discovered that Johnson had tampered with his text he erupted. In June 1795 he recorded in his diary that his book was 'marr'd entirely': the result was 'a hot quarrel with Johnson.' Johnson agreed to reprint the first volume and entered into negotiation with Stedman about how much of the text could be re-set. Stedman dined twice at St Paul's Churchyard, pronounced himself reconciled with his publisher, and then took himself off to Blake's house, where he persuaded Blake to act as his London agent. Although Johnson agreed to alter the text Stedman still chastised him as 'uncivil all along.'[37] In August he broke his ankle and was confined to bed for five weeks but as soon as he could walk again he limped along to St Paul's Churchyard to resume the row. In his diary he wrote that Johnson was drunk and had written 'from his wine an insolent epistle.'[38] In December Stedman sent a conciliatory goose to his publisher, although he repented of the gesture when he received in return 'a blurr'd index – such as, the book good for nothing.'[39] Blake also received a goose in recompense for the trouble Stedman and Johnson were causing him.[40]

In the spring of 1796 Stedman sent multiple letters to both Johnson and Blake. He charged his printer not to let Johnson – 'who I would now not save from the gallows' – anywhere near the papers.[41] To Johnson himself he sent two further letters, 'and damn him in them.'[42] Despite his exhortations to both printer and publisher he was unable to protect his manuscript from further alterations. 'Johnson, the demon of Hell, again torments me by altering the dedication to the Prince of Wales', he wrote in May. He had only one explanation for Johnson's conduct: 'he being a d–mn'd eternal Jacobin scoundrel.'[43]

Stedman poured his heart into his *Narrative*. The years he spent in Surinam were formative and his account, in both its edited and unedited forms, bore powerful testimony to the reality of an abhorrent practice. In the published text the combination of image and textual detail offered an eyewitness account of raw power. Thomson may have stripped out the polemic of the *Narrative* because he disagreed with its politics, but he left in details that did the work of the abolitionists far more effectively. Johnson had published texts arguing both sides of the slave-trade debate but in *Narrative of a Five Years Expedition* he produced a volume which gave the reader no choice but to look directly at the reality of the institution. In September 1796, in its lead review, the *Analytical* gave a definitive assessment of the import of Stedman's account:

Many of the facts are indeed so dreadful, that nothing could justify the writer in narrating them, but the hope of inciting in the breasts of his readers a degree of indignation, which will stimulate vigorous and effectual exertions for the speedy termination of the execrable traffic in human flesh, which, to the disgrace of civilised society, is still suffered to exist and is, even in christian countries, sanctioned by the law.[44]

✤

The drunk, obstreperous and unhelpful Johnson of Stedman's diary may be in part the creation of a hot-tempered author unaccustomed to being thwarted by his publisher. He is certainly at odds with the figure described by others who joined the table for dinner. But he may also be representative of the strains under which Johnson was operating by 1795. Johnson was sixty-three and suffering from asthma when he worked with Stedman, and the number of people who depended on him grew no smaller. Priestley was his oldest friend and nevertheless received a brusque reply when he invited Johnson to invest in his plans for a farm and college in Northumberland. Stedman may well have experienced Johnson's increasing disinclination to conciliate with egotistical authors whose manuscripts were not ready for publication. He appeared at St Paul's Churchyard just as an increasingly polarised political culture resulted in authors who had once discussed their differences with courtesy now rejecting each other's company. Sarah Trimmer found increasingly public ways of articulating her disapproval with the politics of Johnson's inner circle. She was particularly censorious of Barbauld's 'Things by their Right Names', which she attacked in a long review of *Evenings at Home*. The dialogue was 'evidently designed to impress children with the idea that all *warriors* are *murderers*.' But 'to call a battle "a *bloody murder*," when the cause on one side or another is justifiable, is *not* "calling things by their *right names*".'[45] Johnson continued to issue Trimmer's work for the first part of the 1790s but by the end of the decade she had found a publisher with whose politics she felt more sympathy. Trimmer might have left his lists, but Johnson continued to publish educational textbooks and volumes for children in amongst his more eye-catching acquisitions. The Dissenting defences and sermons also continued to appear, even as the Dissenters themselves were singled out for public opprobrium.

In the autumn of 1795 Pitt's government introduced a pair of bills that became known as the 'Gagging Acts'. By December both pieces of legislation had passed through Parliament and received royal assent. The Acts extended the definition of treason to include speaking and writing, even if no treasonable action followed as a result. Booksellers were one of its chief targets. The Acts also prohibited any meeting of more than fifty people without the express permission of a magistrate, which rendered the activities of London's reform societies illegal. The Gagging Acts were extremely effective in quelling the chorus of reformist resistance that had been building throughout Britain since 1789. 'The people of this country are mute', wrote Johnson six months later. 'Even a petition is not mentioned, the cabinet is supposed to be all wise.'[46] Writing on the same day to Priestley, he expressed the same sentiment: 'The people here are as quiet as lambs, hardly any grumbling, no seditions meetings or pamphlets, the minister does what he pleases.'[47] For thirty-five years Johnson had worked to open up conversation in person and in print. In 1795, as the country fell silent, that work appeared to count for little.

PART SIX

CAVE (1792–1799)

James Gillray, 'A peep into the Cave of Jacobinism', for the *Anti-Jacobin Review*, 1798

How, then, to keep talking, as the law of the land is twisted into a gag? In concert with Cowper and Fuseli, Johnson finds one answer to this question in the melding of images with the words of a long-dead poet. Wordsworth finds in poetry a different kind of answer, in the company of a new friend, Samuel Taylor Coleridge. Coleridge is a young Unitarian of whom Lindsey has had high hopes. When he comes to dinner at St Paul's Churchyard he is at a crossroads, poised to leave behind the dubious comforts of family and home in order to travel to a country where he is a stranger. Wollstonecraft also leaves the sanctuary of Johnson's dining room for a period. When she returns it is to build a new kind of bond with a man whose dinner conversation she has, in the past, dismissed. Priestley has gone too but Lindsey is still there, along with Bonnycastle, Fuseli and Rowland Hunter, who is increasingly seen by those at dinner as his proxy uncle's mainstay. Maria Edgeworth and her father Richard dine whenever they are in town; a new writer, Thomas Malthus, spars with Godwin over his veal and rice pudding. In the dying days of the 1790s it still seems as if it is possible for the men and women of the dining room to meet at Johnson's house in safety and security. But to some of those who do not have the privilege of dining under the image of Fuseli's Nightmare, Johnson's dining room appears less a sanctuary than a cave of Jacobin sedition. And, in the shop below, a government spy has just made a purchase that will bring dinner with Joseph Johnson to a sudden and unexpected stop.

2 2

Paradise Lost

Amid the political turmoil of the first half of the 1790s, the work of making and writing offered relief. While many of Johnson's dinner guests drew renewed energy from the legislative assaults of Pitt's Terror, honing their craft in oppositional pamphlets, poems and essays, for others creative labour remained driven primarily by artistic vision, economic necessity and personal need. For Cowper and Fuseli work was central to the business of survival. Cowper depended on the absorption of professional authorship for his sanity and connection to the world. Fuseli's ability to keep a roof over his head hung on the generosity of unpredictable patrons and the tastes of a fickle public. In August 1791 Johnson proposed a project that he hoped would produce contrasting forms of security for both men. The shorthand title of the project was 'Milton'.

Johnson's proposal was bold. Fuseli would paint large-scale images from Milton's work, financed by subscribers; Johnson asked Cowper to take on the task of editing a 'magnificent edition' of Milton's poetry to accompany the images. The concept was borrowed from John Boydell's Shakespeare Gallery but the idea of melding the editorial talents of a popular poet with Fuseli's paintings was Johnson's innovation. There was 'no person so proper as yourself for the task', Johnson told Cowper in a letter outlining his idea. Meanwhile Fuseli 'of all men is certainly the fittest to <u>paint</u> from Milton.' Johnson ended his letter by declining an invitation to visit Cowper at Weston. No further excursion was possible that summer since his two chief adjutants in the shop were ill. His duty, he told Cowper, was 'rather to work double tides than dismiss a servant for the visitation of God.'[1]

Johnson enclosed draft proposals for the Milton project in his letter to Cowper, prompting him to demand more information in return. What, precisely, did Johnson expect of him? Merely, came the reply, 'a correct text', along with 'notes from other writers as deserve to be preserved, & to add such as may occur to yourself illustrative of any part of his works.' And, as an afterthought, 'also translations of his Italian & Latin poems.'[2] Cowper agreed. A triumphant Johnson asked him to begin by editing the proposals. He gave Cowper considerable latitude in how he approached the project and offered a fixed payment of 200 guineas. He also wasted no time in securing the services of his two best engravers for the enterprise. William Blake and Richard Sharp were charged with transforming Fuseli's enormous paintings into book-sized engravings; other engravers also promised their services. Initially Sharp was at a loss as to how to capture the images at full scale. He employed a carpenter to make a roller that was supposed to rise and fall over Fuseli's canvases but the device was a failure. It was Paine, the lover of invention, who came to the rescue. 'Milton goes on', Fuseli told Roscoe:

> Sharpe has had his picture (the picture itself, not a Copy) nearly these two months and is busy in the Aqua-fortis part of both plates. We have contrived a roller for him from the design of Mr. Paine who is a Mechanic as well as a Demogorgon, to enable him to place it, for it is nearly 13 feet high by a width of 10; and though his house is larger than those of most Engravers it was too high to enter any of his rooms.[3]

With Cowper in place as editor, Fuseli as painter and Paine, somewhat unexpectedly, acting as informal technical advisor, the Milton project appeared destined for success. But subscriptions were slow to arrive. Wollstonecraft thought the problem lay both in a surfeit of schemes for illustrated editions started 'with *catch-penny* eagerness' and in Johnson's incorruptible good nature. 'The world contains not a more friendly heart', she told Roscoe. Johnson's workload diverted his attention elsewhere and he 'could not condescend to use the mean arts, had he leisure, which the promoters of other plans, of a similar nature, avail themselves of.' Such goodness was of no use in a 'puffing age.' Moreover, Wollstonecraft continued, 'I still think, I speak without reserve, that it would have been carried on with more spirit had there been a partner or two with money to speculate with.' She was worried about the impact of failure on Fuseli. 'I love the man and admire the artist ... this I mention to you in confidence and make light of it to him, for on this work the comfort of his life, in every sense of the word, seems to depend.'⁴ She was at least convinced that in Milton Fuseli had found the right subject. 'He seems quite at home in hell.'⁵

As subscriptions failed to emerge Fuseli became embroiled in a quarrel with John Boydell, when the latter revealed that he too was preparing a large-scale Milton edition to accompany a biography of the poet from the writer William Hayley. In spite, or because, of the competition, Johnson pressed forward. Fuseli continued to produce paintings for the gallery in between other commissions and Johnson kept Cowper supplied with the books he needed for research. He issued an ambitious advertisement for 'proposals for engraving and publishing by subscription thirty capital plates, [16 inches by 23] from subjects in Milton; to be painted principally, if not entirely, by Henry Fuseli, R. A. and for copying them in a reduced size to accompany a correct and magnificent edition, embellished also with forty-five elegant vignettes, of his poetical works, with notes, illustrations, and translations of the Italian and Latin poems, by W. Cowper. Messieurs Bartolozzi, Sharp, Holloway, Blake and other eminent Engravers have promised their Assistance in the Execution of the Plates.'⁶ The advertisement emphasised expertise across three fields: painting, editing and engraving.

From Weston Cowper wrote with a mixture of pleasure and unease about his new role. The prospect of becoming caught up in a dispute with Boydell worried him but the financial freedom the commission gave him was welcome. Johnson agreed to act as Cowper's banker, holding his earnings and offering an interest rate of 5 per cent. It was better security, Cowper acknowledged to one friend, than that promised by most banks. He told Samuel Rose it was a relief to be called to sit down to work each day. 'You, who know how necessary it is to me to be employed, will be glad to hear that I have been called to a new literary engagement, and that I have not refused it.'⁷ To another acquaintance he wrote that since he had already appeared before the public as an author and translator it seemed right he should appear once more in print as an editor. It was a conceit he repeated several times to different correspondents, suggesting he felt a degree of unease about the impact of the Milton project on his reputation as a poet. Milton's republican politics also presented difficulties, particularly in an era when king-killing appeared to be back in vogue. Cowper read through the four Latin poems on the Gunpowder Plot and informed Johnson that they would best remain untranslated. 'We and the Papists are at present on amicable terms', he explained. 'They have behaved themselves peaceably many years, and have lately received favours from government: I should think, therefore, that the dying embers of antient animosity had better not be troubled.'[8]

Cowper began work with confidence, translating all the poems he considered to be politically palatable and complaining vociferously when Johnson's failure to send books held him up. In March 1792 he received a concerned letter from the biographer Boydell had employed, William Hayley. Hayley sent the letter to St Paul's Churchyard where it languished for six weeks. Cowper was furious that Johnson's neglect had made him appear rude to a fellow gentleman writer and he wrote fulsomely in reply, both of Johnson's failings and Hayley's kindness. 'A Life of Milton is no part of my bargain', he insisted.[9] A productive correspondence unfolded between the two men, focused on the challenges and possibilities presented by Milton. Johnson had sent Cowper an interleaved edition of Milton's verse, so that he could write his annotations next to the relevant lines of poetry. He went to work on the first two books of *Paradise Lost* and in May wrote to Hayley of his disbelief that Milton was so little read. 'It is in fact a wonderful thing and no small disgrace to us English, that being natives of a Country that has produced the finest poem in the world, so few of us ever look into it.'[10] Later that month Hayley made the journey from his home in Sussex to Weston to continue the conversation in person. 'We have formed a friendship', Cowper told his cousin, 'that I trust will last for life.'[11]

Hayley was still in residence at Weston in late May, when Cowper's companion Mary Unwin had a stroke. The attack rendered her speech unintelligible, paralysed her right hand and arm, weakened her legs and made it almost impossible for her to open her eyes. Cowper was devastated and Hayley marched into action. He dispatched letters to London doctors and arranged to borrow an 'Electrical Machine' from a neighbour. The machine sent electrical currents through Mrs Unwin's body. 'We think', Cowper reported, 'it has been of material service.'[12] Mrs Unwin's condition slowly stabilised, although she remained immobile and fragile. Hayley left and Cowper took on the role of chief nurse. The thought of losing Mrs Unwin tormented him. 'My nocturnal experiences are all of the most terrible kind. Death, church yards and carcases, or else thunder storms and lightnings, God angry, and myself wishing that I had never been born.'[13] With his domestic world turned upside down he found it impossible to keep working on Milton. To multiple correspondents he wrote that he was utterly unable to work. 'Who can hope for peace amid such trouble?' he asked Samuel Teedon. 'I cannot. I live a life of terrour.'[14]

In mid-June there was a moment of triumph when Mrs Unwin managed a few independent steps in the garden. Cowper was still unable to focus on Milton but he did turn his gaze briefly towards the literary world. His young cousin Johnny had been to see Johnson and had discussed whether there was merit in producing a new Anglo-Greek edition of Cowper's Homer. Johnson replied decisively that such an edition would be 'bought only by idle folks who are at a loss to know what do with their money' but he was receptive to the idea of a new and improved edition of Cowper's translation itself.[15] A letter arrived from Paine's friend Clio Rickman, to whom Johnson had sent a copy of Homer. 'He is a red-hot Paynite', Cowper told Lady Hesketh, 'and thinking me such also, boasts that ... Tom dines often with him. He commends my Homer and hopes for my correspondence, but I shall not answer him.'[16] Cowper's politics had shifted since the pre-Revolutionary years when he had written of the bleakness of the Bastille in *The Task*. Although he thought reform was necessary the radicalism of Paine and his supporters was an anathema. A year later, when Lady Hesketh reported that Paine was being burnt in effigy, Cowper retorted, only partly in jest, that he objected 'to his being executed in effigy only, and not in reality.'[17]

✝

'Love you?' wrote Cowper to Hayley in June 1792. 'Yes to be sure I do. Do you take me for a stock or a stone that you make a question of it? Have you not taken a more ardent interest in me and my poor Mary than ever man did? Of what materials can you suppose me made, if after all the rapid proofs that you have given me of your friendship, I do not love you with all my heart and regret your absence continually?'[18] William Hayley had a passion for collecting celebrated writers and he went to great lengths to involve himself in the lives of his friends. Some who came into his orbit found him suffocating and domineering; others were grateful to have their problems taken in hand. As a young man he was determined to be a literary personage but his talent lay more in organising the lives of others than in producing original work. Hayley was not the first person to try and rescue Cowper and Mrs Unwin but he was the most masterful. In mid-June he suggested that Cowper and Mrs Unwin should spend the summer at his house at Eartham in Sussex. Despite Mrs Unwin's health and the fact that

Cowper had not left Buckinghamshire for twenty-five years, they accepted Hayley's suggestion.

The invitation injected new optimism into Cowper's letters. By the end of June he was sufficiently engaged in the world of letters to agree to review the complete edition of both parts of Darwin's *Botanic Garden* for the *Analytical Review*. The prospect of the journey to Eartham was alarming: Cowper called it a 'formidable but pleasing enterprize'.[19] He stipulated that Mrs Unwin would need to be able to walk alone, wear her own shoes and cut up her own food before they attempted it. Johnson wrote enclosing Cowper's manuscript translation of Homer and a bound copy of the proofs so that Cowper could get to work on a revised edition and Cowper was touched by the care with which Johnson had preserved the manuscripts from the printer's depredations. Johnson also offered Cowper and Mrs Unwin a bed for the night at St Paul's Churchyard so that they could break their journey to Eartham. Cowper sent a decisive rejection, but he did so with regret that he and Johnson were unlikely ever to meet in person. 'I tell you the truth when I tell you that I should have great pleasure in passing a night under your roof, and Mrs U. and I both feel the obligation of your hospitable offer.' To re-enter London, the city in which he had first seen visions of his own damnation, seemed impossible. 'I have a real horror of London, not as London, but for reasons which would fill a volume.'[20]

Throughout July Cowper and Mrs Unwin remained in limbo at Weston, waiting for the moment when they felt strong enough to travel. On July 8th Cowper wrote in a panic to Johnson that he was not making progress. At home he was performing every role except that of writer: 'electrician' (that is, operator of the electrical machine), 'Escort into the Garden' and nurse. Did Johnson really expect to publish the first part of the Milton project in the spring of 1794? 'I cannot bear to be waited for, neither shall I be able to perform my part of the work with any success if I am hunted.' Cowper's imagery tells its own story. In *The Task* he had described himself amidst the tortures of mental agony as a 'stricken deer'. Now he evoked himself once more as 'hunted' and he warned Johnson that he asked the question 'lest my own distress should increase and should ultimately prove a distress to you.'[21] It took Johnson time to respond, prompting a characteristic barb from Cowper about Johnson's professional status. 'Little men', he told Hayley, 'can be dumb in my concerns as well as great ones.'[22]

At the end of July Hayley sent directions about the route to Eartham and Cowper's cousin Johnny arrived at Weston to superintend the journey.

A coach was hired; letters were sent reserving beds at stopping places along the way. Cowper's tone in his correspondence in the days before the journey was fatalistic. He wrote of his hope that Mrs Unwin would benefit from the change of air and that he would recover his work ethic at Eartham, but he was confident of neither. But on August 5th he wrote to Samuel Teedon from Eartham of his surprise that the journey, so long dreaded, had been accomplished without disaster. He was intimidated by the scale of the Sussex hills and relayed nightmare memories of the noise of the inn at Barnet where they had spent the first of two nights on the road. The route passed through London and although the carriage did not stop it nevertheless took all Cowper's mental strength to withstand the experience. His friend Samuel Rose travelled out to Barnet and joined Cowper, Mrs Unwin and Johnny in the coach for the perilous passage through the capital. As they passed over the river at Westminster Bridge Cowper caught a glimpse of St Paul's Cathedral and was assailed by thoughts of the world from which he had exiled himself. 'In my way hither I saw the cupola of your church,' he told Johnson, 'and thought much of you at the bottom of it. But it was not possible for me to gratify the desire I felt to see you.'[23]

At Eartham Hayley brimmed with confidence that he could reanimate Cowper's work. He instituted a strict schedule, driving Cowper from bed in the mornings for two hours of mutual work on 'Miltonic labours'.[24] Hayley was in his element, with a vulnerable literary celebrity under his eye who was apparently in need of his support and who was working on the same author as Hayley himself. A soothing letter arrived from Johnson saying that he was in no hurry to receive Cowper's work and the combination of Hayley's encouragement and Johnson's reassurances brought Cowper a brief period of respite from anxiety about the project.

Eartham was full of visitors and he enjoyed the unaccustomed sensation of mixing with artistic people. Among the other guests were the painter George Romney and the writer Charlotte Smith. Smith was a prolific and much-admired poet and novelist and Cowper was interested both in her work and in the extremity of her misfortune. When she was sixteen she had married a merchant called Benjamin Smith, by whom she bore eleven children. Her husband was profligate and violent and in the early 1780s she had joined him in a debtor's prison. She left him in 1787 but under English law her earnings remained his property. In consequence her finances were parlous and she enjoyed little security as a result of her literary success. Her novels dealt with the legal injustices suffered by women; her poetry influenced a new generation of young male poets in its presentation of nature as a source of emotional and mental strength during times of difficulty. Cowper thought she was 'interesting both by her manners and her misfortunes.'[25] In the intervals between compulsory work on Milton, Hayley persuaded Cowper to sit for his portrait to Romney. The image that resulted shows the poet in his writer's cap, gazing into the distance. His face is mobile; his eyes are puffy and show the effects of broken nights and unhappiness. Cowper wrote that the drawing 'is agreed by all here to be my exact counterpart' and told Johnson that if he insisted on having an engraving of him included in a new edition of his poems and translations Romney's image would serve as a source.[26]

✢

Cowper and Mrs Unwin returned home at the beginning of the third week of September. In his letter reporting their safe arrival Cowper told Hayley that the chaos of their house on their return matched the Chaos evoked by Milton himself. He nevertheless acknowledged that the adventure had been a success. Within a day, however, the blackness against which he had struggled all summer descended. 'My frame of mind continues such as it was before I went to Eartham, almost always low, and often inexpressibly dejected. My work is still in suspense, or to say truth, not yet begun, nor do I at present see that I am likely to have any leisure for such labours.'[27] At the beginning of October he made a renewed attempt to write, but to no avail. Friends wrote encouragingly; Cowper responded with some frustration that he was unable to convey the depths of the difficulties he was experiencing. On October 28th he told Hayley that Milton had become a grievance: 'I might almost as well be haunted by his ghost, as goaded with such continual self reproaches for neglecting him.'[28] His cousin Johnny visited Johnson and sent a cheering account of the people and conversations he had encountered at St Paul's Churchyard. Cowper responded with an anxious demand to know whether Johnson had commented on his lack of progress. By November he was writing of his wish that he had never consented to Johnson's initial request and he blamed the project for his mental torment. Johnson himself figured in his correspondence alternately as a gentleman saviour and a low-born villain. News reached Cowper that Johnson, who owned the copyright of his poems, was proposing to issue a new edition for the poet's benefit. It was a fair-minded gesture that acknowledged how much Johnson had benefited financially from Cowper's talent.

On November 20th Cowper wrote that he rejoiced in the idea: 'It restores him to his place in my good opinion, and even advances him a little higher than he stood before.'[29] Surely, he continued, it would vindicate Johnson in the eyes of those among his friends who had doubted the bookseller's good intentions. Five days later, however, Johnson was once more 'an idle rogue', although, Cowper conceded, a generous one.[30]

The end of 1792 came and Cowper was still trapped, unable to move forward with Milton or to give up the attempt. On a loose-leaf page, stored amongst an annotated proof of Homer, he wrote fragmentary prayers and responses which veered between hope and despair. 'Apply assistance in my case indigent and necessitous' ... 'I cannot doubt that my God is in earnest with me' ... 'Give us the best edition of Milton.' Sometimes God was consoling: 'I have never left you entirely, though I have often been accused of doing so.' At other times there was little hope, although there were always new discoveries. 'I read Milton now with other eyes than I ever did before. Which with the rest shall be dismissed.'[31] Cowper's eyes were inflamed and he complained that to sit at a desk and write was physically as well as mentally taxing – although he continued to write long letters to his closest confidantes. As he looked back on 1792 he felt that the year had been blighted by the undertaking he had given Johnson. 'Milton is still a mountain on my shoulders, and it seems to me that if the new year brings with it no favourable change for me, either in outward circumstance or mental qualification, I must at last relinquish him.'[32] The scale of the task was insurmountable, but wrestling with Milton's visions of hell produced in Cowper a degree of mental torment that was not accounted for by volume of work alone. Milton wrote of damnation with terrifying clarity and it was almost more than Cowper could bear. 'The year 92 shall stand chronicled in my remembrance as the most melancholy that I have ever known, except the weeks that I spent at Eartham', he wrote at the end of the year. 'Such it has been principally because being engaged to Milton I felt myself no longer free for any other engagement. That ill-fated work, impracticable itself, has made every thing else impracticable.'[33]

✠

In the first months of 1793 references to Milton faded from Cowper's letters. He busied himself as best he could with amendments for the revised edition of Homer and, in January, was anxiously anticipating a review of his translation in the *Analytical Review*. His correspondent James Hurdis had hoped to win the commission but Johnson gave the task of reviewing Cowper's work to Fuseli, who had already commented extensively on the manuscript.[34] Fuseli was complimentary but not uncritical. Cowper was to be congratulated but he was 'often verbose' and some of his lines were unpolished.[35] Cowper worked out that the review was by Fuseli – 'I know him by infallible indications' – but although he took issue with some of the criticism he was relieved to find his work fairly treated.[36] In February he professed himself happy with Johnson's offer of £200, and the retention of the copyright, for the new edition of Homer. Again he wrote of his pleasure that the bookseller had acted in a gentlemanly way. 'What think you of my little book-seller now?' he asked Lady Hesketh, long one of Johnson's chief detractors.[37] In April he was sufficiently moved by Johnson's generosity to write that it almost made up for his own lack of rich ancestors. It was 'an act of liberality which I take every opportunity to blazon as it well deserves.'[38] This sentiment he repeated to Johnson himself: 'A bookseller with a disposition like yours is an author's best patron.'[39] But alongside this blazoning there were frequent complaints which suggest Cowper's deep unease about class and dependence. Could a bookseller – a tradesman – really be the patron of a gentleman? Was he not rather, as Cowper often suggested to his aristocratic correspondents, a servant charged with producing printed pages for a fee? When a bookseller was lauded by mutual friends as a gentleman with his own creative will and voice, or as an astute editor and reader, how was he then to be treated?

In his tangles with these questions, Cowper occasionally resorted to insults. A wanted parcel was delayed at St Paul's Churchyard in March. 'Hang him.'[40] Johnson was usually 'my little Bookseller' or 'My Bookseller': proprietorial formulations through which Cowper asserted his seniority in the relationship. But in spite of the frequency with which he wrote of Johnson as an infuriating tradesman, he recognised Johnson's loyalty and consistently wrote of it, including to correspondents who he knew took a different view. In spite of his protestations it mattered that Johnson thought him worthy of support. Thus, to Samuel Rose: 'I am now satisfied with my Bookseller, as I have substantial cause to be, and account myself in good hands; a circumstance as pleasant to me as any other part of the business, for I love dearly to be able to confide with all my heart in those with whom I am connected, of what kind soever the connection be.'[41]

At the end of November 1792 Johnson brought Cowper's Miltonic labours to an end. Hayley went to St Paul's Churchyard and, in the course of a frank conversation with Johnson, the two men agreed that Cowper was simply unable to complete the work required. Boydell was pulling away with his own project, aided by the industrious and punctual delivery by Hayley of his own life of Milton. Hayley told Cowper that Johnson had decided to postpone publication 'on account of the war, which leaves the world no leisure for literary amusements; Johnson accordingly thinks it would be too hazardous to send forth so expensive a work at present.'[42] There was truth in this assertion, but it also released Cowper from an undertaking he was manifestly unable to fulfil without humiliating him. Gratitude rang through his letters. 'I cannot tell you what a relief I feel it, not to be press'd for Milton'.[43] A week later: 'It is a great relief to me that my Miltonic labours are suspended.'[44] For a brief period he returned to the revision of Homer but the darkness of winter tested his mental stability as it had done for so many winters before. In January 1794 he wrote that he was blinded to the world outside his door. 'Were I less absorbed in miserable Self than I am, the horrid condition of Europe, and especially the affairs of England, would touch me deeply. But, as it is, whether towns are taken and battles won or lost, seems to affect me little.'[45]

✢

Throughout the fourteen-month period in which Cowper wrestled with Milton, Fuseli painted scenes from *Paradise Lost*. Two canvases, each thirteen feet by ten, showed Satan and Death meeting at the gates of Hell, and Satan in Chaos. A third canvas, twelve feet by ten, represented the Vision of the Leper house from Book Eleven. Two pictures depicted Eve, at the moment of her creation and as she saw herself for the first time in the reflection of a stream. There was a further picture of Milton dictating to his daughters, and, from *Paradise Regained*, a representation of Christ in the stormy desert. Fuseli poured himself into the images, which combined the epic scale of his history paintings with an intensely personal imaginative response to Milton's verse.

Fuseli had worked on the paintings without the prospect of secure payment; neither subscribers nor the projected edition of Milton's work had materialised. With Cowper released from his obligations Johnson and Fuseli wrote again to William Roscoe in Liverpool. They wanted a small group of men to unite as supporters of Fuseli in order to pay him a salary in return for a set number of smaller pieces of work, each with a fixed price. Fuseli's backers would be required to wait several years before their investment was repaid with art, since he was determined to reserve three days a week for the Milton project alone. He asked Roscoe to act as guarantor for the scheme, so that his backers could invest in his time in confidence that their money was safe. It was an innovative scheme, which merged the established patronage models of the art world with a newer conception of the artist's time and labour as a tradeable commodity. It arose from Johnson's conviction that even without an accompanying edition, it was possible for Fuseli to live on the proceeds of his remaking of Milton, and that the work might give him the security and independence he so desired. Roscoe was sympathetic to the idea of a subscription to support Fuseli's industry and he authorised Johnson to draw up a formal proposal for investors. Johnson struggled with the text and professed himself dissatisfied with the draft he sent to Liverpool:

> Mr F. having employed the Last two Years almost entirely in executing pictures from Milton for his intended exhibition of a Series of Subjects from that Author in which he had made a considerable progress, Specimens of which may be Seen at his house: finds it necessary to address his Friends for their encouragement in an undertaking so arduous & so expensive, and the more so because a report has gone abroad that he has no Leisure for undertaking anything else. He wishes to inform His Friends, such that, at hours of relaxation, Such as the sustained attention to a great object must at times necessarily require, he should be glad to receive orders for small pictures at 20, 30, 50 Guineas each, half to be paid at the time of giving the commission, & the remainder on receiving the picture.[46]

It was an awkward proposal to couch, but it did result in a few staunch supporters – Johnson among them – coming forward to back Fuseli's efforts. For the most part, though, the financial burden of supporting Fuseli's vision fell to Roscoe alone.

⁺

Fuseli's artistic labours for the Milton project unfolded on a heroic scale. There were vast canvases, epic scenes and untrammelled ambition. There was heroism too in the long months Cowper spent wrestling with his Miltonic mountain, during which he refused to give up the attempt despite domestic crisis and bleak depression. Also heroic on its own terms was

Johnson's determination to bring together his friend and one of his most prized authors in order to make a new kind of book and artistic endeavour, while also easing the difficulties with which friend and author struggled. Publisher, artist and author were all tested by the creative demands of the project. It failed because of public events, but also because Johnson recognised that the human cost of continuing was too high.

Cowper never emerged from the darkness that enveloped him in January 1794. Mrs Unwin's health declined in step with Cowper's mental state to the point that they could no longer care for themselves. In July 1795 they were moved by friends to Norfolk, to the home of Cowper's devoted cousin Johnny. Mrs Unwin died in Norfolk at the end of 1796. Cowper attempted once more to hold the nightmares at bay through the translation of Latin poems, but work could no longer save him. His last surviving letter was dated April 11th 1799 and was to John Newton, who had shown him the way back to God and introduced him to Johnson twenty years before. He wrote to acknowledge the gift of a volume that reminded Cowper of the brief happy period before he learnt of the certainty of his own damnation. The memories of a period when he remained in ignorance of the 'storm ... which in one terrible moment would darken, and in another still more terrible, blot out that prospect for ever' were painful beyond description, but Cowper was nevertheless grateful for the memory of Newton's friendship. 'Adieu Dear Sir,' his letter concluded, 'whom in those days I call'd Dear friend, with feelings that justified the appellation'.[47] A year after writing his last letter Cowper died, aged sixty-eight.

23

Vindication of the Rights of Woman

When Mary Wollstonecraft's first biographer William Godwin came to try and understand the events and experiences that shaped her, he drew attention to three features of the life she made for herself after 1789. First, he wrote of the French Revolution as the formative event in the development of her politics and her political writing. Second, he represented the company she kept at St Paul's Churchyard as central to her burgeoning confidence and intellectual ambition. Third, he positioned her relationship with Fuseli as the trigger for an emotional upheaval which prompted her subsequent actions. In the summer of 1792 the ramifications of all three events and experiences came together to propel Wollstonecraft out of London, in a crisis that shaped the rest of her life.

In the months following the publication of *A Vindication of the Rights of Woman* Wollstonecraft experienced the pleasures of professional recognition. She was the author of a well-known book and she had achieved her ambition to become a professional woman writer. She was just able to pay for lodgings of her own and, through her own exertions and Johnson's friendship, had freed herself from the drudgery of governessing. In letters to her sisters it was professional success that she emphasised: of the turmoil entailed by her connection with Fuseli she was silent. When Godwin wrote of this period of Wollstonecraft's life he went to great lengths to demonstrate that she had no wish to come between Fuseli and his wife. 'She set a great value', he wrote, 'on a mutual affection between persons of an opposite sex. She regarded it as the principal solace of human life.' In other words, he continued, Wollstonecraft believed it should be possible for men and women to establish imaginative and emotional connections with each other without debasing those connections by muddying them with physical or sensual passions. In Wollstonecraft's philosophy it was only as a result of the failings of men that such connections rarely flourished. 'She regarded the manners and habits of the majority of our sex in that respect, with strong disapprobation.' Yet Godwin was also convinced that Wollstonecraft framed her feelings for Fuseli as a matter of the imagination rather than the senses only because the artist was already married. 'There is no reason to doubt that, if Mr. Fuseli had been disengaged at the period of their acquaintance, he would have been the man of her choice.'[1]

Godwin presented Wollstonecraft's belief in the possibility of platonic reciprocal passion between men and women as heroic and deluded. In his explanation, marriage placed Fuseli beyond reach and in response Wollstonecraft deceived herself into thinking a different kind of relationship might be possible. 'She conceived it both practicable and eligible, to cultivate a distinguishing affection for him, and to foster it by the endearments of personal intercourse and a reciprocation of kindness, without departing in the smallest degree from the rules she prescribed to herself.'[2] Godwin's phrasing – 'she conceived' – writes his own scepticism into his narrative. It implies a belief that Wollstonecraft's unruly passions led her into faulty reasoning. What Godwin neglected to mention, possibly because he did not witness it before the complications of other kinds of relationships altered its dynamic, was that Wollstonecraft's friendship with Johnson offered a model for a connection between a man and woman which, like Johnson's own friendship with Fuseli, had no name.

In June 1792 Wollstonecraft, Johnson and Fuseli decided they wanted to witness events in Paris for themselves. They travelled to Dover with Fuseli's wife Sophia, where they waited to set sail for France. Wollstonecraft viewed the prospect of a foreign excursion in the company of Johnson and the Fuselis eagerly. 'I shall be introduced to many people', she predicted to Everina. 'My book has been translated and praised in some popular prints; and Fuseli, of course, is well known; it is then very probable that I shall hear of some situation for Eliza, and I shall be on the watch. We intend to be absent only six weeks, if then I fix on an eligible situation for her she may avoid the Welsh winter.'[3] Wollstonecraft found it easier to justify an international jaunt made in defiance of her sisters' unhappiness by insisting she had their interests and prospects chiefly in mind, but the rhythms of her prose belied her. Paris held many attractions, amongst which securing a position for Eliza hardly figured. Her focus as she contemplated a visit to the French capital was instead on new readers and the glow cast by Fuseli's celebrity.

While Johnson, Wollstonecraft and the Fuselis waited for a ship in Dover news reached them of the French Royal Family's escape and recapture. France suddenly seemed a dangerous place to visit on a whim. The party returned to London briefly, before Wollstonecraft and Johnson departed once more for the country, this time leaving the Fuselis behind. When they returned to London in the autumn they were greeted with rumours that they had married. Wollstonecraft repeated the gossip for Roscoe's benefit. 'Our friend Johnson is well – I am told the world, to talk big, married m[e] to him whilst we were away'.[4]

The idea was sufficiently amusing to be recounted, but Wollstonecraft's letters to Johnson himself reveal that although marriage was out of the question a relationship based on great depths of emotional understanding was not. When Johnson failed to appreciate the extremity of her passions it mattered as much as if the failure was that of a husband or lover. 'I am a mere animal', she told him in one undated letter. 'Instinctive emotions too often silence the suggestions of reason. Your note – I can scarcely tell why, hurt me – and produced a kind of winterly smile, which diffuses a beam of despondent tranquillity over the features.' She wanted recognition of her suffering rather than to have her passions frozen by reason, but in her distress she also reproached herself with her treatment of her friend and chief supporter. 'I blushed when I recollected how often I had teazed you with childish complaints, and the reveries of a disordered imagination. I even *imagined* that I intruded on you, because you never called on me – though you perceived that I was not well.' As she tried to articulate her torment Wollstonecraft pushed at the boundaries of language, searching for a register through which Johnson could be made to bear witness to her difficulties. 'I have nourished a sickly kind of delicacy ... I am a strange compound of weakness and resolution ... I must be content to weep and dance like a child ... We must each of us wear a fool's cap; but mine, alas! has lost its bells.'[5]

At some point in the autumn of 1792 the febrile exchanges between Wollstonecraft and Fuseli came to a head. Fuseli told John Knowles that Wollstonecraft had confronted his wife Sophia and asked to be admitted as a third member of her marriage and that Sophia had ordered her from the house as a result. It was a story that suited Fuseli's idea of himself, as the idol of two women. Johnson may have played a part, compelling Wollstonecraft to confront the impossibility of the kind of idealised relationship of which she dreamt. Wollstonecraft herself may have concluded that to remain in Fuseli's orbit was no longer tolerable. In late November she decided to remove herself from the company of both bookseller and artist. Godwin wrote that she recognised the necessity of parting from Fuseli and took a decisive step to protect herself from the pain of continued meeting. 'She felt herself formed for domestic affection, and all those tender charities, which men of sensibility have constantly treated as the dearest band of human society. She felt herself alone, as it were, in the great mass of her species.' In the face of this reality Fuseli's company offered only pain. 'She conceived it necessary to snap the chain of this association in her mind; and, for that purpose, determined to seek a new climate, and mingle in different scenes.'[6]

In early December 1792 Wollstonecraft told Everina that she had booked her passage to Paris and that this time there would be no turning back at Dover. Everina knew little of her sister's relationships and Fuseli was not mentioned as Wollstonecraft outlined the anxieties that leaving London caused her. To part with Johnson entailed a pain of which it was easier to write. 'My spirits even sink; but I go – yet should any accident happen to my dear and worthy friend Johnson during my absence I should never forgive myself for leaving him.'[7] Wollstonecraft also had more practical worries, prompted by the aggression of France's Revolutionary government and the reaction of the British authorities. She knew herself to be travelling to an unstable country with no guarantee of a safe passage home. Yet she remained determined to break the bonds of her life in London. She secured lodgings with Everina's old Parisian employer and, in a reversal of normal practice, borrowed £30 from her sisters to fund her travels. They were requested to send the money to Johnson so that she could draw on it through his network of Parisian business connections.

�†

On Christmas Eve Wollstonecraft wrote her first letter from Paris. Two days later she watched from her window as Louis XVI was taken to his trial. Opposite she saw that every window was crowded with witnesses, none of whom made a sound. 'For the first time since I entered France', she told Johnson, 'I bowed to the majesty of the people, and respected the propriety of behaviour so perfectly in unison with my own feelings. I can scarcely tell you why, but an association of ideas made the tears flow insensibly from my eyes, when I saw Louis sitting, with more dignity than I expected from his character, in a hackney coach, going to meet death, where so many of his race have triumphed.' It was a sight that showed what was possible if a people rose up to defend their rights, and it served as a reminder that every revolution entailed human suffering. Wollstonecraft told Johnson that it brought before her mind's eye a vision of Louis XIV entering Paris in his pomp, oblivious to the misery endured by his subjects. The downfall of such corruption was a cause for celebration; but in her solitude Wollstonecraft nevertheless felt the Parisian air to be thick with menace. She knew that Johnson would greet such flights of fancy with friendly scepticism. 'Nay, do not smile, but pity me', she told him. 'For, once or twice, lifting my eyes from the paper, I have seen eyes glare through a glass-door opposite my chair, and bloody hands shook at me. Not the distant sound of a footstep can I hear.' Even the kitchen cat had fled to its quarters, taking with it the fleeting comfort of the presence of another animate being. 'I want to see something alive', she concluded. 'Death in so many frightful shapes has taken hold of my fancy. – I am going to bed – and, for the first time in my life, I cannot put out the candle.'[8]

Wollstonecraft's isolation was broken as news of her arrival brought visits from members of the English community who gathered at White's hotel and in the house of Helen Maria Williams. Williams was a friend of both Godwin and Barbauld and a Dissenting writer whose *Letters from France* were providing English readers with a vivid eyewitness account of the unfolding Revolution. In Paris she was among Wollstonecraft's first visitors: Wollstonecraft thought her manners were affected, but 'the *simple* goodness of her heart continually breaks through the varnish.'[9] She renewed her acquaintance with Paine and with Thomas Christie, the original editor of the *Analytical Review*. As her French improved she also made friends with radicals of both nationalities at Helen Maria Williams's *salon*. After Britain declared war on France at the beginning of February the English nationals in Paris found themselves viewed with suspicion by the Revolutionary government. Many of those who Wollstonecraft met through Williams were sympathetic to the Girondins, rather than to Robespierre's Jacobins, and as the Terror took hold their political allegiances as well as their nationality made them suspect.

When Wollstonecraft left London she had intended to be away for only a few weeks. She did not give up her lodgings and she told Johnson her absence would be temporary. But in the spring of 1793 she met an American adventurer called Gilbert Imlay at the house of Thomas Christie. Shortly after their first meeting she and Imlay became lovers. In May the Girondins fell and their English supporters in Paris fled. Wollstonecraft moved out of the capital to the village of Neuilly-sur-Seine, from where she occasionally journeyed with caution into Paris to visit Joel and Ruth Barlow who, like Imlay, were protected from the Jacobins by American citizenship. At Neuilly she began to write a history of the French Revolution, probably at Johnson's urging. She located the fall of the French monarchy in the lascivious corruption of the Court and she celebrated its passing. Writing amidst the chaos of the Jacobin seizure of power, however, she was aware that the success of the Revolution hung in the balance. 'We should guard against inferring, that the spirit of the moment will not evaporate, and leave the disturbed water more clear for the fermentation.' She held fast to the belief that out of the current anarchy a fairer political system would emerge. 'It is perhaps, difficult to bring ourselves to believe, that out of this chaotic mass a fairer government is rising than has ever shed the sweets of social life on the world. – But things must have time to find their level.'[10] In the evenings she wrote to Imlay, whose frequent absences she mourned. 'I obey an emotion of my heart, which made me think of wishing thee, my love, good-night!' ran one early letter. 'You would smile to hear how many plans of employment I have in my head, now that I am confident my heart has found peace in your bosom.'[11] In the early autumn of 1793 she returned to Paris and, during a brief period when they were both in the capital, Imlay registered her as his wife at the American Embassy in order to afford her the nominal protection of his own American nationality. He then left Paris once again, leaving Wollstonecraft alone in his lodgings over the winter.

Gilbert Imlay was one of many commercial opportunists who believed that revolution in France offered scope for fortune-making. He had fought in the American Revolutionary War and called himself Captain Imlay but the surviving records do not confirm if he earned the rank. He was a cosmopolitan, popular figure, with an air of confidence that impressed those who met him. Wollstonecraft believed he represented the ideal for which she had been waiting. By the time of Imlay's autumn departure she was pregnant and her letters home became elliptical about personal matters as well as politics. Her sisters were forced to read between the lines. 'What say you Everina to the <u>Continental</u> air', wrote Eliza in July. 'Is it <u>Love</u>? Ambition or Pity?'[12] In October the English in Paris were arrested and imprisoned, Helen Maria Williams among them. Rumours reached Eliza and Everina that Wollstonecraft was one of those rounded up. 'I hope in

God she is safe', worried Eliza. 'Yet the contrary idea haunts me and makes me forget her few faults. She is certainly in greater danger than a mere insignificant character.'[13] In Wollstonecraft's absence Johnson continued to act as her family's banker and financial advisor and was often a more reliable source of information about their sister's welfare than were her own letters. A mutual friend had been to his shop and reported to Eliza that 'Mr Johnson looked quite cheerful ... he thought M. was quite safe.'[14]

Wollstonecraft was safe but her longed-for domestic contentment did not arrive. During the months of her pregnancy she waited for Imlay to give up his restless travels and join her in a shared home. He did not do so. In the autumn of 1793 she moved back to Paris in the hope of seeing him more regularly and in November wrote from her new lodging to tell him she was expecting a baby. 'Ever since you last saw me inclined to faint, I have felt some gentle twitches, which make me begin to think, that I am nourishing a creature who will soon be sensible of my care.'[15] When Imlay showed no signs of settling in Paris she followed him to Le Havre, where she called herself Mrs Imlay. From Le Havre, in March 1794, she sent Johnson the manuscript of An Historical and Moral View of the Origin and Progress of the French Revolution and settled down to await the birth of her child.

The baby was born in May and was registered as Françoise Imlay. Wollstonecraft called her Fanny and delighted in her. Imlay was still often absent and when he was present he was harassed by the precarious speculations in which he was enmeshed but Wollstonecraft nevertheless clung to prized moments of happiness. With every week that passed her love for Fanny grew. 'When I am sad', she told Imlay, 'I lament that all my affections grow on me, till they become too strong for my peace, though they all afford me snatches of exquisite enjoyment – This for our little girl was at first very reasonable – more the effect of reason, a sense of duty, than feeling – now, she has got into my heart and imagination, and when I walk out without her, her little figure is ever dancing before me.'[16] News reached an astonished Eliza that her sister was married and had borne a child. 'Mary cannot be married!!!' she wrote with incredulity. 'It is mere report it is natural to conclude her protector her husband.' Yet the story came both from Johnson and from Charles in America and 'Johnson does not repeat things at random and that the very same tale should have crossed the Atlantic makes me almost believe – that the once M – is now Mrs Imlay and a mother.' Such news made Wollstonecraft seem a distant figure to her family. 'Are we ever to see the Father and her Babe.'[17] At Johnson's shop

Lindsey saw a letter from Wollstonecraft written in Imlay's company and wondered why she had not changed her professional name on the frontispiece of her history of the French Revolution. Maybe, he mused, 'she thinks she shall be better known and the work have larger encouragement and sale by her old name.'[18] Both Lindsey and Eliza's letters suggest that Johnson assumed that Wollstonecraft had indeed married Imlay. She signed herself Mary Imlay and in her correspondence she kept Imlay's failings hidden from view.

For almost a year after Fanny's birth Wollstonecraft remained in France, waiting for the moment when Imlay would join her and family life could begin. That moment never arrived. Imlay did not return to Wollstonecraft but instead travelled to London. In April 1795 Wollstonecraft packed up her possessions and prepared to return to England, accompanied by Fanny and a nursemaid, Marguerite. She knew nothing of the arrangements Imlay had made so directed French friends to write to her care of Johnson at St Paul's Churchyard. On April 11th she landed on the south coast and wrote to Imlay that she would search for him at a hotel where she believed he had stayed.

Within a few days of arriving in London Wollstonecraft learnt that Imlay had formed a new relationship with an actress. In May she tried to kill herself by swallowing opium. Godwin thought that Imlay found her either before or as she took the dose. Somehow she was revived and a badly frightened Imlay suggested she should travel to Scandinavia on his behalf. A ship he had chartered had gone missing on its journey to Norway, along with its valuable cargo of silver. Imlay's suggestion was borne of a desire to occupy her away from London. He also wanted his cargo back and he had confidence in Wollstonecraft's ability to find it. The suggestion that a suicidal woman should undertake a difficult journey to an unknown country in the company of a toddler and nursemaid in order to retrieve a cargo of dubious provenance was audacious, but Wollstonecraft seized on the opportunity for escape.

In June, just over a week after her suicide attempt, she arrived in Hull to wait for a packet north. Her travels took her all over Sweden, Norway and Denmark. Sometimes she travelled with Marguerite and Fanny but for long periods was compelled to leave them in lodgings while she traversed the most difficult terrain alone. At every stopping place she wrote letters to Imlay that told of her heartbreak while also testifying to the effect of strange landscapes, new conversations and local customs on her spirits. She wrote too of love, as an emotion that, with the exception of the powerful feelings generated by Fanny, seemed to offer nothing but misery. She worked hard on Imlay's behalf, tackling politicians and shipping authorities with determination, writing letters and memoranda as she hunted for information. She received little encouragement in return. By September she was in Copenhagen and wrote that she was 'weary of travelling – yet seem to have no home – no resting place to look to.'[19]

At the beginning of October she arrived back in Dover, the question of her future still unresolved. In his letters Imlay vacillated and told her that she alone must determine their future. But from his tone Wollstonecraft intimated that there were other women in his life and that his protestations of affection were borne of a guilty conscience. She was not prepared to be the kept woman of a bitter man. 'Tell me, that you wish it, and I will cut this Gordian knot.'[20] In London Imlay took lodgings for her and Fanny and made one more assertion of fidelity. In his absence Wollstonecraft quizzed the cook and learnt that he had a new mistress. On October 10th she wrote him a letter with instructions for Fanny's future and went out into the London night. She paid a boatman to take her to Putney Bridge where she walked up and down until her clothes were heavy with rain. Then she jumped. A fisherman pulled her unconscious body from the river and carried her to a local inn where she was revived. The knowledge that she had been snatched back from death caused her acute distress. 'I have only to lament,' she told Imlay, 'that, when the bitterness of death was past, I was inhumanly brought back to life and misery.' She told him that her suicide attempt was an act of reason, and a decision she was entitled to make. 'I am only accountable to myself', she insisted. 'If I am condemned to live longer, it is a living death.'[21]

From the Thameside Inn where she was revived Wollstonecraft was taken to the house of Thomas Christie and his wife. The Christies, like Wollstonecraft, had left Paris when the violence of the Terror escalated and they knew more of Wollstonecraft's unhappiness than her old London friends. Imlay offered money for Wollstonecraft and Fanny which she refused. This time despair made her clear-sighted. She found lodgings for herself and Fanny in Finsbury Place and began the labour of forming an independent family unit of two by taking her furniture out of store. She wrote more letters to Imlay but stuck to a resolution made on the day she moved into a home of her own once more. 'I shall protect and provide for my child.' In the same letter she freed Imlay from the responsibility of keeping her alive. 'I only mean by this to say, that you have nothing to fear from my desperation.'[22] As she looked to the future she made a determined effort to take control of her own story. She asked Imlay to return all her letters and he did so. She made the same request to Fuseli but he refused.

Slowly she picked up the threads of the life she had left behind in 1792. Mary Hays had moved into lodgings nearby and the two women became friends. 'I have promised to dine with Mr. Johnson tomorrow', she wrote to Hays late in 1795. 'He requested me to invite you. If you have no previous engagement, I will call on you about half after four, as the dining hour is five.'[23] She began to work again, commissioning reviews for the *Analytical* on Johnson's behalf. In a series of letters she bade Imlay farewell. She also took the correspondence she had written from Scandinavia and, with Johnson's support, turned it into a book. She called it *Letters Written During a Short Residence in Sweden, Norway, and Denmark* and although in her revisions she blurred personal details and turned her gaze outwards to the landscapes and customs of the countries she visited, she also left a carefully mediated version of personal unhappiness. Johnson published the book early in 1796, alongside a new edition of *Vindication of the Rights of Woman*. The reviews of *Letters* were admiring. Once again Wollstonecraft found herself the subject of talk on the literary scene but this time the conversation was less condemnatory. 'If ever there was a book calculated to make a man in love with its author', wrote Godwin, 'this appears to me to be the book.'[24]

±

Wollstonecraft and Godwin met again in January 1796. Godwin knew of her return to London from Mary Hays, with whom he was in regular correspondence, and it was Hays who reintroduced her mutual friends to each other. Shortly after their meeting Godwin read *Letters from Sweden* and in April, after Wollstonecraft had returned from a visit to friends in the country, she called on him. She had taken new lodgings in Cumming Street, just a short walk from Godwin's home in Somers Town. A day later he returned the visit. Godwin's diary for the summer of 1796 records a pattern of meetings as he and Wollstonecraft took tea together, met each other's friends, visited each other for supper after the day's work was done and bumped into each other at the houses of others. The first letter between them dated from July and was from Wollstonecraft. She enclosed with it a gift of the last volume of Rousseau's *Julie; ou, La Nouvelle Héloïse*, a novel famous for its revolutionary exploration of female emotional and sexual experience. She sent *Julie*, she explained, in order to encourage Godwin 'not to choose the easiest task, my perfections, but to dwell on your own feelings – that is to say, give me a bird's-eye view of your heart.'[25]

This instruction set the tone for a courtship correspondence that at times had the rapier wit of Shakespeare's Beatrice and Benedict and was at other points challenging, combative, affectionate and melancholy. Wollstonecraft was thirty-six in 1796; Godwin forty. Wollstonecraft had confronted the possibility of being broken by her passions and had rebuilt her life in the face of pain. Godwin believed himself to be immune to the tumults and desires experienced by more susceptible men. Each knew the other to be a brilliant thinker and writer, with a public name and reputation. As they sparred their way to an understanding they treated each other as equals with independent intellects and unknown emotional hinterlands. When Wollstonecraft challenged Godwin to write of his feelings he poked fun at his own emotional reserve and her desire for self-expression, but he did not dissemble. 'Shall I write a love letter? May Lucifer fly away with me, if I do! No, when I make love, it shall be with the eloquent tones of my voice, with dying accents, with speaking glances (through the glass of my spectacles), with all the witching of that irresistible, universal passion.'[26] In late July it was Godwin's turn to be absent from London and Wollstonecraft found herself missing him. 'I suppose you mean to drink tea with me, *one* of these days', she wrote at the beginning of August. 'How can you find it in your heart to let me pass so many evenings alone.'[27]

She had written laments of abandonment before, to Imlay, but her mock-chastisement of Godwin demonstrated new confidence in the strength of the connection they were forging. She sent him the manuscript of the self-revealing novel on which she was working. It was provisionally entitled *The Wrongs of Woman* and he read it with care. On August 15th he made a note in his diary: 'chez moi'. The phrase, alongside its companion note, 'chez elle', was shorthand for the fact that Wollstonecraft and Godwin had spent the night together. It appeared in his diary with regularity thereafter. Sometimes he appended a gesture towards description. On August 21st: 'chez moi, toute'. At other points punctuation did the job of expressing the inexpressible: 'chez elle, —'; 'chez moi, —'. They were 'chez elle' more often than 'chez moi', in recognition of the difficulty of leaving two-year-old Fanny in the company of only her nursemaid. The day after their first night together there was a difficult exchange of letters. Both found it easier to communicate on paper than in person and both acknowledged as much. Godwin had talked of roses growing in the path of every life and encouraged Wollstonecraft to embrace happiness: 'I catch at them', she responded, 'but only encounter the thorns.' At the outset of their correspondence she had asked him to describe his own feelings and, after years of rigorous self-containment, he reciprocated with an effusion of emotion she found alarming, even self-indulgent. 'Full of your own feelings, little as I comprehend them, you forgot mine – or do not understand my character.'[28] The pain she had suffered, first over Fuseli and then over Imlay, made her cautious of becoming again the object of transient male passion.

As August came to an end the tumults of high summer gave way to a more settled understanding. Their notes took on a patina of domesticity, as they exchanged work and made plans about where to meet, eat and sleep. Godwin sent fond messages and tiny presents to Fanny, who took to calling him 'Man.' When the weather turned stormy Wollstonecraft preferred to stay at home and dine with him by her own fireside, while Fanny slumbered nearby. Sometimes it was still easier to express emotions on paper. In September she reminded Godwin that her relationship with Imlay had produced a dependent child and required her to earn a living by her writing. Godwin had offered a critical response to work in draft and she read his criticisms as a threat to her ability to keep body and soul together. In an uncharacteristically sharp attack on the two men whose friendship she most valued she intimated that both he and Johnson had underestimated her talent and her worth. But her rediscovered confidence meant that such difficulties were surmountable. While she was out walking with Fanny the child demanded they pay a call on Godwin. 'Go this way Mama, me wants to see Man.' Wollstonecraft related Fanny's plea to Godwin with pleasure at the unconventional family unit they were forming. She was more cautious about the reaction to the relationship of her friends. The response of Mary Hays was of particular concern. 'She has owned to me that she cannot endure to see others enjoy the mutual affection from which she is debarred – I will write a kind note to her to ease my conscience.' But the unhappiness of others was no reason not to further her own chance of joy. 'I shall come to you to night, probably before nine.'[29]

Amidst the fear and exultation of a new and revelatory relationship, the rhythms of ordinary life continued. In September Fanny caught chickenpox and was miserable and clingy. Only her mother's care would console her and Wollstonecraft retreated home, trying to meet deadlines while entertaining an itchy and uncomfortable child. She made brief forays to St Paul's Churchyard to see Johnson but told Godwin to come to her. She scribbled notes while Fanny sat in her lap. 'I have been trying to amuse her all the morning to prevent her scratching her face', ran one letter to Godwin.[30] A day later Fanny was still ill and Wollstonecraft wrote with a maternal weariness that reverberates across the centuries. 'I had full employment yesterday; nay, was extremely fatigued by endeavouring to prevent Fanny from tearing herself to pieces; and afterwards she would scarcely allow me to catch half an hour, of what deserved the name of sleep.' She was in need, she told Godwin, of a nurse herself. 'Are you above the feminine office? I think not, for you are above the affectation of wisdom.'[31]

At scattered points during Fanny's childhood Wollstonecraft wrote of her in a series of *Lessons* for children written in imitation of Barbauld. 'Papa' figures frequently in the *Lessons*. Sometimes Fanny is a baby and 'Papa' is evidently Imlay; at other points she is a toddler and 'Papa' is Godwin. 'When I caught cold some time ago, I had such a pain my head, I could scarcely hold it up', Wollstonecraft wrote in Lesson X. 'Papa opened the door very softly, because he loves me. You love me, yet you made a noise. You had not the sense to know that it made my head worse, till papa told you.' A cross Fanny had protested that she did not know how to think. 'Yes, you do a little', her mother responded. 'The other day papa was tired; he had been walking about all the morning. After dinner he fell asleep on the sopha. I did not bid you be quiet; but you thought of what papa said to you, when my head ached. This made you think that you ought not to make a noise, when papa was resting himself. So you came to me, and said to me, very softly, Pray reach me my ball, and I will go and play in the garden, till papa wakes.'[32]

Throughout the winter of 1796–7 Wollstonecraft and Godwin continued in the pattern established that autumn. They exchanged frequent evening and nightly visits and letters to clear up misunderstandings; they moved forward with lives lived together but also apart. Both continued to dine with Johnson, sometimes on the same evening but often when the other was elsewhere. They were cautious about revealing their romance. Mary Hays found their affection difficult to witness; other more distant acquaintances assumed that Wollstonecraft was married to Imlay and she was wary of their censoriousness. In November Fuseli's friend Joseph Farington recorded gossip about her Putney Bridge suicide attempt in his diary; in January he wrote of her again, in a sign of his curiosity about her mode of existence. 'Johnson, employs Mrs Wollstonecraft; she has abt. £50 a yr. besides. She has a little girl by the American she lived with.'[33] While

Farington collected information about her, Wollstonecraft found herself seized by sickness. She kept working, organising *Analytical* reviews for Johnson and visiting Bedlam in the company of him and Godwin in order to undertake research for her new novel. She went to the theatre with Godwin and endured a visit from her sister Everina. In early February she called on Johnson's old friend, the doctor George Fordyce. There is some suggestion in her letters for this period that she and Godwin had been attempting to use a form of rhythm-based birth control. At the end of January, shortly before she called on Fordyce, she realised that this system had failed. 'Women are certainly great fools; but nature made them so. I have not time, or paper, else I could draw an inference, not very illustrative of your chance-medley system.' The prospect of another pregnancy without the protection of marriage offered little comfort, but she faced its reality head on. 'I spare the moth-like opinion', she told Godwin. 'There is room enough in the world'.[34]

Pregnancy introduced an uncertainty into Wollstonecraft's future which for a while she resisted. Her letters of February and March 1797 were determinedly focused on other things. At a dinner, almost certainly at Johnson's, she met Barbauld's husband Rochemont, who was rude about Mary Hays. 'You are stigmatized as a Philosophess – a Godwinian', she told her friend. 'I assured him that your nove[ll] would not undermine religion.'[35] She continued her practice of farming out reviews for the *Analytical* to Hays, knowing that Johnson needed reviewers and Hays needed money. Sometimes she asked Godwin to take on some of her work for the *Analytical*. 'There is a good boy write me a review of Vaurien.'[36] She delighted in the blossoming affection between Godwin and Fanny but she was an experienced parent and she warned him against over-indulgence. 'Do not give Fanny a cake to day', she reminded in him March. 'I am afraid she staid too long with you yesterday.'[37]

At the end of March Johnson himself became a source of strain. He pressed her for work and was less prepared than usual to settle her family's debts. 'Johnson is either half ruined by the present public circumstances, or grown strangely mean, at any rate he torments me.'[38] The financial arrangements between Johnson and Wollstonecraft were labyrinthine in their complexity and details of their transactions have not survived. He sustained her existence but she never felt free of debt or obligation and, in the early stages of an unexpected pregnancy, the extent of her entanglements increased her sense of vulnerability.

In striking recent work on eighteenth-century women writers as a precarious underclass in literary London, the literary scholar E. J. Clery has suggested that Johnson underpaid Wollstonecraft for her years of continuous work. Clery acknowledges that Wollstonecraft was already in debt when she began working for Johnson, and she also notes that many of the women who earned recognition in literary circles at the end of the century struggled to earn enough to support themselves. Wollstonecraft's history and politics hampered her ability, Clery writes, 'to negotiate the literary marketplace on a secure footing.' Johnson enabled her existence as a professional woman writer but he did not comprehend or address the difficulties she experienced as a result of her dependence on him. 'Reconstruct the asymmetric economic positions', Clery suggests, and 'the strain of the situation is apparent.'[39] In his dealings with Wollstonecraft Johnson was once again both extremely unusual and a man of his time. He created the conditions she needed in order to live, think and do the work that made her famous, and he cared very much about her well-being. But he did not free her from the burden of financial anxiety and he did not pay her more than he thought her writing was worth.

An alternative explanation for Wollstonecraft's indebtedness to Johnson lies in the extent of the financial assistance he provided to her family in order to keep her house and her work free of needy relations. In July he sent a stern letter to Charles Wollstonecraft, reminding him of all he owed to his sister and the difficulties she had suffered. 'It is so long since any of your family have heard from you that they begin to think themselves neglected. Mary especially, her distresses she thought might have drawn from you some ... attention, on this subject she frequently expresses herself with warmth.' Wollstonecraft's difficulties, in Johnson's telling, encompassed 'distresses from the rascals of Imlay' as well as continued anxiety about the financial situation of her unloving father, which represented a burden she was compelled to share with Johnson. 'He has had no one to depend upon for nearly three years but herself, & she has no recourse but to me; of course her account with me, as you may suppose, is in a much worse state than it otherwise would have been.' Johnson required Charles to take on his father's support and made it clear that although the bonds of old friendship would prompt him to continue his financial support of Wollstonecraft he would not assume responsibility for another man's father. His reason was simple. 'I am far from being rich'.[40]

Six days after Wollstonecraft wrote of Johnson's meanness Godwin made a note in his diary. 'Panc'. The word signified his marriage to Wollstonecraft at St Pancras Church, on March 29th 1797. They married as a result of her pregnancy and because she knew too well the difficulties entailed in raising a child outside wedlock. The wedding revealed to casual observers that her marriage to Imlay had been a fiction. Wollstonecraft was hurt by the moralistic reaction of some of those she had thought her supporters but she was most worried about the response of Johnson. She was in his debt financially and she found it difficult to tell her oldest and most reliable friend of the change in her circumstances. Under English law her marriage meant that her debts were now transferred to Godwin and she knew that Johnson would be hurt to have received no prior warning of her intentions. The difficulty she felt was about more than money. Although she moved with Fanny into Godwin's house in Somers Town after the wedding, she and Godwin agreed to maintain separate working spaces, and he accordingly rented a study in lodgings nearby. During the day they thus continued to correspond by letter.

On April 8th she wrote to ask him to visit Johnson and break the news. 'It would spare me some awkwardness, and please him; and I want you to visit him often of a Tuesday.' She wanted her friend and her husband to appreciate each other without her intercession and she undertook to stay away from Johnson's dinners for a period in order to enable their friendship. 'This is quite disinterested – as I shall never be of the party – Do go – you would oblige me.'[41] Later that day Godwin paid a visit to St Paul's Churchyard. 'Call on Johnson', he wrote in his diary. 'Altercation.' It is likely that Johnson had intimated something of Wollstonecraft's romance when she wrote of his strange meanness and that, shut out from her confidence, he was less inclined than usual to help her. Godwin's record of an 'altercation' suggests that Johnson was worried about the predicament in which a new pregnancy and a hasty marriage placed her. If, as seems possible, he was himself unclear about whether or not Wollstonecraft and Imlay had undergone some form of marriage ceremony in France, his anger may also in part have been a response to a sense of betrayal. He stepped back as the manager of her financial and administrative affairs. Before Wollstonecraft's marriage Johnson had settled with tradespeople on her behalf; now she found that, since she did not wish to disturb Godwin, she had to confront her creditors herself. Some were rude but the difficulty was more that 'I am tormented by the want of money.'[42] News of the marriage reached Fuseli and he wrote of it with an acerbity which suggests a measure of wounded pride. 'You have perhaps not heard', he wrote to Roscoe, 'that the assertrix of female rights has given her hand to the *balancier* of political Justice.'[43]

The altercation was smoothed over and Godwin dined again at St Paul's Churchyard. Wollstonecraft and Johnson also resumed their working relationship and he continued to defend her from the demands of her brothers and sisters. Godwin attempted to consolidate her debts, many of which she had incurred as a result of her entanglement with Imlay. She and Godwin continued to experience periods of misunderstanding and difficulty and they wrote frankly of the moments when they had failed or disappointed each other. In June Godwin set off on a tour of the Midlands and during his absence the correspondence between them stretched out once more. His letters were full of new scenes and new people, interspersed with affectionate messages for Fanny and enquiries after their unborn baby, who they called William (both were convinced that the child would be a boy). To Wollstonecraft herself he sent messages of love and sympathy for the discomforts of pregnancy. 'I remember at every moment all the accidents to which your condition subjects you, & wish I knew of some sympathy that could inform me from moment to moment, how you do, & how you feel.'[44] He had promised Fanny to bring her a present from Wedgwood's factory at Etruria and on June 7th he sent a message that he had not forgotten his vow. 'Remember William; but (most of all) take care of yourself. Tell Fanny, I am safely arrived in the land of mugs.'[45]

In Godwin's absence Wollstonecraft's attention turned inwards. She was now six months pregnant and the physical experience of carrying a second child was at times all-encompassing. 'I was not quite well the day after you left me', she wrote on June 6th. 'But it is past, and I am well and tranquil, excepting the disturbance produced by Master William's joy, who took it in his head to frisk a little at being informed of your remembrance. I begin to love this little creature, and to anticipate his birth as a fresh twist to a knot, which I do not wish to untie.'[46] Godwin's journey home took longer than he had anticipated and on June 19th she wrote crossly that she had sat up until midnight waiting for him to appear. After his return they resumed their pattern of dining out together and alone, but at the end of June Wollstonecraft confessed that she felt a prisoner of her changing body. 'When I lived alone', she recalled, 'I always dined on a Sunday, with company in the evening, if not at dinner, at St P's. Generally also of a Tuesday, and some other day at Fuselis.' For a period she had felt unwelcome at St Paul's Churchyard, as her preoccupation with her developing relationship with Godwin drove older connections from her mind, and in the aftermath of Johnson's reaction to the news of her pregnancy and marriage. 'Mr J—s house and spirits were so altered, that my visiting him depressed instead of exhilarated my min[d].' Now that difficulty was done away with, but the walk suddenly seemed unfeasibly far. 'To Mr Johnson – I would go without ceremony – but it is not convenient for me, at present to make haphazard visits.'[47] For his part Johnson overcame his objections to Wollstonecraft's marriage. He continued to worry about her financial situation and the burden imposed by her family but he had observed her relationship with Godwin and of her prospects for happiness he was more confident. 'She is happily married in every sense but one', he told her brother. 'No money on either side, nor the means of procuring it but by literary exertion; she will soon bless Mr. Godwin with one or two and is likely I think to have a large family.'[48]

⚓

On August 30th 1797 Wollstonecraft sent a note to Godwin to tell him she was in labour. The midwife had been sent for and Wollstonecraft was confident of a speedy delivery. 'I have no doubt of seeing the animal to day.' In the meantime, she was bored. 'I wish I had a novel, or some book of sheer amusement, to excite curiosity, and while away the time – Have you any thing of the kind?'[49] The midwife arrived and was sure that the baby was on its way although 'she thinks, I shall not immediately be freed from my load.'[50] A short time later Wollstonecraft sent a third bulletin. 'Mrs Blenkinsop tells me that I am in the most natural state, and can promise me a safe delivery – But that I must have a little patience.'[51] At this point her voice falls silent.

Late in the evening of August 30th she gave birth to a baby girl. She had planned to present the child to Godwin herself and in obedience to her instructions he waited in the parlour to be summoned to her bedroom. In the early hours of September 1st the summons came, not from Wollstonecraft but from the midwife. The placenta was not delivered and she was unable to extract it. Godwin sent for a doctor who removed it in pieces. Wollstonecraft, even though she had now given birth twice, told Godwin that until the manual extraction of the placenta she had 'never known what bodily pain was before.' Godwin dismissed the emergency doctor and, at Wollstonecraft's request, sent for Johnson's friend George Fordyce. What Fordyce did not know was that, despite his assertions to the contrary, the doctor who removed the placenta had not succeeded in extracting the organ complete. As a result of the retained placenta and the trauma of the attempted manual extraction Wollstonecraft contracted septicaemia. Fordyce's initial confidence in her strength gave way to anxiety; on September 2nd a nurse arrived to take charge. On September 3rd Fordyce called twice; in his diary Godwin recorded 'shivering fits.' On September 4th puppies were brought to Wollstonecraft's room to draw off her excess breast milk, since her baby girl was being cared for elsewhere. Mary Hays called but Godwin refused to allow her into the bedchamber. Instead he admitted Eliza Fenwick, an old and experienced friend of Wollstonecraft's, as well as her most trusted servant. A second doctor was summoned: another friend, Thomas Carlisle. He agreed with Fordyce that their only option was to ply Wollstonecraft with wine to dull her awareness and her pain. Old supporters of Godwin gathered in the parlour below, ready to take messages across London at a moment's notice.

Wollstonecraft knew that she was dying. On September 8th Godwin recorded in his diary a 'solemn communication'. On the 9th he asked for her guidance about how he should care for Fanny and the baby, who they called Mary. Wollstonecraft was slipping in and out of consciousness and was unable to issue instructions. 'After having repeated this idea to her in a great variety of forms', Godwin recalled, 'she at length said, with a significant tone of voice, "I know what you are thinking of," but added, that she had nothing to communicate to me upon the subject.'[52] She died on the morning of September 10th. Godwin wrote the time and a series of dashes in his diary. '20 minutes before 8. ———'. Later that day Johnson wrote two letters. One was to Godwin:

> I have had daily notices of what I dreaded to hear, & nothing but Mrs G's strength of constitution left me the faint hope of her recovery, you have a just but not exaggerated sense of her merit; I know her too well not to admire and love her. Your loss is insuperable.[53]

The second letter Johnson wrote was to Fuseli and was two sentences long. 'One who loved you, & whom I respected, is no more. Mrs Godwin died this morning.'[54] When, two days later, Godwin sent Johnson a provisional list of mourners for the funeral, Johnson insisted that Fuseli should be included. In his view the pain occasioned by Wollstonecraft's relationship with Fuseli did not negate its importance. 'In the list you shew'd this morning I did not observe the name of Fuseli, it is true that of late he was not intimate with Mrs Godwin, but from circumstances that I am acquainted with I think he was not to be blamed for it; before this they were so intimate & spent so many happy hours in my house that I may say he was the first of our friends, indeed next to ourselves I believe no one had a juster sense of her worth or more laments her loss.'[55] As he contemplated the relationship between Wollstonecraft and Fuseli, Johnson preferred to dwell on the happy days of early acquaintance than on the particularities of its ending. Fuseli's own response came in the postscript of a letter to Roscoe and was self-consciously elliptical. 'Poor mary!'[56]

On September 15th Wollstonecraft's funeral was held at St Pancras Church. Johnson was in attendance; Godwin appears to have asked his advice about where she should be buried. 'You have known her & her connections long & may by possibility be acquainted with circumstances of which I am ignorant that ought to influence me in that.'[57] The request may have been influenced by Godwin's recognition that in her religious beliefs Wollstonecraft was more closely aligned to Johnson's Unitarian faith than to his own atheism. On the day of the funeral itself Godwin remained at home, too broken to join the mourners. Friends sent news of Wollstonecraft's death to her family but the responses of her sisters have not survived. In the days following September 10th a furious row broke out between Godwin and Mary Hays about the latter's exclusion from Wollstonecraft's deathbed. Godwin was unrepentant. Wollstonecraft had been surrounded by the friends, doctors and servants most able to care for her and in his view nothing else mattered.

Within weeks of her death Godwin began work on a book he called *Memoirs of the Author of A Vindication of the Rights of Woman*. Johnson was his principal source of information for Wollstonecraft's life in London between 1788 and 1795. He also wrote letters to all those who he thought might have information about his wife's early years. He began dining regularly at Johnson's, seeking comfort in the company of a man who had been Wollstonecraft's friend. In late October, six weeks after her death, he attempted to describe how much he had lost. For forty years, he told his correspondent, he had been alone in the world. The brevity of his joy added to his agony. 'I partook of a happiness, by so much more exquisite, as I had a short time before, had no conception of it, or scarcely admitted its possibility, & saw one bright ray that streaked my day of life, only to leave the remainder more gloomy, & (in the truest sense of the word hope) hopeless.' As he surveyed the future, it was Fanny and baby Mary who were his chief concern. 'The poor children! I am myself madam, totally unfitted to educate them. The scepticism, which perhaps sometimes leads me right in matters of speculation, is torment to me when I would attempt to direct the infant mind. I am the most unfit person for this office; she was the best qualified in the world. What a change!'[58]

＋

In the summer of 1797, during the final months of her pregnancy, Wollstonecraft had her portrait painted for a second time by John Opie. In the painting she looks away from the viewer. The props of earlier portraits – book, pen, paper – are gone. There is a bloom on her cheeks, her hair curls out from under her cap and she is dressed in white. But her eyes are as piercing as ever and the line of her mouth is as firm. In A *Vindication of the Rights of Woman* Wollstonecraft defended the ability of women to think and be educated to think. She demanded equality for the sexes and a reframing of the conventions that kept women subjugated. Through the manner in which she lived her life she insisted on the right of women to feel and express their feelings according to experience rather than expectation. She insisted on living on her own terms and made clear her belief that society would only be reformed when all women had the opportunity to follow her example without incurring criticism. In her final work, unfinished at her death, she insisted on the importance of happiness and her right as a woman to claim it. She compared true happiness 'which enlarges and civilises the mind' to 'the pleasure experienced in roving through nature at large, inhaling the sweet gale natural to the clime'. Such happiness stood as a rebuke to 'artificial forms of felicity': a happiness assumed, or modelled only according to the dictates of stale custom. This false happiness she compared to 'gardens full of aromatic shrubs, which cloy while they delight, and weaken the sense of pleasure they gratify.'[59] Wollstonecraft found real and substantial happiness with Godwin, but she also found it in the joy Fanny brought her, and in the sustenance offered by female friendship. She found it too in a relationship with Johnson which proved the truth of her assertion that men and women were capable of supporting and caring for each other in ways that defied definition and convention. Freedom was the right of every woman, but so was the ability to make and keep a friend.

24

Original Poetry

Between 1796 and 1798 France won a series of decisive victories on the
European continent. Under the direction of Napoleon Bonaparte French
soldiers captured swathes of territory in northern Italy and Austria. Spain
fell and British forces withdrew to Gibraltar. French troops landed briefly
on Irish soil and on the Welsh coast but both expeditions were repelled.
In the autumn of 1797 France declared victory against the European allied
forces. The defeated Austrians ceded the Austrian Netherlands to France
and acknowledged the new eastern French border at the Rhine. In October
Napoleon created the Army of England and set his sights on the invasion
of Britain. In February 1798, after French forces took command of
Switzerland and the Papal States, Britain made ready for invasion. Reports
swirled through the British press that the bloodthirsty French, not content
with beheading their own King and Queen with a custom-built machine
of monstrous efficiency, were harnessing terrifying technological developments in order to overcome British defences. Cartoons circulated of an
industrial raft glimpsed off the French coast, powered by windmills attached
to giant paddles, with a deck big enough to transport multiple regiments
of mounted cavalry. In English coastal towns rumours circulated that the
French were amassing a fleet of boats in Channel ports north of Normandy,
and that fishing vessels were being commandeered in preparation for the
onslaught.

In the months leading up to the scare, government spies fanned out of
London to hunt down French sympathisers and informers. One unfortunate
government employee, James Walsh, was dispatched all the way to the
Somerset coast in pursuit of the Treason Trial defendant John Thelwall,
who had left London to visit friends. He found Thelwall consorting with
a ramshackle group of poets and local agitators whose behaviour Walsh

thought highly suspicious. They slept and ate at odd times, went for long walks and treated each other's houses with indecent familiarity. They sat up late talking about complicated, foreign-sounding ideas and although they did not behave like gentlemen of leisure they appeared to have no fixed employment. If any Englishmen were unpatriotic enough to welcome the arrival of French republicans on windmill-powered rafts, it was likely, thought Walsh's employers, to be men such as this.

At the heart of the party on whom Walsh was sent to spy were two poets: William Wordsworth and Samuel Taylor Coleridge. In the spring of 1798 Wordsworth was living at Alfoxden House in the Quantocks, in the company of his sister Dorothy and five-year-old Basil Montagu. Basil was the child of a recently widowed friend who found himself unable to care for his son while earning a living as a lawyer. Three miles away, in the village of Nether Stowey, Samuel Taylor Coleridge had rented a cottage for himself, his pregnant wife Sara and their toddler son Hartley. Coleridge was making his name as a journalist and had published verses in the 'Original Poetry' section of a new periodical edited by John Aikin and published by Johnson's neighbour Richard Phillips in conjunction with Johnson himself, entitled the *Monthly Magazine*.[1]

During his residence at Nether Stowey Coleridge combined writing with preaching at Unitarian chapels. In London Lindsey heard good reports of him and thought he might be an asset to the movement. 'You cannot well conceive how mu[ch] you have raised my opinion of Mr Coleridge', he wrote to his fellow Unitarian John Rowe. 'Such shining lights, so virtuous and disinterested will contribute to redeem the age we live in from being so destitute of apostolic zeal.'[2] At the beginning of 1798 Coleridge was at a crossroads, unsure whether to commit himself to a life of writing or to the Church. Throughout the summer and autumn of 1797 he had walked and talked with the Wordsworths and had written poems that would change the course of English literature. In an isolated farmhouse he had seen visions of Xanadu. Sitting alone in his garden he had written of a lime-tree bower as his prison. During winter evenings he had told assembled friends of a wedding guest and an ancient mariner with a tale to tell. Wordsworth had also been writing throughout 1797. His poems took the 'very language of men' and wrought it as poetry.[3] Together Wordsworth and Coleridge envisaged a volume of poetry that would give voice to the most marginal and extend the possibilities of their form. They called their volume *Lyrical Ballads*. Wordsworth described its contents as 'experiments' and asked readers not to pre-judge the work according to the dictates of outdated custom. In the Advertisement to the volume he issued a warning:

> Readers accustomed to the gaudiness and inane phraseology of many modern writers, if they persist in reading this book to its conclusion, will perhaps frequently have to struggle with feelings of strangeness and awkwardness: they will look round for poetry, and will be induced to enquire by what species of courtesy these attempts can be permitted to assume that title.[4]

⁜

Wordsworth and Coleridge are bit-part players in Johnson's story. Their glancing presence in the world of St Paul's Churchyard reveals that the most influential voices, genres and preoccupations of the literary landscape Johnson shaped were distinct from those subsequently celebrated by posterity. Poetry became the dominant form of the Romantic period through a complex process of posthumous canon formation. But in the 1790s, when Wordsworth and Coleridge produced many of the works for which they are most famous, poetry and poets had to jostle for attention and space. Wordsworth was twenty-three when he arrived in Johnson's shop in 1793. He had little money, no reputation, and had left his French family behind. At St Paul's Churchyard he was a supplicant, one among a crowd of hustling young men who came to listen to the conversation of Priestley and Fuseli and who vied for Johnson's attention. In his unpublished *Letter to the Bishop of Llandaff* he expressed his indignation at the treatment of 'philosophic Priestley', thus allying himself to the cohesive communal outrage at the Birmingham Riots that pervaded Johnson's circle.[5] The two poems Wordsworth published with Johnson that year were reviewed very briefly in the *Analytical* on pages immediately following Cowper's long review of Darwin's *Botanic Garden*. That the poems were reviewed at all was a symptom of Johnson's generosity and of his interest in the voice of a lonely twenty-three-year-old with no literary connections. As the *Analytical* made clear it was Darwin and Cowper, not Wordsworth, who were the great literary celebrities of the age.

On the frontispieces of *An Evening Walk* and *Descriptive Sketches* Johnson felt it necessary to underline Wordsworth's credentials by describing him as 'B.A. of St John's, Cambridge.' In both poems Wordsworth wrote of his own reaction to particular landscapes, in explorations of the self that were enabled by description of the natural world. In *The Task* Cowper had evoked the rhythms and topography of rural Buckinghamshire through painterly details and, in so doing, conjured his world in words. Within that world he situated himself as a stylised figure. Sometimes he was 'the stricken deer'. At other points he was the eye of the poem: out walking, always observing, the agent rather than the subject of the verse. Wordsworth foregrounded his own subjectivity, melding his representation of the Lake District and the Alps with memories that underlaid the description like geological strata. In *An Evening Walk* he made the archaeology of his experience of place apparent:

> While, Memory at my side, I wander here,
> Starts at the simplest sight th' unbidden tear,
> A form discovered at the well-known seat,
> A spot, that angles at the riv'let's feet,
> The cot the ray of morning trav'ling nigh,
> And sail that glides the well-known alders by.[6]

The cyclical process by which Wordsworth excavated self and place in his poems of 1793 unsettled the critic of the *Analytical*. Johnson's reviewer was in no doubt that *Descriptive Sketches* was the product of 'a lively imagination, furnished by actual and attentive observation with an abundant store of materials'. But he was discomfited by the poet's aggressively modern refusal of coherence and by a manipulation of language that left meaning unclear. 'At the same time we must own, that this poem is on the whole less interesting than the subject led us to expect; owing in part, we believe, to the want of a general thread of narrative to connect the several descriptions, or of some episodical tale, to vary the impression; and in part also to a certain laboured and artificial cast of expression, which often involves the poet's meaning in obscurity.'[7]

For two years after he left London Wordsworth drifted. He walked across Salisbury Plain and he may have slipped into France to visit Annette and his daughter.[8] In 1794 he came once more into the orbit of his sister Dorothy. As children Wordsworth and Dorothy had been separated following the death of their mother but after their reunion they became inseparable. Wordsworth still had no home but in Dorothy he found a family. In May they were in Whitehaven on the Cumbrian coast, from where Wordsworth wrote that he was revising his poems of 1793. He told his friend William Matthews that he was 'correcting and considerably adding' to both. 'It was with great reluctance I huddled up those two little works and sent them into the world in so imperfect a state.' He had done so, he explained, out of anxiety that he was failing to prove himself. 'But as I had done nothing by which to distinguish myself at the university, I thought these little things might shew that I could do something.' Now he was writing again and was determined to make money through his pen. The fate of the poems he had abandoned at St Paul's Churchyard suddenly seemed important. 'As I am speaking on this subject, pray let me request you to have the goodness to call on Johnson my publisher, and ask him if he ever sells any of those poems and what number he thinks are yet on his hands.'[9]

By early 1795 Wordsworth had returned to London. Once again he hovered on the fringes of Johnson's circle, meeting Godwin, George Dyer and the other veterans of Pitt's Terror for whom St Paul's Churchyard served as a refuge. He contemplated starting a journal but instead agreed to take charge of his friend Basil Montagu's son. In return for their care of the child he and Dorothy were offered £50 a year and free use of Racedown Lodge in Dorset. On his way there Wordsworth visited Bristol, where he met the bookseller Joseph Cottle, the poet Robert Southey, and Coleridge.

Coleridge was two years younger than Wordsworth and he read *Descriptive Sketches* during his last year at Cambridge. Writing in 1817 he recalled his early certainty of Wordsworth's talent. 'Seldom, if ever, was the emergence of an original poetic genius above the literary horizon more evidently announced.' He described what he saw as the elemental quality of the poem's language. 'There is a harshness and acerbity connected and combined with words and images all a-glow, which might recall those products of the vegetable world, where gorgeous blossoms rise out of the hard and thorny rind and shell, within which the rich fruit was elaborating.'[10] After Cambridge Coleridge experienced a period of aimlessness to match that endured by Wordsworth, during which he briefly enlisted in the army and became friends with Robert Southey. In Bristol he and Southey developed a plan inspired by Priestley's emigration, which they called Pantisocracy. Coleridge and Southey aimed to gather together a small group of like-minded men and women with whom they would form an ideal community in Pennsylvania. One of their number was Thomas Poole, a tanner from Nether Stowey; two other adherents to the scheme were the sisters Edith and Sara Fricker. The plan for Pantisocracy collapsed but Southey married Edith and Coleridge married Sara.

For a period after his marriage Coleridge earned a living lecturing in Bristol and in 1796 he founded a short-lived journal, called the *Watchman*. After their first child was born it became necessary for Coleridge and Sara to trim their expenses and Thomas Poole found them a cramped cottage near his own house in Nether Stowey. Coleridge turned his hand to play-writing, hoping to make money from the stage, but this effort too was unsuccessful. Friends who visited him at Nether Stowey included an essayist and clerk at the East India Company called Charles Lamb, and John Thelwall. In June 1797 Coleridge left Sara and Hartley at home and walked to Racedown in Dorset to visit Wordsworth and Dorothy. He stayed with them for two weeks, during which the novelty of a developing friendship and the exchange of ideas provided relief from his unhappy marriage. In July the Wordsworths moved with Basil to nearby Alfoxden and Wordsworth and Coleridge began working, together and apart, on the poems that would form *Lyrical Ballads*.

In the two and a quarter centuries since its first publication *Lyrical Ballads* has come to stand as the epoch-making volume of English Romanticism. It combined Coleridge's visionary reworking of ancient literary forms with Wordsworth's radically stripped-back immortalisation of the rural poor. It offered an account of nature as a space of retreat, but also as the site of an encounter with inequality in its most barbaric form. It was a radical volume, politically and creatively, that acknowledged tradition while simultaneously presenting poetry anew. Its impact has been such that it is easy to assume the volume published in 1798 was the result of a carefully worked-through manifesto, a detailed collaboration. In fact, its history was much more haphazard and reflected the evolving balance of power between its two poets. Wordsworth was the dominant voice both in the partnership and in *Lyrical Ballads*. By the time the volume was in press with Joseph Cottle in Bristol, the two were drifting apart, physically and emotionally. It was a separation that caused Coleridge much pain.

When Cottle agreed to publish *Lyrical Ballads* his firm was on the verge of bankruptcy. For weeks the volume, which Wordsworth viewed as a crucial statement of his poetic philosophy, languished undistributed. Cottle had the pages set in type but he appeared during the summer of 1798 to be unable to send unbound copies out into the world. In September Wordsworth wrote to ask him to transfer the copyright to Johnson. He insisted that he made the request out of concern for Cottle's well-being, and because he knew he was on the point of closing down his business. Cottle instead transferred the copyright to the rival firm of J. and A. Arch, with whom Wordsworth had no connection. To Johnson he sent an assertion of his right to dispose of the volume as he wished:

> I have received a letter from Mr Wordsworth requesting me to give up my Interest in his Lyrical Ballads to you. By the tenor of his letter I perceive clearly he is influenced, in this request, by an apprehension that the sale may not be such as to answer my purpose in publishing. I however purchased them of him originally with the intention of being their publisher, and I have still the same wish.[11]

Cottle asked whether Johnson had already paid Wordsworth for the volume and if the poet had thus made a commodity of that which was not his to sell. Wordsworth left England the day after he wrote to Cottle and it was not until May 1799 that he learnt his request had not been fulfilled. He was embarrassed by the bluntness with which Cottle had asked Johnson about money and was angered by the professional cost of his publisher's intransigence:

> I must add that I entirely disapproved of his not surrendering his claim to Johnson because as he repeatedly assured me that he published the work for my benefit (and as I only suffered him to have it on this account) he ought to have resigned his claim when I had a so much better prospect before me than I possibly could have if the work continued in his hands.[12]

Johnson was a better-connected publisher than Cottle and Wordsworth was ambitious for the volume and his future work. When he wrote to Cottle himself, having learnt of the bargain struck with J. and A. Arch, he did so in terms of frosty politeness. Clearly the agreement with the Arches made the transfer of the copyright to Johnson impossible but 'I still, however, regret it upon the same grounds as before, namely, that I have lost a good opportunity of connecting myself with Johnson; that I think the poems are not so likely to have a quick sale as if they were in his hands; and also that they must necessarily be separated from any thing which I may here-after publish.'[13]

Wordsworth saw his publishing future with Johnson. He was determined that his work should emerge from the centre of the London literary world, even while he, like Cowper, lived beyond its margins. It was a sign of the provisional, sometimes chaotic nature of the book trade that a collaborative work over which Wordsworth was exerting stringent creative control remained beyond the grasp of his chosen publisher. It was a symptom of Wordsworth's particular sense of the supremacy of the author – as the creative genius responsible for all elements of a book – that the chaos mattered so much.

✢

In the spring of 1798 Coleridge wrote a poem he called 'Fears in Solitude'. Two months after he completed the poem his community in the Quantocks disintegrated. The Wordsworths were told that rumours about their political allegiances meant they were no longer welcome tenants at Alfoxden and in late June they left for Bristol, after a brief and cramped stay with the Coleridges at Nether Stowey. At the beginning of the year Coleridge had still been uncertain about whether he should dedicate his life to poetry or accept a Unitarian ministry. In January he received an offer of an annuity from Tom Wedgwood to support his literary pursuits and, after the Wordsworths left Somerset, he decided to travel to Germany in order to write and study. He convinced Wordsworth and Dorothy that they should travel with him, although he left his own wife and children behind. Early in the autumn Lindsey met Basil Montagu and heard gossip about the young man 'who promised such great things' to the Unitarian cause. 'I began with asking abt Mr Colerige', he reported to John Rowe. The poet had gone to Germany: 'My wife asked if he had taken his wife.' No, came the answer from Montagu. 'What could he do with that clog about his neck.'[14] In London that September, as he prepared to leave England, Coleridge cut an isolated figure. Like Wordsworth before him he took his poetry to Johnson. The poems he showed Johnson were 'Fears in Solitude' and two companion pieces. 'France: An Ode' considered the tragedy of France's descent from freedom to tyranny. 'Frost at Midnight' turned inwards to explore the relationship between self, nature and family. Johnson was quick to see the originality and importance of Coleridge's voice.

During the two-week period in which Coleridge lingered in London Johnson rushed all three poems into print as a pamphlet entitled *Fears in Solitude*. At St Paul's Churchyard Coleridge dined multiple times. Johnson, he told his wife Sara, 'received me civilly the first time, cordially the second, affectionately the third – & finally took leave of me with tears in his eyes. – He is a worthy man.'[15] Johnson gave Coleridge £30 credit to be drawn from the booksellers of Hamburg as payment for the volume. When Coleridge wrote to Sara from Hamburg he was still full of wonder at the books and authors he had encountered at St Paul's Churchyard. He also insisted that the £30 was a gift rather than a transaction, and a token of a bond that would not easily be broken. 'Johnson, the Bookseller, without any poems sold to him; but purely out of affection conceived for me, & as part of any thing I *might* do for him, gave me an order on Remnant at Hamburgh for 30 pound.'[16] It mattered to Coleridge that Johnson was his friend as well as his publisher, and that their relationship was founded on mutual affection rather than commerce. He appeared in St Paul's Churchyard only briefly: not, as Lindsey had hoped, as the newest recruit to the Unitarian cause, but as a poet determined to make his way on the strength of his pen. Johnson offered him a readership and the company of other writers, beyond Wordsworth's shadow. The speed with which Johnson published *Fears in Solitude* demonstrated his belief in Coleridge and his poetry.

The subtitle to 'Fears in Solitude' explained that the poem was 'written in 1798, during the alarm of an invasion.'[17] It opened with an evocation of 'a green and silent spot' amid the Quantocks, 'a small and silent dell' described by Coleridge as 'spirit-healing' for those who have reached an age to repent of early folly and develop self-knowledge. Amidst the ferns the man bruised by life may for a moment lay down his burdens:

> And so, his senses gradually wrapp'd
> In a half sleep, he dreams of better worlds,
> And dreaming hears thee still, O singing lark;
> That singest like an angel in the clouds!

Within this haven the noise of international tumult threatens to drown out the song of the lark. It is impossible for Coleridge's retreating figure to ignore 'What uproar and what strife may now be stirring / This way or that way o'er these silent hills.' The tempests of the sea just beyond the hills are made by man, not nature: screams of war and invasion threaten the essence of Englishness, disrupting the sanctity of the landscape. Coleridge reads the prospect of an invasion as a punishment for a nation that has already betrayed its most sacred ideals. The English have become 'Contemptuous of all honourable rule,' a race content to barter 'freedom, and the poor man's life / For gold, as at a market!' Rapacious colonialism, slavery, greed and vice have debased the country; punishment is visited not just on individuals but also on places which once symbolised peace. Men, women and children have been debased in turn:

> Boys and girls,
> And women that would groan to see a child
> Pull off an insect's leg, all read of war,
> The best amusement for our morning-meal!

As war becomes spectacle, consumed by insentient readers greedy for sensational narrative, language, like place, is emptied of essence and meaning. Wretches who can barely remember the words for prayer become fluent in the language of war, 'technical in victories and defeats, / And all our dainty terms for fratricide'. Against these horrors, Coleridge asks for mercy. He issues a call for an impious enemy, drunk on a corrupted, tyrannical version of freedom, to be driven back across 'the insulted ocean'. But victory does not simply entail the vanquishing of an enemy. It also necessitates triumph over the sins that have degraded the nation and the land. The people of Britain owe as much to the geological formation that sustains and protects them:

> O native Britain! O my Mother Isle!
> How shouldst thou prove aught else but dear and holy
> To me, who from thy lakes and mountain-hills,
> Thy clouds, thy quiet dales, thy rocks, and seas,
> Have drunk in all my intellectual life,
> All sweet sensations, all ennobling thoughts,
> All adoration of the God in nature,
> All lovely and all honourable things,
> Whatever makes this mortal spirit feel
> The joy and greatness of its future being?

As the prospect of invasion threatens all that for which the poet cares, he evokes the relationship between landscape, faith and imagination as symbiotic. The lakes, dales, hills and coasts of Britain produce religious revelation and the poetic imagination. 'There lives nor form nor feeling in my soul / Unborrowed from my country', he declares. These lines epitomise patriotism for a new Romantic age, as an attachment not to stale or jingoistic notions of national power but to the qualities immanent in coastlines, dells and rural vistas.

The year 1798 has sometimes been described as a period of retreat for both Coleridge and Wordsworth, when they withdrew from the hubbub of an alienating national conversation in order to commune with each other and with skylarks. Wordsworth's focus on the poor in *Lyrical Ballads* gives the lie to this reading and in 'Fears in Solitude' Coleridge proclaims a philosophy of place that is at once rigorously intellectual and passionately felt. Poetry is not simply a vehicle for political comment in the hands of either poet. They do not, like Darwin, put stanzas at the service of a greater cause. Instead their poetry, in contrasting ways, has its own politics. It makes the case for a different kind of relationship between people, place and ideas and in its form it holds the possibility of regeneration. The invasion of which Coleridge writes comes partly from a foreign enemy and partly from a collective failure to recognise the importance of protecting a geographically located, organic peace from the corruptions of man. Poetry offers a way to see and counteract those corruptions, as it returns its gaze to the natural vistas from which, in Coleridge's telling, it first emerges.

As 'Fears in Solitude' comes to a close Coleridge turns his gaze away from the vistas of hill, coast and sky towards his own home as, sustained by the memory of a place of verdant peace, the poet re-encounters an idealised version of his own family and the society of other people. Nature equips him with the strength he needs to meet the joys and sorrows of everyday life. It symbolises all that is worthy of protection in the character of the country but it also affords protection against the strains of living for others as well as oneself. 'Fears in Solitude' asks a question about how to live at a time of public and personal turmoil and it offers poetry as the means by which enlightenment can be sought. It is at once a celebration of place and a political poem in the broadest sense. It is avowedly anti-war but its politics is located in more than the search for an answer to the questions of a particular moment. It represents a mode of being in the world which honours the essence of a country and an imaginative and spiritual response to that country while offering a challenge to all the ways in which a nation and its people have been despoiled by war and conquest.

✝

The *Analytical Review* saw in Coleridge a patriot driven away from the country he loved. The reviewer of *Fears in Solitude* made common cause with the poet, identifying him as a fellow Dissenter impugned for his belief that the nation might be reformed. 'Mr C., in common with many others of the purest patriotism, has been slandered with the appellation of an enemy to his country.' Surely, continued Johnson's reviewer, *Fears in Solitude* demonstrated that 'an adherence to the measures of administration is not the necessary consequence of an ardent love for the constitution.'[18] In the poems they brought to Johnson, Wordsworth and Coleridge both asked what it meant to be British when Britain was at war. To defend the landscapes that sustained them as well as all that those landscapes represented, they turned not to mechanised cavalry rafts but to language. They took quotidian experiences and familiar places and re-worked them as poetry in order to illustrate what was at stake in the battle for Britain's soul. In one answer to this question, in 'Frost at Midnight', Coleridge wrote of peace. His, though, was not the peace which came when one army finally vanquished another. It appeared instead as an organic stillness, that descended over country, village, sea and soul like the evening frost:

> The inmates of my cottage, all at rest,
> Have left me to that solitude, which suits
> Abstruser musings: save that at my side
> My cradled infant slumbers peacefully.
> 'Tis calm indeed! so calm, that it disturbs
> And vexes meditation with its strange
> And extreme silentness. Sea, hill, and wood,
> This populous village! Sea, and hill, and wood,
> With all the numberless goings on of life,
> Inaudible as dreams![19]

25

A peep into the Cave of Jacobinism

In James Gillray's 1798 print, 'A peep into the Cave of Jacobinism', Truth appears in light and glory, accompanied by cherubim holding aloft the symbols of Church, King and Judiciary. The monstrous figure of Jacobinism cowers in the darkness of his cave, hiding his eyes from the beam of Truth's torch. His mask of humanity slips from his face as he grasps his liberty cap and his serpent-like limbs are powerless to stop the rays of Truth's light setting fire to his collection of pamphlets. Each pamphlet is emblazoned with a title: 'Libels', 'Defamation', 'Sedition', 'Ignorance', 'Anarchy', 'Atheism' and 'Abuse'. A bottle marked 'Gall' lies useless at his side and the toads who are his only companions are fleeing from Truth's sight into the 'Lethean Stream'. In the opposite corner from the Toads, illuminated by the light cast from Truth's diadem, a journal is open. A flourishing script proclaims its title: the 'Anti-Jacobin Review & Mag.'

The *Anti-Jacobin Review* was founded by a group of young government partisans in July 1798, as a successor to the short-lived *Anti-Jacobin, or Weekly Examiner*, that appeared from November 1797 to July 1798. Its presiding genius was George Canning, then an under-secretary in the Foreign Office. It was edited by John Gifford, enabled by the Piccadilly bookseller James Wright, and sanctioned by Pitt. Gillray's portrait of Truth and the 'Cave of Jacobinism' provided the frontispiece for the first issue. The image proclaimed the *Anti-Jacobin Review* as the proud supporter of Church and King; as a tool in the service of Truth and as a weapon against Jacobinical sedition in all its monstrous forms.

The Prospectus for the *Anti-Jacobin* warned readers that enemies lurked among them. 'The existence of a Jacobin faction, in the bosom of our country, can no longer be denied. Its members are vigilant, persevering, indefatigable; desperate in their plans and daring in their language. The torrent of licentiousness, incessantly rushing forth from their numerous presses, exceeds, in violence and duration, all former examples.'[1] The emphasis on presses and pamphlets in the Prospectus and in Gillray's image was no accident. It was the purveyors of paper who represented the greatest threat to Britain's security. Against that threat the *Anti-Jacobin* presented itself as a bulwark. 'At such time, what friend of social order will deny, that *the Press* requires some strong control? And what control is more effectual than that which *the Press itself* can supply?'

The *Anti-Jacobin* was clear that some elements of the press were more threatening than others. Those journals that maliciously encouraged the spread of seditious foreign ideas were particularly dangerous. The Prospectus presented a riposte to the cosmopolitanism of the *Analytical Review*. Each issue of the *Anti-Jacobin*, it explained, would contain an Appendix reviewing foreign literature. 'We have been induced to make this a part of our plan by the consideration that this department of criticism has long been monop-olized by men who, favouring the views of the French *Economists* and other *Philosophists* of modern times, have facilitated the propagation of principles, subversive of social order, and, consequently, destructive of social happi-ness.'[2] The *Analytical* and other internationally focused journals were little more than a cover for the spread of Jacobin poison throughout the land, but the writers of the *Anti-Jacobin* assured their readers that they stood ready to expose the activities of enemies of the State wherever they appeared.

✝

From the outset the *Anti-Jacobin Review* had Johnson and his circle in its sights. In word and image it presented his shop and home as the Cave of Jacobinism. Gillray's image draws on the Gothic grammar of light and shade established in Fuseli's *Nightmare*, the image under which Johnson's guests dined. The *Anti-Jacobin* presented Johnson as the serpent in Eden, spreading poison through his presses. Chief among his crimes was the conversation he generated. Ignorant men might praise his loyalty but it behoved those men to look more closely at the company he kept. 'We advise, therefore, these critics, in future, to throw off a mask which will no longer conceal their object, and boldly, *if they dare*, pronounce an eulogy on the *loyalty* of this favourite publisher and friend of the PRIESTLEYS, the DARWINS, the GODWINS, and other *unprejudiced* authors, who have kindly taken upon themselves, for the last twenty years, the important task of *enlightening* the public mind.'[3] It was time, the *Anti-Jacobin* declared, for the version of enlightenment practised by Johnson and his ilk to be unmasked. Henceforth, the periodical declared, it would shine the light of Truth on all that was most dangerous and despicable in the world of letters.

As a consequence of attack from without, the figures with whom the *Anti-Jacobin* peopled Johnson's Cave of Jacobinism found themselves ever more closely aligned with his name. Priestley was charged with membership of a confederacy of unpatriotic disloyalty just at the point that geography rendered the consolations of that confederacy for ever beyond his reach. In Philadelphia in February 1796 he took tea with the American President, George Washington, with whom, he told Lindsey, he 'spent two hours as in any private family. He invited me to come at any time, without ceremony.' Priestley was convinced that America had immense potential but his own enjoyment of the country was limited by the knowledge that his friends were unlikely to follow him. 'I wish all my friends, with you, were here, provided they could subsist and be happy.' But, 'great numbers find themselves, on one account or other, disappointed, and return, I understand, with very unfavourable ideas of the country; and for this I see no remedy.'[4] The boxes of books that Johnson sent at sporadic intervals were a lifeline. A delivery in April contained 'a treasure of things'.[5] The books were valuable not just because they enabled Priestley to follow scientific and theological developments but because they offered an opportunity to reconstruct in letters exchanges interrupted by exile. Johnson's boxes prompted letters from Priestley filled with comments on the detail of his reading and when ships arrived from England without parcels on board he found it hard to mask his disappointment. 'We have had no arrivals from England about a month, and are very anxious for news of you', he wrote to the Unitarian minister Thomas Belsham in March. 'We sometimes hope for peace, but I do not expect any that will be stable, and followed by tranquillity within yourselves.'[6]

Priestley's dependence on sustaining news and books from England had its roots in difficulties no amount of American freedom could overcome. In December 1795 his son Harry died aged eighteen, as a result of complications from what Priestley described as a summer 'ague', or malaria. Nine months later, on September 11th 1796, Priestley told Lindsey that Mary was ill in bed with 'a feverish complaint, which is pretty common in this neighbourhood'.[7] On the 19th he wrote again. 'This day I bury my wife. She died on Saturday, after an illness of a fortnight. On Sunday morning she went to my son's, in whose house we have our service, but returned before we had begun, was seized with sickness, followed by a fever, which almost instantly affected her head, so that she had but little sense of anything, and spake but very little till she died.'

After Harry's death Priestley had consoled himself with the thought of God's love. Faced with the loss of Mary he struggled to reconcile the bitterness of his grief with his faith. To face such a loss while separated from his friends seemed impossible. 'I never stood more in need of friendship than I do now.'[8] He had been married to Mary for thirty-four years and for once in his life he saw no clear path forward. With this crisis there could be no rushing into print to set out his position: it was an experience at once more ordinary and unbearable than anything he had ever known. For a short period he toyed with the idea of becoming an itinerant Unitarian preacher, travelling throughout the American continent in search of congregations. Instead he remained in his partially built house in Northumberland, near the homes of his surviving sons William and Joseph, both of whom had married and settled nearby. After Mary's death Priestley moved in with his elder son Joseph and daughter-in-law Elizabeth. He was distressed by intermittent squalls between the brothers and their wives but he told friends in Britain that to return home and leave the graves of Harry and Mary untended was unthinkable. Anna Barbauld, who had been friends with Mary as a young woman, wrote a letter of condolence that prompted in Priestley the recollection of a vanished life. It reminded him of pleasant times past and 'brought a great number of pleasing scenes to mind'. Such memories were all the more precious because so many other prompts to memory were lost. 'If my diaries had not been destroyed in the riots, I should have been able to retrace some of them better than I can do now.' The lost item that Mary mourned most, he told Barbauld, was 'a folio book, into which she had copied all your unpublished poems, and other small pieces, especially the first poem we ever saw of yours, on taking leave of her, when we left Warrington.'[9] Mary's death prompted Priestley to fresh distress at the immolation of the record of his married life in the Birmingham fires. While Mary was alive the loss mattered less but in her absence it reappeared in new form as the theft of testimony to past happiness.

Priestley was sixty-three in the year Mary died. Although his grief was profound he believed he had important work to do in America and he kept writing. He travelled back and forth to Philadelphia, preaching to the city's small Unitarian congregation. In March 1797 he went to pay a farewell visit to Washington at the Presidential House. He was critical of Washington's policies and had high hopes that his successor, John Adams, would impose stronger protections on American merchants against the French, but he was nevertheless fond of the man who had done so much to build America. Washington, he told Belsham, 'seemed not to be in very good spirits. He invited me to Mount Vernon, and said he thought he should hardly go from home twenty miles as long as he lived.' Washington was at least pleased about one element of his legacy. 'The new federal city is within twenty miles of his residence, and that has been a favourite object with him.'[10] He told Lindsey that his own looks were so changed old friends would hardly recognise him. The transformation was chiefly a result of his adopting the unaccountable American habit of leaving off powdered wigs. Luckily, 'I have hair enough to keep me warm in the coldest weather, and as yet it is very little grey.'[11] He found a Philadelphia printer to whom he took his manuscripts, and who was instructed to send the unbound pages to Johnson for sale. It was an imperfect system, since the pages often arrived out of order and Johnson was highly critical of what he regarded as poor-quality American paper. Priestley persisted since it allowed him to correct his work in proof himself and to avoid the risk inherent in entrusting precious manuscripts to sailors voyaging across treacherous seas.

Distance did not spare Priestley anxiety on the part of the friends and family he had left behind. In August 1797 he was worried by news that Hannah Lindsey was ill and was frustrated by his inability to access news that was not months out of date by the time it reached him. Hannah recovered but Priestley wrote that he had begun to feel distanced from everyday life. 'The loss of near friends, and the society to which we have been long accustomed, weans us from the world.'[12] In September word reached him that his daughter Sarah's husband was on the brink of financial ruin. For his son-in-law he had little sympathy, although he acknowledged that he believed him to be guilty of folly rather than vice. For Sarah, who gave birth to another child as disaster unfolded around her, he was deeply concerned. Anna Barbauld took in one of Sarah's children while the family searched for a new home. 'I never felt my distance from England so much as now', Priestley mourned. But, he continued, 'I do not know that I could do them any good if I were with them.'[13]

In June 1798, as news of the invasion scare of the spring filtered through to America, Priestley reported that John Adams and his ministers had lost patience with the French-authorised privateers who were seizing American merchant ships in order to disrupt trade between Britain and America.

France and America embarked on two years of naval hostilities that became known subsequently as the Quasi-War. Once again Priestley attempted to capture the alienating sensation of being ignorant of whether his home country had fallen to enemy hands. 'We are now, in fact, at war with France, and you are threatened, probably by this time more than threatened, with an invasion from the same great power', ran his regular dispatch to Lindsey. The prospect of Britain's defeat led him to thoughts about the actions of Providence, and the strange ways by which God made his will known. 'I find a great disadvantage in being *alone*, having no person whatever to confer with on any subject of this kind', he confessed. He worried that without friends to guide his thinking he would become lost in a maze of speculation and from Lindsey he asked for patience. God's workings would be revealed to them all, he concluded, but only when they finally met their appointed hour.

⚓

A month after Wollstonecraft's death, Godwin wrote to Fanny Blood's widower, Hugh Skeys, to acknowledge Skeys's letter of condolence and to search for information. He was, he explained, 'at present employed upon the papers she left behind, & compiling some materials for an account of her life.' Skeys agreed to help him and undertook to secure him the cooperation of Eliza and Everina. Godwin was grateful but firm about the timetable: he could not wait months for information, even if the alternative was to impose on Skeys's good nature. In defence of this position he explained that Wollstonecraft's manuscripts were already with Johnson, who was pressing the commercial case for speedy publication. In early November Godwin and Johnson called on each other repeatedly as they planned their posthumous celebration of Wollstonecraft. In addition to the composition of a memoir, Godwin went to work on the manuscript of the novel left unfinished by Wollstonecraft at her death, The Wrongs of Woman. He presented it to Johnson with the story unresolved, honouring its provisional nature and Wollstonecraft's authorial authority. His work rate was prodigious and by mid-November he had a draft of the memoir ready for Skeys's comments. From Ireland Skeys wrote anxiously about the boldness of Godwin's account of Wollstonecraft's extramarital relationships, including with Godwin himself. Godwin agreed to tone down passages that related to other people but he would not alter his version of Wollstonecraft's passion. 'There is little or nothing that relates to me, that I should feel any pain in seeing published to the world', he proclaimed. 'You may regard my spirit of frankness, in this respect, as savouring of romantic.'[14]

Johnson also had views on Godwin's manuscript. In January 1798 the two men had a testy exchange over Godwin's characterisation of Fuseli. Godwin responded to Johnson's criticism by asserting his right to describe the man as he saw him, even though he had not been witness, as Johnson had, to his behaviour towards Wollstonecraft before her departure for Paris. 'As to his cynical cast, his impatience of contradiction, & his propensity to satire, I have carefully observed them', he countered. 'You see no faults in your friend: I do not blame you for this: it raises my idea of your temper & character: but (as you justly intimate) I am to state the report, not of your eyes, but of mine.'[15] Having raised his objections, Johnson agreed to publish Godwin's assertion that Fuseli had influenced Wollstonecraft for the worse. In the version of the memoir that he printed in collaboration with the firm of G. G. & J. Robinson, who were Godwin's usual publishers, Fuseli remained a target of criticism. 'Mr. Fuseli is somewhat of a caustic turn of mind', Godwin observed, 'with much wit, and a disposition to search, in every thing new or modern, for occasions of censure. I believe Mary came something more of a cynic out of the school of Mr. Fuseli, than she went into it.'[16] After Fuseli read the *Memoirs* he called on Joseph Farington in a rage and Farington recorded his conversation. 'Godwin was wrong in taking any notice of his conversation or opinion as He has done in his acct. of Mary Wolstonecraft'. Before he left Farington's company Fuseli predicted that the consequence for his own reputation of being allied so publicly with Wollstonecraft's emotional tempests would be severe.[17]

As they wrestled with Wollstonecraft's manuscripts and the production of *Memoirs*, Johnson and Godwin also tangled with her financial affairs. Creditors dating from her connection with Imlay demanded money of Godwin which, for the most part, he refused to produce. 'I was married to her five months', he wrote in explanation, and 'I have taken upon myself the care & support of her two children. More than this, under my circumstances, cannot, I think, be expected of me.' As their relationship disintegrated Imlay had persuaded Wollstonecraft to accept a bond for Fanny, the only form of financial support she would countenance. After her death Imlay sent an agent to Johnson to ask for it back. Wollstonecraft had also died in debt to Johnson himself which worried Godwin more 'because it was the debt of long-tried friendship & attachment, & because the money you advanced might be considered as most immediately advanced upon the mortgage of her future writings'.[18]

In the weeks after Wollstonecraft's death an argument erupted between Godwin and Mary Hays about who had rights to her papers and her story. Hays was angry with Godwin for excluding her from Wollstonecraft's deathbed and mistrustful of his assertion that he had complied with her demand to return all the letters she had written to Wollstonecraft. She succeeded in being the first to write of her friend in public, in an obituary published in the *Monthly Magazine* in late September. Hays presented Wollstonecraft as a martyr to her passions. 'The history of this singular woman (till within a very late period) has been that of one continued struggle with adverse circumstances, cares, and sorrows, combated, in every instance but one (over which humanity sheds its softest tear) with heroic fortitude.'[19] In the longer memoir she subsequently produced for Richard Phillips's *Annual Necrology* she expanded on this allusive reference to Wollstonecraft's Putney Bridge suicide attempt with a detailed description of the measures Wollstonecraft took to kill herself, drawn from the memory of conversations with Wollstonecraft herself. In both the long and short version of her tribute Hays insisted that Wollstonecraft's passing marked a public loss. In the longer piece she sharpened her sense of where that loss fell most heavily. 'Her own sex have lost, in the premature fate of this extraordinary woman, an able champion.' But, Hays insisted, 'she has not laboured in vain: the spirit of reform is silently pursuing its course.' 'Who', she asked, 'can mark its limits?'[20]

Faced with the challenge of marking the limits of reform, the *Anti-Jacobin Review* volunteered its services. Its review of Godwin's *Memoirs of the Author of A Vindication of the Rights of Woman* was so savage it tarnished Wollstonecraft's reputation for a generation. Godwin had written of Wollstonecraft's life as an exemplar; the *Anti-Jacobin* retorted that it offered an example of what not to do. It tied Wollstonecraft's story to that of the *Analytical Review* and it blamed the periodical for infecting 'Mary' with 'anti-hierarchical and anti-monarchical doctrines.' (The repeated use of her Christian name was a ruse, designed to deny her the status of professional authorship for which she fought so hard.) It alighted with delight on Godwin's uncompromising account of Wollstonecraft's emotional story, representing her as a foolish 'amorous lady' who first fell in love with Fuseli in spite of his marriage and then became the 'concubine' of Imlay. It implied that these relationships were only two among many and emphasised that such immoral behaviour made Wollstonecraft a prime example of 'JACOBIN MORALITY'. Wollstonecraft's private 'concubinage' was thus not merely a matter for personal shame but a public threat and an attack on the moral integrity of a nation at war.[21]

The *Anti-Jacobin* attacks worked. As Wollstonecraft's name was made synonymous in the public imagination with loose living and corrupted morality it became almost impossible for the feminist campaigners who survived her to uphold the ideas that were her legacy. The *Anti-Jacobin's* campaign was given succour when one of its writers, Richard Polwhele, produced a poem that pilloried Wollstonecraft, Hays and their contemporaries as *Unsex'd Females*. Polwhele's attack on Wollstonecraft included descriptions of her mounting the 'dazzling dome' to reach Fuseli before fleeing to 'IMLAY and licentious love'. Polwhele quoted liberally from Godwin's *Memoir* in footnotes to his poem, which also included mocking lines describing Wollstonecraft's attempt to drown herself at Putney Bridge:

> And dost thou rove, with no internal light,
> Poor maniac! thro' the stormy waste of night?
> Hast thou no sense of guilt to be forgiv'n
> No comforter on earth, no hope in Heaven?
> Stay, stay – thine impious arrogance restrain —
> What tho' the flood may quench thy burning brain,
> Rash woman! Can its whelming wave bestow
> Oblivion, to blot out eternal woe?[22]

Polwhele's poem appeared in 1798, as did an anonymous work Johnson published to counter the onslaught against Wollstonecraft's feminist legacy. *An Appeal to the Men of Great Britain* has traditionally been credited to Mary Hays, although some literary scholars have queried this attribution.[23] The author of the *Appeal* warned the men of Britain that by holding on to their empire by force, and in the face of reasoned objections, they risked the security of their grip on power. Her remarks, she insisted, 'are indeed directed to you, oh man! clothed with authority of your own assuming, and clothed with strength to maintain what you have assumed. You maintain it by the same law by which the strong oppress the weak, and the rich the poor; and by which the great and powerful crush the friendless, and him who has none to help him.' At least, she continued, 'this is what women suppose to be the real state of the case.' It was for the good of men that she made such an argument. 'For your own sakes therefore, and in support of that character you assume of superior rationality; in the name of every thing that is candid, open, and generous; be persuaded to consider the matter in a fair point of view, as you would any other subject of equal importance.'[24] The *Appeal* was polemical, angry and meticulously argued and it represented a valiant celebration of Wollstonecraft's legacy. The impact of the *Anti-Jacobin* smears and Polwhele's vicious couplets, however, meant that its author could not run the risk of appearing in public, and once the *Appeal* left the confines of St Paul's Churchyard its arguments fell on deaf ears.

Throughout the period in which Godwin, Johnson and Hays worked together and in competition to produce a posthumous version of Wollstonecraft's story, Godwin himself was a frequent visitor at Johnson's table. He did his best by four-year-old Fanny and by baby Mary, working to keep them in the home he had made with Wollstonecraft and to pay the nursemaid who was familiar to them. Wollstonecraft's portrait hung in his study and as they grew older he taught her daughters to read using Barbauld's *Lessons for Children*. At St Paul's Churchyard he found company during a bewildering period and, along with Fuseli and Bonnycastle, he became one of Johnson's most reliable and regular guests. They made a strange quartet: the bookseller, the artist, the philosopher and the math-ematician, but in spite of their divergent intellectual interests they sustained each other.

New faces at the table continued to bring new ideas. In 1798 Godwin met a writer in whom Johnson was interested called Thomas Malthus. In August 1798, when Godwin and Malthus came to dinner, Johnson had just published Malthus's *Essay on the Principle of Population*, a work that took issue with Godwin's philosophy of perfectibility. Johnson was sufficiently intrigued by the *Essay* to press a copy into Coleridge's hands in September as Coleridge left for Hamburg. The morning after the August dinner Malthus joined Godwin for breakfast so that they could continue the debate started the night before. Later that day Godwin wrote a letter underscoring his position with ideas that had escaped him during conversation. Malthus had argued in print and at the table that disease, hunger and social deprivation controlled the population level and were thus necessary correctives to overpopulation. Godwin responded that since every human being was of value a society that cut short the lives of so many of its citizens was abhor-rent. 'Shall I not', he asked, 'then be the irreconcilable foe of the present system of society, which produces so melancholy a consequence, & seems to cut us off from hopes which must be inexpressibly dear to every lover of his kind?'[25] The argument between Godwin and Malthus, started over wine and roasted veal in the candlelight at St Paul's Churchyard, would rumble on in print and in person for decades and would become increasingly acrimonious. In August 1798, however, it marked the point when Godwin's presence at Johnson's table bought him back into the world of letters from which he had been exiled by grief.

✝

The *Anti-Jacobin* review charged Johnson with the crime of befriending Priestley, Godwin and Darwin. Darwin also received the dubious honour of being singled out for solo *Anti-Jacobin* attack in a mock satire published in the journal in 1798, entitled 'Loves of the Triangles'. In the face of politically charged invective Darwin remained exuberantly outspoken. In 1796 he sent Johnson the second volume of *Zoonomia* for publication. It encompassed a thorough catalogue of diseases and treatments and, to his delight, brought him new patients 'from even London, and distant parts of England' as well as new readers.[26] He wrote of himself as an old man but his energy was undimmed. 'What is there in this world to ex[c]ite men of the age at which You and myself are arrived at, to make us wish to continue you in it?' he wrote to his friend James Watt in 1796. 'Activity of mind is the only circumstance which can prevent one from thinking over disagreeable events, which already exist, or are likely soon to exist, in England as well as in other countries devoted to this bloody war!'[27]

Johnson continued in his support of Darwin as increasing scientific parochialism rendered his work unfashionable in some quarters, but he was cautious about the potential risks inherent in taking on new authors. One of Darwin's protégés was warned not to expect great rewards from his work and in letters to friends and business acquaintances Johnson revealed that keeping open house during years of ferment had taken its toll. In August 1796 he complained to William Russell of the scepticism displayed by some young Dissenters towards Priestley's theological arguments. 'Infidelity is making rapid strides among us', he worried. 'Attacks on revelation are read with avidity, defences with indifference, if at all.'[28] As a young man Johnson had enabled Priestley's own overturning of theological orthodoxy, but when the rebellious students of Hackney turned away from Priestley and Lindsey, and towards Godwin, unorthodox thinking took on a more threatening form.

The shop and office were as busy as ever. At one point Johnson had ten compositors at work on a text and in the late 1790s he took on a new informal apprentice, his great-nephew John Miles. Miles was the grandson of Johnson's older brother John and after he turned fourteen in 1798 he was sent to St Paul's Churchyard to learn a trade, following the path laid out by Rowland Hunter before him. Johnson did not forget the needs of the people who worked for him or their dependents and his letters reveal fundraising among friends and fellow booksellers for a printer's widow left in difficult circumstances. That extra help was needed in the shop and back rooms was evident from the complaints of friends, who kept up an exchange of anecdotes about the time Johnson took to fulfil orders and print pamphlets. Lindsey described his old friend as 'a worthy and most honest man, but incorrigibly neglectful, often to his own detriment.'[29]

Johnson might leave letters unanswered and orders unfulfilled but in other respects his command of his empire was absolute. As Cowper's work grew in popularity pirated editions of his poetry threatened Johnson's custody of his copyrights. The Scottish booksellers, who worked under different copyright laws, were particularly casual about work owned by others and in his correspondence Johnson was unapologetic about his right to defend his property. The Scottish bookseller who had attempted to pirate Cowper was told to reprint in such a way as acknowledged Johnson's ownership in order to avoid a lawsuit neither bookseller wanted. It was his right to go to law, Johnson explained, but 'as I am not fond of lawsuits myself so neither do I wish to involve others in them, especially where I see a strong disposition to undo, as far as may be, the mischief that has been done.' In amongst everything else Johnson kept reading new work and new translations and was not above an acerbic comment when hastily produced books failed to meet his own standards. The publisher of a new translation of an older French work was consoled with the information that 'out of mercy to the parties concerned' Johnson would make sure it remained unnoticed by the *Analytical Review*.[30] James Hurdis, who had a higher opinion of his own poetry than did most of his readers, wrote angrily that Johnson's refusal to pay what Hurdis considered to be a fair price for his copyrights was symptomatic of 'Presbyterian' meanness. Hurdis was convinced that Johnson's behaviour was reflective of broader failings in the bookseller's tribe and that it had nothing to do with the quality of his verse. In his anger he elided distinct religious groups in a caricature of Nonconformist ingratitude. 'To dissenters I have always behaved with politeness and moderation,' he complained. 'Yet I have never met with a Presbyterian who did not in the end make me repent that I had ever been connected with him.'[31]

On Johnson's list old friends and old themes remained mainstays. Maria Edgeworth sent a collection of educational children's stories for publication, called *The Parent's Friend*. She was pleased when Johnson decided to publish the stories in the same size and design as *Evenings at Home* but cross when he changed the title of the collection to *The Parent's Assistant* without consulting her. She told her cousin Sophy that the new title made her think of an old and hated arithmetic book called *The Tutor's Assistant*. In 1796 her father Richard Lovell Edgeworth told Darwin that, amongst his many other pursuits (which included an attempt to introduce an early version of telegraph communication to Ireland) he and his daughter were working on a new educational treatise. 'I seriously think, that more good may be done by improving education, than by any other means; and to that we apply our feeble powers with strong good will.'[32] The book on which the Edgeworths were working was called *Practical Education*. It was a parenting guide grounded in the reality of life at Edgeworthstown, where older siblings took charge of younger children and where, throughout the 1790s, there were multiple infants in need of education. The Edgeworths encouraged parents to try the experiments outlined in Priestley's 1772 *History of Vision* with their children, in order to inculcate an early taste for science by making it exciting and entertaining. They warned against pushing children towards too much knowledge too early and they presented a scheme akin to contemporary phonics to aid the teaching of reading. They advocated six months of sound-based reading, at which point the child in question could be permitted to move on to the first book of Barbauld's *Lessons for Children*. They dispensed advice about behaviour and, while they upheld the rights of the child, they were sceptical about the benefits of too much liberty. About tantrums they wrote from bitter experience and of the screaming child they had this to say: 'It is better to stop them by presenting new objects to their attention, than by the stimulus of a peremptory voice.'[33]

The education of very young children had been a central concern on Johnson's list since his publication of the early works of Barbauld and Trimmer. It was a concern taken up by Wollstonecraft in her own early work and carried forward by the Edgeworths. Like Wollstonecraft they were dubious about the value to young women of hours spent acquiring polite and mechanical accomplishments but they were more circumspect than her about the politics of separate female education. Maria Edgeworth was responsible for the chapter 'On Temper' and she explicitly distanced herself from Wollstonecraft's theories. 'We cannot help thinking', she wrote of young women, 'that their happiness is of more consequence than their speculative rights, and we wish to educate women so that they may be happy in the situations in which they are most likely to be placed.' She recognised that young women were liable to suffer more restraints upon their behaviour than their male counterparts but the answer she proposed was to inure them to that restraint rather than equip them to fight it.[34] *Practical Education* did not present a manifesto for changing the world. Instead it offered ways to prepare children of both sexes to face the world as it was: divided, imperfect and unequal. The Edgeworths also emphasised the importance of avoiding retreat at all costs. 'We cannot forbear to advise young people to read the newspapers of the day regularly: they will keep up by these means with the current of affairs.' It was a particularly important lesson for the boys who would be compelled to face a harsh reality as they emerged from the shelter of childhood. 'The sooner boys acquire the sort of knowledge necessary for the conversations of sensible men the better; they will be the less exposed to feel false shame.'[35]

Richard Lovell Edgeworth's third wife Elizabeth died in 1797 after succumbing to tuberculosis. By early 1798 letters were travelling back and forth between Edgeworthstown, St Paul's Churchyard and the home of Frances Beaufort, the daughter of one of Richard Lovell's friends. Frances was a talented draughtswoman and the Edgeworths wanted her illustrations to appear in *Practical Education*. Johnson was reluctant and Edgeworth pleaded with her Aunt Ruxton to break the news to Frances. 'Enclosed is a letter of Johnson's which I wish you would be so good as to shew to dear Miss Beaufort ... I feel very much mortified about the idea that the beautiful little bubble boys are not immediately to make their appearance; but my father seems to think that we must in this instance submit to Mr Johnson's decrees.'[36] In May 1798 Richard Lovell and Frances were married. Six more children followed, to join the six children of Elizabeth who had been under Edgeworth's care during her stepmother's long illness. By June 1798 *Practical Education* was advertised for publication. Three months later the Edgeworths had to flee their home when the violence of the Irish Rebellion reached Edgeworthstown. In 1794 Richard Lovell had prophesied to Darwin that if the oppressed people of Ireland were tormented until they were forced to rise up they would do so with ungovernable brutality. In September the family witnessed the violence of those who had been provoked beyond endurance at first hand. Edgeworthstown was only saved when one of the rebels tasked with razing it identified it as a house in which he had once received kindness. A short while later Richard Lovell narrowly escaped being lynched by a loyalist crowd after he was accused of aiding the rebels. As the rebellion was quashed and the violence subsided Edgeworth wrote to her cousin Sophy to report that they were safely home. 'The scenes we have gone through for some days past, have succeeded one another like the pictures in a magic lantern, and have scarcely left the impression of reality upon the mind. It all seems like a dream.'[37]

When Frances Edgeworth came to write a *Memoir* of her famous step-daughter, she wrote of Johnson with affection. Nevertheless, she thought, 'it was afterwards a disadvantage to Maria that her works were published by the printer of what were considered seditious and sectarian books.'[38] The conviction that Johnson's name was irrevocably tainted by the *Anti-Jacobin* attacks was shared by Joseph Farington, who was of the opinion that Fuseli's long association with Johnson had caused the artist professional harm. In 1799 Farington recorded gossip in his diary that Edmund Burke (who had died in 1797) was an admirer of Fuseli's work and 'would have procured some essential advantages for [him] – but for the opinion entertained of his associating so much with *revolution men* and at Johnsons.'[39] For those who sought physical and mental shelter at St Paul's Churchyard, including Godwin, the Edgeworths, Fuseli and, on his rare London visits, Darwin, Johnson's dining room continued to act as a sanctuary. For Priestley, exiled across the Atlantic, books dispatched from the shop below offered a crucial connection to the debates taking place around the table. But for those who feared the power of reform-minded conversation, or who were determined to undermine it, the spectacle of the assembled company at St Paul's Churchyard offered the chance to elide all those who gathered around Johnson in person and in print into a homogenous band of revolutionary plotters. As the dining room was transformed into the Cave of Jacobinism in the public imagination, the refuge it offered was threatened as never before.

26

The King Versus Joseph Johnson

On February 5th 1798 a stranger called John Hancock walked into Johnson's shop and bought a pamphlet by Gilbert Wakefield. He had already bought another copy at the shop of Jeremiah Jordan, who had previously been prosecuted for selling *The Rights of Man*. The pamphlet Hancock purchased at both shops was entitled *A Reply to Some Parts of the Bishop of Llandaff's Address to the People of Great Britain*. Wakefield arranged his own printing and the pamphlet's primary bookseller was John Cuthell, from whom Johnson ordered copies in response to an advertisement.

The Bishop of Llandaff, Richard Watson, had continued to dabble in the Establishment proselytising that had angered Wordsworth in 1793. In January 1798 he published an Address in which he defended the war with France, proposed that it should be funded through tax increases of a tenth of every man's whole property, and in which he outlined the virtues of different classes remaining in their ordained spheres. In his reply Wakefield pointed out the manifold injustice of a tax increase that might cause rich men like the bishop to make marginal reductions in their discretionary spending while simultaneously driving poor families to destitution. His main objection, however, was to Watson's defence of the war. He charged the bishop with putting his own self-interest above the needs of the country. 'By an essential alteration in the present system of our government, if the result of foreign invasion or intestine anarchy, the Bishop of Llandaff would lose immediately all his *ecclesiastical* offices at least; whose emoluments, if not exorbitant, appear very considerable.'[1] Wakefield then widened his attack to encompass the entirety of Pitt's administration. 'The present ministry', he insisted, 'and the abuses in Church and State, are indivisibly interwoven with each other; and every man alive, who profits by these enormous inequalities, can by no means be esteemed *independent*, but must be considered in the eye of reason as an *interested supporter* of our existing forms.'[2] Pitt and his ministers might claim to desire peace but their characters suggested otherwise. They were 'self-opinionated, arrogant, audacious, defamatory, and despotical' and they delighted in war-mongering.[3] Such men betrayed the founding British principles of constitutional freedom and the corruption with which they dispensed 'their staple commodity, posts and peerages' damaged the nation.[4]

Wakefield warned that the abuses suffered by the British populace had consequences. 'I am fully satisfied,' he wrote, 'that, if the French could land a considerable army in this country, to the number, suppose, of 60,000 or 70,000 men (which, nevertheless, appears to me utterly impracticable, with our present naval superiority) the kingdom would be lost for ever.' Republicans in France had effected revolution as a result of the poverty and wretchedness of millions of desperate people and the same degree of desperation existed in Britain. 'I believe from my soul', Wakefield continued, 'that within three miles of the house, where I am writing these pages, there is a much greater number of starving, miserable human beings, the hopeless victims of penury and distress, than on any equal portion of ground through the habitable globe.'[5] Should the French come, he wrote, they would find him in his study, contemplating matters of antiquarian and theological importance. 'No zeal in support of frontless corruption and "every evil work," shall dip my hands in the blood of MEN!'[6] It was for those who had created the current crisis to defend 'domestic robbers against a foreign spoiler.' He would wait with tranquil resignation for a grand revolution in the country and would play no part in defending corruption. 'When I see all consideration of the public welfare swallowed up in a domineering profligacy, venality, and selfishness; when I behold the most hideous crimes daringly perpetrated under the pretence of preserving regularity and subordination ... when I observe these, and other enormities, which the time would fail me to numerate, committed without scruple and without remorse, to maintain, forsooth! a degenerate constitution of ideal excellence and practical depravity, and am called upon to defend it against invaders; I revolt at such an audacious imposition, and pity the understanding that can be duped by such despicable artifice.'[7] The only possibility for the nation's salvation lay, in Wakefield's diagnosis, in a complete change of ministry, constitutional reform, the abolition of political abuses and through a reasoned and civilised negotiation with the newly emboldened French republic.

John Hancock was a government spy and he bought Wakefield's *Reply* from Jordan and Johnson at the behest of the Crown. The pamphlet was on sale all over London but Hancock only purchased it from selected booksellers. In the third week of February Lindsey reported that Cuthell had been arrested for selling Wakefield's pamphlet. 'The part of Mr W's letter, which I understand has given the most offence, is where he is thought to discourage any efforts being made at the pres[en]t time to repell our invaders; tho' many lawyers think that it is a trifling accusation.'[8]

As soon as word reached Johnson that booksellers were being prosecuted for selling Wakefield's work he ordered his shopman Mr Dale to clear all copies of the pamphlet from the shop. But Hancock had already made his purchases and government law officers had Johnson in their sights. On Saturday February 10th, five days after Hancock's visit, Johnson was presented with an indictment issued under the auspices of John Scott, the Attorney General. He was charged with enabling the circulation of 'several scandalous and seditious libels' during a time of war. The indictment described Johnson as a 'London Bookseller being a malicious seditious and ill disposed person and being greatly disaffected to our said sovereign Lord the King and to the Government and Institution of this Kingdom' who was 'most unlawfully seditiously and maliciously contriving and intending to traduce vilify and bring into hatred and contempt among the liege subjects of our said Lord the King the Government and Constitution of this Kingdom.' His hatred was directed towards 'Church and State as now by Law Established and also our said Lord The King's administration of the Government of this Kingdom and the Persons Employed by our said Lord the King in the administration of the Government of this kingdom.' The desired effect of Johnson's actions, according to the indictment, was to 'withdraw the affection and allegiance of the liege subjects of our said Lord the King from our said Lord the King and his Government and also most unlawfully maliciously and seditiously devising and intending to dissuade and discourage the liege subjects of our said Lord the King from resisting and opposing the said Enemies of our said Lord the King in case the said Enemies should make a hostile Invasion into the Kingdom.'[9]

The indictment charged Johnson with acting in such a way as to turn British citizens against the King and the Government, and to discourage those citizens from defending the country against a declared enemy. It also damned him personally, as the possessor of a 'malicious' and 'seditious' character. The law made booksellers responsible for the content of the books they sold and attributed the politics of particular books to the views of the individuals selling them. In practice many booksellers were not prosecuted for selling work to which the authorities objected and Hancock's shopping expedition provides solid evidence that the government had been waiting for an opportunity to use the libel laws against Johnson. Although Cuthell was arrested first his trial remained unscheduled as Johnson and Jordan were issued with court dates.

In preparation for the trial Johnson enlisted the services of Lord Erskine, who had triumphed as chief defence counsel during the Treason Trials of 1794. Shortly before the trial Johnson was walking through Lincoln's Inn with Bonnycastle. They were on their way to dine with Fuseli when they bumped into Erskine, exercising his pack of dogs. 'Johnson', Bonnycastle heard him shout, 'I have something particular to say to you.' Johnson kept Bonnycastle waiting for fifteen minutes while Erskine talked to him, apparently with great seriousness. As they resumed their walk Johnson asked Bonnycastle to guess the subject of their conversation. 'Doubtless', Bonnycastle replied, 'your forthcoming trial.' '"Not a bit," said Johnson; "he never even alluded to it, and the time was wholly occupied with his opinions about Brothers the Prophet, and in asking questions respecting a book 'on the Revelations,' lately offered me for publication."'[10] Bonnycastle's anecdote captures something of the strange quality of the spring of 1798 at St Paul's Churchyard. While the country waited for an invasion that never came Johnson proceeded as normal, hosting dinners, issuing books, corresponding with friends, authors and booksellers, directing his staff. He did so with the prospect of the trial and a possible prison sentence hanging over him, knowing that the Attorney General's office had finally acted decisively to discredit him.

Jordan and Johnson were tried on the same day, July 17th 1798, at the Court of King's Bench, Guildhall. Johnson's trial was recorded in court transcripts as 'The King versus Joseph Johnson'. The presiding judge was Lord Kenyon, a previous Attorney General under Pitt. At the Treason Trials the prosecution had relied on ordinary juries but for the trials of Jordan and Johnson they selected a 'special jury' of merchants who could be relied upon to support the prosecution position. Jordan's trial was heard first and was over within minutes. Erskine had prepared a lengthy defence but *The Times* reported that just as the jury was sworn in Erskine was obliged to inform the judge 'that a letter had just been put into his hands from Mr. Jordan, stating that he would not give his Lordship and the Jury any trouble in this business.'[11] Kenyon immediately summed up for a guilty verdict and Jordan was found guilty. The speed with which Jordan offered the court his cooperation, and the fact that he did so without informing Erskine of his decision, suggests that he had agreed a plea-bargain in order to lay the foundations for a successful prosecution of Johnson. Jordan was vulnerable to particularly vindictive judicial treatment because he had previously been found guilty of publishing Paine's *Rights of Man* and he may have been subjected to considerable pressure by government agents. Since he could not afford bail he was sent to prison to await sentencing.

Trials before the King's Bench were usually swift affairs, but Johnson's trial, which followed immediately after the conclusion of Jordan's, lasted nearly six hours. It opened with the prosecution barrister making the argument for the decision to charge a bookseller with the crimes of an author. The State's case rested on the position that the efficient administration of government and the country depended on the letter of the law being applied. In short, social ruin would be the result of juries disregarding the law. The rationale for the law was simple: 'because ... the author cannot do the mischief he intends without the publisher.' 'Publisher', in this sense, encompassed anyone who acted so as to disseminate words in print. The Crown called one witness only: John Hancock. In response Erskine attempted to change the legal foundation of the argument in a speech that took several hours to deliver. He insisted that the question at issue was not whether or not a bookseller should be charged as an author, but the much more fundamental matter of free speech.

Erskine opened by citing precedents where juries had objected to the content of books but not found the authors guilty, and he praised Wakefield's integrity. He reminded the jury that Wakefield had not criticised the institution of government but the actions of a specific administration and he drew attention to his own peerage as proof that he had no wish to support arguments designed to destabilise State institutions. The King, he insisted, was separate from his government, and could not be implicated in its successes or failures. He emphasised that it was perfectly possible for moderate men to believe in the need for reform without being guilty of sedition and he denied the suggestion that Wakefield had written in support of a French invasion. If questions of international policy were no longer admissible subjects for consideration by thinking men, then other writers, including Burke himself, were guilty of the charges levelled against Wakefield's publishers. Wakefield's previous writings on theological subjects had given his booksellers no reason to suspect he had turned his attention to political matters and it was a legal nonsense to suggest that booksellers could be made liable for every publication circulated by accident or design through their shops. A guilty verdict, Erskine reminded the jury of merchants, would put a bookseller 'into such a situation that he may be indicted every day of his life if he does not read from the beginning to the end of the whole library he sells.' The indictment charged Johnson with crimes of thought and character as well as of actions and in response Erskine was defiant. He painted the prosecution as an attempt to dismantle the life Johnson had made:

> If you think it is too much to say that a peaceable citizen of London living in Saint Pauls Church Yard – a respectable man known for many years in the literary world – a man connected with honourable persons whom he can bring here in vindication of his moral life and character that because he had unfortunately sold this book that he has done it with the malicious intentions stated and charged upon this regard – Is that an inference of law? ... I say it is a scandal to the statute book if that meant so.

Erskine presented the prosecution as an assault on the world of commerce and city civility from which the jury was drawn. In support of his argument he summoned a procession of witnesses: first Cuthell, who explained how Johnson had placed a routine order for Wakefield's newest work, then George Fordyce, who testified to his old friend's outstanding moral character and to the wide variety of books he published. Fordyce was followed by John Aiken, and then John Hewlett, all of them quick to rally round an ally under siege. Erskine also called Johnson's shopman William Dale, who emphasised the speed with which Johnson ordered him to withdraw Wakefield's work from sale.

During his speech Erskine intimated that Johnson was being prosecuted at the behest of shadowy forces. In reply the Attorney General rebutted the suggestion that he was acting on behalf of others. He argued that if booksellers were set free to publish whatever they pleased the country would be in a dangerous position, in a riposte to Erskine's defence of free speech that argued for the supreme importance of national security. Jordan had offered no defence and been found guilty; it was a legal nonsense that Johnson should be acquitted on the same charge. Were the jury, he demanded, 'prepared to let the energies of the law sleep with respect to checking the licentiousness of the press for the purposes of preserving the liberty of the press?' Such licentiousness, he admonished, did more damage to free speech than any amount of legal control. In his summing up Lord Kenyon made it clear that his patience had been tried by the theoretical basis of Erskine's defence. He wished to hear no more about the war with France, or Burke, or arguments for and against the peerage, or Wakefield's character. Jordan had been found guilty and in his own reading of Wakefield's pamphlet Kenyon found plenty that was libellous and seditious. He was unmoved by the suggestion that Johnson's crime was less because he was not the original publisher. If the jury wanted to defend the country from those who wished it evil it was their duty to find the defendant guilty. It did not matter that Johnson was 'a literary man living with literary people' who had brought illustrious men to speak in his defence: what mattered was 'the rule ... that the Publisher is liable for what he had published.' The libel in question, meanwhile, was 'a very abominable one'. The jury, the court record noted, 'immediately pronounced the Defendant Guilty.'[12]

The court records for the trials of Johnson and Jordan are filled with voices and theatrical gestures. Erskine's rhetoric soared through the court-room in a meditation on free speech, reform and the rights of the individual; the Attorney General countered with a claim that the security of the nation was at stake. Erskine demanded that windows be shut so his voice could better be heard; Fordyce, Aikin and Hewlett provided eloquent testimony to Johnson's virtues. Even Jordan can be heard, promising not to make trouble for the lawyers. Johnson remains silent. His friends speak for him, as does his shopman: his lawyer speaks mostly for himself. Fuseli's biographer John Knowles wrote of Fuseli's anger at Erskine's conduct. The lawyer had, Fuseli thought, 'lost sight of the interest of his client, in the wish to shew his own political opinions, and to make a display of his oratorical powers.'[13] Before Kenyon Johnson was the object of the noise of others, made respon-sible for the words of another by the letter of the law.

After the guilty verdict Johnson was freed on bail to await sentencing and he returned home. Lindsey was away from London and so was compelled to rely on newspapers and an account of the trial sent by Thomas Belsham. Like Fuseli he thought Erskine had let Johnson down. 'It is to be lamented that his case was not set forth with all the force and distinction that was due to it.' The whole affair, he told Belsham, 'makes me tremble more and more for our liberties.'[14] The news took time to reach Priestley and it was not until early November that he acknowledged his friend's fate. 'I feel much concerned for Mr Johnson', he wrote to Lindsey. 'How unequally is justice administered! I wish he had come hither, as he once seemed inclined to do.'[15] The suggestion that Johnson had contemplated following Priestley to America is an intriguing one. The apparatus of Johnson's life and business was grounded in St Paul's Churchyard; to move across continents and start afresh in a foreign market would have been a huge undertaking. Nevertheless, the effort of navigating the commercial and cultural repressions of the 1790s was immense and booksellers were particularly vulnerable. So were international citizens, but Johnson was compelled to stand by as those closest to him were targeted. In August Fuseli had to report to a government office in Marlborough Street to sign a declaration under the Alien Act. Joseph Farington, rather than Johnson the convicted criminal, went with Fuseli to testify to his identity and good behaviour. Fuseli remained steadfast in spite of the conditions placed on his political engagement by the Alien Act. Johnson's family also rallied round. In the diary entry for August 14th in which Godwin noted having met Malthus at St Paul's Churchyard he also recorded the presence at dinner of 'Johnson senr'. This was Johnson's older brother John, who left his brewing business in the hands of his son Joseph in order to visit his brother during a time of trouble.

In one quarter the news of the guilty verdict against Johnson was met with joy. The staff writers of the *Anti-Jacobin Review* professed indignation at the suggestion that a bookseller was not responsible for the books he sold. They asked their readers to conjure in their imaginations a frightful future in which booksellers were able to evade the law by claiming not to know the details of the material they published. '*Ignorance* is a most convenient plea for persons accused of crimes, but it is the duty of every *publisher*, at least, to print no work, that he had not perused.' Were the plea of ignorance to be admitted, 'all prosecution of booksellers would be at an end, and the country might be inundated with treasonable and seditious tracts, (as it is at present with *newspapers* of that description,) for which no person would found to be responsible.'[16] Where the *Anti-Jacobin* did agree with Johnson's friends was in their estimation of Erskine as more concerned with his own image than with the fate of his client. James Gillray provided the journal with a portrait of Erskine as 'Councellor Ego' in which Erskine figured as the letter i, with his dot formed by a liberty cap. In the accompanying dialogue Erskine praises himself in a cascade of Latin cases. Text accompanying the plate made it clear that it represented Erskine in

1798.

Councellor EGO. _i:e:_little i.myself i.

full flight during Johnson's trial. 'The subject of the plate', it read, 'was suggested by a friend, who, as he was walking in Guildhall, on the morning appointed for the trial of Mr. JOHNSON, the bookseller ... overheard the following Soliloquy'.[17]

In the months between his trial and sentencing Johnson worked as hard as ever. It was during this period that he published Coleridge's *Fears in Solitude*; the *Analytical Review* appeared without interruption. In September the *Analytical* carried a review of a book by Arthur O'Connor entitled *The State of Ireland* and of a letter by Wakefield to the Attorney General on the subject of Johnson's trial. Wakefield was awaiting his own prosecution and to write directly to John Scott was an audacious act. Equally audacious was Johnson's acquiescence in the pamphlet being profiled in his in-house journal before his own sentence was pronounced. Wakefield announced himself ready to undergo all the privations judicial tyranny could ordain in defence of free speech. For his bravery the *Analytical* had only praise. 'We here behold a man about to undergo an expensive and perhaps rigorous prosecution on account of his opinions; but we perceive, at the same time, that he is prepared to encounter the menaced hostility, with all the firmness and intrepidity of the christian martyrs!'[18] Both Lindsey and Priestley had been accorded the status of martyr when they were attacked for their adherence to particular religious tenets. Now the same term was accorded to Wakefield and Johnson as they stood ready to withstand the wrath of the law in defence of the liberty of the press.

Arthur O'Connor's tract on Ireland, reviewed in the same issue of the *Analytical*, mounted a defence of the Irish rebels and made the case for Catholic Emancipation and popular representation. The *Analytical's* review was studiedly neutral: 'we forbear to make any observation on this publication, which seems to have been intended as a species of *manifesto*, rather than a political pamphlet.'[19] The *Anti-Jacobin*, however, was incandescent that such a manifestly seditious work should have been afforded a platform by the *Analytical*. The *Anti-Jacobin's* reviewer explained that he had tried to obtain a copy of O'Connor's work, having been alerted that it was inflammatory, seditious and treasonable. 'But, having no connection with traitors, incendiaries, or members of the London Corresponding Society, all our endeavours proved fruitless.' The *Analytical* revealed that others had been more successful. 'Mr. JOHNSON, however, it seems, has been more fortunate, and actuated, no doubt, by a patriotic desire to render service to the community, has determined that the effects of this precious production shall not be totally lost, and has, *therefore*, given an analysis of the same in his admirable Review.'

On November 15th Johnson returned to the Court of King's Bench for a mitigation hearing in advance of sentencing. Once again his case was heard alongside Jordan's, who was brought from prison for the hearing. Erskine opened by reading a series of affidavits, including a joint statement from Fordyce and Aikin in which they drew attention to the dangers a custodial sentence represented for their asthmatic friend. 'From a knowledge of the Defendant's State of health they verily believe that the confinement of a prison would in all probability endanger his life.' Johnson himself provided an affidavit, which represents the only document in the extensive

Treasury Solicitor holdings on his case in which his voice can be heard. In his statement, written in the third person, he described himself as a bookseller of thirty-eight years' standing, who had demeaned himself 'as a quiet peaceable and good subject' all his life. His connections had not been with seditious men, but rather with 'respectable and scientific Writers and his publications generally of a Moral, Philosophical, and Medical Nature.' He insisted he had always avoided publishing any work that threatened sedition and that his aim was to issue publications 'as had a tendency to promote good morals instead of such as were calculated to mislead and inflame the Common people.' Wakefield had published multiple pamphlets, none of which had attracted the attention of the law, and Cuthell, from whom he bought the pamphlet, had a reputation for selling only works of unimpeachable morality. Wakefield's pamphlet had been generally in circulation and available in many bookshops, so he 'did not think it necessary to caution his servants as was his practice in other instances'. He underscored the evidence of his shopman Mr Dale, testifying that as soon as he learnt of the Bill of Indictment issued against Cuthell he had ordered his shelves to be cleared of the work. He reminded the court that he had sold far more copies of the Bishop of Llandaff's original address than he had of Wakefield's reply. 'This Deponent further saith that he is well affected to the Constitution of this Country which he would be very sorry to do any act to injure or bring into contempt.' Lastly, he concluded, in a moment when the rhythms of his speech shine through the formal language of his deposition, 'he had no evil or improper intention whatsoever in not forbidding his servants to sell the said pamphlets sooner than he did and ... he is exceedingly sorry it was sold at all.'

During Johnson's trial in July Erskine had founded part of his defence on the purity of Johnson's intentions and character. 'No man', he had told the court, 'can be guilty unless his mind is guilty.' Johnson's affidavit emphasised his good character and his credentials as a loyal citizen. In response the Attorney General offered the court a different insight into Johnson's mind. In a manoeuvre which demonstrated the extent of the coordination between the officers of the law and the officers of the *Anti-Jacobin*, he presented the September issue of the *Analytical Review* as evidence of Johnson's seditious tendencies. He transformed the journal into an extension of Johnson himself, attributing the views of the works under discussion to the bookseller who had orchestrated their review. By reviewing Wakefield's letter Johnson had allowed a libellous author to continue his assault on the individuals who represented the State; by quoting from the work of O'Connor, Johnson had knowingly broadcast treasonable arguments. Thus arguments made before the Bench and arguments made in the court of public opinion during the course of Johnson's trial melded in a judicial and extra-judicial character assassination.

The Attorney General's decision to introduce new material from the *Analytical* as further evidence against Johnson was sanctioned by Lord Kenyon. It was a development that blindsided Erskine. For once 'Counsellor EGO' stumbled in his defence. 'It comes very much on a sudden upon me I had no conception of it and I certainly very much lament it': Erskine's opening was hardly a rousing defence of the right to free speech. He blustered and played for time, protesting that the *Analytical* aggregated rather than sanctioned the political opinions of others. But his confusion was apparent. Johnson 'has been with regard to this last work in the same condition unfortunately and criminally to a certain extent ... that publishing this Analytical Review he has trusted it to others'. Surely, he protested, Johnson had too much common sense and too much purity of heart to knowingly allow such words to be broadcast, especially when the outcome of his own trial hung in the balance. Erskine found his client 'guilty certainly of culpable negligence' but nothing more 'in permitting this foul performance to make its appearance and to be read against him in the manner it has today.' It was not a ringing endorsement. He concluded by reminding the court that Dr Fordyce and Dr Aikin, friends of Johnson both, had testified to the fact that Johnson's asthma meant that he would be in mortal danger within the confines of a prison. He also reminded Lord Kenyon that Jordan had already served four months and was so impoverished that any fine would subject him to perpetual imprisonment.

In his summing up, the Attorney General asked the judge a question to which, in the eyes of the State, there was only one answer. Would the man who dared to defend Johnson 'tell me whether it is his idea of a moral man endeavouring to demean himself as a peaceable quiet publisher first letting him read this book and secondly letting him read the other books which have been read to your Lordship today to issue such books as these into the world without either giving any instructions to the people he employs or himself taking care to ascertain whether he is to do good or to mischief by it'? The mind of the bookseller could be divined by the books he sold, and by the books he sold Johnson was guilty of crimes of thought and action. 'The Country', the Attorney General concluded, 'cannot be safe unless Booksellers are authoritatively taught that they are answerable for what they publish.'[20] The country, in the person of the judge, agreed. Sentencing was reserved for a later date. The extent of the punishment remained to be determined, but the time had nevertheless come to silence the bookseller. At the close of the hearing on November 15th 1798, Johnson was committed to the King's Bench Prison and escorted out of the Guildhall by a prison marshal.

PART SEVEN

HOUSE (1799–1809)

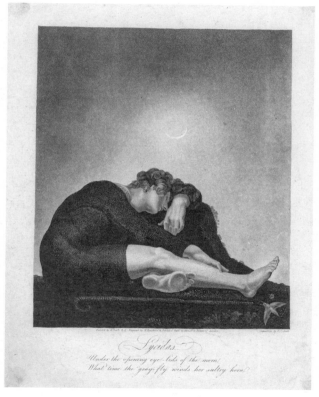

Henry Fuseli, *Lycidas*, engraving after a lost painting for the
Milton Gallery, 1803

For a time the scene shifts, away from the dining room to a prison on the other side of the river. Here the evenings are quieter, although not entirely solitary. When Johnson steps once more into the candlelight of his own quarters, taking up his place at the table again, a new generation attempts to crowd in alongside old friends. Humphry Davy rushes to join the company straight from his laboratory at the Royal Institution. William Hazlitt, son of the Unitarian minister, sends friends to supplicate Johnson on his behalf. In the last months of 1809 Rowland Hunter, now married, brings his new stepson-in-law to dinner, a young journalist who records the conversations of the dining room and subsequently forms his own life around the ideals personified within its walls. There is now also another house, and another dining room, where peace rather than conversation reigns. The ideas forged under the shadow of Fuseli's Nightmare, however, do not fade when the candles at St Paul's Churchyard are snuffed out. They re-form instead in new conversations, held across different tables in different houses, shaping and reshaping the country in which Johnson's dining room stands dark.

27

Idyllium. The Prison

The marshal's carriage took Johnson through the City and across the river to Borough Road in Southwark, the site of the King's Bench Prison.[1] Erskine travelled with them; so did two unnamed friends. Johnson described one of these as his 'oldest friend' and the other as his 'younger friend', descriptions which are best fitted by Fuseli and Rowland Hunter. When they arrived at the prison Johnson's entourage demanded the best accommodation money could buy. The marshal, who had been present in court and knew of Johnson's crime and professional status, showed them to a small house adjoining his own, just outside the main prison precinct. It was occupied by the marshal's coachman and his family but a parlour and bedchamber were free. The marshal offered these to Johnson, along with the domestic services of the coachman's family and use of his own garden.

Johnson's friends were delighted by the thought of him lodged in such comfort. The rooms were comfortable and the younger member of the party, who prided himself on his knowledge of physiognomy, announced that a brief glance at her face proved the coachman's wife to be an excellent woman. Johnson himself asked the price. He did not record the sum but it was evidently extortionate. His supporters negotiated £50 off the total and agreed to pay the remainder immediately, overriding Johnson's objections. The marshal offered to wait until the next day for payment but Johnson had come to court that morning with a large sum of money in his pocket, hoping that he would be fined and discharged. He could see that the marshal himself was the major beneficiary of the arrangement and that it would allay the anxieties of those who cared for him. Johnson was sixty when he went to prison and one of his party had already reminded the marshal of his fragile health. 'All this thought I', Johnson wrote later, 'may be very well for you Mr. Marshal & it may be very agreeable to you my

friends to see me well lodged, but in this case I feel myself a bit of a miser.'
For once, however, he allowed the words of others and his own comfort to
prevail. It was dinner time, and his supporters needed to go to their own
homes. The marshal asked them to keep their counsel about the special
arrangements put in place for Johnson and arranged for the prisoner to be
shown to the parlour he had paid for. The coachman's wife left her own
meal to discuss the menu with her new lodger. 'What would you please to
have for dinner Sir?' Johnson recorded the ensuing conversation for the
benefit of one of his correspondents:

> It grows late, a chop, or anything, what gives the least trouble. We
> are dressing a duck that has been a present of the country, if you
> think you could dine of it. To be sure, nothing can be better. Then
> I am very glad I did not happen to dress it sooner. But I fear I shall
> rob you. O no, we have plenty besides. Dinner being nearly over she
> brought a decanter with some port in it. I am sorry to bring you only
> part of a bottle but it is what was left when I lay in. I wish you may
> be able to drink it, they say it is good, but we never drink wine at
> any other time, & we have no spirit, for my husband drinks nothing
> but small beer or porter. You are right, thought I, Mr. Marshall & my
> young physiognomist, I will listen to you another time.

As the November evening drew in the coachman's wife left Johnson to his
duck and the port left over from her last labour. After a day of court drama,
noise and negotiations, he was at last alone. Through the walls he could
hear the sounds of the coachman's children chattering to their parents. 'It
is,' he wrote, 'a house of order & peace.'[2]

✦

The prison complex to which Johnson was taken dated from 1758. In 1754
the old King's Bench Prison had been declared uninhabitable and the new
site, in St George's Fields, was chosen for the space it offered. The prison
primarily housed debtors. Crown prisoners, of whom Johnson was one, were
heavily outnumbered. The anonymous author of a 1793 publication called
the *Debtor and Creditor's Assistant* warned new inmates that on arrival in
prison they would be put under considerable pressure to pay for the best
rooms the marshal thought they could afford. Those who arrived as the
light faded were most at risk of succumbing. 'When a prisoner comes in at

night, or late in the evening, he has but little time for consideration, and often, through a want of choice, is hurried into an agreement of the most exorbitant kind.'[3] The author reviewed the facilities across the capital's prison estate and proclaimed the glad tidings that those held at the King's Bench were the luckiest inmates in town.

> The King's Bench Prison is by far the most airy and commodious. It consists of one regular building, 100 yards in length, with wings at each end of it, and a spacious parade, the whole being enclosed by a stout thick wall, 25 feet high. It is divided into sixteen different staircases, containing from eight to thirty rooms, the general dimensions of which are 11 feet by 15. Those in the third, or upper stories, are naturally preferred, on account of their commanding a prospect over the walls, and a pleasing view of the Surry and Kentish hills.[4]

Johnson's lodgings in the coachman's house were not sufficiently elevated to have hill views but in letters to friends he nevertheless referred to his accommodation as his 'country house'.[5]

The staff of the prison was tiny. It consisted of the marshal and his deputy, who were responsible for admitting prisoners and allocating rooms, and a very small number of turnkeys who locked the gates each night. The prisoners themselves were primarily responsible for questions of communal governance, which they organised through a 'prisoners' College'. The prison itself received no State support. The marshal and his staff collected their salaries from the fees paid by prisoners and it was thus in their interest to encourage respectable inmates like Johnson to pay as much as possible for more salubrious accommodation. The remit of the marshal exetended beyond the walls of the building to an area of Southwark known as the 'Rules', a collection of streets in which some debtors were allowed to live and work provided they could afford the fees payable for the privilege.

In 1801 a debtor called George Hanger wrote an account of life in the King's Bench Prison. He was a prisoner in 1798, the same year in which Johnson arrived. Hanger was at pains to point out that in spite of its claims to airiness and liberalism the suggestion that the prison was 'a place of mirth, festivity, and joy' was ill-founded. Instead, he reported, it rivalled the brothels of the capital 'in vice, drunkenness, and debauchery; and, setting aside the indulgence of unnatural propensities, may be said to out-Herod Sodom and Gomorrah.' Young men were, he thought, chiefly at risk.

'Unless a man be of a certain age, of a bold and firm mind, and of undaunted resolution to bear with fortitude and manly dignity the oppression and heart-breaking agonies he suffers from his persecutors, he soon sinks into drunkenness and dissipation; and, what is worse, loses every sense of honour and dignity of sentiment ... from the immoral contagion that is to be found in them.'[6]

Hanger's imagery points to sodomy as a fact of prison life; the only recourse for virtuous men was to live apart from the multitude. Repeatedly he compared the vice rampant in the prison to disease:

> This contagion is so great, that, like the plague or the yellow fever, if he does not separate himself from the multitude, and live alone, which, under his circumstances, he must be more than man to do, or contrive to associate with those alone, for such there are, who bring honour and gentlemanly manners with them into their confinement, which is no very easy matter, he soon will be contaminated, and be lost to himself, to his friends, and to the world for ever.[7]

Many of the prisoners were hungry, he continued; many more were ill. As he looked back on his period at the prison he recalled that 'the very air of the place is enough to infect a weak and afflicted mind.'[8]

Johnson followed Hanger's example and kept well apart from his fellow inmates. For much for the time he remained immured in the coachman's house, only venturing outside to take a turn around the marshal's small garden. Several months into his incarceration he complained that he had developed gout in his feet through lack of exercise but still he did not risk exposing himself to the dangers of the main parade ground. It is unlikely, however, that the conditions inside the prison caused him much surprise. Prison reform was among the many subjects with which he had concerned himself before his incarceration. In 1784 he published and sold an updated edition of the penal reformer John Howard's *The State of the Prisons in England and Wales*. Howard did more than any other individual to expose the squalid and dangerous conditions in which the nation's prisoners were held and today his work and name lives on in the activities of the Howard League for Penal Reform. Howard was a great friend of John Aikin who helped edit the first edition of *The State of the Prisons*. In 1792, two years after Howard's death, he published a memoir entitled *A View of the Character and Public Services of the Late John Howard* with Johnson. Johnson also published a new edition of *The State of the Prisons* to accompany Aikin's work. In 1796 Darwin celebrated Howard's endeavours in a poem for the *Monthly Magazine* called 'Idyllium. The Prison'. It depicted the loneliness of the debtor, separated by unjust laws from those he loved:

> O, WELCOME, Debtor! in these walls
> > Thy cares, and joys, and loves forgo;
> Approach; a brother Debtor calls,
> > And join the family of woe!

Darwin depicts the debtor's wife surrounded by weeping children, frantically imploring friends and creditors for help. All turn away from her; she beats 'in vain the closing door'. In the final stanza, however, both the debtor and his wife are presented with a vision of hope:

> Look up, and share our scanty mean;
> > For us some brighter hours may flow;
> Some angel break these bolts of steel,
> > For HOWARD marks, and feels our woe.[9]

Howard's work shed light on an area of social policy where, then as now, campaigners struggled to capture public attention. Darwin's emphasis on the plight of the debtor was not accidental. Upstanding citizens of late-eighteenth-century Britain might feel themselves to be far removed from the Crown prisoners imprisoned for crimes, but in a society without any kind of social safety net only the very richest and most prudent lived free of the threat of a debtor's prison.

Johnson worked throughout his imprisonment and Rowland Hunter kept the shop at St Paul's Churchyard open. Nevertheless Johnson's absence brought changes to the life of his family and his business. Dinner no longer took place in the shadow of Fuseli's *Nightmare*, but in the parlour at the coachman's house. 'Tea Johnson's, K B P, w. Fuseli, Newnum & JJ' read Godwin's diary for November 29th. Three weeks later he was back, dining at the coachman's house alongside Bonnycastle, Johnson's nephew by marriage Henry Newnum and two other visitors. A day later Hannah Lindsey told a mutual friend that Johnson 'is in the Kings bench, a prisoner but not unhappy.'[10] The Lindseys were among Johnson's first visitors. By November 22nd, a week after the court hearing, Lindsey was able to send news of their friend to anxious Unitarians outside London. 'Johnson's fate', he predicted, 'will add to the apprehensions of the trade. For no man could be more free from design to offend the laws or hurt the constitution.' He did however share Johnson's relief at the comfort of his lodgings. 'I have been to visit him you will believe since his confinement, and was rejoiced to find it so airy and convenient, like a country-lodging near Town.' Relief mingled with anxiety, however, since Johnson had not yet been sentenced. 'We are in anxious suspense about him till we know his sentence: the duration of his confinement and the place', Lindsey reported. 'For the lawyers say, he may still be sent to Newgate.'[11] By December gossip about Johnson's arrangement with the marshal had reached the ever-curious Joseph Farington. 'Johnson, the Bookseller, has apartments in Marshalls House in the Kings Bench, but pays very dear for them'. Farington also recorded the view prevalent among Johnson's circle, that he had been punished as much for the *Analytical Review* as for publishing Wakefield.

> Johnson probably would have got off for a fine only, had not an impudent person who reviews for him, on reviewing the trial of Johnson, on mentioning the trial, commented upon it in such a manner, that the Attorney General thought it His Duty to produce it when Johnson was brought up for judgement, observing that though Johnson might plead ignorance of the contents of Wakefield's pamphlet He could not deny a knowledge of his own publication.

The result of such judicial severity was, Farington thought, inevitable. 'It is probable that Johnson will drop the Analytical Review.'[12]

Farington was correct. In December 1798 Johnson issued instructions from the coachman's house for the closure of the *Analytical Review*. The final issue carried a review of *Lyrical Ballads*, and of two recent works that bore Johnson's imprint: *Fears in Solitude* and *Practical Education*. Elsewhere it represented the diversity of Johnson's own interests. It carried reviews under the headings 'Farriery, Anatomy, Medicine, Chemistry, Poetry, Topography, Translations, Voyages, Biography, Education, Engineering, Novels, Political Economy, School Books and Politics' (although for once this section was concerned not with current affairs but with a new translation of Aristotle's *Ethics* and *Politics*). For the last time, under the heading 'Literary Intelligence', the journal aggregated news from learned societies across Europe. The only reference to the closure came with an advertisement bound with the final issue, dated January 1st 1799. 'Speedily will be published a copious index to the twenty eight volumes of this work; to which will be prefixed A PREFACE, and some REVIEWS already prepared, but hitherto not inserted for want of room.'

The conditions under which Johnson was being held left him no choice but to close the journal. The severity of his sentence, both in terms of its length and location, remained to be determined. At the November hearing the prosecution had demonstrated their willingness to use the contents of work reviewed by the *Analytical* against its publisher. The December issue was put together with a great deal of caution, but to produce a fearlessly independent journal was no longer possible. Johnson might declare himself to be comfortably circumstanced and his friends might continue their pattern of regular visiting and conversation in spite of his incarceration but the closure of the *Analytical* still represented a victory for the forces of the State. The writer of the Prefatory Address in the first bound volume of the *Anti-Jacobin* was unable to contain his delight about the way the voices of liberalism had been silenced. 'The ... object of our immediate attacks, the *Analytical Review*, has received its death-blow, and we have more reason to congratulate ourselves upon the share which we have had in producing its dissolution, than it would be expedient here to unfold.'[13]

In a January letter to the political reformer Christopher Wyvill, who had hoped to publish his new work at St Paul's Churchyard, Johnson conceded that the State had succeeded in silencing him. 'It is impossible to guess when my sentence will be pass'd ... And as it would be highly imprudent in me to publish anything offensive before, and you wish to bring out your Pamphlet in Feby there seems to be a necessity for your choosing another bookseller if another can be found.' He was regretful but not apologetic. His answer, he explained, reflected a collective failure to value and protect a free press, rather than any individual lack of courage. 'The liberty of the press was given up by its pretended friends a few years ago when a fair opportunity offered of making a manly & effectual stand.' All that could be done now, with Pitt in his pomp and the nation subdued by fears of invasion, was to wait for the tide to turn. 'Nothing I fear can be done by pamphlets which will not be read, & nothing should be expected from booksellers who have been left without support.'[14]

Three months later Wyvill was still without a publisher, 'no reputable booksellers', Lindsey wrote, 'venturing to undertake the publication. Johnson's fate deters them all.'[15] Habeas Corpus had been suspended the previous April; in January the suspension had been extended until May. Meanwhile Priestley worried that America was showing every sign of adopting the authoritarian practices of Britain. 'I am much concerned for the fate of Mr Johnson', he wrote to Lindsey in February. 'He certainly did not deserve this harsh treatment, but we are following you here in the same steps as fast as we can.'[16] It was a complaint he repeated in June, when he told Lindsey that he was being watched more closely than even Pitt's spies had managed in Britain. It was most unjust, he protested, since he played so little part in American politics. 'But a bad name once acquired is not easily got rid of, and it is taken for granted that I must be a very fractious troublesome person, or I should never have been driven out of England.'[17]

On February 11th Johnson and Jordan were both returned to court to receive their sentence. Johnson swore an additional affidavit testifying that he was ignorant of the contents of Wakefield's pamphlet when he sold it; Erskine reminded the judge of Johnson's moral worth and physical fragility. The Attorney General repeated his assertion that the country would fall into a state of advanced moral depravity were booksellers not held responsible for the material they sold and pronounced himself undaunted by Johnson's status within the trade. A reporter for *The Times* recorded the closing stages of the Attorney General's argument: 'the little pamphlet-seller, in whatever part he lived, who was prosecuted by him, should never have to reproach him that in the discharge of his duty he had forgot the most eminent Booksellers in the country.' The presiding judge, Mr Justice Ashhurst, restated the severity of Johnson's crimes and his own responsibilities. 'It was his duty to see that nothing was contained in it by which the loyalty, the morality, or decency of his Majesty's subjects could be corrupted or put in danger'. That was much more important, he insisted, 'to the well-being of society, than the private gain of any individual.'[18]

Johnson was sentenced to six further months in prison and a fine of £50, a sum roughly equivalent to several thousand pounds today. Prison committal records noted that he was also required to pay £500 as a guarantee of his good behaviour for the next three years. It was a condition that highlighted the extent to which his activities would be watched and curtailed. In one respect the judge heeded Erskine's warnings about the defendant's health. Johnson was not sent to Newgate, as Lindsey feared: instead he was returned to the King's Bench Prison, and to his lodgings in the coachman's house. Jeremiah Jordan, who could not afford to pay a fine and who had already been in prison since the previous July, was sentenced to twelve more months and was required to commit £300 as a surety for his good behaviour. Wakefield's original publisher, Thomas Cuthell, was sentenced to six nights only in prison, in the clearest sign yet that John Hancock's shopping expedition in February 1798 had been politically motivated. Gilbert Wakefield, who insisted on defending himself, received the harshest treatment of the four men. He was sentenced to two years in Dorchester Gaol and a fine of £500. Charles Fox visited him in prison and political reformers from across the country rallied to raise enough money to support his family during his imprisonment. William Shepherd, an acquaintance who visited Johnson in prison, took on the task of caring for and educating one of Wakefield's sons and refused to accept any money for the child's keep. The conditions in which Wakefield was kept, however, meant that there were limits to the support that friends could offer. Four months after his release in May 1801 he died of typhus fever contracted in gaol.

As news spread of the punishments visited on the men charged in connection with Wakefield's pamphlet, Dissenters up and down the country discussed the sentences with anxious avidity. 'But you see it was not Wakefield, that the prosecutor had in view', wrote Samuel Kenrick to his friend James Woodrow in March. The target was instead 'the patriotic bookseller Johnson ... who was singly pitched upon to expiate the crime, while every bookseller in London sold it with impunity.' Johnson's treatment, Kenrick thought, threatened more ill to the country at large than it did to Johnson himself. 'In what a pitiful light must such ministers be contemplated by the impartial world, who can vent the meanest & most rancorous human passions on such feeble & harmless objects.'[19] Johnson might not have thanked Kenrick for labelling him 'feeble' but the King's Bench marshal evidently shared the view that his Crown prisoner was harmless. In April a grander prisoner than Johnson arrived when Lord Thanet was remanded in custody for the part he had played in a demonstration in support of the Irish nationalist Arthur O'Connor. Johnson was required to give up his parlour and bedchamber in the coachman's house for Thanet and was permitted, according to Joseph Farington, to take up temporary residence within the Rules, 'at a friends opposite to the prison.'[20]

When Johnson wrote to Richard Lovell Edgeworth in February 1799 he sought to reassure his friend that he had little opportunity to be lonely. 'I have plenty of work & more visitors than are necessary.'[21] The Edgeworths themselves were among his visitors, as Frances Edgeworth later described in her biography of her stepdaughter. 'All his literary friends made it a point to visit him in his adversity', wrote Frances of Johnson. 'Mr Edgeworth and Maria went to see him in the King's Bench; she had a great regard for Johnson, though his dilatoriness tried her patience in the business of printing and publishing her works; she thought him a generous, able, kind-hearted man, and an excellent critic.'[22] Godwin's diary reveals that he frequently made the journey over to Southwark for dinner, often in the company of Fuseli and Henry Newnum. Fuseli's presence in Johnson's quarters worried some of his friends, who reminded him of his own vulnerability under the terms of the Alien Act. John Knowles recalled that Fuseli shrugged off all warnings. 'His friendship for Johnson was greater than any prudential motives of this nature; and he therefore visited him as frequently as he had previously done in his own house.'[23] Mary Hays called in the company of a younger friend, the diarist Henry Crabb Robinson. Robinson was impressed and a little overawed by Johnson's air of sage resignation. 'He was a wise man', he recalled, 'and I profited from his advice. He spoke well against the practice of indulging in melancholy forebodings. These are at first the effect of dreamy indolence which indisposes to work and produce the evil they deplore – This was called out by what I was then in the habit of doing – And tho' it did not cure me of the fault, it mitigated some of its consequential evils.'[24]

Throughout his time in the King's Bench Prison Johnson kept working, adopting in his own conduct the advice he dispensed to Robinson. A week after receiving his sentence he wrote a second detailed letter to Richard Lovell Edgeworth, focused not on his own situation but on the publicity for *Practical Education*. He explained that he had sent off many prospectuses for the work, including to 'persons who had the care of children but could not well afford to buy it.' Friends and customers with an eye to their own interests made little allowance for the fact that he was compelled to conduct his business from prison. Richard Lovell Edgeworth accused him of being 'lazy', which moved Johnson to defend his own industriousness. The prospect of interesting new work continued to propel him forward. 'Maria', he told Edgeworth's father, 'need not be afraid of overstocking me.'[25] In April he was demanding errata confirmations from Darwin for a new edition of the *Botanic Garden* and, in a sign of the value he accorded his most trusted authors, offering an additional payment to recompense Darwin for the work entailed in revising and improving *Zoonomia* for a new edition. In July he was mulling the most practical way of dividing *Zoonomia* into volumes and, in a letter full of the business of making books he refused the concern of others. 'I am no way anxious about my liberty.'[26]

Johnson might make light of his situation in letters to friends but one aspect of his incarceration worried him considerably. During the months he spent in prison he was required to meet the costs involved in running both the house at St Paul's Churchyard and his prison lodgings. The surviving sources suggest that by 1799 his household comprised a house-keeper named Nancy Lovell and two further servants whose names are not recorded, as well as John Miles, Rowland Hunter and Johnson himself. The business had to sustain the livelihoods of them all, as well as of William Dale and the other unnamed employees who worked in the shop. Johnson was also required to fund a large fine and to raise money to pay the bond required against his future behaviour. Between February and July 1799 he dispatched a series of letters focused on chasing down old debts. Requests for payment made their way from Southwark to booksellers in New York and Philadelphia and to the executors of men who had died with debts outstanding in France and across England. He told Thomas Dobson, a bookseller in Pennsylvania, that the expenses of his conviction ran to £600 and that he could not afford to be as patient as usual in waiting for payment. 'You will not accuse me of being in a hurry with my account or in asking for money', he reminded Dobson. 'I do not address you from St. Paul's Church Yard, my usual place of residence, but from a place of confinement; for having in the course of business had a pamphlet sold in my shop which gave offence to some of our Rulers a prosecution was commenced against me.' Johnson's double-edged account of his trial demonstrates his awareness that his correspondence was being watched. 'The judge pronounced the pamphlet a libel, and the jury very wisely supposing that a libel could not be sold without a bad intention, found me guilty.'[27]

One letter in pursuit of an old debt went as far as Kingston, Jamaica and related to a missing payment dating from 1791. 'During my confine-ment for having sold a political pamphlet that gave offence to Mr. Pitt & his colleagues', Johnson told his correspondent, 'I have in part employ'd myself in looking over letters & papers & destroying what were useless.'[28] His explanation suggests that, for Johnson as well as for his prosecutors, his imprisonment represented a period of reckoning. In the quiet evenings after his visitors had been escorted off the premises he had time to contem-plate his career and go through his papers. Old letters revealed debts unpaid but they also presented Johnson with a version of his professional life. It was a record that he chose, in part at least, to destroy. In prison he turned his attention from his own past to the future of those in his care. 'Life is uncertain', he told the engraver Thomas Holloway. Awareness of his own mortality meant that he would wait for payment no longer. 'We are endangering our family portion, merely because it is not heartily set about, when the longer it be delayed the more difficult it will become.'[29] As his prison sentence drew to a close Johnson turned his attention away from the expense he had incurred towards the legacy he would leave. Rowland Hunter was twenty-six in 1799; John Miles was fifteen. Along with Rowland's sisters they were Johnson's family and the natural heirs to the business he had built. As he readied himself to rejoin the world from which he had been separated it was the interests of the kin who would follow him that he chiefly had in mind.

On August 6th Godwin made his way across the river to Southwark to dine with Johnson in his prison lodgings for a final time. Fuseli was there; so was Johnson's errant engraver Thomas Holloway and so was Rowland Hunter. Three days later the bookseller James Edwards, an old friend of Roscoe, Johnson and Fuseli, told Roscoe that Johnson's release was imminent. 'Johnson comes out tomorrow and I think without any injury to his health from confinement rather the contrary.' Nevertheless, it was evident to all those who cared for Johnson that his experience at the hands of the State had aged him. Fuseli was preparing to take him to Liverpool to recover from his imprisonment and Edwards knew that Roscoe would shortly see both men. He pleaded with Roscoe to use his influence with Johnson for the good. 'If you cd persuade him to relinquish the cares of business it wd add years & health to his life – for he ought not to reckon upon the vigour & exertion he cd in former days.'[30]

28

Essays on Professional Education

Johnson was released from prison on August 10th 1799. He crossed the river and went home. On September 3rd Godwin recorded the first post-prison dinner at St Paul's Churchyard. On September 7th Fuseli wrote to Roscoe to say that he hoped they would be on the road to Liverpool within a week. John Knowles remembered that Fuseli insisted on the excursion, since 'relaxation ... was considered necessary for Johnson's health'.[1] By the time they journeyed home, in early October, Fuseli was still concerned about Johnson. Back in London, on October 14th, he sent a bulletin to Roscoe. 'Johnson dined with me yesterday, he bore the Journey better than I thought he would, is certainly not worse.'[2] A day later Godwin returned to St Paul's Churchyard for tea, where he met Fuseli, Bonnycastle and Johnson's niece Hester among the usual crowd of visitors. Life in the shop and dining room appeared to resume its normal pattern as Johnson shook off the concerns of his friends and went back to work.

✦

In 1809 Richard Lovell Edgeworth wrote a poem in praise of Johnson:

> Wretches there are, their lucky stars who bless
> Whene'er they find a Genius in distress:
> Who starve the Bard, and stunt his growing fame,
> Lest they should pay the value for his name.
> But JOHNSON raised the drooping Bard from earth,
> And fostered rising Genius from its birth:
> His liberal spirit a profession made
> Of what, with vulgar souls, is vulgar trade.[3]

Richard Lovell Edgeworth's compliment echoed that accorded to Johnson almost two decades earlier by Cowper: 'though a bookseller, he has in him the soul of a gentleman.'[4] The divisions between gentleman, professional and tradesman mattered at the turn of the nineteenth century, and the question of where to place Johnson in a hierarchy of gentility was one with which some of his authors – and some of his friends – tangled. Richard Lovell Edgeworth was particularly interested in the question of what constituted a 'profession' and in 1809, the same year in which he wrote his verse to Johnson, he brought out a volume entitled *Essays on Professional Education* under Johnson's imprint. The professions that attracted Richard Lovell's notice were strictly defined. A man might take up a clerical, military, naval or medical profession; equally he might be trained for the profession of country gentleman, lawyer, statesman or prince. Tradesmen and merchants did not figure; neither did authors. Yet Richard Lovell nevertheless drew attention to the increasing professionalism of his own craft, and to the collaborative industry that surrounded it. He aimed for a new level of scientific objectivity in his writing and he was on guard against his own complacency. 'This circumstance is mentioned', he explained, 'to give an unequivocal proof of that industry which never should relax, from an author's becoming more familiar with that press; and of that deference for the publick, which its former favours should exalt into respectful gratitude.'[5]

Richard Lovell's verses in praise of Johnson implied that Johnson transformed bookselling from a trade into a profession through the purity of his character and the generosity of his principles. The same implication underscored Cowper's earlier compliment. Both men suggested Johnson confounded expectations of the tradesman's natural avarice through his own 'gentlemanly' behaviour. Johnson himself gave a different account of his own position in the world. Throughout the 1800s, his fourth decade in business, he referred to himself as a 'tradesman'[6] and he wore the label with pride. But the work he did after his release from prison revealed the extent to which conversations he had created in print and in person at St Paul's Churchyard were changing. Tensions with long-standing collaborators about the best way to make and sell books ran through his correspondence and some of the individuals whose stars had burned brightest during the final decades of the eighteenth century faded from view during the first years of the new decade. Their places were taken by a younger generation of writers who fought for a place at Johnson's table alongside the two young men he was educating in the ways of his house and his trade.

✝

After Cowper's death in 1800 Lady Hesketh was charged, as his literary executor, with choosing from among the crowd of aspirant biographers who clamoured to write his authorised *Life*. From the outset she was determined that the commission should go to Cowper's friend William Hayley, although she exerted strict control over his use of the manuscripts in possession of the estate. When Anna Barbauld heard that Hayley had won the commission she remarked tartly that the results would at least be 'interesting'. 'I should wonder tho how he could draw it out to two Quarto volumes, only that I know Hayley has a good hand at spinning.'[7] For his part Hayley wanted his book to be published by Johnson, who held the copyright of *The Task* and who responded to the news of Cowper's death by preparing memorial editions of his poems and translations of Homer. Johnson travelled to Felpham to negotiate with Hayley and lost a battle over where the work should be printed. Hayley wanted to print it in Chichester at the workshop of his favoured printer, Joseph Seagrave; Johnson was sceptical about Seagrave's workmanship and only agreed to Hayley's demands with the proviso that Seagrave would use paper sent directly from London. It mattered to him that Hayley's biography and his own posthumous editions should be presented to the public as a set, printed on the same paper with the same type, and he insisted on his right to draw on long experience as he questioned Seagrave's experience. 'I write not upon trifling ground', he told Hayley. 'It does not arise from whim or caprice ... but from 40 years exp. of Country printers who are generally employed on smaller matters & seldom upon books.'

Hayley took advice from the bookseller Richard Phillips, who sided with Johnson; and from William Blake, who shared Hayley's belief that both Johnson and Phillips were being unnecessarily patronising about the craftsmanship of a provincial printer. Blake, however, was not a neutral witness in the dispute. Throughout the middle years of the 1790s he kept working on a balance of commercial projects and his own images. His most important commission was for the bookseller Richard Edwards, who employed him to produce designs for a new edition of Edward Young's *Night Thoughts*. Edwards went out of business before the project was completed and in August 1799 Blake complained to a friend that the work that allowed him to feed himself had disappeared. In a letter dated less than two weeks after Johnson's release from prison he blamed his former supporters for his plight. 'Even Johnson

& Fuseli have discarded my Graver.' In the face of such disloyalty he was defiant. 'I laugh at Fortune & Go on & on.'[8]

At the beginning of 1800 Hayley came to Blake's rescue, appearing in his life just as he had blazed his way into Cowper's existence the previous decade. In July Hayley proposed to Blake that he should move his household to a cottage at Felpham, where Hayley himself would employ Blake to undertake a range of projects, the *Life* of Cowper chief among them. Initially Blake was delighted at the prospect of remaking his life outside London. Even an arduous journey, during which he had to transport his great printer's press across the country on a wagon, failed to dent his enthusiasm. In September 1801 he reported from Felpham that the plates for Hayley's *Life* of Cowper took up most of his time but that he was optimistic that the combination of his images, Hayley's narrative and Cowper's letters would produce 'a most valuable acquisition to Literature.'[9] Johnson was pleased about the arrangement. 'Ever since I have had a connection with Mr Blake I have wished to serve him & on every occasion endeavoured to do so', he told Hayley. 'I wish him to be paid for what he is now doing a fair & even liberal price.'[10]

Johnson's letter makes it clear that it was Hayley's decision to commission Blake, and that under the terms of the deal struck between Johnson and Hayley the author's determination to control every aspect of the project, in conjunction with Lady Hesketh, resulted in the publisher effectively subcontracting several production decisions he had in previous projects reserved to himself. But when Blake began to feel the suffocating effects of Hayley's patronage he distributed blame equally. 'My unhappiness has arisen from a source which if explored too narrowly might hurt my pecuniary circumstances', he told a friend. He wanted more than anything to pursue his own visions but 'my dependence is on Engraving at present & particularly on the Engravings I have in hand for Mr. H.' He found, he continued, 'on all hands great objections to my doing any thing but the mere drudgery of business & imitations ... This from Johnson & Fuseli brought me down here & this from Mr H will bring me back again.'[11] Blake's own sense of his spiritual and artistic vocation had sharpened over the years and he resented those who thought of him as little more than the servant of the visions of others. Johnson's letter to Hayley demonstrates his appreciation of Blake's artistry as an engraver and illustrator but his relationship with Blake was always determined by his own sense of the supreme importance of holding a house together and, in company with many of his contemporaries, he appears to have viewed Blake's hand-produced volumes as interesting oddities. In Johnson's view illuminated books that were seen by no one were of limited value: what mattered was to put text and image before as many readers as possible and to earn a decent living in the process. By September 1803 Blake was back in London, on the hunt once more for enough work to pay the rent. 'Mr Johnson the bookseller tells me that there is no want of work', he told Hayley. 'So far you will be rejoiced with me, and your words, *"Do not fear you can want employment!"* were verified.'[12]

Blake's association with Hayley, and his connection with the *Life* of Cowper, prompted in him a tangle of emotions about the man who had both given him a living and hemmed in his vision through years of mechanical drudgery. His letters to Hayley reveal that he resented Johnson's hold on him, which he thought representative of the corrupt power wielded over men of imagination by a cabal of London booksellers. 'Johnson may be very honest, and generous, too, where his own interest is concerned; but I must say that he leaves no stone unturn'd to serve that interest', he wrote in 1804. He had received letters from Johnson over the years which 'called for the sceptre of Agamemnon rather than the tongue of Ulysses' but he viewed the publisher's failings as symptomatic of the city that had made him. In his description of London in *Songs of Experience* of 1794 Blake wrote of the capital as the birthplace of sin:

> I wander thro' each charter'd street,
> Near where the charter'd Thames does flow.
> And mark in every face I meet
> Marks of weakness, marks of woe.

Johnson was, in Blake's view, the product above all of the 'charter'd streets' that gave him power and marked his soul. 'In London', he told Hayley, 'every calumny and falsehood utter'd against another of the same trade is thought fair play. Engravers, Painters, Statuaries, Printers, Poets, we are not in a field of battle, but in a City of Assassinations.'[13] Ultimately Johnson's commercial pre-eminence drove Blake away. In the support extended to Johnson by Richard Phillips and other booksellers in the City, Blake saw a world in which he had no security closing ranks to protect its own. When Fuseli and Joseph Farington gossiped about the great names of their day, 'Blake the Engraver' did not figure in their conversation. Neither did Blake the poet. 'Fuseli thinks Cowper the best of all Poets of his period; above Hayley &c. & even Darwin', wrote Farington in 1803. 'He had imagery and his stile was more perfect and pure ... Fuseli considers Bonoparte a man buoyed up with pride and presumption and of unrestrained passion; and that He must suffer much in the opinion of the world by his conduct and deportment. He thinks the war will be short.'[14]

✢

On November 9th 1799, during the weeks in which Johnson settled back into the rhythms of life at St Paul's Churchyard, Napoleon seized control as First Consul of France in the Coup of 18 Brumaire. The Directory – the committee that had governed France since 1795 – was replaced with the Consulate. Napoleon made himself leader of France five years before he declared himself Emperor. His ascension marked the end of the French Revolution as he gathered power to himself under the ideological auspices of a republican government code. In 1801 French military victories saw Austria compelled to accept peace on terms highly advantageous to France; a year later France and Britain declared peace in the Treaty of Amiens. Those in Johnson's circle who had railed against the folly of war could hardly believe the change in their fortunes. 'I want to wish you joy on the peace, which came at last so unexpectedly', wrote Barbauld to an acquaintance. 'We have hardly done illuminating and bouncing and popping upon the occasion. The spontaneous joy and mutual congratulations of all ranks show plainly what were the wishes of the people, though they dared not declare them.' France, she prophesied, 'will draw every mother's child of us to it. Those who know French are refreshing their memories – those who do not, are learning it; and every one is planning in some way or other to get a sight of the promised land.'[15]

The Edgeworths were among those who sped to France to witness the newly reopened delights of Paris; Fuseli and Farington made the journey in order to enjoy looted Italian paintings at the Louvre. John Opie, who had painted Priestley at St Paul's Churchyard, travelled to Paris for the same reason. By May 1803, however, Britain and France were at war once more in a battle for supremacy over European affairs. In February 1804 Johnson reported to a New York bookseller that the people of Britain again lived under the threat of invasion. 'The French are daily expected in immense force, the weather will decide perhaps whether they land or not.' Faced with the authoritarianism of Napoleon, who appeared to be quelling every representative impulse articulated during the early years of the French Revolution, Johnson's attitude shifted. Should the French succeed in landing, 'we are not unprepared – having 400,000 men in arms.'[16] By October that year the prospect of peace seemed more distant than ever. 'What have we before us,' Johnson asked, 'but continual War?'[17]

☦

In America at the turn of the century, Priestley missed 'philosophical intelligence' more than news of the squabbles of European nations. In September 1799 he told Lindsey he had never been 'so far behind hand' in the former. 'I feel my absence from you and my friends in England more sensibly than ever.' It was a sentiment he had expressed many times before but now 'I fear we shall no more meet on this side of the grave.'[18] Priestley was sixty-seven in 1800 and had already outlived his younger wife by four years. A sense of age as well as the experience of exile shaped his letters home. In rural Pennsylvania there was 'no lunar society, to which I can communicate my observations, & from which I can receive light in return.' But 'at my time of life ... I could not expect to enjoy any society in this world much longer.'[19]

Priestley's letters after 1800 chart the bitterness of his professional and personal disappointment in Johnson. His requests for books were constant: he needed print from Britain as others needed food and water. After his release from prison Johnson was simply unable to keep pace with Priestley's demands and Priestley experienced his failure as a betrayal. In December 1800 the last of the winter ships from London arrived on the eastern seaboard without any packages on board from Johnson. Priestley was devastated at the thought of enduring the long New England winter without books from home. Johnson, he complained to a mutual friend, was 'incorrigible'. Yet Priestley could not bring himself to place his orders with another man. 'When I was first acquainted with him, he was the most active, punctual & intelligent, as well as the most honest man in the trade. But, as I find my own activity much abated with age, so must his.'[20] Ships from London and Liverpool only arrived in America twice a year, in the spring and autumn, and twice a year the Northumberland merchants made their way to Philadelphia to collect their goods. The journey to Philadelphia was no longer one that Priestley himself undertook lightly, so when Johnson's packages failed to arrive in time for collection by local tradesmen they languished in a Philadelphia warehouse for six months. 'I must have some person', he told Lindsey, 'who will not fail to send my packages by the <u>early ships</u>.'[21] But a year after his first complaint he was still angry with his old friend's neglect and still worried about distressing him. 'I intend finally to send my orders to Mr Phillips; but to employ another bookseller <u>immediately</u> might hurt Mr Johnson's feelings more than I wish to do.'[22]

Johnson's failings extended to producing as well as dispatching books. In January 1802 Priestley complained that after a year he had received no acknowledgement of printed pages sent to St Paul's Churchyard for binding and sale, and no response to his request that Johnson would send the type for the Greek alphabet to his Philadelphia printer in order to enable the local printing of his *Letters* on infant baptism. The business of making books in rural Northumberland was exhausting and Priestley knew too well that the processes by which he distributed his work were imperfect. Johnson's silence was a continual concern. 'I cannot get a letter from him', Priestley worried in January 1802. 'If he be offended, it is altogether without reason.'[23] Yet still he was unable to break with him and find a new publisher. 'I do not care to employ any other bookseller, while he continues in business.' Could local friends intercede? 'If you could, by any hints, get him to do better, without offending him, you will oblige me much.'[24]

As Priestley's complaints about Johnson became intemperate, Lindsey was moved to remonstrate with him for forgetting the larger claims of friendship in his preoccupation with his own needs. Priestley was contrite but his letter of apology suggested continued frustration at the failure of his oldest friends to appreciate his plight. 'I am truly sorry if any thing I have written of or to Mr Johnson has hurt him, or you', he wrote in August 1802. 'I am sensible as can be, from long experience, of his moral worth, and his friendship for myself.' Perhaps, after all, it was not Johnson's fault. 'If my disappointment thro the negligence of his servants has made me express some degree of impatience, I hope he will forgive it I hope he will make allowance for my situation.'[25] In September a box arrived from Johnson along with a short note confirming his willingness to publish the pages Priestley was printing and, for a brief period, he was placated. Johnson responded robustly to Priestley's rebukes, chastising him for sending incomplete editions for publication. He had spent hours hunting through packing crates in the Custom House with his broker in search of the material Priestley claimed to have sent and was in no mood to be accused of laziness. Johnson blamed 'sad blundering' in America for his wasted day.[26] A few months later Priestley accused him of blundering in his turn, when a volume arrived in Philadelphia with important plates missing. 'I do not doubt Mr Johnson is a sincere friend, and wishes me well', he wrote to the bookseller's defenders in London, 'but as a <u>tradesman</u> I have great reason to be disappointed with him.'[27]

Between June and December 1803 the strain of making books across the Atlantic during a time of war brought Johnson and Priestley's long friendship to an end. In June Priestley dispatched a letter to Thomas Belsham in which he accused Johnson of ungenerous and mendacious conduct. His usually clear pen slipped in rage as he wavered between describing his friend of four decades as 'dishonourable' and 'dishonest'.[28] Johnson's own patience was exhausted by Priestley's reproaches. He sent a sharp letter to Northumberland informing his friend that the technical production of his latest work was so poor the volumes were fit only to be used as waste paper. Rows over paper and sloppily collated copies continued throughout the summer, as a proxy for the anger and grief attendant on the end of a friendship that was finally unable to survive the strains of exile, imprisonment and age. Priestley knew that the paper on which he was forced to print was not up to Johnson's standards but in a frosty letter to Lindsey he pointed out that he had little choice in the matter. Johnson had written refusing to publish unclean copies; Priestley responded alleging sabotage at Johnson's shop by someone 'no friend to American printing.'[29] It was an allegation he repeated to Lindsey. 'Mr Johnson complains of a prodigious number of <u>imperfect copies</u>. If so, there must have been <u>wilful work</u>, and destruction, IN London.' In the isolation of his anger he demanded proof that his work was unprintable. 'If the sheets were only <u>damaged</u>, let them be produced; for they were certainly sent.'[30]

In December 1803 Priestley finally made the break from St Paul's Churchyard and transferred his book-buying custom to Richard Phillips, although he left Johnson responsible for the publication of his work. He could not bear to write to Johnson himself and instead asked Belsham to undertake the task for him. 'Johnson's negligence is so great, and my want so urgent, in consequence of my having much to do, and little time, and that very uncertain, to do it in, that I cannot bear it any longer.'[31] Johnson kept writing and in January 1804 a shamefaced Priestley reported to Lindsey that a late box of books had arrived on a ship that had just beaten the winter river frosts. He asked forgiveness for his impatience. The box Johnson had compiled 'contains many very interesting and some very splendid works

... I beg you would tell him how much I think myself obliged to him for them.' Again he reiterated that books were his lifeblood, 'especially as my deafness confines me in a manner at home, and my extreme weakness prevents my making any excursions.'[32]

Johnson's last letter to Priestley was dated February 24th 1804. It contained no mention of the arguments of the previous year and was a brief, friendly bulletin containing news of the imminent publication of Priestley's newest work. 'Your last letter to Mr L.', he concluded, 'afforded great relief to all your friends & to none more than Your affec. J. J.'[33] By the time Johnson wrote Priestley had been dead for just over two weeks. His apologetic missive to Lindsey was his last extant letter. He was buried beside his wife and son in Northumberland. Johnson was convinced that Priestley's legacy was the paper he had so valiantly filled in the face of opprobrium and violence. Paper – bad quality paper especially – had almost been their undoing, but it remained the medium on which names were made. When Priestley himself contemplated his future, the memory of the friendships and the faith that shaped his life and work gave him a confidence no amount of public disdain could disturb. He looked forward, he wrote to a fellow former member of the Lunar Society, 'to a state of greater security, & permanency than the present; where no riots will separate us again.'[34]

✢

Others who had once numbered themselves among the Lunar men of Birmingham continued to be more interested in the here and now than the world hereafter. At the turn of the century Darwin was as busy as ever, preparing a long work on agriculture for Johnson's presses. He called his new book *Phytologia* and was convinced that he could revolutionise agricultural practice. In the same letter in which he announced that *Phytologia* was ready for the press he told a New York bookseller that he was also at work on an improved edition of *Zoonomia* and intended 'if I live, to publish another Poem about half the size of the Botanic Garden, which will also most probably go through Mr Johnson's hands to the Public.'[35] The poem was called *The Temple of Nature*. Johnson offered Darwin £500 for the privilege of publishing it and by the end of 1801 had set it up in type with four accompanying illustrations by Fuseli. Then there was a delay. On April 17th 1802 Darwin wrote to Richard Lovell Edgeworth to explain why his work had not yet appeared. 'My bookseller, Mr Johnson, will not begin to print the Temple of Nature, till the price of paper is fixed by Parliament.

I suppose the present duty is paid.' At this point his letter broke off, and another hand appeared in the manuscript:

Sir, This family is in the greatest affliction. I am truly grieved to inform you of the death of the invaluable Dr. Darwin. Dr. Darwin got up apparently in health; about eight o'clock, he rang the library bell. The servant, who went, said, he appeared fainting. He revived again, – Mrs. Darwin was immediately called. The Doctor spoke often, but soon appeared fainting; and died about nine o'clock. Our dear Mrs Darwin and family are inconsolable their affliction be great indeed – being few such husbands or Fathers – & will be most deservedly lamented by all who had the honour to be known to him ... PS this was begun this morning by Dr Darwin himself.[36]

Darwin died as he had lived, in the middle of a project, full of enthusiasm for his work, sharing news of progress. In London a few months later Maria Edgeworth met Johnson at dinner. He appeared worn down by the death of a friend and valued author and for once her father 'had nothing to scold him for & did not scold him: he was as kind to him as possible.' Johnson brought the manuscript of *The Temple of Nature* with him to dinner and left it temporarily in the Edgeworths' possession. 'There are beautiful papers in it', Edgeworth told her brother. 'But the subject seems to me too scientific for poetry & there are too many imitations of himself.'[37]

Darwin's star had waned in the aftermath of the *Anti-Jacobin* attacks but he was still a major figure and Johnson pressed forward with the production of *The Temple of Nature*, publishing the volume posthumously in 1803. Other men who had once published with him found it more difficult to attract his attention. In 1801 Wordsworth told a correspondent who had expressed interest in the genesis of his poetry that the question was best answered by his early poems, *Descriptive Sketches* and *An Evening Walk*. 'They are juvenile productions, inflated and obscure, but they contain many new images, and vigorous lines; and they would perhaps interest you, by shewing how very widely different my former opinions must have been from those which I hold at present.' The difficulty lay in locating a copy of the verses. 'Johnson has told some of my Friends who have called for them, that they were out of print: this must have been a mistake. Unless he has sent them to the Trunk-maker's they must be lying in some corner of his Warehouse, for I have reason to believe that they never sold much.'[38]

Four years later Wordsworth had still not succeeded in tracking down copies of his work. Dorothy did not repeat the suggestion that Johnson had sent remaindered copies of the poems to waste (and therefore to be reused by the trunk-maker) but in her own correspondence she concurred with the suggestion that both poems were lost to the piles of paper in Johnson's warehouse.[39] At the end of 1799, just over a year after its original publication, Coleridge was equally unsure about the fate of *Fears in Solitude*. 'I will speak to Johnson about the Fears in Solitude' he promised his friend Robert Southey on Christmas Eve. 'That dull ode has been printed often enough; and may now be allowed to "sink with dead swoop, & to the bottom go."'[40]

Some contributors to the back catalogue caused more trouble than others. Two years after Gabriel Stedman's death in 1797 Johnson wrote to his widow to propose a new edition of Stedman's *Narrative*. The first edition had nearly sold out and Johnson thought there was 'a prospect of another smaller edition going off at a cheaper price.'[41] The following July Johnson was still trying to untangle Stedman's posthumous account and was unimpressed by the sharp dealing he uncovered. He had allowed Stedman 'necessary expenses incurred in the printing of the work' in addition to a fee of £300, by which he meant 'occasional postage & carriage of parcels.' When he examined Stedman's receipts he discovered that the author had charged a London stay costing £42 to him, as well as putting 'me to an enormous expense in reprint[in]g part of the work from mere caprice'.[42] Johnson refused to be cheated, even by the dead. A month after he uncovered the deception he sent Stedman's executors a formal invoice for £94, 18 shillings and sixpence.

⁓

Cowper, Priestley, Darwin and Stedman were all men of Johnson's generation. In the years following their deaths he appeared as active as ever, issuing posthumous editions of the work of his contemporaries. Yet there were some among his acquaintance who questioned his resilience and the practicability of him continuing in business. The motivation for so doing varied. Mary Hays wrote of Johnson's 'procrastinating and unenterprising habits' but she did so when she was struggling to find a publisher prepared to take her work.[43] Godwin wrote to an acquaintance searching for a publisher for a large-scale dictionary project that 'Johnson ... if he be not a little too old, would have been a likely man.'[44] Johnson himself acknowledged that questions were being asked of his energy and capacity but he was unable to relinquish the thrill of discovering new voices. 'At my time of life when instead of advancing I ought perhaps to withdraw, I may be acting imprudently but I cannot turn a deaf ear to superior merit.'[45] His letters on the state of the book trade grew more assertive as he aged and he dispensed judgements to authors with authority. David Booth, Godwin's dictionary-compiling acquaintance, received a crisp characterisation of the milieu he desired to enter:

> It is unpleasant to a bookseller who can enter into the feelings of literary men to be obliged occasionally to tell some truths. Respecting the work you propose, the tradesman and merchant would say, I have a Dictionary already which answers all its purposes to me ... your book will not enable me to keep my account better, avoid bad debts, or make better bargains, the Physician that it would not help him to rise in his profession, the Lawyer that it would not procure him a client, the Parson a living. Those who read for amusement, the mass of readers, will not be persuaded that it affords any, and will say, you wish to send me again to school. Well then where are we to look for customers? To those who have made language their study, a few writers & public & gentlemen's libraries, a few of the latter only.[46]

The suggestion that the curious ideal reader imagined by the comprehensiveness of the *Analytical Review* was a dying breed appears at various points in Johnson's post-prison correspondence. Nevertheless he remained convinced that the reading public was still capable of improvement. Readers might be facile in their tastes but they were at least less supine in their thinking than at the height of Pitt's Terror. In 1805 he expressed the hope that American readers might one day shed their particular brand of conformist intellectual conservativism. 'The time I hope is not very distant when thinking Men will be as liberal in America as in England, and when it will not be necessary to embrace any set of opinions in order to obtain the good will of the orthodox.'[47] One sure way to improve the ambition of the reading public was to make it possible for the young to access new work in cheap editions. Johnson's commitment to democratic, accessible forms of publication was as strong as ever. In 1805 he informed an American author that concerns over accessibility dictated his publishing strategy. He conceded that his English edition of Benjamin Smith Barton's *Elements of*

Botany was not as 'handsome' as its American counterpart 'but my object was to give a book for students as cheap as possible – a large type and fine paper were not necessary.'[48]

As the voices of Johnson's own generation faded, ambitious young men sought him out. They viewed him as the publisher of new ideas and new ways of thinking, still unbowed by Establishment aggression after forty years in business. In February 1800 he received a letter and a description of a work-in-progress from a twenty-two-year-old chemist called Humphry Davy. Davy had been working with Thomas Beddoes in Bristol on nitrous oxide and his ideas were championed by Coleridge. Johnson was quick to recognise Davy's talents and made a generous offer: £70 for the copyright of Davy's *Researches, Chemical and Philosophical*. Davy was delighted at his good fortune. 'Johnson has bought my work & behaved with great liberality for he offered me 70 £ without seeing it', he told his friend James Tobin in March.[49] In February 1801 Davy moved to London to take up a post at the Royal Institution and shortly after his arrival in the capital he made his way to St Paul's Churchyard to visit his publisher. Godwin met him at dinner at Johnson's on February 17th, where they were joined by Fuseli and Bonnycastle as well as other passing visitors. Thereafter Godwin recorded meeting Davy in Johnson's dining room many times. Fuseli and Bonnycastle were present at all the Johnson dinners at which Godwin met Davy, but at St Paul's Churchyard the chemist was also introduced to Malthus, John Hewlett, John Miles and passing acquaintances of Johnson's from the London book trade. Davy's first biographer, John Paris, who published his *Life* in 1831, recounted stories of Davy rushing from his laboratory to dinner with so little time to spare that instead of changing he simply pulled on a clean shirt over his work clothes as he ran. Paris insisted that at various points Davy had been spotted 'wearing no less than five shirts, and as many pair of stockings, at the same time.' The effect apparently confused those who met Davy at dinner. 'Exclamations of surprise very frequently escaped from his friends at the rapid manner in which he increased and declined in corpulence.'[50]

Aspirant writers whose talents were less apparent than Davy's found it harder to attract Johnson's attention. William Hazlitt was the son of the Unitarian minister of the same name whose work Johnson had published in the 1760s and '70s. In the mid-1790s he was among the group of students at the Hackney Academy who abandoned the path of their Dissenting fathers and teachers to become followers of William Godwin. In 1796 he spent a period trying to make a living as an artist in Liverpool, where he was supported by William Roscoe, and in 1798 he walked from his parents' house in Wem to hear Coleridge preach in Shrewsbury. The meeting with Coleridge led to an invitation to visit Nether Stowey, where he was introduced in turn to the Wordsworths. These were seminal meetings for twenty-year-old Hazlitt, the details of which he later recorded in *My First Acquaintance with Poets*. He also recalled hearing Wollstonecraft and Godwin in conversation with each other, during the period following his departure from Hackney when he had sought out Godwin's company. Many years later the memory of Wollstonecraft was still vivid: 'she seemed to me to turn off Godwin's objections to something she advanced with quite a playful, easy air.'[51]

Hazlitt was among the crowd of English visitors who crossed to Paris during the Peace of 1802; by the time war resumed he was back in London, where he lingered on the fringes of Johnson's circle. Through Godwin he met Charles Lamb, an East India Company Clerk with a love of good company who wrote poetry in snatches of spare time. In 1805 Godwin persuaded Johnson to publish Hazlitt's *Essay on the Principles of Human Action*. Johnson acceded out of fondness for Hazlitt's father but sales were practically non-existent and Hazlitt himself made no money from the volume. Undeterred he tried again, and by 1806 had a second manuscript ready for Johnson. It was an abridgement of Abraham Tucker's *The Light of Nature Pursued* and on early inspection there was little in the manuscript to convince Johnson that the work was commercially viable. Once again Godwin agreed to act as Hazlitt's emissary. The way in which he was received at St Paul's Churchyard indicates the extent to which Johnson's professional practices were changing. 'Godwin went to Johnson's yesterday about your business', Lamb reported to Hazlitt in January 1806. 'Johnson would not come down, or give any answer, but has promised to open the manuscript & to give you an answer in one month. Godwin will punctually go again (Wednesday is Johnson's open day) yesterday four weeks next: i.e. in one lunar month from this time. Till when Johnson positively declines giving any answer.'[52] By 1806 Johnson was no longer at home to all-comers and those who wanted to fight their way onto his list had to present themselves and argue their case on his one public day a week. Godwin's diary reveals that he called on Johnson at least once between January 15th, when he first argued Hazlitt's case, and February 19th, when he returned to hear the verdict, but Johnson was no longer prepared to discuss the affairs of potential authors over dinner. Increasingly he made a distinction between his professional and private lives.

Lamb's second letter to Hazlitt reveals that there remained dangers in the streets of the City that no amount of gatekeeping could prevent. 'Godwin has just been here in his way from Johnson's', Lamb wrote on February 19th. 'Johnson has had a fire in his house, this happened about five weeks ago, it was in the daytime so it did not burn the house down, but did so much damage that the house must come down, to be repaired: his nephew that we met on Hampstead Hill put it out: well, this fire has put him so back, that he craves one more month before he gives you an answer.'[53] The fire of 1806 was nothing like the catastrophe of 1770. Johnson had a lease on warehouse space and on a second small house in the court behind St Paul's Churchyard and, since he was not required to move out of his own home, it is possible that it was one of these secondary buildings that was damaged. Nevertheless, the disruption served as a reminder of the vulnerability of the lives and houses of all City dwellers, including those whose professional security was in all other respects assured.

Johnson did eventually agree to publish Hazlitt's work, and, as with Davy, he paid generously for it. Hazlitt's biographer Duncan Wu has established that in the summer of 1806 Johnson offered Hazlitt £80 for the copyright of the *Abridgement*. It was a huge sum for someone who had never succeeded in making any money from writing and it spurred Hazlitt to devote himself to print instead of art.[54] Johnson was sixty-eight in 1806 and his asthma made daily activities difficult. His contract with Hazlitt reveals that he was still committed to encouraging and establishing young authors in their profession, even if he no longer flung open the doors to his own living quarters so freely. An indication of the volume of work with which he was still dealing comes in a manuscript 'Activity List' for the days between November 4th and 9th 1801. In this five-day period Johnson gave orders for the reprinting of *Olney Hymns*, a collaboration between Newton and Cowper, received and read five submissions and proposals, called on other booksellers, negotiated an appendix for a work-in-progress, corresponded with Richard Lovell Edgeworth about a draft of his latest work and arranged a detailed paper order with the printer who was setting Edgeworth's manuscript in type. The quality, cost and availability of paper was a perennial concern. In February 1800 he sent an order to a paper-maker in Exeter who had supplied a Taunton printer with a satisfactory product. 'You may make me 100 Rm more', he directed. But 'Only so much lighter as will reduce it to the first price, and pray put less blue into it.' If his instructions were heeded he promised his loyalty. 'I am out of humour with the London stationers and if your make give satisfaction may be a considerable customer to you as I have long been to them.'[55]

Paper quality was one among several concerns that dominated Johnson's business correspondence for the 1800s. Late payments were a constant irritant and his demands for prompt settlement of debts grew peremptory. In 1806 a fellow Churchyard tradesman was left in no doubt as to Johnson's determination to settle their account to his satisfaction. 'Called upon as I have lately been by declining strength I find it my duty to settle all old accounts without delay, and am determined to do so. If it will be of service to you I will make the balance of this account £500 upon your giving me good security – failing in this, & also in discharging this account, I shall put it into other hands at the expiration of next July.'[56] Johnson wrote to his neighbour at the end of April, giving him a window of two months to avoid the deployment of bailiffs.

Johnson continued to correspond regularly with American booksellers and in 1803 he wrote to James Madison about an order of books for the newly established Library of Congress. The lackadaisical approach both to copyright and the settlement of debts demonstrated by many of his American contemporaries generated sharp words. In August 1807 he told the New York booksellers T. and J. Swords that most of their London counterparts 'declined' orders on principle because American repayment rates were so bad. He fulfilled their order, despite the fact that the Swordses were more than two years in debt to him, but he told them that their own and their nation's honour was at stake in their prompt repayment.[57] He was irritated when American booksellers reprinted works to which he owned the copyright but he conceded that they at least acted within the confines of their own copyright law. British booksellers who attempted to infringe his intellectual property received shorter shrift. Joseph Cottle, the Bristol bookseller who had ignored Wordsworth's request to transfer the publication of *Lyrical Ballads* to Johnson, was rebuked for reprinting over a thousand lines of Cowper's poetry without permission. Cottle had also reprinted Darwin's work and Johnson accused him of stealing. Other booksellers who had attempted to purloin Cowper's words had settled with Johnson on his terms and he advised Cottle to make good his 'insufferable' behaviour by following their example.[58]

To those in real trouble Johnson remained capable of great kindness. In 1804 he helped a novelist called Phoebe Gibbs make a successful application for financial relief to the Royal Literary Fund. Gibbs had written a novel, *Elfrida*, which Johnson had published in three volumes, but a series of misfortunes had left her totally without capacity to feed herself and her two daughters. Later that year he supported an application to the fund from Grace Parman, the widowed daughter of the *Joineriana* author Samuel Paterson. Parman had been left destitute by the deaths of her husband and father, and near-blindness meant that her own letters to the trustees of the fund were very difficult to read. Johnson wrote to ask that her case be considered favourably and secured a grant of £5 on her behalf. Her relief and gratitude appear in letters that Johnson himself described as 'scarcely legible.'[59] Johnson had sent a 'young gent' to Parman's lodgings with news of the grant: she was sure that the messenger 'must think I looked more like a goast – than a living woman – for indeed my dr friend I was very ill that day but have been worse since – with a Violent Inflammation in my Eyes they are better – and I hope in a few days to thank you in person.' Pain and blindness made it difficult for her to continue. 'Indisposition makes me say no more at present for your kindness to me –, but that may you my Dr Sir, this and every Season enjoy health and happiness is the sincere wish of Dr Sir your most grateful and obliged Servant – G. Parman.'[60]

It is not coincidental that the two individuals Johnson helped to negotiate with powerful institutional structures were both women left destitute by the whims of the literary world. Gibbs and Parman were without connections or independent means of support: no one knocked on Johnson's door or demanded his attention on their behalf. His commitment to improving the lives of women had been evident since the 1770s, when he published Mary Scott's *Female Advocate* and the anonymous *Laws Respecting Women*. In 1804, when his own comfort was assured, he continued to support women living impossible lives on the margins of society.

&

Johnson might describe himself as a tradesman, but neither that term, nor the label 'bookseller' encapsulated his status, power or responsibilities after 1800. Two letters, dating from 1805 and 1806, demonstrate the extent to which his relationships with his authors and his position within the trade had shifted over the course of his career. Both letters also reveal the ways in which Johnson's profession had evolved in his image. In April 1805 he sent a long letter to Samuel Miller, an American historian who wanted Johnson to publish an English edition of his *Brief Retrospect of the Eighteenth Century*. Johnson explained that for many weeks he had been unsure as to how to act, since although the manuscript had plenty to recommend it, it was also riddled with errors. Such errors, he told Miller, would not have occurred if he had worked harder:

> Had you written a work addressed to your own Congregation or party it might have passed, but you have undertaken a History, and the requisites of a Historian will be expected from the intelligent among your readers, they will look for a fair statement of facts and opinions to enable them to form a judgement, and not for oracular dogmatism; that men who have enlarged the boundaries of knowledge and extended the sphere of mental improvement are treated with high respect not disposed of in a Line of Censure.[61]

Johnson did not write to Miller as the servant or instrument of other men's words, equipped only to grapple with matters of production and commerce. He wrote instead as an arbiter of knowledge and as the flagbearer for intellectual standards. Johnson's position had always enabled him to decide who deserved the privilege of a readership but by the mid-1800s he assumed that responsibility as a right endowed by long experience. Johnson would have demurred at the suggestion that he was a literary man, but his power to make literary men and women exemplified a decisive shift in his own position and in his industry. In 1760, when he was freed from his apprenticeship, booksellers were the instruments of production, not arbiters of taste. By 1805 the era of literary patronage was over and it was the booksellers who controlled access to the paper on which was inscribed the literary rhythms of the nation. Johnson's own fate symbolised the change, as his trial and imprisonment revealed more eloquently than could any compliment the extent to which the authorities viewed him as central to the dissemination of dangerous ideas.

In April 1806 Johnson wrote to his competitor Thomas Longman to protest about the ordering of publishers' names on a collaboratively produced edition. Longman had printed his own name ahead of Johnson's, despite the fact that as the recent heir to his father's business he was a new figure in the trade. 'When I came into the business', Johnson told Longman, it was 'governed by certain rules which I felt it my duty to adopt'. Chief among those rules was the placing of booksellers according to the seniority ordained by the length of time they had traded. 'Regulations are necessary to keep bodies of men in order, and what I mete to others in following an established custom I expect shall be meted to me again.' There was no shame in being at the outset of one's career, he insisted. 'Consider also what you will say when you are the oldest bookseller in the trade of young men who place their names before your own.'

Longman was three decades Johnson's junior and he came of age in the heady days of the 1790s, when old hierarchies tumbled in France and survived in Britain. He wanted to make a world where the prize of seniority came with professional success borne of luck and adventurousness rather than experience. Johnson, however, valued experience above all, and he proclaimed his own experience at the helm of his publishing house as the quality that fitted him to head his profession. Yet he also encouraged Longman not to wish his life away. Were he to be granted the opportunities of youth once again he would seize them gladly. 'Few men are fond of age, I certainly am not, & should have no objection to be placed on the bottom of the ladder & to rise by slow degrees as I have already done to the first step.'[62] In that ascent, he told Longman, was all the professional education a man could ever need.

29

Lycidas

Together both, ere the high Lawns appear'd
Under the opening eye-lids of the morn,
We drove afield, and both together heard
What time the Gray-fly winds her sultry horn,
Batt'ning our flocks with the fresh dews of night,
Oft till the Star that rose, at Ev'ning, bright
Toward Heav'ns descent had slop'd his westering wheel.[1]

(Lycidas, 25–31)

One summer's evening in the early 1800s, Fuseli caught sight of a moth in a garden. He watched it entranced, his artist's eye capturing its delicate structure and the gradations of its colours. That summer he was working on a painting for his friend James Carrick Moore, of the shepherd speaker of Milton's *Lycidas*. Fuseli had painted the character before but in the image he presented to Moore, which measured less than a foot in length, he represented the shepherd alongside a shepherdess and added a life-sized image of a moth hovering over their heads.

The painting does not survive apart from in the description by John Knowles, Fuseli's first biographer. Knowles wrote apologetically that the shepherdess – who appears nowhere in Milton's poem – represented 'the licence of a painter' and acknowledged that a life-sized moth on a ten-inch painting dwarfed the human figures on the canvas. At a dinner organised by the doctor John Moore, Fuseli met Edward Jenner, the inventor of the smallpox vaccination. Jenner demanded to be told why the painting was dominated by a giant moth; Fuseli responded that it represented the 'grey-fly' of Milton's verse. "'No, no,'" replied the Doctor, "this is no grey-fly, but a moth, and winds no horn; it is a mute.'" For once Fuseli was silenced by

Jenner's rebuke. 'He knew well its accuracy', Knowles reported, 'and therefore said nothing.'[2] But in defiance of Jenner he added the moth to the
corner of an earlier image of Milton's shepherd, slumbering under a crescent
moon. In this image, which survives only in a later engraving, the moth
hovers at the edge of the frame, observing the sleeping figure at the centre.
It does not dominate the image; instead it glimmers at the edges of both
subject and viewer's consciousness. The moth in the evening light is a
creature gone as soon as it is glimpsed; it vanishes as quickly as it appears.
It appears in Fuseli's image like the dreams that dissipate at the moment
of waking. The shepherd dreams of a lost friend and of a past when 'together
both / ... Under the opening eye-lids of the morn, / We drove a field.' In
sleep comes a refuge from loss and worldly cares, but both return as dawn
breaks and the moth retreats from the glare of the sun.

Milton's *Lycidas* is a lament for his fellow Cambridge undergraduate
Edward King, who drowned in 1637 on his way to visit his family in Ireland.
The poem is a pastoral elegy which incorporates an attack on Church
corruption; a hymn to friendship and an indictment of avaricious clergy.
'Who would not sing for *Lycidas*?' asks the broken-hearted shepherd, as he
summons the gods of sea and river to account for their part in his friend's
death. The shepherd imagines Lycidas's tomb strewn with flowers:

> The tufted Crow-toe, and pale Gessamine,
> The white Pink, and the Pansie freakt with jet,
> The glowing Violet,
> The Musk-rose, and the well attir'd Woodbine,
> With Cowslips wan that hang the pensive hed.

His vision is disrupted by the memory that the body of his friend is lost
beneath the waves:

> Ay me! Whilst thee the shores, and sounding Seas
> Wash far away, where ere thy bones are hurld,
> Whether beyond the stormy Hebrides,
> Where thou perhaps under the whelming tide
> Visit'st the bottom of the monstrous world;

Words, rather than a flower-strewn tomb, have to stand as a memorial for
the dead. Lycidas rises from the ocean bed in the memories of those who

have loved him and through the goodness of Christ, who appears in the poem as 'him that walk'd the waves.'

✢

The garden in which Fuseli saw the moth of his *Lycidas* images was Johnson's. At some point between 1800 and 1804 Johnson took a lease on Dungannon House in the village of Fulham, which at that point stood apart from the Cities of London and Westminster. The writer of a 1795 account entitled *The Environs of London* described it as a village 'situated on the banks of the Thames, at the distance of four miles from Hyde-park-corner': he noted that its parish was comprised largely of market gardens and domestic houses.[3] Johnson rented Dungannon House in order to give himself a country retreat and it heralded a significant change in his life. He did not move out of St Paul's Churchyard but instead alternated between the two houses as business and his breathing required. It was not uncommon for the prosperous merchants of the City to have a second house away from the noise of their commercial premises and for a long time Johnson had been unusual in choosing to remain so closely tied to his shop. But within a year or so of his release from prison it was apparent to both him and his friends that the air of the City was choking him. Most of Johnson's friends referred to his new house by its address: Purser's Cross, or, simply, 'P.C.' The house was in fact half a house: it was the side portion of a grander dwelling with which it shared a wall. One visitor to the house recalled a grand fireplace in one room but no other details about its interior remain. Records of the garden, however, do survive. In a letter to Roscoe, dated June 21ˢᵗ 1804, Fuseli described himself as a delighted visitor at 'Johnson's Subarno.' The garden he characterised as 'a Sweet & peaceful little retreat inbosomed by a wilderness of Shrubs & what I like still better, entomologic weeds; a close & humble neighbour ... undisturbed by any of our Daemons ye classed gardeners.'[4]

The earliest indication that Fuseli was at work on an image inspired by *Lycidas* came in a letter to William Roscoe dated October 1799. Fuseli wrote to reassure his friend and patron that he did not 'sit only before a fire with my hands between my knees, I have begun to prepare the pictures I intend for you.' The 'Twilight Shepherd from Lycidas' was among the images he promised, although he warned Roscoe that it remained unfinished.[5] When Fuseli began work on the image of the slumbering shepherd he was still smarting from the fact that his long-planned Milton Gallery had been a commercial failure. The exhibition opened in Pall Mall in the spring of 1799, while Johnson was in prison. By late May it was clear that the crowds Fuseli needed to attract in order to recoup his costs were not buying tickets. Newspaper critics were ostentatiously uninterested in the work of a painter tainted by Jacobin suspicion and Fuseli spotted conspiracy. 'Silence', he told Roscoe, 'is the weapon of those who dare not damn me.' He was defiant in the face of failure. 'The nation that left Milton poor will not make me rich, but this I knew before.'[6] He was defiant too in the face of visitors who did not show sufficient appreciation for either his work or Milton's. Knowles described how the artist sometimes 'lounged about the Milton Gallery' in order to eavesdrop on the remarks of critics and casual visitors. One day a man asked for enlightenment about the subject of a picture. Fuseli told him it depicted the bridging of Chaos in *Paradise Lost*. 'No wonder I did not know it', responded the man, 'for I never read Milton, but I will.' 'I advise you not', replied Fuseli, 'You will find it a d—d tough job.'[7]

By the time an enlarged version of the exhibition closed in 1800, it was apparent to both Fuseli and his friends that the scheme, so long dreamt of, would not bring him financial independence. Supporters rallied round to buy the paintings and help him meet his expenses. The Countess of Guilford bought an early image of Lycidas and Roscoe purchased work to the value of £300, including some images that Fuseli had thought it best not to exhibit. The Milton Gallery did have one beneficial effect on Fuseli's finances, since it prompted his fellow artists to elect him to the position of Professor of Painting at the Royal Academy. Joseph Farington reminded him of the importance of cultivating supporters in the art world in order to survive. The suggestion prompted a rare moment of vulnerability in Fuseli. 'He told me', Farington wrote in his diary, that 'he avoids company because He cannot sufficiently command himself in it.'[8]

Fuseli features largely in several accounts of Johnson among his friends during the 1800s. In July 1803 the American writer William Austin came to dinner at St Paul's Churchyard and a year later he published a lengthy description of the evening in his *Letters from London*. 'The English don't say much till the first course is finished', he explained for the benefit of his American readers. 'But their manner of eating soon throws them into a gentle fever, which invites to sociability, when they have sufficient confidence in their company.' At Johnson's it was Bonnycastle who initiated the conversation and Fuseli who was 'the life of the entertainment ... his happy combination of language, joined to his emphatic manner, bordering hard on dogmatism, together with his deep insight into human nature, renders him an oracle wherever he goes.' The conversation turned to the work and character of Lavater, subjects on which Fuseli was an acknowledged authority. It also encompassed history and the poetry of Ossian. Fuseli, Austin recalled, was sceptical about the veracity of the Ossian poems, later discovered to be the work of the forger James Macpherson. Fuseli 'seemed to treat the poems with no great respect, and at length let off a shot at the whole clan of Scotch poets, by roundly asserting that, all the Scotch rhymers put together would not amount to half a poet. Fuseli, I discovered, would allow no man to be a poet who is not in the habit of attaining to the sublime.'[9]

Four years later, another visitor to St Paul's Churchyard also witnessed Fuseli dominating the conversation. Alexander Gibson Hunter called at Johnson's shop on his public day and found himself invited to stay for dinner. It is thanks to Hunter that we have a rare glimpse of the food Johnson served: 'a piece of boiled cod, a fillet of veal roasted, with vegetables, for a remove, and then a rice-pudding – a true citizen dinner for eight hungry men.' Hunter found himself sitting down to dinner alongside Fuseli, Bonnycastle, his own companion and two strangers, as well as Johnson's unnamed shopmen. Unlike Austin, Hunter thought little of Fuseli's conversational prowess. The artist, he told his friend Archibald Constable, was 'the most conceited, self-sufficient quiz I ever saw; but clever and well-read – defied and despised all opinions.' Johnson himself Hunter described as 'a true and conceited good old Cockney fellow, who likes a joke and fun amazingly.'[10]

Hunter's description of Johnson sits oddly alongside the austere, self-effacing figure described by other visitors to the dining room. It suggests that, among intimate friends, Fuseli and Bonnycastle above all, Johnson relaxed as he aged. The confidence of the bookseller at the top of his profession comes through in late descriptions of him at ease at his own table. This joking, relaxed Johnson also stands more easily alongside Fuseli, and allows a different view of their friendship. Johnson evidently believed that Fuseli's dominant rapier-wit was to be celebrated and within the confines of his own house he allowed his friend full rein. The change in Johnson himself was remarked upon by Joel Barlow when he returned briefly to London in 1802. 'He is grown fat & careless & happy', he told his wife Ruth. 'He took me by the hand shaking his sides, & the first

word was "well you could not get me hanged, you tried all you could.'"
A 'good deal of fun' was also had at dinner, Barlow continued. 'Johnson
loves to drink toasts, – so he began – Mrs Barlow's health.' Despite the
jollity Barlow wrote of his evening at Johnson's with some melancholy.
Many familiar faces no longer gathered around the table; the old guard
who had written of reform in the 1790s were dead or dispersed across the
globe. 'Did not see ... any other old friends', he told Ruth. 'So much for
to day of London.'[11]

Other friends also wrote of Johnson laughing, but with an ever-present
note of condescension which kept him in his tradesman's place. Charlotte
Edgeworth told her newly married sister Emmaline that Johnson spoke
highly of both her and her new husband, and that he 'laughed heartily' on
hearing that Emmaline had absent-mindedly signed a letter using her maiden
name. 'How I do like that little man', wrote Charlotte of the family bookseller. Nevertheless she took seriously Johnson's approbation of Emmaline's
husband, John King. 'Oh yes says J he is a very excellent man and he writes
extremely well ... this he repeated several times over & with the most
serious look & shake of the head; my father made no remark upon it, but
I will answer for it, that it made no small impression upon it.'[12] Maria
Edgeworth also wrote fondly of Johnson but she was more critical of him
than were her siblings. Politically, she told her cousin Sophy in 1800, 'he
is grown very cautious – a burnt child dreads the fire.'[13]

Joseph Farington left a different kind of record of dinner at Johnson's.
In his diary for July 24th 1805 he sketched a plan of the table. An oblong
box showed Johnson sitting across the table from his nephew. Bonnycastle
and Fuseli sat together at one end; Farington was opposite them, next to
an unnamed 'Young man.' 'We dined at 5', he wrote in a note to accompany the diagram. 'Drank tea at 8 & played at Whist till 10. Not for
money – a weekly custom.'[14] This was a different kind of dinner to the
public affairs open to passing authors and shop visitors. Farington found
himself, courtesy of Fuseli, at an intimate gathering of friends and kin,
where games rather than political or philosophical debate had become the
order of the evening. For men who were growing old together, company
in which no performance was required was a blessing. Lindsey suffered a
stroke in 1802 and for a period was unable to walk. Hannah took over as
the scribe for his correspondence and assumed control over every aspect
of their lives. In July 1803 she reported with relief that Lindsey was sufficiently recovered to 'walk to Johnson's & back after resting.' Lindsey was

eighty in 1803; Hannah a youthful sixty-three. She was suffering from 'Gallstones and bilious misery' but she refused to be cowed by physical frailty. To an ailing correspondent she sent bracing encouragement. 'We trust that the Sea air and bathing, & your recess from business will chear, restore, & purify you all from every remaining atom of disease, and this glorious weather give plenty of everything.'[15]

One more figure who joined the company in Johnson's dining room in the 1800s left a written record of the scenes he witnessed. In January 1807 Godwin recorded meeting Fuseli's biographer John Knowles over dinner, in company as usual with Johnson, Bonnycastle and Fuseli. Knowles himself wrote that for some years after 1800 he dined at Johnson's at least once a week. Knowles remembered Johnson for 'the good sense which he exercised, and the prudence with which he allayed the occasional contests of his irritable guests, many of whom were distinguished men of letters, of various character, and conflicting opinions.' The presence of the biographer at the table lends a depth and tenderness to his account of Fuseli and Johnson sitting alongside each other. 'Fuseli', he wrote, 'was always a favoured guest at this table; when absent, which rarely happened, a gloom for some time pervaded the company; but when present, his acute taste in poetry, oratory, and the fine arts; his original opinions, singular ideas, and poignant wit, enlivened the conversation, and rendered him a delightful companion.'[16] Knowles also remembered that when Fuseli was present Johnson himself subsided into silence, his taste for toasts and jokes forgotten as his moon was eclipsed by Fuseli's sun.

⊹

Godwin was not merely a witness to Johnson's gatherings. After 1800 he depended on Johnson for financial and practical support. In 1801 he remarried. His new wife was his next-door neighbour, Mary Jane Vial. Mary Jane already had two children of her own and in 1803 she and Godwin had a son. In order to make enough money to feed five children Godwin and Mary Jane opened a bookshop and publishing business specialising in work for children. The business struggled to make money and by 1807 Godwin was in crisis. He wrote to Johnson asking for help, invoking the needs of his children. Two years previously Wollstonecraft's sisters had asked for Fanny to be sent to them on condition that they also received financial support for her upkeep. Johnson had exhorted Godwin to keep Fanny in London, in the only home she knew. Now Godwin drew attention to the circumstances of Fanny and Mary: the two girls for whom he knew Johnson felt 'some concern for on account of their mother, independently of any kindness you may be so good as to entertain for me.'[17] In a second letter Godwin reminded the bookseller that, like Johnson, he had suffered for his principles. 'My writings have raised me many enemies', he wrote in April. But 'they have also made me friends – in some cases among persons to whom I am not myself known. You, perhaps, Sir, are acquainted with some of them; some of them you know, might point out others. How far are you inclined to interest yourself in my behalf, an acquaintance of ten or eleven years standing? If you felt the inclination, I would willingly put myself into your hands.'[18]

Godwin's proposal was that Johnson should help him raise a subscription to fund the move to a new premises as well as a new enterprise, a subscription service for children that Godwin called the Juvenile Library. The news that Godwin was in financial trouble did not come as a surprise to Johnson, who had been the recipient in the autumn of 1806 of a string of visits as Godwin attempted to untangle his affairs. Johnson lent Godwin £200 to keep him afloat but he also did his best to move his business venture onto a more secure footing. He called the task of advising Godwin 'a very unpleasant office' but acknowledged it was one he could not refuse. By the spring of 1808 Godwin was £600 in debt to merchants and tradespeople and owed £1,500 to friends who were prepared to wait for payment. Johnson was among those friends and offered to put his own bond in the fire if Godwin's other creditors would either forgive the debt or agree to the suspension of interest payments. With such help and with Godwin's 'frugality & his industry & his talents' he predicted that Godwin had 'as fair a prospect of bringing up his family & providing for them as man ought to wish for ... to say nothing of the useful effects of his writings on the rising gen[eratio]n.'[19] Johnson was Wollstonecraft's friend long before he became Godwin's business advisor and although Godwin dined regularly at St Paul's Churchyard after Wollstonecraft's death the two men never became as close as Wollstonecraft and Johnson, or as intimate as Johnson was with Bonnycastle and Fuseli. Godwin's letters show that he was sincere in his desire to support his children and there is no suggestion in the correspondence of either man that Godwin compelled Johnson's assistance through the cynical manipulation of his family. Nevertheless by 1807 he was in desperate need of Johnson's money and he knew that Johnson's first loyalty was to Wollstonecraft and her daughters, orphaned Fanny above all. When

Johnson came to write his will he formally returned Godwin's bond for £200, on the stipulation that the funds released should be transferred to Fanny for her support.

♣

In Johnson's own family, members of the younger generations jostled for position around him. In August 1800 word reached him that his older brother John had died. He set off for Liverpool, leaving Fuseli the task of arranging a planned 'Venison Party' at a local hotel.[20] John died in financial difficulty, after a fire his son described as 'very destructive' ripped through his Liverpool brewing business. At the time of his death he was still rebuilding houses destroyed by the blaze and bills for the repair work were unpaid. Johnson wrote immediately to John's son and heir Joseph to offer help. In the weeks following John's death Johnson wrote three times to his nephew, encouraging him to draw on him for funds. He insisted he offered the money as a gift, not a loan. 'I can relieve you from the embarrassment you mention, whenever you are so circumstanced, draw upon me, you cannot find it difficult to cash your drafts.'[21]

Although he was not unhappy in his father's trade Joseph Johnson the Younger sometimes looked wistfully at the opportunities offered to Rowland Hunter and John Miles. 'Many years ago', he wrote in 1816, 'had I not known I was usefully employed in my Father's service, I have no doubt that I should have become an assistant to my Uncle, where I should have been as at the fountain head of what I always thirsted after, viz. – Literary pursuits and Literary accomplishments.'[22] Joseph was the same generation as Rowland Hunter, although Rowland was a decade younger than him. John Miles was of the next generation, the son of Joseph's sister Mary. The generational gap mattered in the Johnson family, as splits developed between those who remained tied to Liverpool and those who were given a home and livelihood in London. John Miles was disliked by many of those who knew Johnson, although Johnson himself evidently trusted Miles's financial acumen and relied on his management of the business's finances. Joseph Johnson the Younger detested Miles and was suspicious of his actions and motives. Many years later he accused him of lining his own pockets with Johnson's wealth at the expense of Miles's own mother as the family fought for control over Johnson's affairs. Rowland Hunter was more popular and it was he, rather than Miles, who took on the responsibilities of co-host on Johnson's public days. Joel Barlow was very impressed by 'Young Rowland,

Johnson's nephew.' Rowland 'had got to be one of the best read & most sensible among the republicans, well versed in the philosophy & mythology & political economy of the present English & French schools. but attentive to business & is to be Johnson's successor.'[23] After 1800 Rowland and Johnson were united in sorrow at the early death of his older sister Hester Newnum, who left behind a thirteen-year-old daughter and a four-year-old son. Her widower Henry continued to dine at St Paul's Churchyard after his wife's death and something of Johnson's fondness for Hester can be deduced from the fact that he commissioned Fuseli to paint her portrait. Knowles remembered that the picture was one of only two formal portraits Fuseli completed.

Although Joseph Johnson the Younger made only occasional visits to St Paul's Churchyard, he was in no doubt as to the importance of Fuseli in Johnson's life. His view was that Fuseli brought nothing but joy to Johnson's existence and that their long friendship – longer than his own life – was worthy of respect. In 1804 Fuseli wrote him a letter in which he expressed the hope that the house and garden in Fulham offered the prospect of the restoration of Johnson's breathing, 'could he be persuaded to spend more of his time at it.' To Joseph, Fuseli described the house as 'a sweet retired and healthful spot ... eminently conducive to his health.' But he also indicated that Johnson's friends believed he needed more than a country house to save his life. In an aside which suggests the central role Joseph at one time planned to play in Johnson's world Fuseli expressed the hope that a proposal made to him in person during a summer visit to Liverpool might be fulfilled. 'I hope Mrs Johnson has not forgot her promise, to come and reside and nurse him there, as soon as it is in her power.'[24]

Joseph and his wife did not move their household to Fulham and there is no suggestion in the surviving records that any other Johnson nieces arrived to replace Hester or Elizabeth (of whom there is no trace at St Paul's Churchyard after 1800). Instead it was Fuseli himself who took on the support of his friend. His own household was now based at Somerset House and his wife Sophia made her home there but Fuseli frequently stayed for weeks on end at Purser's Cross, getting up early in the morning to walk into the capital. In the summer of 1805 he was involved in a carriage accident and was physically unable to cover the distance each day. The result was an interlude of peace and stillness as in Johnson's garden he took tentative steps towards recovery. He had, he told Roscoe, 'been for a fortnight past at Johnsons villa to teach my toes to articulate on smooth garden ground & Level greens', without any access to 'political or Literary information.' For once he was unable to work but he wrote of his plight with calm equanimity. 'There are pictures enough in my possession', he told Roscoe, 'what would more than answer your demand had the horse & the wheel that grazed me succeeded in crushing me.'

Happily marooned by an injured foot, Fuseli settled into the role of co-host at Purser's Cross. A mutual friend had left cards for him there and he issued a genial invitation to Roscoe: 'are there any hopes of seeing you here?'[25] Farington noted that Fuseli's accident was more dangerous than the artist himself acknowledged and that he had been 'thrown down by a Coach' passing at speed. Farington called on Fuseli immediately after the accident and found him laid up in bed. Fuseli's subsequent removal to the quiet of Fulham may have been the result of Johnson's insistence and it suggests that the artist's physical care for the bookseller was reciprocated. Sophia Fuseli hardly figures in accounts from this period, although in June 1806 she did make an appearance in Farington's diary when a dispute broke out between her and the housekeeping staff at the Royal Academy. In the ensuing fuss Farington reported that Fuseli had taken the part of the staff rather than that of his wife.[26] Meanwhile those who hoped to meet Johnson found him an ever more elusive figure. When Maria Edgeworth's younger brother called at St Paul's Churchyard in April 1806 he was met with the news that Johnson 'was in the country' and he had to make do instead with the welcome offered by Rowland Hunter.[27] When Godwin embarked on his campaign for Johnson's support he was compelled to rely on letters rather than haunt the shop and dining room at St Paul's Churchyard. In his attempt to secure Johnson's backing he was obliged several times to walk the four miles to Purser's Cross himself.

In December 1806 Joseph Farington entered a caustic observation in his diary. 'I had now fully experienced that Fuseli was incapable of real attachment or gratitude.' Farington resolved 'to act towards Him accordingly', particularly since his manners 'have frequently been such as to make his friends afraid to introduce him into company.'[28] Many of those who met Fuseli would have agreed with this assessment. Yet towards Johnson Fuseli was capable of great gentleness. His care of his friend of forty years pulses through his correspondence for the 1800s. As a young man Fuseli had met Sterne in Johnson's dining room and been disgusted (hypocritically so, perhaps) by the fact that nothing seemed to please Sterne but talking in expletives. When decades later he met Coleridge at St Paul's Churchyard he was equally dismissive – 'thought little of him', Farington reported.[29] But about Johnson himself Fuseli left no traces of criticism. Others might bemoan Johnson's tardiness or lack of attention to detail but theirs was a chorus to which Fuseli never added his voice. By the time the two men shared the idyll of an overgrown country garden both knew that Johnson's life was drawing to a close. The moth from his garden hovers at the edge of the frame in Fuseli's representation of the sleeping shepherd of *Lycidas*. It offers a fleeting glimpse of a commitment that had no name. Milton's shepherd dreams of days before the end of friendship; Fuseli's image celebrates a friend and a home even as it anticipates and acknowledges loss. The closing lines of *Lycidas* itself testify to the enduring power of friendship to sustain and protect, even when the friends themselves have gone.

> Now Lycidas the Shepherds weep no more;
> Hence forth thou art the Genius of the shore,
> In thy large recompense, and shalt be good
> To all that wander in that perilous flood.

30

Beachy Head

In 1807 Johnson published a collection of poems by Charlotte Smith, the writer whom Cowper had met and admired at Eartham in 1792. Smith made her name as a poet in 1784 with the publication of her *Elegiac Sonnets*. In 1798 she had the dubious honour of being ranked alongside Wollstonecraft and Hays as an 'unsex'd female' by Richard Polwhele. In the same year her acquaintance with Godwin blossomed into friendship and through Godwin Smith was also introduced to Coleridge, whom she liked a great deal. At the turn of the century Smith's celebrity was more firmly established than that of Blake, Wordsworth or Coleridge. Johnson's bookselling neighbour Richard Phillips commissioned Mary Hays to write Smith's biography for his *Public Characters of 1800–1801* and Hays subsequently included Smith in her six-volume *Female Biography* of 1803. Smith had no protection from her estranged husband, who had the right to spend her earnings and who contributed nothing to the maintenance of the eleven children she bore between 1767 and 1785. For years she was tangled in a legal dispute with her husband's family which, as Hays noted, brought her new enemies from the ranks of men 'who hated her in proportion as they had injured her.'[1] In her poetry Smith foregrounded her own suffering in an extended process of creative self-revelation which both invited and deflected scrutiny from admirers and critics alike.

By the early 1800s Smith had turned her attention to writing for children in an attempt to increase her earnings. In 1803, after her relationship with her long-standing publisher broke down, she was introduced to Johnson by Cowper's friend Samuel Rose. Johnson encouraged Smith to write more poetry as well as books for children. He was convinced there was a market for Smith's poems, provided Smith herself was willing to produce the volume of material necessary for a saleable edition. He required half as much again, he explained, in addition to the manuscript material he had in hand, for which he was willing to pay half as much more. His request, he insisted, was not motivated by greed. 'You should know I do very much dislike dear books.' But he had to work within the constraints of the market and he knew that readers expected bulk for their money. 'It is our misfortune', he explained, 'that he who wishes to pay a liberal price & publish nothing but what is good, has to combat with many who can easily procure trash for a mere trifle, put a promising title & puffs in the papers in a way that a respectable man cannot, but which must succeed with the mass of the people until the slow operation of time shall decide in his favour.'[2]

In addition to the volume of poems, Johnson commissioned two further children's books from Smith. The first, *Conversations Introducing Poetry*, appeared in 1804. Although she was grateful for his support Smith, like others before her, was frustrated by Johnson's slowness. In March 1804 he heard that she was compelled to sell her library in order to raise funds. He helped her drive up the price by offering the services of an expert in second-hand book valuation and once the books were gone he sent her parcels of new titles whenever he could. When the parcels did not arrive she was desolate. 'Tis misery past compute', she told her friend Sarah Rose, 'to hear of books, & hunger & thirst after them without being able to get them.' It was a sentiment previously uttered by Priestley, but unlike Priestley Smith was close enough to London literary circles to understand Johnson's frailty. His silences left her as worried for him as herself. Was he 'confined by sickness?' she asked a mutual acquaintance in March. 'I do not love to tieze Mr Johnson & cannot help persuading myself he is ill.'[3]

By 1806 Smith was herself ill as a result of the multiple blows she had suffered. Johnson's faith in her work was as important to her as the financial and logistical support he offered, but she was frustrated by his failure to understand the nature of the financial strains under which she operated. Johnson, Smith told Sarah Rose, 'often gives me lectures on oeconomy'. She quoted one of his lectures. 'If you had not been fostered in the lap of prosperity, you wd think your income ample.'[4] Johnson knew what it was to run a large and demanding house and business which sustained the lives of a network of kin, authors and servants but he had no experience of the strain imposed by the arbitrary financial appropriation Smith suffered at the hands of her husband. Her children were dependent on her too, and her sex meant that she had nothing like Johnson's ability to meet the demands of her family. Johnson continued to make exacting demands of

Smith even as he helped her purchase the fixtures and fittings for a cheaper house. 'My Novel finish'd?' she wrote in response to a friend's enquiry. 'Oh no – Johnson throes some cold water upon it: he thought I might do better.'[5]

Smith never fully reconciled herself to the contradictions in Johnson's character. At one point she complained that 'an answer from him is more rare than a comet'. His neglect 'mingled with so much bonhomie that I cannot complain' but she confessed that she found his silences discouraging.[6] By the summer of 1806 she knew she was dying and she wrote to a former patron that she saw no prospect 'of ending my days anywhere but in the County Jail.' She believed she had 'exhausted' the kindness of her bookseller but Johnson confounded her doubts by pressing ahead with the production of her poems. In her last surviving letter to him she acknowledged that she had been mistaken in her assumptions about the nature of his commitment to writing by women. She had never doubted 'your gallantry or what is better your benevolence & good nature' but she had assumed that he treated 'Ladies literature' as had her late publisher James Dodsley 'who, when I offered him my Sonnets in 1783, said, "I suppose now this is all loving stuff about Shepherds and Shepherdesses, & little lambs, & <u>all that</u>."'[7] It was a welcome surprise to be compelled to revisit her opinion and to find in Johnson a bookseller who was free of preconceived ideas about fit subjects for professional women writers.

Smith died on October 18th 1806, aged fifty-seven, the poems she had sent to Johnson still unpublished. At the end of the year he gathered together the material he had and prepared it for the printer. The volume appeared in January 1807 as *Beachy Head: with Other Poems.* Johnson prefaced Smith's poetry with an advertisement in which he characterised the poems as 'the most unquestionable evidence of the same undiminished genius, spirit, and imagination, which so imminently distinguished her former productions.' One poem required additional explanation. 'The Poem entitled BEACHY HEAD is not completed according to the original design. That the increasing debility of its author has been the case of its being left in an imperfect state, will it is hoped be a sufficient apology.'[8]

Johnson placed Smith's unfinished poem at the head of his edition of her poetry; he also borrowed its title for the volume. In its unfinished, experimental state, 'Beachy Head' is one of the masterpieces of English Romantic poetry. It features shepherds but has nothing else in common with the women's magazine verse about which Smith's publisher James Dodsley was so disparaging. It tells the story of the nation through the rocks and prospects of Beachy Head, a documented place of death since the early sixteenth century. 'Beachy Head' is a poem concerned with the lines of history – the way those lines reach back into the geological strata decoded by Darwin, and forward into the unknown. Darwin had written of seashell fossils encased in chalk and Smith takes up his line of questioning:

> Or did this range of chalky mountins, once
> Form a vast bason, where the Ocean waves
> Swell'd fathomless?

She represents the inequalities rampant in modern Britain, contrasting a rich man travelling in gilded splendour along the new network of post-roads with the starving labourer he passes, compelled to doff 'what *was* a hat.' The poem also recalls the happiness of Smith's own childhood, as she follows the chains of memory back to the Sussex Downs of her youth.

The version of 'Beachy Head' that Johnson published ends with the re-telling of the story of Parson Derby. Derby was a curate at a local church during the first years of the eighteenth century and he devoted decades of his life to saving sailors and shipwrecks at Beachy Head. He excavated a cave for himself on the shoreline, from which he watched each night for people in danger. He appears in the poem as an everyman who cares for others more than he cares for himself and who values human life and community over jewels or national jingoism. The draft breaks off with Derby's death in a storm and with the discovery of his body near his cave:

> Those who read
> Chisel'd within the rock, these mournful lines,
> Memorials of his sufferings, did not grieve,
> That dying in the cause of charity
> His spirit, from its early bondage freed,
> Had to some better region fled for ever.

Here the lines of 'Beachy Head' itself are written in the rock as 'chisel'd' memorials. Art becomes part of the geological strata of the nation, a testament to the power of words to endure when the body has returned to the earth. The poem may be unfinished, but in Johnson's celebration of its provisional state the story of a connected country and its people reaches outwards towards an unresolved future.

✝

In the summer of 1804 Maria Edgeworth wrote to Anna Barbauld with a proposal. The two women were connected through Johnson, who in 1804 also facilitated a correspondence between Edgeworth and Smith. Edgeworth's proposal came from her father and was for 'a periodical paper, to be written entirely by ladies.'[9] Barbauld greeted the idea with scepticism. 'All the literary ladies! Mercy on us! Have you ever reckoned up how many there are, or computed how much trash, and how many discordant materials would be poured in from such a general invitation.' She rejected the idea that writing by women had any single defining characteristic other than the gender of its authors. 'There is no bond of union among literary women, any more than among literary men; different sentiments and different connections separate them much more than the joint interest of their sex would unite them. Mrs Hannah More would not write along with you or me, and we should probably hesitate at joining Miss Hays, or if she were living, Mrs Godwin.'[10] Barbauld's rejection of the intellectual comradeship of two of the women alongside whom she had sat in Johnson's dining room underlines the intellectual diversity among the women writers who found a place on Johnson's list. Edgeworth, Hays, Barbauld, Wollstonecraft and Smith had different views about the position of women, although they had more in common with each other than they did with the conservative Hannah More, who published elsewhere. The one characteristic that united them was their determination to be the 'professional woman writer' of Wollstonecraft's vision. Johnson never questioned their professionalism or the range of their interests and, as Smith acknowledged, he rejected narrow generic categorisations founded on the sex of the author.

Johnson shared Barbauld's scepticism about the idea of a journal for and by literary ladies, telling Elizabeth Hamilton (who he believed was involved with Edgeworth's scheme) that the mechanics of the book trade made the financial success of such a venture doubtful. But throughout the 1800s he continued prominently to feature writing by women. Smith and Edgeworth were among his most well-known authors after the deaths of Cowper and Darwin and he reprinted Barbauld's most popular works even when Barbauld herself produced fewer new titles. Priestley's exile and the failure of the long Dissenting campaign for political and religious reform affected Barbauld deeply, and in 1800 she wrote that the country of her youth seemed a foreign land. 'If all that has happened had not happened, or the memory of it could be washed away with Lethe, how usefully and respectably might Dr. Priestley now be placed at the head of the Royal Institution, which is so fashionable just now in London!' She had been to hear a popular lecturer and was struck by the volume of new scientific knowledge that had emerged since her own girlhood in Warrington. 'How much is taught now, and even made a part of education, which, when you and I were young, was not even discovered!'[11] At the beginning of the decade a sense of loss pervaded Barbauld's correspondence, as she spoke of an absence for which no scientific discovery could compensate. 'I wish there were any process, electric, galvanic, or through any other medium, by which we might recover some of the fine feelings which age is so apt to blunt: it would be the true secret of growing young.'[12]

Although Barbauld believed her voice was muted her books continued to sell. Her popularity can be glimpsed not only in the number of editions Johnson issued of *Lessons for Children* and her other nursery staples, but in the way those in Johnson's circle talked of her work. When Godwin travelled to Ireland in 1800, leaving his small daughter and stepdaughter in the care of his friend James Marshall, he explained that he would soon return through a reference he knew the children would understand. 'My visit to Ireland is almost done', he promised. 'Perhaps I shall be upon the sea in a ship, the very moment Marsh{a}l is reading the letter to you. There is about going in a ship in Mrs Barbauld's book.'[13] Both Johnson and his fellow bookseller Richard Phillips also insisted that Barbauld had more to say. In 1804 Phillips contracted her to write and edit a life and letters of Samuel Richardson; in the same year Johnson commissioned her to produce a three-volume selection from the *Tatler* and *Spectator*. She continued to call occasionally on Johnson but domestic strains made excursions difficult. Her husband Rochemont had suffered from mental illness for many years and in 1808 he attacked her with a knife during a fit of mania. She was forced to take refuge with her brother, while her family found a house for Rochemont and a servant (whom Barbauld's niece termed a 'keeper') adjacent to that of his adopted son Charles.[14] Within a short space of time Rochemont had paid his keeper to allow him to leave the house alone and he drowned himself in the New River.

Theophilus Lindsey also died in 1808. He was eighty-five and his end came at home in Essex Street, in the house he and Hannah had built. It was only in the final week of his life that Lindsey was no longer able to make his daily progression to the chair in his study and Hannah told friends that he retained his faculties to the end. On the day he died his speech became imperfect as he uttered the same phrase to Hannah over and over again: 'My Love'.[15] At the end of the year Johnson published Thomas Belsham's sermon on the death of Lindsey, alongside a brief biographical memoir. In his sermon Belsham returned to Lindsey's own words in his *Farewell Address* to the people of Catterick. Lindsey and Belsham spoke for the generation of Dissenting men and women who had suffered for their faith and found it unshakeable. To Lindsey and Hannah, and to Belsham and Johnson, death was not an ending but a stage in a story. 'It is of small concern in what outward circumstances we pass over the short term of life', said Lindsey in 1774, in words Belsham quoted. The manner of death mattered little 'if we can but obtain that blessed approbation in the end, *Well done, good and faithful servant, enter thou into the joy of thy Lord.*'[16]

✠

Johnson's letters from 1805 onwards were the letters of a man who knew that his body was failing. In August that year he declined an invitation on the grounds that 'asthma will not suffer me to go near the sea'.[17] In April 1806 he told a correspondent that he had 'been confined nearly a month' at his house in Fulham.[18] During the period in which he was housebound he told the bookseller Daniel Isaac Eaton that he felt 'the infirmities of Age.'[19] His acerbity did not diminish as he contemplated the prospect of his own death. 'Dispatch is very desirable', he told a desultory fellow publisher. 'I wish to live to see this impression sold.'[20]

For much of 1809 the long-established rhythms of Johnson's life appeared to be uninterrupted. Godwin recorded dinners at St Paul's Churchyard; Johnson continued to advise him about his business affairs. But around the edges there were differences. Farington reported that Fuseli was turning down dinner invitations in order to honour his commitment to dine with Johnson, and when spring came and Johnson retreated to Fulham Fuseli followed him there. Farington wrote admiringly of the physical feat Fuseli's relocation entailed. 'He rose there at 5 this morning, & walked to Somerset House before 7 o'Clock. He said his usual Hour of going to bed when in London is 12 o'Clock at the soonest, often later, as He prefers the night hours for study.'[21] Farington made this diary entry in May; in July the same observation was reported. 'Fuseli told me that He rose this morning at 5 o'Clock & walked from Johnson's House at Fulham, & was at the Academy door at 7 o'Clock & did not feel more than very slightly any fatigue from it.'[22] Fuseli was still a figure of fascination to many of those with whom he came into contact. At the end of 1808 the young artist Benjamin Haydon was delighted to find he had briefly attracted Fuseli's notice. 'When Fuzeli dies, where shall I meet "his like again"?'[23] Johnson himself remained constant in his admiration for Fuseli's mind and work. When Fuseli dallied over the manuscript of a history of painting Johnson told him to increase his work rate. Johnson 'urges for the completion', Farington noted, 'as otherwise He may die before it is finished.'[24]

Throughout 1809 Johnson worked. He continued to take an interest in the fortunes of the London Institution, an early precursor of the University of London devoted to making a scientific education available to citizens of the capital. Johnson was a founder member of the Institution when it opened in 1805 and his involvement testifies to his lifelong commitment to making knowledge available to as many people as possible. He saw the work of Maria and Richard Lovell Edgeworth move through the press and he corresponded with Hayley about a new edition of Cowper's poems. On November 29th he wrote to the chemist William Henry about a new edition of Henry's *Elements of Experimental Chemistry*, as well as about a popular, inexpensive edition of Davy's *Elements of Chemical Philosophy*. His letter to Henry seamlessly combined the personal and the professional. 'I strongly suspect', it opened, 'that I am indebted to your father for a most excellent cheese, & beg you will return him my thanks.' Johnson went on to advise Henry about the corrections needed for his book. 'Let me recommend it to you not to draw up an Appendix but to correct your book throughout.' It was a suggestion motivated by the principle that had underlined his whole career. 'My wish constantly is to give an edition of a book in the best state [it] can be done at the time.'[25]

On December 18th 1809 Godwin called on Johnson twice and was told he was not at home. He called again a day later and received the same answer. Inside the house Johnson was fighting for air. He asked John Miles to read him the most recent letter from Maria Edgeworth and in a series of laboured breaths began to dictate a reply. 'My uncle is so afflicted with spasms & asthmas that he has desired me to acknowledge the rect of your and Mr E's letter. He desires me to say that he should ill deserve the confidence of Miss Edgeworth if he were rigidly to adhere to the contract which he made for her last work Tales of Fashionable Life the sale of which has enabled him to add to the original purchase money four hundred and fifty pounds and place the same to the credit of her account.'[26] It was a characteristic gesture: a punctilious reapportioning of profit according to the principles, as Johnson saw them, of natural justice. On December 20th one of the inhabitants of St Paul's Churchyard sent a message to Fuseli asking him to come to Johnson without delay. As Fuseli raced to a waiting hackney carriage he caught sight of his doctor friend John Carrick Moore, who he swept into the coach alongside him. Fuseli subsequently told John Knowles that when they arrived they found Johnson struggling for breath, with a hardly perceptible pulse. He recognised Fuseli and appeared glad of his presence. 'But', Knowles reported, 'no means which were tried could restore the sinking energies of the vital functions.'[27] Shortly after Fuseli and Moore arrived Johnson died, surrounded by his oldest friend and his nephews.

+

'Joseph Johnson dies', wrote Godwin in his diary for December 20th. A day later Godwin published a short notice of Johnson's death in the *Morning Chronicle*. He captured Johnson with a simplicity that transcended the formal rituals of posthumous praise. Johnson, Godwin wrote, 'was a man of generous, candid, and liberal mind; he delighted in doing good.' He paid tribute too to the 'integrity and clearness' of Johnson's views. 'Though he was the very reverse of every thing assuming and ostentatious, yet those who knew him best, and were most able to estimate his talents, will readily bear testimony, that they never heard him say a weak or a foolish thing.'[28] John Aikin also wrote an obituary of Johnson, for the *Gentleman's Magazine*. There he told the story of Johnson's Baptist origins in Liverpool; his apprenticeship under George Keith, his early endeavours in the trade and the fire of 1770 from which he rebuilt his life. Johnson's list, he wrote, spoke for his talents. 'Many of the most distinguished names in Science and Literature during the last half century appear in works which he ushered to the world.' Aikin described his friend as the possessor 'of a temper the reverse of sanguine, with a manner somewhat cold and indifferent, and with a decided aversion to all arts of puffing and parade.' Johnson's refusal to flatter, however, meant that 'the confidence and attachment he inspired were entirely the result of his solid judgement, his unaffected sincerity, and the friendly benevolence with which he entered into the interests of all who were connected with him.' When Aikin looked at Johnson's life it was the bookseller's kindness that struck him most forcefully. 'His house and purse were always open to the calls of friendship, kindred, or misfortune; and perhaps few men of his means and condition have done more substantial services to persons whose merits and necessities recommended them to his notice.'[29]

On December 29th Godwin was present as Johnson was buried in the churchyard of All Saints, Fulham. Fuseli was there; so were Bonnycastle, Knowles and Fuseli's engraver Moses Haughton, who created the only surviving image of Johnson. Johnson's family organised the erection of a grand tomb and Fuseli provided the epigraph. 'Here lie the remains of Joseph Johnson, late of St Pauls, London, who departed this life on the 20th day of December, 1809, aged 72 years.' In words chiselled on stone, now rendered illegible by two centuries of weather and pollution, Fuseli described Johnson as 'a man equally distinguished by probity, industry, and disinterestedness in his intercourse with the public, and very domestic and social virtue in life; beneficent without ostentation, ever ready to produce merit and to relieve distress; unassuming in prosperity, not appalled by misfortune; inexorable to his own, indulgent to the wants of others; resigned and cheerful under the torture of a malady which he saw gradually destroy his life'.[30]

As the news of Johnson's death spread, those who had gathered at St Paul's Churchyard turned to paper to consider the man who had brought them together. At the beginning of January 1810 Humphry Davy reported 'a great loss indeed in Mr Johnson. There never lived a more amiable or honorable Man.'[31] From Ireland Maria Edgeworth relayed the news of Johnson's death to her Aunt Ruxton in terms that conveyed the subtle class distinctions which saw Johnson always stand slightly apart from some of those who frequented his house. Edgeworth told Mrs Ruxton the details of Johnson's final act of generosity. 'I know you well enough my dear to be certain that this conduct will touch you; tho' it is as some fine folk would say only a bookseller that you will think the person who was capable of it fully worthy of the title of friend – I wish in the highest ranks of life we could always see such generous conduct & such honourable principles.'[32] Two weeks later Edgeworth wrote again with the news that 'poor good Johnson' had died, according to John Miles, 'worth over 50 thousand pounds.' Edgeworth's view was that Johnson was worthy of his riches. 'I wish he had a million of money I am sure he deserved it.'[33] To Anna Barbauld Edgeworth also wrote with the same combination of personal regret, financial speculation and condescension. 'What a loss, what an irreparable loss we have had of our excellent friend Johnson.... I am glad to hear that Johnson's habits of liberality did not injure his fortune, and that his property descends to a representative so worthy of him as Mr Miles.' Edgeworth also thought there was much to admire in Miles's conduct towards Johnson's authors. 'I know', she told Barbauld, 'you have pleasure in hearing of instances of virtue in whatever class or rank of life.'[34]

When Hannah Lindsey wrote of Johnson's death to a friend in March 1810 she assumed that Rowland Hunter and John Miles would inherit the business 'with the ample fortune he has left them.'[35] Miles and Hunter did continue where Johnson had left off, and for a period Godwin and others kept up their habit of weekly dining at St Paul's Churchyard. In May, however, Johnson's will was still unproved as a dispute broke out between rival members of the younger generations of his family about which of two existing versions of the will should be preferred.

The disputed version of the will no longer exists and eventually Johnson's three executors – Rowland Hunter, John Miles and Joseph Johnson the Younger – agreed to vote in favour of the document now on file at the National Archives. Johnson's will offers a rare glimpse into the world he created, as well as a portrait of the people he valued. By the time his will was proved one of his instructions had already been disregarded: 'I desire to be quietly and privately buried where my Executors may assert without funeral pomp.' Joseph Johnson the Younger was left ten thousand pounds; so was his sister, Mary Miles (the mother of John). John Miles received 'all the plate – furniture – Liquors and a portrait of Dr Priestley by Fuseli – in my dwelling house in St Paul's Church Yard also the lease of my house at Purser's Cross Fulham with the furniture – plate – Linen & books and Liquors therein.'

Rowland Hunter 'who has long lived with me' received the 'lease of my dwelling house in St Pauls Church Yard also the lease of a small house and adjoining to it also the stock in trade and fixtures in the first mentioned lease' as well as the lease and contents of a separate warehouse. Rowland's siblings Roger and Elizabeth (the latter of whom had kept house for Johnson in the 1780s and '90s) received £100 each and the comparative smallness of the sum left to Elizabeth suggests that she may have married after she left St Paul's Churchyard and that Johnson considered her comfortably settled. Hester's widower Henry received an annuity of £60. Priestley's son Joseph received £100 and John Opie's portrait of his father, which he was directed to present 'to an American College or Institution for promoting knowledge.' Fuseli and Bonnycastle both received annuities of £50 each;

other authors whose accounts were unsettled received small annuities in lieu of payment for their works. Godwin had his bond for £200 returned to him 'for the use of Fanny Imlay who is under his care'; John Aikin, Anna Barbauld and Maria Edgeworth all received £50. There were small sums for local bookbinders and an annuity of £10 'to my late housekeeper Nancy Lovell'. Two unnamed servants living with Johnson received 'twenty pounds on condition that they put the same out to interest and which I direct my Executors to do for them.'

Johnson's residual estate was to be divided between John Miles, Rowland Hunter, Mary Miles and Joseph Johnson the Younger. Mary Miles and Joseph Johnson received a fifth each and Miles and Hunter shared the remainder 'for the trouble they will have in settling my accounts.'[36] After the will was proved John Miles attempted to wrest control of the estate from his cousins and a long-running argument broke out about the manner in which the annuities of Fuseli and Bonnycastle were to be paid. Fuseli, who by common consent was thought to know more about the wishes of Johnson's heart than any other individual, had spoken in favour of the proved version of the will, but in order for his evidence to be accepted he was obliged to relinquish his own claim on the estate. Joseph Johnson the Younger insisted on Fuseli's right to be paid in spite of the legal manoeuvring necessary to prove the will and in 1817, when the estate was still unsettled, he published the rancorous correspondence between himself, Miles, Fuseli, Bonnycastle and John Knowles as a precursor to a lawsuit against Miles. Rowland Hunter attempted to act as peacemaker in the dispute but in 1815 he and Miles ended their partnership as family loyalty crumbled under the pressure of inherited wealth. Without Johnson to sustain the connections between the men and women he had brought together, the community at St Paul's Churchyard could not survive. Within a few years of his death it had disintegrated completely.

By 1816 Rowland had married and moved his own family to Hampstead Heath, leaving the old house at St Paul's Churchyard standing empty. Rowland's wife had two daughters from a previous marriage, Marianne and Elizabeth. In the summer of 1809 Marianne married a young journalist called Leigh Hunt, who came to dinner at St Paul's Churchyard shortly before Johnson died and then again during the period when Rowland attempted to hold the household together. It is thanks to Hunt that we know that Bonnycastle 'goggled over his plate, like a horse' and it is also thanks to Hunt that it is still possible to hear Fuseli's voice among the snatches of conversation in Johnson's dining room. 'I remember, one day', he wrote, 'Bonnycastle told a story of a Frenchman, whom he had received at his house at Woolwich, and who invited him in return to visit him in Paris.' The anecdote continued with Bonnycastle talking:

The Frenchman told me,' said he, 'that he had a superb local. When I went to Paris I called on him, and found he had a good prospect out of his window; but his superb local was at a hair-dresser's, up two pair of stairs.' 'Vell, vell!' said Fuseli impatiently, (for, though he spoke and wrote English remarkably well, he never got rid of his Swiss pronunciation) – 'Vell – vay not – vay not – Vat is to hinder his local being superb for all thtat?' 'I don't see,' returned Bonnycastle, 'how a barber's in an alley can be a superb local.' 'You doan't! Vell – but thtat is not ththe barber's fault – It is your's.' 'How do you make that out? I'm not an alley.' 'No; but you're coarsedly eegnorant.[37]

In the 1810s Hunt, like Johnson before him, went to prison for libel. The independent ideals of the *Analytical Review* were reborn in Hunt's newspaper, the *Examiner*, although the vision of Europe offered by Hunt's publication was constrained by the continuance of war. Hunt took inspiration from Johnson in other ways too, as he gathered around him some of the brightest figures in the literary landscape of the 1810s. The gatherings Hunt held in his own prison cell, and subsequently at his cottage in Hampstead, reawakened the spirit of the dining room at St Paul's Churchyard, a place in which conversation had the power to remake the world.

⁜

Many of the ideals for which Johnson and his writers worked came to fruition in the decades following his death. The labour of Lindsey's life had its reward in 1828, with the Repeal of the Test and Corporation Acts, a legal watershed that paved the way for Catholic Emancipation a year later. Paine's ideas were taken up by the Chartist movement in the 1830s and '40s, in response to the failure of the 1832 Reform Act to produce universal manhood suffrage. Priestley's work on air laid the foundations for the endeavours of the men who described oxygen; Darwin's proto-evolutionary theories were given substance by his grandson Charles. Barbauld and Edgeworth's insistence on the rights of children echoed through the celebration of the child-reader in the Golden Age literature of the second half of the nineteenth century, as well as in successive reforms to child-labour laws that took place between 1833 and 1867. Sarah Trimmer's work on Sunday schools had a similar effect through a different political trajectory: her campaign for mass Sunday school education culminated in the Education Act of 1870. In the early twentieth century Wollstonecraft's work was rediscovered by the suffragists and, subsequently, by successive generations of feminists who responded powerfully to her articulation of the structural and societal consequences of the disempowerment of women. By the late nineteenth century the young poets whom Johnson had encouraged were recognised as the figures who reshaped the literary landscape of their age; Cowper faded from view. Fuseli's art also fell out of fashion, although his *Nightmare* endured. 'Blake the engraver' became Blake the poet and artist, his reputation waxing as Fuseli's waned.

Between 1760 and 1809 Johnson charted a revolution in ideas, not by chiselling through layers of rock but by printing lines on paper. In his dining room and in the books, pamphlets, tracts, journals and images he published he created a space for new ideas to emerge about childhood, the position of women, religious freedom, science, medicine, Europe, poetry, and domestic and international politics. In the manner in which he worked he was in every respect a man of his time, an upstanding figure who lived as he believed others should. But through the ideas he captured he remains a man for our time too. In his house and dining room he created a family tied by loyalty rather than blood. His story reveals, again and again, the kinship of friends who catch each other when they fall. In actions rather than words he demonstrated the power of kindness and community to challenge systems of social control founded on separateness and division. He worked for a world in which children are recognised as reasonable creatures, entitled to an education and a childhood; and in which professional women are unconstrained by reactionary vitriol. He celebrated a vision of an interconnected Europe and of the nation as more than its politics. He gave space to poets and artists who found new ways of seeing, and to scientists and doctors who saw beauty in new forms of knowledge. He leaves us all this in the conversations he created and the books he made.

Afterword

In January 2020 I sent a first draft of *Dinner with Joseph Johnson* to three brilliant women: Clare Alexander, Clara Farmer and Jenny Uglow. Two weeks later I fainted while at home in Exeter, hitting my head as I fell. I am writing this afterword over a year later, as I continue to navigate a winding path out of what Susan Sontag memorably characterised as 'the kingdom of the ill'. 'Illness', Sontag wrote in 1978, 'is *not* a metaphor, and ... the most truthful way of regarding illness – and the healthiest way of being ill – is one most purified of, most resistant to, metaphoric thinking.'[1]

Two months after I hit my head Britain shut down in response to Covid-19. My children's school closed and their education as well as their health and happiness became a responsibility my husband and I shared not with the State, but with each other only. In Oxford my father, Michael Hay, was locked down in the care home in which he had become resident several years earlier, after he developed Progressive Supranuclear Palsy (a rare neurodegenerative disease) while still in his early sixties. Throughout the spring, summer and autumn of 2020, my mother, sister and I were able to see my father only on an iPad or through a fence. This remained the case until the end of the year when, following a Covid outbreak at the care home, we were allowed to don PPE and sit with him on the December Wednesday on which he died.

My father started his career as a scholar of the eighteenth century. At York University in the 1970s he wrote a DPhil thesis on approaches to mental illness between 1650 and 1800. In his thesis he drew on John Aikin's *Thoughts on Hospitals* (published by Johnson in 1771) to explore the structures of care eighteenth-century physicians built around those suffering from maladies that, like his own illness, damaged or destroyed the brain. He subsequently became a publisher and then a university teacher, whose later work was dedicated to social justice and the eradication of poverty.

Afterword

His influence is everywhere in this book. I share my story of the past year here to honour that influence, and to articulate the ways in which *Dinner with Joseph Johnson* has become, over the past seven years, the most personal book I have written. During the period I have spent in Johnson's company, a period in which my family has simultaneously charted the complex terrain of my father's illness, I have thought a great deal about how to make sense of a life when an individual falls silent amidst those to whom he or she has given voice. In the company of my mother and sister I have confronted the limits of medical science, and gained new appreciation for the work of the doctors who are attempting to push beyond the boundaries of knowledge to a greater understanding of the mysteries – and frailties – of the human frame. In the same period I have given birth to a daughter and watched my son became a reader and writer. I have learnt anew the wisdom of Johnson's insistence that the character of a country can be divined through the seriousness with which it treats the minds of its children. Along with countless others I have contemplated national borders, and I have found in the work of Johnson and his writers a vision of the nation among many in which the free exchange of people and ideas matters more than the creation of new barriers. Rendered stationary by my own illness and the virus that has circled the planet, I have remained at home, and as the boundaries between home and work have collapsed I have been reminded again and again of the exceptional good fortune represented by a house that is also a sanctuary. I have been compelled to no longer take my ability to read and write for granted, and, as a result, have learnt anew that access to the world of print is truly a life-enhancing right and privilege.

Above all, I have learnt the truth of a metaphor I reached for lightly at the end of this book before my accident, when I wrote that Johnson's story 'reveals, again and again, the kinship of friends who catch each other when they fall'. Since my own non-metaphorical fall I have experienced this kinship in ways that have led me towards a new understanding about what constitutes family. To the friends who caught me therefore go my first thanks. In Exeter those friends include, in particular, Sara Gibbs, Sally Hedge, Lucy Powell, Emma Roberts and Mary Woodgate, as well as the many other wonderful women in our village in the city alongside whom I talk and walk and swim and bring up children. Further afield the friendship of the women with whom I have charted my adulthood has sustained me over the past year and for many years before that, and for that I name and thank Eleni Bide, Helen Ewen, Jo Kay, Polly Mackenzie, Ali Russell and

Afterword

Lucy Topping. I know that none of them will mind if I also say that without Aoife Ní Luanaigh the past year would have been immeasurably harder, and that I cannot thank her enough for her support. The same is true of Alexandra Harris, best of friends and readers, who, among much else, kept me thinking and talking about books during the period following my injury when I could not myself read.

For the past twenty years or so students at the University of Exeter have had as their informal catchphrase a line purloined from the world of advertising: 'probably the best university in the world'. I can say without a doubt that, in the Department of English and Film, I have the best colleagues in the world. For the friendship and support of those colleagues at all times, but particularly since my accident, I am beyond grateful. It feels invidious to single out individuals within a community characterised by solidarity, but I nevertheless want to record particular thanks to Pascale Aebischer, Joe Crawford, Jane Feaver, Felicity Gee, Helen Hanson, Johanna Harris, Felicity Henderson, Eddie Jones, Kirsty Martin, Andrew McRae, Ellen McWilliams, Kate Montague, Sinéad Moynihan, Vike Martina Plock, Henry Power, Andrew Rudd, Laura Salisbury, Philip Schwyzer, Jane Spencer, Mark Steven and Tricia Zakreski. To the many inspiring students who have patiently listened to me talk about Johnson over the years I also offer my appreciation and my thanks. Research for this book was made possible by a period of internally funded research leave in 2015, and through the award of a Philip Leverhulme Prize in 2016. For both I am exceptionally grateful, and my thanks for the time to think and write go accordingly to the College of Humanities at the University of Exeter, and to the Leverhulme Trust.

I am grateful to the many scholars whose ideas and expertise have contributed to this book. I have indicated specific acknowledgements in the Notes, but here I want to record in particular my indebtedness to the work of Helen Braithwaite, Leslie Chard, Marilyn Gaull, James Raven, Gerald Tyson and John Barrell. I also want to thank John Bugg for both his superlative edition of Johnson's *Letterbook* and for the transatlantic colleagiality that has characterised our conversations. My thanks for assistance with particular questions go too to John Barnard, Kate Bostock, Pamela Clemit, Emma Clery, Mary Ann Constantine, Nora Crook, Elizabeth Edwards, Mary Fairclough, Rachel Hewitt, Katherine Ibbett, Felicity James, Louise Joy, Valerie Pakenham, James Raven, Sharon Ruston, Matthew Sangster and James Vigus. I will be for ever grateful for the kindness and technological genius of Charlotte Tupman, who brought all her wizardry to the taming of the English Short Title Catalogue, and to two exceptional Exeter students: Madeleine Perry, who translated the German letters of Henry Fuseli, and Katie Snow, who undertook the laborious task of reference checking on my behalf. Hermione Lee has been a beacon of encouragement in both action and example, and I feel very fortunate to be the recipient of her friendship and support. I am grateful to all at Chatto & Windus, and owe a particular debt to Charlotte Humphery and Mary Chamberlain for their meticulous and generous work as the book went into production, and to Vicki Robinson who made the index.

I have been helped throughout my research by librarians and archivists all over the United Kingdom and beyond. My thanks go to the staff of the Guildhall Library, Dr Williams's Library, the British Library, the Bodleian Library, the National Library of Scotland, Liverpool Record Office, the National Archives, the Hackney Archives, the Wren Library at Trinity College Cambridge, the National Library of Ireland, the Huntington Library and the Royal Society. All mistakes are, of course, my own. For permission to quote from manuscript material I gratefully acknowledge the Royal Literary Fund, the trustees of Dr Williams's Trust and Library, Liverpool Record Office, the British Library (correspondence of Sarah Trimmer and the Revolution Society Minute Book), Bodleian Libraries, Oxford and The Master and Fellows of Trinity College, Cambridge. Manuscript material relating to Richard Lovell and Maria Edgeworth is quoted courtesy of the National Library of Ireland.

At various stages in its long gestation this book has been read in draft by my agent, Clare Alexander, my publisher, Clara Farmer, and by Helena Drysdale, Jane Feaver, Alexandra Harris, Amanda Mackenzie Stuart, Lucy Powell, Jane Spencer and Jenny Uglow. At late notice and with huge generosity, Emma Clery scrutinised a set of proofs, endowing the final stages of work on the manuscript with all her scholarly acumen and energy. The imagination, precision and thoughtfulness of all these readers has kept this project alive, including during the periods when I was not able to work. For their time and effort I am more grateful than I can say. Clara Farmer and Clare Alexander have shown nothing but kindness and understanding in response to the long delays that have characterised the later stages of my work. Their patience has made it possible to bring this book to fruition. Jenny Uglow has been my heroine since I first read The Lunar Men in my teens and I still find it hard to believe that I have been accorded the privilege of her intellectual companionship. At the beginning of this book

I suggested that Johnson's professional and personal life was characterised by generosity, and by his belief that acts of kindness contained within them political and ethical significance. My own experiences, as well as the national story that has unfolded over the past year, have only left me more convinced of the truth underpinning that belief.

Kindness is one word that runs through Johnson's story. It has its active counterpart in 'care': another word that characterised his mode of being and which has taken on new significance in public conversation since the advent of Covid-19. The care I have received from my family has made every sentence of *Dinner with Joseph Johnson* possible. For the unstinting support of Paul and Vron Santer I record heartfelt acknowledgement. For the black-humoured magnificence and foul-weather companionship of my sister and mother, Marianna Hay and Amanda Mackenzie Stuart, I give thanks every day. We all know how lucky we are to have with us the gifts my father leaves us. This book is dedicated to his memory. It is also dedicated to my children, Freddy and Eloise, with love and gratitude for the joy they bring to our present and for the promise they bring to the future. Finally, at the end of this long book about words, I am compelled to confront the reality that there are not words enough to describe all that Matthew Santer means and gives to me, or to express the gratitude I feel for the life we have made together. To him instead I can only offer my love.

Bibliography

Primary Reading

Manuscripts and Archives

The Abinger Papers, Oxford, Bodleian Libraries
Aikin Papers, Hackney Archives
Anna Letitia Barbauld Papers, Huntington Library, San Marino, California
Edgeworth Papers, National Library of Ireland
Henry Crabb Robinson Papers, Dr Williams's Library
John Murray Archive, National Library of Scotland
Joseph Priestley Papers, Dr Williams's Library
Joseph Priestley Papers, Royal Society
King's Bench Prison Committal Records, National Archives
Musicians Company Account Book, Guildhall Library
Probate Records, National Archives
Revolution Society Minute Book, British Library
Roscoe Papers, Liverpool Record Office, Liverpool Libraries
Rothschild Collection, Wren Library, Trinity College, Cambridge
Royal Literary Fund Archive, British Library
Sarah Trimmer Correspondence, British Library
Theophilus Lindsey Papers, Dr Williams's Library
Treasury Solicitor Records, National Archives
Underhill Papers, Liverpool Record Office, Liverpool Libraries

Online Archival Resources

Anna Letitia Barbauld Letters to Lydia Rickards, 1798–1815, ed. William
    McCarthy, Romantic Circles
British History Online
Darwin Correspondence Project

Bibliography

Franklin Papers
Joel Barlow Papers, Harvard Library
The Letters of Joseph Priestley to Theophilus Lindsey 1769–94, Queen Mary Centre for Religion and Literature in English
William Godwin's Diary, Bodleian Library

Newspapers and Periodicals

Aldine Magazine
The Analytical Review
Annual Bibliography and Obituary
Anti-Jacobin Review
Critical Review
Gazetteer and New Daily Advertiser
General Evening Post
Gentleman's Magazine
Middlesex Journal or Chronicle of Liberty
The Monthly Magazine
Monthly Review
The Times

Books

Abercrombie, John, *Every Man his Own Gardener* (London: S. Crowder, G. Robinson, W. Goldsmith, J. Johnson, F. Newberry, T. Cadell, T. Evans and W. Davis, 1779).

Aikin, John, *An Address to the Dissidents of England on their Late Defeat* (London: J. Johnson, 1790).

— 'Joseph Johnson', *Gentleman's Magazine*, December 1809, repr. in Edward L. Hard., ed., *Minor Lives: A Collection of Biographies by John Nichols* (Cambridge, MA: Harvard University Press, 1970), pp. 282–6.

— *Thoughts on Hospitals* (London: J. Johnson, 1771).

Aikin, John, and Anna Letitia Barbauld, *Evenings at Home: or, The Juvenile Budget Opened, Consisting of A Variety of Miscellaneous Pieces, For the Instruction and Amusement of Young Persons*, 6 vols (London: J. Johnson, 1792).

— *Miscellaneous Pieces, in Prose* (London: J. Johnson, 1773).

Anon., *Appeal to the Men of Great Britain in Behalf of Women* (London: J. Johnson, 1798).

Anon., *The Debtor and Creditor's Assistant; or, A Key to the King's Bench and Fleet Prisons; Calculated For the Information and Benefit of the Injured Creditor as well as the Unfortunate Debtor: Including Newgate, Ludgate, and the Three Compters. To which are added Reflections on Perpetual Imprisonment for Debt; and Outlines of a Bill for Abolishing the Same* (London: G. Riley, 1793).

Anon., *A Defence of the Act of Parliament Lately Passed for the Relief of Roman Catholics* (London: J. Johnson, 1780).

Anon., *A Defence of the Reverend Theophilus Lindsey from the Attack of William Burgh, Esq., Interspersed with Remarks on Church Authority, on Reason as the Judge, and Self-denial as the Test, of Religious Truth, in Opposition to Him* (London: J. Johnson, 1778).

Anon., *Essays Commercial and Political, on the Real and Relative Interests of Imperial and Dependent States, Particularly those of Great Britain and her Dependencies: Displaying the Probable Causes of, and a Mode of Comprising the Present Disputes Between this Country and her American Colonies* (London: J. Johnson, 1777).

Anon., *The Laws Respecting Women* (London: J. Johnson, 1777).

Anon., *New Discoveries Concerning the World, and its Inhabitants. In Two Parts* (London: J. Johnson, 1778).

Anon., *Observations on the Character and Conduct of a Physician, in Twenty Letters to a Friend* (London: J. Johnson, 1772).

Anon., *A Plan of Reconciliation between Britain and her Colonies* (London: J. Johnson and P. Elmsly, 1776).

Anon., *Reflections on Mr Lindsey's Apology* (London: G. Keith, 1774).

Anon., *The Scripture Doctrine of the Trinity Justified* (n.p., 1774).

Anon., *Views of the Ruins of the Principal Houses Destroyed During the Riots at Birmingham*. Plates engraved by William Ellis after drawings by P. H. Whitton (London: J. Johnson, 1792).

Austin, William, *Letters from London, Written During the Years 1802 and 1803* (Boston, MA: W. Pelham, 1804).

Barbauld, Anna Letitia, *An Address to the Opposers of the Repeal of the Corporation and Test Acts* (London: J. Johnson, 1790).

— *Devotional Pieces* (London: J. Johnson, 1775).

— *A Legacy for Young Ladies, Consisting of Miscellaneous Pieces in Prose and Verse*, ed. Lucy Aikin (London: Longman, Hurst, Rees, Orme, Brown, and Green, 1826).

— *Lessons for Children from Two to Three Years Old* (London: J. Johnson, 1778).

Bibliography

— *Poems* (London: J. Johnson, 1773).

— *Poems*, ed. William McCarthy and Elizabeth Kraft (Athens, Georgia: University of Georgia Press, 1994).

— *Selected Poetry and Prose*, ed. William McCarthy and Elizabeth Kraft (Peterborough, ON: Broadview Literary Press, 2001).

— *Sins of Government, Sins of the Nation; or, A Discourse for the Fast, Appointed on April 19, 1793* (London: J. Johnson, 1793).

— *Works*, ed. Lucy Aikin, 2 vols (London: Longman, Hurst, Rees, Orme, Brown, and Green, 1825).

Barlow, Joel, *Advice to the Privileged Orders* (London: J. Johnson, 1792).

— *The Conspiracy of Kings: A Poem* (London: J. Johnson, 1792).

Barrell, John, and Jon Mee, eds, *Trials for Treason and Sedition, 1792–1794*, 8 vols (Abingdon: Routledge, 2016; first published 2006 by Pickering and Chatto).

Beaume, Antoine, *Manual of Chemistry*, trans. John Aikin (Warrington: printed by W. Eyres for J. Johnson, 1778).

Beloe, William, *Sexagenarian: Recollections of a Literary Life* (London: F. C. and J. Rivington, 1817).

Belsham, Thomas, *Memoirs of the Late Reverend Theophilus Lindsey* (London: Williams and Norgate, 1873).

— *A Sermon Occasioned by the Death of the Rev. Theophilus Lindsey, M.A., Preached at the Chapel in Essex Street, Strand, November 13th, 1808: To Which is Added a Brief Biographical Memoir* (London: J. Johnson, 1808).

Blackburne, Francis, *Works, Theological and Miscellaneous*, 7 vols (Cambridge: B. Flower, 1804).

Blake, William, *Complete Poetry and Prose*, ed. David Erdman (Berkeley, CA: University of California Press, 2008; first published 1965).

Bonnycastle, John, *An Introduction to Astronomy* (London: J. Johnson, 1786).

— *The Scholar's Guide to Arithmetic* (London: J. Johnson, 1780).

Burgh, William, *A Spiritual Confutation of the Arguments Against the One Godhead of the Father, Son, and Holy Ghost, Produced by The Reverend Mr Lindsey in his late Apology, by a Layman* (London: W. Nicoll, 1774).

Burke, Edmund, *Correspondence (July 1768–June 1774)*, ed. Lucy S. Sutherland (Cambridge: Cambridge University Press, 1960).

— *Reflections on the Revolution in France and on the Proceedings in Certain Societies in London Relative to that Event*, ed. Conor Cruise O'Brien (Harmondsworth: Penguin, 1982; first published 1790).

Cappe, Catharine, *Memoirs of the Late Mrs Catharine Cappe* (Boston, MA: Wells and Lilly, 1824).

Coleridge, Samuel Taylor, *Collected Letters*, ed. Earl Leslie Griggs, 2 vols (Oxford: Clarendon Press, 1956).

— *Fears in Solitude* (London: J. Johnson, 1793).

— *The Major Works*, ed. H. J. Jackson (Oxford: Oxford University Press, 1985).

Collins, John, *The Case of the Sugar Colonies* (London: J. Johnson, 1793).

Constable, Thomas, *Archibald Constable and his Literary Correspondents; A Memorial* (Edinburgh: Edmonston and Douglas, 1873).

Cowden Clarke, Charles and Mary, *Recollections of Writers* (London: Sampson Low, Marston, Searle, & Rivington, 1878).

Cowper, William, *The Letters and Prose Writings of William Cowper*, ed. James King and Charles Ryskamp, 5 vols (Oxford: Clarendon Press, 1979–86).

— *The Poems of William Cowper*, ed. John D. Baird and Charles Ryskamp, 3 vols (Oxford: Oxford University Press, 2014; first published 1980). Oxford Scholarly Editions Online.

Darwin, Erasmus, *The Botanic Garden* (London: J. Johnson, 1791).

— *Collected Letters of Erasmus Darwin*, ed. Desmond King-Hele (Cambridge: Cambridge University Press, 2006).

— *Zoonomia; or, The Laws of Organic Life*, 2 vols (London: J. Johnson, 1794–6).

Davy, Humphry, *The Collected Letters of Sir Humphry Davy*, ed. Tim Fulford and Sharon Ruston, advisory eds Jan Golkinski, Frank A. J. James and David Knight, assisted by Andrew Lacey, 4 vols (Oxford: Oxford University Press, 2020).

Dyer, George, *Poems* (London: J. Johnson, 1792).

Edgeworth, Frances Anne Beaufort, *A Memoir of Maria Edgeworth: With a Selection from her Letters*, 3 vols (London: J. Masters and Son, 1867).

Edgeworth, Maria, *Letters from Ireland*, ed. Valerie Pakenham (Dublin: The Lilliput Press, 2018).

— *Letters for Literary Ladies*, ed. Claire Connolly (Cardiff: University of Wales Press, 1993).

Edgeworth, Richard Lovell, *Essays on Professional Education* (London: J. Johnson, 1809).

Edgeworth, Richard Lovell and Maria, *Memoirs of Richard Lovell Edgeworth*, 2 vols (London: R. Hunter, 1820).

— *Practical Education*, 2 vols (London: J. Johnson, 1798).

Elliot, John, *The Medical Pocket-Book* (London: J. Johnson, 1781).

Equiano, Olaudah, *The Interesting Narrative of the Life of Olaudah Equiano, or Gustavus Vassa, The African, Written by Himself*, ed. Werner Sollors (New York, NY: W. W. Norton and Company, 2001; first published 1789).

Farington, Joseph, *The Diary of Joseph Farington*, ed. K. Garlick, A. Macintyre, K. Cave and E. Newby, 17 vols (New Haven, CT: Yale University Press, 1978–98).

Fordyce, George, *Elements of the Practice of Physic*, fifth edition (London: J. Johnson, 1784).

Fuseli, Henry, *Briefe*, ed. Walter Muschg (Klosterberg, Basel: Verlag Benno Schwabe & Co., 1942).

— *Collected English Letters*, ed. David Weinglass (Millwood, NY: Kraus International, 1982).

— *Remarks on the Writings and Conduct of J. J. Rousseau* (J. Johnson, 1767).

Gill, John, *An Exposition of the Book of Solomon's Song* (London: George Keith, 1765).

Glasse, Hannah, *The Art of Cookery, Made Plain and Easy* (London: W. Strahan, J. Rivington and Sons, S. Crowder, J. Hinton, J. Johnson, T. Longman, W. Owen, B. White, T. Caslon, J. Wilkie, J. Robson, G. Robinson, T. Cadell, T. Becket, W. Davies, J. Knox, W. Nicoll, T. Lowndes, R. Dymott, H. Gardner, B. Domville, J. Richardson, T. Durham, R. Baldwin, J. Bew, F. Newberry, W. Goldsmith, Fielding and Walker, J. Wallis and W. Fox, 1778).

Godwin, William, *Caleb Williams*, ed. Pamela Clemit in the *Collected Novels and Memoirs of William Godwin*, ed. Mark Philp (London: William Pickering, 1992).

— *Cursory Strictures on the Charge Delivered by Lord Chief Justice Eyre to the Grand Jury, October 2, 1794* (London: C. and G. Kearsley, 1794).

— 'Joseph Johnson', *Morning Chronicle*, 21 December 1809.

— *The Letters of William Godwin*, ed. Pamela Clemit, 2 vols to date (Oxford: Oxford University Press, 2011–).

— *Memoirs of the Author of A Vindication of the Rights of Woman* (London: J. Johnson and G. G. and J. Robinson, 1798).

Hanger, George, *The Life, Adventures, and Opinions of Col. George Hanger*, 2 vols (London: J. Debrett, 1801).

Harrison, R., *The Catholic Protestant, Part the Last and Third* (London: J. Johnson, 1780).

Haydon, Benjamin Robert, *The Diary of Benjamin Robert Haydon*, ed. Willard Bissell Pope (Cambridge, MA: Harvard University Press, 1960–63).

Hays, Mary, *The Correspondence (1779–1843) of Mary Hays, British Novelist*, ed. Marilyn L. Brooks (Lewiston: NY: The Edwin Mellen Press, 2004).

— *The Idea of Being Free: A Mary Hays Reader*, ed. Gina Luria Walker (Peterborough, ON: Broadview Press, 2005).

— *Letters and Essays, Moral, and Miscellaneous* (London: T. Knott, 1793).

— 'Memoirs of Mary Wollstonecraft' in *The Annual Necrology for 1797–8* (London: R. Phillips, 1800).

Hazlitt, William, *Complete Works*, ed. P. P. Howe (London: J. M. Dent, 1930–34).

— *Selected Essays*, ed. George Sampson (Cambridge: Cambridge University Press, 1917).

Hewlett, John, *Sermons on Different Subjects* (London: J. F. and C. Rivington, C. Dilly and J. Johnson, 1786).

Hewson, William, *Experimental Inquiries*, second edition (London: J. Johnson, 1774).

Holcroft, Thomas, *A Plain and Succinct Narrative of the Late Riots and Disturbances in the Cities of London and Westminster and Borough of Southwark* (London: Fielding and Walker, 1780).

Howell, T. B., ed., *A Complete Collection of State Trials and Proceedings for High Treason and Other Crimes and Misdemeanors*, 34 vols (London: T. C. Hansard for Longman, Hurst, Rees, Orme and Brown, 1816–28), Vol. XXII (1817).

Hunt, Leigh, *Lord Byron and Some of his Contemporaries* (London: Henry Colburn, 1828).

Hunter, Andrew, *Advice from a Father to a Son Just Entered into the Army and About to Go Abroad into Action* (London: J. Johnson, 1776).

Hunter, John, *The Natural History of Human Teeth*, second edition (London: J. Johnson, 1778).

Hurdis, James, *Letters of the Revd. James Hurdis, D.D., Vicar of Bishopstone, Sussex, to William Cowper, 1791–4. Reprinted from the 'Sussex Country Magazine', 1926–7.* (Eastbourne: T. R. Beckett, 1927).

Hutton, William, *The Life of William Hutton, Stationer, of Birmingham: And the History of his Family* (London: Charles Knight and Company, 1841).

Johnson, Joseph, *The Joseph Johnson Letterbook*, ed. John Bugg (Oxford: Oxford University Press, 2016).

— *New Books in Midwifery, Medicine, Experimental Philosophy and Topography* (London: J. Johnson, 1775).

Johnson Jr, Joseph, *References to the Case of Mr. Fuseli's Legacy. Under the Will of the Late Mr. Joseph Johnson, of St Paul's Churchyard* (Liverpool: F. B. Wright, 1817).

Lamb, Charles and Mary, *The Letters of Charles and Mary Lamb*, ed. Edwin Marrs, 2 vols (Ithaca: Cornell University Press, 1975).

Lavater, Johann Casper, *Aphorisms on Man*, trans. Henry Fuseli, third edition (London: J. Johnson, 1794).

Lavoisier, Antoine, *Essays Physical and Chemical*, trans. Thomas Henry (London: J. Johnson, 1776).

Le Breton, Anna, *Memoir of Mrs Barbauld, Including Letters and Notices of her Family and Friends* (London: George Bell and Sons, 1874).

— *Memories of Seventy Years, by one of a Literary Family* (London: Griffith & Farran, 1883).

Lindsey, Theophilus, *The Apology of Theophilus Lindsey, M.A., on Resigning the Vicarage of Catterick, Yorkshire*, with *Farewell Address to the People of Catterick* (London: J. Johnson, 1774).

— *Letters*, ed. G. M. Ditchfield, 2 vols (Woodbridge: The Boydell Press, 2007).

— *A Sermon Preached at the Opening of the Chapel in Essex-House, Essex-Street, in the Strand, on Sunday, April 17, 1774* (London: J. Johnson, 1774).

— *Vindiciae Priestleiane: An Address to the Students of Oxford and Cambridge* (London: J. Johnson, 1788).

Malthus, Thomas, *An Essay on the Principle of Population as it Affects the Future Improvement of Society With Remarks on the Speculations of Mr. Godwin, M. Condorcet and Other Writers* (London: J. Johnson, 1798).

Millar, John, *A Discourse on the Duty of Physicians* (London: J. Johnson, 1776).

Milton, John, *The Riverside Milton*, ed. Roy Flannagan (Boston: Houghton Mifflin, 1998).

Morganwg, Iolo (Edward Williams), *The Correspondence of Iolo Morganwg*, ed. Geraint H. Jenkins, Ffion Mair Jones and Ceri Jones, 3 vols (Cardiff: University of Wales Press, 2007).

Newton, John, *An Authentic Narrative* (London: J. Johnson, 1764).

— *One Hundred and Twenty Nine Letters from the Rev. John Newton, Late Rector of St. Mary Woolnoth, London, to the Rev. William Bull, of Newport Pagnell, Written During a Period of Thirty-Two Years, From 1773–1805.* (London: Hamilton, Adams and Co., 1847).

— *Thoughts on the African Slave Trade* (London: J. Johnson, 1788).

Paine, Thomas, *The Rights of Man* in *Political Writings*, ed. Bruce Kuklick (Cambridge: Cambridge University Press, 1989).

Paterson, Samuel, *Joineriana; or, The Book of Scraps* (London: J. Johnson, 1772).

Percival, Thomas, *Essays Medical and Experimental* (London: J. Johnson and B. Davenport, 1767).

Polwhele, Richard, *The Unsex'd Females; A Poem, Addressed to the Author of the Pursuits of Literature* (New York, NY: W. M. Cobbett, 1800; first published in Britain 1798).

Price, Richard, *A Discourse on the Love of our Country* (London: T. Cadell, 1790).

— Price, Richard, *Observations on Civil Liberty, The Principles of Government and the Practice and Policy of the War with America* (London: T. Cadell and J. Johnson, 1776).

Priestley, Joseph, *An Address to the Protestant Dissenters of all Denominations, On the Approaching Election of Members of Parliament, with Respect to the State of Public Liberty in General, and of American Affairs in Particular* (London: J. Johnson, 1774).

— *An Appeal to the Public on the Subject of the Riots in Birmingham* (London: J. Johnson, 1791).

— *A Chart of Biography* (London: J. Johnson, 1765).

— *A Description of a Chart of Biography; with a Catalogue of all the Names inserted in it, and the Dates annexed to them*, 6th edition (London: J. Johnson, 1777).

— *Disquisitions Relating to Matter and Spirit* (London: J. Johnson, 1777).

— *Essay on a Course of Liberal Education* (London: J. Johnson, 1765).

— *Essay on the First Principles of Government* (London: J. Johnson, 1768).

— *Experiments and Observations on Different Kinds of Air*, second edition (London: J. Johnson, 1775).

— *A Familiar Introduction to the Theory and Practice of Perspective* (London: J. Johnson, 1770).

— *Familiar Letters, Addressed to the Inhabitants of Birmingham* (London: J. Johnson, 1790).

Bibliography

— *The History and Present State of Electricity* (London: J. Johnson, 1767).

— *Letters to the Right Honourable Edmund Burke* (London: J. Johnson, 1791).

— *Life and Correspondence*, ed. John Towill Rutt, 2 vols (London: R. Hunter, 1831).

— *Memoirs of Dr. Joseph Priestley to the Year 1795*, 2 vols (Northumberland, PA: John Binns, 1806).

— *The Present State of Europe Compared with the Antient Prophecies; A Sermon Preached at the Gravel Pit Meeting in Hackney* (London: J. Johnson, 1794).

— *A Sermon on the Subject of the Slave Trade* (London: J. Johnson, 1788).

— *Theological and Miscellaneous Works*, ed. John Towill Rutt, 25 vols (London: G. Smallfield, 1817–1832).

Randolph, Thomas, *A Vindication of the Worship of the Son and the Holy Ghost Against the Exceptions of Mr. Theophilus Lindsey from Scripture and Authority* (Oxford: J. and J. Fletcher, 1775).

Rigby, Edward, *An Essay on the Uterine Haemorrhage* (London: J. Johnson, 1775).

Robinson, Mary, *Elegiac Verses to a Young Lady on the Death of her Brother Who Was Slain in the Late Engagement at Boston* (London: J. Johnson, 1776).

Roscoe, William, *Mount Pleasant: A Descriptive Poem* (London and Liverpool: J. Johnson and S. Crane, 1777).

Russell, Martha, 'Journal relating to the Birmingham riots, by a young lady of one of the persecuted families', *The Christian Reformer* 2 (1835), pp. 293–304.

Scott, Mary, *The Female Advocate: A Poem Occasioned by Reading Mr. Duncombe's Feminead* (London: J. Johnson, 1774).

Seward, Anna, *Letters*, ed. Archibald Constable, 6 vols (Edinburgh and London: Archibald Constable and Company, Longman, Hurst, Rees, Orme, and Brown, William Millar and John Murray, 1811).

Smethurst, Gamaliel, *An explanation and use of the constellarium, or, apparent astronomy* (London: printed by W. and J. Richardson, and sold by J. Dodsley, T. Durham, J. Johnson, William Anderson and Heath and Wing, 1771).

Smith, Charlotte, *Beachy Head: with Other Poems* (London: J. Johnson, 1807).

— *The Collected Letters of Charlotte Smith*, ed. Judith Stanton (Bloomington, IN: Indiana University Press, 2003).

— *The Poems of Charlotte Smith*, ed. Stuart Curran (Oxford: Oxford University Press, 1993).

Stedman, John Gabriel, *The Journal of John Gabriel Stedman, 1744–1797*, ed. Stanbury Thompson (London: Mitre Press, 1962).

— *Narrative of a Five Years' Expedition against the Revolted Negroes of Surinam*, ed. Richard and Sally Price (Baltimore, MD: Johns Hopkins University Press, 1998).

Toulmin, Joshua, *The American War Lamented: A Sermon Preached at Taunton* (London: J. Johnson, 1776).

Trimmer, Sarah, *An Easy Introduction to the Knowledge of Nature, and Reading the Holy Scriptures. Adapted to the Capacities of Children*, tenth edition (London: T. Longman and C. Rees, G. G. and J. Robinson, J. Johnson, F. and C. Rivington, 1799).

— *The Guardian of Education*, ed. Matthew Grenby, 4 vols (Bristol: Thoemmes Press, 2002).

— *The Oeconomy of Charity*, 2 vols (London: J. Johnson, 1801; first published 1787).

— *Some Account of the Life and Writings of Mrs. Trimmer, with Original Letters and Meditations and Prayers, Selected from her Journal*, 2 vols (London: F. C. and J. Rivington and J. Johnson and J. Hatchard, 1814).

Wakefield, Gilbert, *An Enquiry into the Expediency and Propriety of Public or Social Worship* (London: J. Deighton, 1791).

— *A Reply to Some Parts of the Bishop of Llandaff's Address to the People of Great Britain* (London: J. Cuthell, 1798).

Walker, George, *On the Doctrine of the Sphere, in Six Books* (London: J. Johnson, 1777).

Wollstonecraft, Mary, *Collected Letters*, ed. Janet Todd (New York, NY: Columbia University Press, 2003).

— *Mary* and *The Wrongs of Woman*, ed. Gary Kelly (Oxford: Oxford University Press, 1976).

— *A Vindication of the Rights of Men* and *A Vindication of the Rights of Woman*, ed. Sylvana Tomaselli (Cambridge: Cambridge University Press, 1995).

— *A Vindication of the Rights of Woman*, ed. Miriam Brody (Harmondsworth: Penguin, 1972).

— *Works*, ed. Janet Todd and Marilyn Butler, 7 vols (London: Pickering and Chatto, 1989).

Bibliography

Wordsworth, William, *Descriptive Sketches. In Verse. Taken During a Pedestrian Tour in the Italian, Grison, Swiss, and Savoyard Alps* (London: J. Johnson, 1793).

— *An Evening Walk. An Epistle; In Verse. Addressed to a Young Lady, from the Lakes of the North of England* (London: J. Johnson, 1793).

— *The Major Works*, ed. Stephen Gill (Oxford: Oxford University Press, 2000; first published 1984).

— *The Prose Works*, ed. W. J. B. Owen and Jane Worthington Smyser, 3 vols (Oxford: Oxford University Press, 1974).

Wordsworth, William and Dorothy, *The Letters of William and Dorothy Wordsworth*, ed. E. De Selincourt, and Alan G. Hill, 8 vols, second edition (Oxford: Oxford University Press, 2000).

Secondary Reading

Acosta, Ana M., 'Spaces of Dissent and the Public Sphere in Hackney, Stoke Newington, and Newington Green', *Eighteenth-Century Life* 27.1 (2003), pp. 1–27.

Aikin, Lucy, *Memoir of John Aikin. With a Selection of his Miscellaneous Pieces, Biographical, Moral and Critical*, 2 vols (London: Baldwin, Cradock, and Joy, 1823).

Barrell, John, *Imagining the King's Death: Figurative Treason, Fantasies of Regicide, 1793–1796* (Oxford: Oxford Univeristy Press, 2000).

— *The Spirit of Despotism: Invasions of Privacy in the 1790s* (Oxford: Oxford University Press, 2006).

Bentley, Gerald, ed., *Blake Records* (Oxford: Oxford University Press, 1969).

— *The Stranger from Paradise: A Biography of William Blake* (New Haven, CN: Yale University Press, 2001).

Braithwaite, Helen, *Romanticism, Publishing and Dissent: Joseph Johnson and the Cause of Liberty* (Basingstoke: Palgrave Macmillan, 2003).

Bray, Alan, *The Friend* (Chicago, IL: University of Chicago Press, 2003).

Buel Jr, Richard, *Joel Barlow: American Citizen in a Revolutionary World* (Baltimore, MD: Johns Hopkins University Press, 2011).

Bugg, John, *Five Long Winters: The Trials of British Romanticism* (Redwood City, CA: Stanford University Press, 2014).

Butler, Marilyn, *Maria Edgeworth: A Literary Biography* (Oxford: Clarendon Press, 1972).

Bygrave, Stephen, '"I Predict a Riot": Joseph Priestley and the Languages of Enlightenment in Birmingham in 1791', *Romanticism* 18.1 (2012), pp. 70–88.

Carey, Brycchan, 'Introduction' in Olaudah Equiano, *Interesting Narrative*, ed. Brycchan Carey (Oxford: Oxford University Press, 2018).

Cappe, Catharine, 'Memoirs of Mrs Lindsey', *The Belfast Monthly Magazine* 8.45 (1812), pp. 282–91.

Chard, Leslie F., *Joseph Johnson: Father of the Book Trade*, (New York, NY: New York Public Library, 1975).

— 'Joseph Johnson in the 1970s', *Wordsworth Circle* 33.3 (2002), pp. 95–100.

Clemit, Pamela, 'Charlotte Smith to William and Mary Jane Godwin: Five Holograph Letters', *Keats–Shelley Journal* 55 (2006), pp. 29–40.

Clery, E. J., 'Revising the Professional Woman Writer: Mary Wollstonecraft and Precarious Income', *Huntington Library Quarterly* 84.1 (2021), pp. 27–38.

Coleman, Deirdre, 'Firebrands, Letters and Flowers: Mrs Barbauld and the Priestleys' in Gillian Russell and Clara Tuite, eds, *Romantic Sociability: Social Networks and Literary Culture in Britain, 1770–1840* (Cambridge: Cambridge University Press, 2006), pp. 82–103.

Constantine, Mary-Ann, *The Truth Against the World: Iolo Morganwg and Romantic Forgery* (Aberystwyth: University of Wales Press, 2007).

Cox, Jeffrey N., and William Gaperin, 'Joseph Johnson', *Wordsworth Circle* 40.2/3 (2009), pp. 93–95.

Darton, F. J. Harvey, *Children's Books in England: Five Centuries of Social Life* (Cambridge: Cambridge University Press, 1958).

Davis, Keri, 'Miss Bliss: a Blake Collector of 1794' in *Blake in the Nineties*, ed. Steve Clark and David Worrall (Basingstoke: Palgrave Macmillan, 1999), pp. 212–30.

Ditchfield, G. M., 'Hannah Lindsey and her Circle: The Female Element in Early British Unitarianism', *Enlightenment and Dissent* 26 (2010), pp. 54–70.

— 'The Priestley Riots in Historical Perspective', *Transactions of the Unitarian Historical Society* 20.1 (1991), pp. 3–16.

— 'A Unitarian Saint? Theophilus Lindsey 1728–1808, *Transactions of the Unitarian Historical Society* 24.2 (2008), pp. 81–99.

Earland, Ada, *John Opie and His Circle* (London: Hutchinson and Co., 1911).

Bibliography

Erdman, David, *Blake: Prophet Against Empire* (Princeton, NJ: Princeton University Press, 1954).

Esterhammer, Angela, 'Continential Literature, Translation, and the Johnson Circle', *Wordsworth Circle* 33.3 (2002), pp. 101–4.

Fallon, David, 'Joseph Johnson' in Nancy E. Johnson and Paul Keen, eds., *Mary Wollstonecraft in Context* (Cambridge: Cambridge University Press, 2020), pp. 29–38.

Fletcher, Loriane, *Charlotte Smith: A Critical Biography* (Basingstoke: Palgrave Macmillian, 1998).

Freeman, Elizabeth, 'Queer Belonginings: Kinship Theory and Queer Theory' in George E. Haggerty and Molly McGarry, eds, *A Companion to Lesbian, Gay, Bisexual, Transgender and Queer Studies* (Oxford: Blackwell Publishing Ltd, 2007), pp. 295–314.

Gaull, Marilyn, 'Joseph Johnson: Literary Alchemist', *European Romantic Review*, 10 (1999), pp. 265–78.

— 'Joseph Johnson: Webmaster', *Wordsworth Circle* 40.2/3 (2009), pp. 107–110.

— 'Joseph Johnson's World: Ancestral Voices, Invsible Worms, and Roaming Tigers', *Wordsworth Circle* 33.3 (2002), pp. 92–4.

Gill, Stephen, *William Wordsworth: A Life* (Oxford: Oxford University Press, 1989).

Gilchrist, Alexander, *Life of William Blake*, 2 vols (London: Macmillan and Company, 1863).

Gordon, Lyndall, *Mary Wollstonecraft: A New Genus* (London: Little, Brown, 2005).

Good, John Mason, *Memoirs of the Life and Writings of the Reverend Alexander Geddes* (London: G. Kearsley, 1803).

Goodwin, George, *Benjamin Franklin in London: The British Life of America's Founding Father* (London: Weidenfeld and Nicholson, 2017).

Grenby, Matthew, *The Child Reader, 1700–1840* (Cambridge: Cambridge University Press, 2011).

Haggarty, Sarah, '"The Ceremonial of Letter for Letter": Wiliam Cowper and the Tempo of Epistolarly Exchange', *Eighteenth-Century Life* 35.1 (2011), pp. 149–167.

Harris, Alexandra, 'Cowper Away: A Summer in Sussex', *The Cowper and Newton Journal* 8 (n.p., 2018).

Haywood, Ian and John Seed, eds, *The Gordon Riots: Politics, Culture and Insurrection in Eighteenth-Century Britain* (Cambridge: Cambridge University Press, 2015).

Holmes, Richard, *The Age of Wonder: How the Romantic Generation Discovered the Beauty and Terror of Science* (London: HarperCollins, 2008).

— *Coleridge: Early Visions* (London: HarperCollins, 1989).

Hazlitt, William Carew, *Memoirs of William Hazlitt*, 2 vols (London: Richard Bentley, 1867).

James, Felicity, *Charles Lamb, Coleridge and Wordsworth: Reading Friendship in the 1790s* (Basingstoke: Palgrave Macmillan, 2008).

— 'Writing the Lives of Dissent: Life Writing, Religion and Community from Edmund Calamy to Elizabeth Gaskell', *Life Writing* 14.2 (2017), pp. 185–97.

James, Felicity and Ian Inkster, eds, *Religious Dissent and the Aikin-Barbauld Circle, 1740–1860* (Cambridge: Cambridge University Press, 2011).

Janowitz, Anne, 'Amiable and Radical Sociability: Anna Barbauld's "free familiar conversation"' in Gillian Russell and Clara Tuite, eds, *Romantic Sociability: Social Networks and Literary Culture in Britain, 1770–1840* (Cambridge: Cambridge University Press, 2006), pp. 62–81.

Jenkins, Geraint H., ed., *A Rattleskull Genius: The Many Faces of Iolo Morganwg* (Aberystwyth: University of Wales Press, 2009).

Johnston, Kenneth, *The Hidden Wordsworth: Poet, Lover, Rebel, Spy* (New York, NY: W. W. Norton and Company, 1998).

— *Unusual Suspects: Pitt's Reign of Alarm and the Lost Generation of the 1790s* (Oxford: Oxford University Press, 2013).

Keane, John, *Tom Paine: A Political Life* (London: Bloomsbury Publishing, 2009; first published 1995).

Kelly, Gary, *Women, Writing and Revolution 1790–1827* (Oxford: Oxford University Press, 1993).

King, James, *William Cowper: A Biography* (Durham, NC: Duke University Press, 1986).

King Hele, Desmond, *Erasmus Darwin: A Life of Unequalled Achievement* (London: Giles de la Mare, 1999).

Klancher, Jon P., *The Making of English Reading Audiences 1790–1832* (Madison, WI: University of Wisconsin Press, 1987).

Knight, David, *Humphry Davy: Science and Power* (Cambridge: Cambridge University Press, 1998).

Knowles, John, *The Life and Writings of Henry Fuseli*, 3 vols (London: H. Colburn and R. Bentley, 1831).

Krawczyk, Scott, *Romantic Literary Families* (Basingstoke: Palgrave Macmillan, 2009).

Labbe, Jacqueline M., *Charlotte Smith: Romanticism, Poetry and the Culture of Gender* (Manchester: Manchester University Press, 2003).

Lau, Beth, 'William Godwin and the Joseph Johnson circle: the Evidence of the Diaries', *The Wordsworth Circle* 33.3 (2001), pp. 104–8.

Lee, Debbie, 'Johnson, Stedman, Blake, and the Monkeys', *Wordsworth Circle* 33.3 (2002), pp. 116–18.

Levy, Michelle, *Family Authorship and Print Culture* (Basingstoke: Palgrave Macmillan, 2008).

Mandell, Laura, 'Johnson's Lesssons for Men: Producing the Professional Woman Writer', *Wordsworth Circle* 33.3 (2002), pp. 108–12.

Mason, Eudo C., *The Mind of Henry Fuseli* (London: Routledge and Kegan Paul, 1951).

Makdisi, Saree, *William Blake and the Impossible History of the 1790s* (Chicago, IL: Chicago University Press, 2003).

Mayhew, Robert J., *Malthus: The Life and Legacies of an Untimely Prophet* (Cambridge, MA: Harvard University Press, 2014).

McCarthy, William, *Anna Letitia Barbauld* (Baltimore, MD: Johns Hopkins University Press, 2008).

— 'The Celebrated Academy at Palgrave: A Documentary History of Anna Letitia Barbauld's School', *The Age of Johnson: A Scholarly Annual*, 8 (1997), pp. 279–392.

McGann, Jerome J., 'The Idea of an Indeterminate Text: Blake's Bible of Hell and Dr. Alexander Geddes', *Studies in Romanticism* 25.3 (1986), pp. 303–324.

Mee, Jon, *Conversable Worlds: Literature, Contention and Community 1762–1830* (Oxford: Oxford University Press, 2011).

— *Dangerous Enthusiasm: William Blake and the Culture of Radicalism in the 1790s* (Oxford: Clarendon Press, 1994).

— 'Radical Publishers' in Nancy E. Johnson and Paul Keen, eds, *Mary Wollstonecraft in Context* (Cambridge: Cambridge University Press, 2020), pp. 95–101.

Nicolson, Adam, *The Making of Poetry: Coleridge, the Wordsworths and Their Year of Marvels* (London: William Collins, 2019).

Oliver, Susan, 'Silencing Joseph Johnson and the "Analytical Review"', *Wordsworth Circle* 40.2/3 (2009), pp. 96–102.

O'Malley, Andrew, *The Making of the Modern Child* (London: Routledge, 2003).

Bibliography

Paris, John Ayrton, *The Life of Sir Humphry Davy* (London: Henry Colburn and Richard Bentley, 1831).

Perry, Seamus, 'In Praise of Puny Boundaries', *Wordsworth Circle* 33.3 (2002), pp. 116–18.

Phillips, Michael, *William Blake: The Creation of the Songs from Manuscript to Illuminated Printing* (London: The British Library, 2000).

Porter, Roy, *Flesh in the Age of Reason* (London: Penguin, 2003).

Raven, James, *Bookscapes: Geographies of Printing and Publishing in London before 1800* (London: The British Library, 2014).

— *The Business of Books* (New Haven, CN: Yale University Press, 2007).

Richardson, Alan, 'Erasmus Darwin and the Fungus School', *Wordsworth Circle* 33.3 (2002), pp. 113–16.

Rickman, Thomas Clio, *The Life of Thomas Paine* (n.p., 1819).

Roe, Nicholas, *Wordsworth and Coleridge: The Radical Years*, second edition (Oxford: Oxford University Press, 2018; first published 1988).

Sangster, Matthew, *Living as an Author in the Romantic Period* (Basingstoke: Palgrave Macmillan, 2021).

Schofield, Robert, *The Enlightened Joseph Priestley: A Study of His Life and Work from 1773 to 1804* (Philadelphia, PA: Penn State University Press, 2004).

Seed, John, *Dissenting Histories: Religious Division and the Politics of Memory in Eighteenth-Century England* (Edinburgh: Edinburgh University Press, 2008).

Seward, Anna, *Memoirs of the Life of Dr Darwin: Chiefly During his Residence at Lichfield: With Anecdotes of his Friends, and Criticisms on his Writings* (London: J. Johnson, 1804).

Smyser, Jane Worthington, 'The Trial and Imprisonment of Joseph Johnson, Bookseller', *Bulletin of the New York Public Library* 77 (1974), pp. 418–35.

St Clair, William, *The Godwins and the Shelleys: A Biography of a Family* (Baltimore, MD: Johns Hopkins University Press, 1991).

— *The Reading Nation in the Romantic Period* (Cambridge: Cambridge University Press, 2004).

Tomalin, Claire, *The Life and Death of Mary Wollstonecraft* (Harmondsworth: Penguin Books, 1992; first published 1975).

Tomory, Peter, *The Life and Art of Henry Fuseli* (London: Thames and Hudson, 1972).

Tyson, Gerald, *Joseph Johnson: A Liberal Publisher* (Iowa City, IA: University of Iowa Press, 1979).

Bibliography

Uglow, Jenny, *The Lunar Men: The Friends Who Made the Future* (London: Faber and Faber, 2002).

Walker, Gina Laura, *Mary Hays (1759–1843): The Growth of a Woman's Mind* (London: Routledge, 2006).

Waters, Mary A., '"The First of a New Genus": Mary Wollstonecraft as Literary Critic and Mentor to Mary Hays', *Eighteenth-Century Studies* 37.3 (204), pp. 415–34.

Watts, Ruth, *Gender, Power and the Unitarians in England, 1760–1860* (London: Longman, 1998).

Weinglass, D. H., 'Henry Fuseli's Letter of Enquiry to Paris on Behalf of Mary Wollstonecraft's Sister, Everina', *Blake Illustrated Quarterly* 21.4 (1988), pp. 144–6.

West, William, 'Letters to my Son at Rome: XI: Mr. Johnson, of St Paul's Church-Yard, and His Literary Connections', *Aldine Magazine* 1 (1839), pp. 201–05.

White, Daniel, *Early Romanticism and Religious Dissent* (Cambridge: Cambridge University Press, 2009).

Wu, Duncan, *William Hazlitt: The First Modern Man* (Oxford: Oxford University Press, 2008).

— 'William Hazlitt (1737–1820), the Priestley Circle, and "The Theological Repository": A Brief Survey and Bibliography', *Review of English Studies* 56.227 (2005), pp. 758–66.

Wykes, David, 'The Spirit of Persecution Exemplified: The Priestley Riots and the Victims of the Church and King mobs', *Transactions of the Unitarian Historical Society*, 20.1 (1991), pp. 17–39.

Yarde, D.M., *The Life and Works of Sarah Trimmer: A Lady of Brentford* (London: Hounslow and District History Society, 1972).

Zachs, William, *The First John Murray and the Late Eighteenth-Century London Book Trade* (Oxford: Oxford University Press, 1998).

List of Illustrations

Plate section I

List of Illustrations

Photo; Henry Fuseli, *Joseph Priestley* © Heinrich Zinram Photography Archive/Bridgeman Images; John Opie (attrib.), *Reverend Joseph Priestley* © Harris Manchester College, University of Oxford. Reproduced under CC BY-SA 4.0 • John Chapman, *Anna Letitia Barbauld (née Aikin)* © National Portrait Gallery, London; Anna Aikin (Anna Barbauld), 'Map of the Land of Matrimony and the Ocean of Love'. © British Library Board. All Rights Reserved/Bridgeman Images • John Opie, *Mary Wollstonecraft* (c. 1790–91) © Tate; John Opie, *Mary Wollstonecraft* (1797) © National Portrait Gallery, London.

Plate section II

Henry Howard, *Sarah Trimmer* © National Portrait Gallery London; George Romney, *William Cowper* © Granger Historical Picture Archive/Alamy Stock Photo • Joseph Wright of Derby, *Erasmus Darwin*: Bridgeman Images (public domain); Frontispiece to Olaudah Equiano's *The Interesting Narrative of the Life of Olaudah Equiano* (public domain); William Sharp (after George Romney), *Thomas Paine* © National Portrait Gallery, London; William Williams (Ap Caledfryn), *Iolo Morganwg (Edward Williams)* © Llyfrgell Genedlaethol Cymru/The National Library of Wales • 'Sedition and atheism defeated' (published 1790) © The Trustees of the British Museum; P. H. Witton Jr, 'The Rev Dr Priestley's House and Elaboratory, Fair-Hill' © SSPL/UIG/Bridgeman Images • Henry Fuseli, *Satan and Death with Sin Intervening* (public domain); Adam Buck, *The Edgeworth Family* © Estate of Michael Butler. Photograph © National Portrait Gallery, London.

Notes

INTRODUCTION: DINNER WITH JOSEPH JOHNSON

1 Eliza Bishop to Everina Wollstonecraft, 07/07/1794. Oxford, Bodleian Libraries, MS Abinger b. 4, fols 68–9.
2 James Hurdis to William Cowper, 31/07/1791. J. F. Tattersall, ed., *Letters of the Revd. James Hurdis, D. D., Vicar of Bishopstone, Sussex, to William Cowper, 1791–4*, p. 11.
3 Alexander Gibson Hunter to Archibald Constable, 05/03/1807, quoted in Thomas Constable, *Archibald Constable and his Literary Correspondents: A Memorial*, I, pp. 94–5.
4 Diary of Joseph Farington, 07/11/1799. *Diary of Joseph Farington*, IV, p. 1299.
5 Leigh Hunt, *Lord Byron and Some of his Contemporaries*, p. 293.
6 William Godwin, *Memoirs of the Author of A Vindication of the Rights of Woman*, p. 95.
7 James Hurdis to William Cowper, 07/02/1792. J. F. Tattersall, ed., *Letters of the Revd. James Hurdis, D. D., Vicar of Bishopstone, Sussex, to William Cowper, 1791–4*, pp. 16–17.
8 Diary of Joseph Farington, 24/06/1796. *The Diary of Joseph Farington*, II, pp. 588–9.

PART ONE: FIRE (1760–1770)
CHAPTER ONE: AUTHENTIC NARRATIVE

1 The complex background of eighteenth-century dissent is discussed at length in John Seed, *Dissenting Histories: Religious Division and the Politics of Memory in Eighteenth-Century England*; Ruth Watts, *Gender, Power and the Unitarians in England, 1760–1860*, and, more recently, by Felicity James in 'Writing the Lives of Dissent: Life-Writing, Religion and Community from Edmund Calamy to Elizabeth Gaskell'.
2 Musicians Company Account Book, Guildhall Library, MS 3088/1, p. 6. This document gives the earliest textual evidence for the shape of Johnson's professional life. Johnson has been the subject of book-length attention from Gerald

Tyson (*Joseph Johnson: A Liberal Publisher* (1979)) and from Helen Braithwaite (*Romanticism, Publishing and Dissent: Joseph Johnson and the Cause of Liberty* (2003)). Scholarly articles by Leslie Chard, Angela Esterhammer, Marilyn Gaull, Laura Mandell, Alan Richardson, Debbie Lee, Seamus Perry, Jeffrey Cox and William Galperin, Jane Smyster and Susan Oliver have also contributed substantially to scholarly understanding of his work. For full details see Bibliography. I am indebted to all those who have contributed to knowledge of Johnson's life and work, and, in particular, to Marilyn Gaull for her pioneering scholarship in this area, and to Helen Braithwaite for her meticulous reconstruction of Johnson's career.

3 Sample indenture from 1797; Guildhall Library, CLC/L/ME/C013.
4 James Raven, *The Business of Books*, p. 4. For more on the geography of bookselling London, see James Raven, *Bookscapes: Geographies of Printing and Publishing in London before 1800*.
5 Musicians Company Account Book, Guildhall Library, p. 29.
6 John Newton, *An Authentic Narrative*, pp. 22–3.
7 Ibid., p. 192.
8 Details of Davenport's varied career are given in Leslie Chard, *Joseph Johnson: Father of the Book Trade*, p. 56.

CHAPTER TWO: DOMESTIC OCCURRENCES

1 *Blake Records* (1969), p. 53.
2 John Knowles, *The Life and Writings of Henry Fuseli*, I, pp. 30–1. For full accounts of Fuseli's life and work see Peter Tomory, *The Life and Art of Henry Fuseli* and Eudo C. Mason, *The Mind of Henry Fuseli*.
3 'You wish I had not "put on airs with my fellow countrymen around the Englishman,"' wrote Fuseli to Lavater in 1766. Fuseli to Lavater, 12/1766. Henry Fuseli, *Briefe*, p. 132. All translations from this volume are by Madeleine Perry, to whom I am greatly indebted.
4 Patrick Murdock to Sir Andrew Mitchel, 12/06/1764. *Fuseli Letters*, p. 5.
5 Claire Tomalin, *The Life and Death of Mary Wollstonecraft*, pp. 96–7.
6 'Beckett, a bookseller in London, is trying to make a name for himself by publishing German books, but he has neither taste nor someone to advise him, so he will be Germany's undoing. Apart from me, there was not a single person in London who would be sufficiently proficient in both English and German to be able to write in both languages.' Fuseli to Bodmer, 1777. Henry Fuseli, *Briefe*, p. 124.
7 Fuseli to Lavater, 23/06/1769. Henry Fuseli, *Briefe*, pp. 146–7. For illuminating scholarly approaches to reading male friendship, as well as relationships which more generally do not conform to heteronormative models, see Alan Bray, *The Friend* and, more recently, Elizabeth Freeman, 'Queer Belongings: Kinship Theory and Queer Theory'.

8 Henry Fuseli, *Remarks on the Writings and Conduct of J. J. Rousseau*, n.p.

9 Ibid., p. 13.

10 Ibid., p. 48.

11 Ibid., p. 97.

12 Ibid., p. 117.

13 Ibid., p. 27.

14 William Austin, 'Dinner at Johnson's', quoted in *The Joseph Johnson Letterbook*, p. 169.

15 Henry Fuseli, *Remarks on the Conduct of Rousseau*, n.p.

CHAPTER THREE: THE ENQUIRER

1 William Hazlitt, 'The late Dr. Priestley', *The Atlas*, 14/07/1829, in P. P. Howe, *The Complete Works of William Hazlitt*, pp. 20, 236–8.

2 'The Enquirer', *The Monthly Magazine*, 1 (1796), pp. 2–5 (p. 2).

3 William Hazlitt, 'The Late Dr. Priestley', p. 236.

4 Anna Letitia Barbauld, née Aikin, *Poems* (1773), p. 41.

5 Joseph Priestley, *Essay on a Course of Liberal Education*, p. 22.

6 Ibid., p. 11.

7 Priestley, *Essay on a Course of Liberal Education*, pp. 35–6.

8 Ibid., p. 67.

9 William Hazlitt, 'The late Dr. Priestley', p. 237.

10 The phrase was Erasmus Darwin's, and was repeated frequently in the letters of Darwin's grandson Charles. See, for example, Charles Darwin to J. D. Hooker, 11/05/1859. Darwin Correspondence Project.

11 For an account of the life and work of William Hazlitt the elder, in particular his relationship with Priestley, see Duncan Wu, 'William Hazlitt (1737–1820), the Priestley Circle, and "The Theological Respository": A Brief Survey and Bibliography'.

12 Priestley to the Rev. Caleb Rotheram, 14/02/1766. MS 12.57 (fol 45), Dr Williams's Library.

13 Priestley to Richard Price, 08/03/1766. MS 12.54 (fol 44) Dr Williams's Library.

14 Priestley, *Memoirs*, II, p. 443.

15 Priestley to Franklin, 25/03/1766. *Franklin Papers* (online).

16 Johnson to Franklin, 04/11/1766. *The Joseph Johnson Letterbook*, p. 3.

17 Ibid., II, p. 450.

18 Ibid., pp. 578–9.

19 Ibid., p. xiv.

20 Priestley, *Essay on the First Principles of Government*, p. 25.

21 Ibid., p. 44.

22 *The Poems of Anna Letitia Barbauld*, pp. 133–4.

23 Ibid., p. 26.
24 Priestley, 'Sermon on the Death of the Reverend R. Robinson' in *Theological and Miscellaneous Works*, XV, pp. 418–19. Anna Aikin's friendship with the Priestleys, and its influence on her work, receives extensive attention in Deirdre Colman, 'Firebrands, letters and flowers: Mrs Barbauld and the Priestleys'.
25 Priestley to Anna Aikin, 13/06/1769. *Memoir of Mrs Barbauld*, pp. 34–6.
26 Priestley to Theophilus Lindsey, 18/12/1769. *Life and Correspondence*, ed. Rutt, I, pp. 104–5.

CHAPTER FOUR: LONDON

1 *General Evening Post*, 06/01/1770–09/01/1770, Issue 5646, p. 2.
2 *Middlesex Journal or Chronicle of Liberty*, 06/01/1770–09/01/1770, Issue 121, p. 3.
3 *Gazetteer and New Daily Advertiser*, Tuesday, 09/01/1770; Issue 12748, n.p.
4 Fuseli to Lavater, 14/06/1770. Henry Fuseli, *Briefe*, pp. 152–3.
5 Ibid., p. 155.
6 Ibid., p. 154.
7 Fuseli to Lavater, 02/11/1770. Ibid., p. 161.
8 Fuseli to Lavater, 23/06/1769. Ibid., pp. 146–7.

PART TWO: RIOT (1770–1780)
CHAPTER FIVE: JOINERIANA

1 John Aikin, quoted in William West, 'Letters to My Son at Rome: XI: Mr. Johnson, of St Paul's Church-Yard, and his Literary Connections', p. 202.
2 John Underhill, MS Collections for a History of Liverpool. Liverpool Record Office, Liverpool Libraries, 942 UND 3 (Vol 3, pp. 141–3).
3 The details of the transactions Johnson appears to have engaged in during this period are laid out by Gerald Tyson: 'Johnson's pressing financial problem – setting up a permanent shop – was also eased by divesting himself of copyrights or selling shares he had in various works. An example of the latter may have been volume two of Thomas Amory's *Life of John Buncle, Esq.*, which Johnson had originally published in October 1769, three months before the fire. A year later, however, "a new and neat edition" was published by Becket & Co. and Thomas Cadell. Similarly, Bruckner's *Philosophical Survey of the Animal Creation*, which Johnson had originally published, was now issued in a second edition by G. Robinson. Johnson also sold his share of a popular political piece by the Reverend James Murray titled *Sermons to Asses* (1768; 2nd ed. 1769). Its successor, *New Sermons to Asses* (1773), appeared under the imprint of S. Bladon, and Johnson published no further editions of the *Sermons*.' Gerald Tyson, *Joseph Johnson: A Liberal Publisher*, p. 35.
4 William West, 'Letter to my Son at Rome', pp. 204–5.

5 Alexander Gilchrist, *Life of William Blake*, p. 92.
6 William West, 'Letter to my Son at Rome', p. 204.
7 Johnson to Anon., 28/10/1797. *Joseph Johnson Letterbook*, p. 48.
8 Marquess of Rockingham to Edmund Burke, 01/06/1774. *The Letters of Edmund Burke*, pp. 540–1.
9 Samuel Paterson, *Joineriana*, I, p. 30.
10 Ibid., I, pp. 38, 52.
11 Ibid., I, pp. 67–8.
12 Ibid., I, p. 80.
13 Ibid., I, p. 82.
14 Ibid., I, p. 83.
15 Ibid., I, p. 157.
16 John Murray to William Enfield, 14/09/1775. MS.41900 ff. 217–18, John Murray Archive, National Library of Scotland. I am indebted to William Zachs, *The First John Murray and the Late Eighteenth-Century London Book Trade* for details of Murray's career.
17 Ibid.

CHAPTER SIX: FREETHINKER

1 Lindsey to William Turner, 21/12/1771. *Letters of Theophilus Lindsey*, I, 122. For an analysis of Lindsey's career see G. M. Ditchfield, 'A Unitarian Saint? Theophilus Lindsey 1728–1808'. The life of Hannah Lindsey is considered in G. M. Ditchfield, 'Hannah Lindsey and Her Circle: The Female Element in Early British Unitarianism'. Many of the details relating to the Lindseys' first lodgings in London come from Catharine Cappe's *Memoirs of Mrs Lindsey*. Cappe visited the Lindseys in London after they left Catterick and saw their makeshift furniture at first hand.
2 Ibid.
3 See *Reflections on Mr Lindsey's Apology*, pp. 1–2; 4–5.
4 Anon., *A Defence of the Reverend Theophilus Lindsey from the attack of William Burgh*, p. 394.
5 Priestley to Richard Price, 27/09/1772. *Life and Correspondence*, I, p. 183.
6 Priestley to Richard Price, 11/11/1772. *Life and Correspondence*, I, pp. 184–5.
7 *The Scripture Doctrine of the Trinity Justified*, pp. 9–10.
8 Lindsey to unknown recipient, April 1774. *Letters of Theophilus Lindsey*, I, p. 182.
9 Lindsey to John Jebb, post 11/04/1774. *Letters of Theophilus Lindsey*, I, p. 183.
10 Lindsey to John Jebb, 18/04/1774. *Letters of Theophilus Lindsey*, I, p. 184.
11 Thomas Randolph, *A Vindication of the Worship of the Son and the Holy Ghost against the exceptions of Mr. Theophilus Lindsey*, p. 164. The reference to 'poison' comes in Anon., *The Scripture Doctrine of the Trinity Justified*, p. 24.

12 Lindsey, *A Sermon preached at the opening of the chapel in Essex-House, Essex Street, in the Strand, on Sunday April 17, 1774*, pp. 17–18.

13 Priestley, *Memoirs*, pp. 88–90. See George Goodwin, *Benjamin Franklin in London: The British Life of America's Founding Father*, for a vivid account of this phase of Franklin's career.

14 Priestley, *An Address to the Protestant Dissenters*, pp. 3, 5, 14.

15 Benjamin Vaughan to Franklin, before 07/12/1779. *Franklin Papers* (online).

16 Priestley to William Turner, *Life and Correspondence of Priestley*, I, p. 267.

CHAPTER SEVEN: ESSAYS MEDICAL AND EXPERIMENTAL

1 Thomas Percival, *Essays Medical and Experimental*, pp. 46–7.

2 Anon., *Observations on the Character and Conduct of a Physician: In Twenty Letters to a Friend*, p. 15.

3 John Millar, *A Discourse on the Duty of Physicians*, p. 25.

4 John Aikin, *Thoughts on Hospitals*, pp. 71–2.

5 Edward Rigby, *Essay on the Uterine Haemorrhage*, p. 121.

6 John Aikin, *Thoughts on Hospitals*, p. 58.

7 George Fordyce, *Elements of the Practice of Physic*, p. 1.

8 Joseph Johnson, *New Books in Anatomy, Midwifery, Medicine, Experimental Philosophy and Topography*, p. 1.

9 William Hewson, *Experimental Inquiries: Part the first*, p. 8.

10 George Walker, *On the Doctrine of the Sphere, in Six Books*, p. x.

11 Antoine Beaumé, *A Manual of Chemistry*, trans. John Aikin, p. 1.

12 Joseph Priestley, *Experiments and Observations on Different Kinds of Air*, p. xiv.

13 Roy Porter, *Flesh in the Age of Reason*, p. 18.

14 Joseph Priestley, *Disquisitions relating to matter and spirit*, p. xvi.

15 Joseph Priestley, *Experiments and Observations on Different Kinds of Air*, pp. vi–vii.

16 Ibid., pp. xix–xx.

17 Priestley to Lindsey, 20/11/1777. *Life and Correspondence of Joseph Priestley*, I, p. 301.

CHAPTER EIGHT: PAINT AND WASHES

1 Samuel Paterson, *Joineriana*, II, p. 138.

2 Ibid.

3 Ibid., p. 141.

4 Anna Seward to Mary Scott, 29/03/1786. *The Letters of Anna Seward*, I, p. 133.

5 Mary Scott, *The Female Advocate*, pp. v–vi.

6 Ibid., p. viii.

7 *The Monthly Review*, 51 (1774), pp. 387–90 (pp. 387, 389).

8 Quoted in *The Poems of Anna Letitia Barbauld*, ed. William McCarthy and Elizabeth Kraft, p. 245.

9 Anna Barbauld to John Aikin, ?1774/5. *Works of Anna Letitia Barbauld*, II, p. 9. Valuable readings of the life and work of Barbauld and her circle are given in William McCarthy, *Anna Letitia Barbauld*, Scott Krawczyk, *Romantic Literary Families*, Daniel White, *Early Romanticism and Religious Dissent*, Felicity James and Ian Inkster, eds, *Religious Dissent and the Aikin-Barbauld Circle, 1740–1860*, Michelle Levy, *Family Authorship and Print Culture* and Anne Janowitz, 'Amiable and Radical Sociability: Anna Barbauld's "free familiar conversation"'.

10 *Critical Review* 35 (1773), pp. 192–95 (p. 194).

11 *Monthly Review*, Feb 1773, pp. 133–137 (p. 137).

12 Ibid.

13 William McCarthy, *Anna Letitia Barbauld*, p. 116.

14 J. and A. L. Aikin, *Miscellaneous Pieces in Prose*, p. 39.

15 Barbauld's authorship of this publication has been established by William McCarthy, who notes that in 1773 Johnson advertised the map together with the second edition of Barbauld's *Poems*. See *Anna Letitia Barbauld*, p. 125 and note.

16 *The Poems of Anna Letitia Barbauld*, p. 88.

17 Lindsey to William Turner, 17/01/1775. *Letters of Theophilus Lindsey*, I, p. 205.

18 Anna Barbauld to John Aikin, 21/04/1784. *Works of Anna Letitia Barbauld*, II, p. 24.

19 Anna Barbauld to John Aikin, n.d. [1776]. *Works of Anna Letitia Barbauld*, II, p. 11.

20 Anna Barbauld to Martha Aikin, 1776. *Works of Anna Letitia Barbauld*, II, pp. 13–14.

21 Anna Barbauld to John Aikin, June 1777. *Works of Anna Letitia Barbauld*, II, pp. 17.

22 Anna Letitia Barbauld, *Lessons for Children from two to three years old*, Advertisment. For further reading on eighteenth-century attitudes to children and on children's publishing see, in particular, F. J. Harvey Darton, *Children's Books in England: Five Centuries of Social Life*, M. O. Grenby, *The Child Reader, 1700–1740* and Andrew O'Malley, *The Making of the Modern Child*.

23 Anna Letitia Barbauld, *Lessons for Children from two to three years old*, p. 31.

24 Anna Barbauld to John Aikin, 19/01/1778. *Works of Anna Letitia Barbauld*, II, p. 19.

25 Anna Letitia Barbauld, *Lessons for Children from two to three years old*, Advertisement.

26 Anna Barbauld to John Aikin, n.d., 1778. *Works of Anna Letitia Barbauld*, II, p. 21.

27 Anna Letitia Barbauld, *A Legacy for Young Ladies*, p. 165.

28 Ibid., p. 176.

29 Ibid., pp. 167–8.
30 Anon., *The Laws Respecting Women*, p. vi.
31 Ibid., p. xii. For further information on Johnson's role in the growth of eighteenth-century women's writing see also Laura Mandell, 'Johnson's Lessons for Men: Producing the Professional Woman Writer'.

CHAPTER NINE: THE AMERICAN WAR LAMENTED

1   Lindsey to William Turner, 28/02/1775. *Letters of Theophilus Lindsey*, I, p. 208.
2   Lindsey to William Turner, 26/01/1775. *Letters of Theophilus Lindsey*, I, p. 206.
3   Lindsey to William Turner, 12/12/1775. *Letters of Theophilus Lindsey*, I, p. 219.
4   Lindsey to William Turner, 15/03/1775. *Letters of Theophilus Lindsey*, I, p. 222.
5   Lindsey to William Turner, 04/10/1778. *Letters of Theophilus Lindsey*, I, p. 271.
6   Lindsey to John Lee, 06/10/1783. *Letters of Theophilus Lindsey*, I, p. 394.
7   Andrew Hunter, *Advice from a Father to a Son, Just Entered into the Army*, pp. 54, 80.
8   Mary Robinson, *Elegiac Verses to a Young Lady, on the Death of her Brother, who was Slain in the Late Engagement at Boston'*, pp. 10–11.
9   Joshua Toulmin, *The American War Lamented*, p. 19.
10 Richard Price, *Observations on the Nature of Civil Liberty*, p. 27.
11 Ibid., pp. 120–1.
12 Ibid., p. 154.
13 Anon., *Essays Commercial and Political, on the Real and Relative Interests of Imperial and Dependent States, Particularly Those of Great Britain and her Dependencies*, pp. 61–2.
14 William Roscoe, *Mount Pleasant*, p. 14.
15 Ibid., pp. 14–15.
16 *Critical Review*, 44 (1777), p. 311.
17 J. and A. Aikin, *Miscellaneous Pieces in Prose*, p. 61.
18 Lindsey to William Tayleur, 25/03/1778. *Letters of Theophilus Lindsey*, I, p. 254.
19 Lindsey to William Tayleur, 30/06/1778. *Letters of Theophilus Lindsey*, I, p. 261.
20 Hannah Glasse, *The Art of Cookery, Made Plain and Easy*, Frontispiece.
21 John Abercrombie, *Every Man his Own Gardener*, Frontispiece.
22 Anon., *New Discoveries Concerning the World, and Its Inhabitants* (1778), Advertisement.

CHAPTER TEN: THOUGHTS ON THE DEVOTIONAL TASTE

1   Thomas Holcroft, *A Plain and Succinct Narrative*, p. 32.
2   Ibid., p. 33.
3   Lindsey to William Tayleur, 10/06/1780. *Letters of Theophilus Lindsey*, I, p. 317.
4   For a valuable recent articulation of this argument, see *The Gordon Riots: Politics, Culture and Insurrection in Late Eighteenth-Century Britain*, ed. Ian Haywood and John Seed, passim.

5 Lindsey to William Tayleur, 10/06/1780. *Letters of Theophilus Lindsey*, I, p. 317.
6 R. Harrison, *The Catholic Protestant, Part the Third and Last*, pp. 8–9.
7 *A Defence of the Act of Parliament Lately Passed for the Relief of Roman Catholics*, pp. 40–1.
8 Anna Letitia Barbauld, *Devotional Pieces*, p. 6.
9 Ibid., p. 36.
10 Priestley to Barbauld, 20/12/1775. *Life and Correspondence of Joseph Priestley*, I, p. 280.
11 Ibid., I, p. 285.
12 Ibid., I, pp. 285–6.
13 Quoted in *Life and Correspondence of Joseph Priestley*, I, p. 286.
14 Anna Letitia Barbauld, *Devotional Pieces*, p. 3–4.
15 For particularly valuable accounts of Blake's relationship with Johnson see Saree Makdisi, *William Blake and the Impossible History of the 1790s*, Jon Mee, *Dangerous Enthusiasm: William Blake and the Culture of Radicalism in the 1790s*, G. E. Bentley Jr., *The Stranger from Paradise: A Biography of William Blake* as well as David Erdman's classic biographical study, *Blake: Prophet Against Empire*.
16 John Bonnycastle, *An Introduction to Astronomy*, pp. iii–iv.
17 Ibid., p. vi.
18 Leigh Hunt, *Lord Byron and Some of his Contemporaries*, p. 293.
19 John Knowles, *The Life and Writings of Henry Fuseli*, III, p. 59.
20 Leigh Hunt, *Lord Byron and Some of his Contemporaries*, p. 291.
21 *Morning Chronicle*, 21/12/1809.

PART THREE: REVOLT (1780–1789)
CHAPTER ELEVEN: THE TASK

1 William Cowper, 'Adelphi', in *The Letters and Prose Writings of William Cowper*, I, p. 28. For further details of Cowper's life and career see James King, *William Cowper: A Biography*.
2 William Cowper, 'Adelphi', p. 39.
3 Cowper to John Newton, 12/07/1780. *Letters of William Cowper*, I, p. 367. For an illuminating reading of Cowper's correspondence see Sarah Haggery, '"The Ceremonial of Letter for Letter": William Cowper and the Tempo of Epistolary Exchange'.
4 Ibid., p. 366.
5 Cowper to John Newton, 27/11/1780. *Letters of William Cowper*, I, p. 413.
6 Cowper to John Newton, 02/12/1780. *Letters of William Cowper*, I, p. 418.
7 John Newton to William Bull, 20/01/1781. *One Hundred and Twenty Nine Letters from the Rev. John Newton . . . to the Rev. William Bull*, p. 107.
8 Cowper to Johnson, 15/01/1781. *Letters of William Cowper*, I, pp. 433–4.
9 Cowper to John Newton, 18/03/1781. *Letters of William Cowper*, I, p. 459.
10 Cowper to William Unwin, 01/05/1781. *Letters of William Cowper*, I, p. 469.

11 Cowper to William Unwin, 23/05/1781. *Letters of William Cowper*, I, p. 480.
12 Cowper to John Newton, 07/07/1781. *Letters of William Cowper*, I, p. 495.
13 Cowper to William Unwin, c.01/07/1781. *Letters of William Cowper*, I, p. 494.
14 Cowper to Johnson, 03/09/1781. *Letters of William Cowper*, I, p. 516.
15 Cowper to John Newton, 16/02/1782. *Letters of William Cowper*, II, p. 20.
16 Cowper to Johnson, 17/02/1782. *Letters of William Cowper*, II, p. 22.
17 'Newton's Preface to *Poems*, 1782, in John D. Baird and Charles Ryskamp, eds, *The Poems of William Cowper, Vol 1: 1748–1782*. Oxford Scholarly Editions Online.
18 Johnson to Cowper, 18/02/1782. *Joseph Johnson Letter Book*, p. 4.
19 Cowper to William Unwin, 24/02/1782. *Letters of William Cowper*, II, p. 23.
20 Cowper to John and Mary Newton, 14/03/1782. *Letters of William Cowper*, II, pp. 36–7.
21 Cowper, *Poems* (1782). In *The Poems of William Cowper, Vol, 1: 1748–1782*. Oxford Scholarly Editions Online.
22 *Monthly Review*, 67 (1782), pp. 262–5.
23 *Critical Review*, 53 (1782), pp. 287–90.
24 Cowper to Joseph Hill, 24/03/1782. *Letters of William Cowper*, II, p. 41.
25 *The Task*, III, pp. 108–9, in *The Poems of William Cowper, Vol 2: 1782–1785*. Oxford Scholarly Editions Online.
26 *The Task*, I, pp. 730–8.
27 *The Task*, IV, pp. 346, 397–8.
28 *The Task*, I, pp. 73–89.
29 *The Task*, II, pp. 5–7.
30 *The Task*, III, p. 198.
31 *The Task*, VI, pp. 1000–1005.
32 Cowper to William Unwin, 20/10/1784. *Letters of William Cowper*, II, p. 286.
33 Cowper to John Newton, 30/10/1784. *Letters of William Cowper*, II, p. 291.
34 Cowper to William Unwin, 01/11/1784. *Letters of William Cowper*, II, p. 292.
35 Cowper to William Unwin, 29/11/1784. *Letters of William Cowper*, II, p. 305.
36 Ibid.
37 Cowper to William Unwin, 28/02/1785. *Letters of William Cowper*, II, p. 352.
38 Cowper to William Unwin, 30/04/1785. *Letters of William Cowper*, II, p. 345.
39 Cowper to Newton, 25/06/1785. *Letters of William Cowper*, II, p. 358.
40 *Monthly Review*, 74 (1786), pp. 416–25 (p. 416).
41 Cowper to John Newton, 10/12/1785. *Letters of William Cowper*, II, p. 420.
42 Cowper to Lady Hesketh, 23–24/12/1785. *Letters of William Cowper*, II, p. 429.
43 Cowper to George Colman, 27/12/1785. *Letters of William Cowper*, II, p. 436.
44 Cowper to Johnson, 25/01/1786. *Letters of William Cowper*, II, p. 468.
45 Cowper to Johnson, 01/02/1786. *Letters of William Cowper*, II, p. 472.
46 Cowper to Lady Hesketh, 09/02/1786. *Letters of William Cowper*, II, p. 474.
47 Cowper to Johnson, 08/03/1786. *Letters of William Cowper*, II, pp. 490–1.

48 Cowper to William Unwin, 13/03/1786. *Letters of William Cowper*, II, p. 497.
49 Cowper to Johnson, 02/09/1786. *Letters of William Cowper*, II, p. 588.
50 Cowper to Johnson, 09/01/1787. *Letters of William Cowper*, III, p. 9.
51 Cowper to Johnson, 18/10/1787. *Letters of William Cowper*, III, p. 41.
52 Cowper to Robert Smith, 07/12/1787. *Letters of William Cowper*, III, p. 64.
53 Cowper to Walter Churchey, 13/12/1786. *Letters of William Cowper*, II, p. 617.
54 Cowper to Lady Hesketh, 12/10/1785. *Letters of William Cowper*, II, pp. 382–3.

CHAPTER TWELVE: TRADE WINDS
1 Priestley to Joseph Bretland, 19/03/1781. *Letters of Joseph Priestley*, I, p. 350.
2 Jenny Uglow, *The Lunar Men*, p. xx.
3 *Autobiography of Joseph Priestley*, p. 120.
4 Quoted in William McCarthy, 'The Celebrated Academy at Palgrave', p. 357.
5 Lindsey to William Tayleur, 14/05/1785. *Letters of Theophilus Lindsey*, I, p. 469.
6 Lindsey to William Tayleur, 25/06/1787. *Letters of Theophilus Lindsey*, I, p. 514.
7 Ibid.
8 Priestley to Johnson, 26/02/1783. MS 12.58 (fol 36), Dr Williams's Library.
9 Priestley to Johnson, 28/08/1787. MS 12.58 (fol 48), Dr Williams's Library.
10 Anna Seward, *Memoirs of the Life of Dr Darwin*, pp. 1–2. For full details of Darwin's life and career see Desmond King-Hele, *Erasmus Darwin: A Life of Unequalled Achievement* and Jenny Uglow, *The Lunar Men*. For further reading on Darwin's working relationship with Johnson, see Alan Richardson, 'Erasmus Darwin and the Fungus School'.
11 Darwin, *Loves of the Plants (The Botanic Garden*, Part II) III, pp. 55–62; 73–7.
12 Darwin, *Loves of the Plants*, 1st Interlude.
13 Darwin, *Loves of the Plants*, Advertisement.
14 Darwin to Johnson, 23/05/1784. *Letters of Erasmus Darwin*, p. 235.
15 Ibid., p. 236.
16 Barbauld to Johnson, 03/06/1783. 'Celebrated Academy at Palgrave', pp. 331–2.
17 Barbauld to Johnson, September 1783. Huntington Library, MSSHM 1605.
18 Barbauld to Johnson, 29/04/1784. 'Celebrated Academy at Palgrave', pp. 338–9.
19 John Murray to Johnson, 02/01/1784. MS.41904, ff. 270–1, John Murray Archive, National Library of Scotland.
20 Darwin, 'Winds' in *The Economy of Vegetation (The Botanic Garden*, Part I). Note to IV, pp. 13–24.
21 Lindsey to William Tayleur, 24/04/1784. *Letters of Theophilus Lindsey*, I, p. 425.

CHAPTER THIRTEEN: THOUGHTS ON THE EDUCATION OF DAUGHTERS

1 William Beloe, *Sexagenarian: Recollections of a Literary Life*, II, p. 253; I, p. 345.

2 Sarah Trimmer to Joseph Johnson, 19/04/1784. British Library MS RP 6222. Further details of the life and work of Sarah Trimmer are given in D. M. Yarde, *The Life and Works of Sarah Trimmer: A Lady of Brentford*.

3 Beloe, *Sexagenarian*, I, p. 346.

4 Sarah Trimmer, *An Easy Introduction to the Knowledge of Nature, and Reading the Holy Scriptures. Adapted to the Capacities of Children*, pp. 89, 79.

5 Sarah Trimmer to Hannah More, quoted in Matthew Grenby ed., *Guardian of Education*, I, ix, n. 8.

6 Sarah Trimmer, *The Oeconomy of Charity*, I, pp. 84–6.

7 Wollstonecraft to Everina Wollstonecraft, c. mid-November 1787. *Collected Letters of Mary Wollstonecraft*, p. 141. Mary Wollstonecraft's working relationship with Johnson has been the subject of recent scholarly attention in *Mary Wollstonecraft in Context* (2021). See in particular essays by David Fallon ('Joseph Johnson') and Jon Mee ('Radical Publishers'). Mary A. Waters's earlier '"The First of a New Genus": Mary Wollstonecraft as a Literary Critic and Mentor to Mary Hays' gives a particularly illuminating account of Wollstonecraft's professional activities.

8 Sarah Trimmer to Mrs. M., 12/07/1792. *Some Account of the Life and Writings of Mrs. Trimmer*, I, pp. 354–5.

9 Wollstonecraft, *Thoughts on the Education of Daughters* in *Works*, IV, p. 10.

10 John Hewlett, *Sermons on Different Subjects*, p. 3.

11 Wollstonecraft, *Thoughts on the Education of Daughters* in *Works*, IV, p. 5.

12 Wollstonecraft, *Thoughts on the Education of Daughters* in *Works*, IV, p. 26.

13 Wollstonecraft to Johnson, 05/12/1876. *Collected Letters of Mary Wollstonecraft*, p. 96.

14 Wollstonecraft, *Thoughts on the Education of Daughters* in *Works*, IV, p. 25.

15 Wollstonecraft to Johnson, 14/04/1787. *Collected Letters of Mary Wollstonecraft*, p. 119.

16 Johnson, 'A Few Facts', in *The Joseph Johnson Letterbook*, p. 165.

17 Wollstonecraft to Everina Wollstonecraft, 07/11/1787. *Collected Letters of Mary Wollstonecraft*, p. 139.

18 Wollstonecraft to Everina Wollstonecraft, c. mid-November 1787. *Collected Letters of Mary Wollstonecraft*, p. 141.

19 Johnson, 'A Few Facts', p. 165.

20 Wollstonecraft to Everina Wollstonecraft, 07/11/1787. *Collected Letters of Mary Wollstonecraft*, p. 139.

21 Wollstonecraft to William Godwin, 12/01/1797. *Collected Letters of Mary Wollstonecraft*, p. 391.

22 Wollstonecraft to Johnson, 13/09/1787. *Collected Letters of Mary Wollstonecraft*, p. 133–4.

23 Wollstonecraft to Johnson, 20/09/1787. *Collected Letters of Mary Wollstonecraft*, p. 137.

24 Wollstonecraft to Everina Wollstonecraft, 07/11/1787. *Collected Letters of Mary Wollstonecraft*, pp. 139–40.

25 Wollstonecraft to Everina Wollstonecraft, c. mid-November 1787. *Collected Letters of Mary Wollstonecraft*, p. 140–2.

26 Wollstonecraft to George Blood, 03/03/1788. *Collected Letters of Mary Wollstonecraft*, p. 149.

27 Wollstonecraft to Johnson, ?early 1789. *Collected Letters of Mary Wollstonecraft*, pp. 159–60.

28 Wollstonecraft, *Original Stories*, in *Works*, IV, p. 360.

29 Wollstonecraft, *Original Stories*, IV, p. 359.

30 Wollstonecraft to Johnson, c. late 1787–early 1788. *Collected Letters of Mary Wollstonecraft*, pp. 142–3.

31 Eliza Bishop to Everina Wollstonecraft, 07/07/1794. Oxford, Bodleian Libraries, MS Abinger b. 4, fols 68–9.

32 Henry Fuseli to Heinrich Füssli, 15/01/1788. Quoted in D. H. Weinglass, 'Henry Fuseli's Letter of Enquiry to Paris on Behalf of Mary Wollstonecraft's Sister, Everina, *Blake Illustrated Quarterly*, p. 146.

33 Joseph Johnson to Everina Wollstonecraft (postscript), 22/03/1788. *The Joseph Johnson Letterbook*, p. 5.

34 Wollstonecraft to Johnson, ?late 1788–early 1789. *Collected Letters of Mary Wollstonecraft*, p. 159.

CHAPTER FOURTEEN: THE PAPER AGE

1 Barbauld to John Aikin, 31/01/1787. *Works of Anna Letitia Barbauld*, II, p. 150.

2 Priestley, *Letter to the Right Hon. William Pitt* in *The Theological and Miscellaneous Works of Joseph Priestley*, ed. Rutt, XIX, pp. 134, 128.

3 Lindsey, *Vindiciae Priestleianae*, p. 343.

4 Revolution Society Minute Book, British Library Manuscripts. Add MS 64814.

5 Darwin, *Loves of the Plants*, p. 117.

6 Darwin to Josiah Wedgwood, 13/04/1789. *Letters of Erasmus Darwin*, p. 338.

7 Barbauld to John Aikin, Feb 1788. *Works of Anna Letitia Barbauld*, II, p. 156.

8 Priestley, *A Sermon on the Subject of the Slave Trade*, p. 11.

9 Ibid., p. 8.

10 Cowper to General Cowper, 27/03/1788. *Letters of William Cowper*, III, p. 133.

11 Cowper to Samuel Rose, 29/03/1788. *Letters of William Cowper*, III, p. 137.

12 Cowper, 'The Negro's Complaint', in Cowper, *Poems*, Oxford Scholarly Editions Online.

13 Cowper to Lady Hesketh, 31/03/1877. *Letters of William Cowper*, III, p. 140.

14 Olaudah Equiano, *Interesting Narrative*, p. 41. For a full discussion of Equiano's biography, and the uncertainty surrounding his early life, see the extensive work by Brycchan Carey, summarised in the Introduction to *Interesting Narrative*, ed. Brycchan Carey (Oxford: Oxford University Press, 2018).

15 *Interesting Narrative*, p. 176.

16 For details of the influence of Geddes on Blake, see Jerome J. McGann, 'The Idea of an Indeterminate Text: Blake's Bible of Hell and Dr. Alexander Geddes'.

17 Knowles, *The Life and Writings of Henry Fuseli*, I, p. 74. Details of Geddes' life and career are given in John Mason Good, *Memoirs of the Life and Writings of the Reverend Alexander Geddes*.

18 Prospectus, *Analytical Review*, 1 (1788), pp. i–vi.

19 Wollstonecraft to Johnson, c. July 1788. *Letters of Mary Wollstonecraft*, pp. 156–7.

20 *Analytical Review*, 1, (1788), p. 333.

21 Wollstonecraft to Johnson, ?late 1788–early 1789. *Letters of Mary Wollstonecraft*, p. 158.

22 *Analytical Review*, 1, (1788), n.p.

23 *Analytical Review*, 2, (1788), p. 7.

24 *Analytical Review*, 2, (1788), p. 170.

25 *Analytical Review*, 2, (1788), p. 385.

26 *Analytical Review*, 2, (1788), pp. 223–4.

CHAPTER FIFTEEN: APHORISMS ON MAN

1 Johann Caspar Lavater, *Aphorisms on Man*, p. 108.

2 John Murray to Johnson, 08/10/1787. MS.41905 ff.198, John Murray Archive, National Library of Scotland.

3 Lavater, *Aphorisms on Man*, pp. 11–12.

4 Wollstonecraft to Joshua Cristall, 19/03/?1790. *Collected Letters of Mary Wollstonecraft*, p. 167.

5 Wollstonecraft to George Blood, 16/4/[89]. *Collected Letters of Mary Wollstonecraft*, p. 162.

6 Wollstonecraft to Johnson, ?1790. *Collected Letters of Mary Wollstonecraft*, p. 166.

7 Johnson, 'A Few Facts', in *The Joseph Johnson Letterbook*, p. 165.

8 Cowper to Samuel Rose, 08/08/1789. *Letters and Prose Writings of William Cowper*, III, p. 308.

9 Frederica Lock to Frances Burney, 17–21/06/1789. *Collected English Letters of Henry Fuseli*, p. 44.

10 Priestley to Lindsey, 22/07/1789. *Correspondence of Joseph Priestley*, II, p .26.

11 Lindsey to William Frend, 10/08/1789. *Letters of Theophilus Lindsey*, II, p. 16.

12 Priestley to Lindsey, 20/07/1789. *Correspondence of Joseph Priestley*, II, p. 26.

PART FOUR: RUINS (1789–1791)
CHAPTER SIXTEEN: ON LIBERTY

1 Wordsworth, *The Prelude*, X, 692–700 in *The Major Works*, p. 550.
2 Charles and Mary Lamb, *Recollections of Writers*, p. 12.
3 George Dyer, 'On Liberty', in *Poems*, pp. 34–6.
4 Ibid., p. 32.
5 Ibid., p. 36.
6 Barbauld to Miss Dixon, August 1789. *Works of Anna Letitia Barbauld*, II, p. 82.
7 Priestley to Lindsey, 10/12/1789. *Life and Correspondence of Joseph Priestley*, II, pp. 49–50.
8 Priestley to Lindsey, 21/09/1789. Ibid., II, p. 33.
9 Lindsey to William Frend, 14/11/1789. *Letters of Theophilus Lindsey*, II, p. 26.
10 Lindsey to William Frend, 02/01/1790. *Letters of Theophilus Lindsey*, II, p. 30.
11 *Analytical Review*, 5 (1789), pp. 148–9.
12 *Declaration of the Rights of Man and the Citizen*, reprinted in Richard Price, *A Discourse on the Love of our Country*, Appendix, pp. 6–8.
13 Price, *A Discourse on the Love of our Country*, p. 3.
14 Ibid., p. 10.
15 Ibid., pp. 11–12.
16 Ibid., p. 28.
17 Ibid., p. 49.
18 Ibid., pp. 50–1.
19 Priestley to Lindsey, 10/12/1789. *Life and Correspondence of Joseph Priestley*, II, p. 49.
20 Lindsey to William Tayleur, 10/02/1790. *Letters of Theophilus Lindsey*, II, p. 39.
21 Priestley to Lindsey, 13/05/1790. *Life and Correspondence of Joseph Priestley*, II, p. 64.
22 Priestley, *Familiar Letters to the Inhabitants of Birmingham*, pp. 5–6.
23 Ibid., p. 37.
24 Ibid., p. 156.
25 John Aikin, *An Address to the Dissidents of England on their Late Defeat*, p. 6.
26 Anna Letitia Barbauld, *An Address to the Opposers of the Repeal of the Corporation and Test Acts*, p. 6.
27 Ibid., pp. 11–12.
28 Ibid., p. 12–13.
29 Ibid., p. 21.
30 Ibid., p. 30–1.
31 Ibid., pp. 35–6.
32 Sarah Trimmer, *Life and Writings*, I, p. 241.

CHAPTER SEVENTEEN: ORIGINAL STORIES

1 Wollstonecraft to Eliza Bishop, c. late 1790. *Collected Letters of Mary Wollstonecraft*, pp. 181–3.

2 This account of Blake's printing process is based on the work of Michael Phillips. See Michael Phillips, *William Blake: The Creation of the Songs from Manuscript to Illuminated Printing*. For an account of the critical debates that surround Blake's process, the review of this title by Alexander S. Gourlay in *Blake: An Illustrated Quarterly* 32.2 (2002) offers a useful summary.

3 William Blake, 'Prospectus' in *Complete Poetry and Prose*, p. 692.

4 G. E. Bentley, *Blake Records*, p. 39.

5 Diary of Joseph Farington, 24/06/1796. *The Diary of Joseph Farington*, II, pp. 588–9.

6 Richard Twiss to Francis Douce, 25/09/1794, quoted in Keri Davis, 'Miss Bliss: a Blake Collector of 1794' in *Blake in the Nineties*, p. 216.

7 Blake, 'The French Revolution' in *Complete Poetry and Prose*, p. 286.

8 Wollstonecraft, Advertisement to *Elements of Morality* in *The Works of Mary Wollstonecraft*, II, p. 5.

9 Anna Le Breton, *Memories of Seventy Years*, p. 96.

10 *Analytical Review*, 9 (1791), p. 102.

11 Darwin to James Watt, 20/11/1789. *Letters of Erasmus Darwin*, pp. 353–4.

12 Johnson to Darwin, 23/07/1791. *Joseph Johnson Letterbook*, p. 7.

13 Darwin to Josiah Wedgwood, 04/03/1790. *Letters of Erasmus Darwin*, pp. 360–1.

14 *Analytical Review*, 15 (1793), 289.

15 Richard Lovell Edgeworth to Darwin and vice versa, n.d. 1790. *Memoirs of Richard Lovell Edgeworth*, II, p. 134.

16 Fuseli to William Roscoe, 25/11/1789. *English Letters of Henry Fuseli*, p. 46.

17 Cowper to Johnson, 07/09/1790. *Letters of William Cowper*, III, p. 410.

18 Cowper to Johnson, 30/10/1790. *Letters of William Cowper*, III, p. 426.

19 Cowper to Lady Hesketh, 26/06/1791. *Letters of William Cowper*, III, 534.

20 Cowper to Samuel Rose, 06/07/1791. *Letters of William Cowper*, III, p. 538.

21 Cowper to Lady Hesketh, 11/07/1791. *Letters of William Cowper*, III, p. 543.

22 Cowper to Johnson, 03/07/1791. *Letters of William Cowper*, III, p. 537.

23 Cowper to Lady Hesketh, 11/07/1791. *Letters of William Cowper*, III, p. 542.

24 Cowper to Joseph Hill, 12/07/1791. *Letters of William Cowper*, III, pp. 544–5.

25 Ibid., p. 544.

26 Wollstonecraft to Johnson, ?early 1790. *Collected Letters of Mary Wollstonecraft*, p. 169.

27 The fragments of Wollstonecraft's letters to Fuseli are quoted in Knowles, *The Life and Writings of Henry Fuseli*, pp. 163, 167.

28 Lyndall Gordon, *Mary Wollstonecraft: A New Genus*, p. 179.

29 E. J. Clery, 'Revising the Professional Woman Writer: Mary Wollstonecraft and Precarious Income', p. 37.

30 Wollstonecraft to Johnson, ?summer 1790. *Collected Letters of Mary Wollstonecraft*, pp. 172–3.

31 Wollstonecraft to Anon., ?summer 1790. *Collected Letters of Mary Wollstonecraft*, pp. 174–5.

32 Jane Roscoe to William Roscoe, 06/04/1791. *English Letters of Henry Fuseli*, pp. 64–5.

33 Jane Roscoe to William Roscoe, n.d. Roscoe Papers, Liverpool Record Office, Liverpool Libraries 920 ROS 3507.

34 William Roscoe to Jane Roscoe, n.d. Roscoe Papers, Liverpool Record Office, Liverpool Libraries 920 ROS 4212.

35 Fuseli and Johnson to William Roscoe, 17/08/1790. Roscoe Papers, Liverpool Record Office, Liverpool Libraries 920 ROS 1601.

CHAPTER EIGHTEEN: VIEWS OF THE RUINS

1 Edmund Burke, *Reflections on the Revolution in France*, p. 164. For an illuminating reading of events covered in this chapter see Stephen Bygrave, '"I Predict a Riot": Joseph Priestley and Languages of Enlightenment in Birmingham in 1791' and G. M. Ditchfield, 'The Priestley Riots in Historical Perspective'.

2 Treasury Solicitor Documents relating to the Society for Constitutional Information, National Archives. TS 11/951/3495.

3 *Reflections on the Revolution in France*, p. 87.

4 Ibid., p. 90.

5 Ibid., p. 93.

6 Ibid., p. 94.

7 Ibid., p. 119.

8 Ibid., p. 159.

9 *Analytical Review*, 8 (1790), pp. 295–307.

10 Wollstonecraft, *A Vindication of the Rights of Men*, p. 5.

11 Ibid., p. 17.

12 Ibid., p. 25.

13 *Analytical Review*, 8 (1790), pp. 417.

14 Priestley to Lindsey, 23/12/1790. *Life and Correspondence of Joseph Priestley*, II, p. 97.

15 Priestley, *Letters to the Right Honourable Edmund Burke*, p. 115.

16 Ibid., p. 143.

17 Priestley to Price, 27/01/1791. *Life and Correspondence of Joseph Priestley*, II, p. 99.

18 Barbauld to Miss Dixon, 07/05/1791. *Works of Anna Letitia Barbauld*, II, p. 84.

19 Lindsey to William Tayleur, 10/11/1790. *The Letters of Theophilus Lindsey*, II, p. 79.
20 Paine, *The Rights of Man, Part I*, p. 143.
21 Ibid., p. 63.
22 Lindsey to William Tayleur, 23/02/1791. *The Letters of Theophilus Lindsey*, II, p. 97.
23 John Keane, *Tom Paine: A Political Life*, pp. 304–5.
24 Priestley to Lindsey, 11/03/1791. *Life and Correspondence of Joseph Priestley*, II, p. 105.
25 Lindsey to Russell Scott, 24/03/1791. *The Letters of Theophilus Lindsey*, II, p. 107.
26 Lindsey to William Tayleur, 09/04/1791. *The Letters of Theophilus Lindsey*, II, p. 111.
27 *Analytical Review*, 9 (1791), pp. 312–13.
28 Clio Rickman, *Life of Thomas Paine*, p. 8.
29 John Scott to Thomas Cooper, quoted in Gerald Tyson, *Joseph Johnson: A Liberal Bookseller*, p. 124.
30 Priestley to Lindsey, 14/03/1791. *Life and Correspondence of Joseph Priestley*, II, p. 106.
31 Cowper to Lady Hesketh, 27/05/1791. *Letters of William Cowper*, III, p. 519.
32 Priestley to Lindsey, 07/03/1791. *The Letters of Joseph Priestley to Theophilus Lindsey 1769–94*, Queen Mary Centre for Religion and Literature in English (online).
33 Lindsey to William Tayleur, 21/05/1791. *The Letters of Theophilus Lindsey*, II, p. 124.
34 Priestley to Lindsey, 29/06/1791. *Life and Correspondence of Joseph Priestley*, II, p. 114.
35 See Robert Schofield, *The Enlightened Joseph Priestley*, p. 285.
36 Martha Russell, 'Journal Relating to the Birmingham Riots', p. 301.
37 William Hutton, *The Life of William Hutton*, p. 60.
38 Lindsey to William Tayleur, 16/07/1791. *The Letters of Theophilus Lindsey*, II, p. 135.
39 Johnson to Darwin, 23/08/1791. *Joseph Johnson Letterbook*, 23/07/1791.
40 Darwin to Josiah Wedgwood, 25/07/1791. *Letters of Erasmus Darwin*, p. 386.
41 Cowper to John Newton, 22/07/1791. *Letters and Prose Writings of William Cowper*, III, p. 546.
42 Lindsey to William Tayleur, 04/08/1791. *The Letters of Theophilus Lindsey*, II, p. 142.
43 Priestley to William Russell, 29/07/1791. *Life and Correspondence of Joseph Priestley*, II, p. 124.
44 Ibid.
45 Priestley, *An Appeal to the Public on the Subject of the Riots in Birmingham*, pp. 83, 91–2.

46 Ibid., pp. 112–13, 115.
47 Priestley to William Russell, 08/08/1791. *Life and Correspondence of Joseph Priestley*, II, p. 137.

PART FIVE: REFUGE (1791–1795)
CHAPTER NINETEEN: EVENINGS AT HOME
1 Lindsey to Samuel Shore III, 16/08/1791. *Letters of Theophilus Lindsey*, II, p. 145.
2 'At this time Priestley was Joseph Johnson's guest in St. Paul's Churchyard, and was requested to sit for his portrait, that it might remain in the house which he was accustomed to frequent, and in which he enjoyed the society of such men as Fuseli, Opie, Price, Geddes, Wakefield, Aikin, and Bonnycastle. After Johnson's death, the portrait passed into the hands of Mr. John Miles, a relation, at West End, Hampstead. He allowed it to remain in a state of neglect at the top of his house, until, in 1828, Mr. Rowland Hunter, who was Johnson's nephew and successor, persuaded him to give it to Dr. Williams's Trustees. It belongs to them, and is preserved in the Library, 49, Redcross Street.' James Yates, *Memorials of Joseph Priestley. From the* Christian Reformer, *A.D. 1860, With Numerous Corrections and Additions*, pp. 5–6, in *Memorials of Joseph Priestley*, Royal Society MS 654/1, fol 2.
3 The location of the sittings for Opie's portrait of Priestley is given in Ada Earland, *John Opie and His Circle*, in a catalogue entry: 'Priestley, Joseph, LLD (1783–1804) – Painted at the residence of Mr. J. Johnson, Dr Priestley's publisher and friend'. (p. 309).
4 19/09/1791. *Letters of Theophilus Lindsey*, II, p. 148.
5 Priestley, 'Preface' in *The Present State of Europe Compared with the Antient Prophecies*, pp. v–vi. For the significance of Hackney in Dissenting circles during this period see Ana M. Acosta, 'Spaces of Dissent and the Public Sphere in Hackney, Stoke Newington and Newington Green'.
6 Details of these attacks, and others experienced by Dissenters elsewhere on the anniversary of the Birmingham Riots, are in David L. Wykes, 'The Spirit of Persecution Exemplified: The Priestley riots and the victims of the Church and King mobs', *Transactions of the Unitarian Historical Society*, p. 27.
7 Priestley to William Withering, n.d., quoted in *The Enlightened Joseph Priestley*, p. 294.
8 Priestley, *An Appeal to the People of Birmingham*, p. 41.
9 John Aikin and Anna Letitia Barbauld, *Evenings at Home*, I, pp. 1–3.
10 Hannah Lindsey to Russell Scott, 01/07/1793. *Letters of Theophilus Lindsey*, II, p. 233.
11 Wollstonecraft to Everina Wollstonecraft, 14/09/1792. *Collected Letters of Mary Wollstonecraft*, p. 203.

12 Eliza Bishop to Everina Wollstonecraft, 29/03/1792. Oxford, Bodleian Libraries, MS Abinger b. 4.

13 John Knowles, *The Life and Writings of Henry Fuseli*, I, p. 166.

14 All quotations from Godwin's diary are taken from William Godwin's Diary, Bodleian Library (online). For an analysis of Godwin's diary in the context of Johnson's life and work see Beth Lau, 'William Godwin and Joseph Johnson: The Evidence of the Diaries'. See also William St Clair, *The Godwins and the Shelleys* for details of Godwin's life and career, including as a publisher and bookseller of children's literature.

15 Godwin, *Memoirs of the Author of A Vindication of the Rights of Woman*, pp. 95–6.

16 Maria Edgeworth to Sophy Ruxton, 23/02/1794. *A Memoir of Maria Edgeworth*, I, pp. 48–9. For full details of Maria Edgeworth's life and work see Marilyn Butler, *Maria Edgeworth: A Literary Biography*.

17 Johnson to Maria Edgeworth, 05/10/1795. *Joseph Johnson Letterbook*, p. 17.

18 Maria Edgeworth to Mrs Ruxton, 08/05/1794. *A Memoir of Maria Edgeworth*, I, p. 50.

19 Maria Edgeworth, *Letters for Literary Ladies*, pp. 54–5.

20 Iolo Morganwg to Peggy Williams, 30/10/1793. *Correspondence of Iolo Morganwg*, I, p. 613. For further information on the extraordinary life and career of Iolo Morganwg see Mary-Anne Constantine, *The Truth Against the World: Iolo Morganwg and Romantic Forgery* and Geraint H. Jenkins, ed., *A Rattleskull Genius: The Many Faces of Iolo Morganwg*.

21 Ibid., I, p. 612.

22 Iolo Morganwg to Johnson, ?September 1795. *Correspondence of Iolo Morganwg*, I, p. 772.

23 Fuseli to William Roscoe, 01/10/1791. *English Letters of Henry Fuseli*, p. 72.

24 Roscoe to Jane Roscoe, 04/02/1793. *English Letters of Henry Fuseli*, p. 87.

25 John Mason Good, *Memoirs of the Life and Writings of the Reverend Alexander Geddes*, p. 282.

26 John Knowles, *The Life and Writings of Henry Fuseli*, I, pp. 406–7.

27 William West, 'Mr Johnson of St Paul's Churchyard', p. 204.

28 Johnson to Edward Moor, 18/06/1796. *Joseph Johnson Letterbook*, p. 22.

29 Priestley to the Members of the Lunar Society, 16/11/1793. *Life and Correspondence of Joseph Priestley*, II, p. 210.

30 Priestley to Lindsey, 09/04/1794. *Life and Correspondence of Joseph Priestley*, II, p. 230.

31 Lindsey to Robert Millar, 17/04/1794. *Correspondence of Theophilus Lindsey*, II, p. 277.

32 Priestley to Lindsey, 15/06/1794. *Life and Correspondence of Joseph Priestley*, II, pp. 255–6.

33 Mary Priestley to Thomas Belsham, 15/06/1794. *Life and Correspondence of Joseph Priestley*, II, p. 235.

34 Johnson to Priestley, September 1795. *Joseph Johnson Letterbook*, p. 12.
35 'The Manufacture of Paper' in *Evenings at Home*, II, pp. 140, 148.

CHAPTER TWENTY: THINGS AS THEY ARE

1 Godwin, 'Preface' to *Caleb Williams*, p. 279. The events covered in this chapter have received extensive scholarly attention. See, in particular, John Barrell, *Imagining the King's Death: Figurative Treason, Fantasies of Regicide, 1773–1796*. Invaluable accounts of the 1790s more generally include John Barrell's *The Spirit of Despotism: Invasions of Privacy in the 1790s* and John Bugg's *Five Long Winters: The Trials of British Romanticism*.
2 See John Keane, *Tom Paine: A Political Life*, p. 324.
3 John Knowles, *The Life and Writings of Henry Fuseli*, I, p. 375.
4 'The Trial of Thomas Paine' in Howell, *State Trials*, XXII, p. 402.
5 Paine, *The Rights of Man*, in *The Thomas Paine Reader*, p. 265.
6 *Critical Review*, 3rd Series, V (1792), p. 353.
7 Knowles, *The Life and Writings of Henry Fuseli*, I, p. 375.
8 Gilchrist, *Life of William Blake*, p. 97.
9 Lindsey to William Tayleur, 15/02/1792 and to Russell Scott, 21/02/1792, in *The Letters of Theophilus Lindsey*, II, 168–9.
10 Wakefield, *Enquiry into the Expediency and Propriety of Public or Social Worship*, pp. 18, 41.
11 Mary Hays, *Cursory Remarks on an Enquiry into the Expediency and Propriety of Public or Social Worship* in *A Mary Hays Reader*, pp. 123, 124–5. Full details of Mary Hays's work are given in Gina Lauria Walker, *Mary Hays (1759–1843): The Growth of a Woman's Mind*.
12 Lindsey to Russell Scott, 27/11/1794. *Letters of Theophilus Lindsey*, II, p. 310.
13 William Wordsworth to William Matthews, 19/05/1792. *Letters of William Wordsworth*, I, pp. 77–8.
14 Wordsworth, *A Letter to the Bishop of Llandaff* in *The Prose Works of William Wordsworth*, I, p. 48.
15 Darwin to Richard Dixon, 25/10/1792. *Letters of Erasmus Darwin*, p. 409.
16 Iolo Morganwg to Peggy Williams, 28/05/1794. *Correspondence of Iolo Morganwg*, I, p. 672.
17 Iolo Morgangwg to Hugh Jones, 04/06/1794. *Correspondence of Iolo Morganwg*, I, pp. 676–7.
18 Kenneth R. Johnston, *Unusual Suspects*, p. 15.
19 Iolo Morganwg to William Owen Pughe, 20/05/1795. *Correspondence of Iolo Morganwg*, I, p. 760.
20 Godwin, *Cursory Strictures*, pp. 25, 18.
21 Trial of Thomas Hardy in Howell, *State Trials*, pp. 24, 512.
22 See 'Introduction' to John Barrell and Jon Mee, *Trials for Treason and Sedition, 1792–1794*, p. xxxv.

23 Johnson to Priestley, 25/09/1795. *Joseph Johnson Letterbook*, p. 15.
24 Ibid., pp. 15–16.

CHAPTER TWENTY-ONE: THINGS BY THEIR RIGHT NAMES

1 Aikin and Barbauld, *Evenings at Home*, I, pp. 150–2.
2 Mary Hays to Godwin, 14/10/1794. *Correspondence of Mary Hays*, p. 383.
3 Joel Barlow, *The Conspiracy of Kings*, p. 6.
4 Joel Barlow, *Advice to the Privileged Orders*, Advertisement. For a full account of Barlow's life and work see Richard Buel Jr, *Joel Barlow: American Citizen in a Revolutionary World*.
5 Barbauld, *Sins of Government*, pp. 27–8.
6 Ibid., pp. 12–14.
7 Wollstonecraft to William Roscoe, 06/10/1791. *Collected Letters of Mary Wollstonecraft*, p. 190.
8 Wollstonecraft, *A Vindication of the Rights of Woman*, p. 112.
9 Ibid., p. 170.
10 Ibid., p. 325.
11 Ibid., pp. 327–8.
12 *Analytical Review*, 12 (1792) pp. 248–9.
13 *Critical Review*, 4 (1792), p. 389.
14 Wollstonecraft to William Roscoe, 14/02/1792. *Collected Letters of Mary Wollstonecraft*, I, p. 197.
15 Godwin Diary, 09/03/1792.
16 Godwin Diary, 15/03/1792.
17 Wollstonecraft to Everina Wollstonecraft, 23/02/1792. *Collected Letters of Mary Wollstonecraft*, p. 198.
18 Wollstonecraft to Hays, 25/11/1792. *Collected Letters of Mary Wollstonecraft*, p. 209.
19 Mary Hays, *Letters and Essays*, p. 17.
20 Lindsey to Hays, 15/04/1793. *Letters of Theophilus Lindsey*, II, p. 221.
21 Wollstonecraft to Hays, 25/11/1792. *Collected Letters of Mary Wollstonecraft*, II, pp. 210–1.
22 Ibid., II, p. 211.
23 Lindsey to John Rowe, 23/12/1796. *Letters of Theophilus Lindsey*, II, p. 414.
24 John Elliot, *The Medical Pocket-Book*.
25 Darwin to Richard Dixon, 15/10/1792. *Letters of Erasmus Darwin*, pp. 409–10.
26 Darwin, *Zoonomia*, p. 2.
27 Ibid., p. 1.
28 *Analytical Review*, 19 (1794), p. 225.
29 Darwin to Robert Darwin, 18/08/1794, *Letters of Erasmus Darwin*, p. 451.
30 John Aikin to Anna Barbauld, 28/11/1791. M3710, Hackney Archives.

31 Maria Edgeworth to Sophy Ruxton, 09/03/1791. *Memoir of Maria Edgeworth*, I, p. 31.

32 See also John Newton's *Thoughts on the African Slave Trade* (1788) and Barbauld's *Epistle to William Wilberforce* (1791).

33 John Collins, *Case of the Sugar Colonies*, pp. 16–17.

34 William Thomson obituary, *Annual Bibliography and Obituary*, 2 (1818), pp. 74–117 (p. 108).

35 Richard and Sally Price, 'Introduction' in *Narrative of a Five Year's Expedition*, p. lxv.

36 William Thomson obituary, p. 110.

37 *Journal of John Gabriel Stedman*, pp. 385–90.

38 *Journal of John Gabriel Stedman*, p. 391. In the published edition of Stedman's diary the word 'wine' is reproduced as 'w——'. Richard and Sally Price, who have consulted the manuscript original, note in their edition of Stedman's *Narrative* that the word in the manuscript is clearly wine. *Narrative of a Five Years Expedition*, p. xxx.

39 *Journal of John Gabriel Stedman*, p. 392.

40 For further discussion of Johnson, Blake and Steadman see Debbie Lee, 'Johnson, Stedman, Blake, and the Monkeys', passim.

41 Ibid., p. 394.

42 Ibid., p. 395.

43 Ibid.

44 *Analytical Review*, 24 (1796), pp. 225–6.

45 Sarah Trimmer, *Guardian of Education*, p. 308, quoted in Anna Letitia Barbauld, *Selected Poetry and Prose*, p. 292.

46 Johnson to William Russell, 24/08/1796. *Joseph Johnson Letterbook*, p. 25.

47 Johnson to Priestley, 24/08/1796. *Joseph Johnson Letterbook*, p. 27.

PART SIX: CAVE (1792–1799)
CHAPTER TWENTY-TWO: PARADISE LOST

1 Johnson to Cowper, 22/08/1791. *Joseph Johnson Letterbook*, p. 8.

2 Johnson to Cowper, 31/08/1791. *Joseph Johnson Letterbook*, p. 9.

3 Fuseli to William Roscoe, 30/05/1792. *Collected English Letters of Henry Fuseli*, p. 81. The word 'nearly' is deleted in the manuscript.

4 Wollstonecraft to Roscoe, 14/02/1792. *Collected Letters of Mary Wollstonecraft*, p. 196.

5 Wollstonecraft to Roscoe, 03/01/1792. *Collected Letters of Mary Wollstonecraft*, p. 194.

6 Milton Gallery Advertisement, *Blake Records*, p. 44.

7 Cowper to Samuel Rose, 14/09/1791. *Letters of William Cowper*, III, p. 572.

8 Cowper to Johnson, 30/10/1791. *Letters of William Cowper*, III, p. 583.

9 Cowper to William Hayley, 17/03/1792. *Letters of William Cowper*, IV, p. 29.

10 Cowper to William Hayley, 09/05/1792. *Letters of William Cowper*, IV, p. 75.
11 Cowper to John Johnson, 20/05/1792. *Letters of William Cowper*, IV, p. 78.
12 Cowper to Lady Hesketh, 24/05/1792. *Letters of William Cowper*, IV, p. 80.
13 Cowper to Samuel Teedon, 05/06/1792. *Letters of William Cowper*, IV, p. 93.
14 Cowper to Samuel Teedon, 05/06/1792. *Letters of William Cowper*, IV, pp. 93–4.
15 Cowper to William Hayley, 19–20/06/1792. *Letters of William Cowper*, IV, p. 124.
16 Cowper to Lady Hesketh, 21/06/1792. *Letters of William Cowper*, IV, p. 127.
17 Cowper to Lady Hesketh, 01/06/1792. *Letters of William Cowper*, IV, p. 344.
18 Cowper to William Hayley, 07/06/1792. *Letters of William Cowper*, IV, p. 101.
19 Cowper to William Hayley, 27/06/1792. *Letters of William Cowper*, IV, p. 134.
20 Cowper to Johnson, 29/06/1792. *Letters of William Cowper*, IV, p. 139.
21 Cowper to Johnson, 08/07/1792. *Letters of William Cowper*, IV, p. 144.
22 Cowper to William Hayley, 15/07/1792. *Letters of William Cowper*, IV, p. 147.
23 Cowper to Johnson, 21/08/1792. *Letters of William Cowper*, IV, p. 177.
24 Cowper to Lady Hesketh, 11/08/1792. *Letters of William Cowper*, IV, p. 167. For an illuminating reading of Cowper's visit to Sussex see Alexandra Harris, 'Cowper Away: A Smmer in Sussex'.
25 Cowper to Samuel Rose, 13/08/1792. *Letters of William Cowper*, IV, p. 172.
26 Cowper to Johnson, 21/08/1792. *Letters of William Cowper*, IV, p. 178.
27 Cowper to Samuel Teedon, 22/09/1792. *Letters of William Cowper*, IV, p. 197.
28 Cowper to William Hayley, 28/10/1792. *Letters of William Cowper*, IV, p. 225.
29 Cowper to John Johnson, 20/11/1792. *Letters of William Cowper*, IV, p. 239.
30 Cowper to William Hayley, 25/11/1792. *Letters of William Cowper*, IV, p. 242.
31 Cowper MS. Rothschild 693 (kept inside front cover of RW.31.8). Wren Library, Trinity College, Cambridge.
32 Cowper to Samuel Teedon, 21/12/1792. *Letters of William Cowper*, IV, p. 264.
33 Cowper to William Hayley, 26/12/1792. *Letters of William Cowper*, IV, p. 265.
34 'I thought to have drawn up a comparative view of your merits as translators, & even applied to Johnson that I might be your Critic in the Analytical Review. But that office is I believe assigned to someone else, perhaps to Fuseli, who is well qualified for the undertaking, & who, tho' I have often been tempted to laugh at the extravagance of his ideas in painting, has much astonished me with his erudition.' James Hurdis to William Cowper, 13/09/1791 in J. F. Tattersall, ed., *Letters of the Revd. James Hurdis, D. D., Vicar of Bishopstone, Sussex, to William Cowper, 1791–4*, p. 13.
35 *Analytical Review*, 15 (1793), pp. 1–16 (p. 4).
36 Cowper to Samuel Rose, 17/02/1693. *Letters of William Cowper*, IV, p. 294.
37 Cowper to Lady Hesketh, 10/02/1793. *Letters of William Cowper*, IV, p. 291.
38 Cowper to John Johnson, 11/04/1793. *Letters of William Cowper*, IV, p. 321.
39 Cowper to Johnson, 28/03/1793. *Letters of William Cowper*, IV, p. 314.

40 Cowper to William Hayley, 19/03/1793. *Letters of William Cowper*, IV, p. 308.
41 Cowper to Samuel Rose, 27/03/1793. *Letters of William Cowper*, IV, p. 313.
42 Cowper to John Johnson, 30/11/1793. *Letters of William Cowper*, IV, p. 435.
43 Cowper to Samuel Rose, 29/11/1793. *Letters of William Cowper*, IV, p. 434.
44 Cowper to William Hayley, 08/12/1793. *Letters of William Cowper*, IV, p. 439.
45 Cowper to Samuel Rose, 02/01/1794. *Letters of William Cowper*, IV, p. 443.
46 Fuseli to William Roscoe, 30/04/1794. Roscoe Papers, Liverpool Record Office, Liverpool Libraries 920 ROS 1616.
47 Cowper to John Newton, 11/04/1799. *Letters of William Cowper*, IV, p. 466.

CHAPTER TWENTY-THREE: VINDICATION OF THE RIGHTS OF WOMAN

 1 William Godwin, *Memoirs of the Author of A Vindication of the Rights of Woman*, pp. 91–2.
 2 Ibid., p. 92.
 3 Wollstonecraft to Everina Wollstonecraft, 20/06/1792. *Collected Letters of Mary Wollstonecraft*, pp. 200–1.
 4 Wollstonecraft to William Roscoe, 12/11/1792. *Collected Letters of Mary Wollstonecraft*, p. 208.
 5 Wollstonecraft to Johnson, ?October 1792. *Collected Letters of Mary Wollstonecraft*, pp. 205–6.
 6 Godwin, *Memoirs of the Author of A Vindication of the Rights of Woman*, p. 98.
 7 Wollstonecraft to Everina Wollstonecraft, c. early December 1792. *Collected Letters of Mary Wollstonecraft*, p. 212.
 8 Wollstonecraft to Johnson, 26/12/1792. *Collected Letters of Mary Wollstonecraft*, pp. 216–17.
 9 Wollstonecraft to Everina Wollstonecraft, 24/12/1792. *Collected Letters of Mary Wollstonecraft*, p. 215.
10 Wollstonecraft, *An Historical and Moral View of the Origin and Progress of the French Revolution*; in *Works of Mary Wollstonecraft*, VI, p. 47.
11 Wollstonecraft to Gilbert Imlay, c. August 1793. *Collected Letters of Mary Wollstonecraft*, p. 228.
12 Eliza Bishop to Everina Wollstonecraft, 14/07/1793. Oxford, Bodleian Libraries, MS Abinger b. 4, fol 51.
13 Eliza Bishop to Everina Wollstonecraft, 05/11/?1793. Oxford, Bodleian Libraries, MS Abinger b. 4, fols 54–5.
14 Eliza Bishop to Everina Wollstonecraft, 30/01/1794. Oxford, Bodleian Libraries, MS Abinger b. 4, fols 60–1.
15 Wollstonecraft to Imlay, c. November 1793. *Collected Letters of Mary Wollstonecraft*, pp. 232–3.
16 Wollstonecraft to Imlay, 19/09/1794. *Collected Letters of Mary Wollstonecraft*, p. 258.

17 Eliza Bishop to Everina Wollstonecraft, 15/08/1794. Oxford, Bodleian Libraries, MS Abinger b. 4, fols 70–1.

18 Lindsey to William Tayleur, 29/09/1794. *Letters of Theophilus Lindsey*, II, p. 305.

19 Wollstonecraft to Gilbert Imlay, 06/09/1795. *Collected Letters of Mary Wollstonecraft*, p. 320.

20 Wollstonecraft to Gilbert Imlay, 04/10/1795. *Collected Letters of Mary Wollstonecraft*, p. 324.

21 Wollstonecraft to Gilbert Imlay, c. October 1795. *Collected Letters of Mary Wollstonecraft*, p. 327.

22 Wollstonecraft to Gilbert Imlay, c. November 1795. *Collected Letters of Mary Wollstonecraft*, p. 331.

23 Wollstonecraft to Mary Hays, c. late 1795. *Collected Letters of Mary Wollstonecraft*, p. 337.

24 Godwin, *Memoirs of the Author of A Vindication of the Rights of Woman*, p. 129.

25 Wollstonecraft to Godwin, 01/07/1796. *Collected Letters of Mary Wollstonecraft*, p. 342.

26 Godwin to Wollstonecraft, 13/07/1796. *Letters of William Godwin*, I, p. 171.

27 Wollstonecraft to Godwin, 02/08/1796. *Collected Letters of Mary Wollstonecraft*, p. 345.

28 Wollstonecraft to Godwin, 17/08/1796. *Collected Letters of Mary Wollstonecraft*, pp. 348–9.

29 Wollstonecraft to Godwin, 10/09/1796. *Collected Letters of Mary Wollstonecraft*, pp. 359–60.

30 Wollstonecraft to Godwin, 17/09/1796. *Collected Letters of Mary Wollstonecraft*, p. 366.

31 Wollstonecraft to Godwin, 19/09/1795. *Collected Letters of Mary Wollstonecraft*, p. 366.

32 Wollstonecraft, *Lessons*, in *The Works of Mary Wollstonecraft*, IV, pp. 473–4.

33 Diary of Joseph Farington, 22/01/1797. *Diary of Joseph Farington*, III, p. 755.

34 Wollstonecraft to Godwin, 27/01/1797. *Collected Letters of Mary Wollstonecraft*, p. 394.

35 Wollstonecraft to Mary Hays, c. early 1797. *Collected Letters of Mary Wollstonecraft*, p. 400.

36 Wollstonecraft to Godwin, 17/03/1797. *Collected Letters of Mary Wollstonecraft*, p. 402.

37 Wollstonecraft to Godwin, 11/03/1797. *Collected Letters of Mary Wollstonecraft*, p. 402.

38 Wollstonecraft to Everina Wollstonecraft, 22/03/1797. *Collected Letters of Mary Wollstonecraft*, p. 403.

39 E. J. Clery, 'Revising the Professional Woman Writer: Mary Wollstonecraft and Precarious Income', pp. 31–2.

40 Johnson to Charles Wollstonecraft, 15/07/1797. *Joseph Johnson Letterbook*, p. 42.

41 Wollstonecraft to Godwin, 08/04/1797. *Collected Letters of Mary Wollstonecraft*, p. 406.

42 Wollstonecraft to Godwin, 11/04/1797. *Collected Letters of Mary Wollstonecraft*, p. 407.

43 Fuseli to William Roscoe, 25/05/1797. *English Letters of Henry Fuseli*, pp. 169–70.

44 Godwin to Wollstonecraft, 05/06/1797. *Letters of William Godwin*, I, p. 210.

45 Godwin to Wollstonecraft, 07/06/1797. *Letters of William Godwin*, I, p. 214.

46 Wollstonecraft to Godwin, 06/06/1797. *Collected Letters of Mary Wollstonecraft*, pp. 416–17.

47 Wollstonecraft to Godwin, 25/06/1797. *Collected Letters of Mary Wollstonecraft*, p. 423.

48 Johnson to Charles Wollstonecraft, 15/07/1797. *Joseph Johnson Letterbook*, p. 42.

49 Wollstonecraft to Godwin, 30/08/1797. *Collected Letters of Mary Wollstonecraft*, p. 436.

50 Wollstonecraft to Godwin, 30/08/1797. *Collected Letters of Mary Wollstonecraft*, p. 437.

51 Wollstonecraft to Godwin, 30/08/1797. *Collected Letters of Mary Wollstonecraft*, p. 437.

52 Godwin, *Memoirs of the Author of A Vindication of the Rights of Woman*, p. 192.

53 Johnson to Godwin, 10/09/1797. *Joseph Johnson Letterbook*, pp. 45–6.

54 Johnson to Fuseli, 10/09/1797. *Joseph Johnson Letterbook*, p. 46.

55 Johnson to Godwin, 12/09/1797. *Joseph Johnson Letterbook*, p. 46.

56 Fuseli to Roscoe, 24/09/1797. *English Letters of Henry Fuseli*, p. 175.

57 Godwin to ?Joseph Johnson, 11–12/09/1797. *Letters of William Godwin*, I, p. 240.

58 Godwin to ?Charlotte Smith, 24/10/1797. *Letters of William Godwin*, I, p. 263.

59 Wollstonecraft, *The Wrongs of Woman*, in *Mary* and *The Wrongs of Woman*, p. 193.

CHAPTER TWENTY-FOUR: ORIGINAL POETRY

1 For further information on the *Monthly Magazine* see Jon Klancher, *The Making of English Reading Audiences 1790–1832*. Full details of the lives of Wordsworth and Coleridge can be found in Stepehen Gill, *William Wordsworth: A Life* and in Richard Holmes's two-volume biography of Coleridge. Volume I, *Coleridge: Early Visions*, covers the events that are the focus of this chapter. These events also receive extensive attention in Nicholas Roe's seminal *Wordsworth and Coleridge: The Radical Years* and in

Adam Nicholson's wonderful *The Making of Poetry: Coleridge, the Wordsworths and Their Year of Marvels*. For illuminating readings of the poetry detailed in this chapter see also Felicity James, *Charles Lamb, Coleridge and Wordsworth: Reading Friendship in the 1790s*.

2 Lindsey to John Rowe, 13/02/1798. *Letters of Theophilus Lindsey*, II, p. 445.
3 Wordsworth, 'Preface' to *Lyrical Ballads* in *The Major Works*, p. 600.
4 Advertisement to *Lyrical Ballads* in Wordsworth, *The Major Works*, p. 591.
5 Wordsworth, *Letter to the Bishop of Llandaff* in *The Prose Works of William Wordsworth*, I, p. 38.
6 Wordsworth, *An Evening Walk*, in *The Major Works*, p. 2.
7 *Analytical Review*, 15 (1793), p. 294.
8 See Kenneth Johnston, *The Hidden Wordsworth*, for a full exposition of this suggestion.
9 Wordsworth to William Matthews, 23/05/1794. *Letters of William and Dorothy Wordsworth*, I, p. 120.
10 Coleridge, *Biographia Literaria* in *The Major Works*, pp. 199–200.
11 Joseph Cottle to Johnson, 02/10/1798. *Letters of William and Dorothy Wordsworth*, I, p. 675.
12 Wordsworth to Richard Wordsworth, 23/05/1799. *Letters of William and Dorothy Wordsworth*, I, p. 260.
13 Wordsworth to Joseph Cottle, 02/06/1799. *Letters of William and Dorothy Wordsworth*, I, p. 263.
14 Lindsey to John Rowe, 15/10/1798. *Letters of Theophilus Lindsey*, II, p. 459.
15 Coleridge to Sara Coleridge, 03/10/1798. *Letters of Samuel Taylor Coleridge*, I, p. 255.
16 Coleridge to Sara Coleridge, 18/09/1798. *Letters of Samuel Taylor Coleridge*, I, p. 254.
17 Samuel Taylor Coleridge, 'Fears in Solitude' in *The Major Works*, pp. 92–8.
18 *Analytical Review*, 28 (1798), p. 591.
19 Samuel Taylor Coleridge, 'Frost at Midnight' in *The Major Works*, pp. 87–9.

CHAPTER TWENTY-FIVE: A PEEP INTO THE CAVE OF JACOBINISM

1 'Prospectus', *Anti-Jacobin Review*, 1 (1798), p. 1.
2 Ibid., pp. 4–5.
3 *Anti-Jacobin Review*, 1 (1798), pp. 85–6.
4 Priestley to Lindsey, 15/02/1796. *Life and Correspondence of Joseph Priestley*, II, pp. 332–3.
5 Priestley to Lindsey, 08/04/1796. *Life and Correspondence of Joseph Priestley*, II, p. 336.
6 Priestley to Thomas Belsham, 05/03/1796. *Life and Correspondence of Joseph Priestley*, II, pp. 335–6.

7   Priestley to Lindsey, 11/09/1796. *Life and Correspondence of Joseph Priestley*, II, p. 353.

8   Priestley to Lindsey, 19/09/1796. *Life and Correspondence of Joseph Priestley*, II, p. 354.

9   Priestley to Barbauld, ?late 1796. *Life and Correspondence of Joseph Priestley*, II, p. 364.

10 Priestley to Thomas Belsham, 14/09/1796. *Life and Correspondence of Joseph Priestley*, II, p. 373.

11 Priestley to Lindsey, 29/05/1797. *Life and Correspondence of Joseph Priestley*, II, p. 381.

12 Priestley to Lindsey, 04/11/1797. *Life and Correspondence of Joseph Priestley*, II, p. 386.

13 Priestley to Lindsey, 14/09/1797. MS 12.13.42, Dr Williams's Library.

14 Godwin to Hugh Skeys, 20/11/1797. *Letters of William Godwin*, I, pp. 269–70.

15 Godwin to Johnson, 11/01/1798. *Letters of William Godwin*, II, p. 7.

16 Godwin, *Memoirs of the Author of A Vindication of the Rights of Woman*, p. 89.

17 Diary of Joseph Farington, 03/08/1798. *Diary of Joseph Farington*, III, p. 1043.

18 Godwin to ?Johnson, 02/01/1798. *Letters of William Godwin*, II, p. 3.

19 Mary Hays, Obituary of Mary Wollstonecraft, *Monthly Magazine* IV (Sept 1797), p. 233.

20 Mary Hays, 'Memoirs of Mary Wollstonecraft', *Annual Necrology for 1797–8*, p. 459.

21 *Anti-Jacobin Review*, 1 (1798), pp. 94–101.

22 Richard Polwhele, *The Unsex'd Females*, pp. 31, 34, 35–6.

23 See, for example, Gary Kelly, *Women, Writing and Revolution 1790–1827*, p. 113.

24 Anon., *Appeal to the Men of Great Britain*, pp. 28–9.

25 Godwin to Malthus, 15/08/1798. *Letters of William Godwin*, 15/08/1798. Malthus made the arguments to which Godwin objected in *An Essay on the Principle of Population*, published by Johnson earlier that month. For details of Malthus's life and career see Robert J. Mayhew, *Malthus: The Life and Legacies of an Untimely Prophet*.

26 Darwin to Thomas Brown, 12/01/1797. *Letters of Erasmus Darwin*, p. 509.

27 Darwin to James Watt, 21/06/1796. *Letters of Erasmus Darwin*, p. 500.

28 Johnson to William Russell, 24/08/1796. *Joseph Johnson Letterbook*, p. 25.

29 Lindsey to William Turner, 20/10/1796. *Letters of Theophilus Lindsey*, II, p. 406.

30 Johnson to Messrs Morrison, 07/12/1796. *Joseph Johnson Letterbook*, p. 37.

31 James Hurdis to William Cowper, 29/01/1793. J. F. Tattersall, ed., *Letters of the Revd. James Hurdis, D. D., Vicar of Bishopstone, Sussex, to William Cowper, 1791–4*, p. 29.

32 Richard Lovell Edgeworth to Darwin, n.d., 1796. *Memoirs of Richard Lovell Edgeworth*, II, p. 156.
33 Richard Lovell and Maria Edgeworth, *Practical Education*, I, p. 284.
34 Ibid., I, pp. 258–9.
35 Ibid., II, p. 707.
36 Maria Edgeworth to Mrs Ruxton, n.d. 1797. Edgeworth Papers, National Library of Ireland, MS 10, 166/7, Microfilm Pos 9027.
37 Maria Edgeworth to Sophy Ruxton, 09/09/1798. *Maria Edgeworth's Letters from Ireland*, p. 59.
38 Frances Edgeworth, *A Memoir of Maria Edgeworth*, I, p. 99.
39 Diary of Joseph Farington, 29/10/1798. *Diary of Joseph Farington*, III, pp. 1077–8.

CHAPTER TWENTY-SIX: THE KING VERSUS JOSEPH JOHNSON

1 Gilbert Wakefield, *Reply to the Bishop of Llandaff*, pp. 3–4. For valuable readings of Johnson's trial see Jane Worthington Smyser, 'The Trial and Imprisonment of Joseph Johnson, Bookseller' and Susan Oliver, 'Silencing Joseph Johnson and the "Analytical Review"'.
2 Ibid., pp. 6–7.
3 Ibid., p. 11.
4 Ibid., p. 14.
5 Ibid., p. 18.
6 Ibid., p. 21.
7 Ibid., p. 22.
8 Lindsey to Russell Scott, 22/02/1798. *Letters of Theophilus Lindsey*, II, p. 449.
9 Joseph Johnson Indictment. National Archives TS 11 456/1511.
10 Knowles, *The Life and Writings of Henry Fuseli*, p. 203.
11 *The Times*, 17/07/1798, Issue 4233, p. 2.
12 All quotations from Johnson's trial come from Treasury Solicitor Records held by the National Archives at TS 11 456/1511.
13 Knowles, *The Life and Writings of Henry Fuseli*, p. 202.
14 Lindsey to Thomas Belsham, 01/08/1798. *Letters of Theophilus Lindsey*, II, p. 454.
15 Priestley to Lindsey, 01/11/1798, MS 12.13.52, Dr Williams's Library.
16 *Anti-Jacobin Review*, 1 (1798), p. 83.
17 *Anti-Jacobin Review*, 1 (1798), p. 355.
18 *Analytical Review*, 28 (1798), p. 316.
19 *Analytical Review*, 28 (1798), p. 307.
20 All quotations from Johnson's mitigation hearing come from Treasury Solicitor Records held by the National Archives at TS 11 456/1511. Johnson's affidavit is also quoted in full in Gerald Tyson, *Joseph Johnson: A Liberal Publisher*, pp. 160–161.

PART SEVEN: HOUSE (1799–1809)
CHAPTER TWENTY-SEVEN: IDYLLIUM. THE PRISON

1 The location of the first part of Johnson's prison residence, between November 1798 and February 1799, has been the subject of some confusion among scholars of his life. All the friends who visited him during this period recorded that he was lodged at the King's Bench Prison, but it has also been suggested that during this period he was held instead at the nearby Marshalsea Prison. Johnson's own description of his reception at the King's Bench Prison before he received sentence confirms his whereabouts. The confusion may arise because of the legal terminology of the King's Bench Prison Committal Records, which recorded in November and February that he was 'Committed to the Custody of the Marshal of the Marshalsea of this Court.'(King's Bench Prison Committal Records, National Archives MSS: Pris 4, entry number 545.) The Marshalsea and the King's Bench Prison were located close to each other but by 1799 the Marshalsea was in such an advanced state of disrepair that the decision was taken to close it and rebuild it nearby. In 1777 John Howard recorded that the deputy marshal was primarily responsible for the daily running of the Marshalsea and that legally the marshal of the Marshalsea was responsible for the good conduct of prisoners at the King's Bench Prison. Rules for the latter establishment, quoted in the edition of Howard's work published by Johnson in 1792, stipulated that the 'Marshal of the Marshalsea of this Court' (King's Bench) was responsible for searching visitors to the King's Bench Prison for unlicensed liquor (*The State of the Prisons* (1792), p. 248). I am indebted to Lucy Powell for her expert knowledge of London's eighteenth-century prisons and for her help in resolving the question of Johnson's whereabouts in the months before sentencing.

2 Johnson to Richard Lovell Edgeworth, 18/02/1799. *Joseph Johnson Letterbook*, pp. 51–2.

3 Anon., *The Debtor and Creditor's Assistant*, pp. 40–1.

4 Ibid., p. 2.

5 Johnson to Richard Lovell Edgeworth, 19/02/1799. *Joseph Johnson Letterbook*, p. 52.

6 George Hanger, *Life and Opinions*, II, p. 281.

7 Ibid., II, pp. 282–3.

8 Ibid., II, p. 284.

9 Darwin, 'Idyllium. The Prison' in the *Monthly Magazine* 1 (Feb 1798), p. 54.

10 Hannah Lindsey to Russell Scott, 30/11/1798. *Letters of Theophilus Lindsey*, II, p. 462.

11 Lindsey to William Turner, 22/11/1798. *Letters of Theophilus Lindsey*, II, p. 460.

12 Diary of Joseph Farington, 16/12/1798. *Diary of Joseph Farington*, III, p. 1113.

13 'Prefatory Address', *Anti-Jacobin Review* 1 (1798), pp. iv–v.

14 Johnson to Christopher Wyvill, 23/01/1799. *Joseph Johnson Letterbook*, p. 50.

15 Lindsey to William Turner, 01/04/1799. *Letters of Theophilus Lindsey*, II, p. 468.

16 Priestley to Lindsey, 14/02/1799. *Life and Correspondence of Joseph Priestley*, II, pp. 414–15.

17 Priestley to Lindsey, 25/06/1799. MS 12.57.58, Dr Williams's Library.

18 *The Times*, 12/02/1799, p. 4.

19 Samuel Kenrick to James Woodrow, 16/03/1799. MS 12.157, Dr Williams's Library.

20 Diary of Joseph Farington, 31/05/1799. *Diary of Joseph Farington*, IV, p. 1231.

21 Johnson to Richard Lovell Edgeworth, 18/02/1799. *Joseph Johnson Letterbook*, p. 52.

22 Frances Edgeworth, *A Memoir of Maria Edgeworth*, I, pp. 98–9.

23 Knowles, *The Life and Writings of Henry Fuseli*, I, p. 202.

24 Henry Crabb Robinson, 'Reminiscences', Dr Williams's Library MS, 4 vols, vol 1 (for 1799), f. 118. I am indebted to James Vigus and Timothy Whelan for allowing me to quote from this transcription, to be published in their forthcoming edition of the *Reminiscences*, which supersedes previously published versions of this text.

25 Johnson to Richard Lovell Edgeworth, 19/02/1799. *Joseph Johnson Letterbook*, p. 53.

26 Johnson to Darwin, 20/07/1799. *Joseph Johnson Letterbook*, p. 60.

27 Johnson to Thomas Dobson, 17/07/1799. *Joseph Johnson Letterbook*, p. 58.

28 Johnson to Ballard Beckford Nembhard, 23/07/1799. *Joseph Johnson Letterbook*, p. 61.

29 Johnson to Thomas Holloway, 23/07/1799. *Joseph Johnson Letterbook*, p. 62.

30 James Edwards to William Roscoe, 09/08/1799. Roscoe Papers, Liverpool Record Office, Liverpool Libraries 920 ROS 1423.

CHAPTER TWENTY-EIGHT: ESSAYS ON PROFESSIONAL EDUCATION

1 Knowles, *The Life and Writings of Henry Fuseli*, p. 203.

2 Fuseli to William Roscoe, 14/10/1799. Roscoe Papers, Liverpool Record Office, Liverpool Libraries 920 ROS 1663.

3 Quoted in *Memoir of Richard Lovell Edgeworth*, II, pp. 335–6.

4 Cowper to Lady Hesketh, 26/06/1791. *Letters of William Cowper*, III, p. 534.

5 Richard Lovell Edgeworth, *Essays on Professional Education*, p. viii.

6 See, for example, Johnson to Elizabeth Hamilton, 16/01/1807. *Joseph Johnson Letterbook*, p. 138.

7 Anna Barbauld to Lydia Rickards, 29/12/1802. *Anna Letitia Barbauld Letters to Lydia Rickards, 1798–1815* (online).

8 Blake to George Cumberland, *Complete Poetry and Prose of William Blake*, p. 704.

9 Blake to Mr Butts, 11/09/1801. *Complete Poetry and Prose of William Blake*, p. 716.

10 Johnson to Hayley, 04/01/1802. *Joseph Johnson Letterbook*, p. 82.

11 Blake to Thomas Butts, 10/01/180[3]. *Complete Poetry and Prose of William Blake*, p. 724.

12 Blake to William Hayley, 07/10/1803. *Complete Poetry and Prose of William Blake*, p. 738.

13 Blake to William Hayley, 28/05/1804. *Complete Poetry and Prose of William Blake*, pp. 750–1.

14 Diary of Joseph Farington, 28/05/1803. *Diary of Joseph Farington*, VI, 2040.

15 Barbauld to Mrs Carr, October 1801. *Works of Anna Letitia Barbauld*, II, pp. 119–20.

16 Johnson to T. and J. Swords, 24/02/1804. *Joseph Johnson Letterbook*, p. 101.

17 Johnson to James Edwards, 13/10/1804. *Joseph Johnson Letterbook*, p. 108.

18 Priestley to Lindsey, 12/09/1799. *Life and Correspondence of Joseph Priestley*, II, p. 421.

19 Priestley to Samuel Galton, 01/02/1800. MS 12.57.59, Dr Williams's Library.

20 Priestley to ?Thomas Belsham, 26/12/1800, MS 12.57.61(a), Dr Williams's Library.

21 Priestley to Lindsey, 28/05/1801. MS 12.57.75, Dr Williams's Library.

22 Priestley to Thomas Belsham, 30/01/1802. MS 12.57.62, Dr Williams's Library.

23 Priestley to Thomas Belsham, 19/01/1802. MS 12.57.36, Dr William's Library, 12.

24 Priestley to Thomas Belsham, 10/03/1803. MS 12.57.64, Dr Williams's Library.

25 Priestley to Lindsey, 28/08/1802. MS 12.57.89, Dr Williams's Library.

26 Johnson to Priestley, 20/09/1802. *Joseph Johnson Letterbook*, p. 87.

27 Priestley to Thomas Belsham, 02/04/1803. MS 12.57.42, Dr Williams's Library.

28 Priestley to Thomas Belsham, 04/06/1803. MS 12.57.44, Dr Williams's Library. The word in question is partially illegible but the words to which it bears the closest resemblance are 'dishonourable' and 'dishonest'.

29 Priestley to Thomas Belsham, 24/09/1803. MS 12.57.48, Dr Williams's Library.

30 Priestley to Lindsey, 12/03/1803. MS 12.57.101, Dr Williams's Library.

31 Priestley to Thomas Belsham, 23/12/1803. MS 12.57.49, Dr Williams's Library.

32 Priestley to Lindsey, 16/01/1804. *Life and Correspondence of Joseph Priestley*, II, pp. 522–4.

33 Johnson to Priestley, 24/02/1804. *Joseph Johnson Letterbook*, p. 103.

34 Priestley to Samuel Galton, 01/02/1800. MS 12.57.59, Dr Williams's Library.

35 Erasmus Darwin to Elihu Hubbard Smith, ?1799. *Joseph Johnson Letterbook*, p. 155.

36 Darwin/Anon. to Richard Lovell Edgeworth, 17/04/1802. Edgeworth Papers, National Library of Ireland, Ms 10,166/7, Microfilm Pos 9028.284.

37 Maria Edgeworth to Charles Sneyd Edgeworth, c. October 1802. Edgeworth Papers, National Library of Ireland, Ms 10,166/7, Microfilm Pos 9028.308.

38 Wordsworth to Anne Taylor, 09/04/1801. *The Letters of William and Dorothy Wordsworth: The Early Years*, I, pp. 327–8.

39 See Dorothy Wordsworth to Lady Beaumont, 16/06/1805. *The Letters of William and Dorothy Wordsworth: The Early Years*, I, pp. 602–3.

40 Coleridge to Robert Southey, 24/12/1799. *The Letters of Samuel Taylor Coleridge*, I, p. 552

41 Johnson to Adriana Stedman, 25/10/1799. *Joseph Johnson Letterbook*, p. 64.

42 Johnson to Nicholas Dennys, 09/07/1800. *Joseph Johnson Letterbook*, p. 71.

43 Hays to William Tooke, May 1803. *Correspondence of Mary Hays*, p. 331.

44 Godwin to David Booth, 27/12/1802. *Letters of William Godwin*, II, p. 264.

45 Johnson to Sydney Owenson, 05/04/1806. *Joseph Johnson Letterbook*, p. 132.

46 Johnson to David Booth, 13/03/1806. *Joseph Johnson Letterbook*, p. 130.

47 Johnson to Samuel Miller, 14/08/1805. *Joseph Johnson Letterbook*, p. 125.

48 Johnson to Benjamin Smith Barton, 14/08/1805. *Joseph Johnson Letterbook*, p. 126.

49 Humphry Davy to James Webbe Tobin, 21/03/1800. *The Collected Letters of Sir Humphry Davy*, I, p. 44. For Davy's life and career see David Knight, *Humphry Davy: Science and Power* and Richard Holmes, *The Age of Wonder: How the Romantic Generation Discovered the Beauty and Terror of Science*.

50 John Ayrton Paris, *The Life of Sir Humphry Davy*, pp. 184–5.

51 William Hazlitt, 'My First Acquaintance with Poets' in *Selected Essays*, p. 7.

52 Charles Lamb to William Hazlitt, 15/01/1806. *Letters of Charles Lamb*, II, pp. 199–200.

53 Charles Lamb to William Hazlitt, 19/02/1806. *Letters of Charles Lamb*, II, p. 208.

54 See Duncan Wu, *William Hazlitt: The First Modern Man*, pp. 109–10. Wu's source for this figure is the manuscript diary of Henry Crabb Robinson, held at HCR bundle 6.VIII, Dr Williams's Library. Wu says of his discovery: 'It reveals that Johnson was the first London publisher to comprehend Hazlitt's potential as an author, to the extent of investing seriously in him.'

55 Johnson to Oxenham & Co., 18/02/1800. *Joseph Johnson Letterbook*, p. 65.

56 Johnson to Thomas Wilkie, 26/04/1806. *Joseph Johnson Letterbook*, p. 135.

57 Johnson to T. and J. Swords, 13/08/1807. *Joseph Johnson Letterbook*, p. 145.

58 Johnson to Joseph Cottle, 06/12/1804. *Joseph Johnson Letterbook*, p. 111.
59 Johnson to Charles Symmons, 18/04/1804. *Joseph Johnson Letterbook*, p. 109.
60 Grace Parman to Johnson, 11/12/1804. Royal Literary Fund Files, British Library, RLF 1/159/7.
61 Johnson to Samuel Miller, 08/04/1805. *Joseph Johnson Letterbook*, p. 117.
62 Johnson to Thomas Norton Longman, 09/04/1806. *Joseph Johnson Letterbook*, pp. 132–3.

CHAPTER TWENTY-NINE: LYCIDAS

1 All quotations from *Lycidas* in this chapter are taken from *The Riverside Milton*, ed. Roy Flannagan, pp. 100–107.
2 Knowles, *The Life and Writings of Henry Fuseli*, pp. 362–3.
3 Daniel Lysons, 'Fulham' in *The Environs of London: Volume 2, County of Middlesex*. British History Online.
4 Fuseli to William Roscoe, 21/06/1804. Roscoe Papers, Liverpool Record Office, Liverpool Libraries 920 ROS 1693.
5 Fuseli to William Roscoe, 14/10/1799. Roscoe Papers, Liverpool Record Office, Liverpool Libraries 920 ROS 1663.
6 Fuseli to William Roscoe, 12/06/1799. Roscoe Papers, Liverpool Record Office, Liverpool Libraries 920 ROS 1660.
7 Knowles, *The Life and Writings of Henry Fuseli*, p. 236.
8 Diary of Joseph Farington, 07/11/1799. *Diary of Joseph Farington*, IV, p. 1299.
9 William Austin, *Letters from London*, pp. 237–41.
10 Alexander Gibson Hunter to Archibald Constable, 05/03/1807, quoted in Thomas Constable, *Archibald Constable and his Literary Correspondents: A Memorial*, I, pp. 94–5.
11 Joel Barlow to Ruth Barlow, 12/07/1802. Barlow Papers 394.
12 Charlotte Edgeworth to Emmaline King, n.d. 1802. Edgeworth Papers, National Library of Ireland, MS 10, 166/7, Microfilm Pos 9028.297.
13 Maria Edgeworth to Sophy Ruxton, 07/05/1800. Edgeworth Papers, National Library of Ireland, MS 10, 166/7, Microfilm 9028.250.
14 Diary of Joseph Farington, 24/07/1805. *Diary of Joseph Farington*, VII, pp. 2593–4.
15 Hannah Lindsey to Christopher Wyvill, 11/07/1803. *Letters of Theophilus Lindsey*, II, p. 585.
16 Knowles, *The Life and Writings of Henry Fuseli*, pp. 301–2.
17 Godwin to Johnson, 21/03/1807. Oxford, Bodleian Libraries, MS Abinger c.18, 90–3.
18 Godwin to Johnson, 29/04/1807. Oxford, Bodleian Libraries, MS Abinger c.18, 96–7.
19 Johnson to Richard Sharp, 21/03/1808. *Joseph Johnson Letterbook*, p. 148.

20 Fuseli to James Heath, ?22/08/1800. *English Letters of Henry Fuseli*, p. 219.
21 Quoted in Joseph Johnson Jr, 'Explanatory' in *References to the Case of Mr. Fuseli's Legacy*, p. 8.
22 Ibid., Section One, p. 13.
23 Joel Barlow to Ruth Barlow, 12/07/1802. Barlow Papers 394.
24 Fuseli to Joseph Johnson Jr, n.d., 1804. *Life and Writings of Henry Fuseli*, p. 285.
25 Fuseli to Roscoe, 05/06/1805. Roscoe Papers, Liverpool Record Office, Liverpool Libraries 920 ROS 1695.
26 Diary of Joseph Farington, 23/06/1806. *Diary of Joseph Farington*, VII, p. 2792.
27 Charles Sneyd Edgeworth to Mrs Ruxton, 30/04/1806. Edgeworth Papers, National Library of Ireland, Ms 10, 166/7, Microfilm Pos 9029.513.
28 Diary of Joseph Farington, 10/12/1806. *Diary of Joseph Farington*, VIII, p. 2923.
29 Diary of Joseph Farington, 26/03/1804. *Diary of Joseph Farington*, VI, p. 2277. Knowles describes Fuseli's meeting with Sterne on p. 373 of his memoir.

CHAPTER THIRTY: BEACHY HEAD

1 Mary Hays, 'Charlotte Smith', *Female Biography*, quoted in *A Mary Hays Reader*, p. 277. For full details of the life and work of Charlotte Smith see Loraine Fletcher, *Charlotte Smith: A Critical Biography*, and for an illuminating reading of 'Beachy Head' see Jacqueline M. Labbe, *Charlotte Smith: Romanticism, Poetry and the Culture of Gender*.
2 Johnson to Smith, 25/11/1803. *Joseph Johnson Letterbook*, p. 98.
3 Smith to Sarah Rose, 05/03/1804. *Collected Letters of Charlotte Smith*, p. 611.
4 Smith to Sara Rose, c. August 1805. *Collected Letters of Charlotte Smith*, p. 702.
5 Smith to Sarah Rose, 14/02/1805. *Collected Letters of Charlotte Smith*, p. 681.
6 Smith to Sarah Rose, 02/07/1805. *Collected Letters of Charlotte Smith*, pp. 689, 690.
7 Smith to Johnson, 12/07/1806. *Collected Letters of Charlotte Smith*, p. 742.
8 'Advertisement' to *Beachy Head: with Other Poems*, pp. vi–vii.
9 Maria Edgeworth to Barbauld, 22/07/1804. *Memoir of Mrs Barbauld*, p. 84.
10 Barbauld to Maria Edgeworth, 30/08/1804. *Memoir of Mrs Barbauld*, pp. 86–7.
11 Barbauld to Miss Belsham, n.d., 1800. *Works of Anna Letitia Barbauld*, II, p. 67.
12 Barbauld to Mrs Beecroft, 14/01/1802. *Works of Anna Letitia Barbauld*, II, p. 91.
13 Godwin to James Marshal, Fanny Imlay and Mary Godwin, 03/08/1800. *Letters of William Godwin*, II, p. 159.
14 *Memoir of Anna Barbauld*, p. 122.
15 Hannah Lindsey to Robert Millar, 15/11/1808. MS 12.46.60, Dr Williams's Library.

16 Thomas Belsham, *A Sermon Occasioned by the Death of the Rev. Theophilus Lindsey*, M.A., p. 2.

17 Johnson to William Henry, 14/08/1805. *Joseph Johnson Letterbook*, p. 124.

18 Johnson to Adam Clarke, 25/04/1806. *Joseph Johnson Letterbook*, p. 135.

19 Johnson to Daniel Isaac Eaton, 26/04/1806. *Joseph Johnson Letterbook*, p. 136.

20 Johnson to Murray & Cochrane, 19/01/1807. *Joseph Johnson Letterbook*, p. 141.

21 Diary of Joseph Farington, 10/05/1809. *Diary of Joseph Farington*, IX, p. 3452.

22 Diary of Joseph Farington, 03/07/1809. *Diary of Joseph Farington*, X, p. 3503.

23 Diary of Benjamin Robert Haydon, 12/12/1808. *Diary of Benjamin Robert Haydon*, I, p. 37.

24 Diary of Joseph Farington, 25/03/1808. *Diary of Joseph Farington*, IX, p. 3245.

25 Johnson to William Henry, 29/11/1809. *Joseph Johnson Letterbook*, p. 151.

26 Quoted in Maria Edgeworth to Mrs Ruxton, 26/12/1809. Edgeworth Papers, National Library of Ireland, Ms 10, 166/7, Microfilm Pos 9029.722.

27 Knowles, *The Life and Writings of Henry Fuseli*, p. 299.

28 *Morning Chronicle*, 21/12/1809, p. 3.

29 John Aikin in the *Gentleman's Magazine*, December 1809, reprinted in John Nichols, *Minor Lives: A Collection of Biographies*, pp. 286–6 (pp. 283–4).

30 Quoted in Knowles, *The Life and Writings of Henry Fuseli*, p. 302.

31 Humphry Davy to Thomas Rackett, 03/01/1810. *The Collected Letters of Humphry Davy*, II, p. 44.

32 Maria Edgeworth to Mrs Ruxton, 26/12/1809. Edgeworth Papers, National Library of Ireland, Ms 10, 166/7, Microfilm Pos 9029.722.

33 Maria Edgeworth to Mrs Ruxton, 09/01/1810. Edgeworth Papers, National Library of Ireland, Ms 10, 166/7, Microfilm Pos 9029.726.

34 Maria Edgeworth to Anna Barbauld, 18/01/1810. *Memoir of Mrs Barbauld*, p. 138.

35 Hannah Lindsey to Robert Millar, 27/03/1810. MS 12.46.61, Dr Williams's Library.

36 Joseph Johnson Will, National Archives, PROB 11/1513.

37 Leigh Hunt, *Lord Byron and Some of his Contemporaries*, II, pp. 32–4.

AFTERWORD

1 Susan Sontag, 'Illness as Metaphor', *New York Review of Books*, 26/01/1978.

Index

Index

Index

Index

Index

291, 348–9, 361; continues to go to Johnson's 353, and visits him in prison 375, 380; at the first post-prison dinner 383; recommends Johnson for a dictionary project 394; meets Humphry Davy 396; persuades Johnson to publish Hazlitt's *Essay on the Principles of Human Action* 397, 398; his financial dependence on Johnson 409, 410–11, 413, 421; remarries 409; his children 409–10; proposes a Juvenile Library 410; and Johnson's death 422, 423, 424; continues the habit of dining at St Paul's Churchyard 425; in Johnson's will 426

Works

'Cursory Strictures' 266(n20)

An Enquiry into Political Justice 245, 271–2

Memoirs of the Author of A Vindication of the Rights of Woman 177, 178, 246(n15), 306–7, 309(n6), 313, 315, 324(n52), 325, 344–5, 346–7

Things as they Are: or, The Adventures of Caleb Williams: 'Preface' 255

Good, John Mason: *Memoirs of . . . Reverend Alexander Geddes* 250

Gordon, Lord George 102, 104

Gordon, Lyndall: *Mary Wollstonecraft . . .* 211

Gordon Riots (1780) 102–6, 117, 125, 219

Grafton, August Fitzroy, 3rd Duke of 35, 36, 39, 128

'Great Ejection, The' *see* 'Black Bartholomew's Day

Grierson, Constantia 77, 78

Guilford, Susan North, Countess of 406

Hackney: New College/Academy 226, 231, 259, 260, 349, 396; Gravel Pit Meeting 239

Hamilton, Elizabeth 419

Hamilton, Sir William 203–4

Hancock, John 354, 356, 357, 358, 379

Hanger, George: *Life and Opinions* 373–4

Hardy, Thomas (shoemaker) 262, 264, 265–6, 267–8

'Harrison, R.': *The Catholic Protestant* 105–6

Hartley, David 73

Haughton, Moses 424

Hawkes, Thomas 228

Hawkesworth, John: *New Discoveries . . .* 100

Haydon, Benjamin 422

Hayley, William 295, 296, 297, 298–300, 302–3, 385, 386; correspondence with Cowper 296, 297, 298, 300, 301(n33), 302(n40), 303; his *Life* of Cowper 385–7

Hays, Mary: publishes her reply to Gilbert Wakefield 259–60, 278; meets Johnson and Lindsey 260; sends her *Letters and Essays* to Lindsey 277; at Johnson's dinners 237, 419; and William Godwin 260, 272, 278–9, 318; and Mary Wollstonecraft 260, 276–8, 279, 315, 317, 318, 319; excluded from Wollstonecraft's deathbed 324, 325; clashes with Godwin over rights to Wollstonecraft's papers 346; writes her obituary and 'Memoirs' 346; pilloried by Richard Polwhele 347, 415; visits Johnson in prison 380; critical of him 394

Index

Riots 104, 105; at Johnson's dinners 111, 161; and Barbauld 111; worried by Johnson's agreement to publish Priestley's *History of Early Opinion* 136–7; his idea of happiness 142; with Priestley in the House of Commons 162; and Priestley's sermon on the slave trade 165; stays with him at Fair Hill 178; and the French Revolution 179, 183, 185, 188, 189, 226, 227; immortalised by George Dyer 186; and Richard Price 191; mobilises against legislation 191–2; caricatured as lackey of the Devil 192; at Revolution Society meeting 219; and publication of Paine's *Rights of Man* 224, 258; supports the opening of New College, Hackney 226; and attacks on Priestley 226, 229, 230; at Revolution dinner 227; with Johnson 237, 243, 253; retires from his Essex Street ministry 243; and Priestley's emigration 251; and William Godwin 260, 271–2; finds himself short of theological reading material 260; and transportation of Thomas Fyshe Palmer 263; approves of Hays' *Letters and Essays* 277, 279; and Coleridge 291, 328, 334; and Mary Wollstonecraft 313; and Wakefield's pamphlet 356; and Johnson's trial 360; his status as martyr 363; visits Johnson in prison 375–6; on Christopher Wyvill 377; defends Johnson against Priestley 390; suffers a stroke 408–9; death

420–21; and Repeal of Test and Corporation Acts (1828) 427; Priestley's letters to 74, 179(n12), 187(n8), 191, 192–3, 221, 224(n24), 225(n30), 226(n32), 227(n34), 251, 252, 341–2, 343, 344, 361, 378, 389–90, 391–2

The Apology . . . on resigning the vicarage of Catterick . . . 56, 57–8

Farewell Address to the people of Catterick 421

A Sermon preached at the opening of the chapel . . . 61(n12), 62

Vindiciae Priestleiane 163

Linnaeus, Carl 139

Liverpool 15, 16, 26, 31, 97, 98, 99, 110, 153, 389, 397;
    Baptists 15, 18, 423; Benn's Garden Chapel 28, 98

Livery Companies 15, 16

Llandaff, Bishop of see Watson, Richard

Lock, Frederica 178

Lock Hospital, London 117

Locke, John 89

London Corresponding Society (LCS) 262–3, 264, 265, 268, 363

London Evening Post 41

London Institution 422

London Magazine 251

Longman, Thomas Norton 52; Johnson to 401–2

Louis XVI, of France 179, 187, 190, 216, 226, 261, 262, 309–10

Lovell, Nancy 381, 426

Lowhill, Everton 13

Lunar Society, Birmingham 135, 137, 138, 205, 240, 251, 392

Macaulay, Catharine 78

McCarthy, William: *Anna Letitia Barbauld* 83

Index

Index

and the burning of the New Meeting and his home, Fair Hill 227–8, 229, 239, 363; escapes to London 229–30, 233, 237; and William Russell 230, 231, 234; dines with Sheridan 231; his account of the Birmingham riots published by Johnson 231–3; has his portrait painted by Opie 239; elected to fill Price's place as minister 239; rents house in Clapton 239–40, 241; private papers salvaged from Fair Hill 240–41; and the Lunar Society 240, 251; emigrates to America 251–3; and Wakefield's *Enquiry into ... Worship* 258, 259; Johnson rejects his invitation to invest in farm and college 268–9, 286; and Wordsworth 329, 331; attacked by the *Anti-Jacobin Review* 340, 341, 349; and George Washington 341, 342–3; dependent on news and books from England 341, 343, 353, 416; and death of his son and wife 341–2; and war with France 343–4; young Dissenters turn from 349; and Johnson's sentence 360–61; final break with Johnson 389–92; death 392

Works

Address to the Protestant Dissenters 62–3

An Appeal to the Public on the Subject of the Riots at Birmingham 231–3, 241

Disquisitions relating to matter and spirit 73, 73(n14)

Essay on a Course of Liberal Education 27, 29–31

Essay on the First Principles of Government 35–6

Experiments and Observations on Different Kinds of Air 73, 74

Familiar Letters to the Inhabitants of Birmingham 193

History and Present State of Electricity 33, 34–5, 37

History of Early Opinion 136–7

History of Vision 351

Institutes of Natural and Revealed Religion 58

Letter to the Right Hon. William Pitt 162–3

Letters to the Right Hon. Edmund Burke 221

The Present State of Europe ... : 'Preface' 240(n50)

'Sermon on the Death of the Reverend R. Robinson' 38(n24)

A Sermon on the Subject of the Slave Trade 164–5 see also *Theological Repository*

Priestley, Joseph (son) 228, 251, 342, 435

Priestley, Mary (*née* Wilkinson) 29, 37, 59, 80, 228, 229, 230, 251, 252–3, 341–2, 389

Priestley, Sarah see Finch, Sarah

Priestley, William 187–8, 228, 251, 342

Protestants/Protestantism 13, 14, 62, 76, 78, 84, 102, 221

Pughe, William Owen: Iolo Morganwg to 265(n19)

Purser's Cross, Fulham 405, 412–13, 421, 425

Quakers 15

Rackett, Thomas: Humphry Davy to 424(n31)

Ramsgate, Kent 213

Index

Index

Scott, Russell: Hannah Lindsey to
243(n10), 375(n10); Theophilus
Lindsey to 224(n25), 260, 356
Scott, Sarah 75
Seagrave, Joseph 385
Seward, Anna 76
Memoirs of the Life of Dr Darwin 137–8
Shakespeare Gallery, London 213,
214, 293, 295
Sharp, Richard 294, 295; Johnson to
410(n19)
Shelburne, William Petty, 2nd Earl of
58–9, 73, 74, 128, 135
Shepherd, William 379
Sheridan, Richard Brinsley 231
Shore, Samuel: Lindsey to 239(n1)
Skeys, Fanny (*née* Blood) 147, 344
Skeys, Hugh 344; Godwin to 344–5
slavery and slave trade 19, 97–9, 161,
164–8, 281–2
Smith, Benjamin 299
Smith, Charlotte 3, 299–300, 415,
419; Johnson to 415–16
Works
Beachy Head: with Other Poems 417;
'Beachy Head' 417–18
Conversations Introducing Poetry 416
Elegiac Sonnets 415
Emmeline 171
Smith, Elihu Hubbard: Darwin to
392(n35)
Smith, Robert: Cowper to 133(n52)
Society for the Abolition of the Slave
Trade 98
Society for Constitutional Information
(SCI) 217, 225, 262, 263, 268
Society for the Reformation of Man-
ners 16
Society of Antiquaries 108
Southey, Edith (*née* Fricker) 331–2
Southey, Robert 331; Coleridge to 394
Spectator, The 420
Spence, James 69

Spencer, Benjamin 227
Stamp Act (1765) 33–4, 35
Stationers' Company 18
Stedman, Adriana: Johnson to 394
Stedman, Gabriel 283–5, 286, 394
*Narrative of a Five Years Expedition
against the Revolted Negroes of
Surinam* 284–6, 394
Stedman, Joanna 283
Stedman, Johnny 283
Sterne, Laurence 413
Stevenson, Margaret 70
Stothard, Thomas 108
Sulzer, Johann Georg 22
General Theory of the Fine Arts 22
Swords, T. and J.: Johnson to
389(n16), 399

Talleyrand, Charles-Maurice de 274
Tatler 420
Tayleur, William: Lindsey to 99(nn18,
19), 99, 104(n3), 105(n5),
137(nn5–7), 141(n21), 142,
191–2(n20), 222(n19), 223,
224(n26), 226(n33), 230(n38),
231–2(n42), 258(n9), 313(n18)
Taylor, Anne: Wordsworth to
393(n38)
Teedon, Samuel: Cowper to 297(n13),
297, 299, 300(n27), 301(n32)
Test and Corporation Acts 14, 28, 35,
62, 162, 172, 191, 192, 427
Thanet, Sackville Tufton, 9th Earl of
379
Thelwall, John 264, 268, 327–8, 332
Theological Repository (journal) 32, 58,
136
Thomson, William 284
Times, The 231, 357–8, 378
Tobin, James Webbe: Humphry Davy
to 396
Tomalin, Claire: *The Life and Death of
Mary Wollstonecraft* 23

Index